The Politics of
the Developing Areas

The Politics of the Developing Areas

EDITORS

GABRIEL A. ALMOND

JAMES S. COLEMAN

COAUTHORS

JAMES S. COLEMAN

LUCIAN W. PYE

MYRON WEINER

DANKWART A. RUSTOW

GEORGE I. BLANKSTEN

GABRIEL A. ALMOND

PRINCETON, NEW JERSEY

PRINCETON UNIVERSITY PRESS

1960

FOREWORD

THIS book sets out to do two things. The first is to construct a theoretical framework that makes possible, for the first time, a comparative method of analysis for political systems of all kinds. The second is to offer a comparative analysis of the political systems of those areas of the world in which dramatic social and political changes are taking place—Asia, Africa, and Latin America.

The first of these objectives is covered by Professor Almond in his introductory essay on "A Functional Approach to Comparative Politics." This reflects the very large amount of thought and invention that have gone into the construction of the analytical framework of the enterprise. The significance of this conceptual scheme goes far beyond the areal scope of the volume and indicates that we may be approaching a revolution in the study of comparative politics.

The second objective—the comparative analysis of the political systems of the developing countries—has assumed considerable importance in this period of falling empires and emerging nations. If we want to know what to expect from the new political entities, we need some means for describing their properties in functional categories and making some general statements about them. Our past knowledge about them has been largely couched in a legal and institutional vocabulary that effectively conceals the factors and interests influencing political behavior in concrete situations. The areal chapters of the book and Professor Coleman's final chapter summarizing the modal characteristics of the political systems covered indicate what can be done with a functional approach.

The book had its origin several years ago in long informal discussions which Professor Almond had with some members of the Princeton Center of International Studies and later with the members of the Committee on Comparative Politics of the Social Science Research Council, of which Professor Almond has served as chairman. Both the Center of International Studies and the Committee on Comparative Politics have extended research facilities and financial aid to the project and the book is presented under their joint sponsorship.

FREDERICK S. DUNN
Director

Center of International Studies
Princeton University
December 1, 1959

v

PREFACE

THIS book had its beginnings several years ago in a series of informal discussions among three of the coauthors of the present volume—Lucian W. Pye, Dankwart A. Rustow, and myself—then all at Princeton University. The discussions had been stimulated by some of the work of the Committee on Comparative Politics of the Social Science Research Council which had stressed the importance of moving from an "area studies" approach to the study of foreign political systems to a genuinely comparative and analytical one. At the initiative of the two members of this trio who were members of the Committee on Comparative Politics, a series of area memoranda were commissioned with the requirement that a common framework and set of categories be used in the area political analyses.

The theoretical approach of the undertaking had its beginnings in a conference on "The Comparative Method in the Study of Politics" held in June 1955 at Princeton University under the sponsorship of the Committees on Political Behavior and Comparative Politics of the Social Science Research Council. Two of the papers presented to the Conference, one by Francis X. Sutton entitled "Social Theory and Comparative Politics" and one by myself entitled "Comparative Political Systems," were experiments in the application of sociological and anthropological theories and concepts in the comparison of political systems.

During my fellowship year at the Center for the Advanced Study in the Behavior Sciences in 1956-1957 I had an opportunity to experiment further with the problem of political comparison. I met with a group of anthropologists in a series of seminars dealing with primitive political systems. The group included John Whiting, Beatrice Whiting, Kimball Romney, John Roberts, and E. E. Evans-Pritchard. With this small seminar providing opportunities for occasional discussion, John Roberts and I met together daily over a period of several months, during which we attempted to spell out the properties which primitive and modern political systems had in common. The project we were then planning—to prepare a small collaborative volume on primitive political systems—has not as yet borne fruit, but the ideas and concepts stimulated by these seminars and discussions have been assimilated, elaborated, and modified in the theoretical introduction to this book. The functional approach to political comparison which we use here developed in these discussions, although its beginnings go back to collaborative efforts of Bernard C. Cohen and myself to grapple with the foreign-policy-making process in the United States in 1952-1953.

With this small stock of theoretical categories in hand, clumsy and ill-defined as they were, the co-authors of the present volume met together at Princeton University, first in the fall of 1957 and again in the spring of 1958, at the invitation of the Center of International Studies. During these planning and editorial sessions the functional categories were discussed and the structural categories of interest groups and party systems were developed. First drafts of the area memoranda were criticized and revised. Meanwhile James Coleman agreed to serve as co-editor of the volume, and to prepare a concluding chapter which would treat the common characteristics of non-Western political systems, the various types of political systems to be found in these areas, and the relationship between levels of economic development and political characteristics.

The theoretical chapter was elaborated from a memorandum which had been distributed to the co-authors before our first meeting. Much of its content was developed after the area sections were completed. As a consequence, the functional theory presented in the first part of the book has not been fully applied in the individual area chapters. Nevertheless these functional categories provide the concepts in terms of which the actual performances of the political systems of the various areas are analyzed.

Still another shortcoming of the book calls for explanation. Both in the theoretical and in the area sections, far more stress is placed on the political functions and structures than on the governmental ones. This is mainly justified on the grounds that constitutions and formal governmental institutions in these areas change so frequently and typically bear so remote a relation to actual performance that detailed description would be of little help in predicting the behavior of these systems. These political systems of the underdeveloped areas are in rapid process of change. If we are to improve our capacity for explaining and predicting the directions of political change, and in particular the prospects of democratic modernization in these areas, it is more important to analyze their traditional cultures, the impact of Western and other influences on them, their political socialization and recruitment practices, and their political "infrastructures"—interest groups, political parties, and media of communication.

The co-authors have substantial reasons to be grateful to the members of the Committee on Comparative Politics who did not collaborate in this particular venture. Many of the concepts we use here have been

discussed in Committee meetings or in Committee-sponsored conferences in which Taylor Cole, Sigmund Neumann, Guy Pauker, Roy
Macridis, George McT. Kahin, and Walter Sharp—all of whom served
on the Committee as this project was maturing—and Pendleton Her-
ring and Bryce Wood of the Social Science Research Council Staff
participated actively. As in any creative group activity, it is difficult
to give credit to those who may have been first in giving expression
to an idea or a concept. On the other hand, the responsibility for the
formulations which appear in the individual parts of the book is that
of their authors. We also wish to acknowledge our appreciation to the
Center of International Studies and to its Director, Frederick S. Dunn,
and Associate Director, Klaus Knorr, for making the Center's facilities
and resources available for the completion of this undertaking.

GABRIEL A. ALMOND

December 1, 1959

CONTENTS

The Politics of
the Developing Areas

INTRODUCTION:
A FUNCTIONAL APPROACH
TO COMPARATIVE POLITICS

GABRIEL A. ALMOND

THIS book is the first effort to compare the political systems of the "developing" areas, and to compare them systematically according to a common set of categories. To accomplish this it has been necessary to experiment with the conceptual vocabulary of political science. The old rubrics served us fairly well during the long era of political dominance of the Western European culture area. As long as scholars carried in the backs of their minds the history and anthropology of the area, the gross changes in the functional characteristics of governmental institutions which occurred in the nineteenth and twentieth centuries placed no great strain on the existing vocabulary. They corrected as they went along, adding empirical functions and questioning normative ones, making comparisons from one country to the next and offering causal explanations based upon inferences from historical experience and social structural and cultural differences.

But despite this apparent good health of the discipline of comparative government in its special area of competence, the conceptual scheme of political science steadily lost its capacity to grapple even with the phenomena of Western European politics in the course of the last fifty years. The concepts of separation of powers and of representation had arisen at a time of a relatively narrow suffrage, when public office was the monopoly of aristocratic or middle-class notables, when party and interest groups were informal and relatively limited phenomena, and when the "public" was limited to men of substance and culture. Since that time suffrage has become universal, political recruitment has lost its class character, political parties have developed formal and mass organization, associational interest groups have emerged, universal education and the media of mass communication have developed. These enormous changes in the political cultures and political structures of the West have not been accompanied by thoughtful conceptual adaptations. Until recent experiments began, we were endeavoring to handle the complexity of the political phenomena of the modern world with a legal and institutional vocabulary.

To find concepts and categories appropriate for the comparison of

3

political systems differing radically in scale, structure, and culture—to say nothing of dealing adequately with the familiar phenomena of Western Europe—we have had to turn to sociological and anthropological theory. Some of the concepts we use in this book, such as *political system, political role, political culture, political structure*, and *political socialization*, have acquired a certain currency among scholars in the field. Perhaps their utility may be said to have been tested. The additional categories which we introduce here have had only a preliminary trial in the area analyses of this present group of collaborators.

It ought also to be pointed out that the search for new concepts reflected in these terms is not an *ad hoc* matter. It reflects an underlying drift toward a new and coherent way of thinking about and studying politics that is implied in such slogans as the "behavioral approach." This urge toward a new conceptual unity is suggested when we compare the new terms with the old. Thus, instead of the concept of the "state," limited as it is by legal and institutional meanings, we prefer "political system"; instead of "powers," which again is a legal concept in connotation, we are beginning to prefer "functions"; instead of "offices" (legal again), we prefer "roles"; instead of "institutions," which again directs us toward formal norms, "structures"; instead of "public opinion" and "citizenship training," formal and rational in meaning, we prefer "political culture" and "political socialization." We are not setting aside public law and philosophy as disciplines, but simply telling them to move over to make room for a growth in political theory that has been long overdue.

If we pause for a moment and consider the interconnection among these terms, how they all rest on an "action" or a "behavioral" base, how one suggests another, and how open they are to the other components of the social process, it becomes evident that we are not simply adding terms to an old vocabulary, but rather are in the process of developing or adapting a new one. And, to put all of our cards on the table, this is not only a matter of a conceptual vocabulary; it is an intimation of a major step forward in the nature of political science as science. The joyous barks of the few formal logicians who have emerged in political science may still be worse than their bites, but there can be no doubt that we are moving slowly forward toward a probabilistic theory of politics. The concepts used here contribute to this ultimate goal, as we shall attempt to show at the conclusion of this chapter.

I. THE POLITICAL SYSTEM

If the concept of political system is to serve the purpose to which we wish to put it—that is, separate out analytically the structures which perform political functions in all societies regardless of scale, degree of differentiation, and culture—we shall have to specify what we mean by politics and the political system. Without such a sharp definition we will be unable to compare the differentiated modern political systems with the relatively undifferentiated primitive ones, the secular modern systems with the traditional and theocratic ones. The definitions of politics which identify it with such general societal functions as "integration" and "adaptation" fail us from this point of view. It is of course true that political systems typically perform the functions of maintaining the integration of a society, adapting and changing elements of the kinship, religious, and economic systems, protecting the integrity of political systems from outside threats, or expanding into and attacking other societies. But to identify politics with social integration and adaptation is a regressive step, scientifically speaking. It represents a return to a dull tool, rather than an advance to a sharper one, for if in pursuit of the political system we follow the phantoms of integration and adaptation, we will find ourselves including in the political system churches, economies, schools, kinship and lineage groups, age-sets, and the like.

If we consult the current literature for adequate definitions of politics and the political, we find considerable variety and some help. Weber's celebrated definition is of the "state," rather than of the political system in our sense of the term: "Today, however, we have to say that a state is a human community that (successfully) claims the monopoly of the legitimate use of physical force within a given territory. Note that 'territory' is one of the characteristics of the state. Specifically, at the present time, the right to use physical force is ascribed to other institutions or to individuals only to the extent to which the state permits it."[1] Schapera's point that the Weber definition would rule out as political systems small, undifferentiated societies in which there is no *monopoly* of the legitimate use of physical force is well taken. On the other hand, Schapera himself simply sets aside Weber's definition of the state, and does not offer an alternative definition, even though he insists that the Bergdama and Bushmen, for example, have political organization.[2] He throws away

[1] Max Weber, "Politics as a Vocation," in Gerth and Mills, *From Max Weber*, New York, 1946, p. 78.
[2] I. Schapera, *Government and Politics in Tribal Societies*, London, 1956, p. 119.

one tool but does not offer another. Levy's definition is not confined to the state: "Political allocation for the purposes of this study has been defined above as the distribution of power over and responsibility for the actions of the various members of the concrete structure concerned, involving on the one hand coercive sanctions, of which force is the extreme form in one direction, and, on the other, accountability to the members and in terms of the structure concerned, or to the members of other concrete structures."[3] But what these coercive and other sanctions are is left in doubt, as are the structures which perform these sanctions. Hence, the definition points indecisively in all directions in the society and does not enable us to pick out a specific system which we can relate to other systems and properties of a given society, or compare with the political systems of other societies.

Definitions of the sociologically inclined political scientists are suggestive, but still leave something to be desired for comparative purposes. Lasswell and Kaplan define political power in these terms: "Power is a special case of the exercise of influence: It is the process of affecting policies of others with the help of (actual or threatened) severe deprivations for non-conformity with the policies intended."[4] Here again, "severe deprivations" does not distinguish the political system from other social systems. David Easton[5] offers a definition with three components: (1) The political system allocates values (by means of policies); (2) its allocations are authoritative; and (3) its authoritative allocations are binding on the society as a whole. Elaborating on the meaning of "authoritative," Easton points out: ". . . a policy is clearly authoritative when the feeling prevails that it must or ought to be obeyed . . . that policies, whether formal or effective, are accepted as binding."[6] The difficulty with this definition, as with the others, is that "authoritativeness" as defined by Easton does not differentiate political systems from churches, business firms, and the like. But his combination of comprehensiveness of application plus "authoritativeness" comes close to the kind of tool we need in the work of comparing political systems of differing scales and degrees of differentiation. We may sharpen Easton's definition by turning his conception of authority into "legitimate physical compulsion"—in other words, building back into the definition the

[3] Marion Levy, Jr., *The Structure of Society*, Princeton, N.J., 1952, p. 469.

[4] H. D. Lasswell and Abraham Kaplan, *Power and Society*, New Haven, Conn., 1950, p. 76.

[5] David Easton, *The Political System: An Inquiry into the State of Political Science*, New York, 1953, pp. 130ff.

[6] *Ibid.*, p. 133.

explicitness of Max Weber's formulation—at the same time that we broaden the Weber definition in order to be able to include types of political organization other than the state. Certainly the comparative politics of modern times must be in a position to handle primitive and traditional systems which are political but are not states in the sense of Weber's definition, as well as transitional and revolutionary systems in which there may be no "monopoly of the legitimate use of physical force within a given territory." What we propose is that the political system is that system of interactions to be found in all independent societies which performs the functions of integration and adaptation (both internally and vis-à-vis other societies) by means of the employment, or threat of employment, of more or less legitimate physical compulsion. The political system is the legitimate, order-maintaining or transforming system in the society. We use the term "more or less" to modify legitimacy because we do not want to exclude from our definition political systems, like the totalitarian ones, where the degree of legitimacy may be very much in doubt; revolutionary systems, where the basis of legitimacy may be in process of change; or non-Western systems, in which there may be more than one legitimate system in operation. We use the term "physical compulsion" since we believe that we can distinguish political systems from other social systems only by such a specific definition, but this is by no means the same thing as reducing politics to force. Legitimate force is the thread that runs through the inputs and outputs of the political system, giving it its special quality and salience and its coherence as a system. The inputs into the political system are all in some way related to claims for the employment of legitimate compulsion, whether these are demands for war or for recreational facilities. The outputs of the political system are also all in some way related to legitimate physical compulsion, however remote the relationship may be. Thus, public recreational facilities are usually supported by taxation, and any violation of the regulations governing their use is a legal offense.

With the conceptions of input and output we have moved from the definition of "political" to that of "system," for if by the "political" we mean to separate out a certain set of interactions in a society in order to relate it to other sets, by "system" we mean to attribute a particular set of properties to these interactions. Among these properties are (1) comprehensiveness, (2) interdependence, and (3) existence of boundaries. The criterion of comprehensiveness means that when we speak of the political system we include all the interactions—inputs as well as out-

7

puts—which affect the use or the threat of use of physical coercion. We mean to include not just the structures based on law, like parliaments, executives, bureaucracies, and courts, or just the associational or formally organized units, like parties, interest groups, and media of communication, but *all of the structures in their political aspects*, including undifferentiated structures like kinship and lineage, status and caste groups, as well as anomic phenomena like riots, street demonstrations, and the like.

By "interdependence" we mean that a change in one subset of interactions (e.g., the electoral reforms of 1832 in England) produces changes in all the other subsets (e.g., the characteristics of the party system, the functions of parliament and cabinet, and so forth). Or, to borrow from an earlier comment on the interdependence of the political system: ". . . the emergence of pressure groups in the present century produced certain changes in the party system and in the administrative and legislative processes. The rapid expansion of executive bureaucracy was one of the factors that triggered off the development of legislative bureaucracy and pressure group bureaucracy. Changes in the technology of communication have transformed the electoral process, the characteristics of political parties, the legislature, the executive. The concepts of system and of interdependence lead us to look for these changes when any specific role changes significantly. It suggests the usefulness of thinking at the level of the system and its interdependence rather than in terms of discrete phenomena, or limited bilateral relationships occurring only within the formal-legal role structure."[7]

By the existence of a boundary in the political system, we mean that there are points where other systems end and the political system begins. We may illustrate this point in the following way. The murmurs and complaints in the bazaar in Baghdad are not in the political system until they break out, for example, in an act of violence—an anomic act of interest articulation—or when Haroun-el-Rashid, disguised as a water bearer, overhears the murmurs and translates them into political claims. As the diffuse and inarticulate murmur is translated into a claim on the use of "public authority," it passes the boundary and enters the political system as an act of "interest articulation."

In a more modern setting the police agent or informant in the Soviet Union observes a decline in labor productivity in a particular plant. He may overhear conversations and read cues in faces that lead him to infer

[7] Gabriel A. Almond, "Comparative Political Systems," *Journal of Politics*, Vol. XVIII, No. 3, August 1956, pp. 395-396.

that the decline is due to a special shortage of consumer goods. The conversations themselves and the cues from which motive was inferred are not in the political system. They pass the boundary into the political system when the agent translates them in his report to higher authorities into claims for public policy or bureaucratic action.

While we can say that the religious organization and the social stratification of a society influence the political system, we would not say that they are part of it. Only when a religious group makes claims upon the political system through religious authorities, or through specialized structures such as religious interest groups, religious political parties, or a religious press, do the intermittent political actions of the clergy, or the regular action of the specialized religio-political structures, become part of the political system. What kinds of structures man the boundaries of the political system is of the utmost importance in the functioning of the political system. These structures process the inputs, establish and maintain the contact between the polity and the society.

The boundaries between the society and polity differ from political system to political system. In a primitive society the shift from economy to church to polity may in one case be hardly perceptible. It may involve only a change of insignia or location of the action. But even in the "omnifunctional" primitive band some signaling occurs. On the other hand, the boundaries between the political and other social systems of primitive societies may be most sharply marked, as in war dances, sacrificial rites, and dramatic changes of costume. When we talk about good and bad boundary maintenance, we must use criteria appropriate to the system. In one case diffuseness and intermittency may be appropriate boundary maintenance; in another specialized secular structures are appropriate. We shall return to this concept of boundary maintenance when we deal with the functions of the political system in detail.

II. THE COMMON PROPERTIES OF POLITICAL SYSTEMS

The Universe of Political Systems

We suggested above that the discipline of political science until recent years has been working in a limited sector of man's experience with politics—the modern, complex, primarily Western states. Thus out of the many thousands of experiments with politics which have occurred in history and exist today, political science derives its generalizations from the study of a relatively small number. Furthermore, the political scientist is not aware—nor can he be—of how special and peculiar are the political forms and processes which he does study, since he is not aware of the composition of the total universe, of the range of complexity, and the kinds and frequencies of patterns to be found in it. The capacity to identify the peculiar properties of a particular species of politics, and the conditions with which it is associated, is dependent upon the variety of contrasting species with which one can compare it.

Even in the absence of this compelling scientific justification for broadening the scope of comparative politics, practical policy motives have forced the modern political scientist to concern himself with the whole range of political systems which exist in the modern world—from African kingdoms and tribal organizations to traditional oligarchies such as Saudi Arabia, and transitional, modernizing systems such as Burma and India.

An extraordinary enrichment of the discipline of political science is bound to result from the inclusion of these non-Western systems. For while the interdependences of the different components of the political system and of the political system with other social systems may elude us when we focus on the modern, specialized political systems of the West, they are inescapable when we examine them in the context of the less fully differentiated non-Western systems.

An illustration or two may make this point clear. Political scientists know in a general way that political control in a society is just one of a number of social control systems, such as religion, the family, the economic organization, and the like. What he is less likely to be aware of is the fact that the form and content of the political system in a society will vary with the form and content of the religious, family, and other systems in a society. Thus a society in which threats to social order are handled largely through a witchcraft system may have a less differentiated political system than one which does not. The essential point here is that crucial interrelations which we may miss when we examine the fully differentiated, more or less autonomous political systems in the West stand out more clearly in primitive and non-Western contexts.

If we are to extend the boundaries of the universe of comparative politics and include in it the "uncouth" and exotic systems of the areas outside Western Europe, it will be useful to specify the properties which all the individuals in this universe have in common. We shall have to break through the barriers of culture and language and show that what may seem strange at first sight is strange by virtue of its costume or its name, but not by virtue of its function. What are the common properties of all political systems? What makes the Bergdama band and the United Kingdom members of the same universe? We would suggest that there are four characteristics which all political systems have in common, and in terms of which they may be compared.

1. First, all political systems, including the simplest ones, have political structure. In a sense it is correct to say that even the simplest societies have all of the types of political structure which are to be found in the most complex ones. They may be compared with one another according to the degree and form of structural specialization.

2. Second, the same functions are performed in all political systems, even though these functions may be performed with different frequencies, and by different kinds of structures. Comparisons may be made according to the frequency of the performance of the functions, the kinds of structures performing them, and the style of their performance.

3. Third, all political structure, no matter how specialized, whether it is found in primitive or in modern societies, is multifunctional. Political systems may be compared according to the degree of specificity of function in the structure; but the limiting case, while specialized, still involves substantial multifunctionality.

4. Fourth, all political systems are "mixed" systems in the cultural sense. There are no "all-modern" cultures and structures, in the sense of rationality, and no all-primitive ones, in the sense of traditionality. They differ in the relative dominance of the one as against the other, and in the pattern of mixture of the two components.

The Universality of Political Structure

There is no such thing as a society which maintains internal and external order, which has no "political structure"—i.e., legitimate patterns of interaction by means of which this order is maintained. Furthermore, all the types of political structures which are to be found in the modern systems are to be found in the non-Western and primitive ones. The interactions, or the structures, may be occasional or intermittent. They may not be clearly visible, but to say that there are no structures would be to argue that the performance of the political function is random. What may be involved are intermittent actions of the oldest male of a band in response to situations, or an informally formulated consensus by the group dealing with some serious threat to internal order, or some problem of external relations. The articulative, aggregative, communicative, rule-making, and rule-application functions may spill over into one another without formal partitions between them, as a part of a single continuous action. But this is not a case of no political structures, but of a special kind of political structure. In other words, we are arguing that the classic distinction between primitive societies which are states and those which are not should be reformulated as a distinction between those in which the political structure is quite differentiated and clearly visible and those in which it is less visible and intermittent. We are dealing with a continuum and not a dichotomous distinction.

This rejection of the "state and non-state" classification, which is found throughout the anthropological, sociological, and political science literature is not simply a verbal quibble. It is a matter of theoretical and operational importance. Such a dichotomous classification could come only from an approach to politics which identifies the political with the existence of a specialized, visible structure, and which tends to restrict the political process to those functions performed by the specialized structure. With this approach an analysis of the politics of a non-Western or primitive society may begin and end with a description of the properties and functions of a specific chieftainship or kingship which in the visible sense may perform only the functions of legislation and administration. The articulative, aggregative, and communicative functions may be performed diffusely within the society, or intermittently through the kinship or lineage structure. An adequate analysis of a political system must locate and characterize all of these functions, and not simply those performed by the specialized political structure. Indeed, it is this emphasis on the specialized structures of politics which has led to the stereotyped conception of traditional and primitive systems as static systems, since the political structures most likely to be differentiated are executive-legislative and adjudicative structures. The mechanics of political choice are there as well, but in the form of *intermittent* political structures. The rule to follow which we suggest here is: If the functions are there, then the structures must be, even though we may find them tucked away, so to speak, in nooks and crannies of other social systems.

The Universality of the Political Functions

But if all the structures which are to be found in specialized Western systems are also to be found in the non-Western, we are able to locate them only if we ask the correct functional questions. It is true that political systems may be compared with one another structurally, all the way from the intermittent political system of a primitive band like the Bergdama of Schapera and the Eskimo of Hoebel to the modern Western state system. But structural comparison is of only limited utility.

It is like a comparative anatomy without a comparative physiology. It is like comparing an amoeba and a mammal strictly in structural terms— saying that this one is multicellular and that one is unicellular; this one has specialized organs and that one does not have them. We have not compared them as functioning, living organisms. To do this, we have to ask functional questions—e.g., how is the motility function performed? how is the sensory-nervous function performed? how is the digestive function performed? how is the reproductive function performed?

In other words, in comparing political systems with one another, we have made only a beginning when we describe the specialized structures. Furthermore, we may be misled if we follow structural lines in our comparative efforts. Suppose we take interest groups as an example, and attempt a comparison of American interest groups with those of Indonesia. We might say that the United States has many formally organized, large-membership interest associations. Indonesia has relatively few; they are poorly organized, inadequately financed, have highly fluctuating memberships, and so forth.

Suppose we put the problem the other way around, and ask a functional rather than a structural question. Suppose we ask in regard to both countries: how are interests articulated? what structures are involved? how do they articulate interests? These questions open our minds to the whole range of interest phenomena in a society. We are not structure-bound. Thus we find in Indonesia that the few and relatively poorly organized trade unions or business associations are not the important interest-articulating structures, that we have to look at the bureaucracy, status groups, kinship and lineage groups, and anomic phenomena to discover how interests are articulated. Only when we ask this functional question are we led to an accurate representation of a dynamic process.

If we then look to the theory of political science for help in formulating these functional questions, we find ourselves gazing into a stagnant pool. Nothing much has happened to the functional theory of politics since the doctrine of separation of powers and the lively discussion of it in the great era of constitution-making in the United States. Between the Federalist Papers and Frank J. Goodnow's *Politics and Administration*, published in 1900, no formal theoretical attack on the functional theory of politics was undertaken. In the Federalist Papers only the authoritative governmental, or output, functions are treated. The political, or input, functions are treated generally as a representation or election function with little indication of the problems which have to be solved in

13

the political process. The Federalist theory of authoritative governmental functions emphasized the inherent inequality of governmental functions and stressed the necessity for mingling powers among the structures if they were to be kept separate and autonomous.

Goodnow's critique of the separation-of-powers theory[8] rejects the possibility of locating any single function in a single structure. It is a positivist critique of the legal conception of division of powers among the authoritative governmental structures. Goodnow argues that there are two functions of government, politics and administration. The function of politics, which is concerned with constitution-making, legislation, the selection of governmental officers, and the control over administration, is performed by a variety of structures, including parties, parliaments, bureaucracies, and courts. "It is impossible to assign each of these functions to a separate authority, not merely because the exercise of governmental power cannot be clearly apportioned, but also because as political systems develop, these two primary functions of government tend to be differentiated into minor and secondary functions."[9]

These systematic and creative leads of Goodnow were not followed up in later work. Functional theory in political science followed an unsystematic course. Students of political parties developed theories of the party which rejected normative notions and stressed empirical, implicitly probabilistic ones. Students of the courts and of constitutional law stressed the legislative as well as the adjudicative powers of the courts. Students of bureaucracy stressed the legislative and judicial functions of administration. Students of parliaments and legislatures stressed the decline of the legislative function of these bodies.

But no one in political science, prior to very recent and very provisional efforts, confronted the problem of political function and structure in a direct and systematic way. Two interesting recent efforts are David Easton's "An Approach to the Analysis of Political Systems"[10] and Harold D. Lasswell's *The Decision Process*.[11] Easton elaborates his conception of the political system by distinguishing "inputs," which he divides into "demands" and "supports," and "outputs," which are authoritative decisions or policies. The conceptual simplicity of Easton's model, with its three functions—demands, supports, and policies—will not carry us very far in our efforts at political comparison. It is still too

[8] Frank J. Goodnow, *Politics and Administration*, New York, 1900.
[9] *Ibid.*, p. 17.
[10] *World Politics*, Vol. IX, No. 3, April 1957, pp. 383ff.
[11] Bureau of Governmental Research, University of Maryland, 1956.

close to the generic model of a system, with its interdependence, its boundaries, and its inputs and outputs, to be particularly discriminating in the political field. But certainly Easton's work is moving in the general direction of systematic functional theory.

While Easton's functional approach is derived from general systems theory, Lasswell's approach arose out of empirical efforts at comparing judicial processes, and out of dissatisfaction with separation-of-powers "functional" theory for these purposes. The specific categories of functional analysis which Lasswell developed were tested in ". . . studies of comparative political science and jurisprudence."[12] Lasswell makes no claims for the definitiveness of his seven categories: "Classifications are serviceable when they are tentative and undogmatic, and when they guide scholarly activity in directions that are presently accepted as valuable."[13] He also makes the point made by Goodnow as to the multi-functionality of all political structure, a point which we will develop in some systematic detail below.

Lasswell's seven categories of functional analysis are as follows:

(1) Intelligence—Information, prediction, planning
(2) Recommendation—Promoting policy alternatives
(3) Prescription—The enactment of general rules
(4) Invocation—Provisional characterizations of conduct according to prescriptions
(5) Application—The final characterization of conduct according to prescriptions
(6) Appraisal—The assessment of the success or failure of the policy
(7) Termination—The ending of prescriptions, and of arrangements entered into within their framework.[14]

It is quite clear from an examination of these categories that they were designed primarily for governmental and particularly judicial comparison. Thus the political or, in Easton's terms, the input functions are handled in two rather formal categories, "intelligence" and "recommendation"—gentle concepts which hardly do justice to the vigor of politics. Nevertheless, this is to be expected. If functional categories are to be instrumental to research, they must be adapted to the particular kind of comparison which is contemplated. Research on the foreign-policy-making process in the United States also illustrates the difficulties which arise in trying to develop a set of categories of functional analysis

---

[12] *Ibid.*, p. 1.   [13] *Ibid.*, p. 2.   [14] *Ibid.*, p. 2.

which may be used for all kinds of comparisons. In a series of studies[15] which were intended to describe the functions performed by the Executive, the Congress, pressure groups, and the press in the making of foreign policy, some eight more or less distinctive activities or functions developed from the coding of interview responses. These were initiation, authorization, modification, vetoing, representation, communication, advocacy, and interpretation. Initiation, communication, and advocacy were the main foreign-policy-making functions attributed to the Executive. Initiation, authorization, modification, vetoing, and representation were the main functions attributed to the Congress. Representation, communication, advocacy, and interpretation were attributed to pressure groups; and communication, advocacy, and interpretation to the press.

These examples make clear that the functional categories which one employs have to be adapted to the particular aspect of the political system with which one is concerned. This is not to reject the possibility that in time some consensus may develop as to appropriate categories for functional comparison. But we are certainly far from such a mature theoretical position today. The particular functional categories which we employ in this book were developed for the purpose of comparing political systems as whole systems; and particularly for comparing the modern Western ones with the transitional and traditional.

They were derived in a very simple way. The problem essentially was to ask a series of questions based on the distinctive political activities existing in Western complex systems. In other words, we derived our functional categories from the political systems in which structural specialization and functional differentiation have taken place to the greatest extent. Thus the functions performed by associational interest groups in Western systems led us to the question, "How are interests articulated in different political systems?" or the *interest articulation* function. The functions performed by political parties in Western political systems led us to the question, "How are articulated demands or interests aggregated or combined in different political systems?" or the *aggregative function*. The functions performed by specialized media of communication in Western political systems led us to the question, "How is political information communicated in different political systems?" or the *political communication function*. The existence in all political systems of methods of political recruitment and training led us to the question, "How are people recruited to and socialized into political roles and

---

[15] Conducted by graduate students of the Woodrow Wilson School of Princeton University under the supervision of Bernard C. Cohen and myself.

orientations in different political systems?" or the *recruitment* and *sociali-zation function*. Finally, the three authoritative governmental functions, *rule-making, rule application*, and *rule adjudication*, are the old functions of "separation of powers," except that an effort has been made to free them of their structural overtones—rule-making rather than "legisla-tion," rule application rather than "administration." Indeed, this taking over intact of the three functions of "separation of powers" reflects the political bias of this undertaking. It was the conviction of the collabora-tors in this study that the political functions rather than the govern-mental ones, the input functions rather than the output, would be most important in characterizing non-Western political systems, and in dis-criminating types and stages of political development among them.

Our functional categories therefore are as follows:

A. Input functions
   1. Political socialization and recruitment
   2. Interest articulation
   3. Interest aggregation
   4. Political communication

B. Output functions
   5. Rule-making
   6. Rule application
   7. Rule adjudication

The Multifunctionality of Political Structure

The differences between Western and non-Western political systems have generally been exaggerated. This is in part due to the fact that the "limiting case" models of the Western system, on the one hand, and of the traditional and primitive systems, on the other, have been greatly overdrawn. The model of the Western system has overstressed the functional specificity of political structure, while that of the traditional system has overstressed the undifferentiated and diffuse character of political and social structure. If we examine the literature of political science in the past forty or fifty years, we find that one of its great accomplishments has been the demonstration of the multifunctionalism of modern political institutions. Thus it has shown that the courts not only adjudicate but also legislate; that the bureaucracy is one of the most important sources of legislation; that legislative bodies affect both administration and adjudication; that pressure groups initiate legislation and participate in administration; and that the media of communication represent interests and sometimes initiate legislation. In the American system this multifunctionalism is partly intended (legally based), as in the "checks and balances" doctrine of the framers of the American Constitution, and partly an inescapable consequence of the nature of the political system. It is impossible to have political structures in relation to one another in a common process without multifunctionalism. What we mean when we speak of modern systems as being specialized is that certain structures emerge which have a functional distinctiveness, and which tend to perform what we may call a regulatory role in relation to that function within the political system as a whole. Thus the development of a modern party system means that the performances of the political recruitment function by other structures, such as interest groups and the media of communication, tend to pass through and be processed by the party system before they emerge as acts of political recruitment. The development of specialized associational interest groups means that there is a tendency for the articulations of interest which are performed by such structures as legislatures, bureaucracies, informal status and lineage groupings, and institutions such as churches and corporations to pass through and be processed by the associational interest groups before they emerge as acts of interest articulation. Although acts of interest aggregation on the part of political parties, interest groups, media of communication, and the bureaucracy may take the form of legislative projects which are enacted unchanged by legislatures or parliaments, they must pass through the legislative body before they become acts of "rule-making."

The development of these specialized regulating structures creates the modern democratic political system and the peculiar pattern of boundary maintenance which characterizes the internal relations between the sub-systems of the polity and the relations between the polity and the society. But this is by no means the same thing as saying that the relation between structure and function in the modern system is of a one-to-one order. What is peculiar to modern political systems is a relatively high degree of structural differentiation (i.e., the emergence of legislatures, political executives, bureaucracies, courts, electoral systems, parties, interest groups, media of communication), with each structure tending to perform a regulatory role for that function within the political system as a whole.

At the other extreme, our impressions of primitive and traditional systems have exaggerated their compactness and lack of differentiation. Even the simplest ones contain political systems. It is no more correct to think of the primitive band as a kinship group, a religious system, or an economy than it is to think of it as a polity. Indeed, it is all of these things and no more one than any of the others. At the extreme limit of simplicity, societies tend to be "omnifunctional structures" which are intermittently family, economy, church, and political system. While it is true that primitive, traditional, and transitional systems have more intermittent political structures, the modern ones have them, too. A few examples illustrating the relation between intermittency and level of differentiation and specialization of political structure may be in point.

In the Eskimo community it would appear that, with the possible exception of the headman, all the political structures are intermittent.[16] At a higher level of differentiation, executive, legislative, and adjudicative structures may have developed in specialized form, but the political functions of communication, interest articulation, and aggregation may be intermittently performed by lineage, status, religious, and similar groupings. At an even higher level of differentiation and specialization, as for example in "modernizing" or transitional systems, we may find differentiated governmental and political structures operating along with traditional and intermittent ones. The traditional and intermittent structures are not regulated by the modern ones, but continue to operate inside and outside the bureaucracy, parliament, parties, interest groups, and media of communication. The traditional and intermittent structures are not penetrated by or fused to the modern ones. They continue to function autonomously and legitimately. Unlike the modern system, their performance of political functions is not regulated by the differentiated and specialized structures. The modern political system does not eliminate intermittency and traditionality; it tends to regulate and control it. Diffuse and primary structures perform governmental and political functions within the modern structures. Other social systems and structures in the society—such as the family, the church, the educational system, the economy—are parts of the political system as intermittent political socializers, recruiters, interest articulators, and communicators. No political system, however modern, ever fully eliminates intermittency and traditionality. It can penetrate it, regulate it, translate its particularistic and diffuse impacts into the modern political language of interest articulation, public policy, and regulation.

[16] E. Adamson Hoebel, *Law of Primitive Man*, Cambridge, Mass., 1954, pp. 67 ff.

The Culturally Mixed Character of Political Systems

The final point in our argument as to the homogeneity of the universe of political systems is that certain kinds of political structure which we have usually considered to be peculiar to the primitive are also to be found in modern political systems, and not as marginal institutions, but having a high functional importance. Perhaps the best way to develop this argument is to refer to a recent body of research which is illustrative—the discovery in *The People's Choice* and subsequent studies[17] of the great importance of informal opinion leadership and face-to-face communication in the processes of individual decision-making. What is most interesting is the point made by Elihu Katz about the research design of the first of these studies, *The People's Choice*: ". . . the design of the study did not anticipate the importance which interpersonal relations would assume in the analysis of the data. Given the image of the atomized audience which characterized so much of mass media research, the surprising thing is that interpersonal influence attracted the attention of the researchers at all."[18] In other words, the emergence of the specifically modern media of mass communication had so captured the imagination of scholars that they had developed a model of the communications process which counterposed a society or an electorate consisting of atomized individuals to a system of mass media which were assumed to monopolize the communication process. It is a tribute to the faithful empiricism of this research undertaking that their findings did not confirm this model, but uncovered a face-to-face communication and interest articulation system below the mass media of communication and the interest group system—a "particularistic," "diffuse," and "ascriptive" system very much like that described in studies of the politics of primitive societies. The typical opinion leader was found to be a trusted individual whose political influence was often a diffuse consequence of other roles.

[17] Paul F. Lazarsfeld, Bernard Berelson, and Hazel Gaudet, *The People's Choice*, New York, 1948; Robert K. Merton, "Patterns of Influence: A Study of Interpersonal Influence and Communications Behavior in a Local Community," in Paul Lazarsfeld and Frank N. Stanton, eds., *Communications Research, 1948-1949*, New York, 1949; Paul F. Lazarsfeld, Bernard Berelson, and William N. McPhee, *Voting: A Study of Opinion Formation in a Presidential Campaign*, Chicago, 1954; Elihu Katz and Paul F. Lazarsfeld, *Personal Influence: The Part Played by People in the Flow of Mass Communications*, Glencoe, Ill., 1955.

[18] Elihu Katz, "The Two-Step Flow of Communication: An Up-to-Date Report on an Hypothesis," *Public Opinion Quarterly*, Vol. XXI, No. 1, Spring 1957, pp. 61ff.

Subsequent studies have suggested hypotheses as to how these two systems of communication and influence are interrelated, and how they affect one another. The "two-step flow of communication" hypothesis is one of these. In Katz's words: ". . . it is the opinion leader's function to bring the group into touch with this relevant part of the environment through whatever media are appropriate. In every case, influentials have been found to be more exposed to these points of contact with the outside world. Nevertheless, it is also true that, despite their greater exposure to the media, most opinion leaders are primarily affected not by the communication media but by still other people."[19] Given our present state of knowledge, we can conclude tentatively that, in modern political systems, the specialized structures of interest articulation (interest groups), aggregation (political parties), and communication (the mass media) exist in relation to persisting non-specialized structures which are certainly modified by the existence of the specialized ones, but are by no means assimilated to them. In other words, the modern, mass, bureaucratically organized, political party has not supplanted the informal coteries of notables which preceded it, but combines with this "more primitive" type of structure in what amounts to a mixed system. Similarly, the distinctively modern associational interest groups have not supplanted informal groupings of a status or interest kind, but are combined with them in a mixed system, just as the mass media of communication combine with the primary communication system.

Studies of the importance of the primary group and informal organization in governmental and industrial bureaucracies are too well known for detailed comment here.[20] Though research on the informal organization of Western parliaments and legislative bodies is only in its beginnings, certainly here, too, one would expect to find an informal primary-group system combined with the legal normative structure. This combination of formal-legal structure and diffuse and particularistic primary structure is not too different from the situation which obtains in many non-Western parliaments where, within the formal framework of parliamentary norms, there exists a normative structure and decision system based on kinship and status groups. There

---

[19] *Ibid.*, p. 77.

[20] For a summary of the literature on the primary group, see E. A. Shils, "The Study of the Primary Group," in Daniel Lerner and Harold Lasswell, eds., *The Policy Sciences*, Stanford, Calif., 1951, pp. 44ff. See also Sidney Verba, "The Experimental Study of Politics" (Ph.D dissertation, Department of Politics, Princeton University, 1959), pp. 17ff.

are significant differences, without question, between Western and non-Western parliaments, but both of them contain informal, primary groups.

If this general proposition regarding the "cultural" dualism of political systems is correct—and the evidence suggests that it is—then it brings into question certain applications of Parsonian social theory to the study of political systems. Some of Talcott Parsons' theoretical work[21] has as its point of departure the central concepts of Max Weber—in particular, his types of social action.[22] The "pattern variables" of Parsons build in large part on Weber's four types of social action—the affectual, the traditional, the instrumentally rational, and the absolute-value rational. Indeed Parsons' "diffuseness-specificity," "ascription-achievement," and "universalism-particularism" variables are specifications of some of the elements of Weber's general concepts of "rationality" and "traditionality." In the sense that an accurate specification of the elements of general concepts is a step in the direction of precision, the elaboration of the "pattern variables" from Weber's "traditionality" and "rationality" represents an interesting and promising theoretical development. However, certain uses of these pattern variables in the construction of models of political systems create serious problems if the position advanced in this chapter as to the persistence of "primitive" or "pre-modern" political structure in modern systems is a correct one.

There have been two recent efforts at constructing conceptual models of political systems from Parsons' pattern variables, one by Francis X. Sutton,[23] and a later one by Fred W. Riggs,[24] which is specially concerned with comparative administration. Both Sutton and Riggs develop models of industrial and agricultural political systems in which three of Parsons' pattern variables are the more important discriminating concepts. The industrial type of political system is characterized by universalistic, achievement, and functionally specific norms and struc-

---

[21] See in particular Talcott Parsons' introduction to Max Weber, *The Theory of Social and Economic Organization*, trans. by A. M. Henderson and Talcott Parsons, New York, 1947, pp. 8ff., and Talcott Parsons and Edward A. Shils, *Toward a General Theory of Action*, Cambridge, Mass., 1951, pp. 53ff.; Talcott Parsons, *The Social System*, Glencoe, Ill., 1951, pp. 58ff.

[22] See Weber, *The Theory of Social and Economic Organization*, *op.cit.*, pp. 115ff.

[23] "Social Theory and Comparative Politics," a paper prepared for a conference of the Committee on Comparative Politics, Social Science Research Council, held at Princeton in June 1954.

[24] "Agraria and Industria—Toward a Typology of Comparative Administration," in W. J. Siffin, ed., *Toward a Comparative Study of Public Administration*, Bloomington, Ind., 1957, pp. 23-116.

tures and the agricultural type of political system is characterized by particularistic, ascriptive, and functionally diffuse norms and structures. Put in other terms the industrial model is characterized by law, social mobility, and the differentiation of specialized structures, while the agricultural systems are characterized by custom, status, and the relative absence of specialization. Sutton suggests the usefulness of these two models of political systems in the following terms: "The major societies of the modern world show varying combinations of the patterns represented in the ideal types I have sketched out. Some stand close to the model of industrial society; others are in various transitional states which hopefully may be understood better by conceptions of where they have been and where they may be going."[25]

There can be little question of the usefulness of these theoretical efforts, but if the dualism hypothesis which we have advanced is correct, it would appear that the "pattern variable" concept has led to an unfortunate theoretical polarization. A model appropriate for the analysis of modern political systems would have to take into account the interrelations between the differentiated, specialized structures of parliaments, bureaucracies, courts, political parties, interest groups, and media of communication, and the "pre-modern" structures which persist as political structures of great importance. One would have to argue that the modern "industrian" system, to use Riggs' term, never exists by itself, but always has an "agrarian" system inside it.

This dualism of political structure is not only characteristic of modern Western political systems but of non-Western and primitive ones; i.e., there are both primary and secondary structures in primitive and traditional political systems and the secondary structures have modern (specific, universalistic, and achievement) features.

If both Western and traditional systems are dualistic in this sense, in what respects do they differ? Verba suggests that there are two main differences. First, in modern Western systems the secondary structures and relationships are far more differentiated and significant; and, second, the primary structures in modern systems tend to be affected by (modernized by) the secondary ones.[26]

To illustrate we may refer again to our comparison of a Western and a non-Western legislative body. Both have formal and informal structures. But in the Western parliament, the loyalty of the parliamentarian to the formal parliamentary norms would be greater in

---

[25] "Social Theory and Comparative Politics," *op.cit.*
[26] Verba, *op.cit.*, pp. 21ff.

comparison to his loyalty to the norms of his primary groups than would be the case in the non-Western parliament. The secondary structure, in other words, would be more effective. Second, and perhaps more important, the informal structure of a non-Western parliament would be of a different kind than that found in a Western one. In the non-Western parliament, the informal structure may be based on extended aristocratic family ties, on caste, on religious sect. In a very real sense these groupings, rather than legislative committees or party factions, may constitute the decision-making structure of the parliament. In a Western parliament, the informal structure would tend to be adapted to the formal structure; i.e., it would tend to be more modern in its culture (more specific, universalistic, achievement-oriented). The informal groups might take the form of interest or regional blocs, informal leaders of party groups and their followings, friendships based on common interest or residence, and the like. Thus the dualism of the non-Western parliament may really amount to a subversion of the formal by the informal; the dualism of the Western, to a penetration and domestication of the informal by the formal.

But while such a sweeping differentiation between Western and non-Western dualism may be true in general, a simple pair of models such as this may be quite misleading and tend to exaggerate the differences between Western and non-Western systems. It is quite clear that no political system is ever quite modern or Western in the sense in which we have been using the term, just as in the same sense no individual is ever fully "mature" and emancipated from primary ties and diffuse dependences. All political systems—the developed Western ones as well as the less-developed non-Western ones—are transitional systems, or systems in which cultural change is taking place.

We may distinguish among them according to the kind of relationship which exists between the "modern" and the "traditional" components. Let us take as an example the British political system. The relation between the diffuse, affective, particularistic, and ascriptive elements of the British political culture and the more universalistic, specific, instrumental elements tends to be one of *fusion*. In other words, all the way from right to left among the British public, the modern and the pre-modern attitudes are combined in such a way as to produce a homogeneous political culture, secular and traditional in content. In addition, British political structures—interest groups, political parties, parliament, cabinet, and monarchy manifest the same fusional dualism.

What is so interesting in Robert McKenzie's recent book[27] on British political parties is his demonstration of the fact that the British Labor Party, antitraditional and rationalistic in ideology and formal organization though it may be, has actually tended to take on the same pattern of traditional-rational fusion which is characteristic of the Conservative Party.

In contrast, in a country such as France there is a polarization of political culture, with some elements and regions manifesting traditionality and others manifesting rationality. According to our analysis, both subcultures of France are dualistic; but the traditional "areas" would manifest the kind of dualism which we attributed to non-Western societies above, while the other components would manifest the modern form of dualism.

Thus the French political culture is not fusional in its acculturative characteristics. Traditionality and modernity are not uniformly distributed, but are concentrated in different parts of French society. The relationship between these components has tended to be isolative. In some non-Western countries where a modern culture has been introduced in the cities and large-scale modernizing efforts have been introduced in the villages, we may speak of an *incorporative* pattern—i.e., the modern and pre-modern elements have not combined, or fused, and at the same time they are not sharply antagonistic. The two systems exist side by side; the acculturative process continues, and the outcome may turn out to be fusional or isolative, depending on events.[28]

What is useful in these concepts of multifunctionalism, cultural dualism, and political acculturation is that they set aside once and for all the geographic, cultural, and analytical polarizations which have plagued our efforts at social and political comparison. We have been talking of "modern" and "pre-modern," "developed" and "underdeveloped," "industrial" and "agrarian," "Western and non-Western"; or the Parsonian syndromes of universalism-specificity-achievement-affective neutrality, versus particularism-diffuseness-ascription-affectivity. The universe of political systems is less tractable to simple contrasts than we have supposed. We need dualistic models *rather than* monistic ones, and developmental *as well as* equilibrium models, if we are to understand differences precisely and grapple effectively with the processes of political change.

[27] Robert T. McKenzie, *British Political Parties*, London, 1955, pp. 581ff.
[28] I have taken these three models of culture contact and change from Evon Z. Vogt's "The Navaho," in Edward H. Spicer, ed., *New Perspectives in American Indian Culture Change* (forthcoming).

III. THE FUNCTIONS OF THE
POLITICAL SYSTEM

Political Socialization and Recruitment

In his recent book on political socialization, Hyman comments on the relative imbalance of research in the field of political behavior, the emphasis on motivational and emotional factors, and the relative neglect of cognitive elements. He states: "men are urged to certain ends but the political scene in which they act is perceived and given meaning. Some cognitive map accompanies their movement towards their ends."[29] Hyman's own treatment of political socialization views it as a continuous learning process involving both emotional learning and manifest political indoctrination, and as being mediated by all of the participations and experiences of the individual and not simply by early family experiences.[30]

Actually Hyman is criticizing only one of the prevailing theories of political socialization—the one which has stemmed from the psychoanalytic theory of personality and psychoanalytically oriented anthropology. This theory in turn was a reaction against the rational voluntarist theory of man and citizenship of the Enlightenment and liberalism, a theory which stressed political and social history and formal educational and propaganda practices in the development of the political attitudes and "civic spirit" of nations and peoples. Furthermore it is hardly accidental that psychiatrists, psychologists, and anthropologists should have developed a theory of political socialization which stressed unconscious or latent attitudes and the family as the primary mediators of the basic political "learning process." The libido theory and the unconscious were, after all, the great discoveries of psychoanalytic psychology. And the kinship group was clearly the central institution of primitive societies. A theory of political socialization stemming from specialists in unconscious psychological processes and primitive societies could hardly avoid being a "latent, primary group" theory, just as a theory of political socialization stemming from the study of intellectual and social history and political ideology could not avoid overstressing the manifest, rational, indoctrinative aspects of political socialization.

With Hyman, our own conception of political socialization endeavors to combine these two intellectual tendencies. It is a conception that

[29] Herbert Hyman, *Political Socialization*, Glencoe, Ill., 1959, p. 18.
[30] *Ibid.*, p. 25.

recognizes both the latent and the manifest components of the process of induction into citizenship roles and orientations, and which examines the later as well as the earlier and more primary "socializing" institutions and influences.

What do we mean by the function of political socialization? We mean that all political systems tend to perpetuate their cultures and structures through time, and that they do this mainly by means of the socializing influences of the primary and secondary structures through which the young of the society pass in the process of maturation. We use the qualifier "mainly" deliberately, since political socialization, like learning in general, does not terminate at the point of maturation, however this is defined in different societies. It is continuous throughout life. A great war or a depression, an experience like Italian Fascism or German Nazism, is an enormous learning experience which is not mediated through any particular social institution. Nevertheless the early participations tend to define the limits of later adult learning experiences. Thus it is striking that, with all the learning that attended the collapse of Nazism, so much of the earlier political culture of Germany survives into the present.

In a sense the socialization experiences of childhood and early adulthood—family, church, school, work group, voluntary associations—are pre-political citizenship experiences. The individual is inducted into a sequence of decision-making systems with particular authority and participation patterns, and with particular kinds of claim or demand inputs and policy outputs. It need not follow that all of these pre-political citizenship patterns are consistent with one another and with the adult citizenship pattern which emerges. That they influence one another there can be no doubt.

A second qualification to our definition of political socialization is necessary. When we say that all political systems tend to perpetuate their cultures and structures through time, we do not intend to convey a static impression. Insofar as the culture and structure are adapting and changing, the socialization patterns are likely also to be changing. But again this is a matter of degree and involves differences in the rates of change in the various subsystems of the society. One of the most important factors making for resistance to social and political change is the conservatism of primary groups and the early family socialization process.

Political socialization is the process of induction into the political culture. Its end product is a set of attitudes—cognitions, value standards, and feelings—toward the political system, its various roles, and role incumbents. It also includes knowledge of, values affecting, and feelings toward the inputs of demands and claims into the system, and its authoritative outputs.

In comparing the political socialization function in different political systems, it becomes necessary to examine the structures which are involved in the function and the style of the socialization. Thus, in a modern Western political system such as the United States, family, church, peer group, community, school, work group, voluntary associations, media of communication, political parties, and governmental institutions all share in the function of political socialization, and the associations, relationships, and participations of adult life continue the process.

The socialization may be manifest or latent. It is manifest political socialization when it takes the form of an explicit transmission of information, values, or feelings vis-à-vis the roles, inputs, and outputs of the political system. It is latent political socialization when it takes the form of a transmission of information, values, or feelings vis-à-vis the roles, inputs, and outputs of other social systems such as the family which affect attitudes toward analogous roles, inputs, and outputs of the political system.

The psycho-cultural school of political socialization is quite correct when it argues that latent or "analogous" political socialization is the first and undoubtedly the most basic stage of the political socialization process. The first years of life in the family, the experience of authority and discipline and of the family "political process" and "public policy" constitute the most rapid and binding stage of socialization. More of an impact occurs here than at any other point in the process. But the way in which the family citizenship analogy affects adult citizenship is quite complex and rarely, if ever, takes the form of a direct repetition of early childhood patterns.

As the child matures, the rate of latent political socialization drops off as the rate of manifest political socialization accelerates. Thus, in the early family, latent or analogous socialization is most important, and manifest or explicit political socialization is relatively unimportant. In the school, latent and manifest political socialization takes place, with the latter becoming of increasing importance in the higher educational levels. In later experience via work relationships, participation in voluntary associations and political parties, exposure to the media of communication, and to government, manifest socialization is of much greater importance, although latent socialization continues. In other words, even in later life there is a carryover into political citizenship patterns of the analogous citizenship patterns of the adult family, work group, church, and voluntary association memberships.

The style of the political socialization may be specific or diffuse, depending on the extent of differentiation and specificity of the political structure. Thus, in the Bergdama band, socialization into family authority and participation patterns is hardly separated from socialization into the political system, the religious community, or the work group, just as the boundaries of the various social systems of the society are not sharply drawn. It is easy to see how anthropologists, concerned as they have been with societies of only a slightly higher order of complexity than the simple band, should have produced a theory of homogeneity of authority and "public policy" patterns in cultures. Where the boundaries of the social systems of a society are diffuse, their capacity to generate significant differences in culture and structure are greatly limited. Where the boundaries are sharply drawn, autonomous development becomes possible. Thus a modern society may have one form of authority and participation in the family, another in the economy, and still a third in the political system. Each one of these involves a separate socialization process and, while they affect one another, they do not determine one another. At the primitive level, socialization into authority and participation is diffuse and hence more alike from one system to the next.

The political socialization function in different societies may be compared according to the way in which particularistic and universalistic elements are combined. In a modern Western society, political socialization is both universalistic and particularistic. It produces kinsman, friend, religious communicant, member of a status group, as well as interest group member, party member, and citizen with a set of explicit rights and duties. Each one of these roles makes its separate claims, and the most general role of all—that of citizen—under certain circumstances may take precedence over all of them. In many primitive societies, even though there may be membership in a political system constituted on the basis of territorial jurisdiction—in other words, a kind of "subject" or citizenship status with general obligations to the political system—kinship, lineage, or village tends to constitute the dominant group membership, and membership in the larger political system tends to be constituent—i.e., membership in the kinship, lineage, or village group—rather than individual and direct. Kinship or narrow local affiliations tend to define the most enduring political relationships, the basic units of jurisdiction with claims on loyalty more powerful than general membership in the larger political system. In other words, political socialization tends to be to the particular kinship, lineage, or village group as a subsystem of the larger territorial jurisdictional system, rather than directly to the larger system. In larger, more complex societies, caste and religious community, along with village and other local affiliations, may constitute particularistic subsystems; and membership in the larger territorial system and political socialization into it may be via these subsystems. What is unique in the modern political system is a political socialization function which creates a distinct loyalty and membership on the part of the individual in the general political system, and a tendency to penetrate and affect the socialization processes of other social systems, such as the family and church, so that they introduce general citizenship content into their socialization processes.

Finally, the political socialization function in different societies may be compared according to the way in which affective and instrumental elements are combined. All political socialization involves an affective component—the inculcation of loyalty to, love of, respect for, and pride in the political system—and often, perhaps usually, negative affect of differing kinds and intensities for other political systems. The systems differ in the way in which these affective elements are combined with instrumental components. Thus, in a primitive political system, love of the polity tends to be a simple and direct affective attachment with relatively little cognitive discrimination and instrumentalism—i.e., policy preferences, strategies of influence, and the like. But it would be a great mistake to minimize the extent to which instrumental attitudes and strategies of influence enter into even the most primitive political system. The love felt by the citizen for the modern political system is more of a civic love. The affect may be strong even unto death, when the chips are down, so to speak. But it combines with affective ties for other groups, with an instrumental attitude toward the behavior or policy of the loved object, and with rationally calculated strategies of influence.

We may conclude this treatment of the political socialization function by pointing out that in a certain sense in political development, as in biological development, political ontogeny recapitulates phylogeny. That is to say, the early stages of the political socialization process are the same in all political systems, regardless of their degree of complexity. It is essentially a latent, primary process—diffuse, particularistic, ascriptive, and affective. Political socialization in primitive societies tends to stop at this stage or, rather, involves only to a relatively limited extent secondary and manifest socialization into specialized political roles. In the modern system, political socialization continues beyond latent, analogous political socialization into a whole sequence of manifest political socialization experiences via the primary and secondary structures of the society. But no citizen of whatever modern political system ever fully escapes from the effects of his latent primary socialization experiences, or can ever fully suppress his needs for the intimacy and the stability of primary group relationships which bring into human proportion the secondary structures of the secular mass society. Hence the cultural and structural dualism of the modern political system.

The analysis of the political socialization function in a particular society is basic to the whole field of political analysis, since it not only gives us insight into the pattern of political culture and subcultures in that society, but also locates for us in the socialization procesess of the society the points where particular qualities and elements of the political culture are introduced, and the points in the society where these components are being sustained or modified. Furthermore, the study of political socialization and political culture are essential to the understanding of the other political functions. For, if political socialization produces the basic attitudes in a society toward the political system, its various roles, and public policy, then by studying political culture and political socialization we can gain understanding of one of the essential conditions which affect the way in which these roles are performed, and the kinds of political inputs and outputs which these roles produce.

The relationship between the political socialization function and the *political recruitment function* is comparable to the relationship between Linton's "basic personality" and "status" or "role" personality.[31] All members of societies go through common socialization experiences. Differences in the political cultures of societies are introduced by differences in the political socialization processes in the subcultures of that society, and by differences in socialization into different status groups and roles.

The political recruitment function takes up where the general political socialization function leaves off. It recruits members of the society out of particular subcultures—religious communities, statuses, classes, ethnic communities, and the like—and inducts them into the specialized roles of the political system, trains them in the appropriate skills, provides them with political cognitive maps, values, expectations, and affects.

[31] Ralph Linton, *The Cultural Background of Personality*, New York, 1945, pp. 125ff.

In comparing the political recruitment function in different political systems, we have again to consider—as we did in the analysis of the political socialization function—the social and political structures which perform the function and the style of the performance. We have to examine in each political system the role of family, kinship, and lineage in recruitment to specialized political roles, status and caste, religious community, ethnic and linguistic origins, social class, schooling and training institutions. We have to examine the structures affecting specific induction patterns—political parties, election systems, bureaucratic examing systems, "in-role political socialization," and channels of recruitment and advancement within the political and authoritative governmental structures. The recruitment function, in other words, consists of the special political role socializations which occur in a society "on top of" the general political socialization. They include orientation to the special role and the political system of which it is a part, and to political inputs and outputs.

Styles of political recruitment may be compared according to the way in which ascriptive and particularistic criteria combine with performance and universalistic criteria. Thus, in a modern Western political system, recruitment is affected both by ascriptive and by performance criteria. Kinship, friendship, "school ties," religious affiliation, and status qualities affect recruitment in various important ways, but the more thorough-going the political modernization, the more these ascriptive criteria are contained within or limited by achievement criteria—educational levels, performance levels on examinations, formal records of achievement in political roles, and the like. But the recruitment pattern is both structurally and culturally dualistic. Similarly, in the primitive or traditional political system the recruitment function is dualistic, but the achievement or performance criterion is less explicitly and generally applied. A chief or headman is selected because of his place in a lineage. He may be removed for poor performance according to either sacred or secular norms. He is replaced again by ascriptive criteria.

Similarly, particularistic and universalistic criteria are combined differently in the performance of the recruitment function in modern and traditional systems. While, in a formal sense, in modern systems political recruitment is open to all members of the society fulfilling certain general requirements, particularistic structures such as family, friendship, religion, status, and informal groupings in the specifically political and governmental structures enter into the recruitment function throughout the political system. In traditional systems, while particularistic criteria are relatively more important in the performance of the recruitment function, general criteria enter in as well, as in the allocation of members of the society to social and political roles according to age and sex.

Interest Articulation ✓

Every political system has some way of articulating interests, claims, demands for political action. The function of interest articulation, as we have already pointed out, is closely related to the political socialization function and the patterns of political culture produced by it. Among the input functions, interest articulation is of crucial importance since it occurs at the boundary of the political system. The particular structures which perform the articulation function and the style of their performance determine the character of the boundary between polity and society.

In characterizing the interest articulation function in a political system and in comparing it with that of other political systems, we have to discover first what kinds of structures perform the function and, second, the style of their performance. Four main types of structures may be involved in interest articulation: (1) institutional interest groups, (2) non-associational interest groups, (3) anomic interest groups, and (4) associational interest groups.

By institutional interest groups we have in mind phenomena occurring within such organizations as legislatures, political executives, armies, bureaucracies, churches, and the like. These are organizations which perform other social or political functions but which, as corporate bodies or through groups within them (such as legislative blocs, officer cliques, higher or lower clergy or religious orders, departments, skill groups, and ideological cliques in bureaucracies), may articulate their own interests or represent the interests of groups in the society.

By non-associational interests we have in mind kinship and lineage groups, ethnic, regional, religious, status and class groups which articulate interests informally, and intermittently, through individuals, cliques, family and religious heads, and the like. Examples might be the complaint of a tribal chief to a paramount chief about tributes or law enforcement affecting his lineage group; a request made by a landowner to a bureaucrat in a social club regarding the tariff on grains; or the complaint of an informal delegation from a linguistic group regarding language instruction in the schools.

The distinguishing characteristic of the institutional interest group is the fact that a formally organized body made up of professionally employed officials or employees, with another function, performs an interest articulation function, or constitutes a base of operations for a clique or subgroup which does. The distinguishing characteristic of the non-associational interest is that the structure of interest articulation is intermittent and often informal.

By anomic interest groups we mean more or less spontaneous breakthroughs into the political system from the society, such as riots and demonstrations. Their distinguishing characteristic is their relative structural and functional ability. We use the term "relative" advisedly, since riots and demonstrations may be deliberately organized and controlled. But even when organized and controlled they have the potentiality of exceeding limits and norms and disturbing or even changing the political system. Though they may begin as interest articulation structures, they may end up performing a recruitment function (i.e., transferring power from one group to another), a rule-making function (i.e., changing the constitution, enacting, revising, or rescinding statutes), a rule application function (i.e., freeing prisoners, rescinding a bureaucratic decision), a rule adjudication function (i.e., "trying" and lynching), an aggregative or a communication function (drawing other interest groups to it, or publicizing a protest).

Associational interest groups are the specialized structures of interest articulation—trade unions, organizations of businessmen or industrialists, ethnic associations, associations organized by religious denominations, civic groups, and the like. Their particular characteristics are explicit representation of the interests of a particular group, orderly procedures for the formulation of interests and demands, and transmission of these demands to other political structures such as political parties, legislatures, bureaucracies.

The performance of the interest articulation function may be manifest or latent, specific or diffuse, general or particular, instrumental or affective in style. A manifest interest articulation is an explicit formulation of a claim or a demand. It is latent when it takes the form of behavioral or mood cues which may be read and transmitted into the political system. The demand or claim may be specific or diffuse. It is specific when it takes the form of a request for a particular piece of legislation or a subsidy; it is diffuse when it takes the form of a general statement of dissatisfaction or preference (i.e., "We need a change," "The political system is rotten," "We need socialism," and the like). Demands and claims may be general or particular. They are general when they are couched in class or professional group terms (i.e., "The rich ought to be taxed more," "The big estates should be divided"), particular, when they are couched in individual or family terms (i.e., "I'll give you my vote or something of value if you lower my taxes"). Finally, the articulation of interest may be instrumental or affectively neutral or affective. It is instrumental when it takes the form of a bargain with consequences realistically spelled out (i.e., "If you don't vote for this law, we'll campaign against you in the next election"); it is affective when it takes the form of a simple expression of gratitude, anger, disappointment, and the like.

The structure and style of interest articulation define the pattern of boundary maintenance between the polity and the society, and within the political system affect the boundaries between the various parts of the political system—parties, legislatures, bureaucracies, and courts. For example, a high incidence of anomic interest articulation will mean poor boundary maintenance between the society and the polity, frequent eruptions of unprocessed claims without controlled direction into the political system. It will affect boundary maintenance within the political system by performing aggregative, rule-making, rule application, and rule adjudication functions outside of appropriate channels and without benefit of appropriate process.

A high incidence of institutional interest articulation is also an indication of poor boundary maintenance between the polity and the society and within the political system. Thus the direct impingement of a church (or parts of a church) or of business corporations on the political system introduces raw or diffuse claims and demands difficult to process or aggregate with other inputs into the political system. Within the political system a high incidence of interest articulation by bureaucratic or military groups creates boundary difficulties among rule application, rule-making, articulative, and aggregative structures, and may indeed result in their atrophy. A high incidence of non-associational interest articulation—in other words, the performance of the interest articulation function intermittently by individuals, informal groups, or representatives of kinship or status groups, and so forth—similarly may represent poor boundary maintenance between the polity and the society. We have in mind here modern or transitional political systems, and not simple, primitive ones where this form of interest articulation is appropriate. Finally, a high incidence of associational interest articulation may indicate good boundary maintenance between society and polity and may contribute to such maintenance within the subsystems of the political system. Good boundary maintenance is attained by virtue of the regulatory role of associational interest groups in processing raw claims or interest articulations occurring elsewhere in the society and the political system, and directing them in an orderly way and in aggregable form through the party system, legislature, and bureaucracy.

With regard to the style of interest articulation, the more latent, diffuse, particularistic, and affective the pattern of interest articulation, the more difficult it is to aggregate interests and translate them into public policy. Hence a political system characterized by these patterns of interest articulation will have poor circulation between the rest of the society and the political system, unless the society is quite small and has good cue-reading authorities. On the other hand, the more manifest, specific, general, and instrumental the style of interest articulation, the easier it is to maintain the boundary between the polity and society, and the better the circulation of needs, claims, and demands from the society in aggregable form into the political system. A political system with an interest articulation structure and style of this kind can be large and complex and still efficiently process raw demand inputs from the society into outputs responsive to the claims and demands of that society.

It may be useful for illustrative purposes to describe the interest articulation function in a number of types of political systems. In the British political system we begin with a homogeneous, fusional (i.e., mixed secular and traditional) political culture. As a consequence, the members of the society and the political elites are homogeneously oriented toward the polity, and the orientation combines "civility" (from the secular component) and deference (from the traditional component). Though institutional, non-associational, and even (on rare occasion) anomic interest groups are present,[32] there is a thoroughly elaborated system of associational interest groups which regulates the impact of the other interest structures, and mitigates their particularistic, diffuse, ascriptive, and affective impacts, translates these into explicit, general, and bargaining demands for public policies, and works out strategies of influence and access.

In the British political system, ". . . the functions of interest groups and political parties are sharply differentiated. Interest groups articulate political demands in the society, seek support for these demands among other groups by advocacy and bargaining, and attempt to transform these demands into authoritative public policy by influencing the choice

---

[32] Even anomic interest articulation tends to be domesticated in the British political system. Hence "Hyde Park" and the exaggerated concern that the most extreme and unpopular of claims and ideas have a protected opportunity and place for expression.

of political personnel, and the various processes of public policy-making and enforcement. Political parties tend to be free of ideological rigidity, and are aggregative, i.e., seek to form the largest possible interest group coalitions by offering acceptable choices of political personnel and public policy. Both the interest group systems and the party systems are differentiated, bureaucratized, and autonomous. Each unit in the party and interest group systems comes into the 'market,' so to speak, with an adjustive bargaining ethos. Furthermore, the party system stands between the interest group system and the authoritative policy-making agencies and screens them from the particularistic and disintegrative impact of special interests. The party system aggregates interests and transforms them into a relatively small number of alternative general policies. Thus this set of relationships between the party system and the interest group system enables choice among general policies to take place in the cabinet and parliament, and assures that the bureaucracy will tend to function as a neutral instrument of the political agencies."[33] Thus in the British political system a differentiated, secular system of associational interest groups contributes to effective boundary maintenance between the society and the polity, and among the subsystems of the polity.

We may take a second illustration of the performance of the interest articulation function from the French political systems of the Third and Fourth Republics. First, the French political culture is not a homogeneous, fusional culture. Traditional and rational components are distributed in different proportions in the society. The rational part of the culture takes the form of an absolute-value rationality rather than a bargaining, instrumental rationality. Its rationality tends to be apocalyptic rather than civic or pragmatic; and this has been as true of French Catholic intellectuals as it has been true of French Radicals, Socialists, and Communists.

While associational interest groups exist in large numbers and with large memberships in France, institutional and anomic interest groups are of far greater importance than in England. In fact, the significance of institutional and anomic interest groups is directly related to the uneven effectiveness of associational interest groups, the absence of an effectively aggregative party system, and its fragmented or isolative political culture. Parties and interest groups in France do not constitute

[33] Gabriel A. Almond, Rapporteur, "A Comparative Study of Interest Groups and the Political Process," *American Political Science Review*, Vol. LII, No. 1, March 1958, p. 275.

differentiated, autonomous political subsystems. They interpenetrate one another. There are some parties which more or less control interest groups (e.g., the Communist Party and the Communist-dominated trade unions, and to a lesser extent the Socialist Party and the Socialist trade unions). The most powerful institutional interest group, the Catholic Church, controls other interest groups (e.g., the CFTC) and strongly influences political parties (e.g., the MRP).

"When parties control interest groups they may, and in France do, inhibit the capacity of interest groups to formulate pragmatic specific demands; they impart a political-ideological content to interest group activity. When interest groups control parties they inhibit the capacity of the party to combine specific interests into programs with wider appeal. What reaches the legislative process from the interest groups and through the political parties thus are the 'raw,' unaggregated demands of specific interests, or the diffuse, uncompromising, or revolutionary and reactionary tendencies of the Church and the movements of the right or left. Since no interest group is large enough to have a majority, and the party system cannot aggregate different interests into a stable majority and a coherent opposition, the electoral and legislative processes fail to provide alternative, effective choices. The result is a legislature penetrated by relatively narrow interests and uncompromising ideological tendencies, a legislature which can be used as an arena for propaganda, or for the protection of special interests, by veto or otherwise, but not for the effective and timely formulation and support of large policy decisions. And without a strong legislature, special interests and ideological tendencies penetrate the bureaucracy, and undermine its neutral, instrumental character."[34]

Thus the absence in France of an autonomous, secular interest group system is one of the factors contributing to poor boundary maintenance between the society and the political system, and among the various parts of the political system. The high incidence of anomic interest articulation (*"Poujadism"*) reflects the incapacity of the associational interest groups to receive demands from the society, assimilate them and transform them into aggregable claims, and transmit them to the party system, legislature, cabinet, and bureaucracy from which they may emerge as impacts upon public policy and regulation.

The Function of Aggregation

Every political system has some way of aggregating the interests, claims, and demands which have been articulated by the interest groups

[34] *Ibid.*, p. 276.

of the polity. Aggregation may be accomplished by means of the formulation of general policies in which interests are combined, accommodated, or otherwise taken account of, or by means of the recruitment of political personnel, more or less committed to a particular pattern of policy. The functions of articulation and aggregation overlap, just as do those of aggregation, recruitment, and rule-making. In certain political systems, such as the authoritarian and the primitive ones, the three functions of articulation, aggregation, and rule-making may be hardly differentiated from one another. In what appears to be a single act, a headman of a primitive society may read cues in his people, aggregate different cues and complaints, and issue an authoritative rule. We might say that he is intermittently interest articulator, aggregator, and rule-maker in the course of this process. In other systems, such as the modern Western ones, there are partitions in the process and separate structures or subsystems with boundaries take a distinctive part. Certainly, in the Anglo-American mass democracies this threefold division in function maintains the flow from society to polity and from polity to society (from input to output to input again) in an especially efficient manner. Thus, to attain a maximum flow of inputs of raw claims from the society, a low level of processing into a common language of claims is required which is performed by associational interest groups. To assimilate and transform these interests into a relatively small number of alternatives of policy and personnel, a middle range of processing is necessary. If these two functions are performed in substantial part before the authoritative governmental structures are reached, then the output functions of rule-making and rule application are facilitated, and the political and governmental processes become calculable and responsible. The outputs may be related to and controlled by the inputs, and thus circulation becomes relatively free by virtue of good boundary maintenance or division of labor.

The distinction between interest articulation and aggregation is a fluid one. The narrowest event of interest articulation initiated by a lineage head in a primitive political system, or the smallest constituent unit of a trade association, involves the aggregation of the claims of even smaller groups or of individuals or firms. Modern interest groups—particularly the "peak" associations—carry aggregation quite far, sometimes to the point of "speaking for" whole classes of the society—"labor," "agriculture," "business."

In our definition we reserve the term "aggregation" for the more inclusive levels of the combinatory processes, reserving the term "articulation" for the narrower expressions of interest. This is not the same thing as identifying interest articulation with "pressure groups" and aggregation with "political parties," though again in the developed modern systems these agencies have a distinctive and regulatory relation to these functions.

Actually the aggregative function may be performed within all of the subsystems of the political system—legislative bodies, political executives (cabinets, presidencies, kingships, chieftainships), bureaucracies, media of communication, party systems, interest groups of the various types. Parties, factions, blocs in legislatures; cliques or factions in political executives and bureaucracies; individual parties or party coalitions outside the legislature; and individual interest groups (in particular the civic or "general interest" groups) or *ad hoc* coalitions of interest groups —all perform an aggregative function, either by formulating alternative public policies or by supporting or advocating changes in political personnel.

But again it is the party system which is the distinctively modern structure of political aggregation and which in the modern, developed, democratic political system "regulates" or gives order to the performance of the aggregative function by the other structures. Without a party system the aggregative function may be performed covertly, diffusely, and particularistically, as in a political system such as Spain. Spain has associational, institutional, and non-associational interest groups, but aggregation occurs under the surface by cliques in the Falangist Party, the bureaucracy, army, or in the staff of the Caudillo. The relationship between interest articulation and aggregation is obscure and partly latent, the result of "deals," the reading of cues from unarticulated interests, and the like.

In the five area analyses which make up this book, party systems are classified under four headings (1) authoritarian, (2) dominant non-authoritarian, (3) competitive two-party systems, and (4) competitive multiparty systems. Authoritarian party systems may in turn be classified into the totalitarian and authoritarian varieties. Totalitarian parties aggregate interests by means of the penetration of the social structure of the society and by the transmission and aggregation of demands and claims through the party structure. Overt interest articulation is permissible only at the lowest level of individual complaints against the lower-echelon authorities. Above this level, interest articulation and aggregation are latent or covert. The democratic critique of totalitarianism as a political system lacking in any interest articulation and aggregation is not correct. We know of the existence of interest groups ("families," bureaucratic cliques advocating policies and allocations) and of factions in the party which aggregate interests into alternative policies or advocate political personnel changes. What is true of totalitarian systems is that they are characterized by a high rate of coercive social mobilization. The output of authoritative policy is not paralleled by, but only somewhat mitigated by, the input of demands and alternative policies. Nevertheless there is an upward flow of significance and, while difficult to characterize, it is essential that we be aware of it if we are to avoid misleading polarizations.

Authoritarian parties such as the Republican People's Party after the Turkish revolution have some of the properties of totalitarian parties, except that the penetration of the party into the social structure is less complete and some interest groups are permitted to articulate demands overtly. Hence there is more of an upward flow of claims and demands, more of an overt performance of the input functions. The absence of a free party system and an open electoral process usually reduces the aggregative function to the formulation of policy alternatives within the authoritarian party and authoritative governmental structures such as the bureaucracy and army. Where a religious group is powerful, as in Catholic Spain, the Church may perform an aggregative function as well as an interest articulation function.

Dominant non-authoritarian party systems are usually to be found in political systems where nationalist movements have been instrumental in attaining emancipation. Most of the significant interest groups, associational and non-associational, have joined in the nationalist movement around a common program of national independence. In the period following emancipation the nationalist party continues as the greatly dominant party, opposed in elections by relatively small left-wing or traditionalist and particularist movements. This type of party system is a formally free one, but the possibility of a coherent loyal opposition is lacking. Hence the dominant party is confronted by a complex problem of interest aggregation. Since highly dissimilar groups (traditionalist, secularist, socialist, conservative, and so forth) are included in the nationalist movement, it is difficult to adopt a policy which aggregates their interests effectively. The cohesion of the party is difficult to maintain. In order to avoid divisive issues, decisions are postponed, and policy proposals take the form of diffuse programs selected more for their unifying symbolism than for their effective coping with demands emanating from the society or the various political elites. Thus circulation and boundary maintenance are poor in these party systems. Much will depend on the purposes of the political elites of these parties. They may have the goal of political modernization and seek to introduce functionally specific associational interest groups and a loyal, coherent opposition party, and to perform the political socialization function in such a way as to modernize the political culture. Where they do this, we call these systems "tutelary democracies." Where they fail to do so, a dominant non-authoritarian party may turn into an authoritarian party and transform the system into an oligarchy either of a modernizing type (e.g., Turkey between the wars) or of a conservative type (e.g., Poland between the wars).

The third type of party system is the competitive two-party system exemplified by the United Kingdom, the members of the old Commonwealth, and the United States. Here a homogeneous, secular, bargaining political culture and an effective and autonomous system of associational interest groups introduce claims into the party system, legislature, political executive, and bureaucracy which are combinable into responsive, alternative public policies. Boundary maintenance between society and polity and among the articulative, aggregative, and rule-making structures is good. The whole process tends to be overt and calculable and results in an open circulatory flow of inputs and outputs.

Multiparty systems may be divided into two classes—the so-called "working" multiparty systems of the Scandinavian area and the Low Countries, and the "immobilist" multiparty systems of France and Italy. In the Scandinavian version of the multiparty system, some of the parties are broadly aggregative (e.g., the Scandinavian Socialist parties, the Belgian Socialist and Catholic parties). Secondly, the political culture is more homogeneous and fusional of secular and traditional elements. Hence the relations between parties and interests are more consensual, which makes stable majority and opposition coalitions possible. "Thus though the party systems fail to aggregate interests as thoroughly as in the British case, the public policy-making function of the legislature is not undermined to the same extent as in the French and Italian cases. What appears to happen in the Scandinavian and the Low Countries is that the function of interest aggregation and general policy formulation occurs at both the party and parliamentary levels. The parties are partly aggregative of interests, but 'majority-minority' aggregation takes place finally in the coalition-making process in the legislature. This coalition-making process may be organized by parties in the formation of cabinets and the enactment of legislation or it may take the form of interest coalitions organized around issues of public policy. The capacity for stable majority-minority party coalitions and for relatively flexible issue-oriented interest coalitions is dependent upon the existence of a basic political consensus which affects both parties and interest groups. These appear to be the properties of the so-called 'working multi-party systems.' "[35]

The characteristics of the "immobilist" type of multiparty system have been referred to in the discussion of the articulation function above. In comparison to the working multiparty system, with its relatively homogeneous political culture, the political socialization processes in countries such as France and Italy tend to produce a fragmented, isolative political culture, and as a consequence the relations between interest groups and parties are not of an instrumental bargaining kind. The boundaries between the articulative and aggregative functions are poorly maintained. The aggregation performed by the parties is relatively narrow, and coalitions are fragile because of the cultural differences between political movements. The poor circulation of inputs from the society into the polity, and the difficulty of combining different inputs into outputs of rules and rule applications produces an alienation between the society and the polity which is general throughout the society, but is usually marked among particular groups (e.g., workers, obsolescent economic groups, and so forth).

We may also compare the performance of the aggregative function in different political systems in terms of its style. We may distinguish three different kinds of parties from this point of view: (1) secular, "pragmatic," bargaining parties; (2) absolute value-oriented, *Weltanschauung* or ideological parties; and (3) particularistic or traditional parties. The secular, pragmatic, bargaining type of party is instrumental and multivalue-oriented and its aggregative potential is relatively high. It is capable of generalized and adaptive programs intended to attract the maximum of interest support. Parties such as this may be broad- or narrow-based. Thus, in some Latin American countries, parties may emerge only at election time as the small following of a single politician or group of politicians. Without penetrating the countryside, they may bargain for the support of interest groups and then go out of business between elections. Or, a pragmatic party may develop its own structure in the countryside and be in a position to mobilize voters directly through its own organization. Naturally such a party can aggregate

[35] Almond, "Comparative Interest Groups," *op.cit.*, pp. 276-277. See Dankwart Rustow, "Scandinavia: Working Multiparty Systems," in Sigmund Neumann, ed., *Modern Political Parties*, Chicago, 1956, pp. 169ff.

more effectively, since it is not as thoroughly dependent on interest groups as a narrow-based *ad hoc* party.

The *Weltanschauung* or ideological party is absolute value-oriented and is usually revolutionary, reactionary, or oriented toward national independence or power. The Fascist and Nazi versions of this type of party combined all three ideological elements. In their earlier manifestations ideological parties have an appeal among alienates or cultural deviants in the society, usually consisting of small coteries of intellectuals and agitators. In other words, they are narrow-based. In their full-blown version they become the "parties of total integration" of Sigmund Neumann.[36] In this form they penetrate deeply into the society, almost replace all other social structures and, once securely rooted, are most difficult to dislodge by means short of violence.

The "particularistic" party is limited in its aggregative potential by being identified completely with the interests of a particular ethnic or religious group. Just as the totalitarian version of the ideological party is an integrator and general social mobilizer rather than an aggregator, the particularistic party is more of an interest articulator than an aggregator. In this sense, functionally it is like the interest group of the West, differing primarily in the fact that it presents candidates in elections as well as advocating policies. Development toward a modern political system will reduce the particularistic party to an associational interest group, properly speaking.

The mode of performance of the aggregative function is crucial to the performance of the political system as a whole. Thus the aggregative function in the British political system is distinctively performed by the party system. Interest aggregations occurring in the bureaucracy are controlled and to some extent assimilated into the aggregative processes of the party system. The parties are broad-based and hence can maintain their boundaries distinct from interest groups. Because of this autonomy and their secular bargaining culture, they can effectively aggregate these interests into general policy alternatives. The consequences of these structural and cultural patterns for the performance of the aggregative function in the British political system are the following. A high degree of interest aggregation occurs in the British system. This aggregation occurs in large part prior to the performance of the authoritative governmental functions and hence renders responsibility for outputs unambiguously clear. The pragmatic-instrumental quality of the aggregative process regulates the impact of latent, diffuse, particularistic, and affective

---

[36] Neumann, *op.cit.*, p. 405.

components in the political system. It contributes to a relatively high mobility in the aggregative process, i.e., a relatively free movement of interest groups among political parties.

In a transitional country such as India there is a relatively low degree of interest aggregation through the party system as such. The boundaries between party, legislature, and bureaucracy are poorly maintained by virtue of the fact that much of the aggregative function is performed within the bureaucracy in a process which does not separate aggregation, rule-making, and rule application. In the party system the aggregative function is performed in some measure particularistically, diffusely, symbolically, and ideologically, rather than pragmatically. Hence circulation from social needs and demands to articulation, to aggregation, to rule-making, to rule application, and back to society is not a fully open, responsive, and responsible process. The particularisms and ideological tendencies in the party and interest group systems ("communal" movements, linguistic-ethnic interests, traditional groups, sectarian socialist movements) produce relatively low mobility of interest groups in the party system, and a relatively low potential for stable coalitions among political parties.

The Political Communication Function

All of the functions performed in the political system—political socialization and recruitment, interest articulation, interest aggregation, rule-making, rule application, and rule adjudication—are performed *by means of* communication. Parents, teachers, and priests, for example, impart political socialization through communication. Interest group leaders and representatives and party leaders perform their articulation and aggregation functions by communicating demands and policy recommendations. Legislators enact laws on the basis of information communicated to them and by communicating with one another and with other elements of the political system. In performing their functions, bureaucrats receive and analyze information from the society and from various parts of the polity. Similarly, the judicial process is carried on by means of communication.

At first thought, it might appear that there is no political communication function as such, that communication is an aspect of all of the other political functions. But a view such as this comes into conflict with the fact that in the modern political system differentiated media of communication have arisen which have developed a vocational ethics of "neutral" or objective communication. This ethics requires that the dissemination of information ought to be separated from the other political functions such as interest articulation, aggregation, and recruitment.

The separating-out of the communication function is not unique to modern political systems. The Greek Pantheon had a specialized communicator in Mercury; the Old Testament had its dusty messengers, usually carriers of tragic news, who frequently failed to survive the act of communication. Primitive political systems have their drummers and runners, medieval towns had their criers, noblemen and kings their heralds. Even when there is no specialized political communicator, we can distinguish in the combined performance of, for example, the interest articulation and communication function the articulative event from the event of communicating the act of articulation. Thus a labor news medium may both advocate a trade union policy and communicate the content of that policy.

Failure to separate out the political communication function from the other political functions would deprive us of an essential tool necessary for distinguishing among political systems and characterizing their performance. It is not accidental that those political systems which have homogeneous political cultures and autonomous and differentiated structures of interest articulation and aggregation—the United Kingdom, the old Commonwealth, and the United States—also have to the greatest extent autonomous and differentiated media of communication. Nor is it accidental that the political systems with fragmented political cultures and relatively undifferentiated structures of interest articulation and aggregation—France and Italy, for example—also have a "press" which tends to be dominated by interest groups and political parties. The whole pattern of function in these political systems is affected by and tends to sustain a fragmented political culture. The control over the media of communication by parties and interest groups means that the audience for political communications is fragmented.

Thus it is essential in characterizing a political system to analyze the performance of the communication function. Just because of the fact that all the political functions are performed by means of communications, political communication is the crucial boundary-maintenance function. When there is an autonomous system of communication, covert communications in the bureaucracy, the interest groups, and political parties may to some extent be regulated and controlled by publicity. Similarly latent interests in the society may be made explicit through neutral media of communication. Autonomy in the media of communication makes possible a free flow of information from the society to the polity and, in the polity, from political structure to political structure. It also makes possible an open feedback from output to input again. One may liken the communication function to the circulation of the blood. It is not the blood but what it contains that nourishes the system. The blood is the neutral medium carrying claims, protests, and demands through the veins to the heart; and from the heart through the arteries flow the outputs of rules, regulations, and adjudications in response to the claims and demands.

The general specialization of political structure in modern political systems, the autonomy and regulatory role of the individual structures with respect to individual functions, rests on a neutral system of communications. While associational interest groups in the modern democratic political system perform a regulatory role both in the polity and in the society with reference to the articulation function, the communication function in turn regulates the interest articulation function. Thus it facilitates the articulation of latent interest independently of the associational interest groups, and communicates the articulations of interest emanating from political parties, legislatures, and bureaucracies, which can thereby correct actions of the associational interest groups. Similarly it limits the regulatory power of the political parties in the performance of the aggregative function; that of the legislature and political executive with respect to the rule-making function; that of the bureaucracy with respect to the rule application function. An autonomous communication system "regulates the regulators" and thereby preserves the autonomies and freedoms of the democratic polity.

One might even argue that the crucial control in the totalitarian political system is not coercion—although it is essential—but the monopoly of the media of communication. By means of it coercion may be limited to occasional events of anomic interest articulation or incidental to acts of mobilization. Totalitarian communication directs the inflow of information to a single political structure, and limits the outflow of communication to the purposes of the Communist elite. Thus only that elite has the necessary information on the basis of which it can calculate, devise strategies, control and eliminate anomic potentialities. The dependence, the instrumental character of other political structures are maintained by controlling the information available to them. Only the bureaucratic apparatus of the Communist Party at the very top level has a complete switchboard. All other structures plug in only to the central, where their communications can be received, monitored, and relayed at the discretion of the central. Effective political action must be based on rational calculation, which in turn requires information. A democratic system provides for a relatively free, multidirectional flow of information, thus making it possible for all the structures to calculate and to act effectively.

In particular, an autonomous, neutral, and thoroughly penetrative system of communication is essential to the development and maintenance of an active and effective electorate and citizenship. The effective performance of the recruitment function by an electorate (i.e., choosing candidates in relation to needs and demands) is dependent on an open and multidirectional flow of communications reporting on the performance of the other functions by the incumbents of the authoritative offices to the mass of citizens. There is still another aspect of the communication function in a democratic polity which calls for comment. The availability of neutral information about the functioning of the political system tends to create an informed stratum of citizens— public policy-oriented, rather than interest-oriented in the narrow sense —a stratum which sustains the regulatory role of the media of communication in the polity. For the existence of an "attentive" informed audience is not only sustained by an adequate system of communication; it in turn provides an audience or market for high-quality political information. In other words, it creates and sustains a sector in the communication elite which carries on an analytical, open, and informed discussion of public policy issues within the polity as a whole, more or less independently of interest groups, parties, legislators, executives, and bureaucrats. In addition, this attentive stratum constitutes a special political subculture in which special kinds of interest groups thrive— interest groups concerned with general policy problems rather than with special interests.

The performance of the communication function in different political systems may be compared according to the structures performing it and the style of its performance. We have already pointed out that all of the political structures—governmental agencies, parties, interest groups, media of communication—and all of the social structures— families, kinship and lineage groups, face-to-face groups, neighborhoods, communities, villages, caste, status and class groups, ethnic and linguistic groups—may be involved in the performance of the communication function. What distinguishes a modern political system from a traditional or primitive one is the fact that in the modern system the specialized communication structure is more elaborate, and that it penetrates the unspecialized or intermittent structures of political communication. Thus Katz's point referred to above as the "two-step flow of communication" is a demonstration of the penetration of the informal and intermittent structures of political communication by the specialized mass media. Traditional or primitive political communication is performed intermittently by kinship, lineage, status, and village groups. Specialized media of communication are present only to a limited degree, if they are present at all.

Political systems may also be compared according to the ways in which they combine communication styles. Styles of political communication may be distinguished according to whether they are manifest or latent, specific or diffuse, particularistic or "generalistic," affectively neutral or affective. A manifest political communication is an explicit message; a latent one is a mood readable only from behavioral or expressive cues. A specific message is a statement of a political event or potential event which separates the political from the non-political and involves explicit cognitive discrimination. A specific political event is reported as having occurred, as occurring, or as likely to occur, with the estimate of probability, and sometimes with the consequences, spelled out. A particularistic message is one which by virtue of its language, or of its esoteric properties, cannot be easily transmitted throughout the polity as a whole. It requires political interpreters if it is to be transmitted at all beyond the limits of the esoteric audience. A general or universal message is one that is so couched as to be more or less transmissible throughout the entire communication network of the polity. An affectively neutral communication is an objective report of an event or events which may be combined with other reports and other data and be the ready object of analysis and inference. An affective communication creates difficulties in analysis and inference. It cannot be as readily appraised or weighed, and fed into the stream of political inputs and outputs.

But here, as in the treatment of the other functions, we have to avoid polarizations. The political communication networks of modern political systems are full of latent, diffuse, particularistic, and affective messages. But with the existence of autonomous and specialized media of communication, associational interest groups, and aggregative parties these traditional messages tend to get translated into modern ones. Furthermore, in this process of translation the messages tend to get placed in envelopes with the correct political addresses.

In order to illustrate this mode of analysis of the political communication function, it may be useful to compare its performance in a modern Western system such as the United States with its performance in a transitional political system such as India. The comparison may be made in four respects: (1) the homogeneity of political information; (2) the mobility of information; (3) the volume of information; (4) the direction of the flow of information.

With respect to the homogeneity of political information, the point has already been made that the existence of autonomous and specialized media of communication and their penetration of the polity as a whole in modern Western political systems do not eliminate latent, diffuse, particularistic, and affective messages but only tend to afford opportunities throughout the political system for such messages to be couched in a manifest, specific, general, and instrumental language of politics. There is, in other words, a system whereby these messages are made manifest and homogeneous. If what has been written about the opinion leader in the United States is correct, a modern political system does not eliminate esoteric communication; it works through a system of widely distributed interpreters which tend to penetrate these primary communication cells and connect them with the secondary media of communication. In contrast, in a transitional political system the messages in the communication network are heterogeneous. In the urban, relatively modern areas, specialized media of communication are to be found, but they tend to be organs of interest groups or political parties. Even in the cities, among the illiterate and uneducated elements of the urban population, the impact of the specialized media of communication is relatively limited. The illiterate and certainly the newly urbanized elements of the population tend to persist in a traditional, rural-type network of communication, with kinship, lineage, caste, and language groupings performing the political communication function intermittently, diffusely, and particularistically.

Although here too there are interpreters standing between the modernized and the non-modernized sectors of the urban populations, the problem of interpretation is much more difficult than in the modern Western system. The opinion leader in the United States receives information from the mass media and interprets it for his "opinion followers." These opinion followers tend to speak the same language, share the same values, and have cognitive maps similar to the ones conveyed in the mass media. The politician or interest group leader in an Indian urban area faces a far greater gap between the communication content of the literate modern sector of the Indian city and the illiterate and traditional sector. The gap is one of culture; it may include language in the specific sense, values, and cognitive maps differing radically in amount and specificity of information and in the range of political objects which they include. What has been said of the communication gap in the urban areas of a country like India is true to an even greater extent of connections between the urban and rural and village areas. Here, the problem of interpretation is a massive one. The interpreter, whether he be a bureaucrat, interest group leader, or party leader, cannot readily find equivalents in language, values, and cognitive material to make an accurate translation. There is a genuine block in communication between the urban central and the rural and village periphery. No real penetration by communication is possible, and the audience of the polity consists of a loosely articulated congeries of subaudiences.

This takes us to the second major point of contrast between a modern Western and a transitional system of political communication—the mobility of information. In a modern Western system, neutral information flows freely throughout the polity, from the initiators of information into the neutral secondary media of communication, and into the capillaries of primary communication. In a transitional system, information circulates relatively freely in the urban areas, but never penetrates fully the diffuse and undifferentiated networks of the traditional and rural areas. Obstacles to mobility exist in both the input and the output process.

Third, in the modern Western system, the volume of political information passing through the communication network is far greater than in a transitional system. A differentiated and autonomous system of communication creates information, by bringing covert communication into "the open," by making latent information manifest. Its very mobility creates animated discussion and controversy among the various political role incumbents. Thus a large volume of information is pumped rapidly throughout the polity. The assimilation of information is rapid, and calculations may be made relatively quickly and accurately. The volume of flow in a transitional system is uneven. Much information remains covert and latent, and it is consequently difficult to make political estimates accurately and quickly.

Finally, there are important differences in the direction of the flow of information. The output of messages from the authoritative governmental structures in a transitional system tends to be far larger than the input of messages from the society. The government employs the mass media and operates through its own media as well. To be sure, governmental messages cannot be accurately transmitted to "tribesmen," "kinsmen," and "villagers." They may hear the messages over the radio, but they cannot register their meaning precisely. Nevertheless the messages get there physically. On the input side, much important information regarding the needs of the base and periphery of the society never gets explicated, and cannot therefore be fully taken account of by other elements in the political system.

This brief comparison of the communication function in a modern and a transitional political system is sufficient to suggest how important the communication function is in the operations and cohesion of political systems. An examination of other systems, such as the varieties of traditional ones, and the various forms of authoritarianism and totalitarianism in terms of the communication function, would be useful not only in gaining a more precise understanding of their functioning but in developing a more adequate theory of political communication.

The Governmental Functions: Rule-Making, Rule Application, Rule Adjudication

In the individual area analyses which follow, far greater stress has been placed on the political functions than on the governmental. The primary reasons for this are the indeterminacy of the formal governmental structures in most of the non-Western areas, and the gross deviations in the performance of the governmental functions from the constitutional and legal norms. Most of these political systems either have had, have now, or aspire to constitutions which provide for legislatures, executives, and judiciaries. In the distribution of legal powers they follow either the British, the American, or the French model. But it is the exceptional case in which these institutions perform in any way corresponding to these norms. A careful examination of governmental structures and their formal powers would have yielded little of predictive value.

On the other hand, a careful examination of the political culture of these political systems, the factors making for change, the political socialization processes, patterns of recruitment into politics, and the characteristics of the infrastructure—interest groups, political parties, and media of communication—yield some insight into the directions and tempo of political change. Hence our emphasis on political structure and function both in the theoretical discussion and in the area analyses.

In a recent paper Shils[37] classifies the "new states" of the non-Western world into five groups: (1) political democracies, (2) "tutelary" democracies, (3) modernizing oligarchies, (4) totalitarian oligarchies, and (5) traditional oligarchies. Although these are classes of *political systems*, they each imply a particular state of governmental structure.

The political democracies are those systems with functioning and relatively autonomous legislatures, executives, courts, and with differentiated and autonomous interest groups, political parties, and media of communication. In the non-Western areas, Japan, Turkey, Israel, and Chile are examples which approximate this type.

Tutelary democracies are political systems which have adopted both the formal norms of the democratic polity—universal suffrage, freedom of association, and of speech and publication—and the structural forms of democracy. In addition, the elites of these systems have the goal of democratizing their polities even though they may be unclear as to the requirements—in particular, the requirements in political infrastructure and function. In reality, as Shils points out, these systems are characterized by a concentration of power in the executive and the bureaucracy. The legislature tends to be relatively powerless, and the independence of the judiciary has not been fully attained. A country such as Ghana comes close to this model.

Modernizing oligarchies are political systems controlled by bureaucratic and/or army officer cliques in which democratic constitutions have been suspended or in which they do not exist. The goals of the elites may or may not include democratization. The modernizing impulse usually takes the form of a concern for efficiency and rationality, and an effort to eliminate corruption and traditionality. Modernizing oligarchies are usually strongly motivated toward economic development. The governmental structure of modernizing oligarchies concentrates powers in the hands of a clique of military officers or bureaucrats who are usually placed in control of the chief ministries. Turkey under Atatürk and contemporary Pakistan and the Sudan are examples of modernizing oligarchies.

Totalitarian oligarchy such as exists in North Korea and Viet Minh differs from modernizing oligarchy by the degree of penetration of the society by the polity, the degree of concentration of power in the ruling elite, and the tempo of social mobilization. There have been two types

[37] Edward Shils, *"Political Development in the New States"* (mimeographed paper prepared for the Committee on Comparative Politics, Social Science Research Council, 1959).

of totalitarianism—the Bolshevist and the traditionalist, such as Nazi Germany and Fascist Italy. Two criteria distinguish the Bolshevist version from the traditional version. National Socialism and Fascism left some autonomy to other institutions, such as the Church, economic interest groups, and kinship and status groups. In addition, its goals took the form of an extremely militant and charismatic nationalism. The Bolshevist version is more thoroughly penetrative of the society, and its goals are revolutionary and global.

Traditional oligarchy is usually monarchic and dynastic in form, based on custom rather than constitution or statute. The ruling elite and the bureaucracy are recruited on the basis of kinship or status. The central governmental institutions control local kinship, lineage, or territorial units only to a limited extent. The goals of the elite are primarily maintenance goals; the capacity and mechanisms for adaptation and change are present only to a limited extent. Nepal, Saudi Arabia, and Yemen are examples of traditional oligarchy.

Shils distinguishes the traditional regime from the "traditionalistic"[38] or traditional "revival" regime. These are conservative reactions against modernizing tendencies or threats. But because they are reactions against modernizing tendencies or threats which require mobilization and modernization, these traditionalistic systems tend to rationalize the governmental structure and mitigate the autonomies of kinship, status, and local units. In other words, the traditionalistic regime cannot avoid some modernization and consequently tends to overlap with the modernizing oligarchy. It is distinguished from it primarily by its "defensive" and limited modernization.

The most frequent types of political systems to be found in the non-Western areas are tutelary democracies and modernizing and traditionalistic oligarchies. From a functional point of view, the tutelary democracy tends to concentrate—to a far greater extent than is true of developed democracies—the rule-making function and the rule application function in the executive and the bureaucracy. Because of the rudimentary character of the party system, the interest group system, and the modern media of communication, the executive and the bureaucracy are far more dominant in the performance of the political functions than they are in developed democracies. Furthermore, the cultural dualism of the tutelary democracy is either "isolative" or "incorporative," rather than "fusional," in character. Nevertheless the

[38] *Ibid.*, p. 53.

54

elites of the tutelary democracies have in their goal system, more or less clearly spelled out, the functional properties of the modern differentiated, fusional political system, with its autonomies and its boundary maintenance pattern.

The modernizing oligarchies are characterized to an even greater extent by the concentration of functions in a ruling clique and in the bureaucracy, and by the absence of a competitive party system. The activities of associational interest groups, to the extent that they exist, are greatly limited, and the media of communication are controlled. But though the activities of interest groups are limited, there is an overt, pluralistic system of interest articulation in which local communities, informal status and lineage groups, and institutional groups take part. Like the tutelary democracy, the modernizing oligarchy is characterized by an incorporative or isolative dualism. Particularistic, diffuse, and ascriptive groups perform the political functions, along with groups that are characterized by "modern" styles although not necessarily penetrated by them.

The development of modern structure in traditionalistic oligarchies is defensive. Thus only the army, the police, and parts of the civil bureaucracy are rationalized in order to control or prevent modernizing tendencies in the society. Thus, while a modernizing oligarchy may use an authoritarian party as an instrument of mobilization and aggregation, this is less likely in a traditionalistic oligarchy where the aggregative, articulative, and communication functions are usually performed by the bureaucracy and/or the army, as well as by kinship or tribal units, status groups, and local units such as villages.

While there is justification for having underplayed the governmental structures in this study, their neglect in the development of the theory of the functions of the polity represents a serious shortcoming in the present analysis. The threefold classification of governmental or output functions into rule-making, rule application, and rule adjudication will not carry us very far in our efforts at precise comparison of the performance of political systems. The experiments referred to above in the development of more adequate functional categories make this clear. Cohen and Almond in their studies of the American foreign policy-making process[39] found it necessary to break down the rule-making function into three sub-functions—initiation, modification, vetoing. This threefold breakdown resulted empirically from efforts at coding the contents of responses of individuals who regularly participated in

[39] *Supra*, p. 16.

the foreign policy-making process. Lasswell in his work cited above[40] uses five functions to break down the governmental functions. Two of these—prescription and termination—are divisions of the rule-making function; two—invocation and application—are subdivisions of the rule application function; and two—rule application and appraisal—are subdivisions of the rule adjudication function. Neither of these experiments in functional categorization satisfies our need for a set of conceptual tools which can bring out the differences in the performance of governmental functions in different kinds of political systems. Perhaps we shall have to work empirically in a sequence of bilateral comparisons until a more generally useful classification emerges.

In characterizing the governmental functions in a political system, we have to specify the structures performing the functions, the style of their performance, and the way in which the problem of cultural dualism is solved. We have already illustrated this mode of analysis briefly in our functional comparison of tutelary democracies and oligarchies. In the performance of the rule-making function we may have a division among executive, legislature, and courts, as in the United States; or it may take the parliamentary form, with cabinet and parliament being dominant in the performance of the function, and the courts having far less general rule-making importance. Similarly, the division of the rule-making function may be confederal, federal, or unitary. In each case some rule-making is performed by local governmental structures, but the degree of autonomy varies.

A federal system, in the constitutional sense, is different from a traditional system, in which kinship, lineage, ethnic, and local groups may enjoy great autonomy. The traditional system tends to be particularistic, diffuse, and ascriptive. Thus to the extent that the local unit coincides with lineage, or a group of lineages, there is no general citizenship. Similarly, the penetration of the rule-making of the central authorities may be limited to taxation, tribute, the obligation to military service, or an external contact through the local authorities. In all other respects, rule-making in both process and content may be limited to the specific local unit, and may differ substantially from one local unit to the next, particularly if there are significant differences among them in culture and social structure.

A constitutional or legally based federal system is characterized by a penetration of the local political systems by the central one, and by the existence of general rules governing the distribution of powers

[40] *The Decision Process* (see note 11).

among the central and the local units. A legal federal system is more particularistic than a legal unitary one. However, it is a "particularism" within a "universalism"—that is, the powers of the local units are exercised within a framework of general rules distributing powers. Furthermore, the central system works directly in the local units within its competence, and not outside it and through the authorities of the local system.

The particularism of pluralistic traditional systems may involve a particularism to the point of closure. The central authorities may differ in culture and structure from the local ones and they may operate only through the local authorities, with no direct contact with the individuals of the local units. There is an obvious parallelism with confederal systems, but again there are differences which it is not necessary to go into here.

Perhaps the best way to illustrate the functional approach to the comparison of governmental structure is to contrast modern Western democratic systems with transitional non-Western ones from this point of view. On the whole, it would be correct to say that boundary maintenance tends to be good in modern Western democratic systems such as the United States and England and relatively poor in transitional ones. In the United States the Congress and the Presidency in its legislative role tend to regulate the rule-making activities which are delegated to and performed by the bureaucracy. Thus, even though quantitatively many more general rules may be made by the bureaucracy, they are usually made within grants of power from the Congress and the President. The grants of power may be rescinded or modified. In the British cabinet-parliamentary system, the boundaries are drawn differently, but nevertheless there is a similar regulatory control by the cabinet and parliament over the rule-making function performed by the bureaucracy. In both the British and American systems the boundaries between the courts and the other governmental structures are maintained effectively. The courts in both countries have a regulatory role with reference to the performance of the adjudicative function by other governmental structures. Again the pattern differs as between the United States and the United Kingdom. Through the power of judicial review in the United States, the courts may exercise a generally regulatory role with reference to the performance of the rule-making, rule application, and rule adjudicative functions by the other federal structures, and also regulate the division of powers between the central government and the states. In the British system, the regulatory role of the courts tends to be confined to the performance of the adjudicative function.

In both the British and the American political systems there are informal primary structures within the formal ones. The informal structures take the form of diffuse, ascriptive, and particularistic relationships which may be quite important in the performance of the governmental functions. But these informal structures tend to be penetrated by and acculturated to the primary and secondary formal structures.

In contrast, in transitional political systems, boundary maintenance between governmental structures is less effective. The legislative bodies are far less effective in regulating the performance of the rule-making function by the bureaucracy. The rule-making function tends to be performed by the executive and the bureaucracy. Furthermore, within the governmental structures and particularly at the provincial or local levels, informal, primary groups are of the "communal" kind—i.e., based on lineage, caste, and language. It would not be correct to say that the formal secondary structure has penetrated this informal structure. Rather they tend to operate with equal legitimacy, with the result that the universalistic, specific, and affectively neutral political culture of the modern structures is stalemated by the particularistic, diffuse, and affective political culture of the traditional ones.

Finally, there is a serious problem of continuity between the central governmental structures and the local ones. Village government tends to be assimilated to the traditional lineage, caste, and status structure. Thus, though a mayor may wear the trappings of his formal office, it may really be a caste leader or a headman who is speaking. A modern system of local courts may be subverted by a traditional system of adjudication, as for example by the Koranic interpreters. Thus a transitional system has not as yet eliminated the planes of cleavage which exist both within the central governmental structures and between the central governmental structure and the local units.

IV. TOWARD A PROBABILISTIC THEORY
OF THE POLITY

In recent years there has been growing interest among political scientists in the possibilities of applying formal logic and mathematics to the study of politics. This impulse toward rigor and precision is a sound and constructive one, even though some of the first efforts have not produced impressive results. Perhaps the most serious problem confronting efforts of this kind is the absence of a theory of the political system specifying its properties in such form as to lend itself to statistical and mathematical formulation.

The functional theory of the polity which we have elaborated above does specify the elements of the polity in such form as may ultimately make possible statistical and perhaps mathematical formulation. What we have done is to separate political function from political structure. In other words, we have specified the elements of two sets, one of functions and one of structures, and suggested that political systems may be compared in terms of the probabilities of performance of the specified functions by the specified structures. In addition, we have specified styles of performance of function by structure which makes it possible for us at least to think of a state of knowledge of political systems in which we could make precise comparisons relating the elements of the three sets—functions, structures, and styles—in the form of a series of probability statements.

If this appears to be too rash a projection into the future, the point should be made that the statements about politics now to be found in the political science literature are codable into such functional-structural statements of probability. Dahl has already shown that it is possible to take propositions in political theory, translate them into statements of probability, develop operational indices, and test them against empirical data.[41] It is similarly possible to take the monographic literature on political and governmental institutions and code much of their content into statements of probability of performance of function by structure. Much of what David Truman has to say about interest groups in the political process takes the form of statements about the functions performed by interest groups, the conditions facilitating the performance of these functions, and the effect of the performance of these functions on other functions and the political system as a whole.[42] Similarly V. O. Key's comments on parties and pressure groups may be coded into statements of probability of performance of functions by structures.[43] But these statements tend to be implicit probabilistic statements. The estimates take the form of qualifiers such as "by and large," "in general," "with great frequency," "with increasing (or decreasing) frequency." Similarly, the propositions about the performance of func-

---

[41] Robert A. Dahl, *A Preface to Democratic Theory*, Chicago, 1956.
[42] See *The Governmental Process*, New York, 1951, in particular Ch. 16.
[43] V. O. Key, Jr., *Politics, Parties, and Pressure Groups*, New York, 1958, pp. 142ff.

tion by structure in the body of the present theoretical chapter are estimates of "more or less," or of "increases" and "decreases."

What we are suggesting is that great advantage would be gained if we were to make explicit the essentially statistical nature of our propositions about the structures, functions, and styles of the polity. This is by no means pedantry, as an example or two may make abundantly evident.

When we say that pressure groups in the United States perform certain functions in certain ways, we are saying in effect that there is a universe of pressure group actions—i.e., performances of functions by pressure groups—and that in this universe there is a given probability that these functions will be performed by pressure groups with certain frequencies and in certain ways. A significant step is taken in the direction of precision by the simple recognition of the statistical nature of the proposition, for it immediately and explicitly brings to bear on the problem the theories of sampling and of probability. It is now no longer possible to leave diffuse the evidential nature of the proposition. If such a proposition implies a universe of events, then we must specify the limits and content of the universe. We can examine our evidence and ask of it, to what extent does it sample this universe?

We know that each member of this universe—each performance of function by pressure groups—is a unique individual; but like human populations it has a stratification (e.g., age, sex, occupation, education, and so forth). The stratification of the universe of pressure group events is affected by the nature of the policy issue, its place or salience in the context of public policy issues, the urgency of the issue, its novelty and controversiality, as well as a number of other conditions. If we simply look at our evidence from the point of view of these evidential requirements, we can at least become aware of how imprecise we are and must be in view of the enormity of the research implied. But to explicate our imprecision is in itself a step in the direction of precision.

We will also have discovered that there are ways of sampling this universe. Once we set up the problem in a statistical matrix, our knowledge and intelligence can help us select the probable well-populated cells, and eliminate the empty and poorly populated ones. Thus our sampling of the universe can proceed in an orderly way, step by step, and gradually develop a rigorous theory of interest groups or any other political structure with which we might be concerned.

We do not minimize the problem of finding quantities to place in the cells of our matrices, but, once having thought of the problem in these terms, we have at least liberated our capacities to look for appropriate indices and establish the problems, costs, and values of quantification. Indeed we may conclude that, at least at the present state of our knowledge and resources, we cannot establish quantitative values. Nevertheless statistical thinking is still of great value and may produce greater precision, if not quantitative precision.

We may take as an illustration of this the strategy of case studies of public policy decisions. Quite a library of such case studies, both political and administrative, have accumulated in the last decade or so. But we still do not know how to use them for the purpose of developing political theory. What is a case study, anyway? It is an effort at reconstructing, by documentary research and interviewing of informants, a public policy individual. In this public policy individual will be found the specific performances of political and governmental functions by the structures of the polity. Once we think of case studies in these terms, our capacity to draw from the case study hypotheses or theories of the functioning of the polity, and our capacity to devise a strategy of case studies, have been liberated. The first question we would ask is, what stratum of our universe of public policy decisions does our case study purport to represent? How well does it represent it? What other strata must we sample before we can formulate a theory of the polity which is actually representative of its population? The earlier work of Cohen and Almond referred to above illustrates the method. Thus in order to characterize the foreign-policy-making process in the United States in the post-World War II period eight case studies were made, each one being selected because it tapped a different cell in the foreign policy matrix. This kind of case study approach enables us to develop a typology of foreign-policy-making and a set of "if-then" propositions respecting the conditions which affect forcign-policy-making profiles.

Thus, regardless of the possibilities and costs of quantification, making explicit the statistical basis of our science provides us with far better canons than have guided us in the past. It is this aspiration, rather than rashness or fanaticism, which leads us to conclude our discussion of the functions of the polity with a statement of some of the problems which would have to be solved in the development of a probabilistic theory of the polity.

Throughout this chapter we have been suggesting that political systems may be compared with one another in terms of the frequency and style of the performance of political *functions* by *political* structures.

The set of political functions which we have proposed is most preliminary. We cannot really say that we have developed a set of functional categories which will prove satisfactory for purposes of analyzing and comparing political systems. We must be even more tentative about the structural categories. Here we have simply used the nomenclature of political and social institutions without pretending to have arrived at clearly defined, universally applicable categories of structure. Finally, in comparing styles of performance of function by structure we have relied in the main upon the pattern variable concepts of Parsons and Shils.[44]

Assuming that we had solved the problem of categorization of function, structure, and style, our next problem would be to form the product of these three sets, which would give us a matrix with several hundred cells. If we were then to attempt to sample the actions of a number of polities over a given period of time in order to arrive at precise comparisons of these polities in terms of frequencies of performance of function, by structure, by style, we would have set ourselves a research task of ridiculous proportions.

The point should be clear, however, that the intellectual exercise of thinking of the polity as being representable by a set of frequencies recorded on a series of matrices is not a research design. It simply states the problem in its fully explicated form. It makes explicit the operational assumptions of what many of us have been pretending to be able to say about the political systems of the United Kingdom, the United States, France, Germany, and the many other polities with which political scientists are concerned. With this explication of assumptions in mind, we are in a better position to judge the adequacy of the evidence that we have to support these propositions.

Thus, in having specified the elements of these sets of functions, structures, and styles, we have taken a step in the direction of a probabilistic theory of the polity, but perhaps it is only a small step. Theoretical imagination may enable us to select a limited number of indicators of the performance of function by structure, and research ingenuity may enable us to get quantitative evidence of these performances. The election studies carried on in the United States have yielded quantitative evidence of the relative importance of primary, diffuse, and particularistic communication structures as compared with secondary, specific, and universalistic mass communication structures, in the

---

[44] Talcott Parsons and Edward Shils, *Toward a General Theory of Action*, *op.cit.*, pp. 53ff.

performance of the function of political recruitment. It should be possible to make similar studies of the recruitment function in other polities.

It is conceivable that a well-executed series of case studies in a number of countries of the performance of the interest articulation function by different kinds of structures, and with different kinds of styles, would enable us to spell out what we mean by the forms of cultural dualism to which we have referred above, and might also enable us to specify what we mean when we say that in the United Kingdom and the United States associational interest groups regulate the performance of the interest articulation function, while in other countries such as France and Italy they fail to do so. It is only through such approximative research undertakings, carried on, however, within the framework of a statistical model of the polity, that we will be able to settle the question of which aspects of the polity are susceptible of quantitative representation, and which are not, and what the costs and problems of such operations are likely to be.

There is an even more challenging prospect which this approach to the study of the polity holds out. In our presentation of the functional theory, we have continually stressed the point that all political structure is multifunctional, and all political culture is dualistic. The peculiar properties of "modernity" of structure and culture are a particular mode of solution of the problems of multifunctionality and cultural dualism. In the modern Western system, each of the functions has a specialized structure which regulates the performance of the particular function by other structures. We have characterized this "modern" solution of the problem of multifunctionality as a regulation of the performance of the function within the polity by a specialized autonomous structure with a boundary of its own and a capacity to "enforce" this boundary in the system as a whole. We have characterized the "modern" solution of the problems of cultural dualism as a penetration of the "traditional" styles of diffuseness, particularism, ascriptiveness, and affectivity, by the "rational" styles of specificity, universalism, achievement, and affective neutrality.

If somehow the problem of finding reliable indicators for these concepts of functional regulation and cultural penetration can be solved, we may be able to take a step along the way toward the development of a formal theory of political modernization, a step which would improve our capacity to predict the trend of political development in modernizing states from carefully selected indicators.

To be able to do this implies a state of knowledge of the performance of modern Western polities far beyond what we have attained today. It also implies the obsolescence of the present-day divisions of the study of politics into American, European, Asiatic, Middle Eastern, African, and Latin American "area studies." The political scientist who wishes to study political modernization in the non-Western areas will have to master the model of the modern, which in turn can only be derived from the most careful empirical and formal analysis of the functions of the modern Western polities. In his efforts at predicting what might happen, or in explaining what did happen, he will not only have to know the properties of the systems we call modern, but should be able to call upon, with relative freedom, the experience of the polities of the other non-Western areas as a means of gaining insight into the processes of change in those areas in which he specializes.

The magnitude of the formal and empirical knowledge required of the political scientist of the future staggers the imagination and lames the will. We have been accustomed to working in a dim and fitful light. As we learn that a stronger and steadier illumination is possible, our first reaction is to blink and withdraw in pain. And yet as those who carry on the traditions of one of the most ancient of sciences, which is intended to maximize man's capacity to tame violence and employ it only for the humane goals of freedom, justice, and welfare, we cannot hesitate in the search for a greater illumination. Suppose many of the problems of developing a formal theory of the polity prove intractable and their solution eludes us for generations to come. Casting our problems in terms of formal theory will direct us to the kind and degree of precision which are possible in the discipline, and will enable us to take our place in the order of the sciences with the dignity which is reserved only for those who follow a calling without limit and condition.

THE POLITICS OF

Southeast Asia

LUCIAN W. PYE

....

I. BACKGROUND

THERE IS A QUALITY OF NEWNESS about Southeast Asia. The very term "Southeast Asia" came into common usage only with World War II and the creation of the South-East Asia Command. The end of colonialism and the rise of Communist China has caused the world to take a new interest in tropical Asia. The sense of the new and the contemporary stems also from the region being composed of newly emergent countries with youthful leaders who are striving to bring their peoples out of the old world of traditionalism and colonialism and into the modern world. The quality of newness in Southeast Asia comes also from a generation of peoples seeking to live without a history and with only hopes. Lacking a common store of memories, the people cannot look to the past for strength and guidance. They must look the other way, and in doing so they can see only a tentative present and an unsure future. The region is in such a state of flux that both outsiders and Southeast Asians find it difficult to gain perspective and hence the temptation to seek reality in immediate problems.

This emphasis upon the new and the contemporary is not entirely misplaced, for a fundamental characteristic of Southeast Asian societies is their involvement in a process of social change as a result of their exposure to the West. For all of the countries in the region, except Thailand, the Western impact included a period of colonial rule. Indeed, the modern history of Southeast Asia is largely a matter of various forms of colonial practices stimulating changes in all aspects of traditional societies which in time led to the development of nationalistic movements. With the emergence of seven new states in the postwar period, the dominant theme of Southeast Asia is the effort of the leaders of these new countries to create modern nation-states out of their transitional societies. These leaders have committed their peoples to the task of establishing representative institutions of government and developing more productive modes of economic life. Although enthusiasm for these goals has not been lacking, it is difficult to estimate their chances of being realized, for it is still hard to discern even the outlines of the political and social systems that are evolving in Southeast Asia. The possibility of failure is great, and leaders and citizens can be troubled with self-doubts. Already the tendency toward more authoritarian practices is widespread: for example, armies are coming to play roles that were originally reserved for democratic politicians.

The challenging task for the student of Southeast Asia is that of trying to determine the forces which will shape the future of the region.

The Physical and Human Setting

Southeast Asia consists, first, of a band of loosely organized and relatively underpopulated societies along the southern fringe of the massive and overpopulated East Asian continent, and, second, of the two island countries of Indonesia and the Philippines. The region is about as large as all of Europe and its adjacent seas. There are few regions as large as this with so uniform a climate, not only over the entire area but throughout the year. Except for parts of upper Burma and northern Thailand, and a few variations due to altitude, the average monthly temperatures for the entire region are within ten degrees of 80° at all seasons. In over ninety years Java has never had a temperature recorded above 96° or below 66°.

The population of Southeast Asia is rapidly approaching 180,000,000 (see Table 1). Only a century and a half ago there were barely 10 million people in the region, and since the First World War the population has grown by nearly 100 million. The population of the region is distributed extremely unevenly, so that congestion and empty spaces are found side by side. Java, one of the most densely populated areas of the world, has a total of over 800 people to the square mile and in some areas there are over 3,000 people living on each square mile. The other crowded areas are Lower Thailand and the Red River Delta with densities of over 1,500 people per square mile, and Lower Burma, Central Luzon, and the Lower Mekong with over 750 persons to the square mile. The rest of Southeast Asia is relatively underpopulated: only 8 per cent of Vietnam and Cambodia is cultivated and settled; Sumatra has less than 50 people to the square mile; and the general average of Burma, Malaya, and Thailand is less than 100 persons per square mile.

Indonesia, with over 78 million people, is the largest country of Southeast Asia, and its 3,000 islands stretching for over 3,000 miles

TABLE 1

Country	Area (sq. miles)	Pop. Density (1955: per est. sq. km. in millions)		Religions (per cent)	Ethnic Groups (per cent)
Burma	261,610	19.4	29	Buddhist 82 Moslem 7 Hindu 5 Christian 2	Burmese 75 Indians 9 Chinese 5 Karens, Shans, Chins, Kachins, 5 Others 6

Cambodia	88,780	4.3	25	Buddhist 85	Khmers 85
					Annamese, Laos,
					  Malays,
					  Chinese

Indonesia	735,865	81.9	55	Moslem 98 Christian 1 Buddhist .5	Javanese 45 Sundanese 14.2 Madurese 7.5 Coastal Malays 7.5
Java	50,745	75.0	401		Macassarese- Buginese, 4.2 Minangkabau 3.3 Balinese 2 Batak 1.7 Atjehnese 1.3 Others 13.3
Laos	69,480	1.4	6	Buddhist 85	Laos 95 Khmers, Annamese
Malaya	52,286	6.0	46	Moslem 50 Confucian- Taoist 40 Hindu 10	Malays 49 Chinese 39 Indian 10
Philippines	115,600	21.8	74	Christians 93 Moslem 4	Malay, Chinese, Spanish
Thailand	200,000	20.3	39	Buddhist 94 Moslem 3	Thais 85 Karens, Khmers (Cambodians) Malays Chinese 9.5
Vietnam	127,380	26.3	80	Buddist ⎱ Confucianist ⎰ 85 Moslem 2 Christian 1	Annamese 88 Khmers, Chinese, Malays

along the Equator cover a territory somewhat larger than that of the United States, while the total land area of the islands is equal to about one-fourth the area of the United States. The Philippines consist of over 7,000 islands, of which eleven make up over 95 per cent of the total land area. The Philippines, Burma and Thailand each have populations approaching 20 millions; Vietnam has about 28 millions, Cambodia 3.3 millions, and Laos has anywhere from 1 to 2½ millions.

SOUTHEAST ASIA

0   300   600 miles

PHILIPPINES

CHINA

BURMA

NORTH VIET NAM

LAOS

THAILAND

CAMBODIA

SOUTH VIET NAM

MALAYA

INDONESIA

Southeast Asia is relatively rich in natural resources. Europeans were first attracted to the region by the spice trade, and later the West introduced such commercial crops as rubber, copra, sugar, and coffee. Now the region produces nearly 90 per cent of the world's rubber, 53 per cent of its tin, 75 per cent of its copra, 55 per cent of its palm oil, and 20 per cent of its tungsten. However, agriculture is the dominant way of life in Southeast Asia, and the region is the only major food-exporting area of Asia. The vast majority of Southeast Asians are peasants who are relatively self-sufficient.

The division between the production of raw materials for world trade and the peasant agriculture has created what is generally referred to as dual economies in Southeast Asia. One sphere of the economic life of these countries is closely tied in with world trade, while the other is still largely based on agricultural self-sufficiency. The development of exports was largely the work of Europeans during the colonial period, and since independence most of the countries have indicated a desire to diversify their economies and initiate more industrial activities. However, the pressing problem in much of Southeast Asia is still that of raising production to prewar levels. In spite of the setbacks that came with the war and the breakdown of law and order in some countries after independence, Southeast Asians generally have a higher standard of living than is common to the rest of Asia. For example, in comparison with the per capita income of India, the Malayans are nearly five times as well off and the Thais and Filipinos are about three times as well off.

From this brief introduction to the Southeast Asian scene, it will be apparent that almost every phase of life in the region has been strongly influenced by the Western impact. However, in order to appreciate the full significance of the interaction between the traditional aspects of Southeast Asian societies and the Westernization process, it is first necessary to outline the character of Southeast Asia before the arrival of the West.

Traditional Culture

It is peculiarly difficult to settle on what should be taken as the "traditional" indigenous cultures of Southeast Asia, for historically one of the most distinctive characteristics of the region is the extent to which it has been subjected to external influences. From the beginning of recorded history the area has received waves of migration bringing new religions and new cultures. The Portuguese and the Spanish, the English and the Dutch, the French and the Americans have been only the latest to leave their stamp on different parts of the region. Before the West arrived, Southeast Asia was already a melting-pot of diverse cultures. Indeed, as Cora Du Bois has suggested, "There is probably no other area of the world so richly endowed with diverse cultural strains."[1] And certainly there are few areas that provide a better opportunity for studying the process of cultural diffusion.

The spread of these various earlier cultures did not always occur in clearly separated stages so that one impact could be fully absorbed before the arrival of the next. Rather, in many cases it was only with the appearance of a new cultural impact that the immediately preceding one became deeply ingrained and thus appeared to be a part of the "traditional" culture. For example, we know that as early as 1292, when Marco Polo visited Sumatra as the ambassador of the Emperor of China, a small town at the northern tip of the island had been converted to Islam. However, the final stages of the spread of Islam through Malaya, Indonesia, and on to Mindanao in the Philippines were not completed until the sixteenth and seventeenth centuries, when the West was just beginning to appear in the region.[2] As Western power expanded in the area, the hold of Islam was strengthened rather than weakened. This was particularly the case in the Indies, where the position of Islam was largely consolidated only after the introduction of Dutch rule. And, although the Muslim religion in Indonesia never completely replaced the earlier religions and cultural attitudes, it is significant that the roots of Indonesian nationalism are to be found first culturally in the Modern Islamic movement and then politically in Sarekat Islam, a nationalist organization founded in 1912.[3]

Even before the advent of Islam and the West, the history of Southeast Asia centered on the movement of peoples and cultures into the region. The extent to which there was movement outward from Southeast Asia is far from clear. There is the possibility that *Pithecanthropus*, or "Java Man," may have moved northward into continental Asia while

[1] Cora Du Bois, *Social Forces in Southeast Asia*, Minneapolis, Minn., 1949, p. 27.

[2] Islam was brought to Southeast Asia not by the sword but by Arab traders and teachers, who were a strong influence for peace and stability. In contrast, Christianity was introduced in violent form by the Portuguese, who combined the spirit of the "freebooter" with a traditional animosity toward Islam that went back to the struggles with the Moors. For a profound, yet lively, comparison of the spread of Islam and Christianity, see Sir George B. Sansom, *The Western World and Japan: A Study of the Interaction of European and Asiatic Cultures*, New York, 1950, Part I.

[3] The best discussion of the origins of Indonesian nationalism and its ties to Islam is to be found in George McT. Kahin, *Nationalism and Revolution in Indonesia*, Ithaca, N.Y., 1952, pp. 37-100.

evolving into *Sinanthropus*.[4] Also, it has been hypothesized that the pre-Aryan cultures of India may have originated within Southeast Asia.[5] The dominant theme, however, has always been movement inward, and it is generally accepted that the waves of migration of different human types—the Australoid, Negrito, Melanesoid, and finally the Indonesian or Austronesian—all came into the area from continental Asia. This last physical type, which is divided between the Deutero-Malay, the general Malay type common to present Southeast Asia, and the Proto-Malay, now represented by most of the Dayaks of Borneo, the Jakun of Malaya, and a few other small groups, probably moved into the region between 2500 and 1500 B.C.[6]

The beginning of recorded history finds Indian and Chinese influences already a major factor in the religious and political development of the region. It has been customary to divide Southeast Asia into two principal cultural areas: one consisting of Tonking, Annam, and Cochin-China, where Chinese influences have dominated since the fall of the Indianized kingdom of Champa in the fifteenth century; and the other consisting of the rest of the region, where Indian influences had mastery.[7] It has also been customary to say that Indian influences were more cultural than political, while Chinese influences were predominantly political.

This generalization, however, requires a great deal of qualifying. It is true that the Chinese explicitly saw in Indo-China, and to a lesser extent in Java, Sumatra, and parts of Burma, areas of possible political domination toward which they applied their principles of suzerainty. These principles rested, however, upon assumptions about the superiority of Chinese culture and its relations to less civilized peoples. Thus, wherever Chinese political influences dominated, Chinese culture also made inroads, and in Annam Confucianism became the state ideology and the traditions of a Mandarinate were well established. On the other hand, the Indian states did not see in Southeast Asia an area for imperial expansion and direct political control. However, Hindu and Buddhistic influences did have a profound political effect on the development of the early Southeast Asian state. Indeed, it was these influences which

---

[4] D. G. E. Hall, *A History of South-East Asia*, New York, 1955, pp. 5-6.

[5] For a balanced discussion that leaves the question open as to whether the common features of pre-Aryan India and early Southeast Asian cultures are to be explained by a movement from Southeast Asia or an early pattern of Indian influence in the regions, see George Coedes, *Les Etats hindouises d'Indochine et d'Indonesie*, Paris, 1948, p. 24.

[6] Brian Harrison, *South-East Asia: A Short History*, London, 1954, p. 5.

[7] The Philippines were largely untouched by either Indian or Chinese cultural contacts, and this fact provides the basis for much that distinguishes the Philippines from the rest of Southeast Asia.

produced the Indianized states that were the important empires of early Southeast Asia, and in some cases the states were actually established by Indians. In contrast, the Chinese, in spite of the numbers who ventured into the region and their advantages as representatives of a superior culture, did not attempt to create independent governments, except for a few abortive efforts by Chinese freebooters in Borneo.[8]

The nature of Chinese culture probably acounts for its failure to influence deeply the peoples of Southeast Asia. Chinese culture was an integrated whole in which the Confucian code of ethics and social behavior, and a basic philosophy of life, were all inextricably interwoven with the fabric of the Confucian state. In Southeast Asia, except where the Chinese directly imposed their own form of government, the necessary framework for an acceptance of Chinese culture was lacking. In contrast, Indian culture was based on religion and thus it could spread among peoples regardless of the political structure and in time provide the bases for the subsequent creation of Indianized states.

It would be difficult to exaggerate the importance of Hindu and Buddhistic influences on the political and court life of the early states of Funan, Khmer, and Angkor in present-day Cambodia; Srivijaya on Sumatra; Sailendras, Singhasan, and Majapahit on Java; and the Pagan and Pegu states of Burma.[9] However, the peoples of Southeast Asia had their own civilizations, which were only slightly modified by Indian influences, and except for some questions of religion, and the need of providing manpower for warfare and wealth for the court, the lives of the common people were little affected by the development of the Indianized states.

[8] These ventures, which must be called attempts at creating governments since they involved selling security at monopolistic prices, were not the first manifestations of a phenomenon which in time became endemic, and which was known to some as supporting one's ruler and to others as piracy. Nature, of course, had provided a happy setting for such enterprises, and the Sea-Dayaks of Borneo and their Malay rulers were not backward in recognizing their opportunities. Indeed, the political history of parts of Borneo might well be called "the politics of piracy," for the ties between Malay sultans and Sea-Dayak subjects, as well as the factional disputes among the sultans' "governors," were largely a matter of such activities. The problem of piracy was also the central theme in the story of British influence in the area which began with the private anti-piracy campaigns of Sir James Brooke, who was so successful that the Sultan of Brunei made him the Raja of Sarawak and thus established the "Brooke dynasty," which ruled Sarawak until the Japanese occupation.

[9] Although Indian influences dominated in these early states, there were also Chinese contacts, and it is in the early Chinese records that we find the most complete accounts of these states. Indeed, it would seem that one of the likely consequences of further research will be to show that Chinese influences were far greater than is now generally supposed. For a pioneering study along this line, see Herold J. Wiens, *China's March toward the Tropics*, Hamden, Conn., 1954.

For our purposes it is not necesary to become involved with the histories of these early Southeast Asian states and empires. Our concern is with the general characteristics of their societies, and in particular we are interested in those features of their social structures and patterns of political control which are relevant for understanding the current scene. It should be noted that a conscious awareness of the early historical period has played little part in shaping contemporary developments. Indeed, it is possible that much of the early history of Southeast Asia would have been forgotten had it not been for the work of a small group of European historians and archaeologists.[10] In spite of the remarkable achievements of these scholars, it must be said that most of the historical research on Southeast Asia is still at the stage of focusing on dynastic and chronological questions with a secondary emphasis upon religions and the development of those art forms which have survived to this day. Work on broader social, economic, and political problems has hardly begun and progress is likely to be exceedingly slow, not only because of the inherent difficulties but because contemporary studies attract more attention.[11] This means that there are many gaps in our knowledge and that in seeking to depict the general features of Southeast Asian cultures it is necessary on many points to advance only tentative generalizations. Although this cannot be emphasized too strongly, it would be tedious to repeat the qualification at every turn.

We may begin on solid ground by observing that the social structure general to Southeast Asia was once characterized by a sharp division into two main classes—an aristocracy and a peasant population—which had

[10] Some of these careful and dedicated scholars have not hesitated to point out that the present leaders of the newly independent states, in seeking to recapture the traditions and symbols of earlier days, have found themselves largely indebted to this group of Europeans. However, it must be aded that, inescapably, their historical research tends to reflect a European-centered orientation with respect to basic assumptions and value judgments and this state of affairs is likely to continue until more Southeast Asian scholars engage in critical examination of their region's history.

[11] A serious setback in this development was the early death of J. C. van Leur, who was engaged in pioneering work on the economic history of Southeast Asia. His collected works in English translation have appeared as J. C. van Leur, *Indonesian Trade and Society: Essays in Asian Social and Economic History*, The Hague, 1955. It should also be noted that in general Dutch scholarship has been outstanding in its emphasis upon broader social questions and its use of social science methodology. For example, Schrieke's work still represents the best studies of the problems of cultural diffusion and social change. See *Indonesian Sociological Studies: Selected Writings of B. Schrieke*, The Royal Tropical Institute, Amsterdam, *Selected Studies on Indonesia by Dutch Scholars*, Vol. II, The Hague, 1955. In contrast, British scholars have focused more on chronological and court histories, and physical and cultural anthropological research. French scholarship has tended to emphasize the fields of linguistics, philosophy, and traditional custom.

a common tie in religion. Ruler and ruled to some degree shared a similar view of the world and they could believe that they received the highest statement of values from the same source. However, on closer examination it appears that theirs was a common religion only in general form, because in all cases the peasants lived with a more vulgarized and restrictive version, while the aristocracy possessed a more esoteric version which to some degree they could alter and manipulate according to their needs.

Aside from the worship of the god-king and formal acceptance of the state religion, the peasantry believed in forms of animism which stressed local deities and the worship of ancestors. Their mythology reflected a cosmological dualism: the mountain as against the sea, mountain people opposing sea people, winged beings opposing water beings, etc.[12] The priests and diviners were local people who gave order to the community and provided a link with the capital and its god-king. Although the religions of the aristocracy also preserved the cult of the god-king, they tended to reflect Buddhistic and Brahmanist influences.[13]

Agriculture was the primary basis of life, and the demands of rice cultivation determined in large part the way the societies were organized. For the peasant masses, life centered around small, compact villages in which there were complicated patterns of interpersonal relations. The experiences of the individual were largely limited to his face-to-face relations with no more than a few hundred people. The requirements of rice production and fishing imposed a need for a communal basis for most critical activities. Before the West arrived, the region was not faced with problems of overpopulation and people worked as much land as their primitive technology permitted.

Redfield's general model of a peasant community describes remarkably well the ethos of the majority of the population.[14] A distinctive

[12] A general discussion of Southeast Asian mythology as well as other pre-Indian features of the cultures are to be found in Coedes, *op.cit.*, pp. 26ff., and Ralph Linton, *The Tree of Culture*, New York, 1955, Ch. xv.

[13] Although the Indian influence on Southeast Asia consisted of both Hinduism and Buddhism, it was the latter that came to dominate at a very early stage, probably because of the difficulties of accepting the caste system basic to Hinduism. However, some non-Buddhist influences from India are still to be found in Southeast Asia. For example, in Burma the astrologers who set the propitious minute for inaugurating the independent state at the awkward time of 3:40 a.m. were not Buddhist monks but Brahmanites. (John F. Cady, "Religion and Politics in Modern Burma," *Far Eastern Quarterly*, Vol. xii, No. 2, February 1953, p. 156.) Likewise in Cambodia, another Buddhistic state, the court of the king still retains three Hindu priests who are responsible for the more traditional and intricate ceremonies.

[14] Robert Redfield, *Peasant Society and Culture*, Chicago, 1956.

feature of the peasant world of Southeast Asia was the strong emphasis that it placed on the importance of women; in Burmese culture, the sense of sexual equality was a strong factor in qualifying the influence of Hinduism, and in some extreme cases, as with the Minangkabau in Sumatra and their colonists in Negri Sembilan, Malaya, descent and inheritance were by the maternal line, a tradition which withstood even conversion to Islam in spite of its shocking implications for most followers of the Prophet. Another distinctive feature was the development of elaborate legal codes that covered every possible phase of social intercourse. It is extremely significant that these codes were supported by social convention and not by supernatural sanctions.

The world of the aristocracy contrasted sharply with that of the peasant, and not just in terms of material wealth and splendor. Instead of the pattern of communal life and a high valuation of cooperation, the life of the aristocracy revolved around issues of rank and status in a hierarchy of power. In the earlier period as well as under the Indianized states, the aristocrats tended to center their activities around a central court rather than fragmented estates. Thus the development was toward a type of structure that was more bureaucratic and imperial than strictly feudal. Representatives of the king were usually stationed in the various villages, but they did not hold title to all the lands and the peasants were not strictly their serfs. For this, as well as other reasons, it would be inappropriate to apply the term "feudal" to traditional Southeast Asia.

The life of the aristocracy provided a setting which encouraged complicated and involved intrigues both within and among the various courts. Although the position of the aristocracy as a whole, and of the kings in particular, rested on their symbolizing a divine order, their activities were marked by an extraordinary degree of vicious scheming. (In the peasant world there was considerable malevolent magic, and poisonings were fairly commonplace.)[15] The strong emphasis upon splendor in the court helped to advance the arts, particularly architecture. Since virility was viewed as an important manifestation of the spiritual power of the state, there was great concern with the recruitment and maintenance of harems. There was also considerable development of the arts of war and frequent use of them.[16] The emergence of the more centralized

[15] Linton, *op.cit.*, p. 216.

[16] For the state of the military arts and of Chinese and Indian influences, see H. A. Quartich Wales, *Ancient South-East Asian Warfare*, London, n.d.

states had the effect of reducing intervillage warfare and making possible interregional conflicts among the more important rulers.

The relationship between the world of the influential and that of the villagers, although fundamentally based on the ties of religion, also had other dimensions. First of all, the life of the courts was something the peasant could identify with, but on no more intimate terms than he could identify with the lives of his gods. However, as Cora Du Bois has said, "In Southeast Asia, but certainly not in Europe, the wealth and the sexual potency of the ruler, the splendor of the court and the temples were projected and sublimated expressions of cultural well-being. The lords seem to have been less masters of serfs and more an expression of the peasantry's greatness. The state was not the exclusive, aggressive structure of European nationalism but was rather the symbol of world order, and the expression of a system of proprieties in human and super-human relations."[17]

Secondly, there were certain possibilities for upward social mobility. Although the position of the aristocracy was largely guaranteed by ascriptive considerations, there was usually some slight opportunity for intelligent and able men of peasant stock to make their way into the ranks of the select. In particular, intellectual activities offered such possibilities, and what might pass as the intelligentsia of these societies were always closely related to the realm of government. This, of course, was particularly the case in Annam after the establishment of the Chinese system of imperial examinations for admittance to the Mandarinate. In addition, however, the folklore of all these societies contained stories of young men of humble origin suddenly rising to positions of influence and gaining half a kingdom by displaying some prized skill or solving some problem, maybe just a riddle, which had bedeviled his intellectual and social betters. And, of course, there was always the possibility of an entire family benefiting through a charming daughter who had caught the fancy of an official.

Thirdly, relations between the aristocracy and the peasantry were reinforced by the efforts of the former to control and limit the activities of merchants and traders. Although these Southeast Asian states were never as successful as the Chinese or Indian Empires in restricting the role of the merchant, they still tried to maintain a distinction between officially controlled trade and the activities of private merchants. The officials usually assiduously propagated the notion that independent merchants and others who conspicuously sought wealth outside the ranks

[17] *Op.cit.*, p. 31.

of officialdom were lowly and mean people, deserving of little respect. This was apparently not a particularly difficult thing to do because, first, the intellectuals, who were skilled in spreading ideas, were largely identified with officialdom, and second, the peasant population as a whole was deeply predisposed to believe that the game of the merchant was cheating the customer. Success in accumulating wealth alone did not usually bring respectability and influence: it was more likely to bring infamy.

On the basis of this very brief description of early Southeast Asia, we can make some observations that seem relevant for understanding present-day developments in the area.

First, we may note that throughout their entire histories Southeast Asian societies have been sharply divided into a small elite class and a peasant population. Even more significant, this division has been exaggerated to some degree by the phenomenon of cultural diffusion, which has strengthened the tendencies toward sharp differences between the outlooks of the elite and the mass—tendencies which still persist to this day, insofar as the elite in most Southeast Asian countries is composed of people who are more acculturated than the masses to outside influences. This situation encouraged authoritarian practices on the part of the ruling aristocracies.

Secondly, the process of cultural diffusion, while providing the elite with many advantages that strengthened its power base, also made it difficult, then as now, to develop strongly integrated political systems. Indeed, the uneven pattern of cultural diffusion tended to set up barriers to the development of homogeneous political states. The control of the various states could expand with the spread of cultural and religious influences, but the results were empires that were defined by a loose form of suzerainty. Local and regional cultural differences have always operated against the development of strongly centralized states in Southeast Asia. In the past the tie of religion was adequate for many purposes, but it did not provide an effective means for mobilizing human and material resources for sustained political objectives. Much the same may be said about the ties of ideology and nationalism at present. Thus, it would seem that the fragile quality of relations within Southeast Asian societies which has made them peculiarly vulnerable to new outside influences has also impeded the growth of social cohesion.[18]

This is only to say that Southeast Asia has been characterized by

---

[18] For a general discussion of the lack of social cohesion in Southeast Asian culture, see Du Bois, *op.cit.*, Ch. II.

plural societies of one form or another throughout most of her history. The term "plural society" has been customarily used only in reference to the heterogeneous populations that developed under the colonial period, but it is significant that the earlier processes of migration and cultural diffusion resulted in none of the Southeast Asian societies having a homogeneous population even before the arrival of the West. Now all the countries in the region have problems of minority groups. A conspicuous index of the extent to which these states are so divided is the diversity of languages spoken in each of the countries. In Burma there are 126 dialects,[19] which can be classified under 11 main language groups. In the 3,000 islands that make up Indonesia there are 10 major languages[20] and 16 major "ethnic" groups which give emphasis to the problem and the aspiration expressed in the Indonesian national slogan of "Bhinneka Turrggal Ika," meaning "Unity in Diversity." Malaya is divided almost equally between Malays and Chinese, with an Indian minority of nearly 10 per cent of the population. Even the tiny colony of Brunei, consisting of only 30,000 people and 2,500 square miles, not only has the ubiquitous problem of unassimilated Chinese and Indians; its indigenous Malays are divided between "coast peoples" and the "inland" cultures as well.

In traditional Southeast Asia these divisive tendencies were largely countered by the ties of religion which provided a sense of cohesiveness. As we shall observe, the Western impact tended to weaken this political and social function of religion, and at present the bond of religion between the politically influential and their peasant masses has in most places been harshly broken and is only gradually being replaced by more secular considerations. To some extent the emergent nationalist ideologies perform some of the same functions that the old religions did, and hence it is worth comparing some of the distinctive features of the early religions with the new ideologies.

One important feature of the early religions was that they stressed the importance and validity of the values and customs basic to the smallest and most direct units of social organization: the family, the clan, and the village. This meant that the aristocrats, much as they might personally despise and seek to avoid excessive contacts with the peasants, felt called upon to proclaim continually the virtues of village customs. Thus, the way of life of the masses was sanctified and given

[19] John L. Christian, *Modern Burma*, Berkeley, Calif., 1942, p. 11.
[20] Stephen W. Reed, coordinating editor, *Area Handbook on Indonesia*, Human Relations Area Files, Inc., New Haven, Conn., 1956, Ch. VI.

some degree of dignity and respectability. In contrast, the new ideologies focus on the largest unit of social organization, the nation, and although they may praise the common man in the abstract, they usually do not explicitly give dignity and respectability to the customs and practices of the villages. Thus, although the elite may feel compelled to honor the ideal of village life, it is not as necessary to respect the actual practices of the peasants, which the new ideologies often suggest, at least implicitly, are legitimate sources of national shame.

A second common feature of the traditional religions of Southeast Asia was that they offered only a very dim picture of an ideal earthly society, while bringing into very sharp focus the ideal personal characteristics of those who occupied the various stations in the existing society. They usually provided quite elaborate definitions of the qualities of the good king, the good official, the good soldier, the good head of the household, the good peasant, and the like. In contrast, they generally had very little to say about what might be evil in the structure of society and what might be a more ideal way of ordering it. These characteristics, along with many other considerations, meant that one of the functions of politics—that of devising policies in the light of a normative view of the world—tended to be underemphasized, while another and possibly more basic function of politics—that of maximizing personal prestige—tended to be exaggerated. Once the primary objectives of state action were established and had become standardized and ritualized, men did not have to spend their time looking for new problems to be solved or disagreeing over what new policies might be needed to ensure a better world; they could devote their energies to seeking prestige and power. Thus, these early religions tended to encourage and even sanctify the view that power and influence were end values that could be sought for their own sake, and not simply means for achieving other values, and particularly socially defined values.

In sharp contrast, the new emerging secular ideologies in Southeast Asia tend to place primary stress on how the societies should be reconstituted, and the ideal society of the future, if not the precise means for achieving it, has become the dominant theme. The old emphasis on the ideal standards of individual behavior and of interrole relationships has disappeared; the qualities of the good official and the good citizen seem vague, except to the extent that they are viewed as being instrumental to the realization of the good society. Thus Southeast

Asian officials still seem to feel free to act according to more traditional definitions of their roles even as they advance novel policies.

A third political function of all the early Southeast Asian religions was to give legitimacy not only to the status of the elite but to the distinctive culture of the elite society as well. These religions went beyond providing the rulers with a sense of security so that they need not feel they had to rely upon force alone; they suggested that only those with certain social and cultural characteristics could advance legitimate views about public policy. Thus the notions and opinions of the elite had to be treated as statements of what we would now call the "national interest," while the views of those who did not share the elite culture were suspected of representing only parochial and private interests. This meant that in a sense the early religions sanctified the view that only those who had become acculturated to the elite society could properly participate in the making of public decisions, and the attitudes of the non-elite could be ignored except as warnings of possible disruptive activities.

The present secular ideologies seem to support a somewhat similar view: they are largely premised on the assumption that only those who have to some degree become urbanized, modernized, or Westernized can fully appreciate and understand their content and the goals they suggest for the society. Thus only those who have become acculturated to the present elite societies are in a position to define the "national interest" in terms of the new ideologies. The views of those who are not acculturated to the elite's way of life are still seen as representing parochial and lowly interests which are likely to compromise and even disrupt the plans for a new society.

These general observations suggest that the early Southeast Asian societies had many problems—such as those relating to the process of cultural diffusion and the existence of a distinct elite society and a mass peasantry—that are not unlike the current problems of these countries. It would therefore seem that although the current Southeast Asian societies belong within the general category of transitional societies in which traditional forms are interacting with Western influences, the region has had long experience in reacting to outside influences. Of course, modern Western influences differ greatly from the early cultural impacts, but the fundamental processes and problems seem remarkably similar. In particular, the early societies, like the present ones, seem to have had great difficulties in creating strong and stable governmental institutions. The ambitions of the early rulers were to create in their societies governments that were comparable to the most powerful ones known to them—those of India and China. Similarly, the present-day leaders of Southeast Asia have strived to pattern their governments after the most powerful ones they know.

It might well be said that a central theme running throughout most of the history of Southeast Asia is that the process of cultural diffusion has, on the one hand, compelled rulers to try to establish states modeled after foreign practices, while, on the other hand, the very process that gave them these ambitions has created divisions and encouraged centrifugal forces within the societies which have compromised the attempts. Before turning to current efforts at nation-building in the region, we must investigate the general nature of the Western impact on Southeast Asia.

Patterns of Western Impact

The Western impact, assuming different forms at different stages, has brought changes to nearly every phase of life in the relatively loosely organized societies of Southeast Asia. The pattern of change, however, has been an uneven one. In some spheres the changes have been of revolutionary proportions, in others they have been less extreme, and in still others there have been only slight alterations in what remain essentially traditional modes of behavior. The lack of uniformity has been matched by a lack of continuity. The West did not bring simply more efficient means for realizing existing values, as is the case when change is continuous. Rather, novel modes of behavior were introduced which were strange to the traditional order and which are still strange to much of the village-bound population of the region.

Viewed in broad terms, the Western impact first introduced new roles which were hardly related to the system of roles basic to the traditional societies. In time, these new roles proliferated until they constituted new economic, political, and social spheres which disrupted the traditional system of roles without displacing them. Thus, first through commercial expansion and then through the production of raw materials for the world market, the Southeast Asian societies came to have administrative systems modeled along Western lines, while at the same time at the local village level many forms of traditional control remained. The most dramatic social changes came out of the trading centers that grew into cities, thereby introducing all the complex patterns of urban existence to a region in which the vast majority of the people continued to center their social lives around units no larger than the village.

The Western impact, in spite of bringing divisions and new tensions into Southeast Asian societies, also provided the basis for larger and more integrated units of social and political life. The West introduced both the concept and the framework of the nation-state. It created clearly defined territorial units, and, in response to the social changes and the ideas it introduced, the West inevitably stimulated the emergence of various forms of nationalism. And, except in the case of Siam, it introduced through its colonial administrations the basic structure around which the Southeast Asian societies are now striving to create modern nation-states.

This process of change was marked by different historical periods during which different aspects of the West affected different levels of the traditional societies. The region was first introduced to the West in the fourteenth and fifteenth centuries by adventurers, traders, and missionaries. It is significant that the activites of the early traders had more profound consequences in Europe than in the economies of Southeast Asia. Fortunes were to be made in single shiploads of pepper and spices, teak and ivory. In organizing for the quest of the riches of the Indies, the Dutch in particular developed novel financial arrangements which were to play an important role in the growth of the European economies. On the other hand, the Portuguese and the early Dutch traders seem to have disrupted the economic and social life of the region only in very marginal ways.[21] Although the early traders soon became involved in local rivalries, they left the political initiative largely to the local leaders and did not seek to impose new patterns of authority.[22]

In contrast, where the Western impact came primarily in the form of the spread of Christianity there were significant social changes from the very beginning. This was most clearly the case in the Philippines,

[21] On the limited nature of the early Western commercial impact on the economies of Southeast Asia, see van Leur, *op.cit.*

[22] Indeed, among the more extraordinary characteristics of these early Westerners were the alacrity and zeal they displayed in throwing themselves into local wars. It was while supporting the ruler of Cebu in a struggle against a neighboring island that Magellan met his death in April 1521, and in November of the same year, when the two remaining ships of his squadron reached the Moluccas, they immediately gave their support to Tidore in its permanent feud with Ternate. In the struggle between the Burmese and the Siamese, both sides received the support of Western soldiers of fortune. Of course, at a somewhat later date, the Western powers, in a far more systematic fashion, used local rivalries to extend their influence in the region, but this was a somewhat different phenomenon.

where the Spanish immediately sought to make Catholics out of the Filipinos and limited trade to the annual visit of the "Manila galleon." The spread of Christianity combined with the pattern of Spanish colonialization directly challenged and altered the traditional structure of authority. Philippine society had been organized around small settlements called *baranguys* after the boats which had brought the original migrants from Malaya and Sumatra. Each of these units was under the control of a *datu*, or headman, and, as we have observed, in spite of attempts by warfare and conquest the Filipinos had had little success in creating larger units of government. The Spanish pattern of colonization produced a feudal system of land tenure much as in Spanish America, and the peasantry largely became hacienda peons under the domination of *cacuques*, or chiefs, who owned the estates and replaced the traditional *datus*. Above this was the structure of Spanish administrative control. With the replacement of the localized patterns of authority by the dual but closely related hierarchies of the Church and the Spanish administration, Philippine society by the end of the fifteenth century had undergone a fundamental change which still stands out as one of the most remarkable examples of the acceptance of Western culture by an Asian people. The result was not only the sole Christian country in Asia—93 per cent of the Filipinos are now Catholics—but also a social structure that is conspicuously different from all other Asian societies. In many respects the Philippines today still seem to be an extension of Latin America.

The traditional Southeast Asian societies were seriously affected by Western commercial activities only after the establishment of the English East India Company in 1600 and the Dutch United East India Company (VOC) two years later. The companies, anxious to ensure higher standards of law and order so as to protect the flow of trade, came to assume more and more quasi-governmental functions. In some cases this meant establishing ports which grew into commercial centers under direct company rule; in other cases it involved treaty arrangements with local rulers under which the companies indirectly took on many governmental functions. In all cases, however, the old patterns of authority were disrupted and the doors were opened to extensive social changes.

The rate of change up to the Napoleonic Wars was not as rapid as might have been expected in the light of the great differences between Western civilization and the traditional Asian cultures. In large part, this was the case because the British and the Dutch East India

Companies generally employed various forms of indirect rule. The initial consequences of Western rule were thus primarily limited to the sphere of the traditional elite. Although the ruling aristocracies often received greater revenues and more security under their treaties with the companies, in time they found that in their relations with their subjects they were being gradually ignored and replaced by European officials who, however, sought in the main to conform largely to the traditional customs of the area. Consequently, for the mass of the populations the introduction of indirect rule did not bring about dramatic changes in their ways of life.

As the various European powers advanced their positions in Southeast Asia, they tended to follow different policies according to their particular interests and the local conditions that they encountered. The British tended to emphasize law and order and laissez-faire concepts of economic growth. The Dutch adopted far more paternalistic policies toward traditional Indonesian customs and through the institutions of indirect rule encouraged the development of a dual economy. In the Indo-Chinese states the French vacillated between the ideal of assimilation and that of association—that is, between drawing the Indo-Chinese into French culture and preserving the traditional culture on terms that might lead to cooperation. In the Philippines the Americans placed less stress on the administrative structure of rule than any of the other colonial powers and emphasized education and the development of political parties to a much greater extent.

In spite of differences in emphasis, it seems that the pace and scope of social change directly attributable to governmental policies depended in large part upon the rate and extent to which the colonial rulers (1) introduced rationalized administrative practices, (2) established fixed and standardized taxation in place of tributes in kind, *corvées* of labor, etc., (3) established secular and codified legal systems, (4) encouraged liberal economic policies, and (5) provided the people with a Westernized educational system. By and large, all five of these developments took place more rapidly and more intensively under direct colonial rule than under indirect rule, and hence the broader processes of social change were stimulated more by direct than by indirect rule. The pattern of indirect rule, however, tended to be far less stable, since under it there were usually constant pressures to create more rationalized administrative agencies. In turn, this generally led to more standardized methods of taxation and more formally codified legal systems, and finally these developments tended to produce an environment more attractive to foreign capital. Hence the practice of indirect rule produced many of the same social changes as direct rule, but usually at a slower rate.

Direct and indirect rule also had different consequences in regard to introducing new concepts about the nature of political authority. Where direct rule was employed, the Westerners introduced radically new standards for the behavior of authority and it was necessary for the people to adopt quite new images as to the proper role of those in power. The drastic elimination of the old structure of authority and the introduction of new images of authority, combined with the more rapid process of general social change induced by direct rule, often produced acute tensions and strains in a wide range of social relationships. In these situations the traditional order tended to disintegrate at a faster rate than it was possible to introduce a new system of role relationships into the society. Paradoxically, however, those administering systems of direct rule often displayed genuine appreciation for features of the traditional culture—features, that is to say, which did not compromise the new authority system. The sum effect of this process seems to have been an eventual acceptance of the new and essentially Westernized concepts of the proper character of political authority, but under such conditions as to encourage the attitude that the effective operation of such a system of authority is consistent with, and even necessary for, the preservation of that which still seems to be most precious in the traditional culture.

Developments under indirect rule in Southeast Asia tended to be of a less extreme nature, but resulted in a highly ambiguous view as to the proper character of authority. The process of change was less sharply disruptive, since traditional patterns of behavior were not broken down before new modes of life had been clearly established. Many of the social consequences of change were postponed, but this did not always mean that when they eventually had to be faced, they were any less painful. Indirect rule, however, did not generally provide a clear image of a new type of political authority. Although the processes at work under indirect rule usually led to the creation of bureaucratic structures and the undermining of traditional authority, they did not introduce into the societies unmistakably clear concepts of the relevant standards for guiding, and for judging the performance of, those with power. In Southeast Asia the practices of indirect rule have tended to produce highly ambiguous attitudes toward the character of political authority. With the termination of colonial controls, leaders and citizenry alike seem to have been unsure about the essential characteristics of political leadership.

The effects of colonial rule in stimulating social change, and particularly the differences related to direct and indirect rule, can be seen from a brief comparison of British practices in Burma and Malaya and Dutch policies in Java.

The conditions under which British control was introduced in Burma precluded the use of indirect rule. During the period when the West was advancing into Southeast Asia, Burma was the only country, aside from Siam, with a centralized political structure that resembled the Western nation-state. Indeed, at the beginning of the nineteenth century the Burmese kingdom was at the height of its power. Thus, early European relations with Burma revolved around questions of trading rights, much as in the case of early Western dealings with China. The three Anglo-Burmese wars which led to the eventual incorporation of all of Burma into the British Empire were more like interstate conflicts than the common pattern of Western penetration of other areas in Southeast Asia. The first Anglo-Burmese War of 1824-1826 stemmed from border conflicts between Burmese forces and the British East India Company at Chittagong and eastern Assam in India. In the peace treaty the Burmese kingdom lost territory adjacent to India and agreed to receive a British resident at its capital at Ava as a diplomatic representative. Conflicts over the role of the resident and the regularizing of commercial relations led to the Second Anglo-Burmese War of 1852 and gave the British control of parts of Lower Burma. In 1885 the kingdom of Burma came to its end when the British, fearing French domination of upper Burma and dissatisfied with relations with the last Burmese king, occupied the rest of the country.

At no stage was it possible for the British to utilize any of the traditional institutions of central government, and when they began to administer Burma as a province of India, they also ignored the traditional unit of local government, the *myo* or circle, and the *myothugyis* or *taipthugys* or circle headmen, placing responsibility directly on village headmen. The circle was not strictly a territorial unit; rather, the circle headmen had jurisdiction over groups of families who formed their "regiments." There were, broadly speaking, three types of "regiments": those liable for military service to the king, those liable for other kinds of specific and often highly personal services to the king, and those who paid a land tax in lieu of personal service. Members of different circles might reside in the same area, so the territorial units of local government introduced by the British destroyed the traditional hierarchy of authority.

British policy was largely guided by the belief that the primary function of government was to maintain law and order and respect the spirit of economic liberalism. Traditional customs and practices were not to be tampered with, except as they conflicted with these two principles of government. However, the support of these apparently limited objectives meant that in practice much of the traditional order was violently disrupted. An essentially British legal system that was slightly modified by Indian experience and local customs was arbitrarily introduced and came to replace the communal modes of adjudicating disputes even among the village populations. Law and order required the establishment of a highly centralized system of administration, in which the local authorities became the agents of the British administration and not the representatives of local interests and aspirations. The creation of a secular legal system and a rationalized administration greatly weakened the position of Buddhism and the authority of the priesthood. Traditionally the Buddhist hierarchy had been intimately related to the monarchy, but with the British policy of separation of Church and State there was a sharp decline not only in the moral influence of the monasteries but also in the discipline of the priesthood.

Above all else, British rule, particularly in Lower Burma, represents a dramatic example of the explosive consequences that a policy of economic liberalism can have on a traditional society. The introduction of a strictly moneyed economy, of a legally supported credit system, of the principle that land can be alienated, brought great changes to the peasant world. Burma soon became a major rice exporter not only to other parts of Asia, but to Europe as well after the opening of the Suez canal in 1869. The number of acres under rice in Lower Burma expanded from 66,000 in 1830 to nearly 10,000,000 in 1930, and there was over a tenfold increase in rice exports during the same period. Expansion in production and acreage kept ahead of a sixfold growth in population. The capital for this development came largely from Indian money lenders of the Chettyar caste of Madras. However, the Burmese peasant, unaccustomed to the notion that land, which had always been ancestrally held, could be alienated, found it easy to grasp the principle of borrowing for the purchase of land but difficult to believe that foreclosures might follow the failure to meet payments. Consequently, in spite of economic growth, indebtedness and tenancy tended to rise; by 1938 half the agricultural lands of Lower Burma were owned by Burmese and Indian money lenders, and as early as 1929 the Indian Chettyars had investments worth four times the value of all British interests in Lower Burma.

In the political sphere the deepest change was the replacement of the traditional hierarchy of loyalties by a civil service. The standards of the civil service were initially established by British and Indian officials. The establishment of the University of Rangoon at the end of the First World War provided a training ground for Burmese administrators as well as a focus for political activities. It first appeared that the rising interest in self-government in India during the World War had not touched Burma. However, when the Montagu-Chelmsford Committee recommended that Burma be excluded from the Indian experiment with dyarchy, there was a strong Burmese reaction that took the form of a boycott of government schools. The British responded quickly by introducing the dyarchy system into Burma in 1921. Under this system, half of the members of the governor's cabinet were selected by, and responsible to, the legislative council and the other half were responsible to the governor himself. In this way the British retained direct control of such key functions as finance and the police, while transferring others to a representative government. In some respects the Burmese government was given more reseponsibilities than the Indian: in Burma 80 per cent of the members of the legislative council were elected, as compared with 70 per cent in India, and the Burmese were given control of the important Forest Department which directed one of the key industries of the country.

These events led to a far more active interest on the part of the Burmese in the political development of their country. The British responded to this growth in political interest by proposing in 1935 that Burma be separated from India and given a new constitution. The Burmese opposed this suggestion, fearing that it might mean moving toward self-government at a slower pace. The British held firm, however, and insisted that Burma should have its separate constitution and no longer be ruled as a province of India. The constitution which came into effect in 1937 provided for a parliament of two houses with general legislative and budgetary powers. The lower house was popularly elected by all males over eighteen years of age who paid taxes, while half of the Senate was appointed by the governor and half elected by the House of Representatives. This introduction of representative institutions led to the emergence of political leaders and the formation of political factions and embryonic parties directed toward parliamentary activity. However, the war and Japanese occupation intervened before these developments had become fully institutionalized.

In summary, direct rule in Burma brought many sharp and even harsh changes in Burmese society, but it also gave to the Burmese a clearly defined picture of the type of government they would like to create once they gained independence. Although the Burmese did not lose respect for many of their traditional values, there was no demand that the country revert to her precolonial form of government. The Burmese thus gained from their experience with direct rule an unambiguous image of the form of political life that they have been striving to create since independence, and it is only within these institutions that they have sought to deal with conflicts between traditional and Western values. In spite of all the criticism of British rule during the prewar period, as contrasted particularly with the more paternalistic and sympathetic rule of the Dutch, the ultimate effects have been that Burma seems to be more fully committed to the principles of representative government and the rule of law than many of the other Southeast Asian states, which only since independence have come to experience the shocks of being a part of the modern world. At the same time, however, the British provided an image of authority that was primarily relevant to administrative rule and not to that of popular politicians. Hence, when the Burmese ran into difficulties and frustrations under a government of politicians, there was widespread acceptance of a return to administrative government under the leadership of the army.

Prewar Malaya provides in itself a comparative study of three types of colonial rule: direct rule in the three Straits Settlements of Singapore, Penang, and Malacca; a centralized form of indirect rule in the four Federated Malay States; and classic examples of indirect rule in the five Unfederated States. Although Penang became a possession of the East India Company in 1786 and Singapore was ceded in perpetuity in 1824, it was not until the 1870's that Britain began to assume the role of protector of the Malay States and not until 1914 that relations with Johore were regulated by treaty. It was intended that the British would assume the same responsibilities and functions under all the treaties. However, in the cases of Perak, Selangor, Negri Sembilan, and Pahang, the British officer was called a "Resident" and in the other treaties he was called an "Adviser," and in time the Residents began to assume a much more direct role in creating administrative services than did the Advisers. The persistent trend was toward greater centralization in order to increase efficiency and in 1895 the four states with Residents were constituted a Federation. The desire to respect the status of the rulers under the treaties and to encourage local self-government kept alive the ideal of greater decentralization, but the demands of administrative efficiency proved more forceful. Indeed, much of the history of British rule in Malaya revolved around an endless effort to prevent the need for rational efficiency in administration from compromising the need to preserve Malay customs, and particularly the position of the Malay rulers, who were protected by the treaties.[23]

The rate and scope of social change were greatest in the Straits Settlements under direct rule and least in the Unfederated States. This was, of course, not entirely the consequence of different patterns of administration. The discovery of tin in Perak and Selangor attracted Chinese immigrants, who in turn created tensions among the Malays and a considerable amount of disorder and lawlessness around the tin fields. Consequently, the Malay rulers of these states requested their British Residents to adopt more forceful administrative roles. The subsequent introduction of more direct rule produced higher standards of law and order which, however, brought even greater influxes of Chinese. Thereafter, the British began to protect Malay culture and the interests of the Malay rulers by gradually adapting them to the demands of the modern world.[24]

[23] For the details of British policy, see S. W. Jones, *Public Administration in Malaya*, London, 1953; Richard Winstedt, *Malaya and Its History*, London, 1948; L. Richmond Wheeler, *The Modern Malay*, London, 1928.

[24] There was a heroic as well as an anachronistic side to the British efforts to minimize the shock effects of bureaucratization and the British legal system on the customs and practices of the Malays. Consider what this involved in dealing with the matriarchal democracy of the Minangkabau colonists in Negri Sembilan. This was a culture which proudly held to its matriarchal traditions, which insisted that all its chiefs and rulers be elected, and which protected the rights of all. It had, however, one almost fatal flaw: it was firmly wedded to the principle of unanimity in all elections and in all the decisions of its various councils. At times a fair amount of violence and bloodshed was necessary in order to achieve this unanimity. Often no decisions could be taken, but so far as the election of the functionally important chiefs of the matrilineal tribes was concerned, this likelihood was forestalled by the rule that someone had to be unanimously elected before the deceased chief could be buried.

The Minangkabau colonists were ready to accept many features of other cultures so long as these did not affect the principle of unanimity. For example, in defining the role of their chief ruler, or *Yang di-Pertuan*, they reflected their exposure to Indian culture by conceiving of him as one whose ancestors had been the incarnation of Hindu gods, and in deference to their Islamic religion they thought of him as the shadow of Allah on earth, but because of their own traditions they gave him no authority—he could collect no taxes except fees at cockfights. Sir Richard Winstedt, noting the

Although the inescapable trend in all the Malay States was toward greater bureaucratization and a greater reliance upon British concepts of law, this process was mediated and made less harsh by the principles of indirect rule. The result was that gradually an ideal of political development emerged which was essentially consistent with the ideals of representative government. There was not the sharp break that occurred in Burma; tradition in many forms could be respected, but the goal was clearly one that would be consistent with the modern world. On the other hand, it may be questioned whether the protection that the Malays have received from many of the harsher aspects of modern life has prepared them fully to cope with contemporary problems.

Indirect rule as practiced by the Dutch in Indonesia was quite different from that of the British in Malaya. The Dutch did not attempt to introduce a completely Westernized legal system, but relied far more on traditional institutions. In time the Dutch created a dual structure of government, much as they encouraged the development of an extreme form of dual economy. The pattern of rule which the Dutch followed in Indonesia was largely established by the Dutch East India Company, and it slowly evolved over time and under the peculiar circumstances of the remarkably gradual expansion of Dutch control. The Dutch East India Company first gained a definite foothold on Java in 1619 at Jacatra (which they named Batavia and which is now renamed Jakarta), and it was not until 1830 that Dutch administrative control extended to all parts of Java.

The initial approach of the Dutch was to work through the traditional authority structure by preserving and strengthening the position of the Javanese aristocracy. Through their formal and informal relations with the aristocracy, the Dutch gradually reshaped the pattern of traditional relationships in Javanese society in the direction of a more sharply defined hierarchy. The sultans and lords came to assume more

---

awkward position that the *Yang di-Pertuan* traditionally occupied, observed: "He was supreme arbiter and judge, if the territorial chiefs chose to invite him to adjudicate, which they never did. He was Caliph or head of the Muslim theocracy in any territory where the local chief did not arrogate the title for himself—and he always did" (*op.cit.*, p. 83). Theoretically he presided over a state council but this body rarely met, largely because the prospects for unanimity were so dim. Eminent British constitutional theorists made several fruitless attempts to figure out how Minangkabau customs could be harmoniously adjusted to Anglo-Saxon legal principles. In practice this problem was largely dealt with by the individual district officers who, in resolving matters relating to Minangkabau customs, followed the approach of "patiently elucidating the nature of common sense." A mark of, if not a tribute to, the British achievement in this area is the fact that when Malaya gained its independence, it was the *Yang di-Pertuan* of Negri Sembilan who was elected by the other rulers to be the first Paramount Ruler of the new country.

authoritative control over the lesser nobility, who in turn came to exercise more direct control over the village headmen. The result was an efficient structure for exacting deliveries in kind from the peasantry which profited both the lords and the Company.

This system was largely followed after the Dutch government replaced the Company in 1798. In the brief period that the British were in control of Java during the Napoleonic Wars, Sir Stamford Raffles introduced reforms in the direction of economic liberalism and a more direct and rational system of administration. After the Indies were restored to Holland, the Dutch maintained many of Raffles' reforms but, when faced with fiscal difficulties, they introduced the "culture system," under which all the villages on Java were required to devote a certain proportion of their land to the raising of commercial crops for the government's use. In theory, the system was supposed to affect only from three to four per cent of the land, upon which no taxes were to be levied, and the principle of requiring the Javanese peasant to turn to commercial crops was a sound one. However, in practice the culture system worked great hardships: forced labor was necessary to transport crops to warehouses, the government's demands increased, and the production of food for local consumption fell behind the needs of a rising population. Partly as the consequence of these hardships and partly as the consequence of liberal attitudes in Holland, the system was largely discarded in 1877, although some features remained in effect until 1915. Thereafter, there was a strong revulsion against governmental interference in economic matters. Increasingly the Dutch came to adopt a paternalistic approach which was dedicated to preserving basic features of the traditional way of life.

The subsequent pattern of indirect rule tended to emphasize, on the one hand, the preservation of traditional values and customs in spite of changing economic conditions, and, on the other, an increasingly centralized bureaucracy for the efficient preservation of traditional aspects of the society. The rights of the family and the village or *desa* were respected, *adat* or customary law was retained or adjusted to Western legal concepts wherever possible, more social services than usual in colonial Southeast Asia were introduced, and the peasant's claims to his land were guarded. Java was the one area of Asia in which the introduction of a moneyed economy did not result in increasing concentrations of land holdings and large numbers of landless peasants.

By adhering to the principle of "like over like," the Dutch produced a dual administration in which the European and the Indonesian officials had different functions. Although often technically equals, the Dutch official was always in practice the superior of his Indonesian counterpart. In outward form, the traditional sultans and aristocrats still ruled, but in fact it was an increasingly centralized administration that made the decisions. At all levels the assumption appears to have been that the Indonesians could not get along, even in maintaining their traditional customs, without the guidance of the Dutch. The popular characterization of the system, repeated by the Dutch themselves, was that "A villager cannot scratch his head unless a district officer gives him permission and an expert shows him how to do it."

For the Dutch there were essentially two respectable worlds, that of traditional Indonesian culture and that of the European. More than any other colonial power, the Dutch had a concept of cultural relativism. However, in the Dutch scheme there were only the standards that went with these two worlds; there was no room for the transitional man, the man who sought to become Westernized without necessarily losing all of his traditional values. Thus, for example, if an Indonesian wanted to become a doctor, a lawyer, or an engineer, he would be expected to meet the high standards of the universities in Holland. In contrast, for the British there was only one way of doing things, the "proper way," and all peoples were encouraged to follow it to the best of their abilities; they might not succeed and the transitional individuals, the "babu Indians," might be annoying people, but at least they were understandable and they had a place. For the Dutch there was no place, no recognition, for the counterpart of those within the British territories who could identify themselves with some pride as "Oxon, B.A. (failed)."

Before World War II, it was commonly held that the Dutch-administered government not only was the most sympathetic in Asia but also closely represented a model colonial policy.[25] Now, however, it appears that the Dutch system of indirect rule left the Indonesians with a highly ambiguous image of the desirable qualities of political authority. Present-day Indonesians seem more unsure of what their standards of political behavior should be than most Southeast Asians. More important, they also seem to have a high degree of insecurity

[25] In the classic comparative study of British and Dutch role in Southeast Asia, *Colonial Policy and Practice* (Cambridge, Eng., 1908), J. G. Furnivall found much more of merit in the Dutch approach than in the British. It should be noted, however, that he was seeking to influence British postwar policy and thus he was particularly interested in criticizing prewar policies in Burma.

and gnawing doubts as to their own abilities. Although other considerations, including some features of traditional Indonesian culture, contribute to this state of affairs, much of it seems to be related to the Dutch system of indirect rule.[26] Since independence there has been more uncertainty over the goals of the society and the standards of political conduct in Indonesia than in any other Southeast Asian country. This has been the case in spite of the fact that more people have had administrative and political experience in Indonesia than in several of the other countries.

In the case of Indo-China, the Western impact came in a considerably later period, but was relatively more encompassing than in either Burma or Indonesia. In 1787 France established treaty relations with the king of Annam, but aside from the activities of missionaries, the French, first, because they had lost out to the British in India, and, second, because of the Napoleonic Wars, were in no position to extend their influence in Southeast Asia. It was only with Napoleon III that France became a serious colonial power in the region. The persecution of missionaries in 1858 occasioned the dispatching of a French fleet to Saigon. The Annamese emperor was forced to cede three provinces of Cochinchina to the French in 1862. The following year Cambodia became a protectorate, and four years later the three remaining provinces of Cochinchina were annexed. As the result of interventions in Tongking, further treaties were obtained in 1883 and 1884 in which both Annam and Tongking became French protectorates.

Much of the difficulties that the French had in imposing their authority stemmed from their mistaken view that Tongking was a separate country forcibly ruled by the Annamese court. Once they recognized that the area was one country and established friendly relations with the Court of Hue, most of the Indo-Chinese opposition ceased. Thereafter the French relied very heavily upon the mandarins and

[26] The intensity of Indonesian feelings toward the Dutch at present is hard to account for simply in terms of the way in which the Indonesians had to struggle for independence. Many factors have, of course, complicated the recent history of Indonesian-Dutch relations, but fundamental to all of them appears to be a deep feeling on the part of the Indonesians that while they must strive to realize the standards the Dutch respected, they may not be successful. In a sense, the Indonesians realize that the Dutch know them too well and they find it difficult to get the Dutch off their minds. The passing of time, especially since it has been accompanied by obvious difficulties, has only intensified the problem. Elsewhere in colonial Southeast Asia, where the Western rulers were more distant and less concerned with the daily lives of their subjects, the people had at least the advantages of greater privacy, and thus while they might feel that their virtues and strengths were not fully appreciated, they also to some degree could keep their foibles and weaknesses to themselves.

the traditional literati, gradually changing them from members of an essentially Chinese form of bureaucracy into functionaries and officials of civil service in the French tradition.

It is significant for comparative purposes that Indo-China was the one area of Southeast Asia which had a strong and highly developed traditional system of government at the time that it came under colonial rule. The Burmese monarchy was on the decline when the British arrived, and elsewhere in the region colonial rule was introduced to peoples with only petty rulers and memories of greater days. The Annamese, however, still had a strong sense of identity with Confucian civilization and their Sinofied pattern of government. In accepting the French as protectors, they initially expected a relationship somewhat comparable to the one that they had had under Chinese suzerainty. The Vietnamese had a justifiable pride in their civilization and they could see the possibilities of a reciprocal relationship with the French under which they would gain many of the benefits of Western civilization without losing their traditional identity.

French policy, in vacillating between the ideals of assimilation and the goal of association, produced a far broader and more diffuse cultural impact than either British or Dutch colonial policy. The idea of making Indo-China an extension of France in Asia, which guided the earlier phases of French rule, opened the way to a remarkably rapid emergence of a large group of highly Westernized Vietnamese. In responding to this invitation to participate in French culture, the Vietnamese proved to be the most successful of Southeast Asians in adapting to Western standards; of all the peoples of the region, the Vietnamese alone have produced men who have successfully followed careers within Europe as professors and scientists and as members of other professions. This is a reflection not only of French policy but also of the fact that the Vietnamese are the products of a sophisticated traditional civilization that placed high value on intellectual attainment and the disciplining of the mind.

In spite of a few conspicuous successes in Europeanizing the Indo-Chinese, the French ideal of assimilation was completely unrealistic in terms of the bulk of the population. The alternative French goal of association was equally unattainable, for no class was produced that could serve as the foundation for a Franco-Asian relationship. The Westernized Vietnamese who had lost the claim to leadership of the traditional elements in their society could only reestablish such a claim by conspicuously rejecting their affiliations with the French.

The peculiar emphasis of French rule helps to explain why the present leadership of South Vietnam, probably the most Westernized in all Southeast Asia, places the most emphasis upon recapturing features of the traditional culture. To the extent that it can be said that the French left the Vietnamese unprepared for independence, it was for almost precisely the opposite reasons that the Dutch may have left the Indonesians unprepared for the modern world. For, if it can be said that the Dutch sought to preserve traditional Indonesian culture under hothouse conditions, then it would seem appropriate to say that the French sought to develop a Europeanized culture under hothouse conditions.

We have already noted the profound impact of Spain on the Philippines, particularly in the sphere of religion. The few decades of American rule exposed the Philippines to quite a different kind of Western impact. Indeed, the American approach differs not only from that of Spain but also from that of all the other European powers. Even before the United States had established its rule, thought was being given to eventual independence. In contrast to the other colonial powers, the American government did not seek economic gain from its colony, but rather assumed many of the expenses which colonial peoples have generally had to bear. In making more explicit than the European colonial powers the goal of independence, the Americans sought to emphasize aspects of Western life that were stressed to a lesser degree elsewhere in Southeast Asia. This led, for example, to the American focus on public education. Within three years after the United States assumed control, over 1,000 American schoolteachers had been recruited to teach in the Philippines, and within twenty-five years there were, in proportion to their respective populations, eight times as many people receiving high-school educations in the Philippines as in their former mother country, Spain.

The most distinctive feature of American rule, however, was that it made constitutional issues and the development of legislative and political processes a primary goal of policy. Everywhere else the Western impact in the sphere of government had centered on the development of administrative rule. For all the other colonial powers, the first priority was the creation of an administrative structure; a civil service and a rationalized bureaucracy had to be established before any attention was given to the development of politicians and of an open political process. In the Philippines the American concept of rule required the emergence of elected representatives of the people at the earliest possible moment. Although the Americans brought radical changes in all spheres of government, introducing a civil service based on merit, establishing a supreme court and an independent judiciary, their greatest impact was in the realm of constitutional and popular politics.

Even before American rule was fully established, the Filipinos were encouraged to create political parties. The first party was the Federalist, which championed the goal of eventual statehood, a goal which the Americans first saw as praiseworthy but later as rather embarrassing. In February 1901 the second party, the Partido Conservador, was formed; it opposed annexation and favored a liberal government that would reflect the Spanish heritage of Philippine society. Several other parties were formed by the time the first elections were held in 1907, but only the Nationalista Party, which won 59 of the 80 seats, was to have an enduring history.[27]

The American approach meant that the Filipinos were introduced to the idea that the relationship between the people and the government rested primarily upon the politician and not upon the administrator. Since all political parties could proclaim independence as their objective, none found it necessary or desirable to champion gross nationalistic ideologies. Instead, the image of leadership that evolved in the Philippines was clearly that of the politician who looked after the particular interests of voters. Elsewhere the pattern of the Western impact under colonialism gave emphasis to the role of the rational administrator who apparently operated according to principles of efficiency and who was not supposed to be influenced by political pressures within the society. Consequently, when the politicians emerged in these societies, they tended to become the champions of nationalistic ideologies and even the enemies of the rational administrators. As we shall see, only slowly is the role of the politician becoming that of the representative of the various interests of the public in these countries, and in most cases an effective working relationship between the role of the politician and that of the administrator is yet to be achieved. The Philippines have been spared many of these problems, but on the other hand it cannot be said that the Western impact has given the Filipinos an efficient administrative machinery.

Although in Southeast Asia colonialism was the primary agent of the Western impact, there remains Thailand, the one country that did not

[27] The remarkable stability and continuity of the Nationalista Party, which at present is the dominant party, were in large part due to the political skills of two of its founders, Sergio Osmena and Manuel L. Quezon, who as speaker of the House and president of the Senate, respectively, shaped the path to Philippine independence.

experience European rule. In this case, the Western impact came largely under the auspices of the traditional elite. The Siamese court, in struggling to maintain its independence, found it necessary to introduce many Western ideas and practices. Under the remarkable reforms of King Mongkut and King Chulalongkorn, the traditional Siamese machinery of government was gradually transformed into a modernized bureaucracy. The traditional aristocracy came to assume new roles and responsibilities as officials in the departments of government set up by advisors from numerous Western countries.

The effect of the Western impact on Thailand was less drastic than in the colonial regions and large numbers of people were not violently jarred out of their traditional modes of life. The effect, rather, was to change the character of the elite; the monarchy in time lost its autocratic powers and authority gravitated into the hands of three groups of the transformed elite: the military, the bureaucrats, and the students who had returned from studying abroad.

These three groups were all the products of the changes that the monarchy introduced; they were the most Westernized elements of Thai society. However, since the rest of the society had not changed as drastically, they came to occupy a somewhat autonomous position, in that they did not have strong roots in the larger society and thus relations among themselves came to dominate the politics of the country. Under these circumstances, the military became the key group because of their command of the means of violence, and the *coup d'état* became the main device for testing changes in relative power.

The fact that Thailand was the one country in Southeast Asia that did not experience colonial rule makes it possible to distinguish the general effects of the Western impact from the effects of colonial rule. To a remarkable extent, Thailand seems to have many characteristics in common with the former colonial countries of the region, and thus many developments which have generally been associated with particular policies of the colonial government may in fact have been related to the more basic process which societies are likely to undergo in breaking out of their traditional forms.

The characteristics of this process will be analyzed in the next section, and it is only necessary to note here that the most conspicuous differences between Thailand and the other Southeast Asian countries are: (1) the Westernization process was much slower and has not touched as deeply the bulk of the population in Thailand; (2) the Thais have not as yet had to make as many fundamental social and economic adjustments and thus they are just beginning to experience some of the problems of the other countries; (3) although traditional institutions have been greatly weakened, there is a less vigorous demand in Thailand for the adoption of democratic forms and the stimulation of economic development; and (4) the Thais appear to have a less complicated emotional reaction to the West.

In summarizing the Western impact on Southeast Asia, we may note that the different forms and auspices under which Western influence was introduced to the various countries set the stage for significantly different patterns of subsequent political development. In particular, in Southeast Asia it is possible to perceive striking differences that depend upon whether the Western impact had its greatest effect on the formal, authoritative structure of government, on the non-authoritative social processes of the entire society, or on both in about equal degree. In those cases where direct rule was employed, there were drastic changes in the formal structure of government which ran far ahead of the changes in the societies at large. For example, Burma and Malaya came to have governmental institutions which were far more rationalized and modernized than any other institutions within their society.

In the case of indirect rule, the formal structures of government were not the leading innovators or examples of modern practices, but rather social changes tended to take place at a faster pace. Often under indirect rule changes in the authoritative structures of government occurred only in order to keep up with changes in the social or economic patterns of life. In most cases where indirect rule was practiced, the formal structures of government have been inadequate to the task of guiding or controlling the pattern of change even during the post-colonial period.

In Thailand, and to a lesser degree in Laos and Cambodia, change was mediated through an indigenous elite, with the result that it was more gradual, more evenly balanced between the realms of the formal authoritative structure of government and the societies at large, and both government and people have been less intensely committed to achieving a modern way of life.

II. PROCESSES OF CHANGE

The pattern of the Western impact in Southeast Asia, which was most conspicuous in the form of colonial rule, dislocated the fundamental bonds of the traditional societies and set in motion several processes of social change. It has been customary to relate these changes and the problems they created to the policies of the colonial powers. As important as public policy was under governments that emphasized administrative rule, it would be a gross exaggeration of the powers of government to identify all change with colonial policy. Indeed, to do so would be to give an inordinate degree of primacy to the political realm in human societies. It is often convenient for purposes of analysis to relate the social changes in Southeast Asia to particular policies of colonial government, but to do only this is to overlook many of the fundamental problems that traditional societies encounter in adjusting to the modern world and to obscure the types of problems that these countries now face. Attention must be given to some of the types of fundamental changes that have arisen and are still arising in Southeast Asia.

Urbanization

In traditional Southeast Asia, as we have noted, the village was the primary unit of social life and towns existed largely as centers of court life. With the arrival of the West, trading centers were established which grew, first, in response to the needs of defense, and then as administrative centers. The city is a relatively new phenomenon in Southeast Asia; all the large cities of the area were either non-existent or only small towns when Boston was already a city with worldwide connections.

It is extremely significant that the rapid growth of all the cities in the area occurred with almost no encouragement from industrial development. In the West the modern city is a function of industrialism; in Southeast Asia the basis of the city has been commercial and administrative activities. Yet in Southeast Asia people are being attracted to the cities with the expectation that they will be able to find a way of life and a standard of living that are dependent upon industrial development. Also, of course, people are being pushed toward the cities because of the bankruptcy of the peasant economy under the pressures of population growth and commercialization. The cities have become the centers of the Southeast Asian countries in the sense that they produce the national leadership and the people who are now most influential in defining the expectations of the nation as a whole.

The process of urbanization has been the strongest factor in breaking the ties of Southeast Asians to their traditional modes of life (see Table 2). It has produced, on the one hand, the new elite society that

TABLE 2

Country	Literate % of Pop. (estimate 1956)	Urbanized % of Pop. (estimate 1956)	Per Capita Income $US	Rate of Population Increase %
Philippines	62.1	24.1	201	1.9
Malaya	30.8	26.5	310	2.3
Thailand	18.0	9.9	130	1.5
Vietnam	23.0	11.0	100	1.8
Burma	56.4	8.0	72	1.7
Indonesia	46.2	15.0	100	2.1
Cambodia	20.0	5.0	70	1.3
Laos	20.0	2.0	50	1.3

dominates the politics of the various countries. Indeed, the national politics of most of the countries is largely limited to the pattern of relationships of those within the capital city. As the most Westernized elements of the society, they are the ones most concerned with the shaping of their countries' future.

On the other hand, the urbanization process has produced large masses of uprooted people who have not found economic or social security. They have been either lured to the city or driven to it, and in the process they have seen the possibilities for a much better way of life than they have realized in actual fact. The result has been a high degree of restlessness.

The problem of urban growth without industrial development is at present a pressing one: Jakarta has recently been attracting nearly 500 people a day, Bangkok and Rangoon nearly 250. Since the need for labor has not been expanding much, the result has been an inefficient use of manpower and persisting low wages. At the same time the rapid increase in urban population has generated inflationary pressures. It is largely these newly urbanized elements who, dissatisfied with their lot, are now turning increasingly to political activities.

The process of urbanization has thus produced the two groups who are now the most important elements in Southeast Asian politics: the current Westernized leadership and the restless aspiring elite. This has led to the extraordinary phenomenon that Southeast Asia has one of the most urban-centered political processes in the world, while the bulk of the population is still village-based and peasant-oriented.

Restratification

In traditional Southeast Asian societies, the bulk of the population was divided between peasants and aristocracy. The marginal groups consisted largely of artisans, soldiers, and merchants. The process of change, and particularly urbanization, has produced new social groupings and a new stratification of the society. The basic division in Southeast Asia is now between the urbanized classes and the rural population.

A distinctive feature of social stratification in this region is that many of the economic changes introduced by the West did not produce new classes of Southeast Asians, but rather the necessary functions were performed by other Asians, particularly Chinese and Indians. With the opening of mines and plantations, it was found to be more efficient and economical to recruit Chinese and Indians for the labor force, even when this involved paying for their transportation. Even more significant has been the fact that with the introduction of a moneyed economy the Chinese and Indians were the most successful in developing retail trade and the credit market. The traditional Southeast Asian aristocracy generally avoided commercial activities and clung to its historic manner of life. For example, in Indonesia, although the wives of the *prijaji* class have engaged in some genteel commercial activities, largely connected with the sale of *batik* cloth, the men have generally turned to commerce only as clerks in European firms, an occupation which is seen as being compatible with the traditional role of the bureaucratic official.

The functions that the Chinese and Indians came to perform in the region hindered the development of a Southeast Asian middle class. In Indonesia the existence of large numbers of Eurasians was a further obstacle to the achievement of middle-class status, since this group tended to fill many of the middle ranks in the civil service.

There are some differences in social stratification among the Southeast Asian countries. In the Philippines the traditional land-owning upper class has responded to the opportunity to engage in industrial and commercial entrepreneurial activities. Indeed, most of the entrepreneurs who have been introducing new enterprises come from the established families of Spanish days. A second class is that produced by educational opportunities and consists largely of lawyers, teachers, other professional people, and politicians.

In Indonesia, the traditional aristocracy was not land-based but dependent upon government office; consequently it has lacked the capital and the inclination to turn to modern forms of entrepreneurship. Education in Indonesia has greatly increased the number of people seeking careers in government; it has not produced a class concerned with leadership in the commercial or industrial field. Government and politics have remained the principal answer to social advancement.

Traditionally, Burmese society was a highly mobile one; even peasants with wits and good fortune might become members of the court. Security could always be found in the monastery. Like the Indonesians, the Burmese were slow in turning to commercial activities; the Indians, and, to a lesser extent, the Chinese assumed many of the economically beneficial functions made possible by colonial rule. The educated classes in Burma have tended to look to careers in government and reject private industry. As elsewhere in Southeast Asia, the fact that more Burmese are being trained than the government can absorb has produced a class of underemployed intellectuals.

The lack of advanced industrial development in the region has retarded the emergence of a stable laboring class. Western enterprises, concentrating mainly on extractive industries, have tended to rely upon other Asians for their skilled labor and upon Southeast Asians as unskilled laborers. Peasants in moving to the mines and oil fields and onto plantations have generally retained the expectation of returning to the land and the village. The high degree of expected, if not actual, mobility back and forth between unskilled jobs and village life has impeded the development of attitudes and commitments common to an industrial labor force. The growth of the trade union movement is still largely a reflection of the interests of a non-laboring class leadership.

In general, it may be said that in the transitional societies of Southeast Asia the Western impact has been sufficient to disarrange the traditional stratification of the societies, but as yet change has not gone far enough to permit the emergence of a social order more appropriate to the modern world. The two main traditional classes of Southeast Asia—the aristocracy and the peasantry—have been slow in rejecting their traditional roles. The urbanization process, which is the main factor in reshaping the social order, has not as yet produced a stable pattern of urban life. As a consequence, sharp class lines have not emerged, and the gap between the rich and the poor is at best filled with people who are unsure of their social identity.

Secularization

As we have observed, religion was the basic bond between rulers and subjects in traditional Southeast Asia. The introduction of Western rule, whether direct or indirect, weakened and eventually destroyed this tie. It cannot, however, be said that the political and social life of Southeast Asia is now dominated by secular attitudes. In the Islamic countries of Indonesia and Malaya there are important elements advocating that government should be based on religion. More generally, much of the emphasis that national leaders have given to ideological matters represents an attempt to establish new emotional bonds between official and citizen.

In numerous respects the Western impact has narrowed the social and political scope of religion. Secular education, the weakening of family ties, the change from village to city life, have all contributed to a decline in the formal position of religion in the lives of Southeast Asians. On the other hand, religion still remains one of the principal bases for social identification, playing an important part in defining the communal groups in most of the countries. The nationalist movement in Indonesia and Burma first took the form of religious activities. All the countries of the region, except the Catholic Philippines, have had political parties based on religion. In a few cases, these parties have been headed by religious leaders, but more often the leadership has been hardly less secular than that of the other parties.

Thus, although secular institutions have been replacing religious ones as the dominant sources of social control, religion remains an important factor in the political and social life of Southeast Asia. Both Islam and Buddhism are still highly dynamic forces. Indeed, they provide the clearest and most authoritative statements of basic human values in societies which have not passed through an era in which such values have been articulated in more secular terms. Thus, while Southeast Asians have adopted many institutions and forms which in the West were of a secular nature and which were imbued with secularized values, they have introduced into them their own religious values. This continued reliance upon historic religions represents one of the most successful ways in which Southeast Asians have given meaning, in terms of their own particular heritages, to their new forms and structures of political life.

Commercialization

The process of urban growth, the changes in social stratification, and the emergence of more secular norms of behavior all reflect in large part the impact of Western commercial and economic institutions on the region. It is significant that the pattern of Western economic activities in Southeast Asia has been one in which the merchant and trader were followed by those involved in extractive enterprises—in mining, oil, and plantation crops—but this did not lead to a higher stage of industrial production. By creating dual economies in most of the Southeast Asian societies, this pattern of Westernized economic activity gave the peoples of the region a sense of the possibility of having a higher standard of living, but it did not provide an adequate basis for an expanding economy which might have improved the lot of everyone in the region. The psychological effects of Western commercial development were mainly to give the people a false impression of the difficulties inherent in economic development. It seemed to many Southeast Asians, especially the nationalists in Indonesia and Burma, that the European lived well on the basis of his managerial activities, that he must be exploiting the Asians, and that his position depended entirely upon the colonial administration. Thus, with independence many of these Southeast Asian leaders expected that there would be an automatic rise in standards of living, and, since the interests of the industrialized European colonial powers were no longer represented in government policy, that there should be a rapid expansion of industrialization. In fact, of course, independence brought very few changes in the structures of the Southeast Asian economies: in the last decade only in the Philippines has much advance been made in the tremendously difficult task of bringing more industrialized activities into a Southeast Asian society.

Westernized Education

We have already had occasion to note the emphasis American policy gave to education in the Philippines. Elsewhere in Southeast Asia the colonial powers were considerably slower and less enthusiastic about introducing Western educational systems. In Burma and Malaya the pressure for establishing British schools came largely from the need for clerks and lower-level administrators. The Dutch were extremely conservative about providing opportunities for Western education, and at a remarkably early period they were sensitive to the problems that might follow from creating numbers of unemployed Westernized intellectuals. The French, with their stress on the cultural dimension, led all the European powers in encouraging the growth of Western educational facilities in their territories.

There was considerable difference in the content of the Western education provided by the various colonial powers. In the Philippines the curriculum was adapted from American public school materials, with special emphasis placed upon citizenship training, American history, and democratic ideals and ethics. The British, confident of the merits of their educational traditions, made almost no concessions to local conditions in introducing their school systems. In Burma and Malaya a Westernized education meant preparing for the English universities, to which only a very few ever went, and concentrating on the humanities. Although Raffles College in Singapore began with a medical faculty, most of the British-sponsored training did not lead to a specialization. However, the trend, as in India, was in the direction of encouraging students to look to careers in the law. Thus most of the political leaders in both Malaya and Burma received legal training. In Indonesia legal training involved considerable work in traditional Adat law, and medical and engineering training, which the Dutch emphasized, constituted the most Westernized and the most elite forms of education. It is significant that whereas in Burma and Malaya those with legal training led the independence movements, such leadership in Indonesia came from the students of the medical and engineering schools.

In spite of these differences in emphasis and in substance, the general effects of Western education were the same in all Southeast Asian cultures: it produced the leadership elements for all the nationalist movements and for all the newly independent governments. Indeed, Westernized education has been more important than class, occupation, or income in determining recruitment to the ranks of the political elite in Southeast Asia. In all of the countries, those with Westernized educations have dominated the national political scene, and there are only an exceptional few without such an education among the leaders.

The Westernized schools have thus become centers for creating expectations about future careers of power and influence. A Western form of education is viewed by many Southeast Asians as providing an opportunity to enter into a new world in which power, wealth, and comfort are available to all. This attitude has served to introduce the idea that status should depend in some degree upon effort and achievement. It has also, however, encouraged the belief that success in school should bring substantial material rewards. Consequently, the Westernized schools of Southeast Asia have been the recruiting grounds not only for the political elite of the region but also for some of the most frustrated and disillusioned members of these transitional societies.

National Unification and International Pressures

For most of Southeast Asia, all these various processes of social change took place within the administrative framework of colonial governments; thus they all contributed to the development of a sense of common identity among the people under each separate government. The result was a growth of nationalism that did not always coincide with the traditional, precolonial divisions among Southeast Asians. For example, Dutch rule gave to the people of the Indies a sense that to some degree they belonged to a common nation and that all the territories governed by the Dutch should be brought together in the state of Indonesia. The ideal of a united nation-state which colonial administrations provided tended to stimulate nationalistic ambitions that were often divorced from the realities of local sentiments. Nationalism in Southeast Asia, which often began out of respect for traditional religious values, tended increasingly to center on a demand for control of the authoritative instruments of government and not on the diverse values of the popular cultures. Consequently, nationalism was able to produce unity in seeking control of the offices of government, but it was generally less successful in producing agreement as to appropriate norms for the political process itself. Nationalist leaders were thus often unaware of the harsh and deep divisions that ran through their people and that only began to appear once the unifying power of the colonial authority was removed. In general, it can be said that in Southeast Asia, just as colonialism tended to produce an authoritative structure of government that was far more modernized than the rest of the society, so it also encouraged a kind of nationalism that focused more on that authoritative structure than on the operations of social and political processes throughout the society at large.

There were, of course, exceptions to this pattern. In Malaya demands for national unity were muffled by the fear of each other felt by ethnic groups, and pressure for national independence could take place only after the leaders faced up to the problems that divided them. In the Philippines unity came from the day-to-day operations of the political process rather than from a desire for uninhibited control of the organs of state.

Although it is far from clear how the forces of social change might have reshaped the Southeast Asian societies, it is certain that the process would have been a more gradual and possibly a more planned and rational one if the Second World War and a period of Japanese occupation had not intervened. The defeat of the Western powers and the appearance of Japanese-sponsored regimes not only stimulated nationalist sentiments throughout the region, but also destroyed the political bases of most of the Southeast Asians who had been leading their peoples to national development. The violence of the war and of the Japanese occupation provided opportunities for new elements and new leaders of more limited political experience. The pace and scope of change were thus violently accelerated and given new directions.[28] The nationalist movements that emerged out of this period of conflict were the ones that directed their countries through the difficult first years of independence. Often those who had the appropriate skills and talents for providing leadership during a period of confusion and excitement seemed to be peculiarly lacking in the skills necessary for leadership during the more difficult but less dramatic phase of trying to create a new nation.

Social Change and the Political Process

Social change is still the dynamic factor that governs the character of much of the politics of Southeast Asia. In all the countries of the area, the general commitment is one of advancement toward all that is associated with the modern world, and in none is there a significant clash between the old and the new. The difficulty, however, is that change has been very uneven, producing some harsh discontinuities. That is, change has not meant simply an increase in the technological efficiency with which the people realize their values; rather, it has meant that new values and interests have been introduced in a random and unsystematic fashion. Change has involved the acceptance of new values and new practices with respect to some spheres of life but not to others.

For both the individual and the society, change has been uneven. As we have noted, urban growth has far exceeded industrial development, and thus people are forced to adapt themselves to conditions of living for which the functional basis is missing. Possibly even more serious is the prospect that urban growth will continue to exceed the resources for urban development. Although at one time many of the major cities in the region—Singapore, Jakarta (or Batavia, as it was then), Manila, and Rangoon—had capital overhead investments well in advance of the pressures of population, it is questionable now whether in the foreseeable future any of these large cities will be able to provide the sewerage, water, and paved streets expected in a modern city. It has been estimated that if the total capital investments in all of the Philippines for one year were to be devoted to elementary urban overhead in the city of Manila, it would not be adequate for even the sewerage needs.

---

[28] Unfortunately, very little work has been done on the effects of the Japanese occupation on the various countries of Southeast Asia. The pioneering studies have been Willard H. Elsbree, *Japan's Role in Southeast Asian Nationalist Movements, 1940 to 1945*, Cambridge, 1953; Harry J. Benda, "Indonesian Islam under the Japanese Occupation," *Pacific Affairs*, Vol. XXVIII, December 1955, pp. 350-362; and Harry J. Benda, "The Beginnings of the Japanese Occupation of Java," *Far Eastern Quarterly*, Vol. XV, August 1956, pp. 541-560.

Social change has caused people to go to the city; it has not, however, provided them with a modern urban dweller's way of life. Similarly, social change has given Southeast Asians modern structures of government and expectations about the functions such government might serve, but it has not provided the social bases necessary for these structures to operate as expected in modern societies. There is thus a great gap between the modern forms of government and the more traditional patterns of life, between the world of the Westernized leaders and that of the less Westernized populations. In most of the countries, neither level of the society is in a position to support the other; rather, each tends to frustrate and impede the other's effective functioning. Thus, as we shall see, many of the Westernized structures do not perform the same functions in Southeast Asian societies as they do in the West, while many of the functions of the political process are not performed by the type of group or organization which would perform them in a Western society.

III. POLITICAL GROUPS AND POLITICAL FUNCTIONS

Political Groups

(1) *Parties and party systems.* The only political parties with any notable historical tradition are those in the Philippines, for as we observed the Americans were unique in stressing the development of political leaders and party politics in the colonial era. Elsewhere in Southeast Asia the few political parties that existed before the emergence of the nationalist movements were either little more than the personal followings of individual leaders or modified communal associations. For all their organizational weaknesses, these parties did have the virtue of a highly pragmatic approach, since they saw themselves essentially as groups seeking power and positions of authority for their leaders. The prewar Burmese parties were of this type, and so were the first parties in Malaya.

The rise of the nationalist movements did more than merely broaden and intensify popular interest in political events; it introduced an essentially ideological framework for much of the political life. There are several considerations which may account for the ideological emphasis in the nationalist movements, particularly those in Indonesia and Burma. First, these movements, in spite of their secular objectives, generally began as religious associations—in Indonesia it was the Serekat Islam movement and in Burma the Young Men's Buddhist Association—and thus they have a tradition of posing questions and discussing them in theological and philosophical terms. Second, the communal basis of much of the social life in the region seems to have contributed to the belief that each political association should represent a distinct way of life. Third, the lack of consensus on the very fundamentals of politics in these transitional societies seems to have encouraged the more articulate intellectuals and politicians to elaborate on ideological matters in the hope of clarifying the popular vision of the future society.

Thus in general the political parties of Southeast Asia tend to profess concern for ideological matters, and seek, with varying degrees of success, to provide their members with a total orientation toward life. Often they represent a distinct sociological, ethnic, or religious group. The principal exceptions are the parties in the Philippines and the embryonic parties in Thailand, Cambodia, and Laos, which are at the stage of being little more than the followings of individual leaders.

Indonesia has the most complicated array of political parties of any Southeast Asian country, a fact which reflects in part the cultural diversity of the country and in part the use of proportional representation. More than forty groups ran candidates in the one general election the country has had, but only four parties proved to be of national significance: the Nationalist (PNI), Masjumi (Moslem), Nahdatul Ulama (Moslem Teachers), and the Communist (PKI).

The Nationalist Party, with 57 of the 226 seats in parliament, emerged from the September 1955 elections with the largest popular vote. The party had great prestige because of the role of its leaders in the independence movement; Sukarno is generally considered to be a Nationalist. The party is divided between a "left" and a "right" wing, the former favoring close collaboration with the Communists, the latter being more pro-Western in sympathy. Before the 1955 elections it was widely assumed that Masjumi, with its longer history and its ties with Islam, would prove to be the most popular party in the country, but it received slightly fewer popular votes than the Nationalists, although gaining the same number of parliamentary seats. However, the importance of religion was not overestimated, because Nahdatul Ulama, or the Moslem Teachers' Party, won 45 seats. Both Masjumi and Nahdatul Ulama were organized in the 1920's, and both played important roles during the Japanese occupation. Both profess the same goal of being the political arm of Islam, and there has been intense rivalry between their leaders. In 1945 Masjumi "absorbed" Nahdatul Ulama, so that the latter did not have its strength accurately reflected in the provisional parliament. Nahdatul Ulama's strength lies at the village level and it is more conservative and more nationalistic than Masjumi. Masjumi is the more urbanized party, and indeed it is considered to be composed of the most socially mobile people of Indonesia.

The Communists emerged from the 1955 elections as the fourth largest party, with 39 seats, but since then they have proved themselves in local elections to be the dominant party on Java. The Communists are the best organized and the richest party in Indonesia. They have the largest number of full-time professional workers and a substantial number of front organizations, which include the largest trade unions.

Among the lesser parties is the Indonesian Socialist Party (PSI), the party of the Westernized intellectuals. Basically it is a party in favor of rationality, and therefore opposes the more irrational aspects of nationalism and the more doctrinaire features of Marxism. As an announced champion of intelligence and good sense, it has had little appeal for Indonesians, but its leaders have had considerable influence. Among the other minor parties of national significance are the Christian Party (Parkindo) and the Partai Katholik.

Except for the Communists, none of the Indonesian parties has a well-developed party organization. Although just before the 1955 elections the various parties did seek to establish local organizations and "grass-roots" support, they are primarily instruments of intra-elite competition. The divisions among the parties are far deeper than mere ideological and pragmatic issues; they include in particular a history of twenty or more years of intense personal conflicts among the members of the country's political elite. Thus, the Indonesian parties, in spite of the confusing emphasis they give to arguments about the nature of Utopia, do in fact provide a fairly realistic breakdown on the fundamental question of who among the Indonesian elite gets along well enough with whom to be able to share power effectively.

The parties in Malaya represent the extreme development of communal associations. There have been various widely praised attempts to establish non-communal parties, such as the Labor Party and the Independence for Malaya Party, but in spite of all the good will and kindness shown them, such efforts have not taken root. Apparently in the Malayan environment people prefer to denounce the pernicious qualities of communalism from a secure position within a communal party. The dominant parties in the country are the United Malays National Organization (UMNO) and the Malayan Chinese Association (MCA); during the election preceding independence the two banded together, along with the Malayan Indian Congress, to form the Alliance. The Alliance, still composed of its separate ethnic parts, has been the one political force controlling government since independence. The banding together of UMNO and MCA has meant that intercommunal questions can be handled informally within the Alliance by the leaders of the three ethnic groups. However, the creation of the Alliance has also meant that Malaya lacks a powerful and responsible loyal opposition party. The only other significant party in the country is the illegal Malayan Communist Party, which for over a decade has been employing violence and terror against the Malayan government.

It is still not clear where an effective opposition party will arise in Malaya. The various minor parties either lack appeal because of their non-communal character or tend to be extremist, particularly on communal issues. If an opposition were to come from a dissolution of the Alliance, then, of course, Malayan politics would become frankly based on the communal divisions.

Burma is another of the countries which gained independence without a significant opposition party. The Anti-Fascist Peoples' Freedom League (AFPFL) was, as its name suggests, a group that was formed with Communist participants during the Second World War. It was essentially an association of various political groupings in which the Marxists dominated. With independence the Communists broke away from the League and turned to insurrection. Aside from the personality of U Nu, the dominant factor in shaping the AFPFL was the Socialists, who for a time represented the inner council of the party. Other groups affiliated with the AFPFL include the Burma Muslim Congress, the Kachin National Congress, the Union Karen League, the Chins' Congress, and the United Hill People's Congress. During the early days of the AFPFL, when its leaders were anxious to make it appear the spokesman of all Burmese groups, it also included the All-Burma Fire Brigade, the St. John's Ambulance, the All-Burma Teachers' Organization, the All-Burma Women's Freedom League, and other such urban middle-class associations.

Until it split into two rival factions in June 1958, the AFPFL was a large, loose confederation that encompassed much of the diversity that is Burma. Its lack of homogeneity had been obscured by the articulateness of its ideologists. At the national level, the AFPFL included some of the leading administrators, intellectuals, and businessmen in Burma; it numbered devoted Buddhists and ardent Marxists; at the local level, it had some of the toughest-minded and most uncompromising political workers in all Asia. Although for several years U Nu spoke of the need to eliminate corruption and remove all bullies from the party, the position of the local AFPFL leaders was little affected. Indeed, the AFPFL was one of the rare non-Communist political parties in Asia with a strong organization at the local level, so strong that in some districts everyone, including bureaucratic and even elected officials, acknowledged the complete authority of the AFPFL representative on all matters relating to government. Given the diversity of views and the differences in political orientations in the AFPFL, it has been remarkable that the movement somehow held together for nearly a decade. In large measure the explanation for the unity that the AFPFL was able to maintain lies in the fact that in spite of all the ideological pronouncements the Burmese place great value on pragmatic calculations. These pragmatic considerations gave the party unity for so long; the same considerations led to the split in the AFPFL.

It is extremely difficult to classify the party systems which are emerging in the various countries of Southeast Asia because the parties themselves are generally so unstable. However, we may distinguish, first, the essentially one-party systems. Burma, while the AFPFL still dominated the scene, had what might best be called a comprehensive, nationalist, one-party system. Aside from the opposition, which came from the extremist movement that had turned to violence, the AFPFL dominated the Burmese political scene. Although it is difficult for the Western mind to classify Cambodian political practices, the kingdom probably belongs in the same category: the Sangkum (Popular Socialist Community), a creation of Prince Sihanouk, won all 91 seats in the National Assembly in 1955, in the first election ever held in Cambodia, and then all 62 seats which were contested in 1958. (After the first election Prince Sihanouk felt compelled to apologize for his "too complete success." After the second election it was announced that four of the five candidates of the Communist-front People's Party, the only other party that contested the election, did not receive a single vote. Apparently the People's Party dropped its request for a recount when the government suggested that unless the local Communists stopped disturbing the tranquility of the land, Cambodia might be forced to reconsider its neutralist foreign policy, which has included the acceptance of Communist Chinese aid).

Another type of one-party system found in Southeast Asia is that of North Vietnam, in which the Communist Vietminh exercises dictatorial control. It is the one area in Southeast Asia where, since the Geneva conference of 1954, a Communist party has been able to gain governmental control. Although North Vietnam conforms closely to the model of a Communist dictatorship, South Vietnam (Republic of Vietnam) cannot be said to be a model of a democratic republic. In bringing unity and order to the anti-Communist Vietnamese, President Ngo Dinh Diem felt compelled to destroy the various organizations which were potential political parties. These included the Binh Xuyen, which controlled all forms of vice and also the police in Saigon; the Cao Dai, a religious sect with a pope, an impressive array of saints including Victor Hugo, and a private army; and the Hoa Hao, another secret quasi-religious sect with its own private army. With the elimination of these groups through military action, Diem established the Movement for National Revolution (MNR), which has been largely a propaganda organization for the Diem government. Most of its members are to be found in the national ministries and the provincial administrations, members of the civil bureaucracy which is a prime source of Diem's power.

Malaya is another country possessing a one-party system with a dominant non-dictatorial party. In a separate category are the countries with competitive party systems, including the Philippines, Indonesia, Thailand, and Laos. There are, however, considerable differences among these competitive party systems. In the Philippines the parties are highly pragmatic, and in spite of the importance of personalities, they are fairly wide-based. In contrast, the Thai parties, which are also pragmatic, are quite narrow-based, often being little more than the personal following of a particular leader. In Laos the competition is between the Communist-oriented Neo Lao Hak Xat (Patriotic Front, which was the former Pathet Lao movement) and two parties of the government, one of which is known as the Independents and the other as the National Government Party. This competition between an ideological movement and pragmatic parties is complicated by the fact that Prince Souphandu Vong, the leader of the Communist-front group, is a half-brother of the Premier, Prince Souvanna Phouma. Although other members of the royal family (lower branch) have taken a lead in organizing parties with different degrees of anti-Communist orientations, the Communists have steadily expanded their influence.

The Indonesian party system is one in which ideological parties have tended to dominate the scene and in which compromises and adjustments have been extremely rare, in spite of the Indonesian propensity for discussing the virtues of cooperation.

(2) *Interest groups and interest group systems.* Political parties, ex-

cept where they have been all-embracing social movements, have not generally been the key units in the political processes of the Southeast Asian countries. Except for the Communists, none of the parties in the region has a strong organizational structure. The Philippine parties, for all their historical continuity, still represent primarily the network of personal ties and obligations of the Filipino politicians of the moment. Even in Indonesia, where much of the parliamentary struggle is accomplished in the name of political parties, not even the largest can be said to have well-developed and stable organizations. In Thailand, South Vietnam, Laos, and Cambodia the non-Communist parties are mainly propaganda and public relations organizations which serve as fronts for the real political actors who control them.

Who are the actors who are most influential in shaping the political processes of these countries? For most of the region, authoritative institutional groups dominate the political scene. In Thailand real power resides mainly in the army and, to a lesser extent, in the civil bureaucracy. Although the professional politician is more important in Indonesia, the army is also a crucial factor in the day-to-day politics of the island republic. In South Vietnam those who follow in the long tradition of the mandarinate and of the French bureaucracy have a commanding political role. Only in the Philippines can it be said that the authoritative institutional groups do not dominate the political process.

Political development in the region has thus followed a pattern in which the Western impact introduced relatively highly developed administrative and governmental structures, and now these institutional groups have become the main active elements of politics rather than the neutral instruments of public policy. Instead of the political parties and associational interest groups making policy decisions for the administrators and soldiers, the latter have generally taken the initiative. In several of the countries, their course of political development has resulted in the bureaucracy and the army becoming the only effectively organized and relatively modernized groups in the entire society capable of political action.

In Burma and South Vietnam, the authoritative institutional groups are committed to using their relative political freedom to encourage social and economic development. In some of the other countries, those in command of such power groups have been less anxious to encourage development. In both situations, a tendency toward authoritarian practices has resulted.

The lack of well-developed associational interest groups in most of

Southeast Asia means that an important source of restraint on such an authoritarian tendency is missing. As we shall see, the process of social change in Southeast Asia has not yet produced large numbers of functionally specific interest groups. Consequently there are relatively few formally organized groups that are seeking to differentiate and articulate particular interests. More often than not, those Westernized organizations which do claim to represent specific interests—such as trade unions and peasant associations—are the agents of some other group, like the nationalist movement, the Communists, or a particular ethnic group.

In all the Southeast Asian countries, non-associational interests have a significant influence on the political process. Indeed, popular participation comes less from specific interest groups and more from ethnic, religious, and status groupings which often lack any formal organization and usually represent very diffuse interests. As we have observed, the process of cultural change has produced divisions in all the societies of the region which are fundamental to their political life. In Malaya and to a lesser extent in Burma, ethnic differences provide the basis for some of the most fundamental political divisions. Much of the political behavior of the Indonesians is governed by their sense of identity with various regional groupings.

The latent characteristics of most special interests, and the prevalence of non-associational and essentially communal groupings with diffuse interests, contribute to the periodic appearance of anomic movements in some of the Southeast Asian countries. These movements represent attempts to advance raw, unaggregated demands which have not been systematically articulated. They are thus movements without programs that are usually produced by the tensions and frustrations that stem directly from the process of social change. In Southeast Asia these anomic movements are generally composed of newly urbanized people who have been forced off the land, and who thus lack a clear position in either the traditional society or the newly emerging one.

For example, in Singapore relatively little leadership and organizational effort have produced rather extreme mob actions. Although such demonstrations and attempts at direct political action cannot be considered spontaneous movements, they have taken form readily because significant elements of the Chinese population have felt that their interests are not represented in the open political process. Indonesia has also been plagued with anomic movements, and even more with the general expectation that sudden political outbursts are highly likely. In the rural areas, particularly in West Java, the northern end of Sumatra, and South Celebes, armed gangs have been engaging in acts of violence ever since independence, all in the name of Dar-ul Islam and the vague objective of an Islamic state. Within the large cities a comparable urban element exists which can be readily mobilized for street demonstrations. Although many of these young people are professional demonstrators, ready to perform for pay, the fact remains that in Indonesia people expect outbursts from those who feel politically neglected.

In order to understand the character of political group behavior in Southeast Asia, it is necessary to analyze in particular the problems that exist when a transitional society seeks to cope with the tasks of articulating the diverse interests of its people and then aggregating these interests into policies that are consistent with the basic requirements of public administration and the national interest. We must thus turn to an analysis of Southeast Asian political processes, giving special attention to how certain essential functions are performed.

Political Functions

The dominant characteristic of all the political systems of Southeast Asia is that they are still, as in the traditional and the colonial periods, sharply divided between the ruling few, who possess a distinctive outlook and culture, and the vast majority of the population, who are oriented to village units and the peasant's way of life. There have been, however, great changes in the values and culture of the ruling groups, for they now tend to represent the most urbanized and the most Westernized segments of the population.

None of the countries of Southeast Asia has an integrated and coherent political process, for in all of them the uneven pattern of acculturation has left some of their peoples deeply attached to what they see as a modern life while the others have hardly been shaken from their traditional outlook. Indeed, in Southeast Asia it is useful to think of the countries as possessing not a single and integrating political process but many only loosely related political processes. There is, of course, the dominant process at the national level which is based on the city and the administrative organs of the central government and which reflects the attitudes and values of those who belong to the society of the ruling groups. This process usually reflects the needs of those who envisage their loosely organized societies becoming modern nation-states. At the local level, however, there are other political processes, and since the countryside throughout Southeast Asia is highly fragmented in parochial groupings, it contains many nearly autonomous political processes.

This situation is a reflection of the fact that as yet there has not emerged in any of the Southeast Asian countries a distinct sphere of political relations that is clearly separated from the more basic patterns of social and personal relations. On the contrary, questions of social status, ethnic identity, and personal associations tend to determine the patterns of political loyalties and behavior.

The political processes of Southeast Asia represent essentially mixed systems that reflect the multi-dimensional divisions that run through these societies. Behind the main division separating the urbanized and the peasant-oriented segments lie other divisions. These include the gaps between ethnic and religious communities, between parochial cultures, and between those whose visions of a modern world stem from quite different sources. Under these circumstances, the leaders of the Southeast Asian countries are faced with a dual task: first, they are seeking to create a viable system of intra-elite role relationships; second, they are called upon to encourage the development of new systems of non-elite role relationships for the bulk of their peoples.

To the extent that these new systems of role relationships emerge, the countries will be moving in the direction of more coherent and interrelated political processes. The problem of arriving at a generally recognized and accepted pattern of inter-elite relationships has proved extremely difficult in all the countries, particularly so in Indonesia. However, unless those who now have control of the formal agencies of government can arrive at a consensus on the norms of political leadership, the goals of their societies, and the permissible choice of political means, it is doubtful whether the bulk of their peoples will be able to participate effectively in transforming their societies into modern nation-states. At present the mixed system common to Southeast Asia tends to produce anachronistic and conflicting patterns of behavior, such as a high reliance on democratic symbols coupled with authoritarian practices, and frequent proclamations of popular aspirations combined with denials of broad participation in the making of decisions.

In all cases, the leaders of the Southeast Asian countries who are trying to create new and stable patterns of political roles must operate in terms of the peculiar characteristics of the existing political processes of their societies. In seeking to comprehend their problems and to understand better the evolving shape of political life in Southeast Asia, we will find it helpful to isolate the key functions of the political process.

(1) *Interest articulation.* As the dynamic factor governing the character of Southeast Asian societies, the uneven course of cultural change has produced a paradoxical situation with respect to the articulation of interests. It must be remembered that over 85 per cent of the people of the region depend upon agriculture and yet the interests of agriculture are hardly to be heard. Rather, Southeast Asia has one of the most urbanized forms of politics to be found anywhere, and what might be assumed to be the voices of special interests generally speak in terms that are usually associated with urban life. This is, of course, only another way of emphasizing the extent to which the political processes of Southeast Asia are divided between the urban-dominated national level and the more traditional village-oriented levels.

The reasons why the diverse potential interests of the peoples of Southeast Asia are not better articulated are, of course, largely related to the circumstances that determine the recruitment process and the structure of communication in their societies. However, historical considerations and the tendency for societies in crisis to rely upon ideological expressions are also important in accounting for the inarticulateness of specific interests.

Under colonialism, attempts were made in almost all cases to recognize either legally or informally the existence of special interests. In Malaya the Legislative Council contained a few members who were specifically designated as the representatives of the leading industries, of labor, and of the minority ethnic groups. To a lesser extent, the British followed a similar policy in Burma. In Indo-China the French created the Grand Council of Economic and Financial Interests. The Dutch relied on various groups that were viewed as representing particular interests in Indonesian society. On the informal level such organizations as the chambers of commerce and the associations of the Overseas Chinese were generally able to express their interests to appropriate officials. Of course, the interests that were best received were those that represented the groups related to the more commercial and the more modern segments of the economies.

With the emergence of agitational politics, many of these earlier groups were viewed as being too closely associated with the colonial rulers. Even more important, as we have noticed, agitational politics in Southeast Asia tend to take the form of ideological movements. A common assumption of the nationalist leaders in the area was that they and their parties were capable of representing in themselves all the legitimate interests of their societies. Thus, in articulating their views as to the future character of their countries, they felt that they were speaking for all the interests of their people. The existence of factions within the nationalist movements only served to encourage all groups to expand their claims of representativeness.

Once the nationalist movements set the tone, the other groups tended to follow suit by also speaking in broad ideological terms. In part this process represents an attempt to produce a new political consensus. The focus has largely been on what should be the future character of each society. Rather than to articulate the current interests of the various segments of the society, the general approach has been to stress the idea that all groups will be taken care of in the new world of the future. Even since the nationalist parties in Burma and Indonesia failed to realize their new worlds and were replaced by the military as the dominant political force, the practice has still been to suggest that the common interests of all are represented in the decisions of the national leadership.

The failure of special interest groups to adopt more limited goals related to the peculiar problems of their membership is, of course, partly a function of the changing character of Southeast Asian societies. New interests are just coming into existence with the structural changes in the societies, and interests that are a function of the more traditional order have not lost their basis of power. Given a high degree of uncertainty about the institutionalized patterns of the future, all groups feel it appropriate to have ambitions that go beyond just representing their particular functional interests in the current society. For example, so long as trade union leaders see themselves as occupying a position from which they can move into the ranks of the national elite, they will tend to articulate not the specific problems of workers but the demands and ideas which will make them appear to be appropriate members of the national elite.

These considerations have impeded the emergence of functionally specific interest groups in most of Southeast Asia, so that informal associations still operate as such groups did during the traditional and the colonial periods. Historically, Southeast Asian societies did not have as rich a variety of informal groups and associations as many traditional societies did. Instead of tribes, there were the village and the clan organizations; instead of guilds, there were confederations of traders—but the associations that did exist were essentially communal ones, in the sense that they were the focus of most of the social life of their members. Their functions were not limited to advancing specific objectives, since they sought to protect their members against all outsiders. Their behavior was governed by the atittude that only the king and his court could legitimately decree governmental rules and regulations, but that it was appropriate to seek exemptions from lower officials in the application of such rules. They thus chose to proceed quietly, not articulating any demands in the making of laws; and in seeking special treatment in the application of laws, they had to employ particularistic considerations.

The rapid growth of urban centers during the colonial period produced a great increase in the number of informal associations in Southeast Asia, but the basic situation remained much the same. The colonial authorities in all the countries generally followed the practice of recognizing either formally or informally the existence of such groups. In dealing with the informal associations, the authorities felt they had a channel for communicating policy information to various segments of the population and for receiving popular reactions. The leaders of even the more modern groups like the trade unions and the trade associations and chambers of commerce, however, found that they had little influence on shaping general policy. Thus, within the limited area where they could be effective, it was still to their advantage to reason quietly with the appropriate officials, to try to protect any and all of the interests of their following, and not to articulate broadly any special interest. The effectiveness of the leaders usually depended upon the extent to which they avoided making themselves a nuisance and accepted the general outlook of the officials. Consequently, it was generally the more Westernized officials who were given the best reception, but these were usually the very people who were most likely to lose a sense of identity with the concrete interests of their followings. As Asians they came to represent and articulate what was accepted as "Asian opinion," but which, in fact, was the opinion of only a segment of the society defined in terms of the acculturation process. Their interests were those of a stratum of the total society that was seeking admission into the culture and society of the national elite. Their demands of course became increasingly nationalistic as they sought control over their governments. This process, in producing the new elites of the region, worked against the articulation of the specific economic or social interests of all the elements of the existing societies. In short, even when the emerging nationalist leaders began their climb to power from positions of leadership in what might appear to have been interest groups, they tended to champion the interests of the new Westernized strata of the society and not so much the particular and more limited interests of functionally distinct groups. They generally adopted the position that, in supporting the cause of independence, they were in fact advancing the most basic interest of all groups.

Thus we see that throughout the political history of Southeast Asia various factors have worked against the development of highly articulate interest groups. However, if we examine the emerging patterns of development in the region, we find signs that increasingly specific interests are demanding open recognition. In spite of their ideologically oriented approach, the nationalist leadership has had to respond quietly to the strong demands of many interests in their society. During the immediate post-independence period they tended to treat these responses as though they were only expediencies, but with time and experience they have found it increasingly necessary to heed the immediate and pressing interests of important elements of their societies which have not been satisfied by nationalistic slogans.

In Indonesia the delicate balance of power among the leading parties has forced all of them in varying degrees to seek gradually broader support in terms of interests rather than ideologies. In one sense, the crisis in Indonesia has been brought on by a decline in the effectiveness of ideological and nationalistic appeals without a concurrent rise in the effectiveness of interest group representation. This course of development has been particularly apparent in the demands of the Outer Islands for a greater degree of autonomy. President Sukarno, in responding to these demands with his "concept" of a "guided democracy," charged that the political parties had failed to represent the real interests of the society. In proceeding to create a national council composed of representatives of the various social and economic interests that would supersede parliament, President Sukarno was opposed by all parties, except the Communists and a wing of the Nationalists, on the grounds that his conception of a corporate state would end the hopes for representative government and bring about a reversion to an essentially colonial method of dealing with the various interests. Thus, at present Indonesia is caught up in the problems of moving away from a nationalistic-ideological form of politics toward a political process in which different interests can compete while at the same time maintaining the necessary degree of national unity.

The situation in Burma has been in some respects similar, although not as extreme. Political articulation under the Anti-Fascist People's Freedom League took a largely nationalistic and ideological form, but increasingly the numerous factions within the AFPFL came to establish informal but highly significant ties with particular interests. These practices created tensions and strains, and, although it is clear that functionally specific interest groups are developing and will be demanding greater recognition, it is still difficult to forecast the consequences for national unity. The establishment of the government of General Ne Win in October 1958 has produced a reunifying of the country under army auspices which may have checked, at least temporarily, the trend toward more specific interest groups. It would seem, however, that over time the policies of the army will cause an increase in autonomous interest groups. In Vietnam the same problem is almost certain to arise in a few years, particularly since the highly centralized and controlled administration of the Diem government goes against an earlier tradition of numerous groups with informal ties to special interests. Although Malayan politics have not had a strongly nationalistic and ideological nature, an analogous situation in this newest Southeast Asian country is that the communal problem of the Malays and Chinese has been such an overriding factor as to inhibit the articulation of potentially more specific interest groups. Again we confront the question of whether there exists enough sense of national unity to meet a rising need for competing interest groups to articulate openly their conflicting demands on government policy.

Only in the Philippines do we find a markedly different situation, since the Filipino political parties have never had strong ideological orientations. In contrast to the rest of Southeast Asia, the Filipino politicians and parties from early in the period of American rule have proceeded under the assumption that their key function is that of accommodating different social and economic interests. This, however, has not meant that Philippine politics has been characterized by large numbers of highly articulate interest groups, for the Filipino politicians have sought to deal with interests in the society on an individual and personal basis. In a sense they have usurped the role of leaders of interest groups by establishing relations directly with those who want to make demands on government policy. Changes in Philippine society will lead to more diversified interests, which will probably mean that the Filipino politicians will find it increasingly difficult to deal directly with them. It thus seems quite probable that Philippine politics is moving in the direction of highly articulate interest-group politics along the lines of the American model.

(2) *Interest aggregation.* Our discussion of the interest articulation functions in Southeast Asian politics has foreshadowed and indeed intruded upon the question of the ways in which interests are aggregated in these traditional societies. We have noted how those involved at the national level tend to conceive of themselves as shaping a new future for their societies and hence as representing the interests of all the people. Since specific and limited interests are generally not effectively articulated, it is extremely difficult for the national leaders to cast themselves explicitly in the role of political brokers engaged in aggregating different specific interests. The lack of functionally specific interest groups makes it almost impossible for the Southeast Asian political leaders to measure even crudely the relative support behind one potential interest as against another.

Consequently, the Southeast Asian political leaders cannot easily adapt their political postures according to estimates of the advantages of favoring some particular interests more than others. Finding it necessary to reach relatively undifferentiated audiences, they tend to speak in terms of the largest possible aggregations of interests, which generally means adopting highly nationalistic themes and avoiding issues that might divide the people. This situation also causes the national leaders to employ the same methods for mobilizing support irrespective of the importance they attach to a particular objective or issue. That is to say, the leaders find it necessary to act as though they were aggregating the interests of all the people on all issues; thus, regardless of whether it is a major question of national interest or a more limited problem, they must adopt the same approach.

To the extent that the national leaders of Southeast Asia seek to act as representatives of all their peoples and not as brokers aggregating specific interests, they perform in much the same manner as did the dominant leaders in traditional Southeast Asian societies. It will be remembered that historically the rulers in the region were conceived of as embodying all the interests of their peoples. The great changes in Southeast Asian societies have not yet affected as sharply as might be expected the essentially communal basis for aggregating interests. At the village level, the pressures of custom and conformity still work to suppress the development of more explicit methods of aggregating separate and distinct interests. The demand for harmony and cooperation common to most of the villages of Southeast Asia is an expression of the view that within a communal context all interests can be readily accommodated with a minimum of explicit institutions for aggregating them. The extension of the communal basis of politics to the national level—first, in the form of the urbanized elite society and, second, in the communally oriented political groups—results in much the same lack of emphasis upon explicitly structured means for isolating and then aggregating specific interests. The belief that all interests can and should be aggregated in a communal or fraternal spirit and on the basis of ideological pronouncements has no doubt contributed to the sense of anxiety with which Burmese and Indonesians have watched personal divisions emerge in the ranks of their nationalist leadership. This attitude has probably also contributed to the willingness of these people to accept the political intervention of the military, who speak in terms of a higher national interest and of the aggregation of all special interests through the sentiments of patriotism.

If we explore more deeply into the political processes common to Southeast Asia, we find that the function of aggregating interests is handled largely by highly personal and informal practices. The patterns of social and personal relationships provide the channels through which many interests are communicated and they have to bear much of the strain of aggregating and accommodating the various demands. Consequently the common practice is for those with power and influence to provide protection and security for all those who identify with them and accept them as leaders. Often those with conflicting interests have personal and social associations with the same political figure or group, which then is placed in the position of a mediator. It is here that we find practices which are likely to develop into a more explicit brokerage process as interests become more sharply defined. These developments seem to be relatively slow in most Southeast Asian societies, and in part this is because, as we shall observe, the focus of political activities in Southeast Asia is not concentrated on questions of policy or of formal rule-making. There is thus little expectation that conflicts have to be resolved by decisions about public policy which might favor some interests over others.

The principal exception to these general characterizations of the aggregating function in Southeast Asian politics is the Philippines, where we find a much more open process of accommodating conflicting interests. The Filipino politicians, with their strongly pragmatic and anti-ideological orientations, quite explicitly perform as brokers. The political parties in the Philippines are so actively involved in trying to aggregate various interests that they place little value on distinguishing themselves in ideological terms. The constant need of the individual congressmen and senators to aggregate successfully the various demands of their constituencies leads to weak party discipline, except during election, and to highly fluid alignments in congressional voting.

The vigor with which the Filipino politicians carry out the aggregating function without the benefit of explicitly organized, and hence responsible, interest groups means that many of them go beyond the role of political brokers and become fixers. The result is not only the frequent reports of what are euphemistically referred to as "anomalies" in the press, but also an undercurrent of demand for reform candidates and higher standards of personal integrity among public officials. The substance, if not the vigor, of the Filipinos' criticisms of their politicians is reminiscent of the muckraking era of American politics, when our politicians were seeking to aggregate the diverse interests of a new urban population. However, the very fact that honesty and personal morality have become popular issues reflects a degree of awareness about the essential standards for representative government that is not common to most of Southeast Asia. Also, the intensity with which elections are conducted reflects the extent to which Filipino politicians have come to perform a significant role in aggregating interests. The Philippine electorate seems to recognize that the most fundamental question in politics is who is going to control the government, and thus, while the parties have not had to expend much effort in trying to distinguish themselves ideologically from each other, the expenditures of money on political campaigns in the Philippines are probably the highest in proportion to per capita income of any country in the world.[29]

Although at present the pragmatic approach of the Filipinos to the problem of aggregating interests would appear to be conspicuously different from the pattern common to the rest of Southeast Asia, it is not unlikely that in time other countries in the region will develop along the same lines. In spite of the numerous attempts to rely upon ideologies for the aggregating function, it seems that after a decade of independence there has been a conspicuous decline in the role of formal ideologies in Southeast Asian politics. Although the parties in Indonesia have attempted to employ ideological frames of reference, the decisive considerations in political actions have become increasingly pragmatic. In

[29] Although estimates of campaign expenditures are notoriously difficult to make, it would seem on the basis of the best available estimates that the Philippines spent nearly four times as much, in proportion to per capita income, on its 1957 presidential campaign as was spent on the American presidential campaign of 1956.

Burma, after a decade of elaborate ideological debates within the AFPFL, the final split in the movement came from issues of personality and pragmatic policies, and not from a clash over ideological matters. Indeed, in both Indonesia and Burma it has become increasingly apparent that if these countries are to realize more integrated political systems, there will have to be fewer artificial attempts to base their articulate politics on ideological considerations and a frank recognition that they are likely to perform the aggregating function more effectively if they adopt a more pragmatic approach.

(3) *Political socialization and recruitment.* During the colonial period, Southeast Asians were introduced to administrative rule. Many became aware of the ideals of democracy, but only a very few felt any sense of participation in government. During this period of relatively stable rule, little was done to establish a sense of citizenship. Instead, the process of political socialization was dominated primarily by the unpredictable consequences of the forces of social change. The political attitudes of the Southeast Asians of the current generation were formulated largely by their experiences with all the aspects of social change which we have noted. Above all else, Southeast Asians were jarred into political involvement by the harsh effects of the Second World War and the Japanese occupation. The only element of coherence in this socialization process was the appeal of nationalism. Nationalist movements thus became the principal shapers of the political socialization of Southeast Asians.

Since independence none of the countries of the region has successfully developed a means of giving its population a shared view of its national political life. This lack of continuity and of common direction in the socialization process stems mainly from the absence of agreement on the fundamental ideals and goals of the state. When the people of a nation do not have a common sense of identity and a shared self-image, they cannot be expected to have a common pattern of political socialization. On the other hand, until a pattern of socialization is created that will provide the necessary minimum agreement on the role of the citizen, there can be little hope for a coherent and integrating political system.

Much can be learned about the character of Southeast Asian politics from an examination of the social and educational backgrounds and careers of those who have obtained positions in the political sphere. The national leaders of the various countries have remarkably homogeneous backgrounds. Those who have gained access to the national level of politics have come largely from the recently urbanized segments of the population who have received the most extensive Westernized education. Status within this urbanized and Westernized society has generally been more important than competence in any particular profession or civilian occupation. Thus, although the majority of people in the ruling groups have had some form of professional training, few have applied this training in civilian roles before turning to political roles.

Under the colonial governments, political activities, especially careers in the civil service, did provide some avenues of social mobility. A basic attitude common to most of Southeast Asia during both the traditional and the colonial periods was that most socially respected values—prestige and status, recognition and security, wealth or honor—could best be realized in the realm of government. At present, as in the past, this attitude has made Southeast Asians look to politics as the main avenue for gaining greater social status.

The development of agitational politics during the preindependence years greatly increased the opportunities for rapid advancement to positions of influence and recognition. With a few exceptions, the men who formed the first governments and served as cabinet ministers in Burma were still in their thirties; in Indonesia the mean age of the comparable group of men was just under forty. The picture is much the same in Vietnam, Laos, and Cambodia, although in these countries independence did not result in as extreme a recruitment of new personnel into politics. The more gradual transition to independence in Malaya has not, as yet at least, caused any shift of power to a younger generation. In the Philippines it was men who had had a lifetime of political experience who assumed responsibility with independence; but the war did take a heavy toll of those who would have been their immediate political heirs, and as a result there has been a rapid movement upward by men in their early thirties since independence.

The view that government and politics are the main source of social recognition and mobility gave an added degree of vigor and vitality to the independence movements. Commitment to the ideal of independence was reinforced by personal career commitments. However, this view also contributed to the speed with which the unity of the independence movements has been weakened by social conflicts. With social status and personal advancement so closely associated with political fortune, any threat to one's political position can arouse severe anxieties, and political disappointments can readily be turned into disaffection and disillusionment. The same considerations have encouraged those in a fortunate position to seek unashamedly the elimination of competitors.

In spite of the extraordinary youthfulness of the leadership in much of Southeast Asia, there seems to be a great gap between the political attitudes of the current leaders and the next generation, particularly in Indonesia and Burma. In part this is due to the fact that the two generations have been introduced to politics under quite different conditions. Those who were involved in the independence movement feel that their views and their positions should not be questioned even though the problems their societies face have changed greatly. On the other hand, the new generation, with different experiences and somewhat different aspirations, seems peculiarly impatient. The telescoping of the generations in these two countries has, of course, intensified this problem. College students have become accustomed to seeing those only a few years their senior in power and they realize that they cannot hope for comparable successes at the same stage in their lives. For many of them, the position of those in power is not based upon their achievements in the independence movement but upon ascriptive considerations. Thus in spite of all the challenging problems of nation-building, the students of Indonesia and Burma have shown less enthusiasm for their national leaders than might be expected in newly independent countries. Many have begun to fancy themselves as a lost generation, while others are beginning to think for the first time of careers outside of government. Elsewhere in Southeast Asia this problem is not as acute, but it may become so if the expanding student bodies continue to look on government as the most promising means of advancement. It is estimated by the Philippine Planning Board that for every opening in public life projected for the next five years, there are now eleven students planning such careers.

The rapid expansion of agitational politics through the independence movements has also affected the process of recruitment into bureaucratic service. During the colonial period the civil service, the police, and the army provided the main opportunities for those who sought careers in public life, and many of those recruited into these services developed not only a nationalistic outlook but a sense of loyalty to their service and hence to their nation. However, the nationalist movements, particularly in Indonesia and Burma, tended to distrust such administrators and officials because they were assumed to be too closely associated with the colonial rulers. Immediately after independence there was a sharp drop in the status and prestige of administrative officials which led to widespread demoralization within the various services. In Burma high officials who had family traditions of public service encouraged their sons to look elsewhere for careers. The typical attitude of the new nationalist leaders toward their compatriots in the administrative services is illustrated by a speech U Nu made in September 1949 to an audience composed of Burmese officials, in which he first identified them as having been "instruments in suppression of all nationalist movements" under the British, and then warned them that "those who would not fall in line with the new order of things had better quit" and that they were "a body of servants whose work is liable to be brought at any moment under the master's eye."[30]

Such threats as these in both Burma and Indonesia tended to make officials hesitate in assuming initiative and seek only the safety of bureaucratic routine. However, in spite of these threats to the status and security of the civil servants, careers in the administrative service remain a principal channel for participating in public life. This has been the case largely because of the tendency of the politicians to close their own ranks to any newcomers.

This situation, combined with the ambitions of the new governments to reach more extensively into the life of their societies, has led to a dramatic expansion of all the bureaucracies of Southeast Asia. Prewar Burma was administered through 10 departments which have now expanded to 25 ministries responsible for over 40 departments as well as various boards and corporations. In Indonesia there has been more than a fourfold increase in the number of civil servants, who now total over a million.[31] The proliferation of bureaucrats has tended to lower the

---

[30] U Nu, *From Peace to Stability*, Ministry of Information, Government of the Union of Burma, Rangoon, 1950, pp. 27-36. Quoted by Hugh Tinker, *The Union of Burma*, London, 1957, p. 153.

[31] One reason for the rapid expansion of the bureaucracies in both Indonesia and Burma was an exaggerated expectation as to the number of government jobs that would be available after independence, especially since it was assumed that with the replacement of high-salaried Europeans more people could be employed at lower salaries. Apparently a widespread Javanese belief, related to the *Abangan* religious ethos, is that the number of people that should be employed in any enterprise, whether a private concern or government itself, ought to be determined not by questions of efficiency or productivity but rather by what is generally felt to be a "fair" or "correct" number. Clifford Geertz found that Javanese entrepreneurs felt powerless to limit the numbers on their payrolls according to economic considerations so long as people desiring employment felt that their enterprises "looked as though" they could support more. ("Religious Belief and Economic Behavior in a Central Javanese Town: Some Preliminary Considerations," *Economic Development and Cultural Change*, Vol. IV, No. 2, January 1956, p. 143.) The non-economic view of how many people should make a living off any enterprise produces an extraordinarily high incidence of bankruptcy and some hardships while people await the establishment of a new enterprise. Geertz found this pattern of "shared poverty" in both agriculture and trading, where instead of increasing production or expanding the enterprise to meet a rise in population, the economic pie was divided into smaller and smaller shares. For example, Geertz observed

standards of the civil services markedly, but it has increased the numbers of people who feel they are participants in the political process.

In spite of all these obstacles, the competent officials throughout Southeast Asia have quietly fulfilled their duties and have been a main factor in holding their respective countries together. As a result there has been a gradual shift in power back to the administrators. Indeed, it now appears that the assumption that those who were trained by colonial regimes to guide their countries would be rejected by the nationalist leaders may have been premature, and that they may yet play the major role in building their nations. U Nu, in a speech to senior officials in November 1954, reflected this shift in attitudes when he said: "Politicians will rise and fall on the wishes of the people, but you stay on for ever. Politicians should cooperate whole-heartedly with Government servants in this joint endeavor [of building a new nation]."[32] The establishment of an army-dominated government in the fall of 1958 represented a further step in the direction of restoring the influence of the administrators as against that of the politicians.

Thus, in differing degrees, there has been an extreme fluctuation in the pattern of recruitment to both the national political and the administrative elites. In the case of the political elites, rapid recruitment occurred during the period of the independence movement, while the expansion of the administrative services usually occurred after independence. The general trend in both cases, however, has been toward greater and greater restrictiveness. The extent of these fluctuations depended largely upon the initial size of the educated strata and the intensity of the struggle for independence. Where the transition toward independence proceeded according to plan, as in the case of Malaya, the Philippines, Laos, and Cambodia, the pattern has been one of only modest fluctuations. Where there was a conflict over independence and a relatively small educated elite, as in Indonesia, the fluctuations have been greatest. Although there was no serious struggle for independence in

that Javanese traders, rather than moving goods from their Chinese wholesalers directly to customers, tend to circulate the goods among themselves so that each can get a nibble at the profit margin before letting the goods pass into the hands of the customer. Given this moral obligation to cut others in on a good deal, it is not surprising that once they gained control of their government the Indonesians found it difficult to limit the number of government employees. It should be noted that this attitude is a concrete expression of what the Indonesians hold to be among their highest cultural values: "cooperation" (*gotong rojong*) and "mutual assistance in a family fashion" (*ramah-tamah*); and the Indonesians are quite correct in claiming that these values are unique to their culture, for "cooperation" and "mutual assistance," of course, have quite different meanings in all other cultures, especially in those that also prize rationality.

[32] Quoted by Tinker, *op.cit.*, p. 157.

Burma, there was a high degree of emotionalism and expectation of extreme changes with independence and thus there has been a highly unstable pattern of recruitment. In Vietnam the events leading to independence produced a great expansion of agitational political action during the early phase, but a quick contraction after the Diem government gained control and sought to reduce its domestic opposition. At the same time, owing to the mandarinate tradition and the large number of Westernized officials, the bureaucratic expansion in Vietnam has followed a more orderly pattern than elsewhere.

The tendency increasingly to restrict admission to the ranks of the national elite throughout Southeast Asia has brought these societies back again to their historical structure of a relatively small and socially distinctive elite controlling the national political life. However, the continuing processes of social change are constantly producing new elements seeking admission to the political process.

To some extent, this pressure from those in non-elite roles has been reduced by the development of new associations common to a modern society. These have included trade unions, peasant associations, student unions and, possibly in the same category, armies. As we have noted, in Southeast Asia these associations are meeting needs unrelated to the functions that similar structures fill in the West. For example, the trade union movements in Southeast Asia are generally more highly developed than the industrialized segment of these economies.[33] Since the concept of such organizations came from the West, it is not surprising that their leadership has tended to come from the more Westernized and urbanized strata of the societies. In a sense they have provided opportunities for political action for members of the elite elements of the society who have not gained access to the inner circles of either the nationalist movements or the administrative services. Since their leadership has generally come from the elite society, it is not surprising that these organizations have tended, first, to be adjuncts of the nationalist movements, and then supplementary administrative organs of the new governments. However, at present in most of the countries these associations are becoming centers of political tension as new leaders rise from within the ranks of the organizations, demanding that the organizations cease being simply agents of the national leadership and become the spokesmen for the special interests of their membership. Within the armies there is a

[33] For a discussion of the problems of trade unions in Southeast Asia, see George E. Lichtblau, "The Politics of Trade Union Leadership in Southern Asia," *World Politics*, Vol. VII, No. 1, October 1954, pp. 84-101.

similar pattern of younger officers seeking to become more active in determining political developments.

These organizations are thus providing new channels of recruitment to the political process. They are still, however, largely channels for the advancement of individual political careers. Only as a secondary consequence are they providing general citizenship training for their members.

The problem of inducting the masses into the political process by creating a general concept of citizenship has not been effectively met in any of the Southeast Asian countries. This is largely the case because the process of cultural change has prevented the emergence of any general consensus on what should be the nature of the state. So long as there is no agreement on the ends and means appropriate to political action, it is difficult to create a clear image of the good citizen. At best, the public in most of Southeast Asia is being asked to respect the authority of its current leaders and to support the notions of these leaders about public policy.

Even these added opportunities for political participation have not been able to meet the demands for political participation. The extraordinary phenomenon of rapid urban growth with almost no encouragement from industrial development has produced increasing numbers of restless people who have broken the ties of their traditional village-bound life and who are now seeking satisfaction, security, and personal identification by trying to turn to political action. This process has been stimulated by the traditional belief in Southeast Asia that the realm of politics is the realm of the elite and the secure. These people are seeking political participation in order to resolve intensely personal problems.

This creates a serious source of instability, for it is clear that whenever political behavior is primarily motivated by intensely personal and private considerations, there is no logic that can relate the specific needs of the individual to any specific goals of public policy. One policy program is as good as another. It is, of course, true that in all societies one of the basic functions of politics is to provide an outlet through which people can resolve personal crises. The therapeutic powers of political action are enormous, for through it people can find a sense of identity and break the bonds of loneliness; discover new and less confining roles to play and overcome the grip of emotional inhibition; learn socially respectable ways of expressing aggressiveness and hostility; actively seek respect and deference, power and adoration, the security of subservience or the elation of command, as well as a host of other forms of gratification. However, once these considerations come to dominate political behavior, as they have with many of the newly urbanized peoples of Southeast Asia, any rational relationship between articulated policy objectives and personal motivation is broken, and meaning can be found only in the act of participation and not in the objectives of policy.

People guided by such considerations are now being recruited to the various deviant movements in Southeast Asia, and particularly to the Communist parties.[34] The attitudes and predispositions of such urban elements are constantly a potential threat to the more stable patterns of political relationships. Often unexpected issues can trigger apparently spontaneous and extreme actions. Strikes and student demonstrations can violently disrupt the society, and although they may soon lose their momentum, the problem of increasing numbers seeking participation in their nation's political life remains.

In summary, it appears that there has been a constant expansion of the recruitment process into the political systems of Southeast Asia, but this has been accompanied by increasing restrictions on admittance to the ranks of the political elites. The aspiring elites see these restrictions as arbitrary and not as a means for providing order and a sense of responsibility. Consequently, as new groups of actors seek admission to the national level of politics, they cannot avoid the appearance of being disruptive elements. The rise in the political influence of army officers in Indonesia, for example, has opened a new channel of recruitment to positions of political influence, but so long as it is unclear what role they will occupy and what values they will represent, the effect is to reduce predictability about the political process and increase the sense of political instability. Given the scope of social change in Southeast Asian societies, it would be premature to expect the institutionalization of certain set patterns of recruitment into politics. The prospects for the development of more generally recognized and accepted patterns and channels of recruitment depend, first, upon the emergence of more widespread agreements as to what should be goals of political development; second, upon the interests that will increasingly be demanding representation in the process. The problem of achieving a greater degree of consensus about the future shape of the political sphere is largely dependent upon the workings of the communication process in each country. The second problem is closely associated with the manner in which interests are going to be articulated and aggregated in each of the political processes.

(4) *Political communication.* The structure of the communication processes in Southeast Asia mirrors accurately the uneven pattern of

---

[34] See Lucian W. Pye, *Guerrilla Communism in Malaya*, Princeton, N.J., 1956.

cultural change in the region, the lack of common national languages, and the sharp divisions between the urban-centered elite society and the village-oriented masses. None of the countries in the area have a single, unifying communication process capable of providing for the masses of the people a common basis for understanding, interpreting, and evaluating political developments in their society. Rather, in all the countries there are many newly autonomous communication systems which largely coincide with the various atomized political processes.[35]

Throughout Southeast Asia the media of mass communication are closely related to the urban centers and based on Western technology. They tend to serve the more Westernized elements of the society and are generally very closely related to the dominant or national sphere of politics. Outside these urban centers, the communication process is still largely dependent upon the traditional level of technology, and in its operations it serves the needs of the more local and less formally structured political processes.

It is significant that, even after the end of colonialism, the European language presses have retained their elite status. This is, of course, another indication of the extent to which the more Westernized elements have been able to dominate the political life of Southeast Asia. The Western language press in the region can be divided into three types: a minority which conceives of itself as the "conscience" of the society, a second minority which seeks to avoid any active political role, and a majority which is closely identified with a particular political group or party or with the government itself.

In Burma and the Philippines there has developed the concept of an independent press acting as critic and evaluator of the behavior of political leaders. The Manila press regularly reports cases of "anomalies" in the conduct of those in public life. In Rangoon, the *Nation* and the *Guardian* have exposed and criticized a government that has not been accustomed to having an articulate opposition.[36] In these two countries, the press has to some extent become an active and independent actor in the national political process; indeed, in Burma during the decade of

[35] For a discussion of the general characteristics of the communication processes common to non-Western societies, see Lucian W. Pye, "Communication Patterns and the Problems of Representative Government in Non-Western Societies," *Public Opinion Quarterly*, Vol. xx, No. 1, Spring 1956, pp. 249-257.

[36] Until 1950 the problem of insurrections caused the Burmese government to maintain strict censorship over the press, and as late as 1953 an editor was arrested and his paper closed down for "inaccurate" reporting of police conduct. In 1954, after the government had used its overwhelming majority to push through the lower House a bill that would have drastically limited the freedom of the press, the Burma Journalists' Association organized enough effective opposition to cause the government to drop the measure.

AFPFL domination the press, for all its weaknesses, represented the most effective loyal opposition in the country.

The more common pattern in Southeast Asia is for newspapers to serve as the organs of individual politicians or political groups. In Vietnam the French tradition has been followed, in the sense that most newspapers seem to represent the interests of particular political groupings or the government. The problem of censorship and the dominant role of a semi-official news agency have produced a relatively docile press even in the cases of those papers controlled by opposition parties.

The vernacular press of Southeast Asia includes a large number of newspapers, each with a particular but limited audience. This is especially true of those in the minority languages. Weak financial backing and a shortage of advertisers have been major factors in preventing the development of dailies with large mass circulations, and this in turn has made it difficult to establish a tradition of vigorous and independent reporting. Most of the vernacular papers rely heavily on government press releases and are either undeviating supporters of the government or the organ of a particular political group. As such, they do serve the function of indicating the public stance of those involved in inter-elite relationships. With their limited audiences, their principal aim is to maintain the loyalty of those already committed politically. Those attempting to follow more independent courses generally adopt a non-political position.

Outside the urban centers, the communication process is even more intimately related to the structure of social and personal relations. Indeed, since the main method of transmitting information around the countryside is by word of mouth, the communication process tends to coincide with the patterns of personal relationships. Information about events is often disseminated with extraordinary rapidity throughout the village population of Southeast Asia. This is the case partly because other social institutions have traditionally been endowed with an added communication function; the merchants in the market place, the itinerant peddler, the traveler, the villager returning from a trip to the town are all viewed as sources of information. Also in Indonesia and Burma there have been long traditions of viewing the activities of the elite as a main subject for gossip.

Since the communication process serving the vast majority of Southeast Asians is an adjunct of other social functions, it is not structured to differentiate "political" from other forms of information. Those participating in the network are not "professional" communicators performing a single role, but men who have become communicators because of their other social roles. Thus the setting in which communication takes place tends to obscure what are generally considered the differences between the political and the social and private spheres of life. The relative social position and the personal relationships of those involved in the process become important factors in giving significance to what is communicated. In particular, this seems to mean that the source of information has greater influence on behavior than does the content of a message.

Thus at the village level the communication process serves a much broader function than just that of providing information: it helps to define and give coherence to a wide range of social relationships. The effect on the political process is to impede the emergence of a clearly recognized and distinct political sphere where ideas and judgments can freely compete irrespective of their sources. Rather, the structure of the communication system reinforces the tendency toward many nearly autonomous political processes that follow ethnic, religious, regional, or parochial lines.

The communication structure at both the urban and the village level can be seen as generally supporting the atomized political processes common to Southeast Asia and not as providing the basis for a single, unifying political process. There are, however, some developments which may in time result in a more unified communication process in some of the countries in the region. The most important of these developments is the spread of literacy, which not only makes it possible for people to break from the restricting pattern of face-to-face communication but also, by leading to a greater demand for the printed word, can stimulate the emergence of professional communicators. Moreover, radio, especially in the Philippines, Vietnam, and Malaya, has become a significant medium in creating a new image of the citizen as a critic of politics. However, although radio has the advantage of being able to introduce new ideas while preserving some of the intimacy of face-to-face relations, it does not provide a basis for group action. Except in the Philippines, where there are private stations, broadcasting is generally under the control of government bodies. As such, it does fulfill the function of providing symbols and slogans of national identification and an introduction to the vocabulary of national politics.

These changes in the communication pattern can all be viewed as part of the process by which the urban cultures of Southeast Asia are gradually reaching out to encompass more and more of the rural masses. The extent to which these changes will lead to a more unifying political process depends largely on the rate at which new social elements emerge that are capable of bridging the gap between the urban and the rural worlds of Southeast Asia. Already it is possible to discern in some of the countries rising leaders who might be conceived of as a new provincial elite. These are mainly people who have functions that are largely defined in terms of the urban society, but whose position and influence depend mainly upon expanding their relations with the village people. Such people are beginning to perform a mediator's role in relating the urban and the village levels of politics.

For example, in the Philippines this role is being increasingly performed by a class that includes provincial lawyers, educators, leaders in the community development projects, and even some members of the landed gentry. This group is beginning to serve as something of a check on the older administrative chain of command and communication from the center to the rural areas. In breaking the monopoly that the urbanized officials formerly had over the presentation of policy to rural audiences, this group not only has expanded the amount and the variety of information the *barrio* people receive about national developments but also, and more importantly, is beginning to be a major means of communicating upward the views and interests of the rural people. This has taken place primarily within the context of the relations between the new provincial elite and the congressmen and other elected representatives. There is thus beginning to emerge in the Philippines a new communication network that can provide a tie between the congressman and his constituency.

Elsewhere in Southeast Asia the position of the provincial elite is somewhat different. In Vietnam, during the period leading to independence, there emerged many different groups, including the sects, which had urbanized leaders but were still closely tied to the masses. Since independence, however, many of these groups have been eliminated and the remaining provincial elite has tended to associate itself with the administration and thus serves as an adjunct to the government's means of communication. In Indonesia, the provincial elite has generally been denied access to the world of the national elite. As the pattern of political communication in the country is reshaped, these provincial leaders may in time provide local and regional interests with a great enough sense of security with respect to relations with the central government so that the islands will not become completely divided.

Thus we see that the question of what role the emerging provincial elites of Southeast Asia will fill in creating new patterns of political communications depends largely upon what interests they will be articulating.

IV. GOVERNMENTAL STRUCTURES AND AUTHORITATIVE FUNCTIONS

Governmental Structures

In the above sections we discussed the four basic political functions. Now we can turn to a discussion of how the governmental structures and the authoritative functions of the political process have influenced the course of political development in Southeast Asia. In the case of Western societies, it is usually assumed that the formal structures of government are an end product of the political process. It is thus assumed that the ways in which the process functions are performed will largely determine the ways in which the authoritative functions are performed, while the authoritative functions have some influence, but not as great, on the process functions. In Southeast Asia, however, the Western impact was generally greatest at the level of the formal structure, and although the Westernized institutions which were introduced have not been fully accepted, they have had considerable influence in shaping the political process. Thus, it would be incorrect to assume that the formal governmental structures of the various Southeast Asian countries have been shaped by the forces within their political processes. At the same time, it would be equally incorrect to assume that these authoritative structures are simply façades and are lacking in influence.

Since the Western impact was usually strongest at the governmental level, it is not surprising that the formal governmental structures of the newly independent countries of Southeast Asia are remarkably similar to those of their former mother countries. Opposition to Western rule did not include opposition to the institutions introduced by the West. Indeed, one of the dynamic forces in the region is the desire among many of the leaders for their countries to employ Westernized institutions in a manner more consistent with Western practice.

The Philippine presidential system is closely patterned after its American model, except that it is considerably more centralized. In spite of numerous municipal and provincial bodies, local government is not highly developed, and the authority of the central government is exercised quite directly in local matters. The American system of checks and balances between federal and state authorities and between the executive and legislative has not been fully followed in the Philippines. (The concept of an independent judiciary has, however, been fairly well accepted.) American interest in encouraging the development of political parties and legislative activities did not remove the need for a centralized administration in the islands, and with independence this administrative structure was made directly responsive to the office of the president.

In Burma, Malaya, and Indonesia independence brought parliamentary government with executive power vested in a prime minister and his cabinet. The constitution of the Union of Burma provides for a parliament consisting of a Chamber of Deputies and a Chamber of Nationalities, both elected every four years by universal suffrage of all over eighteen. (The constitution grants a degree of autonomy to the Shan, Kachin, and Karen states, and the minority people actually have a majority of the seats in the Chamber of Nationalities.) The president of the Union is elected by both chambers of parliament, and has a role very similar to that of the French president. Constitutionally the prime minister is responsible to a majority of the Chamber of Deputies, but the role of the prime minister has been defined less by the lower chamber than by the personality of U Nu, who occupied the office during the greater part of the first ten years.

In Malaya, the constitution calls for the election in 1959 of a parliament of two chambers that will follow in the British tradition, even though they are to be known as the House of Representatives and the Senate. The government will be responsible only to the lower House. The Senate, modeled somewhat after the House of Lords, will be in part a chamber of the constituent states of the Federation, and in part a chamber of experts and nominated members with notable qualifications. A unique feature of the Malayan constitution is that His Majesty, the *Yang di-Pertuan Agong,* or Chief of State, is "elected" for a term of five years by his fellow rulers.[37] Theoretically the *Yang di-Pertuan Agong* is supposed to act much like a constitutional monarch, but he may come to play a more openly political role since he has been given the responsibility of upholding the special Malay rights and preserving the status of Islam as the state religion.

The draft constitution of Indonesia calls for a cabinet system of

[37] The procedure by which the Council of Rulers "elects" one of its members requires that the choice be determined by seniority, unless the senior ruler declines the office or unless five of the nine rulers decide the senior ruler to be unsuitable, by reason of infirmity of mind or body, or for any other cause. In the first "election" the senior ruler, the Sultan of Johore, who had previously announced that the British were making a great mistake in forcing independence on Malaya, declined the honor, which would have demanded his residence in Malaya for five years. The Council of Rulers then declared the second rûler in seniority, the Sultan of Pahang, to be "unsuitable," and finally settled on the ruler of Negri Sembilan, as we have noted earlier.

government and a president who is a symbol of the state.[38] In practice, the Indonesian government has been so weak and so much at the mercy of a multiparty parliament that the office of the prime minister has not emerged as a forceful one. On the other hand, President Sukarno has not limited himself to a non-partisan role, as intended by the draft constitution, but has been active in shaping policies and creating cabinets. The key constitutional question since independence has been the extent to which the Outer Islands should be autonomous. The Dutch before finally conceding independence insisted on the rights of the non-Javanese to be bound to Jakarta only within a federal system, but once the Dutch influence was removed the nationalists replaced the federal structure with a unitary one and changed the name of the country from the United States of Indonesia to the Republic of Indonesia.

The three countries of Southeast Asia that have been the least profoundly affected by the Western impact—Thailand, Laos, and Cambodia—all have constitutional monarchies in which the power of the throne and government are united both in theory and in fact. In Thailand the creation of a national assembly and the development of parliamentary practices first took place with only appointed members, and then with a partially elected and partially appointed body. Although Thailand still has a majority of nominated members in its national assembly, much as the other countries had under colonialism, it has had more experience with national elections than any of the other countries of the region, with the exception of the Philippines.

The constitutions and formal structures of government of the Southeast Asian countries reflect not only their past associations with the West but also their aspirations for the future. Indeed, sections of most of the constitutions can be understood better if viewed as statements of ambitions and not as binding regulations on current behavior. The Burmese constitution, for example, sets forth explicitly "Directive Principles of State Policy," which include the right to work, the right to rest and leisure, the right to maintenance in old age and during sickness, and other features of a welfare state which the Burmese economy will be unable to support at any time in the foreseeable future.

In none of the countries of Southeast Asia do the formal Westernized structures of government perform the authoritative functions usually

---

[38] The fact that Indonesia is the only country in the region that has not accepted, at least formally, a permanent constitution is an indication of the political instability and lack of consensus within the country. It also reflects the strongly legalistic attitudes of the Javanese, which will be discussed below.

associated with such structures. Thus, with respect to such functions, we must broaden our analysis to include many informal and more traditional practices.

Authoritative Functions

(1) *Rule-making*. As might be expected, the transitional societies of Southeast Asia have not fully incorporated the view common to rational-legal systems of authority that the appropriate goal of politics is the production of public policy in the form of laws. In spite of the legalism of the colonial period and the current efforts to create modern nations, there are still many manifestations of the traditional Southeast Asian belief that power and prestige are values to be fully enjoyed for their own sake and not rationalized into mere means to achieve policy goals. There is thus some ambivalence as to whether the fundamental function of politics is to make rules or to provide opportunities for gaining honor and recognition.

In large part, the reason that the formal constitutional processes of law-making have not become more significant in Southeast Asian politics is that to a large extent custom and convention still govern social relations. Formal law-making is generally associated with the various efforts to build the societies of the future. In many cases, this means that laws are adopted that would be relevant in more industrialized societies but as yet have little meaning in terms of existing conditions. Thus, surprisingly advanced legislation is often found on the statute books. The labor legislation in Thailand may be a source of national pride, but it does not appear to serve any other purpose.

The legislatures and parliaments of Southeast Asia do not generally act as though they conceived of themselves as deliberative bodies devoted to the initiating and making of laws. Where one party or group dominates the political process, as in Burma, Malaya, Thailand, and Vietnam, there is a strong tendency for the legislatures to act as "rubber stamps" for government-proposed bills. Even the factional struggles common to some of these countries without a responsible and powerful opposition are not generally reflected in open legislative maneuvering; agreements are usually reached before legislation is formally introduced.

Even in the Philippines, congressmen and senators take very little initiative in developing and introducing major bills. In most sessions of Congress, they limit their activities to action on the administration's proposals for legislation. Congressional committees have not become the center of legislative planning and review, and they do not have an influence comparable to that of their American counterparts. This is partly because the Filipino congressmen and senators tend to be highly individualistic and partly because of constitutional limitations on congressional action. The Philippine Congress does not have the same powers of investigation as the American Congress, and it cannot make any cuts in the administration's budgets. The greatest initiative the Filipino legislators take in rule-making is in the field of private bills; the closing hours of any session of the Philippine Congress are usually characterized by such an extraordinary degree of confusion that it becomes impossible to determine whether all the bills that are claimed to have been passed were properly enacted.[39] This situation makes it possible for the administration to claim after Congress has adjourned, without much fear of contradiction, that most if not all of its legislative program was accepted.

The situation in Indonesia is rather different from that in the rest of Southeast Asia with respect to the behavior of the formally constituted law-making body. The complicated and delicate balance among the various parties and factions in parliament makes it necessary for the Indonesian law-makers to devote most of their time and energy to trying to form, reconstitute, or bring down the cabinet. The result is near-paralysis so far as initiative in law-making goes.

This immobilism of the Indonesian multiparty parliament is further exaggerated by an apparently deep-seated Indonesian attitude toward law. Indonesians generally display a high sense of regard for and even awe of law, in that they tend to view laws in much the same way as they traditionally viewed custom and convention. Laws are not to be made or changed simply in response to changes in society, for one must proceed slowly and cautiously in dealing with such an important matter. The introduction of the Dutch spirit of rigid and uncompromising respect for legal principles into a society that had traditionally been bound by the elaborate structure of *adat* law seems to have produced a spirit of legalism in which the idea of legal innovation evokes a sense of danger. In the eyes of the Indonesians, rather than to change the law in the face of new circumstances, it is better either to seek escapes within the existing body of law, such as those found in the standard emergency regulations, or to ignore widespread violations.[40]

[39] Willard H. Elsbree, "The Philippines," in Rupert Emerson, ed., *Representative Government in Southeast Asia*, Cambridge, Mass., 1955, p. 98.

[40] This legalistic attitude is to be found in the behavior of both the central government in Jakarta and the authorities in the Outer Islands in their controversy over foreign trade regulations. The central government has been extremely hesitant to innovate new

To a lesser degree, this spirit of legalism which stems from an attitude toward law that is more traditionalist than rationalist is to be found in the rest of Southeast Asia. It might have been expected that when new nationalist elites replaced the old colonial authorities, the result would have been sweeping legal changes. Yet precisely the opposite has happened, as the newly independent countries of the region are still operating with essentially the same legal codes that were introduced by their former colonial rulers.

In general, it may be said that in the traditional societies of Southeast Asia the formally constituted law-making bodies have not as yet become the focus for the rule-making function. The usual practice is for the dominant group to issue essential decrees or initiate administrative regulations which may affect the entire society. For example, in Thailand the cabinet performs the role of making public the decisions of the particular clique of military officers generally recognized to have the dominant power. In Indonesia the cabinets have increasingly taken guidance from the military and the president, and much of the new rule stems technically from the powers granted to the military under a decree of martial law. In Vietnam conscious efforts at rule-making are left largely to the office of the president, which is in control of the civil administration.

(2) *Rule application.* Again it must be recognized that in the transitional societies of Southeast Asia the grip of custom and convention is still strong and is decisive in many areas of rule enforcement. For the village-oriented masses of the population, rules are still largely enforced by the demands of conformity and through the offices of headmen, magistrates, or administrative officials. Throughout Southeast Asia there is generally very little problem of rule enforcement within those spheres of life where custom, precedence, and routine are still applicable.

The major problem of rule enforcement arises in those areas where social change and the demand for a new society have produced novel

---

regulations which might reduce the demand for "extra-legal" trade, while the Outer Islands maintain that they are engaging not in smuggling but in "barter" arrangements that do not affect the foreign exchange regulations. Although this particular situation is, of course, complicated by deep political considerations, many other illustrations of the Indonesian spirit of legalism could be cited. For example, in spite of the widely articulated demand for economic development, the Indonesian government has not repealed the regulatory legislation introduced by the Dutch during the depression for the purpose of restricting new economic ventures which under the circumstances would have only intensified the problems of surplus production. These regulations make little sense under present inflationary conditions and seriously impede the development of new Indonesian entrepreneurial activities, and yet the government hesitates to alter the laws. The spirit of Indonesian legalism in this case seems to be reinforced by a fear of losing "control" over the economy.

conditions. In particular, it may be said that all the countries of the region have had varying degrees of difficulty in enforcing rules with respect to, first, the behavior of those with dominant power, and, second, the conditions essential for creating a new basis of integration for their societies. The actions of government officials often appear to be arbitrary, and administrative regulations are frequently used to control the behavior of citizens more than that of officials. In large part, this is a reflection of the basic fact that in much of Southeast Asia the bureaucracy and the army are positive actors in the political process and not neutral instruments of policy.

The extraordinary sense of legalism that we have noted in discussing the rule-making function is also a dominant feature in the application of rules by civil officials in Southeast Asia. The colonial governments, in seeking to encourage the ideal of an impersonal system of authority, generally advanced the view that decision-making involved only the mechanical application of regulations. This approach was premised on the notion that the administrative codes were so complete that for every particular problem there was certain to be a general regulation. Every office in the British, Dutch, and French territories was armed with a small library of books of regulations, and in all these areas large numbers of clerks were trained in the special skill of locating the regulations that were applicable to each problem as it arose.

In actual practice, the systems did not work in an entirely mechanistic fashion. The colonial officials generally made what they considered the appropriate decision in conformity with the spirit of the regulations as they understood them. The skill of the clerks, more often than not, was that of finding suitable regulations to support the decisions of their superiors. In a sense, these colonial officials stood slightly aloof from the machinery of administration, so that they could reach in and tinker with the machine in order to ensure that it operated in an efficient and effective manner.

Since independence, the common belief that good government depends upon the mechanical application of rules has not altered in Southeast Asia. The same books of regulations are still being used in Burma, Malaya, Indonesia, and Vietnam. However, the administrative organs for applying the rules are generally seen as being extremely inefficient and lacking in initiative. Much of the trouble is due to the fact that there are no longer those officials who expedited the smooth operation of the government machinery. The concept of a mechanistic application of rules is peculiarly inappropriate for societies undergoing basic social changes. The result has been administrations which have shown great efficiency in maintaining routine operations but little competence in dealing with novel situations. The frustrations that this state of affairs produces have frequently made some of the governments willing to adopt extra-legal and arbitrary practices.

Thus the continued belief in a mechanistic approach to rule application has had the paradoxical effect of encouraging more authoritarian practices at one level and, at another level, of limiting initiative and fostering a narrow view of one's authority. Although, as we have noted, the Southeast Asian bureaucracies have expanded greatly since independence, it is significant that very little of this growth has been caused by "bureaucratic empire building." On the contrary, officials have tended to take such a limited view of the range of their responsibilities that they hesitate to assume new duties that would lead to an expansion of their authority. As a result, new ministries or departments have had to be created to handle new problems.

The rapid growth in the size of the bureaucracies has affected communication within the administrative organs of government, and this in turn has had consequences for rule application. Imperfect communication has led to imperfect division of responsibility. Government organizations have become much more complicated and officials are often confused about the limits of their jurisdiction. It is sometimes extremely difficult to determine what office has responsibility for a particular problem. Problems which are referred to offices which do not recognize their competence to deal with them may never reach the appropriate authority.

In part, this difficulty arises from the fact that all the colonial governments in Southeast Asia tended to be highly centralized and thus officials came to believe that it was appropriate—and certainly the safest course—to refer all problems that were slightly out of the ordinary to a higher authority. In the past, however, the colonial officials at the lower levels made many decisions despite the centralization of government. At present, for various reasons that range from lack of experience and self-confidence to fear of political reprisals for making decisions displeasing to their superiors, low-ranking officials have tended to avoid all but routine decisions and refer matters about which there is any question to higher authorities. As a consequence, throughout Southeast Asia petty problems and major issues are all being dealt with by the same machinery, and important officials are often absorbed in insignificant matters while major problems have to await their turn.

(3) *Rule adjudication.* One of the most radical features of colonial rule in Southeast Asia was the introduction of the concept of a rule of law supported by an independent judiciary. The legal systems of the Western powers were adopted in varying degrees in the respective colonial areas; and possibly because they represented such radical departures from traditional practices, the spirit and practices of court proceedings have generally been closer to their Western counterparts than has been the case with many other structures that were introduced from the West. In most cases, under colonial rule, stress was placed on maintaining the independent integrity of the courts, with the result that these Southeast Asian countries have long traditions in this sphere.

The strength of these traditions stems largely from two sources. First, the general historical pattern was one in which initial adjustments were made to local customs and conditions and thereafter stress could be placed on developing the principles of integrity and justice. Secondly, this development was greatly facilitated by the training of relatively large numbers of Southeast Asians in the law and the subsequent employment of many of them as judges and magistrates. Before independence a remarkably high proportion of the judges and assessors in the court systems were Southeast Asians who often displayed a deep appreciation and understanding of their profession. In fact, those who performed many of the crucial functions in the court systems were generally among the most highly Westernized people in their societies.

This tradition of the courts may be one of the most important factors in encouraging stable political development in the region. In some cases, the courts have performed the important function of serving as the main restraint upon and as loyal opposition to the dominant political party. In Burma the Supreme Court on several occasions effectively held the Anti-Fascist People's Freedom League accountable for the highest standards of justice and of the national interest. Similarly court decisions in the Philippines and even in Vietnam have checked the otherwise unrestrained power of the dominant political leaders.

Possibly there is no better illustration of the extent to which Southeast Asia is the product of cultural diffusion than the records of their court decisions. In arriving at their decisions, justices frequently refer back to precolonial traditions, judgments of the colonial courts, and the entire legal tradition of the Western country which formerly ruled them, and treat all these traditions as their common legal heritage. For example, Philippine courts consider with equal relevance not only pre-Spanish customs and the legal decisions of the Spanish and American periods, but also the entire tradition of Spanish law, both the pre- and post-Napoleonic code, Anglo-Saxon common law, and past as well as contemporary decisions of United States federal and state courts. The richness of their legal tradition means that not infrequently a Philippine court, in citing precedence for its decision, will quote in the same passage the words of Coke and Blackstone, the opinions of an American Supreme Court Justice and those of a judge of a state court, and the views of, say, a thirteenth-century Spanish court. In the light of this, it may be surprising that so many Filipinos claim to have legal training, but it is not surprising that many older Filipino justices feel that most of these are not well read in what they consider to be the Law.

Although Westernized legal systems have been remarkably well received in much of Southeast Asia, the extent to which these formal structures for rule adjudications can significantly shape political development is still open to question. They hardly touch those spheres of life still close to tradition in which ancient modes of adjudication prevail. Even the more urbanized and Westernized elements have been hesitant in utilizing the courts to decide civil cases; and the notion that a citizen might turn to the courts for protection from his government is not widespread. In the day-to-day life of most Southeast Asians, problems of rule adjudication are resolved by informal procedures more than by formal ones. Each of the subsocieties in the various countries has its own practices, which are largely dependent upon the kind of authority that society recognizes in its communal life: the village elders, the religious teachers, the heads of clans, the leaders of chambers of commerce and the other protective associations become the adjudicators for those who feel bound to them.

The great difficulty is that in the political processes of the transitional societies of Southeast Asia there are few recognized methods for adjudicating conflicts between the subsocieties that fragment these countries. Conflicts between the urbanized and rural elements, between minority ethnic groups and the society of the national elite, between the central authorities and provincial communities usually cannot be referred to commonly accepted bodies for adjudication. Until the process of cultural change has produced a higher degree of national integration, appropriate rules for such conflicts and appropriate means of adjudicating such rules cannot be developed.

V. POLITICAL INTEGRATION

Now, as throughout most of history, the phenomenon that dominates the life of Southeast Asia is the process of cultural diffusion. On the one hand, this process has given the region a richness of cultural heritage and a wealth of social and political practices, but on the other it has produced serious problems for the building of viable states in the modern world. The process of cultural change has fragmented and divided the various societies in the region to such an extent that significant barriers have been raised to the integration of these societies into new national communities. The scope of the Westernization process has been broad enough to produce in all the countries important elements that are emotionally and intellectually committed to modernizing their entire societies, but it has not been broad enough to permit the vast majorities of the populations to share the same visions of the future.

The process of change has not produced a state of general social disintegration in the region, and it would be incorrect to say that chaos and confusion are found throughout these societies. A more accurate picture would reveal almost communal groupings within each society, each oriented around ideas and practices that can be placed at different points on a continuum from traditional to modern urban life.

With respect to national integration, a fundamental problem is that, in spite of the intensity of their separate orientations, very few of these groupings are able to translate their orientations into effective action. Although traditional patterns of thought and action are still strong at the village level, rural conditions throughout Southeast Asia are no longer those of the traditional era. Traditions and customs which were functional for sparsely populated communities are still being preserved in spite of tremendous increases in population density.[41] The introduction of a moneyed economy, the possibilities for alienating ancestral lands, and improvements in transportation have all altered the conditions under which village traditions developed. Indeed, the persistence in clinging to many customs which once offered security now seems to be a major contributing factor to the economic bankruptcy of much of rural Southeast Asia. At the other extreme, there are, of course, those who feel themselves committed to a modern urban way of life, and yet they

---

[41] For example, the principle of unanimity means one thing in a small closely knit community and quite another in a larger and hence more impersonally organized one; this can be clearly seen by contrasting traditional Javanese life with the attempts to cling to the principle in contemporary Java.

too find that current conditions in their societies do not provide the necessary substructure for the fulfillment of their ambitions. The extraordinary Southeast Asian phenomenon of cities growing up and continuing to expand with almost no encouragement from industrial development has produced large numbers of people whose orientations are appropriate to an industrial society. They, as much as the tradition-bound peasant, find that their views of what this world should be like are constantly being challenged by what is to them a hostile reality.

In short, in spite of all the changes that have come about, most of the peoples of Southeast Asia, irrespective of where they stand in the continuum from traditional to modern, find that in spite of the changes they have incorporated in their lives, they are still being called upon to make further painful adjustments.

This basic problem complicates the more obvious one of bringing together and integrating into a common national community the diverse elements with their separate orientations. Had the impact of cultural change touched all spheres of life with uniform intensity, then, of course, the task of reintegration would have been much simpler. Indeed, under such conditions the societies of Southeast Asia might be in the happy position of being able to choose freely what they consider to be the best features of two worlds: their own traditional one and that of the industrial West. However, the very nature of the process of cultural change produces too many divisions, each with intense emotional overtones, to make possible such a rationalistic approach to the problem of creating a national consensus.

In Thailand, Vietnam, Laos, and Cambodia there is a strong sense of continuity which enables their peoples to relate their current national institutions to their historic institutions. Religion—for example, Buddhism in Burma, Thailand, and Cambodia, Islam among the Malays and Indonesians, and Catholicism for the Filipinos—still provides one of the strongest bonds of community. However, as we have observed, the concept of a nation-state came largely from, first, the administrative unity introduced by the various colonial governments, and, second, the desire to control these institutions of government. The politics of the various independence movements provided a sense of national integration during the latter days of colonialism.

Since independence the problem of national integration has become more conspicuous in most of the Southeast Asian nations. To a very great extent, the basis of national integration was the personality and views of the dominant leaders in the independence movement. In some cases, the appeal was essentially of a classical charismatic nature, as with Sukarno in Indonesia and U Nu in Burma; in other cases, it was an accurate reflection of the power of a single man, as with Prince Norodom Sihanouk in Cambodia and Premier Ngo Dinh Diem in South Vietnam. In either event, the need to rely upon individual personalities has provided an unstable and impermanent basis for national unity.

The fundamental problem of creating a sense of national unity in the newly independent states has affected the vocabulary of politics in Southeast Asia. Most of the national leaders find it necessary to concentrate in their public statements on appeals to national unity. The result is a nationalistic type of oratory appropriate to ceremonial occasions and national holidays, and an avoidance of serious discussion of the issues that divide their people. The national leaders feel compelled to direct attention to what differentiates their country from all that is foreign rather than to the differences existing within their country.[42]

In all societies, national leaders are, of course, expected to provide the slogans and symbols of national unity. Leaders under a representative system of government, however, are also called upon to articulate the real interests that may divide their peoples, so that in seeking compromises they can create a firm basis for national integration. In Southeast Asia, because special interests are not clearly articulated, the national leaders cannot base their appeals to national unity on a framework of actual compromises that might serve as the fundamental basis of national unity. Since they are forced to speak to an undifferentiated public, their appeals to national unity often seem to be attempts to avoid facing up to the difficult problems that must be resolved if there is to be genuine political integration.

The fact that most of the countries of Southeast Asia, as we have observed, do not have a national political process in which all important interests are clearly articulated and aggregated means that the patterns of domestic political relations cannot perform an integrating function for the entire society. For the more traditional elements, the lack of such a political bargaining process has not affected their sense of identity with their national leaders. These elements have not been accustomed to expecting governments to respond to their interests; instead, they have always felt it appropriate for the powerful to lead a dramatic

---

[42] In some cases, the extent to which the national leader focuses on the foreign rather than the domestic scene is simply a reflection of his strategy for strengthening his internal political position. If the leader can successfully portray himself as playing an important international role and bringing worldwide recognition to his country, then his domestic opponents are forced into the position of appearing to threaten the national interest by challenging him.

life surrounded with pomp and circumstance. In their eyes, much of the behavior of their current leaders is consistent with their image of traditional authority. Without a rationalistic understanding of politics, they do not expect power to be used to advance public policy; it is enough for them that their leaders are acting as leaders should, by appearing to be their intellectual and moral betters and not interfering with their own private lives.

For the more urbanized and literate elements, however, who do have interests that are not being politically satisfied, the lack of a coherent political process affects their sense of identity with the national leaders. For them, the appeals of national unity seem to be a request that they accept an unsatisfactory situation. This is particularly the case with those who had high hopes for a new society after independence but are now becoming increasingly disillusioned. For them, the symbolic appeals of national unity have lost much of their potency, while they cannot find another basis for becoming an integrated part of their nation.

Thus, paradoxically, one often finds that in Southeast Asia, in spite of the gap in outlook between the national leadership and the more traditional elements, it is precisely this latter group, with its non-rationalistic view of politics, which has the strongest sense of identity with the country's leaders. On the other hand, it is often those who best understand the outlook of the national leaders, but who feel they are not participants in a responsive political process, who are the most disaffected. In the future it can be expected that dynamics of social change will produce increasing numbers of Southeast Asians who will feel a need to identify themselves with a modern society, and, if they cannot find a way to be recruited into an integrated political process in which their interests are represented, they may become increasingly dissatisfied with the slogans and symbols which provided a common basis for an earlier generation and its independence movements.

The alternative to the development of receptive and integrating political processes is the growth of various authoritarian movements and particularly Communism. Already the Communist parties in the region pose serious problems for national integration. Vietnam, of course, is a country divided between the Communists and the non-Communists. Elsewhere in the region the Communists constitute in varying degrees a serious menace to national unity. Since the Communists are now seeking respectability, they are prepared to appear as supporters of the various appeals for national unity, although in fact they are not prepared to support an open, competitive political process.

2. THE POLITICS OF

South Asia

MYRON WEINER

··

I. BACKGROUND

The Physical Setting

SOUTH ASIA has been rightfully called a "subcontinent." It is massive in its area and population, prominent in its geographical position, and overwhelming in its problems. The subcontinent, consisting of India, Pakistan, Ceylon, and the secluded Himalayan states to the north—Nepal, Bhutan, and Sikkim—is a thousand-mile projection, dividing the Indian Ocean and the land mass of southern Asia in two. Older images of the region—elephants and snakes, maharajas and Nizams, fakirs and spiritualism, sola topees and sahibs, non-violence and Gandhi, untouchables and Brahmans—are rapidly being replaced with new images—socialism and neutralism, political disorder and violence, Nehru and planning, generals and military dictators, and, above all, poverty and underdevelopment.

Poverty and underdevelopment are the most overwhelming images. Ceylon, the most prosperous of the three major countries considered in this study, has a yearly per capita income of only $110. In all three countries, population density on arable land is high (see Table 1). Two-thirds of the people live directly from the soil, and cultivated area is under one acre for each rural dweller. Low agricultural productivity per man and per acre is the most striking feature of the economy of the subcontinent. Large areas are unsuitable for cultivation and irregular water supply in other areas makes production irregular. Land is the greatest natural resource of the subcontinent and upon its future development and use depends much of the economic growth of the region. But other resources are available, too—more so in India than in resource-poor Pakistan. India ranks seventh among the coal producers of the world, and her reserves are substantial. India's high-grade iron ore reserves are among the world's largest and she is rich in manganese,

TABLE 1

Population Distribution in
South Asia

Country, State or Unit	Area (thousands of sq. miles)	Population* (millions)	Density (per sq. mile)	Capital
INDIA (1951)	1,266.9	361.1	312	New Delhi
States				
Andhra Pradesh	106.0	31.3	295	Hyderabad
Assam	85.0	9.0	176	Shillong
Bihar	67.1	38.8	572	Patna
Bombay	190.9	48.3	253	Bombay
Jammu & Kashmir	85.8	4.4	51	Srinagar
Kerala	15.0	13.5	901	Trivandrum
Madhya Pradesh	171.2	26.0	152	Bhopal
Madras	50.1	30.0	598	Madras
Mysore	74.3	19.4	261	Bangalore
Orissa	60.1	14.6	244	Bhubaneswar
Punjab	47.4	16.1	340	Chandigarh
Rajasthan	132.0	16.0	121	Jaipur
Uttar Pradesh	113.4	63.2	557	Lucknow
West Bengal	33.9	26.3	775	Calcutta
Territories	27.3	4.1	—	—
PAKISTAN (1951)	364.7	75.8	208	Karachi
Units				
East Pakistan	54.5	42.1	777	Dacca
West Pakistan	310.2	33.8	109	Lahore
CEYLON (1953)	25.3	8.1	320	Colombo

* Population estimates for mid-1956 are: India, 387.3 million; Pakistan, 83.6 million; and Ceylon, 8.9 million. See United Nations, *Statistical Yearbook 1957*, p. 25.

mica, and many other minerals. Pakistan's strength is in her fibers—jute, cotton, and wool—but she is poor in power and in minerals.

But if land and resources are the basic facts of life in South Asia, an equally important fact is its geographic position. South Asia stands between Southeast Asia to the east, and the Middle East and sub-Sahara Africa to the west. The subcontinent not only divides the land mass of southern Asia, but historically has extended its influence to and been influenced by the regions that border upon it. This relationship to the outside world continues to shape the cultural, social, and political life of those who live in the subcontinent.

The northern part of the subcontinent—consisting of west Pakistan and northern India—historically has been ruled by land-oriented powers with strong linguistic, cultural, and military ties to Central Asia and the Middle East. Prior to the Western encroachments on South Asia, all invasions of the region—and there have been many—came through the northwest. The Aryans, a Central Asian people whose exact origin is still uncertain, moved through the passes of the Hindu Kush mountains to the plains of India, having a great impact on the development of Hindu religion and social structure and on the languages which were soon to dominate the north and central portions of the subcontinent.

For whatever the reasons—wars in Central Asia or the desiccation of the steppes—from the time of the Aryans through the Mughal invasions of the sixteenth century, the passes of the Hindu Kush mountains in the northwest served as the gateway for one invader after another. Following the last of these important land invasions, Persian became an official court language, Persian words entered the vernacular languages, and wealthy Hindu families adopted the Muslim purdah system. Most important of all, numerous conversions to Islam took place, and Islam became the majority religion in the northwestern region and in parts of the northeast as well. In 1947 the strong ties of the northern part of the subcontinent with Western Asia were reasserted with the partitioning of the subcontinent into two countries; West Pakistan emerged as the easternmost contiguous extension of the Islamic world.

The southern part of the subcontinent, separated from the north by the Vindhya mountains, has been oriented much more toward the sea and toward Southeast Asia than has the north. In other ways, too—in language, dress, food, and culture—the south has differed from the north. Northern kingdoms seldom extended their sway into the south. Ceylon, still farther to the south, began to be converted to Buddhism during the reign of King Asoka. From South India, and from Bengal especially as a result of the rise of seafaring kingdoms, Hindu and Buddhist ideas and institutions spread throughout Southeast Asia. For five centuries, from the eleventh to the sixteenth, parts of Ceylon were under the control of Tamil rulers.

The Mughal invasions of the sixteenth century served to diversify the subcontinent still further. But they also strengthened North India's ties with the Islamic world to the west, just as the expansion of the South Indian kingdoms toward the east strengthened the subcontinent's ties with Southeast Asia. With the advent of the British, this entire region from the towering peak of K-2 in the Himalayas to Cape Comorin and across the Indian Ocean to Ceylon fell under a single ruler. No other event, with the possible exception of the Aryan invasions some three thousand years ago, had such a profound effect on the entire region.

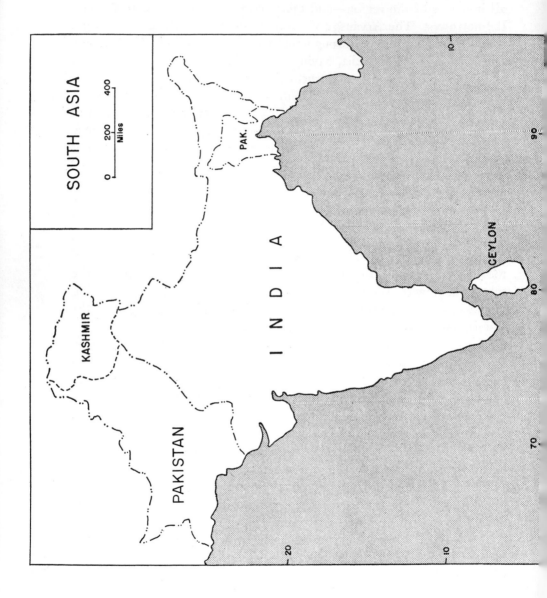

SOUTH ASIA

0 200 400
Miles

PAKISTAN

KASHMIR

PAK.

INDIA

CEYLON

There can be no appreciation of the political developments and problems of South Asia without an examination of the traditional cultures, the impact of the West upon these cultures, and the processes of change which have been set in motion as a result of the interweaving of Western and indigenous patterns.

Traditional Culture

It would be more appropriate to speak of the traditional cultures rather than the culture of South Asia, for this is a region which has fallen under the impact of three distinct and highly developed religions—Hinduism, Islam, and Buddhism. While in the past these religions rarely coincided with political boundaries, today they more or less do. Pakistan is largely Muslim (86 per cent, with the bulk of its Hindu minority in East Pakistan); India is largely Hindu (85 per cent); and Ceylon is largely Buddhist (64 per cent). (See Table 2.) The presence and interaction of these three religious outlooks in the subcontinent call attention to the major distinctive characteristics of the region: the extent to which the area has been subjected to foreign influences and the resulting pluralism in the region with regard to religion, language, race, culture, and social structure.

Greeks, Persians, Afghans, Turks, Arabs, and Mughals all flocked into northern India through the mountain passes. Through the centuries Jews from the Middle East, Christians from the Nestorian community in Syria, persecuted Zoroastrians from Persia, and modern refugees from Fascist Germany have found a home in India. While a few groups have been assimilated into existing cultures, most of them have maintained their own identity, thus making the subcontinent as rich an area in cultural diversity as one will find anywhere in the world. The major religious communities of independent India are Hindu (85 per cent) and Muslim (about 10 per cent), with Christians, Parsis, Jains, Buddhists, and Jews forming smaller minorities. The vastness of the region and its cultural complexity can best be grasped through comparisons with the countries of Europe. There are nearly as many Bengali-speaking people in Pakistan and India (66 million) as there are people in Germany (70 million). Bombay State (48 million) has a greater population than France (44 million), and Uttar Pradesh (63 million) has one greater than Great Britain and Northern Ireland (51 million). There are more Hindus in India and Pakistan (319 million) than Protestant Church members in the entire world (207 million). There are 100 million Muslims in India and Pakistan—about 65 million

TABLE 2

Linguistic and Religious Groups in South Asia*
(in per cent)

India		Pakistan		Ceylon	
LINGUISTIC GROUPS					
Hindi, Urdu, Hindustani, and Punjabi	42.0	Bengali	54.4	Sinhalese	61.4
Telugu	9.3	Punjabi	27.6	Tamil	23.3
Marathi	7.6	Pashtu	6.6	Sinhalese and	
Tamil	7.4	Sindhi	5.1	Tamil	8.7
Bengali	7.0	Urdu	3.2	English and	
Gujarati	4.6	Baluchi	1.2	Sinhalese	2.9
Kannada	4.1			English,	
Malayalam	3.8			Sinhalese,	
Oriya	3.7			and Tamil	1.0
Assamese	1.4			English	.2
RELIGIOUS GROUPS					
Hindu	85.0	Moslem	85.9	Buddhist	64.4
Moslem	9.9	Hindu	12.9	Hindu	19.9
Christian	2.3	Christian	.7	Christian	8.8
Sikh	1.7	Buddhist	.4	Moslem	6.7
Jain	.4				

* These percentages have been computed from figures provided in United Nations, *Demographic Yearbook 1956*, pp. 275, 287, and 290. Figures for India and Pakistan are based on the 1951 censuses. Figures for linguistic groups in Ceylon are based on the 1946 census, and those for religious groups on the 1953 census. The base for India has been taken as 356,610,792, a figure which excludes Jammu and Kashmir and the tribal areas of, Assam, where no census was taken, as well as the settlements of Mahé, Pondichéry, Karikal, and Yanaon, which became part of India on November 1, 1954.

in Pakistan and 35 million in India. This compares with 70 million Arabs and a total of 143 million people throughout the entire Middle East, of whom 90 per cent are Muslim.

About 42 per cent of the Indian population speaks some form of Hindi, but two forms of Hindi may be mutually unintelligible. In addition, Bengali, Punjabi, Marathi, Gujarati, Oriya, and Assamese are all spoken in North India, and although they are derived from some common Aryan source, each is a distinct language. In South India, Tamil, Telugu, Kannada, and Malayalam are all spoken. These derive from a Dravidian, or non-Aryan, source.

Pakistan, which was carved out of the Muslim majority areas of the northeastern and northwestern parts of the subcontinent, is of course united by religion, but by little else. Its two halves are divided by 1,000 miles of Indian territory. Bengal to the east is a tropical, rice- and fish-eating area, where Bengali seems more like a way of life than a language; Western Pakistan, on the other hand, is a dry, wheat-consuming region with large areas of desert, and, unlike East Bengal, is multilingual. Punjabi, Sindhi, Pashtu, and Baluchi are its major languages, and Urdu serves as a lingua franca. The Muslim community of Pakistan is itself divided into the highly orthodox Sunnites, the less orthodox Shi'ites, and the heterodox Ahmadiyas, who are considered by the orthodox to be outside the Islamic fold. Furthermore, Pakistan, like India, has tribal elements which have not been absorbed. The robust Pathan tribes on the Northwest Frontier were always a source of trouble to the British and have continued to be so to the Pakistan government. For many years there has been agitation among the Pashtu-speaking people in neighboring Afghanistan for the creation of a "Pakhtunistan," an independent country of the Pashtu people.

Before the Mughal invasions and large-scale conversions to Islam caused a sharp religious and cultural cleavage on the subcontinent, there was at least a degree of cultural unity in Indian civilization. Ties of religion and of a common classical language, Sanskrit, did much to relate large parts of the subcontinent which were otherwise separated by vernacular languages and local customs. The movement of pilgrims from one part of India to another to visit the sacred places of Hinduism, such as Banaras, Allahabad, Nasik, Rameswaram, and Amarnath, holy rivers and holy temples, inevitably brought people in contact with one another. The wandering Hindu or Buddhist *sadhu* seeking his own salvation also carried with him religious ideas, religious epics, and a classical language which he transmitted across the subcontinent.

But this unity of the higher culture was only rarely overlaid with political unity. It is commonplace but not inaccurate—although perhaps exaggerated—to say that China has had a history of law and order only intermittently broken, while the subcontinent has had a history of disorder and disunity only rarely broken by the creation of a unified state. Indian history is studded with unsuccessful attempts by rulers of the Gangetic Valley to conquer the Deccan plain to the south. Invading forces from Central and Western Asia spread through the northwest portions of India, moved across the prosperous Gangetic Valley, often as far as Bengal, but rarely extended their domain to the deep south. Asoka, a Buddhist king in the third century B.C., the Gupta empire from the fourth to the sixth century A.D., and the Mughal empire from the fifteenth to the eighteenth century did manage to unite large parts of the subcontinent. But none of these northern rulers ever absorbed all the southernmost kingdoms, and whether they actually controlled all the regions that are reported to have been under their suzerainty, or simply had treaties of alliance with many of the petty kingdoms within their domain, is not always clear.

In the absence of either a universal state or a universal church, loyalties in the subcontinent remained parochial. The family, village, and caste became the basic social institutions. While the village was probably never completely self-sufficient, either commercially or socially, the horizons of the villager were limited. Although marriages cut across village lines, caste ties extended beyond the village, and points of pilgrimages lay outside the village, the villager's ties to the state and to the larger society were limited. In many areas village affairs were conducted by *panchayats* (local councils), and the village settled its own conflicts. Only when outside bandits or war threatened the countryside did the state ruler play a more active role in dispensing justice.

State rulers were generally autocratic. The ruler's contact with the villager centered on the collection of land revenue, protection of the village from outsiders, and sometimes provision of certain local services such as irrigation works.

The notion of *dharma*, with its stress on duty, was the central concept guiding relations between the villager and the ruler. Each was to perform his own function; the villager was to be a subject, not a citizen, one who had duties but no rights. According to classical traditions, the function of the ruler was to maintain the system, not to change it. In theory, the warrior-king with the advice of his Brahman priests, was to ensure that each caste performed its duties. The Varna or traditional four-class system drew a sharp line in theory, and the caste system a more or less sharp one in practice, between those who were to rule and wage war (the Kshatriyas), those who were to perform priestly duties (the Brahmans), and those other castes who were to be ruled. The Brahmans might be non-violent, ascetic, and otherworldly, but the Kshatriya's *duty* was to fight and rule.

This sharp division in Hinduism between the functions of the ruler and the functions of the priest provided a basis for a separation of religion and politics which the Islamic religion did not. The Islamic tradition made no distinction between religious and secular life; both state and society must be Islamic. The founding of the Islamic community at Medina by Muhammad and his followers, rather than the prophet's birth, is taken as the first year of Islam. The establishment of secular power, not the revelations to Muhammad, mark Islam's beginning. Islam has been a political theory as well as a religious system. When Pakistan was created in 1947 there were strong cries for creating an Islamic state. The Westernized, largely non-religious leadership which led the preindependence movement was primarily concerned with creating a state with a Muslim majority, free from what they said would be the domination of the Hindu majority in India. They had no desire for an Islamic state. The new state was to possess neither a common language, nor a common economy, nor even a contiguous piece of territory; it could possess only a common religion, a religion which made no distinction between religion and politics. The Westernized leadership, as Wilfred Cantwell Smith has written,[1] was modern and therefore capable of creating a viable state, but it was not religious and therefore incapable of creating an Islamic state. The *ulama*—religious leaders of Islam—offered themselves as an alternative to the present leadership and have thus far presented a much greater challenge to the secular nature of Pakistan than have the orthodox Hindus to the secular nature of India.

Hinduism has no poetic equivalent to the Christian doctrine, "Render unto Caesar the things which are Caesar's, and unto God the things that are God's," but the basic principle of the separation of religious and secular spheres of authority is nevertheless part of the Hindu tradition. Not only did the Kshatriya and the Brahman each have his own sphere of authority, but since Hinduism has no church, the power of the Brahman was that of an individual rather than of an institution. He could hardly challenge the authority of secular society even if he chose to. The Hindu tradition of the separation of royal and religious power may have provided a sounder basis for the rise of a secular leadership than did Islam.

The rise of nationalism in the West meant a break with the religious tradition of the Universal Catholic Church, whose very comprehensive character stood as an obstacle to the creation of distinct national units. India and Ceylon could utilize the religious tradition as an instrument of nationalism and as a cohesive force against foreign rule without endangering modernization. But Islam, with its tradition of joining religion and politics, could not be used as an instrument of nationalism without at the same time endangering the prospects for modernization. Few voices were raised in the Ceylon or Indian constituent assemblies for a Buddhist or Hindu constitution, but the cry for an Islamic con-

[1] Wilfred C. Smith, *Islam in Modern History*, Princeton, N.J., 1957.

stitution in Pakistan was a powerful enough issue to help delay the ratification of a constitution until March 1956, some nine years after independence. Indian and Ceylonese politicians continue to exploit Hinduism and Buddhism with little fear that an organized Hindu or Buddhist clergy or church will displace them, but Pakistani politicians must handle the religious issue with great care. A few Pakistanis, like General Mirza, the former president of Pakistan, privately and very occasionally in public indicate that a secular state, perhaps along the lines of Ataturk's Turkey, might be the goal toward which Pakistan should aim. But the Jamaat-i-Islami and other orthodox parties with *ulama* support continue to press for the creation of an Islamic state. The role of religion in Pakistan is not yet settled.

Diversity is as characteristic of Ceylon as it is of India and Pakistan. Ceylon, too, was the object of many invasions. The Sinhalese inhabitants of Ceylon[2] were probably Aryan invaders from the north of the sixth or fifth century B.C. In the third century B.C. emissaries sent by King Asoka from India converted the island to Buddhism. Not long after Ceylon became Buddhist, Tamils from the Chola country (now Madras) invaded Ceylon. In the eighth century Arab traders from the Persian Gulf settled in Ceylon. In the eleventh century an invasion from South India resulted in an increase in the settlement of Tamil-speaking South Indians in the Jaffna peninsula in northern Ceylon. In the beginning of the sixteenth century, the Portuguese landed at Colombo and for the next 150 years most of Ceylon was under the domination of Portugal. Since the Portuguese believed in religious conversion and practiced intermarriage, a large Catholic population developed on the island. In 1658 the Portuguese were defeated by the Dutch and for the next 138 years Ceylon lived under Dutch rule. Roman-Dutch law, the emergence of a Burgher community, and some fine old forts in Jaffna constitute the Dutch legacy. In 1796 the English invaded Ceylon but were unable to destroy the power of the Kandyan king in south-central Ceylon until 1815, when for the first time Kandy fell under European control. Under British rule, Tamil laborers from South India were brought in to work on the plantations in the hills of Kandy. British rule lasted until November 1947, when Ceylon became an independent member of the British Commonwealth.

The result of these various invasions and immigrations is a highly diversified mixture of races, religions, languages, and cultures. Ceylon

---

[2] "Sinhalese" refers to the language of and members of the majority community, "Ceylonese" to any native of Ceylon.

thus has a population of Sinhalese (69 per cent); Ceylonese Tamils (11 per cent), whose ancestors reached Ceylon in the thirteenth century; Indian Tamils (12 per cent), who came in the last century and are not to be confused with the earlier Tamil immigrants; Ceylonese Moors (6 per cent), descended from the Arab traders; and a few Burghers and Europeans. Even the Sinhalese are divided; there are the low-country Sinhalese whose early contact with the Europeans gives them a dominant position in the commercial and political life of the island, and the up-country Kandyan Sinhalese whose relative seclusion in the mountains protected them from Western invasion until the nineteenth century. Unlike the more "modern" low-country Sinhalese, the Kandyans retain much of the feudal, peasant, and caste structures of earlier kingdoms.[3]

Patterns of Western Impact

South Asia is the classic home of Western imperialism. By the nineteenth century, India was the heart of the British Empire, the "white man's burden," the land of the nabobs. When in 1947 a partitioned India was granted freedom, it marked the beginning of the end of the era of Western imperialism. After India became free, Ceylon and Burma followed. The Dutch were ousted by the Indonesians, the French by the Indo-Chinese, and movements for independence grew in Africa.

The impact which the West had on South Asia was affected by the duration, intensity, scope, and policies of Western rule.

Duration. Ceylon experienced Western rule the longest, and has consequently been affected by the West more than has either India or Pakistan. As we have seen, the Portuguese settled in Ceylon in the sixteenth century, followed by the Dutch, then by the English at the end of the eighteenth century. Under British rule, Ceylon developed a dual economy in which a plantation system was superimposed on the older subsistence economy. Tea, rubber, and coconuts were produced

---

[3] The 1953 Ceylon Census divided the population into the following races and nationalities:

Low-country Sinhalese	3,464,126
Kandyan Sinhalese	2,157,206
Indian Tamils	983,304
Ceylon Tamils	908,705
Ceylon Moors	468,146
Burghers	43,916
Malays	28,736
Others	44,498
Total	8,098,637

163

for export. Ceylon was also affected at an early period by the introduction of Western education. Christian mission schools were particularly active. Ceylon's literacy rate (65.8 per cent of those over five years of age) is much higher than that of either India (16.6 per cent) or Pakistan (18.9 per cent). Within Ceylon, the duration of Western impact varied considerably. As we have noted, the Kandyan hills were affected later than the low-country region around Colombo or the region to the north around Jaffna. Within undivided India there were also variations in the duration of Western rule. European influence was first felt in Bengal, Madras, the region around Bombay, Kerala and, to a lesser extent, in Karachi. Many of the interior portions were not affected until the nineteenth or the twentieth century.

Intensity. Some portions of the subcontinent were under direct British rule, but in others British rule was indirect. After the East India Company conquered Bengal, the British adopted the doctrine of paramountcy in their relationship to many of the Indian princely states. They assumed control of defense, foreign policy, and generally of currency. They could also intervene to maintain law and order and to rectify an unsatisfactory administration. As in parts of tribal Africa, the effect on the princely areas was to undermine the source of legitimacy of the maharajas. But, even then, areas under princely control with few exceptions were not heavily affected by Western education and British administration. Today, some of these regions are often the least politically organized and the most influenced by loyalties to caste and religion.

Scope. The British brought together regions which had rarely if ever been united before. For perhaps the first time, India from Kashmir to Cape Comorin was united under one rule. By the establishment of a network of railways, a post and telegraph system, a national currency, a central administrative organization, the use of the English language, and a university education system, the basis for a modern national state was created by the British.

Policy. Britain's policy in South Asia changed considerably during its two hundred years of rule. The earliest period of British rule was dominated by the East India Company, which was concerned not with changing Indian society, or even controlling it, but with making a profit. During this early phase, the British were curious about Indian practices, but tried to avoid interfering in local customs. A change in this policy occurred during the early part of the nineteenth century when a conflict arose between the "Orientalists," who wanted to preserve the traditional culture, and those like Macaulay, the Law member of the Governor-General's Executive Council in the 1830's, who supported the introduction of English education. It was through the influence of the utilitarians and missionaries who wanted to destroy the "superstition" of Indian society that such practices as *sati* (widow-burning) were abolished, Protestant evangelicism was increased, and British education introduced. Much of the enthusiasm for reform disappeared with the revolt of 1857, which the British interpreted as a protest against their reforms of Indian society. The passion for reforming India slowed down, and emphasis was placed on proper administration and the training of Indians for participation in the administration of their own country. But whether British policy was guided by a reformist zeal (as it tended to be in the earlier part of the century) or limited to an intent to maintain law and order while encouraging economic liberalism (as in the latter part of the century), it had profound effects on traditional Indian institutions and values.

1. A new administrative and judicial system was introduced which changed the role of the village *panchayats* and reduced the importance of law by custom.

2. The introduction of new systems of land tenure, particularly the *zamindar* (landlord) system in Bengal and in eastern India, regularized the collection of land taxes and ensured a continuous and substantial revenue for the East India Company. The creation of this prosperous intermediary class of *zamindars* between the tillers and the state caused capital that might have been invested elsewhere to be put into the purchase (not the development) of land. Fragmentation of holdings, the introduction of cash crops dependent upon a world market, the growing power of a money-lending class, and increase in tenancy all contributed to the deterioration in the position of the peasant, particularly during the world economic crisis in the early 1920's. It was no accident that at this time the peasantry in India joined in the national movement for independence.

3. The pursuit of liberal economic policies by the British meant the duty-free importation of mill-made cloth from England, and the subsequent destruction of handicraft industries in India. These industries had provided substantial rural employment and supplemented the meager income of the peasantry; their ruin resulted in the further deterioration of rural India. The absence of duties also meant that investment by Indians in Indian industries could not be protected. Furthermore, the train freight rates adopted by the British were aimed at facilitating the movement of goods from the interior to the ports.

Production for internal markets was thereby discouraged, and India and Ceylon both became part of an imperial market. For export to Great Britain, commodities like tea, coconut, coffee, and rubber were produced in Ceylon (coffee later decreased rapidly in importance in the 1870's), and tea, cotton, and jute in India. In fact, the economy of Ceylon became heavily dependent upon her export trade.

4. British policy resulted in a large expansion in the functions of government. This had a profound effect upon the policies of India, Pakistan, and Ceylon after independence. From the mid-nineteenth century on, the British, guided by nineteenth-century Victorian notions about the state freeing the individual from institutional restraints and maximizing his opportunities to grow, introduced functions performed by previous governments only on a limited scale or not at all: the development of education, the building of roads and railroads, and the introduction of social services such as public health programs. These activities were increased during the twentieth century, when governments in Europe were themselves expanding the scope of their activities.

As the functions of government expanded, nationalist leaders called for even more government activity. Such political figures were acutely aware of the poverty of their societies, were eager to win public support for nationalist demands, and looked upon the state as the only institution which could provide the wherewithal for development. In all three countries, although in India more than in Pakistan and Ceylon, nationalist leaders after independence undertook to continue the process of expanding governmental functions which the British had begun.

5. The introduction of a Westernized educational system, with the resultant rise of new social classes and the decrease in importance of other traditional social groups, was one of the most significant British policies, particularly from the political point of view. Paradoxically, while the new educational system facilitated greater social mobility, it also reinforced the hierarchical social system. The traditionally hierarchical society emphasized a superior-inferior relationship dictated partly by secular and partly by ritual (or caste) considerations. By creating new differences in the population based upon such criteria as educational background, dress (trousers versus the dhoti), and alien ideas, colonial rule and its Westernized educational system created a new pattern of hierarchical relations.

6. The large-scale introduction of achievement criteria in all spheres of life in which the British had contact with the population of the

area was another major innovation. Recruitment into the civil services and into British firms was based on educational qualifications rather than on caste status, although high castes obviously had greater access to better education and hence to the new jobs. This is not to say that Indians in a position to recruit personnel were unaffected by loyalties to kin and caste and village, or that recruitment today is always on an achievement basis. But the British practice did introduce new standards which are now widely accepted by the upper elite and which therefore represent a norm against which deviant behavior—in this case, traditional behavior—can be judged and corrected. This halfway house, however, in which ideal standards are in continuous conflict with prevailing practices, leads to considerable concern, cynicism, and sometimes calculation upon the part of younger educated people, who either bitterly denounce the prevailing practices or, in order to survive in the system, cultivate friends and relations who might be of assistance in furthering their careers.

7. Although self-rule was introduced only gradually by the British, they did permit civil liberties. A critical English and vernacular press developed, and Indians and Ceylonese were allowed the right to organize and assemble. The British often placed severe restrictions on the exercise of these rights, but South Asians were inculcated with British conceptions of civil liberty and taunted their rulers with their own teachings. John Locke and John Stuart Mill provided more effective standards of government for educated South Asians than did the Vedas, the Koran, or the Tripitaka.

A rationalized administrative system, a framework in which the government operated according to a rational-legal system, an expanded government, achievement criteria in job recruitment and promotion, and civil liberties all gave to South Asians, or at least to a new rising class of South Asians, a relatively clear framework for the kind of society in which they wanted to live. Even in areas of indirect rule like the princely states, a substantial erosion of old values and institutions occurred. The reduction of princely authority, the introduction of railways and buses, new urban centers, and a new administrative system all had their effect on these regions.

What happened in areas of South Asia where there was no Western rule can be seen from a brief examination of Nepal. Nepal remained independent for centuries, even during the era of Western rule in South Asia. In 1851 Nepal's Prime Minister Jung Bahadur Rana forced the King to sign documents which gave effectual power and title to the premiership to the Rana family. The King of Nepal was thus in a position comparable to that of the Japanese Emperor during the Tokugawa era. Legislative, executive, and judicial powers were in the hands of the Rana rulers. While elsewhere in Asia a native leadership organized to oppose foreign oppressors, in Nepal the oppressors were Nepalese. No university or administrative system and consequently no substantial middle classes developed comparable to those of India, with access to the ideas or practices of democracy and nationalism. When the Rana rulers were overthrown in 1951, the revolt came about largely through individual Nepalis then living in India. The Nepali Congress, which stood for constitutional monarchy, land reform and redistribution, full democracy and friendship with India, proved unable to control the government. Personal conflicts between political leaders prevented the administration from functioning. The government was unable to utilize the Rana-controlled, largely corrupt, administrative system, or to find other personnel to build a new system. In this maze of uncertainty and administrative inadequacy, power has been continually moving back toward the King, who is the only remaining unifying symbol.

In the rest of South Asia where the British did rule, differences centered around the duration of their rule and the type of rule—direct or indirect—which they introduced. Since the initial contact with Europeans took place in the coastal regions, Madras, Calcutta, Bombay, and the Malabar coast were among the first to adopt a rationalized administrative system, and to achieve greater commercialization followed by industrialization, Western education, and the use of the English language. These regions grew in importance in at least two respects. As centers of trade and industry, they came to be the wealthiest regions of the country, producing increased revenue for the central and state government. Then, too, as educational centers and points of Western influence, these regions produced the greatest number of individuals who entered the Indian Civil Service, or assumed the responsibilities of leadership in the nationalist movement. In virtually all spheres—industrial-commercial, administrative, political, and intellectual—the Tamils, Bengalis, Malayalees, Gujaratis, and Maharashtrians, the people near the sea, held dominant positions.

Since the early part of the 1920's, however, a shift in the process of modernization has occurred. The coastal areas are no longer the only developed regions. Educational institutions have proliferated; many are now in central and northern India. The interior regions are now producing a middle class of lawyers, doctors, teachers, and, above all, administrators. The state of Uttar Pradesh (the home of Nehru) has become a pivotal area. Not only are more Westernized Indians emerging from the interior regions to assume positions of leadership, but so are the khaddar-wearing, Hindi-speaking, Hindu-practicing Indians, often with only secondary school education. This latter group gave a religious overtone to the national movement and is today a strong force behind the adoption of Hindi as India's national language. As we shall see later, a comparable group of vernacular-speaking, tradition-minded people have become a powerful force in the politics of Ceylon as well.

Following independence, as soon as universal adult suffrage was introduced and educational institutions multiplied in the interior, the large and heavily populated regions in the center were bound to grow in importance. But the coastal regions resent many of the political consequences. First, there is growing hostility in some of the coastal states toward the introduction of Hindi as the official language, particularly insofar as it gives an advantage to young people from Hindi-speaking areas who apply for administrative posts in government. Unemployment among educated people is great in both Bengal and Madras, and many feel that the introduction of Hindi would further restrict job opportunities. The strongest anti-Hindi movements have developed in these two states. Secondly, the more developed and prosperous coastal states contribute more revenue to the central government than is allocated back to them. The union government distributes funds to the state governments largely on a population basis, so that heavily populated Uttar Pradesh and Bihar receive relatively larger sums than Madras, West Bengal, and Kerala.

Growing center-state conflicts in India, over the question of a national language and over the distribution of revenue by the center, are more complex than the federal-state controversies that frequently develop in any kind of federal system. Such conflicts are built into the regional cultural nature of Indian society and the differential response to modernization by these regional cultures.

It should also be noted that while the Western impact was probably heavier in Ceylon than in undivided India, differences are generally greater within each country than between the countries. In Pakistan, Punjab is far more developed than Sind; in India, West Bengal and Bombay are far more developed than Orissa and Rajasthan; in Ceylon, the low country is far more developed than the up-country Kandyan region. Given this differential in development, communities are becoming increasingly aware as communities, of their "backwardness" in relationship to other communities within their *own* society. Indians are not only underdeveloped compared with Americans, and feel so, but Telugus feel underdeveloped compared with neighboring Tamils. This community sense of underdevelopment adds a new dimension to the problem of planning, for it means that planners, to the extent that they are concerned with the political consequences of their plans, must not only attempt to achieve rational development for the nation as a whole, but must also focus on raising the levels of certain communities. In the relatively underdeveloped state of Assam, for example, pressure upon the central government to build a new oil refinery in that state became so great in 1957 that the government finally agreed, although from the point of view of *national* economic planning other sites might have been as good or better. Public policy in South Asian countries increasingly aims not only at hastening the speed of modernization, but at equalizing internal developments as well.

II. PROCESSES OF CHANGE

It has become commonplace to speak of the extent to which rapid change has affected the newly independent areas of Asia and Africa. It is not, however, that everything is changing faster than in the West. To the contrary, population growth is higher in many Western countries than in many parts of Asia, as is the growth in national income and the rate of urbanization. Many of the changes that we now see in Asia and Africa occurred in the West one, two, or, in some instances, even three centuries ago. What is striking, however, is that these changes are occurring in Asia and Africa at a time when one section of the world is already so far ahead. The result is a sense of urgency and a sense of underdevelopment which the West did not feel during its days of hectic growth. Then, too, growth in the "new" areas occurs in societies where political consciousness is often high, where twentieth-century political structures exist side by side with eighteenth-century social practices, and where universal suffrage and a democratic framework facilitate the organization and expression of discontent.

Population Change

Every minute the population of India increases by ten. Between 1920 and 1940 the population of undivided India increased by 83 million. By 1956 India's annual growth was 1.3 per cent, and that of Pakistan was 1.5 per cent. Ceylon, as a result of a large anti-malarial campaign which has cut the death rate enormously since the war, is now growing at the rate of about 3.1 per cent per year (see Table 3). These rates compare with 1.6 per cent yearly for the United States, .3 per cent for the United Kingdom, 2 per cent for Canada, and 1.1 per cent for Japan. The population growth in India and Pakistan is thus not unusually high, compared with that of many Western countries; what is important is that it is based upon a large rural economy

TABLE 3
Processes of Change

Country	Liter- ates (%)	Rural Pop. (%)	Urban Pop. (%)	Average per Capita Income, 1952-1954 ($ US)	Annual Rate of Popula- tion increase, (1953-1956) (%)
India (1951)	16.6	82.7	17.3	60	1.3
Pakistan (1951)	18.9	89.6	10.4	70	1.5
Ceylon (1953)	65.8*	84.6†	15.4†	110	3.1

* Percentage of population aged 5 years and over.
† Census of 1946.
Source: The above statistics have been derived from several sources, including: (1) United Nations, *Statistical Yearbook 1957*; (2) United Nations, *Demographic Yearbook 1955*; (3) United Nations, *Demographic Yearbook, 1956*; (4) *Economic Almanac 1958*; (5) *India 1957*; (6) *India Census 1951*; (7) *Pakistan Census 1951*; (8) *Ten Years of Pakistan 1947-1951*; (9) *Ceylon Year Book 1956*.

whose population lives close to subsistence. (India's yearly per capita income is about $60, Pakistan's is $70, and that of more prosperous Ceylon is only about $110.)

The introduction by the British, and now by Western-trained public health workers, of various improvements in sanitation facilities, hospitals, and other public health measures has led to a decrease in the death rate throughout South Asia. Infant mortality is still high (estimated at 114 per thousand in India, and 72 per thousand in Ceylon, compared with 26 per thousand in the United States), but the death rate for those who survive birth has dropped enormously. Conditions which in the West have encouraged widespread birth control—secularization, urbanization, industrialization, increased education—have only slightly affected South Asia. Estimates by Coale and Hoover,[4]

[4] Ansley J. Coale and Edgar M. Hoover, *Prospects of Population Growth and Their Implications for Economic Development in India, 1956-1986*, Princeton, N.J., 1958.

based upon varying assumptions of change in the birth rate and death rate, suggest that India's population by 1986 will reach a maximum of 775 million, a minimum of 589 million, with a likely middle-range figure of 634 million.

Given all available estimates for population growth in the subcontinent, several political conclusions can be drawn. First, the increase of population alone has become an economic factor forcing modernization in one form or another. Only wide-scale industrialization, an increase in available agricultural lands, or a rapid growth in agricultural productivity can enable South Asia to cope with the population increase. The decision to *try* to move ahead economically is one that few could oppose politically. Even the ascetic-minded Gandhians favor economic growth; differences of opinion concern the methods and the kinds of growth desired rather than the question of whether growth is needed.

Second, the problem of unemployment or underemployment is already a serious one. There is political pressure for projects which create employment, irrespective of their relative economic advantages. The economists may have a case for developing capital goods industries, but local politicians are urging further investment in small-scale cottage industries which maximize the use of labor. India's second five-year plan called for a public investment of about $425 million in small-scale industries, compared with $100 million in the first plan.

Third, population growth is resulting in greater concentrations in already densely populated rural areas. Without very substantial increases in the amount of cultivable land, or very large increases in production on land already under cultivation—and it is uncertain that either of these measures would be able to keep pace with the growth in population—one of two political consequences will occur: there will be an increase in rural discontent resulting from unemployment and underemployment; or there will be an accelerated population overflow into the already crowded and politically explosive cities. From a political point of view, the case for encouraging the growth of small-scale and cottage industries and the development of such industries in smaller towns and rural areas rather than in the large cities would seem to be a strong one.

Urbanization

The city has always been a center for the diffusion of new ideas. In the subcontinent, pre-British towns and cities were important religious and political centers. Their commercial activities often depended upon their position as political centers. With the shifting of a capital, some of these cities, such as Pataliputra, one-time capital of King Asoka, near the modern city of Patna, disappeared. Pilgrimage centers were centers of trade and commerce as well, but they rarely achieved the independence from feudal or royal power that the late medieval, early Renaissance cities of Europe attained.

The major cities of the subcontinent are relatively new. Calcutta, Bombay, Madras, and Colombo all are new and are thus comparatively free from a restrictive tradition. They are diffusion centers for Western ideas, centers where social change often begins, where new ideas, talent, and the organization to execute ideas often originate.

The rate of decennial urban growth in prepartition India gradually increased from 9 per cent in 1881 to 10 per cent in 1921 and 12.8 per cent in 1941. The growth of cities has been relatively slow—only 41 per cent between 1881 and 1941, compared with 111 per cent for the same period in the United States—but the rate of industrialization has also been slow. India's rate of urbanization is about that of the United States between 1790 and 1850 and only now is entering a period of rapid growth.

The growth which has occurred in the cities has been due less to a natural increase in population than to a large rural migration. More than one-third of the population of the cities of India and Pakistan was born in rural areas. In some large cities, such as Bombay, 75 per cent of the population immigrated from rural areas. Immigration also has been largely masculine. Some cities have 180 males to 100 females, and factory districts of Bombay and Calcutta often have over 200 males to 100 females. Those who do immigrate to the cities come less because of the attractions of urban life than because of the pressures in the rural areas. Villagers go to the cities for work and return to their rural homes when it becomes financially possible. The resulting turnover in the work force is one reason for labor's low productivity, and for the difficulties in building a sound trade-union movement.

Indian and Pakistani cities have enormous population densities, without compensating skyscrapers or multistoried tenements. The population is crowded into one- and two-storied buildings. New York in 1950, with its skyscrapers and multistoried tenements, had 25,000 people per square mile. Calcutta today has about 80,000. Workers live in crowded *bustees*, wooden shacks comparable to and often far worse than the slum housing of nineteenth-century English workers. But in spite of these conditions, the push into the cities from the rural areas continues.

Overcrowding on the land, increases in rural debt, tenancy, and under-employment, and a lack of rural industries to provide alternative sources of employment and income to the villagers all drive the peasant to the city.

Three political consequences are resulting from this urbanization. One is that urban areas are becoming a gutter for overflowing rural tensions. Second, large numbers of rootless, crowded, and often un-married urban workers are easily provoked to violence and readily or-ganized by political groups. Third, the continued ties between the urban worker and the rural area to which he returns for births, wed-dings, and funerals, and in which he settles when he has sufficient in-come, serve to bring urban political ideas and organization to the rural areas.

Commercialization and Technical Innovation

Commercial and industrial growth have become prime targets of all three countries of South Asia. Industrial development in the regions which went to Pakistan in 1947 was negligible. Muslims were not energetic in exploiting opportunities for either Western education or economic development; the commercial and industrial activity which did occur in the Karachi and Lahore regions was largely carried on by Hindus and Parsis rather than by Muslims. The areas that form Pakistan were mainly primary producers for outside markets.

Jute, for example, was grown in eastern Bengal, but the jute mills were in West Bengal, which is now part of India. Since Muslim entre-preneurs were largely in commerce rather than industry, most of Paki-stan's industrial development program is the result of government initiative. Since there were virtually no industries, the percentages of growth in Pakistan appear phenomenal. Considerable attention has been paid to developing cotton and woolen textile mills, jute and sugar mills, the paper industry, ship-building, and the manufacture of fer-tilizers and cement. Limited mineral resources (Pakistan has no pig iron) will very likely restrict Pakistan's efforts to develop large-scale in-dustry.

India today ranks about seventh among the industrial countries of the world, but this is a function of size rather than of development. India's output per capita is a fraction of that of most industrial coun-tries. There is evidence that prior to the eighteenth century India was equal and possibly ahead of Western countries in its technology and volume of manufactures. Indian textiles in particular were superior to what was then produced in the West. "The decline from this position was abrupt, and with the rise of Lancashire and the fall of the princely Courts India collapsed into industrial insignificance, complete but for the hard-hit village crafts. In its external relations the whole Indian economy was geared to that of Britain, whether as market or as source of raw materials. The first steps towards a modern industry were taken a century ago, but on the whole progress has been irregular in time, space, and the internal structure of industry."[5]

Since minerals are abundant in India and have not hitherto been developed, they have received special attention from the government. The Damodar region, with its excellent supply of coal, iron ore, power, transportation, and labor, has become the major center for the development of both steel and heavy engineering. It is often called the Ruhr of India, and perhaps of Asia.

Under British rule, Ceylon, far more than India, developed a dual economy. Since independence the government has been trying to introduce manufacturing industries so as to reduce Ceylon's dependence upon world prices of tea, rubber, and coconut (which make up some 90 per cent of the country's visible exports). Like Pakistan, Ceylon is not well endowed for heavy industry, but some effort has been made to develop the manufacture of matches, textiles, plywood, glass, ceramics, and other products.

In virtually all three countries, economic development has been accompanied by political arguments concerning the relative merits of small-scale industries versus large-scale industries, industrial versus agricultural development, public investment versus private investment, and the role of foreign capital.

Westernized Education

Education has been a major force in acculturating South Asians to the values of the West. The English believed that the educational system should be directed at creating a new class of South Asians, familiar with Western literature and humanities, who would become committed to Western ideas and institutions. Many Englishmen were convinced that only through Westernization could the indigenous cultures be "uplifted." This philosophy fitted in well with the growing need in the late nineteenth century for English-speaking Indians and Ceylonese

[5] O. H. K. Spate, *India and Pakistan: A General and Regional Geography*, New York, 1954, p. 272.

who could step into low-ranking administrative posts in government and business.

The English modeled the Indian universities after universities in England. Emphasis was on Western humanities and liberal arts, with scientific training of secondary importance. Learning to read and speak English was essential. Since nineteenth-century English literature received a special place in the curriculum, the speech of South Asians, even today, has the flavor of Thackeray and Dickens. Correspondence has a formal Victorian touch. "Your humble and most obedient servant" is still a fitting close to a letter.

The creation of the universities at Calcutta, Madras, and Bombay were turning points in India's political development. From them came a new Western-educated class, possessing English as a common language and sharing the liberal notions of the nineteenth-century writers whom they read in and out of the universities.[6] The new universities, and the English language in which they taught, also opened the doors to greater contact with other Western countries. Mazzini's Young Italy movement inspired Lala Lajput Rai, a Punjabi nationalist, to create a Young India movement. The Sinn Fein agitation in Ireland, the Bolshevik Revolution in Russia, and the ideologies which grew out of such movements reached into the subcontinent. Soon new ideologies from the West, often irrelevant to the economic and political scene of the subcontinent, were absorbed and expressed by indigenous elements. Nationalism, constitutionalism, communism, socialism, even religious revivalism were fostered by the graduates of the new universities.

Traditional educational institutions did continue, but they were primarily concerned with imparting religious instruction in Hinduism, Islam, or Buddhism. Orthodox families, especially Muslim families, preferred to send their sons to such religious schools rather than to the Westernized universities. In the latter part of the nineteenth century, in order to keep pace with other communities and at the same time to maintain their tradition of religious education, the Muslims under the leadership of Syed Ahmad Khan created Aligarh University as a center in which both Western and Islamic education would be given. In the 1920's, when many nationalist Hindus were concerned about the extent to which the British educational system tended to weaken the ties of educated Indians to their own tradition, an effort was made

[6] For a first-rate treatment of the effects of the introduction of Western education on a nationalist movement, see Bruce T. McCully, *English Education and the Rise of Indian Nationalism*, New York, N.Y., 1940.

to combine Western with traditional Hindu education. Santiniketan, a university in Bengal, was then founded by the Nobel Prize-winning poet Rabindranath Tagore.

The British created a top-heavy educational system. The emphasis was on universities rather than primary schools. But the British had not developed much of a free primary-school system within their own country during the nineteenth century and were not concerned with utilizing an educational system as a means of creating greater social mobility. By 1951 only 16.6 per cent of the Indian population was literate, with literacy highest among urban males (54.6 per cent) and lowest among rural females (6 per cent). In Pakistan, literacy was 18.9 per cent. In Ceylon, where Christian missionaries had created an extensive primary-school system, 65.8 per cent of the population above the age of five was literate in 1953.

In India, a college degree, or even a few years of college, has become so essential for most white-collar jobs that all who had the opportunity have tried to attend a university. B.A. (Honor) used to be a passport to a job. But the British-created university system has grown with such speed that today, in spite of the great expansion within the government, the universities are producing more graduates than there are jobs. The University Grants Commission has estimated that between 1948 and 1958 the number of university students has increased from 204,000 to 705,000, an increase of 50,000 a year for ten years. Part of the difficulty, too, is that the universities are not equipped to train students for the positions in science and engineering which are opening up as a result of the industrial development programs. More attention is now being given to developing scientific institutions and to strengthening the science and engineering programs of universities.

All three governments are now investing large sums of money in developing primary schools. These schools are conducted in vernacular languages. In the long run, the growth of the primary-school system is likely to result in an increase in economic and social mobility, a growth in the vernacular press and other vernacular communication channels, and more use of the printed word by government and political parties for imparting information and new ideas. Since most of the primary schools are public institutions in secular societies, they do not give traditional religious instruction. Children of different castes and religions may sit side by side. Training is, in the broadest sense, for citizenship. The transmission of traditional culture is left to other institutions. The total effect of the new primary schools is to strengthen the forces for secularization.

Secularization

While many members of the elite of South Asia are secular, religion plays an important part in the lives of most Indians, Pakistanis, and Ceylonese. In societies so much divided by class, caste, and language, even secular-minded politicians have turned toward religion as a force for cohesion. In the interwar period, religious revivalism and an emphasis on the religious tradition was a unifying force among Hindus against British rule. For the Muslim League, the revival of Islam was a counterforce to the Hindus and to the Indian National Congress. While religion thus unified some elements, it divided others. Just as Gandhi's emphasis on Hinduism alienated many Muslims, the League's revival of Islam seemed threatening to Hindus, and the revival of Buddhism in Ceylon was viewed as threatening to Hindu Tamils. Since all three countries have large religious minorities, their leaders have been torn between a desire for secularism, which minimizes religious differences, and religious revivalism, which at least ties the majority community to the new state. Pakistan, with one thousand miles separating its two areas, has accorded a special place to Islam and actually calls itself "the Islamic Republic of Pakistan." But at the same time Pakistan leaders stress the equalitarian attitude of Islam toward religious minorities. Ceylon and India, on the other hand, give no official place to religion, although Ceylonese and Hindu politicians frequently emphasize their Buddhist and Hindu heritage in political speeches. Eager to have the best of both worlds, the Hindu politician castigates his listeners on the one hand for their "castism and communalism," belief in untouchability, superstition, and fatalism, and on the other hand praises the Hindu tradition and the "spiritualism" of the East. On the one hand he is attacking those elements in his tradition which impair national unity and economic and social modernization, and on the other hand he is praising his tradition for the sense of cohesion which it creates.

Religion is so interwoven into the fabric of the cultures of South Asia that almost any change in social institutions has a religious effect. The stratification system, especially in India, has been so legitimized by religious beliefs that changes in stratification invariably have their effects upon religious values as well. Many strictures of caste, especially those connected with touch and food, have almost entirely disappeared in public places. Marriage outside of one's caste is not common, but it does occur, and marriage outside of one's religion occasionally occurs as well. The prohibition against traveling abroad has been relaxed and in most educated families discarded. Caste continues, and the unity of caste may even be increased through the creation of caste associations, the political organization of caste demands, and caste solidarity in elections, but many of the strictures of caste have been eroded, and some of the religious sanctions for caste have been weakened.

Older religious forms are, however, more likely to be modified than replaced by a secular outlook. The growth of *bakti* (devotional worship) appears to be occurring in many parts of India, especially in Madras and Bengal. *Bakti*, or devotion, has always been one accepted path to salvation. But in recent years *bakti* has spread even among the more ritual-minded Brahmans. Its emphasis upon direct relations with God and its equalitarian overtones are reminiscent of the earlier Protestant movement in the West which played such an important part in the development of democratic thought.[7]

Restratification

The major changes which have occurred in the positions of various classes in the subcontinent have resulted from the introduction of a completely new set of criteria for social status. In theory, traditional Hindu society based status upon the ascribed position of caste. Even Buddhism and Islam in South Asia, in spite of the equalitarianism which they preach, have caste systems within them. But, in the last one hundred years or so, increased emphasis has been placed upon the attainment of status by merit. University education is now a major avenue for achieving status. India's first Law Minister, for example, was an untouchable, but a graduate of Columbia University. Educated Indians, wearing Western dress and speaking proper English, can often sidestep caste. When an urban Brahman holds status now, it is more often for his higher education and his government job, or his wealth, than his caste. Caste continues as a source of status, but educational, occupational, political, and economic factors are assuming greater importance. What Bryce Ryan wrote on the changing character of caste in Ceylon holds for India as well: "The revolution which is pervading all Ceylonese institutions cannot leave caste untouched, for caste is a

[7] For a study of the role of *bakti* movements in an urban setting, see Milton Singer, "The Great Tradition in a Metropolitan Center: Madras," *Journal of American Folklore*, Vol. LXXI, No. 281, July-September 1958.

phenomenon integrated with feudal, personalized, and familistic status relationships. Neither the values nor the structure of a secular and economically rational democratic state and economy can support this institution of another era. Many specific trends encompassed in the Ceylonese transformation operate to disrupt the caste system directly, as well as by shattering the social order which supports it. The widening popular, and virtually complete legal, acceptance of equality in opportunity and justice, and belief in the propriety of status by achievement bespeak a value system explicitly contradictory to caste. The joint development of urbanism and economic rationality with their combined effects upon mobility, the growth of contractual relations and impersonality, provide objective circumstances in which strictures of caste are unenforceable. Even more significantly, they establish disparities between traditional birth statuses and economic prestige and power."[8]

It should be noted, however, that the mobility of individuals in the subcontinent is still very limited. The response to the Western impact and to the Western educational system which the British introduced was largely in terms of particular social groups rather than of individuals. Groups are often more mobile than individuals. A low caste as a group may move up the status ladder as a result of a change in its occupation or economic position. The Kayasthas, Boidyas, and Brahmans in Bengal responded to Western ideas and institutions earlier than did other castes in their localities. Tamil-speaking people along the Madras coast responded more rapidly than the interior Telugus, the Bengalis more than the Biharis or Oriyas, the Punjabi and Uttar Pradesh Muslims before other Muslims, and in general Hindus before Muslims.

The advent of the British meant not only the rise of a new class of educated South Asians who filled administrative posts, but also the rise of new commercial classes and the growth in importance of older commercial classes. The Muslim Ismailis, the Tamils and Malays in Ceylon, the Gujaratis, Marwaris, Parsis, and Jains along India's western coast became a new *comprador* class. Ultimately these communities produced industrial classes as well. British rule likewise had its effects upon landowning classes. The British-created permanent settlement in Bengal, which converted Hindu revenue collectors into landlords, meant the growth of a Hindu landlord class; in Ceylon the British-introduced plantation system was also adopted by Ceylonese, and a new plantation-owning class was formed. In 1955, of the total acreage on which rubber

[8] Bryce Ryan, *Caste in Modern Ceylon*, New Brunswick, N.J., 1953, p. 338.

was cultivated, 65 per cent (427,000 out of 661,000 acres) was owned by Ceylonese, most of the rest by Europeans. As early as 1934, it was estimated that about 90 per cent of the capital in coconuts, 55 per cent of that in rubber, and about 20 per cent of that in tea had been invested by Ceylonese.[9]

The growth of new classes in administration, commerce and industry, and land often meant that existing divisions along the lines of religion, language, and caste were intensified rather than mitigated. The landlord class in Bengal was Hindu, the peasants (especially in eastern Bengal) were Muslim. The educated elite of South India was Brahman, while the less educated, and politically, economically, and socially less successful were generally non-Brahmans. Employers in Bombay were largely Gujaratis, while the working class was largely Maharashtrian. The business classes in the south tended to be Tamil, while the consumers were Telugu-speaking. The fact that the new stratification, along the lines of education and economic position, often coincided with community divisions was a major factor in intensifying group conflict.

Two recent trends in restratification should be noted: the emergence of an articulate lower middle class in the small towns, and the rise of new technically skilled classes. These two classes have entirely different traditional backgrounds and represent a source of political conflict.

The small-town lawyers, traditional *ayurvedic* doctors, teachers, shopkeepers, and wealthier peasants generally have a secondary school education or are the product of the smaller district colleges. They speak vernacular languages and are usually religiously oriented. In northern India this element plays an active role in pressing for the use of Hindi as the national language, advocating a ban on cow slaughter, supporting prohibition, and in general emphasizing the importance of tradition. Some of the Hindu communal parties draw strength from this class, but its influence extends beyond the Hindu communal groups to other political parties, including the Congress. In South India, many vernacular-speaking people in the towns of Madras State have become active in the Dravida Munetra Kazagham (the DMK), an organization which opposes Hindi as the national language, is militantly anti-Brahman, and advocates the creation of an independent South Indian state free from North Indian "domination." In Ceylon a new Sinhalese-speaking, Sinhalese-conscious community in smaller towns and villages, supported by the Buddhist *bhikkus* (monks), is now advocating Buddhism as a state

[9] W. Ivor Jennings, *The Economy of Ceylon*, Oxford, 1948, p. 26. Jennings' figures are taken from the *Report of the Ceylon Banking Commission*, 1934.

religion and Sinhalese as the only national language. In Pakistan, the Muslim priests and many vernacular-speaking young people have been actively supporting the Jamaat-i-Islami movement for the creation of an Islamic state.

At the other pole is a small but growing Western-educated, English-speaking, development- and technology-minded class whose members work as administrators and technicians for the new state-built and state-owned enterprises, planners for government agencies, advertising executives, employees of large industrial concerns, engineers, professors and staff for the various scientific and research institutes of the government. This class is rooted less in the tradition of liberal arts and humanities in which the Western-educated nationalists of the nineteenth and early twentieth centuries were trained than in the "harder" sciences of chemistry, physics, engineering, statistics, economics, demography, and personnel management. Thus far it has had little taste for party politics, although its influence on government policy, especially economic planning, is considerable. Among this group one often meets the "commissar" type—the impatient, hard-headed "realist" who places emphasis on physical planning.

Impact of Processes of Change on Political Processes

The major processes of change discussed in the preceding pages, most of which received their impetus from the Western impact, are now being advanced by internal pressures. Government policy may affect the rate of population growth, urbanization, or even secularization, but such policy is indigenous. Foreign aid may play a part in the pace of economic growth, but the major motivation and organization for development come from indigenous government and business. Since independence the pace of change has increased rather than decreased; the new leadership in all three countries is eager to speed national development.

The processes of change are closely interrelated. Greater commercialization and technical innovation are likely to further the process of urbanization; urbanization is likely to affect the stratification system; the pace of secularization and stratification is likely to affect population growth; and population growth is likely to affect the rate of technical and commercial change. In the words of Bryce Ryan: "The contemporary transition of Ceylon is revolutionary. Not only has nationalism become an immediate and necessary goal, but similarly western values of political and economic democracy have become fixed points in governmental policy. Ceylon is emerging from an ancient peasant order, dominated by institutions of feudalism, caste, autocracy, and kinship and local solidarities. These institutional systems were supported by a static technology and a pervasive supernaturalism. Summarily the two-thousand-year-old civilization of Ceylon is being regeared toward the goals of an expanding economy, national solidarity, democratic government based upon an informed citizenry, and maximum equality of educational and economic opportunity at the various caste, class, ethnic and regional levels. Such goals represent antitheses to the orientations of a familistic, feudal, technologically stagnant, society of status. While the new goals may well be distant ones, Ceylon is on the move, and the move is toward a total reorientation of institutions, whether or not this fact is widely realized by those whose life is in flux."[10]

Among the three countries there are differences in the pace of the changes which they are experiencing. Ceylon's population growth is higher than that of India and Pakistan; India's rate of industrial growth is likely to be higher than that of her two neighbors; because of their present lower levels of education, India and Pakistan are likely to have a more rapid development of education than Ceylon. All three areas are subject to a complex of social change which places an enormous burden on political institutions. The national leadership of each of these countries is dedicated to maintaining a unified national state, and is enlarging the productive spheres of society. A growth in secularization, economic and commercial development, urbanization, and the like are likely to improve the position of some social classes and deteriorate that of others; new groups will enter the political arena, new kinds of allegiances will develop, and increased demands on government are likely to arise, all of which will strain the political framework. In fact, it can be argued that the political history of South Asia of the last fifty years has been based upon the emergence of new groups and the effects they have had upon political institutions. Precisely what groups have emerged, and which functions they perform in the political process, will be discussed in the following pages.

III. POLITICAL GROUPS AND POLITICAL FUNCTIONS

It has become commonplace to ask whether newly independent areas of Asia and Africa can successfully adopt Western-type democratic institutions in societies quite different from those in which democratic

[10] Ryan, *op.cit.*, p. 338.

institutions first developed. Will these societies fall back upon some kind of traditionally oriented autocratic system, or will a modern totalitarianism of the left triumph? Will the present democratically oriented leaderships expand in number, or will they lose their *élan* and contract into a small closed group concerned more with holding power than with building a new society? Will the new classes and groups that are entering politics be integrated into the political framework, or will they form an opening wedge for the disorganization and violence which lead to either immobilism or authoritarianism?

That we must ask these questions reminds us how uncertain the political future of these countries is. Built into these questions is the assumption that the political ideas and interests that people have and the way they organize to express those ideas and interests will determine what will happen to the new democratic institutions. To understand how these new political systems operate we must know something of the groups which operate the system, how they recruit people, how they communicate their interests to others, how they organize into interests, and how these interests are aggregated. And, finally, to what extent are the new political institutions actually being utilized? Are rule-making, rule application, and rule adjudication (or, to put it another way, the legislative, administrative, and judicial functions) being carried out within or outside of the formal institutions?

For the purpose of our analysis we shall deal with both political groups and political institutions in a discussion of the way political functions are performed in these societies, thereby making it possible to compare the ways in which the political systems of the three countries we are dealing with operate, as well as the ways in which they are similar to or differ from those of Western countries and of other non-Western regions.

Before turning to the ways in which the functions of recruitment, communication, interest articulation and aggregation, rule-making, rule application, and rule adjudication are carried on, and the role played by political groups in performing these functions, we shall explore the development of group systems in South Asia. We shall examine the kinds of nationalist movements which came into being to deal with alien rule, the break-up of these nationalist movements after independence, and the emergence of a party system. Emphasis will be given to showing that differences in the kind of rule imposed by the British, and the kind of response made by various communities to that rule, affected the character not only of the nationalist movements, but of the party systems which emerged after independence.

Political Parties and Party Systems

(1) *India.* The earliest modern political groups in South Asia can be characterized more as interest groups than as political parties. The Indian National Congress, the Muslim League, and the Ceylon National Congress began as small, narrowly based interest groups primarily concerned with the interests of a small Westernized middle class. In India this class grew out of the university system which the British introduced in 1856. From the universities came a new middle class educated for law, medicine, civil engineering, education, and, above all, government service. An intelligentsia began to emerge which communicated its common interests and shared its ideas through a growing English-language press. Lack of adequate access to civil service posts soon led to the creation of several associations in Calcutta and Bombay which demanded, for example, that the age limit for competitive examinations in the civil service be raised (thereby permitting Indians who had lost time studying abroad to compete with Englishmen), and that native judges be allowed to exercise jurisdiction in cases involving Europeans. In 1885 various associations banded together in Bombay to form the Indian National Congress. The meeting was attended mainly by Hindus, with some Parsis and Muslims. Lawyers, teachers, and journalists predominated. Their aim, as two historians wrote, "may justly be described as an attempt to influence the Government within the existing constitution."[11]

There was considerable unrest during the latter part of the nineteenth and the early twentieth century. Unemployed, educated youths provided the backbone for a strong nativist-*cum*-terrorist movement which grew in Bengal and Maharashtra. The new movement was anti-Western in sentiment and demanded greater independence for India, but it had little success in gaining concessions from the British.

The growth of industry and of a class of factory workers, an increase in urbanism, dislocation in the rural economy, and the growth of anti-British sentiment among Muslims who were disturbed by British intrusions into Turkey resulted in a change in the character of the nationalist movement after World War I. Nationalists in general became aware of the failure of both terrorism and constitutionalism based on the demands

[11] W. H. Moreland and Atul Chandra Chatterjee, *A Short History of India*, London, 1953, p. 427.

of the few, and saw in their societies the basis for a mass movement. While it is a common occurrence, there is nothing inevitable about the conversion of a colonial interest group into a mass movement. As we shall see, among Muslims this did not occur until the late 1930's if ever, and in Ceylon it really never occurred during the period of colonial rule.

The nationalist movement which emerged in India under Gandhi's leadership immediately after World War I was comprehensive in three significant ways. First, the participants in the movement conceived of it as representing the nation as a whole rather than any particular interest or aggregation of interests; second, it grew as a mass organization with roots reaching into the districts, provinces, towns, and villages; third, mass membership and mass support were organized for demonstrations and civil-disobedience movements. The shift from a small interest group to a comprehensive nationalist movement had profound effects on the kind of political party system which emerged in India after independence. For one, it meant that India had a political group with an organization which covered most of the country, from rural to urban areas, from Assam in the northeast to Kerala in the southwest. A second consequence was a growth in mass expectations that an independent India would satisfy the dissatisfactions of a variety of groups. In its effort to build a mass movement, the nationalist leadership organized peasant associations, trade unions, student organizations, "constructive" work groups, and the like. Some of the discontent of these groups was originally directed at Indian employers and landlords, but in the earlier days of the struggle for independence nationalist leaders redirected discontent against British rule. In this way, diverse interests were reconciled within a common national movement.

The mass character and the heterogeneous nature of the national movement also facilitated the growth of a sense of nationality. New symbols, new words, new leaders entered the struggle. Out of diverse societies, a nation was being born. New ideologies emerged. Socialist and Marxist ideas spread among intellectuals in the 1930's. Ideas emerging from the Soviet Union, and even more so from the London School of Economics, had an impact on the younger generation. A concern for how this new mass power of the nationalist movement could be utilized and a sense of frustration over the limited gains of Gandhi's non-violent, civil-disobedience campaigns were reflected in the debates within the nationalist movement. Differences over how to win independence and what to do with it once it was achieved had to be reconciled if the movement was to remain truly comprehensive and national. A leadership and an organizational machinery thus developed which were concerned with reconciling diverse interests. For all the vagueness of the resolutions of the national conventions of the Indian National Congress, the organization did develop a program which represented the aggregated interests within the movement.

The aggregative character of the Congress has been a source of great strength. The Congress Party was able to form a government in 1947, write a constitution for the country, manage and survive two general elections based on universal adult suffrage, create two five-year plans, weather a number of major crises—including the assassination of Gandhi, the influx of millions of refugees from Pakistan, a Communist insurrection in South India, and near-war with Pakistan over Kashmir—and somehow manage to maintain a measure of order and stability which, in a region of great uncertainty, is a model for the rest of Asia.

To one degree or another, each of the three countries of South Asia developed a competitive party system after independence. In each country, a process of disintegration occurred within each of the comprehensive nationalist movements. In Ceylon and Pakistan new political parties became so successful that the comprehensive nationalist parties were displaced from power, but in India Congress has effectively retained control of the central government and of virtually all of the states.

But the Congress Party too experienced a period of disintegration. Shortly before independence the Communists were expelled for their failure to support the national movement during the war. The Socialists walked out of Congress in 1948, and a group of Gandhians, especially in the states of Madras, West Bengal, and Uttar Pradesh, also defected. As a result of these and other break-offs, fundamental changes occurred in the character of the Congress Party. While before independence it was made up of various groups with vastly different conceptions of the kind of society India was to achieve, by 1952 Congress was a party which aggregated many diverse elements united in support of a broad common program—a program centering around the desirability of a secular, democratic state dedicated to economic development and national unity. There were still many varied groups inside Congress— business, unions, Gandhian constructive workers, and diverse local interests concerned with improving the position of their religious group, caste, or locality—but these groups disagreed with one another on specific issues of public policy rather than on gross ideological questions.

As a result of the 1952 general elections, it appeared as if India had a party system in which many parties operated freely within a democratic framework, but that in fact a single party overwhelmingly dominated the entire country. This picture was not a completely accurate one. While Congress did win some 75 per cent of the seats for parliament, it won only 45 per cent of the popular vote. Some seventy or more opposition parties and many independent candidates had so split the opposition vote that Congress won a far greater proportion of seats than of votes. In the second place, in many of the individual states Congress was in a highly competitive situation. In Madras, Travancore-Cochin, and PEPSU, Congress formed very precarious governments. Five years later, in India's second general elections, Congress lost control of Travancore-Cochin (now renamed Kerala) to the Communist Party, and in other states, such as Orissa, Rajasthan, and West Bengal, genuinely competitive party situations developed.

The major parties on the national level—four, including Congress, are recognized by the election commission—are all ideologically oriented. After Congress, the Praja Socialist Party and the Communists follow in order of votes. The Hindu-communal Jan Sangh runs a poor fourth. Several other parties cover large portions of the country. The Hindu Mahasabha and Ram Rajya Parishad, both Hindu communal parties, have strength in some of the former princely states in central India, where the nationalist movement had little opportunity to develop. Several of the ideologically left parties also cut across state boundaries, including the Marxist-left, non-Communist Revolutionary Socialist Party, which is strong in both West Bengal and Kerala.

There are essentially four ideological movements in India which more or less coincide with national parties. One movement is nationalist and socialist, one might even say statist. It is committed to a national state which uses its power to effect changes in the economy and social structure. The Congress, the Socialists to a lesser extent, and some of the smaller regional parties fall into this category. A second movement, consisting of the Communists and Marxist-left parties, can be described as totalitarian. A third movement is Hindu communalist; in a general and vague way it wants to strengthen the Hindu tradition and, more particularly, prevent the state from making intrusions into the social system. Finally, there is a peculiarly Indian, Gandhian movement which is antistate and decentralist. This movement has influence within both Congress and the Praja Socialist Party, but its major organizational expression centers about what is known as the *Bhoodan* movement, a non-party organization that solicits voluntary contributions of land and money which are then redistributed to poor peasants. It advocates social and economic change through non-governmental channels, and emphasizes the importance of decentralized village life.

State parties are often even more particularistic than the ideologically oriented "national" parties and movements. And, as we shall see, the ideologically oriented as well as the more particularistic parties are frequently built upon traditional loyalties. The state of Bihar provides useful illustrations of the way in which particular interests and traditional loyalties affect the organization of local and "national" parties.

The Janata (People's) Party, which received the bulk of its support from the rural gentry, was created by Bihar landlords. In one district another political party was formed and built on the basis of its claim that that particular district, having a Bengali—rather than Bihari—speaking population, should be merged with the neighboring state of West Bengal. This group was so effective that it won the bulk of the seats in the district, and in 1955 the district was in fact merged with West Bengal. In still another area of the state, in what is known as the Chotanagpur division of Bihar, where six million tribesmen live, a young tribesman who was educated in England has created the Jharkhand Party. This party's platform is based upon the demand that the tribal areas of Bihar secede to form a "Jharkhand," or tribal state, within the Indian Union.

Caste disputes too divide Bihar. The Congress Party itself has been badly split between the Kayasthas, a traditional scribe caste, and the Rajputs, or warrior caste. This and other caste divisions (such as the Bhumihar Brahmans and the Maithal Brahmans) have kept the Bihar Congress in a continuous state of factional feuding. Allegiances to landlords, language, tribe, and caste thus enter into and help to proliferate the parties of Bihar.

The situation in other areas is comparable. In other states, princes and landlords have won considerable electoral support in spite of the destruction of princely power and the weakening of landlordism by recent legislation. In Rajasthan, for example, where the bulk of the land has been controlled by some 9,000 *jagirdars*, or landlords, the *jagirdar* association nominated candidates within the various existing parties and nearly displaced Congress as the major party in the state. Villagers have traditionally looked to the *jagirdars* for relief from rent in lean years, aid in financing the wedding of daughters, and protection from bandits; in return, the tenant paid his rent and now he often provides the *jagirdar* with votes. In Orissa, several of the princes of the many princely states which now make up the state have run for office, some on Congress tickets, but many on opposition or independent tickets. Invariably they have won, another testimony to the enormous hold of traditional loyalties.

Caste and other traditional loyalties may be overlaid by ideological differences. The leaders and even the party rank and file may put ideological interpretations on conflicts which for the voter have only a traditional meaning. In the state of Andhra, for example, the Communist-Congress conflict is also a conflict between the Kamma and Reddi castes. Likewise, in Kerala, the Christian community tends to vote Congress, while the high-caste Nayars vote Socialist and the low-caste Izhavas Communist. As Selig Harrison noted,[12] votes for Communist candidates may be as much an expression of caste loyalties as of economic discontent. In Andhra, for example, the Communist-dominated Kamma caste represents a more prosperous peasantry than many peasant groups which do not vote Communist. In Maharashtra (the Marathi-speaking portion of Bombay State), where conflicts between Brahmans and non-Brahmans have been a central feature of the social and political life for several decades, the major opposition party, the Peasants' and Workers' Party, is clearly an anti-Brahman movement. The leadership of the Peasants' and Workers' Party considers itself Marxist and at one time passed a resolution declaring the party to be a "Cominformist" party. The party's struggle against Brahmans, it declared, is a struggle against the bourgeoisie; only the non-Brahmans represent the proletariat. Similar ideological embellishments of community rivalries can be found among other political groups.

Particularistic movements have grown considerably in India since independence. Many of these differences were of course dwarfed by the national movement for independence. Frequently middle-class politicians who failed to win office through Congress have exploited particularistic-traditional loyalties to propel themselves into positions of prominence. Candidates for office find it politically profitable to stress caste or regional and linguistic loyalties. Many a politician who speaks of national development and planning in Delhi speaks primarily of linguistic or even caste matters when back in his constituency. The unequal economic development of castes combined with the growing impact of "modern" ideas

---

[12] Selig S. Harrison, "Caste and the Andhra Communists," *American Political Science Review*, Vol. L, No. 2, June 1956.

have made many groups conscious of their low status and their economic backwardness.

It should also be recalled that India has a hierarchical system in which, even today, mobility has been more in terms of groups than individuals. Demands for aid from government, special educational facilities, and more appointments to government jobs are now being made by caste associations. Politicians from the major national parties have frequently taken up the causes of these groups, if only to prevent their opponents from doing so. Socialist candidates for Parliament and for the legislative assemblies, for example, have often supported the cause of tribesmen and scheduled castes (untouchables) and have even forged electoral alliances with parties from those groups. Congress has frequently nominated landlords and former maharajas to take advantage of their popularity. The Communists too have formed alliances with caste and tribal groups, and have actively supported demands of linguistic groups for the organization of states along linguistic lines.

The extent to which India's parties are broadly based or narrowly based varies considerably from party to party. The Indian National Congress, even since independence, has had a membership in the millions. Of these, tens of thousands are active party workers either in their villages, towns, and districts or in the various front organizations of Congress, such as trade unions, peasant associations, refugee groups, and constructive work organizations. Communist membership is about 250,000 and even at its lowest point exceeded 50,000. The Praja Socialist Party has had as many as 200,000 members. The Rashtriya Swayamsevak Sangh (RSS), a youth organization dedicated to "revitalizing" Hinduism which was active during the partition riots and which later played a part in the creation of Jan Sangh, the largest of the Hindu communal parties, had a membership as high as 600,000 in 1951.

Participation in India's two national general elections has been substantial. About one-half the electorate voted. In the first election alone, there were over 15,000 candidates for only 3,229 state assembly seats, and another 1,800 candidates for 479 seats in parliament.

Some of the smaller state parties constitute no more than personal followings with a small membership and little organization. That such parties exist in a newly independent country is not surprising. Perhaps what is surprising is the durable character of so many of these small parties, the strength of their organizations, even though limited in scope or locality, and the extent to which such parties often do have substantial and active memberships. Group loyalties are strong in India, whether to family, caste, locality, or party. Mergers of parties have occurred and a certain amount of political opportunism exists, but the fact is that the major parties in the center or the states and the small particularistic parties have been remarkably durable.

There is no doubt that many of the membership claims of political parties, trade unions, peasant organizations, and other political groups are exaggerated. There is no doubt either that political participation is greater in the towns and cities than in the rural countryside, among the educated middle classes than among the peasantry, among higher castes than lower castes, and greater in the more Westernized former British areas than in some of the less Westernized princely states of central India. But it is also true that India has become tremendously politicized. Politics has become the avenue for personal advancement in a society in which commercial activities offer little status and administrative posts are relatively few in number. The "dedicated" political worker in no matter what party is often more respected than the businessman or low-ranking administrator. One leftist member of parliament recounted the support he received from a wealthy Marwari businessman who told him that, while he disagreed violently with the MP's Marxist orientation, he had great respect for the man's dedication to his country. The fact that this MP had spent many years in jail for causes he believed in and the fact that he remained a bachelor (in the tradition of the *sanyasin*, or Hindu holy man) marked his dedication. While no doubt an element of insurance enters into the contribution by a businessman to a leftist politician, there is also this other, almost religious, element in the giving of aid to those who are dedicated, whether to the cause of personal salvation or to the nation's salvation.

India's party system is thus characterized by relatively heavy participation in politics by relatively durable political organizations and by parties which are oriented around ideologies and particularistic loyalties. There has thus far been a strong central ruling party, but competitive parties exist which have actually overthrown the ruling party in some states.

(2) *Pakistan*. In contrast to India's Congress Party, Pakistan's Muslim League proved itself unable to maintain effective control of the center and the states, or to maintain stable governments even when it had overwhelming control of the legislative seats. Controversies within the cabinet, between the cabinet and party leaders, and between the prime minister and the governor-general, rather than the failure of the League to win the legislative assembly's support, resulted in the collapse of Pakistan's government. Pakistan has thus far not held any national gen-

eral elections. Not until 1956, after the first Constituent Assembly was dissolved by the governor-general and a new assembly appointed, was the country given a constitution. With the failure of the League to provide orderly and stable government, Pakistan's administrative services and her army have played important political roles. In October 1958 the army took over the country and General Mirza, as president, backed by his newly appointed prime minister, General Ayub Khan, abolished the republic and the constitution, outlawed political parties, established martial law, and arrested several prominent opposition leaders.

The difficulties which the League faced with the creation of Pakistan —an inadequate administrative system, an enormous refugee problem, and a lack of finances, adequate means of communication and roads, or even buildings in which a government could meet—were more colossal than those faced by India. But the inadequacies of the League to meet the tasks can also be traced to the circumstances under which it developed in prepartition India.

The Muslim League entered the political arena somewhat later than the Indian National Congress, but like the Congress it entered as an interest group with limited demands rather than as a comprehensive nationalist movement. The Muslim League was created in 1906 after the Aga Khan led a deputation of upper-class Muslims to the Viceroy, Lord Minto, requesting special favors for Muslims in India. The signing of the petition of the deputation by "nobles, ministers of various [princely] states, great landowners, lawyers, merchants" indicated the narrow base of the movement. Unlike Congress, however, the League did not become a mass movement in the 1920's. Some Muslims became members of Congress, while others took part in the All-India Khilafat Conference, which joined with Congress to agitate against British policy in Turkey. Among the Pathans in the Northwest Frontier Province was the Khuda'i Khidmatgar, a religious-*cum*-social service movement of Pathan nationalists which worked with Gandhi, supported the Congress movement, and later opposed the League's move for a Pakistan state. In Kashmir there was, and still is, the Jammu and Kashmir Muslim Conference (now called the National Conference), which was less a Muslim or even an Indian nationalist movement than a Kashmiri nationalist movement. However, it was pro-Congress, anti-Pakistani, and anti-League, and was generally known to be "radical" in its economic program.

Elsewhere there were other non-League, often anti-League, Muslim groups: the Krishak Praja Party of Bengal under Fazl al Huq, who was to play such an important role in East Pakistan in 1954; the Unionist Party in the Punjab, made up mostly of landed interests who joined the League after 1937; the pro-Congress Sind Nationalist Muslim Party; the anti-League, anti-British Ahrar Party in the Punjab. By 1940, however, most of these groups were defunct. An attempt to bring nationalist Muslims together against the League and for a Hindu-Muslim settlement in 1940 (in the Azad Muslim Conference in Delhi) was unsuccessful.

Until the mid-1930's the League remained a small interest group, largely supported by landlords, high officials, and Muslim princes. With the announcement by the British that elections would be held in 1936-1937, Mohammed Ali Jinnah, the leader of the League, endeavored to undertake a program of mass contact, but failed to organize quickly enough to win Muslim votes. In the 1937 elections the League won only 4.5 per cent of the Muslim vote, but ten years later it won three-fourths of that vote.

It was in the three years between 1937 and 1940 that the League grew from a limited interest group to a vast mass movement which was to win its demand for a Pakistan state of eighty million people. How the League grew during those few years has never been carefully studied, but it was obviously a crucial period. After the 1937 elections, a majority of the Muslim members of the various provincial assemblies were persuaded to join the League. In Assam, Bengal, and the Punjab it attracted enough Muslim assembly members to form governments. Until the late 1930's, the League's strength was among upper-class groups in Uttar Pradesh and Bombay, and in Muslim minority areas in which many Muslims held upper-class positions. In the late 1930's, the leadership of the League reached out into the Muslim majority areas of the country and built constituencies which ultimately enabled the movement to win power. Some Muslim nationalist groups were destroyed; others, like the group led by Fazl al Huq, were absorbed.

The idea of a Muslim state, a Pakistan, was posed by Muhammad Iqbal in 1930 and grew among Muslim students studying at Cambridge. The proposal became popular after 1937 and, at its annual convention in 1940, the League adopted it officially. But even after 1940 the League's program remained vague. Until 1940 the Pakistan proposal itself had remained vague. Jinnah made statements against Communism and Socialism, but never specified the kind of society or government he envisioned for Pakistan. Even the boundaries of the proposed state were undefined. "I say to the impatient youth," declared one League leader, "be not concerned with the details of the scheme. . . . Who knows what shape Pakistan will finally take and in what form it will emerge from the turmoil of the years?"

By 1942 the League was a powerful mass organization. But the turning point in its development was the mid-1930's, when the League, like the Congress, considered itself a "national" community representing the interests of all Muslims. In fact, the League made its recognition as the paramount and sole representative of Muslims a major political demand and refused to recognize the right of Congress to nominate Muslims to assemblies. Congress, on the one hand, considered itself the sole representative of all Indians, irrespective of community, and the League, on the other, considered itself the sole representative of Muslims.

Although the League became "comprehensive" enough to have a mass following, it never built an effective organization. It did virtually no work among trade unions or peasant associations, nor did it encourage constructive work organizations as did Congress. It was "mass" in following, but not in organization.

Unlike Congress, the League failed to develop enduring organizational loyalties. The Congress leaders had been with Congress since the 1920's or early 1930's. The League's leadership emerged in the mid-1930's, and many, like Fazl al Huq, did not join until the late 1930's or early 1940's. Mohammed Ali Jinnah demanded and commanded great personal loyalty, but this loyalty did not extend to the League. This lack of organizational loyalty no doubt facilitated the rapid break-up of the League after independence.

The Indian National Congress was more successful in aggregating diverse interests than was the League. Congress accepted any groups which favored independence, no matter what methods they wanted to use or what kind of society they envisioned after independence; it even permitted them to maintain their identity. Within the Congress were such organized groups as the Communists, Socialists, Marxist-left parties and, in the early years, Hindu communal groups as well. The League tolerated only those groups or individuals who advocated the establishment of Pakistan. Nationalist Muslims who were anti-British and who advocated independence, but not a Pakistani state, were excluded from the League. Many of these groups were *absorbed*, not aggregated, by the League in the 1940's. They were absorbed at the cost of their identity. In short, the League effectively destroyed diverse interests, while Congress permitted them to continue and aggregated them.

This integrative capacity of Congress, first as a national movement, and since independence as a political party, is analogous to the integrative capacity of Hinduism and its notion of many paths to truth; the League's incapacity to integrate diversity and its history of destroying competition are analogous to the schismatic tradition of Islam, which acknowledges only one path to truth, the truth as given by Allah, and the need for submission. But perhaps it would be going too far to imply that this is more than an analogy. Undoubtedly, the position of the League, a minority group uncertain as to whether it would obtain its demands for a separate state from the British, had a profound effect upon its attitude toward diversity.

The relatively conservative character of the League's leadership, combined with the uncertainty as to the outcome of its struggle for a state of its own, inhibited the League from forming any conception of the kind of society for which it was fighting. There might not be a Pakistan, so why plan for it? In contrast, the Congress did develop a program, even if a vague one. As a result of the 1937 elections, it formed governments in six provinces and was forced to pass specific pieces of legislation. The governments were conservative, but leftist forces could fight on relatively specific issues within Congress. Resolutions were put forward and by 1947, when India became independent, one knew more or less that Congress constituted a moderate-reformist, planning-oriented, democratic party. The League in 1947 was faced with the problem of having to construct a program. Personal and factional conflicts and differences in the Constituent Assembly over the role of Islam in the new state and in the relationship between the various provinces, especially East and West Pakistan, were so great that from the very beginning the League floundered. Had Mohammed Ali Jinnah and Liaquat Ali Khan, two of the founders of Pakistan, not died so soon after independence, it is conceivable that out of the League might have come a clear program and a more cohesive organization.

As in India, the comprehensive nationalist movement in Pakistan began to disintegrate after independence. But with Pakistan's Muslim League disintegration went much further. Many more important figures defected from the League than from India's Congress Party, and the League itself is no longer the dominating party in Pakistan's political life. Splits within the League became so severe that, although it retained control of the provincial assemblies, between 1947 and 1954 each of the provinces had anywhere from four (as in the Sind) to seven (as in the

Northwest Frontier Province and in the Punjab) different chief ministers.

So long as no national elections were held, the Muslim League retained control of the Constituent Assembly in Karachi. The Assembly unsuccessfully attempted to draft a constitution for the new state, but disputes over the role of Islam in the constitution, relations between the two halves of the country, and a large number of personal conflicts hampered its efforts. Meanwhile, parties were being organized outside the Assembly. H. S. Suhrawardy of Bengal formed the Awami (People's) League, which took an active part in opposing the Muslim League in the Punjab provincial election in 1951. In 1953, the Krishak Sramik Party (Peasants' and Workers' Party) was formed by A. K. Fazl al Huq in East Bengal. Although it stressed regional autonomy and had a broad "socialist" approach, the party centered chiefly about the figure of its founder, an octogenarian with an incredibly large following among East Bengalis.

East Bengal (East Pakistan) was the first province in which the League was defeated—at the hands of a coalition called the United Front, led by the Awami League of H. S. Suhrawardy (later Pakistan's prime minister) and the Krishak Srimak Party of A. K. Fazl al Huq. The United Front campaigned in East Pakistan's 1954 provincial elections on a platform of, among other things, greater autonomy for East Bengal vis-à-vis the central government, and the establishment of Bengali on a par with Urdu as a national language of Pakistan. The object of the United Front clearly was to destroy the Muslim League and to strengthen the position of East Pakistan in relation to West Pakistan and the central government. In its effort to win the support of diverse groups within East Pakistan, the Front went so far as to promise that it would not pass laws repugnant to the Quran or Sunnah, and that it would abolish the landlord system without compensation. Thus, the United Front in 1954, by assuming the proportions of a "comprehensive" movement of a mass character, assured its victory against the League.

Still other parties entered the political scene. It would be more accurate to say that such parties were "formed" rather than "emerged," since it was largely a matter of existing personnel regrouping themselves. As Keith Callard has written: "The system of political parties in Pakistan bears little resemblance to that of most other democratic countries. Politics has begun at the top. Pakistan has neither a two-party system, in which the political struggle is waged between fairly stable groups, one of which is in office and the other in opposition, nor a multi-party system, in which clear differences of programmes or ideology separate a variety of opponents. In Pakistan politics is made up of a large number of leading persons who, with their political dependents, form loose agreements to achieve power and to maintain it. Consequently rigid adherence to a policy or a measure is likely to make a politician less available for office. Those who lack fixed ideas but who control legislators, money or influence have tended to prosper in political life."[13]

In contrast to India, loyalties to political groups have been poorly developed in Pakistan. The most central issues in Pakistan and, for that matter, among Muslim politicians before 1947 have not been questions of public policy but questions of loyalty. Before 1947, loyalty to Jinnah, to the Muslim League, and to the concept of Pakistan were the issues. After 1947, disputes arose over loyalties to parties, to the president, to the state of Pakistan itself. Men accused one another of subverting the state, of being secretly in favor of rejoining Pakistan to India, or of being loyal to their own narrow selfish interests. To separate facts from fancy in this maze of political accusations is virtually impossible, but what is clear is that few men or groups trusted one another. To what extent this absence of trust can be related to the peculiar developments of the Muslim League and of the Pakistan movement, to the pattern of social relations of Muslims, or to the Muslim ethos is difficult to say without far more data than are available. Whatever the explanation, Pakistan is a clear example of what happens in a political order from which mutual trust is absent. As we have seen, control of government shifted frequently from one group to another. Members of the Assembly shifted party affiliations from day to day. In one provincial assembly, the speaker was beaten and the deputy speaker killed. There were reports that the national flag was desecrated. Municipal elections were fixed through bogus votes. Corruption and black marketeering were widespread. Distrust not only of politicians but of bureaucrats grew. Only the army was absolved from this mistrust. It stood apart from day-to-day political controversies. It stressed loyalty to the state of Pakistan. In a system in which politicians were distrusted, the very "non-political" character of the army made it a powerful political force.

While party loyalties and ideologies have played a minimal role in the major Pakistan parties, it would be incorrect to say that they play no role at all. Pakistan has a number of well-knit Islamic parties based upon a religious ideology. Of these, the Jamaat-i-Islami, led by the

---

[13] Keith Callard, *Pakistan: A Political Study*, New York, N.Y., 1957, p. 67.

fiery Maulana Maudoodi, is the most important. Supported by the *ulama*, the Jamaat takes the position that the function of an Islamic legislature is one of law-finding rather than law-making—that is, its task is to apply the laws of the Koran and Sunnah to the Islamic state of Pakistan. Members of the Assembly need not be skilled in representing and reconciling group interests; rather, they must be specialists in Islamic law. The *ulama* are not concerned merely with the nature and functions of the state, but with its control as well. For the orthodox argue that power must rest in the hands not of "secularists" but of those versed in Islamic law. While the Constituent Assembly made some concessions to this group—mostly on the verbal level, by calling the constitution "Islamic" —by the very nature of their demands, it is not really possible for the orthodox elements to be satisfied with anything less than total victory.

The position that the orthodox elements take at first seems unique. But, in a somewhat different form, it is found among other Pakistan groups as well. As some Pakistanis put it: "In Islam, party politics are an impossibility, there being only one party, the body of Muslims, to which each and every adult Muslim belongs as a matter of right, whose ideology is the Divine Law or Nature, and whose existence is governed and directed by the sober, ineluctable truth of Reality."[14] Keith Callard argues that traces of this conception can be found in the belief in the unity of all Muslims that is shared by many political groups in Pakistan, including the Muslim League.

In India, a similar position—that is, a unitary as opposed to a pluralistic conception—grew out of the nationalist notion that the nation first and foremost must be united in its struggle against the colonial oppressor. Today, it is often felt that unity is necessary for the development of the entire society. Congress, and Nehru, have frequently looked upon opposition groups as merely divisive and destructive of the program of national development through state planning. Congress leaders often find it easier to understand the Communists, who favor an entirely different approach, than to understand the Socialists, whose position they feel is sufficiently close to their own for them to join together. Committed as it is to constitutional and democratic procedures, Congress has made no effort to liquidate any political groups forcibly. It has, however, tried to absorb as many political groups as possible, to gain control of unions, peasant organizations, student groups, and the like, not only to strengthen the Congress Party, but, even more important, to win the

[14] *Ibid.*, p. 223.

participation and cooperation of all groups in the attempt to develop and modernize the country. In this scheme of things, there is little room for the trade union which puts forth high wage demands, or a peasantry which is unwilling to pay high irrigation taxes, or Socialists who are sympathetic with the basic objectives of government but are nonetheless critical of the way things are done.

An "organic" view which speaks of the "nation" rather than of the group interests which need to be reconciled, and which views the state and society as one unit, is of course at the base of all totalitarian ideologies. But it is an ideology which may also be held by non-totalitarian groups that state such views more as an ideal than as a principle for which they are prepared to coerce others. Its application by Soekarno in Indonesia has contributed to civil war in that country. But, thus far, in South Asia it is a full-blown ideology only with the Islamic groups. In moments of crisis, disorder, and inability on the part of organized parties to provide stable government, the desperate need for order and unity could result in what General Mirza, the former governor-general of Pakistan, urged upon his country in its moment of crisis—"controlled democracy."[15]

Of the three countries in South Asia, Pakistan is the least organized politically. Its national and provincial parties are more narrowly based than parties in India and Ceylon. While landlords, especially in West Pakistan, are organized, other kinds of interest groups are weaker than in neighboring India—particularly the trade union movement and peasant organizations. This lack of organization has added a note of unpredictability to Pakistan politics. When provincial elections were held in East Bengal in 1954, few were prepared for the colossal defeat which the Muslim League experienced. *Dawn*, a leading pro-League Karachi newspaper, predicted that the League would win from 75 to 80 per cent of the Muslim seats. Since no party had effective rural organization, and communication from rural to urban centers was highly inadequate, little information existed on which predictions could be based. When the returns were in, the League had won only 10 of the 237 Muslim seats, and the victorious United Front had won 223 seats. Not only are the loyalties of leaders to parties weak in Pakistan; it would seem that the voters' loyalties are weak too.

Pakistan differs from the other two countries of South Asia not only

[15] This statement was made some time before General Mirza abolished the republic. It is apparent now that what he had in mind was control by the army.

in terms of the degree to which it is politically organized, but also in the extent to which parliamentary institutions have functioned successfully. While in India and Ceylon the struggle of the nationalist movements centered about demands for greater participation by Indians and Ceylonese in representative institutions—i.e., the struggle for parliamentary government was part of the struggle for independence—the Muslim League was never eager for the creation of stronger parliamentary institutions in undivided India. Unless the special position of the Muslims was secured and, ultimately, unless the British granted the state of Pakistan to the Muslims, the strengthening of parliamentary institutions meant a weakening of the Muslim position vis-à-vis the Hindu. Or, perhaps more accurately, it meant a weakening of the Muslim League vis-à-vis Congress. The Muslim League was thus not as committed as either the Indian National Congress or the Ceylonese nationalist leaders to parliamentary institutions. Nor, for that matter, did the Muslim League have as much experience in running provincial governments as did the Congress Party, which ran seven provincial governments from 1937 to 1939, or the Ceylon National Congress, many of whose members had been in the Assembly for twenty years and whose leader, Ceylon's first prime minister, had been a minister in the government continuously since the 1930's.

The forms and practices of constitutionalism in Pakistan have also been somewhat different from those in Ceylon and India. Pakistan originally created separate electorates in West Pakistan for her non-Muslim minority,[16] while India and Ceylon opposed any distinctions along communal lines. In Pakistan, the president, with the backing of the military, dismissed a constitutionally selected prime minister and the Assembly when he felt that neither was competent to deal with the tasks facing the country. Then, too, Pakistan has not held a national general election since independence. Ceylon and India have thus far been able to maintain parliamentary institutions on a sounder footing; each has had two national elections, and power has rested in the hands of elected personnel committed to working within the constitutional framework.

(3). *Ceylon.* The major characteristic of the two comprehensive nationalist movements in prepartition India—their mass following—was not shared by the national movement in Ceylon. In Ceylon, an English-

[16] In April 1957 the National Assembly reversed its position and amended the Electorate Act so that a single electorate was introduced throughout the country. The Jamaat-i-Islami and other Islamic groups, however, continued to agitate for separate electorates for non-Muslims.

speaking class developed in the 1880's, when commercial banks, business firms, government services, and the professions needed English-speaking Ceylonese. Nationalist sentiment grew during World War I, and in 1919 the Ceylon National Congress was formed. In 1920, the Ceylonese secured a new constitution, providing for an assembly in which non-governmental members would have a majority. In 1932 a new constitution, the result of the work of the famous Donoughmore Commission, was put into effect and this continued in force until 1948, when Ceylon was given her independence. While the Ceylonese were critical of the new constitution, they chose to work within it, and for some fifteen years they had continuous experience in running a government with limited powers. They attempted to modify the Donoughmore constitution by demanding the reduction of the special powers of the governor, an increase in the council's power, especially with regard to finance, and the substitution of a cabinet for the executive committee system. The war, the entrance of Japan as a belligerent, its spectacular successes, and the need for Ceylon's continued support forced the British to make a specific statement as to Ceylon's future constitutional status. In May 1943, they declared that "full and responsible government under the Crown in all matters of internal civil administration" would be given Ceylon after the war. The Ceylonese pressed for full dominion status, and persuaded the British to grant Ceylon full independence in 1947.

Two striking features of Ceylon's nationalist movement were to have profound effects upon the party system which emerged after independence. The first was the peaceful, constitutional character of the nationalist movement; and the second was the absence of any real party system operating under the Donoughmore constitution. "During the same period," wrote one Ceylonese historian, "in India and Burma the constitutional struggle was characterized by civil disobedience, arrests, communal riots, acts of terrorism, sabotage, fifth column activity, and collaboration with the enemy. No such acts marred Ceylon's progress towards Dominion status. The pressure was exerted chiefly by the passing of reform resolutions in the Council, discussions between Governors and leaders of majority and minority communities, the preparation and publication of memoranda and reform despatches by Governors and ministers, agitation for the purpose of sending deputations to the Secretary of State to place Ceylon's case directly before the Imperial Government, and the introduction and discussion of bills embodying the proposed constitutional reforms."[17] As the British governor of Ceylon said in 1947, "It is a matter for profound satisfaction that Ceylon has reached its goal of freedom without strife or bloodshed along the path of peaceful negotiation."[18]

Not only did no real mass movement develop in Ceylon, but neither did any genuine political parties. Candidates for the State Council stood as independents; ministers too stood without party, so that there was no cohesion in the cabinet or unity of policy during British rule. The Donoughmore constitution provided for a political framework which discouraged the organization of parties. The State Council, or Assembly, was elected by universal suffrage. The State Council divided itself into seven executive committees, each with an elected minister who was a member of the Board of Ministers, or cabinet. These executive committees combined legislative and executive functions, which prevented cabinet responsibility. The political position of each Council member and each minister depended upon his success in carrying through individual schemes in the executive committees of the State Council. Sharing the pork-barrel was the chief means of persuasion. Each man was for himself, and each man struggled to obtain rewards for his own constituency. Rivalry among ministers, lack of unity in the Board of Ministers, and an absence of governmental policy characterized the system. It was not until 1947, after independence was gained and a cabinet system created, that groups banded together to form parties. Prior to 1947 some groups did exist—the Ceylon National Congress and the All-Ceylon Tamil Congress—but they were important more because of the individuals who led them than because of their organization.

The absence of a mass movement and well-organized parties in Ceylon may also be related to the relative success of the Ceylonese national leaders in achieving their goals. Ceylon in the early 1930's was given perhaps the most progressive constitution of any colony—it provided for universal suffrage, considerable power for the legislature, and the abolition of communal electorates. Equally if not more important was the effort made by the British from the early 1930's onward to "Ceylonese" the civil service; all new appointees to the service were Ceylonese unless no competent person could be found. As a consequence, Ceylon did not suffer to the same extent as India from educated unemployment.

[17] S. Namasivayam, *The Legislatures of Ceylon*, London, Faber and Faber, 1951, pp. 127-128.
[18] *Ibid.*, p. 128.

The fact, too, that Ceylon was a small country and that the British governor and his staff were in closer contact with developments there than were the British in India may have contributed to the Ceylonese faith in the essential honesty and good intentions of the British. Unlike the Ceylonese, the Indians, especially during the Second World War, were never sure that the British would in fact give them independence.

The differences in the character of the respective leaderships and of the rank-and-file followers in the two countries may also have been a contributing factor. In Ceylon, the leadership was English-speaking, often English-educated, similar to the liberal nationalist leadership in India in the late nineteenth century. The second-ranking, vernacular-speaking politician who played such an important part in the nationalist movement in India, especially in the "Gandhian belt" from Bihar through Uttar Pradesh and Gujarat, did not emerge in Ceylon until the 1950's. In fact, not until the 1956 elections was the monopoly of the English-speaking, higher-income classes broken in Ceylon.

The conservative, moderate constitutional-minded liberals who led Ceylon to independence created Ceylon's first independent government. D. S. Senanayake, the first prime minister, was the founder of the United National Party, which won both the 1947 and the 1952 elections. In opposition were three Marxist parties (two Trotskyite and one Communist), the social democratic Sri Lanka Freedom Party, and the Tamil Federal Party.

The Sri Lanka Freedom Party, led by S.W.R.D. Bandaranaike, successfully appealed to a developing Sinhalese-speaking, rural-based leadership. Some members of the Buddhist Sangha, or priesthood, teachers in Sinhalese schools, *ayurvedic* doctors, minor officials, shopkeepers, and in general members of the lower middle classes rallied behind the Sri Lanka Freedom Party. The emergence of the Sinhalese-speaking voter also marked the political rise of the low-country Karava and Salagama castes. These two castes had energetically entered new enterprises, professions, and public services in the latter part of the nineteenth century. Their growing political importance was halted in the 1930's with the introduction of universal suffrage which placed the majority Goyigamas in a politically advantageous position. Many Karavas and Salagamas felt that the United National Party was dominated by the Goyigama caste and that they were losing rather than retaining their influence. These two groups thus united behind leftist candidates to oppose the United National Party. Bandaranaike's party had joined with the VLSSP, one of Ceylon's two Trotskyite parties, to create the Mahajana

Eksath Peramuna, or MEP, which defeated the UNP in the 1956 elections. The Sri Lanka Freedom Party proved to be the No. 1 party (having won 40 out of 95 seats).[19]

The victory of the MEP also indicated the growing power of the Buddhist clergy, or *bhikkus*, in Ceylon. The political role of the *bhikkus* is also associated with a strong Buddhist revival in Ceylon. The Buddhist revival was particularly important for the attack it made against Western and especially Christian influence in urban areas. It was the *bhikkus* who led the attack against the leaders of the UNP and charged them with being Western in thought and behavior, meat eaters, drinkers, and under Catholic influence.

The Buddhist priesthood, unlike the Catholic Church, is loosely organized and there is no evidence that the activities of the *bhikkus* represent a systematic organizational move on the part of the "church."[20] For one thing, the Buddhist priesthood has no such hierarchy as the Roman Catholic Church; for another, many of the elder priests view political activity as being out of harmony with their role as priest.

The victory of the MEP over the UNP in 1956 meant an intensification of the revival of the traditional culture. Trousers and coat have been discarded by ministers and MP's in favor of traditional dress; *kiri bath* (rice cooked in coconut milk) has replaced the cocktail at official receptions; and there have been proposals to ban racing, gam-

---

[19] Election results for parliament for the 1952 and 1956 elections in Ceylon were as follows:

1952		1956	
Government coalition		*Government coalition*	
United National Party	54	Mahajana Eksath Peramuna (MEP)	
Labour Party	1	Sri Lanka Freedom Party	40
Tamil Congress	4	Viplavakari Lanka Sama Samaja	
Independents	15	Party (Trotskyite)	5
	—	Independents	6
	74		—
			51
Opposition		*Opposition*	
Sri Lanka Freedom Party	9	"Nava" Lanka Sama Samaja Party	
Republican	1	(Trotskyite)	14
Tamil Federal Party	2	Tamil Federal Party	10
Independent	1	United National Party	8
Communists-Trotskyites	13	Communist Party	3
	—	Independents and other	9
	26		—
			44

[20] There are no research studies on the role of the Buddhist priesthood in the politics of Ceylon. A forthcoming study of Ceylon politics by Howard Wriggins will help fill this important gap: *Ceylon, New Nation in Asia: Problems of Independence*, Princeton, N.J., May or June, 1960.

bling, and alcohol. But, as one writer put it, the process of throwing out things Western and replacing them with things Ceylonese has been highly selective: "Western hairstyles may be taboo for ladies, but no one has suggested that men give up their Western-type haircuts and grow their hair into the *konde* (bun once universal but now seen only in old men, or the younger men from remote areas). Likewise no one has suggested that Ceylon should give up railways or buses or the electric light which now beautifies so many Buddhist temples. No one in the traditionalist group has suggested an end to parliamentary institutions or to the rule of law; and the MEP has embraced socialism, a Western concept indeed."[21]

The orderly transfer of power from the UNP to the MEP in 1956 also indicated that the new constitutional framework was working. In spite of some initial fear that the leftist-oriented MEP would drastically change government policy, considerable continuity has been maintained. The British have been asked to withdraw from their naval base at Trincomalee, but Ceylon remains in the Commonwealth. Tea and rubber plantations have thus far not been nationalized, and the private sector continues to exist. Marxists have had a strong hand in the present government and the threat does exist of further encroachments into state power by Trotskyites and Communists.

But since the 1956 elections the most dramatic issue has been raised by the Ceylon Tamil community, which has felt that neither the present government nor the United National Party has taken up its cause. After independence the ruling United National Party decided that English should be replaced as the official language by both Sinhalese and Tamil. The Sri Lanka Freedom Party, which adopted a "Sinhalese Only" slogan in 1955, soon won the support of the self-conscious, Sinhalese-speaking, Buddhist, lower-middle-class voters, who resented the domination both of the English-speaking upper classes and of the Ceylon Tamils, who held a disproportionate number of public posts. The demands of the Sinhalese became so great that even the United National Party reversed its position and, in the 1956 elections, both major parties took positions unacceptable to the Tamil community, which demanded the maintenance of the system of language parity. In 1956 the new government passed a bill which made Sinhalese the sole official language. Efforts were made by the government to provide some assurances to the minority Tamils—the right to have an educa-

[21] "B.M.," "Social and Political Trends in Ceylon," *The World Today,* Vol. XII, No. 7, July 1956, p. 287.

tion in Tamil, to compete in government examinations in Tamil, and for Tamils to communicate to government in their own language in areas in which they predominate—but ardent Sinhalese forced the government to withdraw these modifications from the legislation and then proceeded to attack the Tamils physically. In mid-1958, hundreds were killed and thousands were made homeless as a result of riots.

The government has become so committed to its Sinhalese electorate that it has not been able to accommodate the Tamils, many of whom now demand not only that Tamil be on a par with Sinhalese as a national language, but that they be given a state of their own within a federal union of Ceylon. A few Tamil extremists have even threatened to separate Tamil areas from Ceylon and join them with the Tamil areas of South India. For the government there is a genuine dilemma. It relies upon the Sinhalese vote for its power, yet the Sinhalese have become so violent that it has not been politically possible for the government to make concessions to the Tamil community. If the government makes concessions to the Tamils, it is in danger of losing Sinhalese votes,[22] but if it fails to make concessions, Tamils resort to civil disobedience and the task of creating a unified national state in a pluralistic society is made more difficult.

This specific controversy in Ceylon calls attention to a more general problem in South Asia: the conflict between recently organized local, particularistic interests, and the more national interests of Westernized leaderships. Populations which are not well organized politically and whose loyalties are often more local than national have been given the power of the ballot. Compared with most Western countries, the countries of South Asia have adopted universal suffrage relatively early in their economic development. In England, for example, an industrial revolution during the eighteenth and nineteenth centuries eroded traditional loyalties and a political consciousness gradually developed among the commercial class, the industrial class, a rising middle class, and finally the working class. As each group became more politically articulate, the electorate was gradually expanded. Meanwhile, existing parties had an opportunity to absorb the new interests, and these new interests had an opportunity to learn to work within the existing framework.

[22] An attempt by the new government to make Tamil the official language of a "national minority" resulted in riots by Sinhalese; when the government reverted to a "Sinhalese Only" position, Tamils in the Jaffna area tore Sinhalese licenses off public buses. In retaliation, Sinhalese in Colombo destroyed Tamil-owned shops. For an analysis of the recent Sinhalese-Tamil disturbances, see Howard Wriggins, "Ceylon's Time of Troubles, 1956-1958," *Far Eastern Survey*, March 1959.

In contrast, universal suffrage was introduced in South Asia at a time when a large part of the population was neither politically conscious nor nationally conscious. A politician advocating modernization may attempt to appeal to the voter on the basis of new values. But he often competes with other politicians who find that traditional loyalties to caste, to village, to religious community, and to language are more important when it comes to cultivating votes than any interest on the part of the voters in national unity, economic development, or social change.

In the West, too, the politician is often torn between local interests (which are also sometimes organized around religious or ethnic identifications) and the interests of the nation. But so long as there are strong loyalties to the nation, so long as there is some widespread notion of the general good, the politician can at least appeal to these national interests over the demands of his constituents. The problem which Burke expounded is most severe in societies which are not well integrated, where local groups feel that their interests are more important than any "national" interests, and where no group feels that the existing political framework provides it with adequate opportunities.

Political Functions

(1) *Interest articulation.* Two kinds of interest are expressed and organized in the subcontinent of South Asia: functionally specific economic interests, such as those of landlords, peasants, trade unions, businessmen, refugees, etc., and interests organized around traditional loyalties to caste, tribe, and community.

Economic interests are probably more highly organized in India than in either Pakistan or Ceylon. The fact that India is more industrialized, and that the nationalist movement assumed such a mass character as to encourage diverse interests to participate in the struggle, are major reasons.

In the preindependence era, business (especially foreign business), associations, and landlord groups (especially plantation owners) were influential in all three countries. Lord Cornwallis, under whose rule the *zamindar* system was established in Bengal, looked upon the creation of a landed gentry along British lines as necessary to establish a sound revenue system, and to provide a solid core of subjects upon whom the foundations of order could be built. British business groups were also exceedingly influential; after all, it was a commercial trading company, the East India Company, which first dominated the region.

Shortly after its dissolution, the British in South Asia formed themselves into Chambers of Commerce, whose influence continued in a less conspicuous form.

Indigenous commercial and later industrial entrepreneurs soon formed various chambers and trade associations. With some exceptions, these groups looked upon British capital as competitive and, more importantly, upon British rule as an obstacle to the pursuit of governmental policies which would strengthen indigenous business. Indian businessmen were among the earliest supporters of the nationalist movement. Support *Swadeshi*—that is, buy home-made goods—was one of the slogans of the Indian nationalists even before World War I.

The landlord community, on the other hand, was so dependent upon British rule that, with a few exceptions, it did not support the Congress nationalists. In addition, with the organization of various peasant associations by Indian nationalists in the mid-1930's, there arose in India a strong movement for abolition of the *zamindari* and for a host of other agrarian measures which fell under the general rubric of "land reform." The Muslim League, however, did win more substantial support from Muslim landlords. For one thing, landlords could give support to the League without being clearly anti-British, since the League's relationship with the British was far friendlier than that of the Congress. Then, too, the League was far less active in organizing peasant associations which would put forth demands for land reform.

Since independence, considerably more land reform legislation has been passed in India than in Pakistan. In West Pakistan in particular, where landlords have been politically strong in almost all the major parties, there had been little such legislation until recently. Since the army took control, it has been reported that extensive land reform measures have been carried out in West Pakistan. East Pakistan's landlords were largely Hindu and, since most of them have fled across the border to West Bengal, it has been easier for East Pakistan to pass radical land reform legislation. In India, too, where land legislation is a state matter rather than the concern of the central government, there is considerable variation from one state to another. In such states as Rajasthan, where *jagirdars* are politically active, land reform has made little or no progress.

Nowhere is the peasantry well organized as such. Many groups claim to speak in the name of the peasants, but few have strong peasant support. India has several peasant associations, some under Communist or Socialist control, but the major political activity of the peasantry is not so much in peasant associations as in existing political parties. The Congress is the party most effectively entrenched among the peasantry. In fact, in spite of the decline of Congress in the 1957 elections, its strength has generally increased in rural areas, its major losses having been in the urban centers. In North India, the Socialists have some rural hold, and in some parts of South India, especially in Andhra, the Communists have an effective rural organization.

Trade unions, like peasant associations, were organized by nationalist leaders and became wings of the nationalist movement and later of political parties, rather than autonomous bodies. Since the nationalists wanted to avoid class conflict within their own societies, strikes were generally aimed at British firms and at the government rather than at indigenous industry. Among the textile workers at Ahmedabad, a center of the Indian-owned textile industry, Gandhi's trade unionists discouraged the use of the strike as an instrument for achieving better wages and working conditions. Business, said Gandhi, was to be a "trustee" of the nation's wealth. Socialist and Communist trade unionists opposed the attempts of Gandhi and other nationalists to minimize class struggle and strikes, but these parties too used unions freely for political purposes.

Peasant agitations in the 1920's were also directed against British plantation owners or against the government for its high taxes rather than against indigenous landlords. Not until the late 1930's, when the Congress formed several provincial governments, did pressure for land reform legislation become strong.

Since independence, trade unions and peasant associations have continued as instruments of political parties. With rare exceptions, they have not produced their own leadership or been able to articulate their interests apart from those of the political parties which control them. India has four national trade union federations, one each controlled by the Congress, the Communists, the Socialists, and the Marxist-left parties. Because of the lack of durable parties and shifting elites, Pakistan trade unions seem to be less firmly associated with or controlled by political parties. But a few political parties, including Jamaat-i-Islami, do organize on the trade union front. Peasant associations in India are also under the control of the Communists (which have the largest association), the Socialists, and the Marxist-left groups. In addition, each party has a student front, a women's front, and, in West Bengal, a refugee front. The Communists also have peace fronts and cultural fronts. The term "front" is used by most political parties and accurately signifies an area organized and controlled by the party in question.

Opposition parties use their fronts as a way of building up popular support to overthrow the government or even the entire political order. The ruling Congress Party organizes such groups not only to strengthen its political position but also to get the groups to participate in development programs. Until 1955 the Congress did not have a peasant association of its own, since its leadership felt that its own rural party organization was itself essentially a peasant body. But since leftist parties have been organizing the peasantry, and directing them against government programs, the Congress leadership has come to feel that more specific peasant organizations should be formed, both as a counterweight to the leftists and as a way of rallying the peasantry around the rural development program. Likewise, Congress withdrew from student activities after independence on the grounds that students no longer should be active in politics but should devote their attention to the studies which would prepare them for contributing to national development. But, again, leftist and rightist groups have been so active among students that the Congress leadership recently started a Congress Youth section. Congress has also been exceedingly active in creating an atmosphere in trade unions which encourages workers to be "disciplined," to avoid strikes and settle disputes through the government's conciliation procedures, and to work hard to increase production.

At a minimum, therefore, Congress and the government hope to prevent trade unions, peasant associations, and student groups from being used to destroy the government, the political system, or the development program, and at a maximum to use such groups for furthering national development. Peasants are urged to give their labor for irrigation schemes and the like, workers are urged to produce more, and students are encouraged to do constructive work in towns and villages.

Business and landlord groups are less easy to control and they have tended to play a more autonomous role. But given the generally unfriendly attitude toward landlords and business in South Asia—an attitude which has been stronger in India and Ceylon than in Pakistan—these groups cannot usually work openly. The associations do pass resolutions but these have only minor effects on government policy. West Pakistan landlords have been actively associated with the provincial governments of West Pakistan and with the major political parties and have thereby influenced policy. Landlords have also been openly active in several Indian states. But more often landlords and businessmen have attempted to influence the administration of policy rather than policy itself. The distribution of government contracts, decisions as to who gets import licenses, and the administration of industrial relations legislation and of land reform legislation have been affected by influential landlords and businessmen acting as individuals or in concert.

If one takes the narrow theoretical position that government's economic policy is simply the reflection of diverse interests being articulated and aggregated by the ruling party and government, it would be impossible to understand the policies of South Asian governments. Businessmen do have some effect on industrial policy and taxation measures, landlords do have some effect on agrarian legislation, and unions do have some effect on industrial relations legislation and wage policy. But the major development programs of the three countries, while they have been influenced by organized interests, seem to be conceived almost independently of those interests. India has a five-year plan not because organized interests demand it but because government wills it.

This leads us to the role of the Westernized intelligentsia which dominates the governments of all three countries and whose orientations dominate the policies of these governments. While there are differences in the policies of the three governments, in general the leaderships of all of them are dedicated to "modernization" in some form or other, to be achieved through government initiative within a democratic framework. These leaderships view themselves and their government, rather than business and other non-governmental associations, as the major catalyst of social and economic change. They often tend to view organized interests as an impediment to rational planning, as interests to be avoided rather than accommodated. But since they are committed to democracy and cannot eliminate organized interests, their efforts are often directed toward controlling them (as in the case of unions and peasant associations) or, where possible, ignoring or discrediting them (as in the case of landlord and business associations).

Interests organized around traditional loyalties to caste, religion, community, and the like are important forces in all three countries. Of these, regional-linguistic-ethnic groups have been the most important. All three countries have been plagued by the demands of various regional groups either for greater autonomy in a federal system or, in some instances, for complete independence. The Naga tribesmen of Assam, the Pathan tribesmen of West Pakistan, the Tamils in Ceylon, and other linguistic groups in both India and Pakistan have been highly articulate. In a few instances—particularly in the case of tribes—the organization is in a genuine sense "traditional," although more often the tribes are led politically not by their traditional leaders, but by a new Western-educated leadership which grows up within the tribe. The Jharkhand Party in Bihar, for example, which demands the creation of a "Jharkhand," or tribal state, is led by an English-educated member of parliament, a tribesman in origin only.

Legislation that gives special assistance to castes and tribes which are considered particularly "backward" has encouraged many such communities to organize themselves and put forward their claims. The growth of transportation and communication systems has facilitated the growth of caste and regional-linguistic associations over large areas. The fact that government now has more powers than ever before has led groups to put forward claims which never would have arisen if government had not expanded. Concern over what language is taught in school, for example, becomes an issue only when the state, rather than the local community or religious institution, runs the school.

As noted before, the clergy are a more active political force in Ceylon and Pakistan than in India. The *ulama* have taken an active part in Islamic parties in Pakistan, and Buddhist monks have worked within the Sinhalese-minded MEP. In contrast, the Hindu Mahasabha and Jan Sangh in India are not built around traditional priestly leadership; in fact, their leadership is often Westernized in education. The Brahmans, the priestly class in India, took to Western education readily and have consequently not been threatened so much by the new order. Prime Minister Nehru, for example, is a Brahman, a descendant of the most orthodox and high-caste Saraswati Brahmans of Kashmir; he was educated at Harrow and Trinity College, Cambridge. In Pakistan, the *ulama* were little drawn to Western education; they have remained largely in their old positions and feel threatened by moves to create a secular state.

The more "traditional" interests not only are organized separately but have often permeated the party system. Caste interests, for example, have led to conflicts within state Congress Party organizations. The West Pakistan Muslim League has been affected by conflicts between Punjabi and non-Punjabi party leaders. Indian local government bodies, the village *panchayats* and municipal councils, are often torn by caste loyalties. Even the organization of economic interests is affected by these community loyalties. In Calcutta, for example, there is the Oriental Chamber of Commerce (made up of Muslims), the Bengal National

Chamber of Commerce (made up of Bengal businessmen), the Bharat Chamber of Commerce (made up of Marwaris), and the Indian Chamber of Commerce (mixed, but largely Marwari). In Bombay, the Gujarati and Maharashtrian language groups each has its own Chamber of Commerce. Factory labor is often recruited along community lines, and while workers of different castes may work side by side, they are generally bound by the proximity of their native villages or the language which they speak. An individual trade union may therefore be homogeneous in its membership.

Apart from economic interests and community interests—both being voluntary associations—there are also institutional interest groups in South Asia. Where voluntary interest associations are poorly developed —i.e., where interest articulation is low, or where such interests are inadequately aggregated into a party system which can govern effectively—institutional interests seem to be particularly important. Of the three countries, it is in Pakistan that the military and administrative services play the most active political role. The failure of the Muslim League and of other parties to provide for orderly government in Pakistan has meant that the services have had to assume responsibilities if law and order is to be maintained. It would be a mistake to attribute the role of the military in Pakistan to the Islamic tradition, although the military has certainly played a major part in Islamic history. In India, with a supposedly non-martial tradition, the army has been employed by the central government when state governments were ineffective. For example, the central government sent the army to the Naga Hills when the government of Assam failed to assuage the demands of the Naga tribesmen. In the states of PEPSU, Andhra, Kerala, Kashmir, and Hyderabad, the central government has had to use the army and/or the administrative services. That the army has not played an autonomous political role in these crises but has remained a neutral instrument of government is largely because India's central government is strong and stable.

The army and administrative services are potential political forces in South Asia for at least three reasons. First, their loyalties are not provincial, but national. Second, they are concerned with maintaining law and order. Third, their orientation is toward modernization and they represent a potential attraction to those who are interested in modernizing the country but are dissatisfied with the way existing parties are carrying on. It should also be noted that in former colonial countries the army and administration are not strongholds of tradition, as they were in China when the Republic was founded, or in much of the Middle East until the postwar era, but were recruited on an achievement basis and often attracted some of the brightest and most "modern" Western-educated young people.

Developments in South Asia seem to indicate that the military and administrative services are so molded by the British tradition of being non-political that, so long as the central government is strong, they are likely to remain instruments of government. But if the center becomes weak and ineffectual (as has happened in Pakistan), both the army and administrative services may play a more active role.

If institutional interest groups, such as the army and administration, are placed at one end of the continuum of organized interest articulation, the anomic movement would seem to be at the other end. In much of the non-Western world, these two types of interest articulation—the formless anomic movement, and the highly organized institutional interest—are often present. The effective organization of voluntary interest associations and their effective aggregation tend to minimize the role of both anomic and institutional interests.

Among non-Western countries South Asia has had its share of mob violence. There have been riots of orthodox Muslims against heterodox Ahmadiyas in the Punjab (Pakistan), riots of Sinhalese against the Tamil minority in Ceylon, violent protest in Bombay over the maintenance of a multilingual state, caste riots in Madras and frequent violence in West Bengal on economic issues. Assassinations, while not frequent in South Asia, have involved important figures: Gandhi, Pakistan's Prime Minister Liaquat Ali Khan, West Pakistan's Chief Minister Khan Sahib, and Ceylon's Prime Minister S. W. R. O. Bandaranaike.

To what extent can mob violence and assassination be considered anomic—formless action without norms? In prewar Japan, assassination was often used by organized cliques as a means of changing governments, a kind of substitute for the ballot. In the West, subversive movements have used individual and mass violence to unseat governments. In the twentieth-century West one assumes that reasonable men do not commit violence for political purposes, except of course in relation to other countries. But in the nineteenth-century era of class conflicts, violence was a basic political tool of organized groups.

Virtually every act of mass violence in South Asia has involved organized groups. The spontaneous completely anomic outburst has been rare. At the other pole, the violence of an insurrectionary movement has also been uncommon—the one major instance having occurred in

1949 and 1950, when the Communist movement in South India hoped to lead a successful revolution against the government. More frequently, mass violence is associated with the mass demonstration of an organized group. These demonstrations are generally aimed at expressing grievances and shaping specific government policies, and are often combined with an attempt to discredit the government. Since violence has been a common feature of political life in Calcutta, we can draw from that city our illustrations of types of situations in which violence has occurred.

Political groups in Calcutta have organized two kinds of demonstrations: those in which violence is planned, encouraged, or anticipated; and those in which the political parties have decided to avoid violence. Leftist parties leading demonstrations may deliberately provoke the police into violence by attacking policemen or police stations, for example, and thereby demonstrate the brutality of the existing government, or may stand by while non-party "rowdies" loot shops, overthrow tram cars, and commit other acts of violence. Once rowdies commit violence, and once the police respond with violence, violence becomes legitimate to the demonstrators and all hell may break loose. Any hated symbols of authority—the British-owned tramways, the shops of big businessmen, government buildings, public statues of one-time British rulers, or the glass show-windows of the United States Information Service—may be attacked. Such "mob" violence— "mob" in the sense of being unorganized and often uncontrollable— may flow from organized demonstrations. This represents the anomic element. Organized political parties may often not anticipate such mob violence, may want to stop it but be unable to; more often, they will attempt to utilize it and profit politically from it.

Some attention should be given to the role of the "rowdies." They are unorganized or loosely organized criminal elements found in many major South Asian cities. They are the pimps, procurers, and pickpockets of the city. Probably because the police are under central and state rather than municipal control, rowdy elements have not been able to establish high-level ties with the police. The well-organized, fabulously wealthy underworld of American cities does not exist. The rowdies, or *goondas* as they are sometimes called, are loosely organized into small groups throughout the city. Available evidence from Calcutta indicates that they are not newcomers, but long-established urban residents. Often, but not always, they are unemployed except for their criminal activities. The rowdies are the major catalyst of any mass violence; they take advantage of the disturbances and excitement which always accompany

any kind of mass activity to attack and loot shops. Given the level of discontent, the lack of adequate organization and machinery to deal with such discontent, and the rootlessness of the population, a large part of which comes from rural areas, the street-dwellers of Calcutta often need only a catalyst to arouse them to violence.

There are, however, demonstrations clearly aimed at being non-violent. Those sponsored by Gandhians during the nationalist era were intended as non-violent movements, but spontaneous peasant outbursts (such as the famous outbreak of violence in a North Indian village which led Gandhi to call off his first non-cooperation movement in the 1920's) or political workers less devoted to non-violence might convert these movements into a blood bath. But where the demonstrations are well organized, even where feelings are strong, it has been possible for political parties to avoid violence. That it is possible indicates the extent to which violence, too, can be controlled by organized groups. In 1955, the West Bengal middle class was incensed by a government proposal to combine the neighboring state of Bihar with the state of West Bengal. The government's intention was to call a halt to the alarming tendency of states to quarrel over border districts and to place linguistic provincialism over national considerations by combining two states which were then in the midst of a boundary dispute. But many Bengalis were concerned lest their region be submerged in the more populous region of Bihar. The leftist parties formed a united front and called for mass demonstrations against the government's proposal. The issue had the makings of mass violence: leftist parties against the government, and a deeply felt controversy involving linguistic-cultural loyalties. But the leftist leaders feared that if the demonstrations were violent, the violence would be directed against the many Biharis living in Calcutta. Such violence, with all its communal overtones, would be disastrous from a humanitarian point of view, and from a political point of view would disrupt the attempts of the leftist parties to win the support of Bihari-speaking factory workers against the ruling Congress government. The police were aware that the leftist demonstrators were eager to avoid violence and would use their authority to restrain their own membership. The police and the government, also eager to avoid violence, avoided arresting any of the leftist leaders, but did arrest hundreds of professional rowdies. These rowdies were rounded up, and released at the end of the demonstrations. The result was a complete absence of violence.

Completely spontaneous demonstrations and outbursts of violence do, however, sometimes occur: refugees from Pakistan in a camp, unemployed workers in a line waiting to apply for a limited number of jobs, and students in schools and colleges have committed sudden acts of violence. Sporadic, unplanned, unorganized outbursts rarely remain unorganized for long. A student protest against an injustice toward an individual student may be organized by political parties into a general attack against the university authorities, or against the government; the violent demands of a few refugees for more government aid may be organized by parties into a general protest against the government's refugee policy.

Were violence in South Asia simply the weapon of political groups who deliberately use it to influence government policy or to overthrow the existing order, strong government and police measures would be all that was necessary to destroy such organizations. Were violence simply unorganized expressions of the discontented, anomic outbursts of strongly felt but unorganized interests, then government could at least expect that such activity would dissipate itself. The unorganized mob, by itself, does not overthrow governments. But it is this combination of organization and anomy that makes the potential for violence so great in South Asia. Where the mob has some organizational guidance, and when its vague demands become the demands of organized groups, government finds that it is fighting something which, like an iceberg, is only partly above water.

The persistence of anomic movements in South Asia indicates that more discontent exists than has thus far been articulated through organized groups. Anomy thus represents an organizational potential. The current struggle of leftist, communal, and democratic forces for the organization of anomic discontent in the urban centers of South Asia ought to be a target for further research.

(2) *Interest aggregation.* Before independence, interests were aggregated on two levels: by the colonial British government and by the nationalist movements. In one sense it can be said that colonial rule is endangered to the extent to which a nationalist movement aggregates the diverse interests in the society. As the nationalist movement grew in size in India and attracted unions, peasants, the middle class, business interests, and the like, its strength grew and by 1946 it appeared to be winning support from within the military services as well. By the late 1930's the Congress Party, in its effort to reconcile diverse movements within it, articulated an ideology emphasizing a broad socialistic outlook which still guides the party. The Muslim League, with its

demand for Pakistan, and the Ceylonese nationalists with their constitutional emphasis tended to be less specific in program or ideology.

After independence, all three countries had the problem of reconciling diverse interests. In India, many of these diverse interests were
aggregated by the Congress Party leadership—or, more accurately, by
the Congress Working Committee and the government's cabinet. The
Congress Party was in power and those who wanted to influence government policy had to turn to the Congress. Autonomous economic
interest groups, such as business and landlords, tried generally to work
within the Congress framework, especially after the 1952 elections. The
demands of various linguistic groups for linguistic provinces focused on
the Congress Party and when the government was faced with making
a decision as to how India's states should be reorganized, the decision
was left to the Congress Working Committee. The Congress Party has
developed a machinery for dealing with diverse interests and reconciling
them: the Congress Parliamentary Board, which selects candidates for
elections, tries to "balance" the party ticket with sufficient numbers, for
example, of Muslims, other minorities, women, and untouchables, in
much the same way that Tammany Hall operates in New York. Congress Party general secretaries serve as trouble-shooters who rush to
provincial capitals when conflicts threaten to injure the local organization. Nehru himself is active in settling disputes within the party organization.

Unlike Congress, opposition parties in India are hardly subjected to
the pressures of various interests. The ideological emphasis of the
national opposition parties, plus their distance from power, makes them
unlikely pressure group targets. The fact that organized interests do
not attempt to influence their policies reinforces the ideological emphases
of these parties. Without the pressure of specific interest groups, they
have little incentive to make their programs more specific. Few of these
national parties, for example, have developed state programs or detailed
election manifestoes.

In Pakistan, where no one party has been capable of aggregating
diverse interests in such a way as to provide stable government, the
few articulate economic interests—for example, landlords—have shifted
from one party to another, whenever and wherever they can be most
effective. In Pakistan, articulated interests are largely linguistic-cultural,
and in the absence of a strong central government and party, there has
been no adequate structure to aggregate these differences. The result
has been a constant shifting and bargaining for position on the part

of various interests, occasional outbursts of violence, and a general uncertainty as to the longevity of government. Conflict within West Pakistan between the various states and the Punjabi group whose domination they feared ultimately resulted in the creation of the single state of West Pakistan. But interests shifted so rapidly that the very groups which had favored the creation of a single state turned against it, and the issue is still a live one.

The Constituent Assembly of Pakistan, under the strong arm of General Mirza, Pakistan's governor-general, did manage to find a solution, although perhaps a temporary one, to the conflicts between East and West Pakistan. Urdu and Bengali were given equal status as national languages, and East and West Pakistan were given equal representation in the National Assembly. The Pakistan Industrial Development Corporation made great efforts to pour development funds into East Pakistan, in order to refute the charge that the central government was developing West Pakistan and making East Pakistan a "colony." But conflicts between East and West Pakistan and within West Pakistan continue. Few groups dare to work closely with the rather substantial Hindu minority in East Bengal for fear of alienating the Muslim-minded voter. A party like the Awami League may build a winning coalition in East Bengal, but find it difficult to build a winning coalition in West Pakistan at the same time. The coalition between Khan Sahib's Republican Party (of West Pakistan) and the Awami League (of East Pakistan) was an attempt to create a coalition which could control the center. Aggregation through coalition, rather than within any single party, was Pakistan's unsuccessful attempt at bringing together diverse interests. When it failed, the army and administrative services took over, to attempt what the parties had not been able to do.

In contrast, Ceylon's stable governments have thus far been built by coalitions of interests in coalitions of parties. The United National Party (essentially a coalition of several parties) governed Ceylon until 1956, when the MEP, a coalition of Marxist leftists and Sinhalese-oriented parties, came to power. In Ceylon, as we have noted earlier, the difficulty has been that while coalitions have been relatively stable, the major political groups have not been able to absorb the interests of the Tamil voters and at the same time satisfy the demands of the majority Sinhalese community. Before the rise of the new Sinhalese educated groups, the interests of the Ceylon Tamils were adequately represented in the United National Party. So long as the Ceylon Tamils were represented in the United National Party, communal harmony was maintained. But the rising Sinhalese educated groups felt that the fair treatment given to the Ceylon Tamil minority was at their expense, and after 1955 even the United National Party had deserted the Tamils for a "Sinhalese Only" position.

More recently, instability in the governing coalition has resulted from the withdrawal of the Trotskyites from the MEP government and the assassination of Bandaranaike by a Buddhist priest. The growth of both communal and ideological conflicts in the politics of Ceylon diminishes the possibility that effective coalitions will be able to run the country.

(3) *Political socialization and recruitment.* Definitions of political roles have undergone great changes in South Asia during the past one hundred years. In the nineteenth century the British sought to induct Indians and Ceylonese into what were essentially "collaborationist" roles. South Asians were trained as clerks, as administrators, as school-teachers, even as legislators and military personnel. These roles were largely modeled after comparable roles in Britain. Civil servants were to be dedicated to their work, concerned with efficiency and rationality, devoid of corruption and nepotism, politically neutral, and, above all, capable of maintaining law and order and collecting revenue. But perhaps the major instrument for creating Anglicized Indians was the new system of university education established in the middle of the nineteenth century. The result of these and other such efforts was the emergence of a liberal, and what was generally called a Moderate, group of Indians (and Ceylonese too) who accepted British values as a model toward which to strive. With less success, the liberal viceroy, Lord Ripon, sought after 1882 to reform and rejuvenate local self-government with the explicit intention of making political education rather than administrative efficiency the primary function of local government.

The emergence in India of religious revivalist movements at the turn of the century and especially the emergence of a mass nationalist movement after the First World War resulted in bitter attacks against those who appeared to accept British-defined roles. Those who worked as administrators for the British were accused of betraying the nationalist cause. British-sponsored values—obedience to law, moderation, and subservience to authority—were increasingly rejected by the newer nationalists. Politicians now joined legislatures, not to make them work but to prove that they could not work. Nationalists advocated civil disobedience against law. Martyrdom, sacrifice, and harassment of authority became desirable forms of behavior. Tension between administrators and politicians grew. Above all, many nationalists, recognizing how potent the

British university system had been in inducting people into British-defined roles, consciously rejected the Westernized educational system. Gandhi urged students to leave schools and colleges to join the nationalist movement. Some nationalists—Tangore at Santiniketan immediately comes to mind—created new "Indian" educational institutions.

With independence, still new adjustments had to be made. Neither subservience nor harassment of authority seemed appropriate to the new governments. While some aspects of the old roles seemed appropriate, others did not. The political neutrality of the administrator was welcomed. But development tasks emphasized by all three governments required a bureaucracy not simply dedicated to maintaining law and order and collecting revenue but capable of administering development programs and arousing public participation. Few administrators had the technical skills necessary to participate in development work. Their pre-independence role as aloof men of authority did not encourage constant collaboration between administrator, politician, and citizen. Resocializing administrators became a major problem. Pakistan organized training programs to impart new skills and attitudes to their civil servants. India established an active Public Administration Institute, as well as special programs for the training of village level workers and other personnel responsible for administering community development projects.

India—particularly because its nationalist movement was more comprehensive in scope than that of Ceylon or of those areas which joined Pakistan—has had the problem of coping with parties and interest groups which appear to operate in accordance with values which (to the governing party at least) were more appropriate to a nationalist movement than an independent nation. Groups still resorted to civil disobedience in spite of the existence of representative institutions. Demands are made which run counter to what government considers to be the national interest—economic development, national unity and, in general, modernization.

How to induct people into an acceptance of the values of the Westernized elites is a major problem in all three countries and each has been developing institutions to achieve this objective. Each country has legally defined citizenship (a particularly difficult problem in Ceylon and Pakistan, with their single prominent minority) and is trying to train citizens. One could study the many new institutions and processes created in South Asia in terms of the ways in which they shape citizenship. Elections, apart from their obvious importance in determining who gets elected and how stable governments are, can be examined in terms of their effects on the development of new attitudes toward government, toward legislators, and toward the individual's role as a citizen. Rural development programs are quite explicitly defined in broader terms than simply increasing agricultural production. The Indians call theirs a "community" not "agricultural" development program. Mass media, especially films, are increasingly being used as an instrument for citizen training, and adult education literacy programs are used, as were "Americanization" programs for immigrants to the United States. Laws too—especially those directed at marriage, divorce, caste inequalities, and inheritance—may change behavior and attitudes.

What is striking about the recent attempts of South Asian governments to socialize people into new roles is the scale of the effort. British efforts were directed at relatively small numbers of people. While the nationalist movement sought to inculcate larger numbers of people into new roles, they lacked the instrumentalities which independence made available. Of the three countries, India has been the most active in this direction. Schools, adult literacy programs, films, community development programs, speeches by ministers and party leaders, interest groups (particularly Congress-sponsored trade unions, farming organizations, and student groups, and also the many Gandhian constructive work organizations) are directed at changing attitudes and behavior. Even traditional instrumentalities for transmitting cultural values are not overlooked. Recently the government organized *saddhus* to explain the government's program to villagers. What impact all these efforts have and their relationship to primary socializing institutions and influences (such as the family) is an important area for field research.[23]

Political recruitment, as well as role definition and the institutions by means of which individuals are socialized into new roles, has also undergone great changes. Who is recruited, the criteria for recruitment, and the channels through which recruitment occurs have all changed. If there is any single factor which accounts for these changes it is the emergence of new social classes in the subcontinent. The Western impact

[23] Additional discussions of socialization in South Asia can be found in the sections dealing with Westernized education, secularization, and political communication. The literature on political socialization in India is not well developed. The role of primary socializing institutions in shaping attitudes in inter-personal relations and self-images, both important aspects of attitudes toward authority, are treated by G. Morris Carstairs, *The Twice Born: A Study of a Community of High Caste Hindus*, London, The Hogarth Press, 1957. But the link between socialization in general and *political* socialization is not considered. A treatment of traditional political values as they relate to contemporary attitudes toward authority can be found in Myron Weiner, "Struggle against Power: Notes on Indian Political Behavior," *World Politics*, April 1956.

and colonial rule, industrial and commercial growth, and the development of an educational system have led to changes in the social structures of India, Pakistan, and Ceylon. Further changes are probable, and predictions as to the kinds of political development and political recruitment which are likely to occur hinge upon our capacity to foresee alterations in social stratification.

Under the Mughal rulers, before the arrival of the Europeans, power in the subcontinent was hereditary. Even administrative posts were often inherited. *Zamindars*, or revenue collectors, were appointed by Mughal rulers, and these men passed on their posts to their descendants. Under Mughal rule, some Hindu princely states continued to exist, especially in the south. Posts beneath the rajahs were often, but not always, shared by members of the same family or community. Maharashtra had Maratha kings, but the prime ministership and the top administrative posts were held by the high-caste Chitpavan Brahmans, who transmitted their offices through their own families.

The European conquerors did not in all cases immediately attempt to displace local rulers. The Portuguese and Dutch in Ceylon failed to conquer the Kandyan kingdom; not until 1815 were the Kandyan rulers subjugated by the British. In India, the British first conquered the areas around present-day Madras, Bombay, and Calcutta, and then spread inland. What started as a commercial venture by the East India Company soon became a military struggle. The British negotiated settlements with local Mughal governors who had assumed virtual power in view of the gradual breakdown of Mughal authority in Delhi. They soon conquered much of northern India, but recognized the wisdom of establishing suzerainty over petty rulers rather than waging further wars which would drain their resources and minimize their capacity for profit. By the middle of the nineteenth century, therefore, and up to 1947, the subcontinent was divided into what was known as British India (about a million square miles)—regions under direct British control, such as the presidencies of Bengal, Bombay, and Madras—and those areas known as the Indian States (about 600,000 square miles) which remained under the nominal control of autocratic Hindu or Muslim rulers. Among the largest of such states were Hyderabad, Kashmir, Baroda, Mysore, and Gwalior.

While in theory these Hindu and Muslim princes retained their positions, in fact they lost most of their power. The British could and did intervene when maharajas failed to provide orderly and financially sound governments. Disputes over succession were settled by the British

Resident in the princely state, and many states were in fact taken over and absorbed into British India.

Between 1947 and 1950, the remaining princely states were integrated into India and Pakistan. Their rulers had been so dependent upon British might for their survival that in almost all cases, with the withdrawal of the British, the successor governments could absorb the states with relatively little difficulty. The maharajas were left without political power and, while some have successfully participated in elections, as a major force they have disappeared in the political life of the subcontinent.

In the latter part of the nineteenth century, new Western-educated middle classes arose to fill posts in the administrative services, British commercial firms, law, journalism, and medicine. These new classes came from the areas around the seaports, especially Madras, Calcutta, Bombay, Cochin, Jaffna, and Colombo. Although there have been exceptions, the new classes were drawn largely from those castes which held high positions before the British arrived—Chitpavan Brahmans in Maharashtra, Kyasthas (a scribe caste) in Bengal, the Nayar caste in Travancore-Cochin, the Goyigama caste in Ceylon, and so on. Virtually all the major nationalist leaders came from the new Westernized classes, and these classes still predominate in positions of leadership in all three countries. Even Bandaranaike, late prime minister of Ceylon and leader of the Buddhist and Sinhalese communities, came from a Western-educated class. An Oxford graduate, one-time secretary of the Oxford Union, and the son of one of Ceylon's richest planters, he was a staunch Buddhist who spoke in Sinhalese and wore a sarong in public (but trousers at home).

Under the Western impact, the business classes developed, too—coming largely from communities traditionally involved in some form of commercial or money-lending activities. Trading classes in western India, possibly because of their proximity to the new western ports and to the caravan routes from Arabia to the prosperous Gangetic plains, have also grown in importance. These include the Jains, Parsis, Ismailis, Gujaratis, and Marwaris.

While the business classes have acquired economic importance—first in commerce, particularly as a *comprador* class, and later in industry—their political importance has not yet equaled that of the business classes in nineteenth- or twentieth-century Europe. Businessmen participated in the national movements by providing funds to the League, to Congress, or to the Ceylon National Congress, but almost none assumed prominent positions in the nationalist organizations. To begin with, the businessman was held almost in social contempt. He often belongs to a lower caste than the professional politician or administrator and is generally less educated. Until recently, for example, the sons of Marwari businessmen did not go to college. Furthermore, the businessman had a reputation for being self-seeking and dishonest. The South Asian intellectual's attitude toward the businessman differed little from that of the nineteenth-century British or American intellectual. The popular image of the pot-bellied Marwari businessman differs little from the picture of the nineteenth-century "robber barons" in America. But while the nineteenth-century American and British intellectual had little power, the South Asian intellectual, by virtue of his leadership in the nationalist movement, holds great power. The graduate of the London School of economics, Cambridge, or Oxford still has a greater potential for political success than a young uneducated businessman.

As we have already noted, the earliest political leadership came from the most urbanized, educated, Westernized elements who had the verbal, intellectual, and administrative skills necessary to deal with the Western rulers. The early leaders were staunch constitutionalists in the nineteenth-century Victorian tradition. In Ceylon this group retained leadership until after independence, but in prepartition India the Congress Party produced a second layer of politicians, less educated and less Westernized, and often less devoted to constitutionalism. There emerged in India a vernacular-speaking, political worker whose ties to the Hindu tradition are far stronger than that of the English-speaking national leadership. This Hindu-minded worker, although he is generally not orthodox, is closer to the villager in his values. Those who come from Hindi-speaking regions generally favor banning the slaughter of cows, support Hindi as the national language, and have rurally oriented notions of economic development.

The vernacular-speaking politician is growing in importance throughout South Asia. As we have seen, his emergence as a force in Ceylon in 1956 was the major factor in the defeat of the preindependence leadership of the United National Party. The *ayurvedic* doctor, Buddhist priest, the village schoolteacher—the rural elites—became politically active and resented domination by the "Colombo people," who speak English and are Westernized. Pakistan has not yet been faced with the vernacular politician on a threatening scale, although the *ulama* and the orthodox elements now supporting Jamaat-i-Islami and other Islamic parties may grow in strength. In India control over the states is often in the hands of less Westernized individuals,[24] but in Pakistan the Westernized leadership is everywhere in office.

The growth in the importance of the vernacular-speaking, less Westernized politician also marks the beginning of a shift in power from the urban to the rural areas. The urban center has been the locus of new ideas and of the organization to carry them out, and it is only natural that the urban politicians—urban in birth, education, and outlook—have thus far played a role in political developments far out of proportion to the size of urban areas. But with the introduction of universal suffrage and with the spread of education and new ideas, the rural areas are increasingly becoming politically conscious. One can anticipate that as a rural elite grows, their political power may grow as well. Already, national planners in Delhi are confronted by state chief ministers who are making demands for projects and for revenue to aid their respective rural districts. Moreover, pressure for roads, tube-wells, community development projects, rural credit schemes, bridges, etc., is coming from the rural areas themselves. Although the basic intention of the national leadership to modernize through large-scale industrialization has not yet been affected, it is not unlikely that the growth in rural pressure in the years to come may have drastic influence upon the whole character of planning.

The geographic centers for political recruitment have also changed in recent years. While political party workers and leaders used to come almost exclusively from the areas which had felt the greatest British impact, such as Colombo, Madras, Bombay, and Calcutta, increasingly politicians are being recruited from the "hinterland." Two of the three leaders of the Hindu communal movement in India were Bengalis and the third was from Bombay. But today neither Bengal nor Bombay are centers of Hindu communal activity. The new centers are in the interior: Rajasthan, Uttar Pradesh, Delhi, and Madhya Pradesh. Likewise, the center of Congress Party strength is now in Uttar Pradesh, while its position in Bengal and Bombay, two states in which Congress had its earliest support, has been declining. Dacca and East Bengal were, until after independence, secondary to the metropolis of Calcutta. Calcutta dominated the intellectual and political life of Bengal as much as Vienna dominated Austria. But today, in independent Pakistan, East Bengal has become a political center.

[24] The chief minister of Madras, for example, speaks only Tamil. South Indian states as well as those in the north have important vernacular-speaking politicians.

So far we have called attention to some of the changes in political recruitment in terms of social and economic classes, educational levels, urban-rural changes, and geographic shifts. There have also been changes in the rate of recruitment and in motives for entering politics.

The major political figures in the three countries of South Asia entered politics during the burst of nationalist activity in the interwar period. The struggle for independence attracted recruits, especially young people, in larger numbers than have the struggles between political parties since independence. Pakistan has had some five prime ministers and as many chief ministers in each of her provinces. But power has been shared by about twenty men who were active in prepartition India as well. In India, the Congress Party has continued controlling the center and most of the states, also with a preindependence leadership. The average age of cabinet members is somewhere near sixty. Ceylon too retains an older leadership in spite of the shift in control of government from one party to another. A second generation of political leadership has yet to arise in South Asia. One disquieting factor is the role being played by the younger people in extremist politics. Communist and Trotskyite parties have attracted young people in all three countries, especially in Ceylon and India. Leftist parties have considerable influence among school and college students, but communal groups are influential, too. In West Pakistan, Jamaat-i-Islami has been particularly successful in winning youthful support; the rigorous philosophies of Maudoodi and of Marx alike have their attractions.

Much of the recruitment into extremist parties has been from among unemployed youth. The lack of correlation between the kinds of training students receive in the universities and the work-force needs of growing economies has resulted in a substantial surplus of educated unemployed. The high urban unemployment rates in Bengal and Kerala have been partially responsible for the growth of left-wing parties in the larger cities of those two states. Pakistan seems to have less of a problem of educated unemployed. The university system was not as well developed in the areas which joined Pakistan, and after 1947 there were not as many educated Muslims to fill available posts in the schools, universities, administrative offices, and business houses as there were Hindus in India. Then, too, many jobs were vacated by the exodus of Hindus from Pakistan. If the joint family system of South Asia did not provide some security for the unemployed, the political consequences of such large-scale unemployment, or underemployment (which is very severe in rural areas), would be disastrous for any government. Nonetheless, the unemployed do provide a continuous source of militant party workers for the extremist parties. Another disquieting element is the fact that unemployment has been increasing in spite of development programs; some large-scale industries, such as steel, do not use large amounts of labor. While national income may grow, unemployment may grow as well. Additional population increases (Ceylon is one of the fastest-growing countries in the world) are likely to increase the unemployment problem unless industry, especially industry employing large amounts of labor, grows very rapidly.

An increase in unemployment is likely not only to affect the leftist and rightist parties but to result in an increase in anomic behavior. Thus far few assassinations have occurred in the subcontinent—although those which have occurred have been important. Interestingly enough, the assassinations of Gandhi, Liaquat Ali Khan, and, more recently, of Khan Sahib, leader of West Pakistan's Republican Party and the first chief minister of West Pakistan, were not calculated maneuvers by political groups like those which occurred in, say, prewar Japan. So far as investigations have shown, these assassinations were committed by discontented individuals acting on their own. Khan Sahib, for example, was assassinated by a dismissed government clerk whom he had refused to reinstate. Mass demonstrations, with mob overtones, are also likely to increase, as they have in Calcutta, where few families do not have at least one unemployed member. Unemployed youths wandering in the streets of a crowded, tense, hot city, with plenty of time on their hands, are an easy catch for leftist political groups eager to utilize their time and their passions.

The motives of those entering party politics have also been changing. In the days of national movements, people joined for reasons of power, prestige, patriotism, rarely for material gain. Entering politics generally meant entering a career, not simply making politics an adjunct of one's professional or business activities. Party workers frequently had no other occupation than politics, and no outside avocations. The worker was often unmarried, a dedicated man with no real group ties outside the party. In every sense of the word, he was a "political" man. Independence brought onto the scene men whose political life was only one of their many activities. The Muslim League and Congress were soon joined by businessmen, landlords, and others who had remained out of the national movements but who now felt that party membership would be to their advantage. The parties have accepted and often welcomed many of these people. In Orissa, for example, Congress nominated and helped elect several former princely rulers, and in Rajasthan a number of *jagirdars* have successfully run on Congress tickets. The Congress Party has also attracted some businessmen, lawyers, and other professionals who, in the tradition of British and American parties, look upon their political work not as a career but as an avocation. The part-time politician, with a job, family, and many group interests, is as characteristically a member of the moderate, pragmatic party as the fulltime unmarried party worker, dedicated completely to his political work, is a central figure in ideologically oriented, extremist parties.

In Ceylon the professional politician had actually been a latecomer. Possibly because the national movement had not been as comprehensive as that of India, Ceylon's moderate politicians had other professions as lawyers, teachers, or in running estates. In the preindependence days Ceylon's politicians were much like that of India prior to the First World War. The growth of Marxist parties in Ceylon meant the entrance into politics of professional politicians. Some of the increasing intensity in Ceylon politics can be attributed not only to the rise of communal and ideological conflicts but also to this increase in professional politicians, dedicating all their energies to political work, and having no outside occupations to which they can return in the event of political defeat.

One final note on the recruitment process in South Asia. Interest groups such as trade unions, peasant associations, refugee organizations, and the like, largely because they are controlled by political parties, are rarely sources of political recruits. The trade unionist does not enter politics. Instead, the politician enters trade union work. "Mass" organizations are channels in which political recruits work, not channels from which they are recruited, except temporarily for demonstrations and civil-disobedience campaigns. Until these interest groups produce a leadership of their own, the question of their being sources of recruitment for political parties will not arise.[25]

(4) *Political communication.* How does a democratic government find out what its people want? How does government assess what the public response to its policies will be? How do people find out what their compatriots are like and what values they share? Without some transmission of information and values, a society can hardly hold together—unless the state resorts to coercion or performs so few functions that

[25] The one exception is the student movement, which continues to provide political recruits. Their education, dismal job prospects, rural ties, and idealism make students an important target for recruitment by political parties.

there is little or no need to reconcile differences within a political framework.

So long as governments in South Asia performed limited functions— that is, collected taxes, maintained a few public works and sometimes law and order—communication needs were not great. The subcontinent was politically and culturally divided for centuries. With states generally limited both in geographical scope and in function, there was little need for the community to communicate with the state, for the state to communicate with the community, or for one community to communicate with another.

The traditional basis for communication in the subcontinent coincided with the network of relationships, which was amazingly large, given the vastness and diversity of the area. There was a network of trade and commerce. Not only did villages trade with other nearby villages and towns, but trade caravans brought goods from one part of the subcontinent to another. Brocades, spices, precious metals, and stones were all transported by caravans across the country and by sea to other parts of the world.

A network of family and caste relationships also tied the villager to the larger world. Villages were and are generally exogamous, so that girls marry outside their villages and brides are brought in from other villages. Wives often return to their village home to give birth, to attend weddings, or simply to visit their families and escape from their in-laws. Familial and caste associations may cover a wide area and persist through generations.

The religious network has been a strong source of ties in South Asia. There are mass pilgrimages and movements or gatherings under the tutelage of professional religious preceptors, and there are religious festivals which bring people together. In a traditional agrarian society, such festivities, whether among Muslims, Buddhists, or Hindus, are major events and points of multitudinous contact. Literally millions of people may attend festivals such as the one held every ten years at Allahabad, where the sacred Jamuna and Ganga Rivers meet. The mosque, too, is a center for continuous contact and for the exchange of information and gossip.

The introduction of a mass communication system has not destroyed the traditional communication network based upon personal relations. It simply means that a new network has been introduced which greatly expands the physical area of communication. What cannot now be communicated by face-to-face contact can be communicated through the mass media. In an industrially advanced society, most people receive their major information through this mass communication network. There is, however, an intermediate stage, when the society is neither so under-developed that the communication network and the network of personal relationships coincide perfectly nor so developed that virtually everyone gets some information from the mass communication network. The sub-continent is at this in-between stage, with some people communicating exclusively through a limited network and others largely through the mass communication network. Villagers are generally in one communi-cation network, the urbanized educated elites in another. As a conse-quence, South Asian governments have difficulty in getting information from the rural communication network. It is extremely hard for them to judge what effects would result from implementing given policies. The governments' capacity for assessing the consequences or social costs of their policies is low.

A second problem arises for these governments as a result of the development of an intermediary network based upon the provincial languages. The break between the English-speaking elites and the ver-nacular-speaking elites has also resulted in a dichotomy in the com-munication systems. Almost every major language has its own vernacular press, and the Tamils, Bengalis, Maharashtrians, and Hindi-speaking peoples each have their own language films.

Regional loyalties are growing in the subcontinent and are due as much to the growth of mass communication as national loyalties were several decades ago. Loyalties to language, caste, tribe, etc., may in fact be strengthened by state policies making the vernacular language the language of instruction in schools and in the universities, and by various measures to encourage regional literatures. Such policies may be necessary and in some instances desirable, but they raise problems of how to relate these regional networks and, more importantly, regional loyalties to national loyalties through some national communication net-work. Since Pakistan, India, and Ceylon have each decided to drop Eng-lish as a national language, the question arises as to whether any one or two vernacular languages spoken within these countries will satisfac-torily tie the various linguistic regions together.

Where discontinuity in the communication network exists, the govern-ment has a real problem in communicating decisions to people and in assessing their potential responses and their political demands. The na-tional politician may not be able to use the mass communication system to break into the regional communication networks, nor is the network of personal relationships readily available to him. There are two ways in which the politician, in or out of government, reaches the electorate. One is through the mass rally. The other is through the party organization.

Almost every opportunity is taken by the politician to speak before vast numbers of people—Republic Day, Independence Day, Gandhi's or Jinnah's birthday, days to commemorate the importance of national freedom or of religious toleration. The opening of a dam, the laying of foundation stones, the opening of school buildings, the sinking of a tubewell, and other projects stressing national reconstruction are all fair game for the political speaker. The Indian prime minister is almost constantly on tour of the country, exhorting large crowds of people to work hard, to abolish "communalism, casteism and provincialism" from their hearts, to study more, and so on. Ministers in state and central governments in all three countries travel constantly, not only to impart information and to win political support, but to collect information as well.

Few party organizations in South Asia cover as extensive an area as intensively as the Congress Party in India. The party is organized around local village units, districts, provinces, and on a national level. This network is not only a vote-getting organization but also a communication network. The local Congress worker, often a prosperous peasant, a schoolteacher, a small businessman, or a petty landowner, has a double function. He communicates the new values of development and national unity from the national to the local level, and in some cases may even mobilize local participation in rural development projects. But he also communicates news from the rural to the district level, such as complaints regarding high taxes, discontent and unrest due to crop failures, sentiment for rural credit aid, tubewells, or roads. When the system works well, there may be extensive two-way communication. When only one part of the network operates, the politician becomes either an agitator or an administrator.

The Congress Party network does not always work well. On some issues, such as in the case of demands for state's reorganization, the top leadership is often inadequately informed as to the intensity of feeling in various regions. In its decision to make Bombay a multilingual state, for example, the center was unaware of the violent reaction this would evoke from the Gujaratis, and especially the Maharashtrians, in the state.

Nonetheless, Congress and the national leadership of India probably have a better "feel" for the public's pulse than any other party in India or elsewhere in South or Southeast Asia. The existence of a relatively effective communication system has made elections in India more predictable than they are in many other newly independent areas. In Pakistan, in contrast, no party is sufficiently well organized to perform the function of effective two-way communication. As a consequence, a degree of unpredictability exists in Pakistan politics which is expressed most clearly in the concern which Pakistan's political parties feel during elections. Not only was the Muslim League literally wiped out as a legislative party in East Bengal's 1954 elections, but, even more striking, no one, not even the triumphant parties, had any idea of the magnitude of the League's impending defeat.

IV. GOVERNMENTAL STRUCTURES AND AUTHORITATIVE FUNCTIONS

In each of the countries of South Asia, some people argued that the nation's traditions should be taken into consideration in framing the new constitution. But the writers of the constitutions had only one political tradition to draw on—that of the West. Few could argue for the return of autocratic rule as experienced under the Mughal rulers or the maharajas or Buddhist kings. The Islamists did call for an Islamic constitution, but the Western-trained lawyers in Pakistan's Constituent Assembly could not see how a constitution shaped out of the precepts of the Koran and Sunnah could allow for the creation of a viable state. The only concessions made to the Islamists were constitutional provisions that the state be called "the Islamic Republic of Pakistan" and that the president be a Muslim. In Ceylon and India the question of a Buddhist or Hindu constitution did not arise.

The machinery of government throughout South Asia closely approximates Western models. Ceylon, India, and, until 1958, Pakistan have all adopted parliamentary systems of the British type. Pakistan and India have modified the British parliamentary structure by building a federal system into it. These federal systems are devices for dealing with the great diversity of the regions. In both India and Pakistan the states have power over land legislation, health, welfare, and education. The administration of many central government projects, including rural development programs, is in the hands of the states. In Pakistan, residual powers not specifically delegated to the states or the center are left to the state governments, as in the United States; in India, residual powers are left to the center.

The existence of a federal system in a parliamentary structure means that the center may be thrown off balance, not because of any loss of its parliamentary majority, but because of political failures within the provinces. The loss of East Pakistan by the Muslim League doomed the League in the center, although it still retained its parliamentary majority. The fact that Pakistan has only two provinces means that the loss of one by the party ruling the center makes continued rule from the center difficult. Likewise, the rise of too many unstable state situations in India represents a threat to the central government. Members of the Council of State (known as the Raj Sabha), one of the two houses of parliament in the center, are elected by the state legislatures. Any party which wins control of the seats for the state legislative assembly is likely to win the seats from that state for the House of the People (Lok Sabha) as well. In a federal parliamentary system, parties must concentrate on gaining control of states before they can hope to win control of the center.

In spite of the federal systems, the central governments are quite strong. The bulk of revenue comes to the central governments rather than to the states. The major development programs, especially in the field of industry, are under central control. Both Pakistan's and India's constitution provide the center with emergency powers to take over states. When riots broke out in East Pakistan in 1954, the central government established "Governor's Rule," or direct rule by the center. When government failed in PEPSU, Andhra, and Travancore-Cochin, India's central government established emergency "President's Rule."

Rule-making

In two of the three South Asian countries, India and Ceylon, rule-making functions have been in the hands of the prime ministers and their cabinets, responsible to popularly elected legislatures. Both countries have a president (India) or governor-general (Ceylon) who, like the English monarch, is a symbol of unity, performing ceremonial functions. Only in Pakistan did the governor-general have substantial power; until 1956, when Pakistan's short-lived constitution went into effect, the country operated on the British Parliamentary Act of 1935 which provided for a powerful British governor-general. In the crises which occurred in Pakistan, the governor-general utilized these powers extensively—so much so that governments were more accountable to him than to any political party or to the Constituent Assembly. It was, in fact, the governor-general, rather than the Assembly, who actually appointed and dismissed prime ministers. Pakistan's 1956 Constitution reduced in theory the powers of the office (by then called the president), but in fact General Mirza, who held that office, continued to be the most powerful figure in the government. It was he who abolished the Republic and turned power over to the army, but it was the army which turned around and forced Mirza out. In late 1958 General Mirza went into exile and executive powers shifted into the hands of the commander-in-chief of the Pakistan army, General Ayub Khan who became Chief Martial Law Administrator and President.

In fact as well as in theory, the prime ministers of Ceylon and India have been the crucial policy-makers. Emergency powers have been evoked, but at the initiative of the prime minister and within the constitutional framework. In India, where the Congress Party has been relatively strong and its leadership relatively well united, the president has played no autonomous political role. Prime minister Nehru and members of the cabinet have been the key decision-makers. In Ceylon, the governor-general placed the country under martial law in 1958 when the Tamil-Sinhalese conflict plunged the country into disorder and violence, but he did so at the request of the prime minister. However, during the 1958 crisis the governor-general was the effective center of the government. It is not unlikely that the governor-general could play a more active role in the event of further political crises.

This is not to say that legislative bodies have had no rule-making functions. Like other parliamentary bodies, the parliaments of South Asia have had the functions of articulating interests and of ratifying government decisions. In both India and Ceylon, although less so in Pakistan, the legislature has often been able to modify government policies. In India this has often taken place in state legislatures, where the Congress assembly members have pressured the chief minister or cabinet members and on several occasions actually forced the chief minister to resign. As a general hypothesis, however, one can say that the more such political conflicts have developed within the states, the more likely it has been that the central government would intervene. A reverse proposition might also be suggested: where the capacity of the central government to make and administer rules is weak, the states and local authorities attempt to assume greater authority. Indian politics provide much evidence for the first hypothesis, and Pakistan, before 1958, provided data for the second.

Rule Application and Rule Adjudication

The functions of rule application and rule adjudication in the subcontinent are performed, in accordance with British tradition, by a highly centralized administrative and judicial system. Each country has a national civil service system. The preindependence Indian Civil Service (ICS) has been converted into the Indian Administrative Service (IAS) and the Civil Service of Pakistan (CSP). Under British rule the key figure in the service was the local district magistrate, or district collector, or—in Ceylon—the district revenue officer. Whatever his title, he was first and foremost responsible for all revenue within his district. As well as being the chief revenue officer, he was the chief administrator and chief judicial officer on the local level. Around the district magistrate was a local administrative staff which could enforce higher decisions at the local levels. It had some concern for welfare activities, but its first attention was given to maintaining law and order and collecting revenue. The ICS men were well educated, administratively efficient, and loyal to their government. Congress politicians before independence looked upon them as conservative and disloyal to their nation. When independence came, some Indian politicians felt that the services were too concerned with maintaining law and order and too authoritarian to be able to adapt themselves to a government concerned with social and economic change and encouraging local participation in its development programs. The local politician especially distrusted the administrator. But the national leaders and political heads of departments, in both the state and the center, soon came to realize how much they had to depend upon British-trained administrative personnel.

Since independence, however, considerable effort has gone into broadening the character of the administrative services and of shifting some of the power of administration to local bodies. Some of the newer development programs, such as the Community Projects and the National Extension Schemes, have not been administered by the district magistrate and his administrative apparatus, but by new government departments. Several Indian states have also passed village *panchayat* legislation which aims at turning over to local village councils powers to develop sanitation and educational facilities, local roads, and so on. But few states have provided local councils with adequate revenue for expanding their functions.

While some change has occurred in the character of the administrative services, the complaint is still heard that the services are authoritarian and conservative in their outlook. Politicians speak of the need for soliciting public cooperation and public enthusiasm for development programs, but complain that administrators dampen enthusiasm and make no effort to encourage voluntary activities. A monument-building complex seems to have affected many bureaucrats (and many politicians as well)—the vision of the big dam, the big irrigation scheme, and the big fertilizer factory. The many smaller and less-expensive irrigation works which can be constructed with local participation are given less publicity and, according to some critics, less attention.

In both India and Ceylon, the functions of rule-making, rule application, and rule adjudication are in reality performed by those institutions of government specified in their constitutions as having responsibility for the performance of those functions. Only in Pakistan, with regard to the rule-making functions, has there been any disparity between theory and reality, but with the collapse of the constitution and the republic, theory has been brought more in line with political realities. In 1954 Pakistan's governor-general dismissed the prime minister and the Constituent Assembly, but this was done within the legal framework and sanctioned by Pakistan's Supreme Court. Not until 1958 did the president and the army feel that the situation had gotten totally out of hand. Why General Mirza decided at that time to abolish the republic, place the country under martial law, and appoint the commander-in-chief of the army as Pakistan's prime minister is not absolutely clear. The government had clearly been unable, if not unwilling, to cope with inflation and rampant corruption, and this may have been, as General Mirza publicly reported, the major factor. Then, too, it looked as if the elections scheduled for 1959 and widely heralded as Pakistan's first opportunity to establish stable rule promised more instability and uncertainty rather than less. The anti-military, leftist-oriented National Awami League and the Muslim orthodox Jamaat-i-Islami were energetically organizing themselves for the coming election campaign, and both represented a substantial threat to the army and to the existing framework. It may very well be that the growing disorder and corruption, combined with the prospect of less rather than greater order, precipitated this move of the army. But whatever the reason, the fact is that Pakistan's political framework was suspended and no political interests were powerful enough to prevent this from occurring. Both in theory and in reality, power was now in the hands of the prime minister and his appointed cabinet, backed by the army and the administrative services, free from responsibility to any legislative body. In the months which immediately followed the rise to power of the army, an effort was made to eliminate corruption, wipe out the black market, and lower food prices. What political framework will ultimately emerge is uncertain, but there can be little doubt that the army is likely to remain a major force in Pakistan politics. In the long run, however, it remains to be seen whether the army can mobilize individuals with the skills and enterprise to undertake the creative task of economic development.

V. POLITICAL INTEGRATION

The maintenance of national unity in the countries of South Asia is perhaps their most severe political problem. The future of representative government is closely related to how well and in what way national unity is maintained. Governmental stability and the capacity of governments to lead a program of modernization will also be affected by the extent to which national loyalties override loyalties toward caste, religion, or linguistic communities. Centuries of invasions and migrations, along with the absence of strong central governments over periods sufficiently long to enable varied cultures to be assimilated into some kind of "national" culture, have left the subcontinent divided.

Ceylon is divided ethnically between Tamils and Sinhalese; geographically, between the Tamil-dominated north and the Sinhalese regions to the south; nationality-wise, between the Ceylonese and the large Indian population; politically and culturally, between vernacular- and English-speaking elites, and between the low-country people along the coast and the up-country people of Kandy; ideologically, between the constitutional conservatives and the radical, totalitarian left.

Pakistan is divided geographically, culturally, and linguistically between its eastern and western halves; and, within West Pakistan alone, differences in language and culture separate the tribal Pathans, the desert-based Sindhis, and the more prosperous Punjabis. Pathan demands for a Pashtu-speaking state, and the ever-present threat of secession by East Bengal, continue to endanger the unity of Pakistan. Within East Pakistan, too, divisions exist between the Muslim majority and Hindu minorities. Schisms between political party elements and the military and administrative groups are bringing about drastic changes in the Pakistan political system; and, finally, an emotionally laden dispute continues between secularists, on the one hand, and Islamic elements, who advocate a more rigorous Islamic state, on the other.

India too has ethnic-linguistic divisions. Maharashtrian-Gujarati conflicts in Bombay, tribal-Hindu conflicts in Bihar and Assam, North Indian-South Indian conflicts in Madras, and Brahman versus non-Brahman conflicts in Madras and Maharashtra all illustrate the various forms of community identification which enter into politics. Here, too, as in Pakistan and Ceylon, conflicts exist between politicians motivated by linguistic, caste, and regional loyalties and politicians with "modern," nationalist, reconstructionist philosophies.

The fact that some of these community conflicts are geographically based means that potential secessionist movements exist. In Southeast Asia, where Chinese and Indian communities play an important role, they do not have a majority in any single region (with, of course, the notable exception of Singapore). The problem of integrating minorities in Thailand, Burma, Indonesia, and the Philippines is no doubt a serious one, but secession of Chinese and Indian minorities is out of the question. Revolution and guerrilla warfare rather than partition movements are conceivable. But, in South Asia, linguistic and cultural groups often demand provinces and, in some instances, countries of their own. We have already noted that the demand of Tamils in Ceylon for greater equality has recently been expressed in a movement for a Tamil-speaking province within a federal Ceylon. In India tribes of Orissa and Bihar have demanded a "Jharkhand" state, while in Assam the Naga tribes have called for an independent "Nagaland," and groups in South India have called for an independent "Dravidistan." In Pakistan, some Pathans have demanded a separate state and East Bengalis seek greater provincial autonomy.

Side by side with community conflicts exist various kinds of class conflicts. Peasant agitations, trade union strikes, demonstrations by educated unemployed, and the growing demands of the lower middle classes are features of South Asian politics. As we have seen, the national movements stimulated the articulation of interests, particularly in India and, since independence, increasingly in Ceylon and to a lesser extent in Pakistan.

South Asia is thus experiencing two revolutions at once. As in Europe between the sixteenth and the nineteenth centuries, the national state in South Asia has to bring together diverse loyalties; and as in the West of the nineteenth and twentieth centuries, new social classes have to be absorbed in the political process. Class war, with its forebodings of revolution, and community warfare, with its forebodings of civil war, are latent features of South Asian political life. Totalitarianism and balkanization are the twin dangers.

Integration is performed on two levels. On the one hand, government through its coercive powers seeks to maintain a unified national state. On the other hand, there is the task of getting the population as a whole and groups within the society to accept a set of rules and political institutions under which differences can be negotiated. India, Pakistan, and Ceylon have all had to use some measure of coercion to enforce unity.

The Indian government, with a national administrative system, a national and loyal army, a dominant political party, and an effective national leadership, has had to use its power to enforce law and order in several states. The central governments' extraordinary powers to take over a state in the event of an emergency have on several occasions been employed.

Pakistan's government shares with India and with Ceylon a British-created administrative system which reaches down into the village and which has, on the highest levels, a staff of educated and trained personnel equal to that of any country. Pakistan, however, is less fortunate than India or Ceylon in that, prior to independence, fewer Muslims entered higher education or the administrative services[26] than did Hindus in India or Buddhists in Ceylon. But Pakistan has developed its administrative services and, with American assistance, enlarged its army, and has used both to maintain a unified national state against pressures from East Pakistan. A strong army on the traditionally well-guarded northwest frontier stands as a bulwark against a secessionist movement, just as the Indian army has thus far crushed a secessionist movement among the Nagas of Assam.

Ceylon, too, has used the coercive powers of the central government to deal with the Sinhalese-Tamil agitation and in 1958 actually established martial law when large-scale violence broke out.

That Pakistan, Ceylon, and India can maintain their national identities through coercion is likely for the present at least, but a question exists as to whether liberal processes can be maintained for long if substantial coercion must continually be employed. While successful secession by any community is unlikely, attempts to secede or to agitate for greater autonomy may occupy the resources of the army, adminis-

[26] Pakistan had only about 100 ICS men at the time of independence. Ten years later, in 1957, the Civil Services of Pakistan had 287 officers.

tration, and government to such an extent that instability in government and ineffectiveness in attempts to develop the economy may result. The question is not only whether there will be national unity, but at what price?

In the long run, the capacity of government for effective rule depends upon widespread acceptance within the society of some basic norms about the ways in which differences can be reconciled. Cultural and political differences are common in most societies; the question is whether there are accepted rules by which to effect this reconciliation.

The subcontinent has no long tradition of democratic institutions or of respect for government and its laws, although several centuries of Western rule have contributed toward the development of such a tradition. Democratic groups in general, and government in particular, play an important role in attempting to develop a sense of national unity and respect for the existing democratic framework. But in all three countries there are groups—Communists, Trotskyites, Islamic sects, Hindus—who are not committed to the basic political framework. During the national movement and now after independence, nationalists in each country have made some effort to utilize religion and other traditional elements as a means of achieving integration. For Pakistan, Islam was of course the major force in bringing together the state, and, while Islam continues as a force to hold Pakistan together, it has also become a source of disunity between orthodox and secular elements. In India, the national leadership of Nehru has looked upon Hindu symbols as imperiling the secular state concept and as threatening to Christian and Muslim minorities. In selecting a national symbol, the leadership turned to the sculptured pillar of lions, the royal symbol of the Buddhist king Asoka, as a symbol drawn from neither Hinduism nor Islam. Postage stamps portray leaders of all religions. Islamic, Hindu, Christian, and Sikh holidays are all national holidays in India, giving India perhaps more national holidays than any country in the world. A small price to pay for national unity! India, Pakistan, and Ceylon each have publicized archeological sites and resuscitated classical learning. In India, the Taj Mahal, Sanchi, Bodh Gaya, and Khajuraho, centers of Islam, Buddhism, and Hinduism, attract Indian tourists as well as foreigners.

Pakistan's attempt to draw upon tradition has been a little more difficult, since as a country it came into existence only in 1947. One book, *Five Thousand Years of Pakistan*, tracing the growth of the culture of the northwestern region of the subcontinent to the prehistory of the Mohenjo Daro civilization, represents an effort to resurrect a tradition of great antiquity. Mughal history is now being researched, studied, and popularly disseminated.[27] Pakistan's ties with the Islamic world are being stressed. Islamic studies are urged upon young Muslim students, as the study of Sanskrit is urged upon the young Indian.

Ceylon, too, has used religious symbols to develop a sense of unity. The Buddhist Jayanthi, the 2,500th anniversary of the passing of the Buddha, was widely celebrated and has contributed to the major Buddhist revival now taking place in Ceylon and in Southeast Asia. But just as the growth of Islam in Pakistan has been of concern to Hindus, so has the growth of Buddhism in Ceylon been of concern to non-Buddhist minorities.

The new dams, steel mills, fertilizer factories, and cement factories also serve as symbols of unity, much like the great architectural achievements of the past. The dams in particular, with their massive concrete structure, their imposing appearance, and their dramatic effect, are major symbols of unity and are carefully exploited as such. The dropping of the first bag of cement at a dam site and particularly the first opening of the sluices are events so important that they call for the presence of the prime minister or the president. Pictures and films are circulated throughout the country. Even tours of villagers to the dam are arranged. From a political point of view, economic projects with a quick and dramatic payoff are important, for they give the country a sense of accomplishment and national purpose which is essential for the growth of national unity.

Foreign policy, too, may be a unifying force and may be utilized as such. Pakistan's antagonism toward India and her efforts to strengthen ties with the Islamic world serve to bring Pakistanis together. Groups which diverge on other issues will unite in opposition to India's position on Kashmir or in support of Pakistan's dispute with India over the use of the rivers which cross the two countries. India's neutralism and Nehru's importance as a world figure have contributed to a sense of national pride in India which cuts across political groups. India's strong stand on Kashmir has been supported by Hindu communal groups who are otherwise critical of government policy. Of the three countries, Ceylon is the only one in which foreign policy has been a major political issue rather than a unifying factor. The United National Party was generally pro-Western, but the Sinhalese nationalist MEP coalition has been neutralist.

[27] See *A Short History of Hind-Pakistan*, Karachi, Pakistan Historical Society, 1955.

Charisma as another symbol of unity decreased in importance in South Asia with the death of Ali Jinnah and Liaquat Ali Khan in Pakistan and D. S. Senanayake in Ceylon. Nehru is the last such major figure in South Asia. He has used his charismatic appeal for building a national state and for inculcating new values in the population. An incredibly large amount of the prime minister's time is devoted to public appearances—making speeches, opening dams, laying foundation stones, attending conferences, and the like. There are regional figures with some measure of charisma, and among the more religious-minded elements charismatic figures have some importance, but these figures do not contribute to the *national* unity of the country.

The task of converting the populations of South Asia to new values of economic development, national unity, the democratic process, and more equalitarian social institutions is pursued on many levels by many institutions. But the growth of these institutions does not ensure the success of the acculturating process. The educational system inculcates new values and new expectations but educated unemployment may direct them into violent and anti-democratic channels. Party workers of national political parties campaigning during elections often instill new loyalties, attempt to minimize the importance of caste and regional ties, and give the voter a sense of his own capacity to influence government through democratic means. But parties and candidates may also strengthen particularistic loyalties to caste and community in an effort to win votes. The media of mass communication extend information and encourage a sense of belonging to the nation—but the regional, vernacular press may be even more effective in cultivating local identification. The growth of an industrial working force and of political consciousness and organization on the part of the peasantry mean the growth of functionally specific, economic-oriented pressure groups seeking to influence government, but also working within its framework. However, such groups may be torn by caste and communal loyalties or may be manipulated by anti-democratic groups concerned with destroying the system.

The growth of mass communication, political parties, popular elections, interest groups, and literacy do not ensure that all the new values will prosper or even that national unity is likely to result. They only indicate that political awareness is likely to grow. Under the pressure of a rising population, rising expectations, and rising organization, modernization in some form is likely to continue. But what form of modernization, at what pace, and under whose auspices? These are the essential questions. Much depends upon the extent to which there is leadership in all segments of society, in government, political parties, trade unions, business, peasant association, newspapers, etc., which supports the leading institutions and emerging values and is committed to their preservation by ties of interest, ideology, or organization. The kinds of leadership which emerge, the values and *élan* which they share, and their relationship to the groups they lead may be as decisive in the success or failure of these countries as the policies pursued by governments.

One cannot easily make predictions as to the success of democratic institutions in South Asia or as to the capacity of governments to main- tain unified national states. No techniques now available—or likely to become available—can tell us whether Pakistan will remain united or India will remain democratic. As stable as the systems sometimes appear (as India's has since 1952, and Ceylon's seemed until 1956), it is im- portant to remember that these are societies in which new groups are constantly emerging into politics, where new leadership arises and old leadership disappears, and where institutions and values are not well entrenched. Splits within a major political party, an assassination, a foolish decision by the government—events which might shake some Western countries but not endanger their very structures of govern- ment—could turn South Asian countries away from national unity and political democracy and toward greater fragmentation or authoritari- anism.

We have described the mixed character of the way political functions are performed in the countries of South Asia. The communication net- work is a discontinuous one. Interests are only partly economically oriented and functionally specific, and partly expressions of communal sentiment. Not all interests are organized and new interests are emerg- ing. Not all interests which are organized are aggregated; some groups feel that the existing structures cannot satisfy their wants. Balanced against the way these process functions are performed are modern po- litical structures which make rules, apply them, and adjudicate them. Thus there is often a discrepancy between the way the political process functions and the way government has been set up to function.

Ever since independence, it has looked as if India and Ceylon were better able than Pakistan to work with the new institutions. In Ceylon and India a functioning party system has operated the democratic struc- tures. In contrast, Pakistan's political parties have not been able to operate the structure and the army and administrative services have had to play a more active political role. So far shared values, aggregation of diverse interests, submission to authority, and coercion have been sufficiently present in all three countries to keep these systems functioning and able in some measure to perform their self-imposed tasks of maintaining national unity and furthering economic development. In a world in which neighbors to the east and west—in Indonesia, Indo-China, Lebanon, and Iraq—have been plunged into civil war, the countries of South Asia have shown a relatively high degree of integration.

3. THE POLITICS OF

Sub-Saharan Africa

JAMES S. COLEMAN

....

I. BACKGROUND

The Physical and Human Setting

IN ITS GEOGRAPHICAL FEATURES, Africa is strikingly unique among the great continental masses of the earth's surface. Among the several unusual characteristics setting it apart from other continents, five stand out: the massive Sahara Desert, the world's largest arid waste, which stretches without a break from the Atlantic to the Red Sea and is nowhere less than a thousand miles wide; the historically impenetrable coastline, virtually devoid of natural harbors and throughout its vast length characterized by strong off-shore winds, sand bars, and inhospitable deserts or mangrove swamp-forests; its tropical character—squarely straddling the equator, three-quarters of its huge bulk lying within either the tropical rain-forest or the tropical savannah (see Map 2); the great African plateau south of the Sahara—a vast and monotonous landscape of level or slightly undulating surfaces broken only by such highland areas as those of Ruanda-Urundi or Kenya; and the African soil, which over large areas is of relatively poor quality. These distinctive features have been crucial, if not decisive, factors which have affected Africa's history, the patterns of political organization, and the interrelationships of its peoples.

The physical characteristics of the African continent largely account for four situations relevant to this study; namely, the historic division between Mediterranean Africa and Sub-Saharan Africa; the isolation of Sub-Saharan Africa and, in the past, the vulnerability of its peoples to exploitation and domination by external groups; the comparative smallness in scale, the variegated political systems, and the instability of the boundaries of traditional African societies; and the poverty and low density of the population. As for the first, there can be little question that the Sahara, a veritable ocean of sand and desolation, has in the

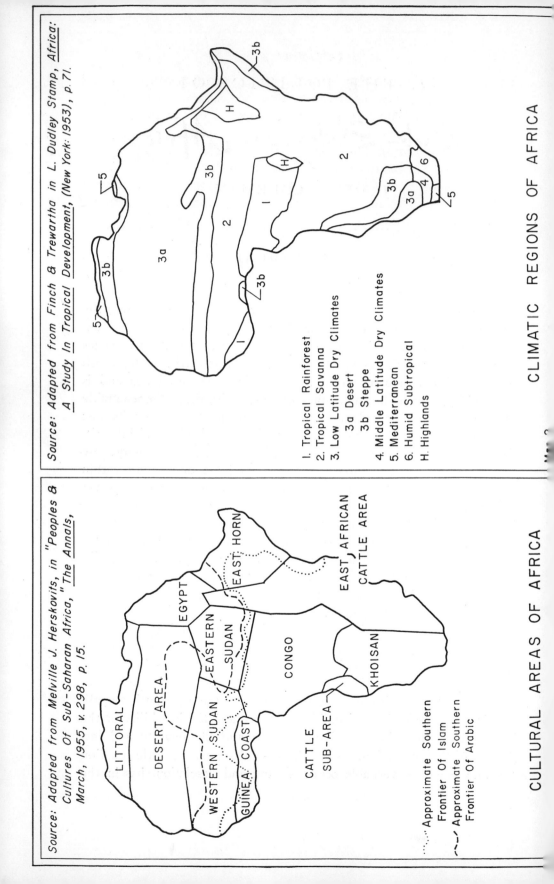

Source: Adapted from Finch & Trewartha in L. Dudley Stamp, *Africa:
A Study In Tropical Development*, (New York: 1953), p. 71.

1. Tropical Rainforest
2. Tropical Savanna
3. Low Latitude Dry Climates
   3a Desert
   3b Steppe
4. Middle Latitude Dry Climates
5. Mediterranean
6. Humid Subtropical
H. Highlands

CLIMATIC REGIONS OF AFRICA

Source: Adapted from Melville J. Herskovits, in "Peoples &
Cultures Of Sub-Saharan Africa," *The Annals*,
March, 1955, v. 298, p. 15.

LITTORAL
DESERT AREA
EGYPT
EASTERN SUDAN
EAST HORN
WESTERN SUDAN
GUINEA COAST
CONGO
EAST AFRICAN CATTLE AREA
CATTLE SUB-AREA
KHOISAN

········ Approximate Southern Frontier Of Islam
── ── Approximate Southern Frontier Of Arabic

CULTURAL AREAS OF AFRICA

past been a formidable barrier to human intercourse. Many scholars, and certainly most existing literature, accept the concept of two Africas— on the one hand, Mediterranean and Saharan Africa, with its historic cultural and religious links with the Middle East and the Muslim world; Sub-Saharan Africa, on the other. The interesting relationship between cultural area and climatic region illustrated by Maps 1 and 2 underscores this basic cleavage which has divided Africa in the past. Increasingly, however, African spokesmen emphasize the unity of Africa.[1]

The historic isolation of most of Sub-Saharan Africa, which continued for over three centuries after its shores were first charted, was the result of an interesting combination of physical barriers—the Sahara, the inhospitable coast which was immediately succeeded by desert, swamps, or forest, and the prevalence of various tropical fevers. Until the Congress of Berlin (1884-1885) European influences were limited to small coastal enclaves; but within the brief span of twenty-five years the whole continent was partitioned among the leading European powers.

Africa's isolation, coupled with the tropical rain-forest and the infertile soil of the great African plateau, also account for the comparative smallness in scale and the instability—and, hence, the vulnerability —of traditional African societies. The lack of intensive and continuous firsthand contact with extra-African cultures meant the absence of the enriching and stimulating effects of cultural infusion, particularly at the material level. The sheer density of the tropical forest in West Africa and parts of central Africa decreed small-scale, closely-knit village societies; and on the vast stretches of the tropical savannah in east, central, and southern areas, the poor soil and the lack of natural boundaries prevented continuous occupation for either agricultural or pastoral purposes—hence the absence of stability of settlement and lack of a continuous history. True, several historic African kingdoms flourished during the eighteenth and nineteenth centuries, but they were heavily concentrated in the great expanses of the Western Sudan.

Finally, the poor soil, the primitive state of technology, the widespread prevalence of human and animal diseases partly explain Africa's poverty and the low density of its population. Although in parts of

---

[1] At the recent conference of Independent African States (Morocco, Tunisia, Libya, United Arab Republic, Sudan, Ethiopia, Ghana, and Liberia) held in Accra in 1958, Prime Minister Nkrumah remarked that the former imperialist powers had been fond of talking about "Arab Africa" and "Black Africa," about "Islamic Africa" and "Non-Islamic Africa," about "Mediterranean Africa," and "Tropical Africa," and then declared: "Today we are one. If in the past the Sahara divided us, now it unites us." The French, of course, have always thought and acted in terms of the unity of the Sahara.

Africa there is considerable pressure of population on land resources (southern Nigeria, the Transkei in the Union of South Africa, southern Uganda, Ruanda-Urundi, and southern Nyasaland), there is no African region of any size in which the population density even approaches that of most of Asia. The continent as a whole, excluding desert areas, is very sparsely populated; according to some authorities, Africa steadily lost ground until recently in its relative world position. This general sparseness of the population has been one of the several factors which have affected the scale and stability of political organization.

The total population of Sub-Saharan Africa is approximately 140,-000,000, which represents about 5 per cent of the world's people. This population is made up of three distinct elements: Africans, 96 per cent; Europeans, 2½ per cent; and other non-Africans (Arabs, Levantines, Asians and Coloureds), 1½ per cent (see Table 1). Two features regarding the 3½ million European inhabitants should be noted. The first is that 80 per cent are concentrated in the Union of South Africa and Southern Rhodesia. Elsewhere they do not constitute more than 3 per cent, and in West Africa they are but a tiny fraction of the population. Secondly, the European groups in the several countries differ in regard to their permanency of residence and in the demands they make upon and expectations they have regarding the political system. In the Union of South Africa, Southern Rhodesia, and Kenya the majority of the Europeans are permanently settled on the land; they regard their country of residence as their home. In the Belgian Congo and Northern Rhodesia the majority of the Europeans have been engaged in industrial, commercial, and mining activities, and, at least until recently, have generally regarded themselves as temporary residents.

The same variations characterize the other non-African groups. The Asians, who make up the largest group, are heavily concentrated in the Union of South Africa, Tanganyika, and Kenya, where they are engaged almost exclusively in retail trade with the African communities. They assume permanency of residence. In the Union they are a segregated minority without political rights; while in Tanganyika and Kenya they have sought, and through the policy of "multi-racialism" the British government has given them, a disproportionate share in the political process. The Coloureds are the product of miscegenation in the Union and the Rhodesias and constitute a minority separate from all other groups. The Arabs are confined mainly to Zanzibar and the coast of Kenya. The Levantines (Greeks, Cypriots, Lebanese, and Syrians) are found mainly in West Africa, where, as traders and com-

TABLE 1
Area, Size, and Racial Composition of Population
of Political Systems in Sub-Saharan Africa

Countries by Type of Political System	Area (in thous. sq. mi.)	POPULATION				
		Total (in thous.)	Density (per sq. mi.)	Race (in %)		
				European	Other Non-African	African
AFRICAN CONTROLLED SYSTEMS						
Historic African States						
Ethiopia	390	12,000	30.8	a	a	a
Liberia	43	2,500	58.1	.04	b	99.96
New African States						
Ghana	92	4,894	53.2	.14	.04	99.82
Sudan	968	8,310	8.6	a	a	a
Nigeria	373	32,571	87.3	.05	b	99.95
Somalia	189	1,000	5.3	.45	b	99.55
Guinea	106	2,261	21.3	.3	b	99.7
Togoland	22	1,030	46.8	.1	b	99.9
Cameroons	166	3,200	18.5	.4	b	99.6
Senegal	81	2,093	25.8	1.6	b	98.4
Sudanese Republic	451	3,347	7.4	.2	b	99.8
Upper Volta	106	3,109	29.3	.1	b	99.9
Dahomey	44	1,535	34.9	.1	b	99.9
Mauritania	416	567	1.4	.1	b	99.9
Niger	495	2,127	4.3	.1	b	99.9
Ivory Coast	123	2,170	17.6	.5	b	99.5
Chad	496	2,253	4.5			
Central African Republic	238	1,082	4.5	.5	b	99.5
Republic of Congo	132	695	5.3			
Gaboon	103	407	3.9			
Emergent African States						
Sierra Leone	30	1,858	61.9	.05	.1	99.84
Uganda	80	5,357	67.0	.1	.9	99.0
TRANSITIONAL SYSTEMS						
Tanganyika	342	8,069	23.6	.3	1.0	98.7
Kenya	220	6,048	27.5	.8	3.0	96.2
Belgian Congo	905	12,666	14.0	.8	b	99.2
Ruanda-Urundi	21	4,111	195.8	.1	.1	99.8
EUROPEAN CONTROLLED SYSTEMS						
Union of South Africa	790	13,066	16.5	20.6	11.2	68.2
Fed. of Rhodesia & Nyasaland	(475)	(7,980)	(16.8)	(3.6)	(.4)	(96.0)
Southern Rhodesia	150	2,290	15.3	7.7	.6	91.7
Northern Rhodesia	288	2,110	7.3	3.1	.3	96.6
Nyasaland	37	2,576	69.6	.3	.4	99.3
Angola	481	4,145	8.6	1.9	.7	97.4
Mozambique	298	5,733	19.2	.9	.7	98.4

a No data available.   b Few; included in "European."

merçants, they constitute but a fraction of the population. Generally they have not assumed permanency of residence, and politically they are accommodationist in their attitudes toward the emergent African leadership groups.

Traditional Culture

The cultural diversity of Africa makes it exceedingly difficult to generalize about *a* traditional African culture.[2] European residents in Africa have either retained the culture of the European homeland from which they or their parents emigrated, or, like the Afrikaners, they have developed a distinctive "European" culture in Africa. Among the other non-African groups, the Levantines and Asians have also adhered to the culture of their national homeland. Indeed, the communal tensions between Hindu, Muslim, Sikh, and Goan groups in Africa are as virulent as in South Asia. The Coloureds in general shun African culture and blindly emulate European culture. The arabs of the northern Sudan and Zanzibar seek to preserve a distinctive way of life built upon Islam and their Middle Eastern heritage. Only the Africans could be regarded as having traditional cultures indigenous to Sub-Saharan Africa.

Culture is a concept applicable to any distinguishable human aggregation ranging from the inhabitants of a continent to a tribal or kinship group. At the most general level, and in contrast with other continental aggregations, one could perhaps loosely speak of a common African culture, at least in the material or technological realm. But such a conception is useless for systematic political analysis, which compels us to recognize Africa's cultural pluralism. Among the several criteria by

[2] According to a classification developed by Dr. C. G. Seligman in his *Races of Africa*, London, 1930, indigenous African peoples are broadly divided into seven main types: the Sudanese and the so-called "True Negroes" of West Africa, the Nilotic peoples of the Southern Sudan and Northern Uganda, the "Hamitic" peoples of the horn of Africa, the Bantu peoples of Central and South Africa, and the Hottentots and Bushmen of Southwest Africa. In terms of physical appearance the Hamites, Hottentots, and Bushmen can be broadly distinguished from the Sudanese, Negroes, Nilotes, and Bantu. The latter four groups constitute the overwhelming majority of the population, and although there are some physical differences among them, they share in common a dark skin, woolly hair, and other distinctive features. Seligman's classification has been subjected to an increasing amount of criticism on the ground that it is inaccurate or inadequate, particularly because the distinctions are made mainly in terms of linguistic criteria. Cf. Joseph H. Greenberg, *Studies in African Linguistic Classification*, New Haven, 1955, pp. 1-61; Lord Hailey, *An African Survey Revised*, 1956, New York, 1957, pp. 28ff. Greenberg has challenged many of the current assumptions about the relationship among culture, language, and race in Africa, particularly including the long-standing implication that peoples speaking languages of a "Hamitic" character are racially superior (pp. 52-54).

which African traditional cultures can be differentiated, three stand out: religion, mode of livelihood, and type of political system. The religious criterion is particularly important because Islamic culture largely provides the basis for the distinction, already drawn, between Mediterranean-Saharan Africa, where it predominates, and Sub-Saharan Africa, where it is largely absent (see Map 1).

The mode of livelihood is the principal criterion employed by Herskovits to classify the traditional cultures of Sub-Saharan Africa (see Map 1) into *pastoral societies*, which predominate in East, Central, and Southern Africa (his East African Cattle Area, Eastern Sudan, and part of the East Horn), and *agriculturally based societies* of West Africa and the Congo Basin (his Congo, Guinea Coast, and Western Sudan cultural areas.[3] In the pastoral societies, wealth, status, and prestige were achieved through the possession of the principal animal herded, although there were important exceptions.[4] Such societies were self-sufficient in food, and, as there was no agricultural surplus, little or no exchange of produce occurred; hence, towns or cities and the institution of the market were unknown. The population tended to be scattered and not permanently settled; hence political structures reflected the importance of the lineage and age grade societies and the prevalence of small locally autonomous groups. By contrast, the agriculturally based societies of West Africa and the Congo Basin had denser and more settled populations producing an economic surplus which permitted a degree of specialization of labor, either on tribal or craft lines. Such specialization facilitated trade, which meant the existence of market centers, towns and cities, and the emergence of a class structure. It is in this region that comparatively stable kingdoms and the medieval empires of the Western Sudan were found.

This broad distinction between the eastern pastoral area and the western agricultural area of Sub-Saharan Africa, advanced by the "culture area" school of anthropologists, is of limited usefulness in the delineation of traditional political cultures. All types are found in both areas. Moreover, it is a classification based exclusively on the mode of livelihood, and, while the latter is an important factor, it has not been the only one determining differences in political organization. For our purposes the character of traditional political systems is a more fruitful

[3] Melville J. Herskovits, "Peoples and Cultures of Sub-Saharan Africa," *The Annals*, No. 298, March 1955, pp. 15-19.

[4] For example, the Ngoni, where the possession of cattle was not the essential element in the prestige system; rather, the "principal index of power was the number of a man's dependents." See J. A. Barnes, *Politics in a Changing Society*, London, 1954, pp. 30ff.

criterion for distinguishing Sub-Saharan cultures. Here the classic distinction is that made by Fortes and Evans-Pritchard between societies having formal and explicit governmental institutions (state systems) and those societies where these are not present (so-called stateless societies).[5] This dichotomous typology has been criticized on many grounds, most particularly the implication it conveys that "stateless societies" are apolitical and do not have any political institutions at all.[6] Space does not permit a detailed examination of these issues here. For our purposes four types of traditional political systems can be usefully distinguished in terms of scale and the degree to which political authority is centralized and operates continuously through explicit institutions of government: (1) large-scale states, (2) centralized chiefdoms, (3) dispersed tribal societies, (4) small autonomous local communities.[7]

The first type is admirably represented by the Hausa-Fulani emirates of northern Nigeria. Here one finds a political elite of alien origin exercising continuous administrative and judicial control on a territorial basis through explicit governmental institutions, possessing a monopoly of military force, and supported by systematic taxation. The territorial organization and the class structure of the society were developed to the point that the kinship structure was completely dissociated from the political system. The elite was buttressed in its power by Islam, and particularly the doctrine *"addinimmu addinin biyayya ne"* (Hausa for "our religion is a religion of obedience"). Although this political pattern is found in its most developed form in northern Nigeria, its general features were characteristic of the several historic kingdoms and empires of the Western Sudan, and with certain variations it is found in other conquest states elsewhere in Sub-Saharan Africa.

The second type of system—the centralized chiefdom—was common

[5] Meyer Fortes and E. E. Evans-Pritchard, eds., *African Political Systems*, London, 1940, pp. 5-11. This typology has been subjected to considerable criticism as being both inadequate and confusing. See Paula Brown, "Patterns of Authority in West Africa," *Africa*, Vol. XXI, October 1951, pp. 261-278; B. Bernardi, "The Age-System of the Nilo-Hamitic Peoples," *Africa*, Vol. XXII, October 1952, pp. 331-332; M. G. Smith, "On Segmentary Lineage Systems," *The Journal of the Royal Anthropological Institute*, Vol. II, No. 86, July-December 1956, pp. 43-55; Phyllis Kaberry, "Primitive States," *British Journal of Sociology*, Vol. VIII, September 1957, pp. 224-234; and John M. Roberts and Gabriel A. Almond, "The Political Process in Primitive Societies," unpublished manuscript.

[6] As Roberts and Almond put it, the distinction "should be reformulated as a distinction between those (societies) in which the political structure is quite differentiated and clearly visible and those in which it is less visible." *Op.cit.*, p. 19.

[7] These categories are drawn in part from those of Daryll Forde in "The Conditions of Social Development in West Africa," *Civilisations*, Vol. III, 1951, pp. 471-489. The first two have formal centralized political structures, the last two do not.

throughout Sub-Saharan Africa. Although societies of this type differed enormously in scale, political power and prerogatives tended to be concentrated in the hands of a hereditary chiefly lineage or clan, usually that of the original leader of the "nuclear community" (i.e., Schapera's term for a ruling group which has conquered and finally amalgamated other peoples often of foreign stocks) or that of the chief of the first people to occupy what later became the tribal homeland. Thus, in origin centralized chiefdoms emerged either from the amalgamation of a number of different ethnic groups into one state through conquest by a ruling group or from the growth of a single tribe largely of one stock under a single chiefly family. In both instances, the ruling elite was recruited from the descendants of the royal lineage or clan and all other clans within the group were ranked in order of precedence, depending upon their relationship to the royal lineage.[8] In fact, the cohesion of the group frequently depended on the continued predominance of the ruling line.

The centralized chiefdoms were not necessarily autocratic; rather, there frequently existed a variety of countervailing forces which acted as checks on the arbitrary exercise of chiefly power. Councils of elders, age-grade or investitive societies, subordinate territorial chiefs, and religious officials were among the several institutionalized restraints upon autocracy. One found the core of the concept of constitutionalism and the assumption of a measure of popular participation—direct or indirect—in the political process.

The political system characteristic of dispersed tribal societies is distinguished from the two preceding types, not by the size of the group concerned—for, like the Tiv of Nigeria or the Nuer of the Sudan, such a society may number in the hundreds of thousands—but rather by the absence of any central organs of government or any individual or institution, such as a royal lineage, which represented and reflected the unity of the society as a whole. The largest political unit, in the sense of continuous submission to political leadership, may have been

[8] "Authority is almost invariably based on descent, whether within the family, the village, the district, or the nation, and the chief of the tribe combines executive, ritual, and judicial functions according to the pattern of leadership in each constituent unit. Like the family head he is a priest of an ancestral cult, believed in many cases to have a mystic power over the land, and he invariably claims rights over his people's labour and produce. . . . The next of kin of the chief may play a definite part in the political organization, may claim rights to territorial chieftainships, or villages, membership of tribal councils or smaller advisory bodies . . . or they may act as a regency council at the chief's death." Audrey I. Richards, "The Political System of the Bemba Tribe," in M. Fortes and E. E. Evans-Pritchard, op.cit., pp. 83-84.

no larger than the compound or the village community. As the Bohannans point out: "The only Tiv group of which one could say 'there must be someone responsible' was the compound."[9] Yet, within societies of this type there were a variety of institutionalized forms of cooperation and linkages operating to maintain a sense of unity among the population as a whole: the assumption of common descent from one original ancestor, the existence of recognized *ad hoc* procedures for the arbitration of disputes between different subgroups, traditions of kinship, pan-tribal associations such as age-grade associations, related religious dogmas, and common ceremonial rites. Thus, as Dike has stated regarding the Ibo, "Beneath the apparent fragmentation of authority lay deep fundamental unities not only in the religious and cultural spheres, but also . . . in matters of politics and economics."[10] The integrative and stabilizing factor in these societies was not a superordinate administrative, juridical, or military structure, but simply the fact, or assumption, of common origin and the ensemble of intragroup relations. The political system of the whole group was found in *ad hoc*, ever-shifting alignments at different levels of the society rather than in hierarchical, continuously functioning structures and institutions.

The fourth type, the autonomous local community, was distinguished from the dispersed tribal society primarily by its small size and the fact that even though it had cultural relations with adjacent groups it remained a distinguishable cultural and political entity. Fortes and Evans-Pritchard describe this type as one in "which even the largest political unit embraces a group of people all of whom are united to one another by ties of kinship, so that political relations are coterminous with kinship relations and the political structure and kinship organization are completely fused."[11] It is a type which existed throughout Sub-Saharan Africa, frequently being found in the interstices between societies of the other three types. The scores of small tribelets found in the pagan Middle Belt of Nigeria and the swamp areas of Northern Rhodesia are representative of this type system.

It is important to distinguish these four types of traditional political culture not only to emphasize Africa's diversity but also because such cultural variants help to explain the differential response of traditional societies to the impact of modernity as well as to recent and contemporary efforts to create larger-scale territorial political systems. The dif-

[9] Laura and Paul Bohannan, *The Tiv of Central Nigeria*, London, 1953, p. 10.
[10] K. Onwuka Dike, *Trade and Politics in the Niger Delta*, London, 1957, p. 246.
[11] *Op.cit.*, pp. 6-7.

ferent patterns of response and adaptation have also been partly determined by policies of colonial authorities toward the traditional political systems. Here the classic distinction is between the British policy of "indirect rule," in which traditional authorities were recognized and permitted to exercise a fairly wide range of customary powers under administrative supervision and statutory regulation on the one hand, and the French policy of "direct rule," in which traditional authorities, if used at all, were regarded only as subordinate officials in a monolithic colonial administration. In theory Belgian policy has been one of indirect rule, but in practice, outside the Watutsi kingdoms of Ruanda-Urundi, the authorities have been inclined toward direct administration. Although the Portuguese authorities have recognized traditional "native authorities," the latter are tightly controlled by a colonial administrative hierarchy. In general, the basic distinction is between the British policy of "differentiation," in which African forms have been given maximum recognition, and the policy of identity followed in varying degrees by the French and Portuguese, in which an effort has been made to create and progressively assimilate an indigenous elite drawn from the African mass. In the British system traditional structures, adapted to the requirements of modernity, were intended to be the principal medium through which Africans would achieve self-government, while, in the latter, Africans could achieve political self-realization only through assimilation to the culture and political system of the imperial country.

Although the British authorities vigorously pursued the policy of working through and developing traditional political systems, there were great differences in its application. In general the policy was most successful where there were identifiable traditional authorities commanding effective control over centralized structures of government as in the Fulani-Hausa conquest states of northern Nigeria; the Hima conquest states (inter-lacustrian kingdoms) of southern Uganda; the centralized chiefdoms of western Nigeria; the northern territories of the Gold Coast (now Ghana) and the protectorate of Sierra Leone; and the Bantu chiefdoms in Tanganyika, Northern Rhodesia, Nyasaland, and the High Commission territories of Swaziland and Basutoland. Considerably greater difficulty was encountered in the case of the dispersed tribal societies, such as the Ibo of eastern Nigeria, and the Kikuyu and Luo of Kenya, for here the traditional political system was less clearly articulated and the political process much more subtle. Indeed, in the case of the Ibo, administrative officers and government anthropologists devoted a decade of research in the quest for the elusive traditional structures.

The policy of indirect rule was affected not only by the variable character of traditional political systems, but also by temporal and areal differences in its application. In several territories (for example, Tanganyika, Nyasaland, and the Belgian Congo), a policy of direct rule was followed for the first several decades of European control, but it was subsequently replaced by a policy of indirect rule.[12] In other territories (for example, the Tribal Hinterland of Liberia and the inland rural areas of Portuguese Mozambique and Angola) the degree of directness or indirectness of central government rule has been determined by sheer expedience—direct rule has been employed in those areas where the government commands effective authority; indirect rule in the case of the more powerful chiefdoms. Thus there are wide differences in the degree to which the policy has been applied to the diverse African groups within a given territory.[13] It is not possible, therefore, to refer uncritically to Nigeria or to Uganda as a whole as an "indirect rule" territory, at least for purposes of systematic comparison and analysis.

The importance of traditional political systems for the study of modern political phenomena in Africa is illustrated by the following propositions:

1. Traditional political systems have largely shaped the political perspectives, orientation to politics, and attitudes toward authority of all but a small fraction (i.e., those one or more generations removed from the conditioning influence of their traditional milieu) of Africans involved in modern political activity. In the conquest states (emirates) of northern Nigeria, where Islam is admittedly a crucial factor, and in the Watutsi kingdoms of Ruanda-Urundi, one finds until recently

[12] During Germany's occupation of Tanganyika a thoroughgoing policy of direct rule prevailed; in 1926 the British administration inaugurated a policy of indirect rule. Indirect rule was not introduced in Nyasaland and the Belgian Congo until 1933. In all such cases it is highly unlikely that the real traditional authorities became part of the new system of indirect rule. In both Tanganyika and the Belgian Congo, for example, the slave trade, internecine wars, and several decades of direct rule had led to the disintegration of several of the traditional systems. Such cases of pseudo-indirect rule must be distinguished from the purer forms which prevailed in nothern Nigeria, southern Uganda, and the Barotse Kingdom of Northern Rhodesia.

[13] Nigeria and Uganda illustrate this point exceedingly well. In each country there are three main types of traditional societies (Hausa, Yoruba and Ibo in Nigeria; Buganda, other Hima States and the northern Nilotic groups in Uganda) to which the policy of indirect rule was differentially applied. The societies are listed in descending order of effectiveness of the policy.

an acceptance of elitism and deferential attitudes toward political authority. In centralized chiefdoms, such as those of the Yoruba in western Nigeria, there is considerable deference but also a deeply ingrained concept of constitutionalism. In the Ashanti states of Ghana, it is not unlikely that the attitudes of youth toward traditional leadership is partly the simple extension in time of the assumption that youth's associations (Asafo societies) have a right to initiate destoolment (i.e., dethronement) proceedings. The pronounced egalitarianism of members of the Tiv and Ibo groups (dispersed tribal societies) is clearly related to patterns of political socialization in traditional Tiv and Ibo culture.[14]

2. Where conquest states and centralized chiefdoms have been recognized and used as units in local administration by colonial authorities they tend to become foci for separatist subnationalisms in the modern territorial system, partly because they provide structures through which status and power can be secured, but also because they are a symbol of cultural continuity and thereby provide the cultural basis for a national sentiment.[15] Where such systems have been ignored or suppressed, as in the old kingdom of Dahomey, this tendency is less in evidence. Even in this category, however, there are some striking examples of the rebirth of tribal nationalisms. Most notable among these are the current efforts of nationalists of the Bakongo tribe in both the Leopoldville area of the Belgian Congo and the Republic of Congo (previously the Territory of Moyen-Congo of French Equatorial Africa) to establish a modern state coterminus with the historic Kingdom of the Congo.

3. The grouping of dispersed tribal societies with other type societies in a territorial system fosters the development of pan-tribal sentiment in the former, partly because of the greater interaction which modernity makes possible, but also because the tribe is the most obvious reference

[14] Note, for example, the observation of the Bohannans regarding the Tiv: "It is dangerous for any man to become prominent; he is immediately the target of mystical and physical malice. Tiv egalitarianism is more concerned with whittling everyone down to the same size than with giving everyone the same chance. A prominent man is considered dangerous; no one has any real confidence that he will not use for his own personal advantage every bit of power he can get." *Op.cit.*, p. 31. Much the same could be said for the Nuer of the southern Sudan.

[15] Also, as David E. Apter has noted: "The greater the degree of organic solidarity of the organized kingdom states, the greater the adaptability to colonial rule, but less to representative parliamentary government because (1) an increase in specialization as a result of westernization must be incorporated into the political hierarchy in the case of the politically well differentiated systems, or else threaten the existence of the hierarchy itself, and (2) in the case of the segmentary systems an increase in division of labor, having no hierarchy to endanger, has greater choice in the recruitment of its leadership, can incorporate more highly diverse goals and circulate elites with less dysfunctional consequences than more highly organized systems." Unpublished manuscript.

group in the competitive struggle for status in a situation of forced coexistence with other groups. This movement toward greater tribal unity, frequently dysfunctional to the development of territorial unity, is strengthened by official colonial policies aimed at the development of central all-tribal institutions, as with the Tiv and Birom of Nigeria, the Chagga and Sukuma of Tanganyika, and the Luo of Kenya.

4. Unless protected by official policy, small autonomous local communities become progressively assimilated to neighboring, culturally dominant, groups. Thus, in northern Nigeria small pagan groups have become assimilated to the dominant Hausa-Fulani culture; the Luo have assimilated small neighboring Bantu groups in western Kenya; and the Bemba of Northern Rhodesia have absorbed peripheral tribelets.

5. In several cases, the most effective nationalist leaders in the modern *territorial* societies have come from smaller tribal societies or autonomous local communities which traditionally have not threatened or do not presently challenge other groups in the emergent territorial society.[16]

Patterns of Western Impact

Mediterranean Africa has for centuries had close and continuous contact with the external world. The striking feature of Sub-Saharan Africa, however, is the comparative recency, unevenness, and intensity of the Western impact upon traditional African societies. The watershed in the Afro-European encounter in this vast area is 1885. In that year the European powers formally launched the scramble for Africa; thereafter territorial claims were legitimate only if there was effective occupation. Within two decades the continent was completely partitioned. For the next half century the whole of Sub-Saharan Africa, except for the historical accidents of Liberia and Ethiopia, was under variant forms of European colonial rule.

Prior to 1885 there were four types of external influences which impinged on African societies:

1. Commencing in the tenth century there was increasing contact via the famous caravan routes between the peoples of Mediterranean Africa—the Maghreb in particular—and those of the southern reaches

---

[16] Dr. Kwame Nkrumah (Ghana), Julius Nyerere (Tanganyika), and Harry Nkumbula (Northern Rhodesia) came from such small groups. By contrast, Dr. Nnamdi Azikiwe (Nigeria) and Joseph Kiwanuka (Uganda) have been handicapped in their claims to territorial leadership in part because of their identification with the Ibo and Baganda respectively.

of the Sahara and the northern savannah areas of the Guinea Coast (a cultural shatter zone known as the Western Sudan). The peoples of the Western Sudan were progressively Islamicized, an active trans-Saharan trade developed, and relatively large, though short-lived, states were formed.

2. At the southern tip of the continent, Dutch settlers (later joined by Huguenots and others) established themselves in the early part of the sixteenth century, and from then on moved northward until they met the Bantu Africans, who at that time were moving south.

3. Except for these early impingements at the extremities, it was the quest for slaves which was the basis for early contacts between Middle Africa and the external world. For several centuries before European governments established formal control, European slave dealers visited the West Coast to meet the heavy demands for slaves in the New World; and Arab slavers, operating south from Egypt (particularly in the southern Sudan), and on the mainland of the East Coast from Zanzibar, supplied the slave marts of the Middle East. These early contacts through the slave trade did not leave a lasting cultural impact (except possibly for the Arabicized portions of the Kenya and Tanganyika coastline, and parts of the Sudan). They were one of the causes, however, of intertribal warfare and the disorganization of the African community which preceded the European intrusion. They also left a legacy of suspicion and distrust of no little significance for an understanding of contemporary political phenomena, and particularly the psychology of nationalism.

4. In the fifteenth century the Portuguese established tenuous control over narrow strips of the coastline of what are now Mozambique and Angola, but the vast hinterland of these territories was not effectively occupied until the end of the nineteenth century.

Thus, until the last quarter of the nineteenth century the peoples inhabiting most of the bulk of Africa had had comparatively little continuous contact with the external world. Since then such contact has been increasingly intensive and widespread. It has taken many forms, however, so that today's political map of Africa presents a mosaic of political arrangements about which few generalizations can be made which are continental in scope.

At the outset it is necessary to distinguish between *traditional* African political systems previously discussed, and the *territorial* political systems which roughly coincide with the boundaries laid down by the imperial powers in their systems in Sub-Saharan Africa. They can be classified into five types falling into three major categories shown on Map. 3. In the category of *African-controlled systems* one finds the following types:

(1) *Historic African states* (the Kingdom of Ethiopia and the Republic of Liberia) in which culturally distinctive African minorities control the political system, ruling over the predominantly tribalized African majority.

(2) *New African states*, which for our purposes include not only those having full independence and membership in the United Nations (Sudan, Ghana, and Guinea), as well as those scheduled for full independence in 1960 (Somalia, Nigeria, Cameroons, and Togoland), but also those eleven former territories of French Afrique Noire which are new autonomous republics in the new French Community (Republics of Congo, Gaboon, Chad, Niger, Dahomey, Upper Volta, and Ivory Coast; the Central African Republic and the Mauritanian Islamic Republic; and the State of Senegal and Sudanese Republic currently linked in the new Federation of Mali).

(3) *Emergent African systems* (Gambia, Sierra Leone, Uganda, and British Somaliland) in which Africans are progressively acquiring increased control over the political system with the firm assurance of some form of self-government or independence.

The *Transitional systems* (Belgian Congo, Ruanda-Urundi, Kenya, and Tanganyika) comprise those territories in which there is a clear trend toward ultimate autonomy under African leadership, a trend reinforced by recent declarations by the colonial governments concerned that self-government is the ultimate goal of policy. In the *European controlled systems* this trend and the goal of African self-government are completely absent. These systems include not only the European oligarchic states of the Union of South Africa and Southern Rhodesia, in which resident European minorities dominate the political system as a result of differentiating legislation (delimitation of separate European and African areas, pass laws controlling movement and residence of Africans, legalized color bar, and the absence of African representation in central organs of government), but also the Portuguese overseas provinces of Mozambique, Angola, and Guinea, which are at present integral units in an authoritarian Portuguese state. Northern Rhodesia and Nyasaland, as constituent parts of the Federation of Rhodesia and Nyasaland, also fall into this same category, although the persistence and spread of autonomist African nationalism in these territories could result in their moving into the transitional category.

Political Systems in Sub-Saharan Africa

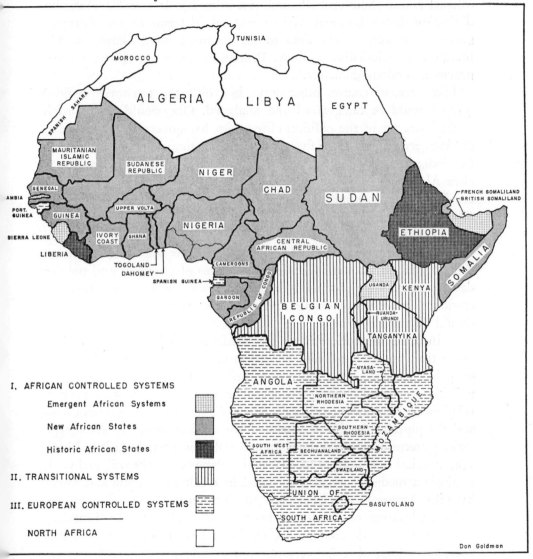

MOROCCO
TUNISIA

ALGERIA
LIBYA
EGYPT

SPANISH SAHARA

MAURITANIAN
ISLAMIC
REPUBLIC

SUDANESE
REPUBLIC

NIGER
CHAD
SUDAN

AMBIA

SENEGAL

PORT.
GUINEA

GUINEA

UPPER VOLTA

NIGERIA

ETHIOPIA

FRENCH SOMALILAND
BRITISH SOMALILAND

SIERRA LEONE

IVORY
COAST

GHANA

LIBERIA

TOGOLAND
DAHOMEY

CENTRAL
AFRICAN REPUBLIC

CAMEROONS

SPANISH GUINEA

SOMALIA

GABOON

UGANDA
KENYA

REPUBLIC OF CONGO

BELGIAN
CONGO

RUANDA-
URUNDI

TANGANYIKA

NYASA-
LAND

ANGOLA

NORTHERN
RHODESIA

MOZAMBIQUE

SOUTHERN
RHODESIA

SOUTH WEST
AFRICA

BECHUANALAND

SWAZILAND

UNION OF
SOUTH AFRICA

BASUTOLAND

I. AFRICAN CONTROLLED SYSTEMS

Emergent African Systems

New African States

Historic African States

II. TRANSITIONAL SYSTEMS

III. EUROPEAN CONTROLLED SYSTEMS

NORTH AFRICA

Don Goldman

This classificatory scheme has certain advantages in that it draws a distinction between radically different types of African systems (Liberia vs. Ghana) as well as variant patterns of development under one colonial power (Southern Rhodesia vs. Nigeria). It avoids the classical distinction drawn between African systems in terms of the European governing power, or according to the legalistic nomenclature used in literature on colonialism (colony, Protectorate, trust territory, overseas province, condominium, etc.).

There are, of course, other ways in which the territorial political systems could be categorized and analyzed. One would be according to the character of the political elite which has governed and mediated the Western impact. Here five types can be distinguished (see Table 2): (1) indigenous African (of which Ethiopia is the only instance), (2) alien African (Liberia), (3) alien European (South Africa and Southern Rhodesia), (4) mixed alien colonial-settler oligarchy (Kenya and Northern Rhodesia), and (5) alien colonial (the remainder of Africa's political entities). These variant modes in which Western ideas, institutions, and forces of acculturation have had their impact upon African societies help to account for differing patterns of economic and political development. Some of these will be illuminated in the subsequent discussion of processes of change. At this point two general propositions should be stated:

1. In those territories where the mediating political elite has been other than an alien colonial bureaucracy, there are three dimensions of political-analysis—the distinctive political realm of intra-oligarchic politics (Americo-Liberian, European settler), the pattern of political relationship between the culturally alien oligarchy and the African mass, and the pluralistic political world of the African mass. In these territories patterns of political development reflect in part the cultural heritage, political ideology, and external relations of the oligarchy. In Ethiopia a medieval monarchy rooted in a culturally dominant minority (the Amharas) has preserved until recently a basically stagnant society, admitting only selected features of modernity. In Liberia, a tiny minority of descendants of ex-slaves has struggled to maintain what has amounted to but tenuous control over a tribalized hinterland mass, and has emulated Western political forms (including techniques of colonial administration) in which until recently only the oligarchy directly participated. In the European oligarchies there has been wholesale importation of Western political institutions and processes mainly for use of the oligarchy, and direct colonial administration of the African

mass. The real difference among these several oligarchic systems is found in the economic realm. While Ethiopia has remained relatively stagnant, and Liberia has only begun to develop economically, the full impact of Western commercialism and industrialism has been felt in the European oligarchic states. This has had profound implications as regards the level of social mobilization and the political aspirations of the African mass.

2. In those territories where the only mediating political elite has been an alien colonial bureaucracy, there has been and is no separate political realm of intra-oligarchic politics. The differential impact of the West, and the resulting variations in political development and the character of politics, have been determined by differences in colonial policies regarding political objectives, mode of administration of the tribalized mass, roles permitted the new African elite, freedom for political activity, and economic development. Some of these differences are shown in Table 2 and will be examined subsequently in greater detail. They all reflect the political theory and institutions prevalent in the metropolitan country, with modifications made necessary by the realities of the African situation. For reasons noted subsequently, African elites have progressively acquired a dominant role in the political process in French and uniracial British territories. Here intra-elite politics is a new and crucial dimension for political analysis.

Another possible basis for differentiating territorial systems is the mode of administration of the tribalized African mass employed by the mediating political elites. Here the distinction would be between direct rule and indirect rule territories. Although in the abstract these two forms of administration may be thought of in a dichotomous sense, they are in reality but polar extremes on a continuum. As previously noted, in practice these forms have not been applied consistently either over time or to the different traditional authority systems within single territories. Moreover, there are tremendous variations in forms of direct and indirect rule. As a consequence, the latter are not suitable criteria for the systematic classification and comparison of *territorial* political systems.

With these reservations, there are certain general propositions which can be stated regarding the political consequences of the application of these variant forms of administration.

1. Where indirect rule has been employed most effectively (e.g., the chiefdoms of northern Ghana, the Hausa-Fulani states in northern Nigeria, the Buganda and other Hima states of southern Uganda, the

TABLE 2

Summary of Selected Features of
African Political Systems

Countries by Type of Political System	Character of Political Elite Mediating the Western Impact	Mode of Government of Tribalized African Mass	Policy toward Westernized African Class
AFRICAN CONTROLLED SYSTEMS			
Historic African States			
Ethiopia	Indigenous	Direct	Assimilation
Liberia	Alien African	Mixed	Assimilation
New African States			
Ghana			Early exclusion;
Sudan		Indirect	subsequent ac-
Nigeria			ceptance as
Somalia			successor elite
Guinea Mauritania			
Togoland Niger			Assimilation; sub-
Cameroons Ivory Coast			sequent ac-
Senegal Chad	Alien colonial	Direct	ceptance as
Upper Volta Gaboon			successor elite
Dahomey Sudanese Rep.			
Central African Republic			
Republic of Congo			
Emergent African States			Early exclusion;
Sierra Leone		Indirect	subsequent ac-
Uganda			ceptance as
			successor elite
TRANSITIONAL SYSTEMS			
Tanganyika	Mixed: alien	Indirect	
Kenya	colonial and	Direct	Exclusion; recent
	European set-		partial accep-
	tler		tance in poli-
Belgian Congo	Alien colonial	Mixed	tical system
Ruanda-Urundi		Indirect	
EUROPEAN CONTROLLED SYSTEMS			
Union of South Africa	European settler	Direct	Exclusion
Southern Rhodesia			
Northern Rhodesia	Mixed: alien	Indirect	Exclusion; recent
Nyasaland	colonial and		partial accep-
	European set-		tance in polit-
	tler		ical system
Angola	Alien colonial	Direct	Assimilation
Mozambique			

266

Watutsi kingdoms of Ruanda and Urundi, and the Barotse Kingdom in Northern Rhodesia) the following results have occurred:

(a) The task of political integration and building new political communities on a territorial basis has been made more complicated and difficult. The traditional African groups concerned have become the foci of separatist movements; they have also provided the ethnic basis for political parties functioning in the territorial political arena. This has been strikingly evident in both Nigeria and Uganda during the past five years.

(b) In the setting up of new institutional structures there has been strong pressure exerted for federal, rather than unitary, systems of territorial government. The federal-unitary issue has been at the heart of the politics of Ghana, Nigeria, and Uganda as they have approached or crossed the threshold of independence.

(c) The tension between traditional elites, preserved under indirect rule, and modernist nationalist leaders, who constitute the new African elite, has been much more in evidence. In some areas there has been open hostility (e.g., in Ghana and northern Nigeria) and in other areas an uneasy alliance (western Nigeria).

(d) There has been a distinctive pattern of nationalist development in that modern agitational activity has been directed against the traditional elites as well as against the colonial power (except, of course, where the latter has affronted the entire group as in the British deposition of the Kabaka of Buganda). Thus, in the Hausa-Fulani states political agitation has been directed primarily at the *Filanin gida* (Fulani aristocracy), in the Buganda Kingdom at the Kabaka's ministers, in the Kingdoms of Ruanda and Urundi at the Watutsi aristocracy, and so forth. The existence of such groups within a territory has militated against the formation of comprehensive nationalist parties in the agitation for territorial independence.

2. Where direct rule has been employed most systematically and effectively, as in French territories, the new African elite has been more cosmopolitan in outlook, more attracted to a unitarian political system, less obstructed by traditional elites, and better able to organize and sustain comprehensive nationalist parties.

In addition to these two factors—the character of the mediating political elite and the mode of tribal administration—there are two other variables crucial to an understanding of the differing patterns of political response and adaptation to the Western impact. Both concern the policy of the mediating political elites, namely: the roles prescribed for the

Western-educated subaltern class (hereinafter called the new African elite), and the degree of freedom allowed for political activity. As for the first, African territories can be divided broadly into those where the mediating political elites practiced assimilation, either as an explicit policy (French and Portuguese Africa) or by accepting it as a fact (Liberia and Ethiopia), and those where they practiced exclusion, either explicitly and completely (Union of South Africa), or implicitly, but to varying degrees somewhat less than absolutely (British and Belgian Africa). Assimilation and exclusion here refer to acceptance or non-acceptance of the new African elite into the ranks of the mediating political elite. In practical terms this has meant participation or non-participation in the higher bureaucracy and central institutions of government of the territories concerned.

Once this broad distinction is made, policy periods (prenationalist and nationalist) should be distinguished. During the early prenationalist stages of British administration it was not anticipated that educated African elites would ever displace the colonial bureaucracy. In British uniracial territories (Ghana, Nigeria, etc.) it was envisaged that after several generations of colonial tutelage African native authorities would be developed sufficiently to perform the local functions of modern government, but the central bureaucratic superstructure would remain indefinitely in British hands. In British multiracial territories (Southern Rhodesia, Kenya, etc.) it seemed natural progressively to devolve control over territorial governments to the "kith and kin" residents (i.e., the settlers), who would thereby inherit the functions of trusteeship over the African mass. In both groups of territories the Western-educated African was destined to be a permanent subaltern in the central government of the country.

The growth of African nationalism during and since World War II—a development which has been, in part, a reaction against such exclusion and role limitation—compelled the British government to reverse their earlier assumptions, provide meaningful political roles to the claimant African elite, and redefine or specify their political goals. Since 1945 in the uniracial territories the British have shifted completely from a policy of exclusion to one of accepting and working with African elites, who they acknowledge to be the presumptive heirs to power. In the multiracial territories the policy of exclusion has been abandoned and a policy of multiracialism affirmed. The latter policy, however, has been rejected by African nationalists and in Uganda ultimate African (uniracial) self-government has been conceded, and according to current developments it is quite clear that it will also be conceded in Kenya and Tanganyika. The real struggle will take place in the multiracial territories of the Federation of Rhodesia and Nyasaland between African nationalists aspiring to the Ghana model and the European settlers ever more attracted to the South African model.

In the Portuguese and Belgian territories, and until recently also the French territories, the new African elite has been just as completely excluded from *effective* participation in the mediating political elite as in British territories. There are, however, three significant differences: (1) the policy of assimilation not only removed the sting of racial inferiority implicit in the British policy of differentiation and exclusion, but it also conferred status; (2) the goal of self-government, repeatedly affirmed but never defined by the British, was not posited by the other powers, hence there were no ambiguities arising from a promise withheld; and (3) the British (and latterly the French) have allowed greater freedom for political activity. The African elites in British Africa have been more conspicuously nationalistic not only because their members were denied status, but also because they were permitted greater freedom to proclaim and to seek their goals.

The impact of, and the African response to, Western institutions and ideas has varied considerably because of differences in the freeness of the milieu. Here one should first distinguish between oligarchic states, in which effective political freedom exists—if it exists at all—only for the oligarchy, and all other systems. In British uniracial territories (now the emergent African states) there has been greater freedom for political activity than elsewhere. In British multiracial territories limitations, both overt and subtle, have been imposed upon African political activity. In French territories there was little political freedom outside of Senegal prior to 1945. Since that year, however, the area of freedom has greatly expanded. In Belgian and Portuguese systems there has been little political freedom permitted, although the Belgians have recently made a few concessions. The implications of these variations for modern political activity will be analyzed subsequently; here the following propositions can be stated: (1) In areas of freedom the formation and development of political groups has followed a more conventional pattern, namely, the formation of comprehensive nationalist parties, which have, in turn, led to competing parties as political concessions have been secured from the colonial power. (2) In areas of limited or no freedom, Africans have been more attracted to messianic and puritanical religious movements, or to terrorism and violence, or they have reconciled themselves to accommodation and conformity to the dominant elements in the society.

These, then, have been some of the factors conditioning the Western impact—the character of the mediating political elite, the form of tribal administration, the policy toward the new African elite, and the freeness of the milieu. These and other considerations have in turn affected the operation of certain basic processes of change, such as urbanization, commercialization of land and labor, and Western education. The latter have led to certain basic changes in the social structure, in dominant values and operative ideals, and in the scale of the political community. These several processes of change will be examined in the following section.

II. PROCESSES OF CHANGE

The striking feature of modern political phenomena in Africa is their transitional character. This compels us in our political analysis to focus upon patterns of change, to employ developmental models rather than equilibrium models. The phenomena are largely the product of the revolutionary changes provoked by the impact of modernity upon the structure of traditional African societies, and upon the values and belief systems of peoples conditioned by an entirely different historical experience. These changes are so complex and variant that it is only the exercise of sheer arbitrariness which permits us to focus upon a limited number of the processes by which these changes have occurred, namely, urbanization, commercialization, and Western education.

Urbanization (see Table 3)

The process of urbanization commands special attention because of two facts: urban centers have been the principal arenas of acculturation, and African politics are primarily urban politics. With few exceptions there were no cities in pre-European Africa.[17] Thus, urban life is a new experience for most Africans. The new cities accelerated the intensification of the division of labor. As urban Africans became increasingly dependent upon their occupational specialties or salaried jobs they lost the economic security of the lineage and the self-sufficient rural community. The impersonality, heterogeneity, and competitiveness of urban life accentuated their personal insecurity as well as their individualism which became more pronounced as they sought status and

[17] Yorubaland in western Nigeria is one of these fascinating exceptions. See William R. Bascom, "Urbanization among the Yoruba," *American Journal of Sociology*, Vol. LX, March 1955, pp. 446-453.

TABLE 3

Urbanization, Literacy, and
Gross National Product in Sub-Saharan Africa

Countries by Type of Political System	Per Cent of Population in Cities of Over		Literacy (in %)	Per Capita Gross National Product (in US $)
	5,000	100,000		
AFRICAN CONTROLLED SYSTEMS				
Historic African States				
Ethiopia	a	2.6	1-5	54
Liberia	1.2	.0	5-10	103
New African States				
Ghana	12.0	3.5	15-20	135
Sudan	a	3.5	5-10	100
Nigeria	9.4	4.3	10-15	70
Somalia	a	.0	1-5	a
Togoland	4.8	.0	5-10	a
Cameroons	5.8	3.8	5-10	a
French West Africa	9.6	1.9	1-5	58
French Equatorial Africa	5.3	2.1	1-5	58
Emergent African States				
Sierra Leone	4.8	.0	5-10	a
Uganda	0.7	.0	25-30 ⎫	
TRANSITIONAL SYSTEMS			⎬	61[b]
Tanganyika	2.7	1.1	5-10 ⎪	
Kenya	4.8	3.4	20-25 ⎭	
Belgian Congo	8.0	4.1	35-40 ⎱	98
Ruanda-Urundi	1.6	.0	5-10 ⎰	
EUROPEAN CONTROLLED SYSTEMS				
Union of South Africa	(23.6)[c]	27.7	40-45	381
Southern Rhodesia	12.8	6.7	20-25 ⎫	
Northern Rhodesia	18.4	.0	20-25 ⎬	134
Nyasaland	1.1	.0	5-10 ⎭	
Angola	6.1	4.3	1-5 ⎱	70
Mozambique	2.8	1.6	1-5 ⎰	

[a] No data available.
[b] Figure is for Uganda, Tanganyika, and Kenya combined.
[c] African population only.

prestige within the urban social structure. The cities were also centers for intensive acculturation, for it was there that Africans came into daily and intimate contact with all aspects of modernity. Urban life gave birth to a new and assertive leadership and to a variable and easily manipulated mass following.

Once these general consequences of urbanization are noted, however, several distinctions and qualifications should be made. As with all other developments in Africa there have been wide variations, depending in particular upon the policy of the mediating political elite and upon the racial character of the population. Four patterns of urbanization can be distinguished. The first, characteristic of the urban centers of French and British West Africa and of Dar-es-Salaam, Tanganyika, is one of uncontrolled immigration into the urban center without tribal segregation as to residence therein. It is in these centers that there has been a relatively unfettered development of nationalist activity and urban politics. The second pattern, characteristic of most British East and Central African cities, is one where European settlers (through their township boards and municipal councils) have exercised complete control over the urban African, allocating his housing (rigidly segregated from European areas), controlling his movements and activity, but not necessarily prescribing tribal grouping. The third pattern, found in the industrial and mining cities of the Union of South Africa and in the mine compounds on the Copperbelt in Northern Rhodesia, is one similar to the second, but with the added prescription of tribal grouping, under headmen imported from the tribal homeland. Ostensibly this policy was meant to minimize the disruptive influence of urban life, particularly since it was not contemplated that Africans would become permanently urbanized. African leaders, however, regard it as a stratagem of divide-and-rule designed to prevent mobilization of a multi-tribal nationalist following. The fourth pattern, distinctive for the Belgian Congo, is one of official control, no tribal segregation, and family stabilization. The Belgians have accepted the inevitability and desirability of permanent African urbanization, and accordingly have concentrated on building housing, stabilizing family life, and creating an urban middle class.

There are four special aspects of urban development which have a direct bearing upon modern political development. The first is that most of the new cities are not agglomerations of "detribalized" and disorganized individuals, as has been popularly assumed. Compensating mechanisms and developments have cushioned the corrosive impact of urban life. Kinship associations and tribal unions have emerged as instruments for maintaining lineage and tribal attachments and also of creating a sense of belonging and relatedness in the city. Moreover, new primary-group identifications have been established. Thus, most urban African aggregations have some form of structure; they are not globs of humanity. And it is upon these structures—the network of tribal and urban associations—that nationalist movements and political parties have been based.

A second consideration is the effect of official policies aimed at Africanizing the ownership and management of business activity in the African residential areas of the new cities. In most urban centers non-Africans have held a virtual monopoly in petty retail trade. On the West Coast it has been the Levantine petty shopkeeper, on the East Coast the Indian. In the Belgian Congo and Southern Rhodesia, however, the governments have excluded this alien middle class as part of a policy of encouraging the development of an African business class. Elsewhere one of the most bitter grievances of the African is the monopoly held by the alien shopkeeper. It is possible that one of the several reasons for the accommodationist and non-political outlook of the Congolese and Rhodesian African merchant in the past has been the opportunity to acquire wealth and prestige through commercial operations in the new cities.

A third factor affecting political development is geopolitical in character: the spatial distribution of urban centers within a territory. On the West Coast and in the Sudan, Uganda, and Tanganyika the epicenter of political life has been a single major city which has also been the territorial capital (Dakar, Bamako, Abidjan, Freetown, Accra, Lagos, Khartoum, Kampala, and Dar-es-Salaam). This permitted effective concentration of political activity at one point, and thus the possibility of mobilizing and maximizing political strength with greater ease. In those territories having two or more major cities, such as Northern Rhodesia (Lusaka vs. the Copperbelt cities), Southern Rhodesia (Bulwayo vs. Salisbury), Kenya (Nairobi vs. Mombasa), and the Belgian Congo (Leopoldville vs. Elizabethville), African political leadership has been dispersed, if not competitive, and it has been far more difficult to organize a comprehensive nationalist party on a territorial basis.

A final consideration in the relationship between urbanization and political phenomena is the special role played by a dominant indigenous group. In many territories, urban politics, and to a certain extent territorial politics, have been conditioned by the special position held, or disproportionate influence exerted, by such a group. Thus, in Freetown, Sierra Leone, it has been until recently the entrenched Creole oligarchy; in Accra and Lagos the "old families"; in Kampala the Baganda, who in fact control the city, and in Mombasa (Kenya) and Dar-es-Salaam (Tanganyika) the Swahili old residents. In the latter case, for example, the Christianized nationalist leaders from the hinterland of Tanganyika have found it necessary to give the Swahili elements a disproportionate role on the central committee of the Tanganyika Africa National Union as a stratagem to ensure effective political influence in Dar-es-Salaam, the capital city.

Commercialization of Land and Labor

One of the most fundamental of the changes now in progress throughout Sub-Saharan Africa is the rapid shift from an almost wholly subsistence economy, based upon the cooperative bonds of the lineage and a variable, but comparatively stabilized system of stratification, to a dynamic money economy based upon the cash nexus, individual profit, and wage employment. This shift has tended to weaken lineage attachments, to give birth to new social classes, to create new values, and to open up new opportunities and methods of accumulating wealth and acquiring prestige. Thus, commercialization in Africa has, in general, accelerated the processes of restratification, of secularization, and of expansion in scale of the political community.

As the data in Table 4 indicate, however, commercialization has not taken place uniformly, nor have its consequences been the same. As with urbanization, there have been variant patterns, of which four can be distinguished. The first, represented by Ethiopia, is quite distinct in that for historical and policy reasons an extremely small percentage of the population has been drawn into the money economy.[18] Commercialization of the oligarchic states of Liberia, Union of South Africa, and Southern Rhodesia (and the territories of Kenya and Northern Rhodesia) follows another quite different pattern, the distinguishing characteristic of which is the disproportionate benefits accruing to the oligarchy (see Table 5). In Liberia, for example, commercialization thus far has operated to strengthen the existing system of stratification, although in time the laborers on the rubber plantations and in the iron ore mines may emerge as a new class which will challenge the present

[18] There are several reasons for this, among which are its self-imposed isolation, the Italian interlude, and the Emperor's apparent opposition, possibly on political grounds, to the emergence of an independent middle class.

TABLE 4

Degree of Commercialization
of African Land and Labor[a]

Countries by Type of Political System	% of Cultivated African Land[b]			% of Adult African Men in Commercialized Sector[c]		
	In Export Crops	*In Crops for Domestic Markets*	*In Subsistence Crops*	*Wage Employ-ment*	*Agri-cultural Pro-duction*	*Subsis-tence Agri-culture Sector*
AFRICAN CONTROLLED SYSTEMS						
New African States						
Ghana	45	30	25	15	64	21
Nigeria	16	25	59	4	39	57
French West Africa	9	10	81	5	18	77
French Equatorial Africa	22	5	73	15	23	62
Emergent African States						
Sierra Leone				8		
Uganda	28	5	67	12	29	59
TRANSITIONAL SYSTEMS						
Tanganyika	7	15	78	19	18	63
Kenya	2	5	93	25	5	70
Belgian Congo	17	25	58	30	29	41
EUROPEAN CONTROLLED SYSTEMS						
Southern Rhodesia	0	15	85	40	9	51
Northern Rhodesia				60[d]		
Nyasaland				34[d]		
Angola				50		
Mozambique				32[d]		

[a] The figures shown do not represent absolute divisions of land or persons between the commercialized and the subsistence sectors. Much land and many Africans are involved in both sectors.

[b] Figures are either those for 1950 (Tanganyika, 1952) or averages for periods covering about 1947-1950.

[c] Figures are for 1950, except Sierra Leone, 1952, and Mozambique, Northern Rhodesia, and Nyasaland, 1953.

[d] Includes migrants working in other territories but not migrants from other territories.

Sources: U.N., Department of Economic Affairs, *Enlargement of the Exchange Economy in Tropical Africa*, New York, 1954, pp. 14, 17 (U.N. Doc. E/2557, ST/ECA/23); "The Development of Wage-Earning Employment in Tropical Africa," *International Labour Review*, Vol. LXXIV, September 1956, p. 242.

TABLE 5

African Participation in the Money Economy[a]

Selected Countries by Type of Political System	African Per Capita Money Income (in $)	Source of African Money Income (in %)		Racial Distribution of Net Geographical Money Income (in %)			Racial Contribution to Geographical Product (in %)[b]	
		Wages	Producers Income	African	Non-African	Public	African Private Enterprise	Non-African Private Enterprise
AFRICAN CONTROLLED SYSTEMS								
New African States								
Ghana	68.2	8	92	67	18	15c	70-75	20-25
Nigeria	20.9	10	90	76	10	14c	75-80	10-15
Emergent African State								
Uganda	21.2	24	76	53	29	18c	60-65	30-35
TRANSITIONAL SYSTEMS								
Kenya	11.3d	74	26	22	74	4	5-10	80-85
Belgian Congo	22.7	63	37	39	60	2	10-15	75-80
EUROPEAN CONTROLLED SYSTEMS								
Southern Rhodesia	35.5	89	11	24	74	2	under 5	85-90
Northern Rhodesia	17.5	95	5	13	86	1	under 5	90-95

a Figures are for 1952, except Ghana and Nigeria, 1950/51, and Kenya, 1951.
b Public contribution omitted.
c Includes profits of marketing boards.
d 1952.

Source: U.N., Department of Economic and Social Affairs, *Scope and Structure of Money Economies in Tropical Africa*, New York, 1955, pp. 14, 18, 19 (U.N. Doc. E/2739, ST/ECA/34).

oligarchy. In the white oligarchic states (including, for present purposes, Kenya and Northern Rhodesia) there has been a tremendous rate of economic growth because of European investment, skill, and enterprise; but among Africans drawn into the commercialized sector there has been a heavy concentration in wage employment, and a correspondingly small percentage in the category of independent producers of cash crops. The rate of economic growth in the Union of South Africa is among the highest in the world, equalling that of Soviet Russia and Japan. For Africa, the rate of growth in Northern and Southern Rhodesia is also high.

A third pattern is that found in British and French West Africa and in Uganda, where a strikingly small percentage of the population has been drawn into wage employment, but a remarkably large percentage is engaged in agricultural production of cash crops for export (cocoa, palm oil, rubber, cotton, etc.). The fourth pattern, unique to the Belgian Congo, stands midway in many respects between the second and third. As in the white oligarchic states there has been a heavy recruitment into wage employment, but unlike those societies the Congolese government has played an active role in fostering the development of the indigenous agricultural economy and in ensuring a wider distribution of the benefits of commercialization and industrialization.[19]

What are the political implications of these variant types of economic development?

1. In the white oligarchic states (including Kenya and Northern Rhodesia) the heavy concentration of Africans in wage employment, and the virtual absence of a mass base of independent agricultural producers, has meant and will probably continue to mean that urban workers constitute the main social basis of political activity. In these territories African labor leaders have played a very prominent if not dominant role in organizational activity and in the articulation of grievances and aspirations.

2. In Uganda and the British West African territories the role of labor leaders and organized labor in politics has been much less pronounced, and certainly not decisive. Here there has been a much heavier political involvement of independent agricultural producers (particularly the cocoa farmers of Ghana and western Nigeria, the palm-oil producers of eastern Nigeria, and the cotton farmers of southern

---

[19] The Belgian Congo and Northern Rhodesia have about an equal number of Europeans; but in the Congo the Africans receive 39 per cent of the net geographical money income, while in Northern Rhodesia the figure stands at 13 per cent.

Uganda), as well as middlemen and traders involved in the export of cash crops.[20]

Western Education

Western education has been the most revolutionary of all influences operative in Sub-Saharan Africa since the imposition of European rule. It has been the instrument for the creation of a class indispensable for imperial rule, but one which invariably has taken the leadership in challenging and displacing that rule. Western education has created the new African elite. Hence, examination of the differing patterns of Western education provides the best insight into the size, composition, and political orientation of that new elite.

It is impossible to discuss Western education in Africa without brief mention of the role of Christian missionary societies. Tropical Africa held a special attraction for the missionary. The heathen was his target, and of all human groups the Africans were believed to be the most heathen. Although missionary societies had been active in Asia for several generations, by 1938 only slightly more than 1 per cent of the population of Asia had accepted Christianity; in Tropical Africa, after but a few decades of Evangelical activity, the figure stood at 7 per cent. By the early 1950's Christians constituted a majority of the population in some areas. When one examines the religious affiliation of members of the new political elites in the emergent African states, the extent of the impact of Christianity is even more striking. In the 1954 Ghana Legislative Assembly, for example, 77 per cent of the elected legislators were Christians, and in eastern Nigeria the figure was even higher. The reason for this is found in the simple fact that until recently missionary societies had a virtual monopoly over the educational system.

Christian missionary societies were carriers not only of a new ethic, the imperatives of which challenged the ethic of colonialism, but also of Western culture in general. The school was their instrument. In the early phases of contact, missionaries assumed that Africans were in the grip of a wicked and immoral system and that only wholesale Europeanization could bring salvation. Except in Muslim areas, such as Northern Nigeria and the Arab north in the Sudan, this assumption was reflected in the school curriculum. Missionaries constituted the vanguard of the forces of acculturation.

---

[20] In the former French territories the labor movement became increasingly active in politics, partly because of the powerful initial influence exerted by metropolitan French labor groups.

Missionaries are also largely responsible for the rapidity of restratification which has characterized the process of social change in many African societies. Although they courted chiefs and chiefly families in order to secure toleration of, if not support for, their activity, missionaries in general were indifferent to the status of their converts in traditional society. Indiscriminate recruitment into the Christian fold (entrance into which meant opportunity for Western education and eventually high status in the emergent territorial society) brought about a status reversal in many societies. Africans drawn from the lowest stratum of traditional society have been elevated, through the activities of missionaries, to the highest strata of the social structure of the larger territorial societies. Thus, one finds in some instances central government officials, frequently of humble origin, placed over chiefs for whom their fathers were slaves. It is doubtful whether in the modern world such rapid vertical mobility has been equalled.

Christianity was not brought to the Africans as a unity; rather, the scramble for Africa occurred as much in the religious as in the political sphere. The religious pluralism of African countries is illustrated by the figures in Table 6. Although the Portuguese, and to a lesser extent the Belgians and French, favored Catholicism, the principal of religious toleration, and international agreements to which imperial governments were committed, resulted in fairly free and intense competition among missionary societies, necessitating, in some instances, the delineation of sectarian spheres of influence. This missionary rivalry is not without significance for African politics. In some instances religious affiliation has been the basis of political party organization: the appearance of Muslim parties in southern Ghana, the development of Protestant and Catholic political parties in Uganda, and the strong suggestions of covert official support of Catholic African groups in the Belgian Congo as a counterweight to the more nationalist-minded Protestant African groups. Where religious and tribal cleavages coincide, the religious factor may in time become even more pronounced in provoking political separatist movements. In general, however, the religious pluralism of the new territorial societies has furthered the principle of religious toleration. In most emergent states African leaders seeking election avoid religious issues or sectarian identification, if for no other reason than that most of them confront a religiously heterogeneous electorate.

As with the other processes, the impact of Western education has been highly varied. The crucial variables are the quantity and character of education offered at the three levels (primary, secondary, and higher)

TABLE 6

Religious Affiliation in Sub-Saharan Africa

(in per cent)

Countries by Type of Political System	Moslem	Protestant	Catholic	Other and Unknown
AFRICAN CONTROLLED SYSTEMS				
Historic African States				
Ethiopia	31	30[a]	*	39
Liberia	20	3	1	76
New African States				
Ghana	5	8	6	81
Sudan	80	*	1	19
Nigeria	34	4	2	60
Somalia	99	*	*	*
Togoland	[b]	3	11	86
Cameroons	3	5	15	77
French West Africa	34	1	2	63
French Equatorial Africa	30	3	7	60
Emergent African States				
Sierra Leone	11	3	5	81
Uganda	3	6	18	73
TRANSITIONAL SYSTEMS				
Tanganyika	19	5	9	67
Kenya	4	6	5	85
Belgian-Congo	*	10	20	70
Ruanda-Urundi	*	[b]	23	77
EUROPEAN CONTROLLED SYSTEMS				
Union of South Africa	*[c]	43[c]	4[c]	53[c]
Southern Rhodesia	*	10	3	87
Northern Rhodesia	*	8	14	78
Nyasaland	9	22	11	58
Angola	*	4	19	77
Mozambique	2	1	3	94

* Less than one per cent.
[a] Coptic Christians constitute 29% of Ethiopia's Protestants.
[b] No data available.
[c] Non-whites only.

Sources: Harry W. Hazard, *Atlas of Islamic History*, 3rd ed., Princeton, 1954, pp. 2-5; *World Christian Handbook*, 1952 ed., London: 1952, pp. 174-211, 265; *The Statesman's Yearbook, 1957*, London, 1957, p. 256.

Note: The Protestant and Catholic figures are based on information supplied by churches and vary considerably from census figures in the very few areas for which such are available; e.g., according to the 1953 Nigerian census Nigeria was 22% Christian, while the Angola 1950 census figures indicated 13% Protestants and 36% Catholics. *See* U.N., *The Demographic Yearbook, 1956*, New York, 1956, pp. 267-272.

and the goals of the educational system as officially conceived. In the Union of South Africa, Southern Rhodesia, and the Belgian Congo education has been widespread at the primary level, limited at the secondary, and highly restricted at higher levels. Few Africans from these countries have been allowed to pursue higher education abroad. Until recently there were no higher educational facilities in the Belgian Congo or the Rhodesias, although Rhodesian Africans were eligible for training in African colleges in South Africa. The curriculum of the latter was designed for a caste society. In the Belgian Congo, however, there has been extensive development of technical and trade schools aimed at creating a class of skilled artisans, clerks, and craftsmen. In British East Africa, educational opportunities have been more limited, although Uganda stands somewhat apart from the other territories. British West Africa is unique in the comparatively large number of Africans who have completed full secondary school and have studied in higher institutions abroad. Ghana and Nigeria have more African university graduates than the rest of Sub-Saharan Africa combined. This is in part the result of the earlier development of educational facilities, a greater freedom to travel abroad, and a larger African middle class whose members could afford to send their children to foreign universities.

French and Portuguese Africa constitute a distinct category because the educational system has been used to further the goals of assimilation, to create a black French or Portuguese citizen. Here the similarity ends, however, for education in Portuguese Africa has been extremely limited, with no provision for higher education; by contrast, in French Africa there has been a steady expansion of facilities and there exists a sizeable group of French Africans who have attended French universities.

These differentials in the character of education and official policies have had, among others, the following consequences for politics:

1. In those territories where opportunities have existed for higher study abroad (the Sudan and the territories of French and British West Africa) a distinct professional class has emerged which commands high prestige in the African community and is confident of its right and capacity to exercise political power. Members of this class have provided the leadership of nationalist movements and political parties and constitute the new political elite in the territories concerned.

2. The assimilationist character of the educational system in French Africa was a crucial factor in creating an African political elite which identified itself with France and French culture, and insofar as the

present generation has been concerned it has been an elite willing, until recently, to seek political self-realization within the framework of some form of permanent Euro-African relationship.

3. The Belgian policy of controlled acculturation, under which the quantity and type of education has been rigorously tailored to the demands and opportunities of a benevolent but paternal colonial system, has been effective until recently in avoiding both an underemployed semi-educated class and a frustrated university-educated class, as developed in British West Africa.

4. The limited degree of education in Ethiopia, Liberia, and Portuguese territories has been an important factor in retarding social mobilization of the African mass and thereby fostering political quiescence.

Two other features of the impact of Western education have relevance for the modern political scene. The first is that there have been wide variations in the impact not only among the several territories, but also within territories. Areal variations in the acquisition of Western education within a given territory have tended to generate new or to aggravate old tensions among groups within the new society. As time passed it became increasingly clear to most thoughtful Africans that Western education brought not only the material delights of modernity and social status but also political power. Western education explains the revolutionary change in power relationships between such historic antagonists as the Kikuyu and Masai in Kenya, the Hausa peoples and Southern Nigerians, and the Creoles and peoples of the protectorate in Sierra Leone. As these territories entered their national era, the disparities between groups in terms of Western education tended to engender tribal or culture-group nationalisms, thus weakening or preventing the growth of territorial nationalisms.[21] There was the obvious apprehension on the part of ethnic and tribal groups whose members were least educated that they would be dominated in the new territorial society by groups whose members had had, for historical or other reasons, greater opportunities to obtain Western education.

The second feature is the elitist mentality which the process of Western education has produced. Apart from the fact that Western education is a requisite for running a modern state, most Africans have

[21] One element in the fear of Baganda domination in Uganda is that there are markedly more educated Baganda. The same could be said regarding the Kikuyu in Kenya, the Bemba in Northern Rhodesia, and the Ewe in Togoland. The uneven impact of Western education is due partly to official policies (e.g., missionaries were excluded from parts of northern Nigeria) and partly to the accidental character of missionary penetration.

regarded it as a grace-giving process. Did not European colonial bureaucrats and settlers rationalize their dominant position in terms of education with which "civilization" was synonymous? In the eyes of missionaries, an educated African was *ipso facto* superior because he was, in most instances, a Christian African. Moreover, throughout Africa the Western-educated class was referred to officially as "the progressive or civilized elements" (British Africa), the "elite," *"notables evolues,"* or *"elite noire"* (French and Belgian Africa), the *"evoluido"* or *"assimilado"* (Portuguese Africa), and the *"emancipado"* (Spanish Africa). This uncritical equating of education with special rights and legitimacy has endowed the educated African with an exaggerated sense of superiority and special legitimacy. Politics have been permeated with the presumably uncontestable assumption that the educated have a divine right to rule.

Restratification

Some of the consequences of the processes of urbanization, commercialization, and Western education have been noted in the preceding analysis. Here we will focus upon two special developments, restratification and secularization. As for the first, we should recognize at the outset that a stratification system is an attribute of a single society. Except for Basutoland and Swaziland, none of the African territories are coterminous with a traditional African society. Thus, there are two levels of stratification analysis: the level of traditional society and the level of the new territorial society. From a purist's standpoint, restratification could occur only in the former; in the latter we are concerned with stratification in an entirely new territorial society. The same people, of course, live, and are ranked, and rank themselves, at both levels. Moreover, the utility of the distinction is lessened by the fact that most traditional societies have been fundamentally altered by colonialism and modernity and could hardly be thought of as ongoing social systems.

In general, the new classes emerging from the Western impact (doctors, lawyers, teachers, businessmen, artisans, traders, clerks, cash crop farmers, etc.) have not only moved into the upper strata in territorial stratification systems; they have also displaced the upper strata in traditional societies. There have been, however, wide variations in this stratification process. Four patterns, illustrative and not exhaustive, can be noted: two at the territorial level and two at the level of traditional society. At the territorial level, the degree to which the new classes have moved into the higher strata of the system has been governed by the racial character of the population and by official policies. In African uniracial territories (emergent African states and most of former French Africa) the new classes have had fairly rapid and free upward movement to the very apex of the territorial stratification system (whether the criteria used are objective or subjective). In the European oligarchies and multiracial territories, however, there have been variable ceilings placed upon the upward mobility of the new African classes. In such areas the upper strata at the territorial level (as defined by income and political or economic roles) are occupied mainly by Europeans and Asians.

At the level of traditional society two patterns of restratification can be distinguished. One is characteristic of the classic indirect rule systems (Hausa-Fulani states, Watutsi Kingdoms, etc.) where the traditional aristocracy has acted as a brake upon the upward mobility of the new classes, either because it has preempted and absorbed the benefits of commercialization, or because of the social and political controls it has imposed upon the emergent claimant groups. At the opposite extreme is another example, characteristic either of traditional societies which were egalitarian and loosely stratified (the Tiv), or customarily provided for considerable upward mobility (the Ibo), or of areas in which traditional societies have largely disintegrated (Ndebele). In this type the traditional system has offered no barriers, if indeed it has not facilitated the entrance of the new classes into positions of prestige, power, and wealth.

Secularization

Another consequence of colonialism and the changes wrought by the Western impact has been the secularization of values, human relations, and institutions. Ironically, one of the most powerful of the forces furthering the process of secularization has been the Christian missionary. Many, if not most, Africans regarded induction into the Christian fold in instrumental terms. Becoming a Christian meant the opportunity to attend school, which in turn meant a clerkship in the urban center. Thus, Christianity has been a vehicle to the secular world. Moreover, the political institutions of colonialism were thoroughly secular in character, including not only the territorial representative institutions but also the structures of indirect rule. Although the latter were intended to preserve what remained of traditional authority and sanctions, it was clear to most—including in particular the traditional authorities—that the ultimate source of legitimacy was the colonial authority.

Perhaps nowhere in the non-Western world is there as passionate an attraction to the Idea of Progress as among Africans affected by modernity. At the core of this idea is the strong conviction that progress is unilinear and inevitable, and that man can creatively master and shape his own destiny through application of the scientific method, the exercise of his ever-accumulating wisdom and ever-growing rationality. It is reflected in party slogans ("Forward Ever, Backward Never," "Freedom and Progress," "Life More Abundant"), names of associations (Calabar Improvement League, African Progress Union), and in many other ways. This almost religious belief in the idea of ceaseless upward progress has been and is particularly pronounced among Africans partly because the main carriers of the Western impact (missionary, educator, settler, and colonial administrator) rationalized their presence and the African's inferior role in terms of a developmental philosophy of history. The literature of modern Africa is saturated with such words as "upliftment," "development," "trusteeship," "progress reports," etc. In general, this has meant a strong orientation toward futurism in popular attitudes and values, and hence in the definition of the issues of politics.

The shift from traditionalism to secularism has occurred very unevenly among different African groups and individuals because of the variable character of traditional culture, the differing official policies toward traditional society, and uneven exposure to the forces of modernity. Since traditionalism and secularism are polar extremes, individual Africans fall somewhere on a continuum between the two. Their values and modes of thought and behavior reflect a complex mixture of both. In certain spheres of activity secularism may predominate; in others there is uncritical acceptance of the traditional. Some of the most acculturated Africans are known to have deep commitments to traditional symbols and sanctions in certain matters. It is this amalgamate character of the individual values and personality structures which makes any measurement of secularity impossible. The extent of commitment to secularism is frequently revealed only in individual situations. Once these qualifications are made, however, there can be little question that most of Africa is being rapidly propelled toward greater secularism.

According to their declared aims, the new African political elites are fully committed to secular values and political institutions. In many instances and in diverse ways, however, they have found it necessary or expedient to employ or to acquiesce in the use of traditional symbols or sanctions. This instrumental use of traditionalism to further the ends of secular politics can be seen in such ways as the acquisition of chiefly titles by modernists, in unanimous voting patterns in certain chiefdoms, and in the pouring of libations, or the performance of some similar ritual, on important political occasions. There have also been instances where modernists have deliberately instigated and manipulated nativistic movements, with their strong traditionalist aim of recapturing the past, or have courted and used leaders of chiliastic movements or syncretistic churches, in order to increase or consolidate their political power. To use a tired cliché, Africa is in transition, and one can expect for some time to come that all aspects of politics will be permeated by both traditional and secular elements.

III. POLITICAL GROUPS

Political Parties and Party Systems

A study of the character and variant patterning of political groups—their structure, leadership, social bases, goals, and interrelationships—is fundamental to an understanding of Africa's political systems, whether independent, emergent, or colonial. These systems can be roughly grouped into four main categories and subtypes as follows (see Table 7 for a detailed listing of political groups in selected territories):

1. *Territories without political parties*
   Ruanda-Urundi
   Portuguese Provinces (Angola, Mozambique and Guinea)
   Ethiopia
   Republic of the Sudan

2. *One-party dominant systems*
   Liberia

   Mauritanian Islamic Republic
   Northern Nigeria

   Ghana   Senegal
   Guinea   Sudanese Republic
   Ivory Coast   Central African Republic
   Republic of Niger Somalia
   Eastern Nigeria

   Federation of Rhodesia and Nyasaland (European Oligarchy)

3. *Comprehensive nationalist* (African population only)
           Tanganyika
           Belgian Congo
           Nyasaland
           Northern Rhodesia
           Southern Rhodesia
           Union of South Africa

4. *Competitive-party systems*

Uganda	Southern Cameroons
Sierra Leone	Republic of Upper Volta
Zanzibar	Republic of the Gaboon
Togoland	Southern Rhodesia ⎱ European pop-
Cameroons	Union of South Africa ⎰ ulation only
Dahomey	
Chad	
Republic of Congo	
Western Nigeria	

Before analyzing briefly the character of political groups in these countries, we should make two observations. One refers to the distinction between the level of the territory and the level of the federation in the following three federal systems: the two autonomous republics constituting the Federation of Mali (the State of Senegal and the Sudanese Republic), the four regions of the Federation of Nigeria (Western, Eastern, and Northern Regions, and the Southern Cameroons), and the three territories of the Federation of Rhodesia and Nyasaland (Northern Rhodesia, Southern Rhodesia, and Nyasaland). If one's frame of reference in each of these instances is the federation, then purely territorial or regional parties such as the NPC (Northern People's Congress) and the URP (United Rhodesia Party) in Southern Rhodesia would be particularistic, while pan-federal parties would be non-particularistic. Considering the fact that the major parties in each of the federations are or endeavor to be pan-federal, we could argue that the federal level should be the focus of analysis. On the other hand, one of the most critical issues confronting political leaders in each of these federations is the question of which political entity—the federation or the region or territory—will become independent and inherit the powers formerly held by colonial authorities. Given the uncertainty on this point, we will here regard the territory (or region) as the basic political unit, with due reference being made to the nature and functioning of parties at the federal level.

The second point is in the nature of a caveat, namely, the patterning

TABLE 7

Party Strengths and Type of Party Systems in Sub-Saharan Africa

Type of Party System	Country and Date of Last Election	Governing Party or Coalition	Legislative Strength (in %)[1]	Other Parties	Legislative Strength (in %)[1]
ONE-PARTY DOMINANT SYSTEMS	Liberia (May 1959)	True Whig Party	100.0	Independent True Whig Party	0.0
	Mauritania (May 1959)	Parti du Regroupement Mauritanien (PRM)	100.0		
	Nigeria, Northern Region[2] (Nov. 1956)	Northern People's Congress (NPC)	80.9	United Middle Belt Congress (UMBC)	9.2
				Northern Elements' Progressive Union (NEPU)	5.3
				Action Group (AG)	3.1
				Bornu Youth Movement (BYM)	1.5
	Ghana (July 1956, revised to Aug. 1959)	Convention People's Party (CPP)	81.7	United Party[3] (Northern People's Party) (National Liberation Movement) (Togoland Congress Party) (Federation of Youth Organizations) (Muslim Association Party)	17.3
	Nigeria, Eastern Region[2] (March 1957)	National Council of Nigeria and the Cameroons (NCNC)	76.2	Action Group (AG)	15.5
				United National Independence Party (UNIP)	5.9

Somalia (March 1959)	Somali Youth League	92.2	Independent Constitutional Somali Party (HDMS)	5.6
			Liberal Somali Youth Party	2.2
Ivory Coast (April 1959)	Rassemblement Démocratique Africain (RDA)	100.0		
Niger (Dec. 1958, revised to Oct. 1959)	RDA: Union pour la Communauté Franco-Africaine (UCFA)	100.0		
Guinea (Sept. 1958)	Parti Démocratique Guinéen (PDG)	100.0		
Senegal (March 1959)	Union Progressiste Sénégalaise (UPS)	100.0	Parti de la Solidarité Sénégalaise (PSS)	0.0
Sudanese Republic (March 1959)	RDA: Union Soudanaise (US)	100.0	PRA[4]: Parti du Regroupement Soudanais (PRS)	0.0
Central African Republic (April 1959)	Mouvement d'Emancipation Sociale de l'Afrique Noire (MESAN)	100.0		
Tanganyika (Sept. 1958 and Feb. 1959)	Tanganyika African National Union (TANU) and TANU supported independents	100.0	United Tanganyika Party (UTP)	0.0
Federation of Rhodesia and Nyasaland (Nov. 1958) (European oligarchy)	United Federal Party (UFP)	83.0	Dominion Party (DP)	15.1
			Constitution Party	0.0

TABLE 7 (continued)

Type of Party System	Country and Date of Last Election	Governing Party or Coalition	Legislative Strength (in %)[1]	Other Parties	Legislative Strength (in %)[1]
COMPREHENSIVE NATIONALIST PARTIES	Belgian Congo			Mouvement National Congolais Parti Solidaire Africain ABAKO (a tribal party)	
(African population only)	Northern Rhodesia			United National Independence Party (UNIP) N.R. African National Congress	
	Nyasaland			African National Congress	
	Southern Rhodesia			African National Congress	
	Union of South Africa			African National Congress	
COMPETITIVE PARTY SYSTEMS	Sudan[5] (March 1958)	Umma	36.4	National Unionist Party (NUP)	26.0
		People's Democratic Party (PDP)	15.6	Liberal Party	11.6
				Federal Party	0.6
				Anti-Imperial Front	0.6
	Uganda (No country-wide elections until 1960)			Uganda National Congress Democratic Party	
	Nigeria (federal level) (Dec. 1959)	Northern People's Congress (NPC)	45.5	Action Group (AG)	23.4
		National Council of Nigeria and the Cameroons (NCNC) and Northern Element's Progressive Union (NEPU)	28.5		

Party System		%	Party	%
Nigeria, Western Region (May 1956)[2]	Action Group (AG)	60.0	National Council of Nigeria and the Cameroons (NCNC)	40.0
			Nigerian Commoners' Liberal Party	0.0
			Nigerian Commoners' Party	0.0
			Nigerian People's Party	0.0
			Dynamic Party	0.0
Nigeria, Southern Cameroons[2] (Jan. 1959)	Kamerun National Democratic Party (KNDP)	53.8	Kamerun National Congress (KNC)	46.2
			Kamerun People's Party (KPP)	0.0
			One Kamerun (OK)	0.0
			Kamerun Unity Party (KUP)	0.0
Sierra Leone (May 1957, revised to Oct. 1958)	Sierra Leone People's Party (SLPP)	71.4	United Progressive Party (UPP)	12.2
			People's National Party (PNP)	10.2
Togoland (April 1958, revised to Oct. 1959)	Comité de l'Unité Togolaise (CUT)	62.0	Union Démocratique Populaire Togolaise (UDPT)	28.3
			Mouvement de la Jeunesse Togolaise (JUVENTO) and Mouvement Populaire Togolais (MPT)	8.7
Cameroons[6] (As of Oct. 1959)	Union Camerounaise (UC) and Action Nationale (AN) coalition	65.5	Démocrates Camerounais (DC)	11.1
			Groupe d'Action Parlementaire pour le Salut National (GAPSN)	11.1
			Intergroupe des Noninscrits (IGNI)	9.7
			Union des Populations du Cameroun (UPC)	0.0

TABLE 7 (continued)

Type of Party System	Country and Date of Last Election	Governing Party or Coalition	Legislative Strength (in %)[1]	Other Parties	Legislative Strength (in %)[1]
COMPETITIVE PARTY SYSTEMS (cont'd)	Chad[7] (May 1959)	RDA: Parti Progressiste Tchadien (PPT)	87.7	PRA: Mouvement Populaire Tchadien (MPT)	12.3
	Upper Volta[7] (April 1959)	Rassemblement Démocratique Africain (RDA)	85.3	PRA: Parti du Regroupement Voltaique (PRV)	14.7
	Dahomey (April 1959, revised to Oct. 1959)	Rassemblement Démocratique Dahoméen (RDD) RDA: Union Démocratique Dahoméenne (UDD)	60.0	Parti Républicain du Dahomey (PRD)	40.0
	Gaboon (March 1957)	RDA: Bloc Démocratique Gabonais (BDG)	44.4	PRA: Union Démocratique et Sociale Gabonaise (UDSG)	38.9
	Republic of Congo[7] (March 1957, revised to Oct. 1959)	RDA: Union Démocratique pour la Défense des Intérêts Africains (UDDIA)	83.6	PRA: Parti Progressiste Congolais (PPC); Mouvement Socialiste Africain (MSA) and MESAN coalition	16.4
	Northern Rhodesia (March 1959)	United Federal Party (UFP)	59.1	Central Africa Party (CAP)	18.2
				African National Congress	4.5
				Dominion Party (DP)	4.5

COMPETITIVE PARTY SYSTEMS (cont'd)			
Southern Rhodesia (June 1958) (European oligarchy)	United Federal Party (UFP) 56.7	Dominion Party (DP) United Rhodesia Party (URP) 43.3	0.0
Union of South Africa (April 1958)	Nationalist Party 66.0	United Party 34.0	
		Liberal Party 0.0	
		Labour Party 0.0	

---

[1] Figures are for the directly elected seats won at the last election, revised to include subsequent by-elections and changes in party affiliations. Where totals do not add up to 100%, the remaining seats are held by independents or minor parties.

[2] Figures are those for elections to the regional houses of assembly.

[3] The United Party was formed after the last election by the union of all opposition parties. The names of the latter, since dissolved, are shown in the table.

[4] Parti du Regroupement Africain.

[5] All political parties were proscribed after the *coup d'état* in November 1958.

[6] The UC, AN, and DC are regional blocs. GAPSN and IGNI are purely parliamentary associations. The UPC, outlawed in 1955, is still active within and outside the Cameroons, although it has never contested an election.

[7] Changes in party strengths during 1959 in the previously competitive party systems of Chad, Upper Volta, and the Republic of Congo have resulted in the emergence of an overwhelmingly dominant party in their respective national parliaments. Because of the history of intense party competition in these countries, however, they have been included in the competitive-party category in the table.

of political groups in each of these countries can be called a "party system" only with very considerable reservation. The existence of a "party system" presumes a relatively stabilized political order, particularly as regards both geographical and juridical boundaries of that order. Moreover, one can make valid judgments regarding the character of a party system only on the basis of an analysis of the structure and interaction of political parties within that order over a reasonable period of time. But throughout much of Africa we have only an extremely short span of time upon which to base our analysis and to make our evaluations; and in many instances the really critical issues determining the alignments of political parties are not fundamental questions of public policy, but those relating to the boundaries and the basic structure of the political system itself. At this stage, for example, it is not at all certain whether Nyasaland will remain a part of the Federation of Rhodesia and Nyasaland or unite with Tanganyika, whether the Republic of the Niger will join the Federation of Mali or unite with Northern Nigeria, whether the Southern Cameroons will remain in the Federation of Nigeria or be integrated with the (French) Cameroons, whether Gambia will unite with Senegal or remain linked to the United Kingdom in a special status, whether the western part of the Belgian Congo will ultimately become part of the Republic of the Congo, whether the non-Yoruba part of Western Nigeria and the non-Ibo part of Eastern Nigeria will have their own regions—and on and on all over Africa. The crucial point here is that at this stage in Africa's political development the patterning of political groups reflects the overriding fact that the systems themselves are indeterminate. This makes it necessary to emphasize again that the most rewarding mode of analysis is that which focusses upon trends rather than upon systems.

The foregoing observations lead to another obvious caveat, namely, that the classification of countries according to "no-party," "one-party," and "competitive-party" systems can be regarded as no more than a "snap-shot" inventory of the patterning of parties at a single point in time. Before November 1958 the Sudan had one of the most competitive party systems in Africa; after the military coup there were no parties. During the past few years Senegalese parties have been highly competitive; recently, for tactical reasons connected with the continuing struggle to define the boundaries of the system itself, the two major parties merged and Senegal in mid-1959 became a one-party state. These examples could be multiplied, but they suffice to illuminate the highly mutable character of Africa's party systems, and to stress the tentativeness of the present classificatory scheme. With these reservations and interpretations, the principal political groups in contemporary Africa will be analyzed under the headings of "one-party" and "competitive-party" systems.

One-party systems. Liberia has been ruled for nearly a century by one party, the present name of which is the True Whig Party.[22] Party activity is confined mainly to the Americo-Liberian oligarchy (including Hinterland Liberians assimilated thereto), and, in general, opposition groups have been ephemeral and factional in character. Break-aways have usually been led by a previous president or party leader. Political groups organized by Hinterland Liberians have been either suppressed or short-lived because of repressive police action or electoral manipulation by the governing party. Apart from a characteristic intolerance toward opposition, the True Whig Party has perpetuated itself in power through extensive patronage (and apart from the Firestone operations the government is the principal source of salaried employment), by heavy campaign expenditures borne mainly by a compulsory levy upon government employees, and by sheer political apathy.

A type of one-party-dominant system characteristic of new polities is found in several territories whose peoples have had variant colonial experiences: Italian (Somalia), British (Northern and Eastern Nigeria, Ghana, and the Federation of Rhodesia and Nyasaland), and French (Mauritanian Islamic Republic, Guinea, Senegal, Sudanese Republic, Ivory Coast and Central African Republic). In each of these the strength of the dominant party, as represented by the number of members in the national legislature, is seventy per cent or more, and the strength of the opposition groups is dispersed and usually sectional or tribal in character. In two of these (the Northern Region of Nigeria and the Mauritanian Islamic Republic) the predominance of one party is explained by several factors: the comparative homogeneity of the population, the common bond of Islam, the strong support the dominant parties have received from traditionalists (emirs and chiefs) as well as the colonial administrations, and the fact that each has been— and Northern Nigeria still is—a less developed and culturally differentiated part of a larger federal system.

In a large measure the dominance and unity of these two parties reflect the fact that the peoples of these two territories are being sud-

[22] The one notable exception was the brief period 1871-1877 during which the Republican party was in power. See Raymond Leslie Buell, *The Native Problem in Africa*, Vol. II, New York, 1928, pp. 711-713.

denly and involuntarily drawn into the vortex of modern political activity in which, because of historical factors, they have been placed, or have felt themselves as being in a disadvantageous competitive position. With the progressive recruitment of non-traditionalist elements into the political arena, and the resultant formation of new political groups, the leaders of these dominant parties will either seek to preserve their present monopoly by repressive actions, or they will be obliged to accommodate themselves to the new forces in what could become an increasingly competitive system. Such developments depend in part, however, upon the relative position of these areas vis-à-vis other areas in the larger federal systems of which they are or may become a part.

The existence of a dominant, non-dictatorial, one-party system in seven of the remaining nine territories is largely the result of the continuing monopoly of influence exercised by what were in origin fairly comprehensive nationalist parties that were in most instances built around and served as instruments of a single dominant personality: in Ghana, the Convention People's Party under Kwame Nkrumah; in Eastern Nigeria, the National Council of Nigeria and the Cameroons under Nnamdi Azikiwe; in Guinea and the Ivory Coast, the Rassemblement Démocratique Africain under Sekou Touré and Felix Houphouet-Boigny respectively; in Senegal, the Union Progressiste Sénégalaise under Leopold Senghor; in the Sudanese Republic, the Union Soudanaise under Modibo Keita; and in the Central African Republic, the Mouvement d'Emancipation Sociale de l'Afrique Noire under the late Joseph Barthélemy. Somaliland is different mainly in that the Somali Youth League has been the vehicle for the assertion of a virulent Somali nationalism in terms not only of extinguishing Italian control but also of creating a Greater Somalia.

As these territories have approached and crossed the threshold of self-government or independence, several of the dominant parties have been subjected to increasing internal stresses and challenges from opposition parties. For several reasons this is, of course, to be expected. One obvious reason is that the struggle for self-government was the only cement linking disparate groups together in the quest for variant concrete goals, all of which were easily subsumed under the abstract goal of self-government. Another is that during the nationalist phase disunity was condemned, if not deemed illegitimate or treasonous; with the assurance of self-government, however, political competition and rivalry are to be expected and in principle accepted, especially since the norms of the new systems are democratic. Thirdly, with the approach of self-government, minority, separatist, and tribal parties become increasingly articulate and claimant: self-government to them means that full power passes from the hands of a neutral colonial bureaucracy to the hands of the leaders of the dominant party, over which a culturally dominant group, in many instances, exercises decisive influence. Fourthly, as the dominant parties progressively acquire unfettered control over public policy, they become vulnerable to popular disenchantment either because of their failure to create the promised brave new world or because of the unpopular measures requisite for rapid economic development. Finally, the charisma of previously dominant personalities tends to evaporate or wear thin, unless new and dramatic external threats can be found, or the image of an uncompleted mission created. The party tends to become increasingly bureaucratized and less sensitive to the claims of new groups entering the political arena;[23] and tensions among factions and cliques in the top leadership ranks become more open and virulent.

Set against these disintegrative tendencies characteristic of comprehensive nationalist parties which have become dominant parties under self-government are factors which operate to preserve their dominance. By far the most important are patronage, reorganization of the functions and structures of local government in order to further central government and party control, and the ensemble of pressures, influences, and coercions which dominant parties elsewhere have successfully employed to maintain their position. The dominant parties concerned are still endowed with an aura of special legitimacy either because of the recency of nationalist victory (as with the CPP in Ghana and the NCNC in Eastern Nigeria) or because they are still primarily instruments for what is claimed to be a continuing struggle against residual colonialism or for the achievement of an advantageous position vis-à-vis other countries in an unstabilized political order (e.g., the new states of the former French West Africa). Leaders of dominant parties seek to promote and perpetuate popular endorsement of their special claim to legitimacy by stigmatizing opposition parties as being not only unnecessary but also dangerous in the pursuit of the unrealized goals of complete independence and modernization. At the present time, how-

---

[23] As David Apter points out regarding Ghana's CPP, "Party headquarters is today a shadow of what it used to be. It is no longer the center of operations for a vibrant and effective nationalist movement. The life of the party is now government, and government handouts, and the party followers are on the political dole, or trying to get on it." "What's Happening in Ghana?" *Africa Special Report*, No. 2, November 1957, p. 12.

ever, it is far too early to evaluate these trends and to generalize from them.

Comprehensive nationalist movements are political action groups characteristic of territories still under colonialism, although they have not been and are not found in all colonial territories.[24] In Kenya, for example, a comprehensive nationalist movement has been prohibited by law. In contemporary Africa they are primarily a phenomenon of the multiracial, European-controlled political systems of East, Central, and South Africa under, or previously under, British control or influence. Here they constitute, however, only one of several types of political groups, the other three types being European, non-European other than African (Asian, Coloured, etc.), and multiracial. The comprehensive nationalist movements organized by Africans in these countries are the product of a common fear, namely, a European oligarchy determined either to maintain permanent white supremacy (Southern Rhodesia and the Union of South Africa) or to perpetuate and to expand its disproportionate influence over public policy (Kenya, Tanganyika, Nyasaland, and Northern Rhodesia). This fear of being permanently imprisoned in a caste society is the cement which binds Africans together and the provocation which galvanizes them to carry out united political action.

In the six countries concerned, however, there are wide variations in the degree of power held by the European oligarchies and, as a consequence, significant differences in the character of the political objectives of African nationalist parties. European oligarchic control is absolute and omnipresent in the Union of South Africa and Southern

[24] It is only with serious reservations that one can refer to comprehensive nationalist movements as "parties" in a "party system." Where a comprehensive nationalist movement has been the vehicle for securing independence, there is a post-independence carryover in which the same leadership and organizational structure constitute the dominant "party" in the new "system." For analytical purposes a distinction should be made between preindependence nationalist movements and postindependence parties. This distinction is based on the conception of a nationalist movement as an "organization formed to achieve self-government," functioning within a status quo which it aims to transform and a conception of a political party as an "organization which competes with other similar organizations in periodical elections in order to participate in formal institutions and thereby influence and control the personnel and policy of government." The dividing line between these two categories is not sharp; insofar as nationalist movements win constitutional reforms, they tend to take on the functions of a party. Thus, TANU (the Tanganyika African National Union) functions both as a nationalist movement pressing for a fundamental transformation in the status quo and as a political party competing with other parties in elections. The distinction may smack of quibbling, but it has certain utility. See my "The Emergence of African Political Parties," in C. Grove Haines, ed., *Africa Today*, Baltimore 1955, pp. 225-227.

Rhodesia; less than absolute, but decisive, in Northern Rhodesia; preponderant, but waning, in Kenya and Nyasaland; and recently has been undermined in Tanganyika. The goals of African parties reflect these variations. In the Union of South Africa and Southern Rhodesia the African National Congresses, like American Negro action groups, have tended in the past to be accommodationist and egalitarian, concerned primarily with the abolition of segregation, discriminatory legislation, and second-class citizenship in societies they acknowledge to be multiracial. African Congress-type movements in Nyasaland, Tanganyika, and Northern Rhodesia, on the other hand, have not only sought the removal of existing racial disabilities, but have envisaged, and recently have openly demanded, ultimate African supremacy.[25] These differences reflect the conditioning effect of the milieu and of the mediating political elite in shaping African expectations and demands regarding the political system. In all instances, however, there has been a progressive radicalization in expectations and demands. African comprehensive movements in their early stages have been egalitarian-accommodationist, but, depending upon the milieu, they have increasingly gravitated to a radical African-supremacist position.[26]

As comprehensive nationalist parties in these territories have shifted to more radical African-supremacist objectives, accommodationist parties have been formed to oppose them. These latter are of two types: uniracial and multiracial. The first type, frequently inspired or supported (openly or covertly) by governments, is represented by the Bantu National Congress (which supports apartheid) in the Union of South Africa, the Nyasaland African Association, and, in certain respects, the former Conference of Chiefs in Tanganyika and the Northern Rhodesia African National Congress after the formation of the Zambia National Congress. These groups seek to recruit traditionalists and so-called

[25] The Mau Mau uprising created a special situation in Kenya. Prior to the "Emergency" the KAU (Kenya African Union) was rapidly gaining strength as Kenya's first comprehensive nationalist party, but at the time of the outbreak of Mau Mau activity it was banned by government. Since the Emergency, government has not allowed the creation of political associations above the district level. Despite this disability, the leaders of the district associations have joined in a common front, for which the African Elected Members' Union serves as their agitational instrument. Thus, a comprehensive nationalist party could be said to exist functionally, but not as a formal organization. As soon as government restrictions on pan-territorial political parties are lifted, it is likely that such a party will be formally created as a capstone to the existing district parties.

[26] Unlike the Sudan and the territories of British West Africa, African supremacy has not usually been explicitly and categorically declared to be an objective by African movements in East, Central, and South Africa; rather, it has been cast in more euphonious language, such as "universal suffrage" or "full democracy," which, if realized, would obviously have the same effect.

"moderates" into active defense of government, or the European oligarchy, or gradualism, against the onslaughts and revolutionary appeals of the more militant comprehensive nationalist parties. The second type is multiracial in character and is represented by the United Federal Party in Southern Rhodesia and the Federation of Rhodesia and Nyasaland, the Central African Party in Northern Rhodesia, the now-defunct United Tanganyika Party, and the several branches of the Capricorn Movement. In this type of party a few European and Asians have joined with so-called "moderate and responsible" African leaders in political action groups which oppose both European supremacy and African nationalism, and support the gradual creation of a "multiracial (or 'non-racial') democracy." Thus far, this type of party has been most successful in Southern Rhodesia. In general, leaders of African nationalist parties regard them as "cooling-off" bodies, and the Africans who join them as either opportunists or "imperialist stooges."

Two other types of political action groups found in most of these territories are, like the African Congress movements, racially communalistic in that they seek to protect the interests, and to maximize the power and influence, of the respective European and Asian elements in the population. Among European parties, however, a distinction should be drawn between those in Southern Rhodesia and the Union of South Africa, where European oligarchies are already in firm control of the government and have a competitive party system, which will be analyzed subsequently, and those in Kenya, Tanganyika, Nyasaland, and Northern Rhodesia, where resident Europeans have not had complete control over government but have had a disproportionate measure of political influence. In the latter areas, European parties have been until recently primarily concerned with expanding their control over government in order not only to advance their economic interests but also to consolidate their position of dominance over the non-European elements of the population. With the recent emergence of a virulent African nationalism in these same areas, and the growing assumption of ultimate African supremacy, there has been a shift in European attitudes and objectives. These range from the advocacy of a final desperate push to establish permanent white supremacy to support for the organization of multiracial political parties and multiracial government.

Asian political groups in East, Central, and South Africa have in general reflected the intense communalism characteristic of southern Asia. Each community—Hindus, Muslims, Sikhs, Ismailis, and Goans—has its own cultural association, which plays variant political roles depending upon the milieu, the size of the Asian community, and government policies regarding their position in society. Here a distinction should be drawn between Kenya, Tanganyika, and Nyasaland, on the one hand, and the Rhodesias and the Union of South Africa, on the other. In the former territories the governments have granted Asians representation in Legislative Councils; in the Rhodesias and South Africa this has been denied them. They have been most successful in organizing comprehensive Congress-type parties in Kenya and the Union of South Africa, partly because they are numerically stronger in those two countries and partly because they have confronted a greater challenge as a total community. In Kenya they struggled for equality in the face of the growing political power of the European settler oligarchy and latterly of African nationalism; in South Africa they have been faced with a government which has imposed upon them increasing liabilities through policies of segregation and exclusion. Elsewhere, at least until recently, their communal associations have played a modest pressure-group role either because the Asians are dispersed or relatively small in number, or because of the absence of a positive threat to their integrity as a group.

In addition to the communal tensions which have militated against sustained and united political action, Asians have been and are politically divided on two other issues. One is the emphasis with which Asian demands are to be advanced. The leadership of the Kenya Indian Congress has been recurrently divided between the extremists advocating non-cooperation and the accommodationists stressing moderation and restraint. In South Africa disagreement on this issue has resulted in the division between the militant Natal Indian Congress and South African Indian Congress, which are political action organizations inclined toward passive resistance and general strikes, on the one hand, and the rival and more moderate Natal Indian Organization and South African Indian Organization, on the other.[27] More recently in Tanganyika a breach has developed between the militant Asian Association which supports African nationalism and other Asian groups inclined toward gradualism and multiracialism.

The second and increasingly important division within the Asian

[27] There are social and communal bases for this division. The Natal Indian Congress, whose leaders have been influenced to some degree by Communism, appeals to urban and agricultural labor and is a predominantly Hindu body; the Natal Indian Organization is predominantly Muslim and represents the wealthier section of the Asian community. The leaders of the pro-African Tanganyika Asia Association are predominantly Hindus, and represent professional groups, particularly barristers.

community concerns the Asian attitude toward the political demands of African nationalist leaders. Although individual Asians have frequently identified themselves with African grievances and aspirations, Asian associations have not heretofore given sustained support to African demands. The one outstanding exception, of course, is the active program of cooperation launched in 1950 by leaders of the African National Congress and the South African Indian Congress. Elsewhere, Asian associations have been comparatively indifferent, if not hostile, to any substantial African advance.[28] Two recent developments, not unrelated, have brought about a change in the Asian position: Prime Minister Nehru's admonition that Asians overseas must become loyal citizens of their country of residence[29] and the emergence of militant African nationalist parties under leaders determined to establish African supremacy in the present generation. In Nyasaland, Tanganyika, and Kenya a section of the Asian community has already openly declared its support of African nationalist demands. As African nationalist parties grow in strength and are able to exact ever larger concessions from colonial governments and European settlers, it is probable that Asians in East Africa, like their compatriots in the new states of former British West Africa, will progressively shift their support to the political objective of African self-government. As a minority heavily dependent upon a favorable government policy toward their economic position in society, they are obliged to be highly opportunistic in politics.

Competitive-party systems. In sixteen of the remaining political entities of Sub-Saharan Africa there have been varying approximations of a competitive-party system. For purposes of analysis these can be usefully divided into the following five categories: (1) Uganda; (2) Sierra Leone and Zanzibar; (3) Togoland, Cameroons, Dahomey, Chad, Re-

[28] There are significant economic reasons for this: except for the wealthier members of their community, Asians would be the first to be displaced by Africans in intermediate positions in the civil service and large business firms, in petty retail trade over which they currently exercise a virtual monopoly, and in skilled and semi-skilled occupations. Although they are co-victims of discrimination, the tensions between Asians and Africans in the economic sphere are among the most acute in contemporary multiracial Africa. Many African nationalists regard the Asians as the most immediate obstacle to their advance in the economic sector.

[29] In a foreign policy debate in the House of the People on September 15, 1953, Nehru said ". . . we have rather gone out of our way to tell our own people in Africa . . . that they can expect no help from us, no protection from us, if they seek any special rights in Africa which are not in the interests of Africa. . . . We have told them: 'We shall help you naturally, we are interested in protecting you, your dignity or interests, but not if you go at all against the people of Africa, because you are their guests, and if they do not want you, out you will have to go, bag and baggage.' "

public of the Congo, and Western Nigeria; (4) Republics of Niger, Upper Volta and the Gaboon, and the Southern Cameroons under British trusteeship; and (5) the European oligarchies of Southern Rhodesia and the Union of South Africa. These will be discussed in the order listed above.

The development of political groups in Uganda has been unique for several obviously related reasons: the existence of several historic kingdoms in southern Uganda whose integrity has been partially preserved under the British policy of indirect rule; the special position of the Buganda Kingdom, which has in the past exercised a cultural hegemony over most other groups in southern Uganda, and which many Baganda feel should in the future exercise political hegemony in the emergent state of Uganda (although the Baganda constitute only 19 per cent of Uganda's population); the much greater economic and educational development and higher per capita income among the Baganda; the cultural cleavage between the Nilotic peoples of the north and the Bantu peoples of the south; the historic struggle mainly between Anglicans and Catholics, and to some extent Muslims, at first confined to the Baganda, but now manifest throughout the territory; and the underdeveloped character of Uganda's central representative institutions. These several factors, individually or in combination, largely account for the pluralism characteristic of modern Uganda political associations.

Until comparatively recently, agitational politics has been largely confined to the Buganda Kingdom and has centered upon political tensions and issues within Buganda society itself.[30] As a consequence of the progressive spread of modernity, the introduction of democratic processes in local and central councils, and the increasing fear of Buganda domination, however, other groups in Uganda have been increasingly drawn into modern political activity. The result has been the appearance of several competing parties divided on a variety of issues, particularly including religion and the role of the Baganda in the Uganda political system. The Uganda National Congress, the first contender for the title of the country's comprehensive nationalist movement, was subsequently opposed by the Uganda Congress Party led

[30] One of the first postwar political parties was an association known as the Descendants of Kintu, whose leaders (traders, clerks, artisans, and some traditionalists) attempted to organize the Baganda against the Mengo ruling classes in the Buganda Kingdom. In 1949, the so-called "nationalist" activity of the Bataka Party and the Uganda Farmers' Union was in large measure directed against the *Kabaka* (king) and certain Saza chiefs. The Uganda National Congress acquired its greatest strength at the time of the deposition of the *kabaka* of Buganda.

by a breakaway faction, composed primarily of Ganda intellectuals. By the end of 1959 the leaders of the parent Congress were divided into three factions, each claiming legitimate control over the organization. Opposing these factions are the Democratic Party, predominantly Catholic in membership and led mainly by Ganda intellectuals, and other minor groups. As all of these parties attempt to territorialize their support and organizational structure, the competition has greatly accelerated the process of political recruitment. In any event, the pattern of party development in Uganda is clearly of a different order than in Tanganyika, Nyasaland, and other British territories in which a single comprehensive nationalist party has focused political energies and perspectives upon the central structure of authority.

The unique feature of party development in Sierra Leone and Zanzibar—which comprise the second analytical category—is the status reversal which has occurred in the relationship between previously dominant and subordinate cultural groups as a result of the advance toward territorial self-government and the introduction of democratic processes and institutions. Until comparatively recently, agitational politics in these territories were largely an affair of the Creole minority of Freetown and the Arab minority of Zanzibar respectively. For special historical reasons each of these culturally dominant minorities exercised a disproportionate measure of political influence, and each tended to assume that in due course it would fall heir to British authority—the Creoles acquiring in Sierra Leone a position not unlike the Americo-Liberians of Liberia and the Arab oligarchy of Zanzibar resuming, in modern garb, the control it had over affairs before the establishment of the British protectorate. With the broadening of representation in territorial legislatures, and the introduction of universal suffrage and elections, however, the center of political gravity has dramatically shifted to the hitherto silent majorities (the hinterland peoples of the Protectorate of Sierra Leone and the Shirazis and Africans of Zanzibar). This was brought about by their political parties, the Sierra Leone People's Party and the Afro-Shirazi Union, respectively, which were overwhelmingly victorious in recent territorial elections. As a consequence of this status reversal in Sierra Leone, political leaders of the previously dominant minority, realizing the futility of organizing communal parties, either joined the majority party or led in organizing a competitive territorial party. In Zanzibar there has been only one election, and therefore the consequences of the status reversal are not yet apparent.

Among the countries in the third category of competitive-party systems there are many differences, but they have in common one characteristic, namely, party alignments reflect the predominance of the communal factor. Parties tend to be primarily, although not exclusively, instruments for the political expression of the interests of distinctive cultural groups defined in terms either of tribe, culture, or level of modernization. The party alignments in Togoland, Cameroons, Dahomey, and Chad reflect a basic cultural division characteristic of the entire Guinea Coast (see Map 1). The division is one between the less-developed, predominantly Muslim, pastoral groups in the northern sections of these countries, and the more developed, more nationalistic, predominantly non-Muslim groups in the southern sections. The CUT (Comité de l'Unité Togolaise) of Togoland, the outlawed UPC (Union des Populations du Cameroun) of the Cameroons, the PRD (Parti Républicain Dahoméen) of Dahomey, and the RDA in Chad have derived the bulk of their support from the southern sections; whereas the principal rival parties have tended to be rooted in and to represent the interests of the peoples in the northern sections. This same cultural cleavage cuts through Nigeria, where it has been a decisive factor in both party alignments and in the adoption of a federal system of government, as well as through the Ivory Coast and Ghana. In the case of the latter two countries, however, the dominant parties centered in the southern sections have been able to transcend this division, the Ivory Coast RDA thus far more effectively than the Ghana CPP.

Political development in Togoland and the Cameroons has been different from that in neighboring British territories because of the French policy of assimilation, and different from other French territories because of their status under the International Trusteeship System. As trust territories they were never completely assimilated into the French system, and they were assured of ultimate self-government or independence by the terms of the United Nations Charter. Their special status has affected party development in at least three respects: (1) being outside the main stream of political evolution in French tropical Africa, Togolese and Cameroonian parties have had a purely territorial focus and no formal link with such transterritorial parties as the RDA or PRA; (2) nationalist parties appeared under militant leaders demanding the fulfillment of the trusteeship objectives, namely, complete independence from France a decade before autonomist demands were made in other French dependencies; and (3) the French administration in the two territories tended to intervene in the political arena far more actively than elsewhere in an attempt to frustrate the growth of such autonomist sentiment and activity by creating and supporting parties (*partis de l'Administration*) favorable to the French connection and opposed to independence. This cleavage of political forces on the issue of the French presence has been reinforced by the previously described cultural cleavage between the anti-independence *partis de l'Administration* of the backward north and the pro-independence southern parties.[31]

Party competition in Western Nigeria and in the Republic of the Congo has been more intense than in most areas of Sub-Saharan Africa. In Western Nigeria the principal contenders for power have been the Action Group and the NCNC (National Council of Nigeria and the Cameroons). The Action Group, which controls the government of the Western Region, draws much of its strength from Yoruba nationalism (strengthened by the fear of Ibo domination via the rival NCNC) and a Yoruba middle class of traders and cocoa farmers. It has tended to stress regional interests and developments against those of Nigeria as a whole. The NCNC, which has its political core area among the Ibo people of the Eastern Region, understandably draws its greatest strength from the non-Yoruba (partly Ibo) areas of the Western Region, but it also commands substantial support among Yoruba youth and labor—a support sufficient to enable it to win the 1958 federal elections in Western Nigeria. The NCNC has been the principal carrier of the idea of Pan-Nigerian nationhood. Although both are particularistic parties in that they are rooted in distinctive cultural groups, party competition for power in a multi-tribal political system has forced them to stress goals and employ symbols that are national in character.

In the Republic of the Congo the two main competing parties also derive their support from distinctive cultural groups. The UDDIA (Union Démocratique pour la Défense des Intérêts Africains) has tended to be the political organ of the Bakonga peoples of the eastern and northern sections, with Brazzaville as their capital, and the PPC (Parti Progressiste Congolais) has tended to reflect the interests of the

---

[31] Official intervention has not been confined to Togoland and Cameroons, though it has been much more pronounced there. The Union Progressiste Mauritanienne and the Union Démocratique Tchadienne, among others, were also *"partis de l'Administration."* The leading pro-independence party in Togoland (Comité de l'Unité Togolaise) draws the bulk of its support from the coastal Ewe people, who are more advanced educationally and economically than the northerners, whose chiefs constituted the leadership of the pro-French Union des Chefs et Peuples du Nord. Thus, tribal antagonisms and the fear of domination have facilitated French intervention and manipulation of party activity. The situation is not dissimilar in the Cameroons, where the proscribed UPC (Union des Populations du Cameroun), which was both pro-independence and pro-communist, drew most of its support from the Douala and other southern peoples, and the pro-French parties were strongest in the Muslim and backward north.

M'Bochi peoples inhabiting the western coastal section, with Pointe Noire as their capital. Until recently, the almost equal strength of the two parties in the national parliament has had the effect of intensifying competition and reinforcing tribal consciousness. Party developments in this small country illuminate the fact that despite the French policies of assimilation and direct rule, and the fact that the two parties are branches of the RDA and PRA, local communal divisions have been the determinative factors in party alignments.

In the case of the Southern Cameroons, at present a region in the Federation of Nigeria, the principal issue dividing the major parties concerns its future vis-à-vis its two larger neighbors. The majority party, KNDP (Kamerun National Democratic Party), advocates secession from the Federation of Nigeria and integration with the Cameroons under French trusteeship in an independent Kamerun state. The opposition party, KNC (Kamerun National Congress), supports continued association of the Southern Cameroons as a self-governing region within an independent Federation of Nigeria. In addition to the issue regarding the future of the political order, however, there are other less evident but nonetheless important bases for party division: the bulk of the support for the KNDP tends to come from the more rural undeveloped areas, while that of the KNC is based mainly upon the southern developed areas; intermixed with this cleavage are tribal factors of no little relevance. In many respects, the situation is not unlike that which existed in British Togoland before its integration with the independent state of Ghana.

In the three remaining African states which have had a competitive-party system (the Republics of Niger, Upper Volta, and the Gaboon) the explanations for party alignments are less obvious and simple. The principal parties in each of these three countries are branches of the RDA (Rassemblement Démocratique Africain) and the PRA (Parti du Regroupement Africain), as is also the case in all but two (Mauritanian Islamic Republic and the Central African Republic) of the other nine new states in the former French Afrique Noire. Indeed, perhaps the most striking and distinctive feature of the French African political scene has been the predominance over the past few years of large parties spanning ten of the twelve territories stretching from Dakar to Brazzaville. In the spring of 1958 the RDA commanded an overwhelming majority and undisputed power in three territories (Ivory Coast, Sudan, and Guinea) and a weaker majority in four others (Chad, Gaboon, Middle Congo, and Upper Volta); and the PRA completely controlled

Senegal and had a weaker majority in Niger and Dahomey. In all of these territories but one (Dahomey), the RDA or PRA, when not in the majority, constituted the principal opposition party. The situation changed very considerably during the fall of 1958 and the spring of 1959, as will be noted subsequently; but it is still in point to inquire (1) why have the political interests of the diverse peoples inhabiting the vast stretches of Afrique Noire been channelled into two major parties, and (2) given such unity what is it that has divided the two parties?

Three explanations are suggested as an answer to the first point. One is that French policies regarding education, assimilation, and direct rule have resulted in, among other things, the creation of a cosmopolitan-minded political elite which until recently was willing to seek self-determination within the broader confines of a Franco-African political community. The second explanation is found in the extreme centralization of authority in metropolitan institutions during the life of the Fourth Republic. This had two consequences: (1) it compelled French African leaders to seek unity in order to maximize their influence upon policy-making in Paris, and (2) it precluded the emergence of the provocative "fear of domination" which elsewhere in Africa has been the single most important causal factor engendering tribalism, communalism, sectionalism, and other fissiparous tendencies. Since no one privileged or well-placed group in French Africa was endowed with, or had the prospects of securing, power over other groups, tribal and communal tensions remained latent.

A third and related consideration was that despite the centralization of authority in Paris, prestigeful political roles were created at all levels of the hierarchy ranging from territory through federation to the metropole. Moreover, most leading members of the African elite played political roles at all three levels simultaneously. This physical dispersion of political roles and the multiple roles played by the leading political actors, coupled with the fact that no single set of structures below the Paris level had been endowed with real power, prevented the build-up of vested interests or political ambitions in political structures at any single level of the hierarchy.

Finally, there was a growing belief among most French African leaders, intensified by burgeoning pressures from a more militant generation of younger leaders entering the political arena, that the time had arrived either to force an immediate redefinition of the nature of the Franco-African political association, placing it on an egalitarian and federal basis, or to opt for independence. Linked with this belief was the conviction that the only way in which the issue could be effectively forced was through a common front. Although efforts made in the spring of 1958 to create a single party were abortive, the two major parties agreed to present a united front vis-à-vis the French government. These developments pointing toward the creation of a comprehensive nationalist movement embracing all of Afrique Noire were interrupted by the dramatic changes which followed the coming to power of De Gaulle and the introduction of the new French constitution in the fall of 1958.

There is no simple explanation for the issues that have divided the RDA and the PRA. The RDA is the oldest transterritorial party, and in a sense its very existence compelled opposition groups to organize an equally comprehensive party if they wanted to compete effectively. The leaders of the RDA resisted merger with the PRA, which sought it in 1958, mainly because they did not wish to abandon the name and the symbol of what they felt to be their special claim to leadership of French Africa's leading comprehensive party.

PRA leaders tended to take a more emphatic and united position on the two major issues that dominated French African politics during 1958 and 1959, namely, the issue of continued association with France versus independence, and the issue of "primary federations" versus territorial autonomy. PRA leaders leaned toward greater African autonomy and the preservation of French African unity through "primary federations," whereas RDA leaders were divided. The holding of the referendum and the introduction of the new constitution in the fall of 1958 forced a decision on these questions. The three main RDA leaders (Sekou Touré in Guinea, Houphouet-Boigny in the Ivory Coast, and Modibo Keita in the Sudan) took opposing positions on one or both of these issues—Touré opted for independence while Houphouet-Boigny and Keita voted to remain within the new Franco-African Community; Keita has been and remains one of the foremost proponents of "primary federations," while Houphouet-Boigny opposes them, favoring direct relations between the territories and France. In other territories positions taken by party leaders on these issues have been similarly contradictory (e.g., the PRA leaders in the Gaboon sided with the RDA leaders in opposing "primary federations"). In sum, the variant decisions made on these fundamental questions, together with subsequent developments, have revealed the extremely tenuous character of the unity of these two parties. They appear now to have been no more than electoral alliances. As one observer put it, "for the PRA as for the

RDA neither a party line nor even a party activity as a whole is worth talking about any more."

The disintegration of the two comprehensive parties is largely a consequence of the process of "territorialization" (i.e., the devolution of legislative and budgetary authority from Paris to the territories) first initiated by the Loi Cadre of 1956, and, except for Community functions, fully consummated by the new French Constitution of 1958. Just as the concentration of authority in Paris called the comprehensive parties into being, so has the dispersion of authority from Paris led to their disintegration and the territorialization of party systems. It seems that once a process of territorialization is launched it acquires a powerful internal dynamic as a result of the ever-increasing number of vested interests (careers, power, prestigeful roles) which become built into the territorial structures. Over against this seemingly inexorable trend are three countervailing forces resisting this process: (1) the belief that continued African unity on a scale larger than a single territory is necessary to ensure absolute equality in the making of Community decisions; (2) the manifest economic advantages of larger polities, recognized most acutely by economically weak states such as Niger and Chad; and (3) the pride and other psychological satisfactions associated with largeness in scale. These are the main ingredients in the rationale for the preservation of transterritorial parties. It is questionable whether they will be strong enough to overcome the powerful centrifugal forces pushing for complete territorialization of both authoritative structures and party systems.

The party systems of the White communities in the two European oligarchic states of Southern Rhodesia and the Union of South Africa represent another distinctive type of competitive system, particularly when contrasted with those analyzed above. They are similar in two respects: participation in the system has been effectively limited to Europeans, and policy regarding relations with the government of the non-European majority is one issue on which parties have been divided. Beyond this, however, party development in the two countries has followed a different course. As Gwendolen Carter states, "the basic division in South African politics has been between the party which, for one reason or another, reflected an exclusive Afrikaner nationalism, and that which held together members of both the English and Afrikaner communities in pursuit of internal and external goals on which both peoples could agree."[32] Virtually every issue in South Africa's

[32] *The Politics of Inequality*, New York, 1958, p. 28.

party struggle has been affected by Afrikaner or English South African nationalism. For the last three decades two principal parties have dominated the political scene, one representing militant Afrikanerdom (the National Party successively under Hertzog, Malan, Strydom, and Verwoerd) and the other representing moderate Afrikaners and most English-speaking South Africans (successively the South African Party under Botha and Smuts and the United Party, first under a moderated Hertzog with Smuts, then under Smuts alone, and finally Jan Hofmeyr). In addition to these two giant parties, which have alternated in power and obtained no less than 70 per cent of the popular vote in all elections since 1921, there have been several minor parties (Unionist, Dominion, Labour, Liberal, Union Federal, and Conservative), only one of which (Labour) has exercised any significant influence on the political process.[33]

In Southern Rhodesia party competition is a rather recent development. Prior to 1923, when the territory became a self-governing colony under a white oligarchy, the settlers were united in their struggle for self-government, their main foe at that time being the British South Africa Company. Between 1923 and the early 1950's there were factional disputes over the issue of union with South Africa and economic policies, but there were no fundamental cleavages leading to the formation of competitive political parties. Since the early 1950's when negotiations commenced for the creation of a Federation of Rhodesia and Nyasaland, however, the question of "native" policy has emerged as the basic issue dividing the European society and determining party alignments. The long-dominant United Rhodesia Party supported the Federation, and the principal of multiracial government which it embodied. With the establishment of the Federation, of which Southern Rhodesia is a constituent and dominant part, there has been an increasing division of European attitudes in Southern Rhodesia on the issue of African advancement. The variant attitudes on this issue have found political expression in three competing parties: the United Rhodesia Party under Garfield Todd, which supports a program of progressive African advance, both economically and politically; the United Federal Party, which accepts the liberal concept of multiracialism but empha-

[33] The Labour Party, unlike its namesakes elsewhere, existed only for the purpose of protecting the interest of white labor against not only management, but also, and particularly, against native labor. Representing the poor-white fear of being displaced by cheap native labor, the Labour Party, though its members were predominantly English-speaking, used the balance of power it held during 1924-1929 to keep Hertzog's Nationalist Party in power.

sizes the need for gradualism and protracted European supremacy; and the Dominion Party, which supports a unitary state made up of the "white" areas of the Rhodesias, with the predominantly "black" areas of Northern Rhodesia and Nyasaland having some form of protectorate status.[34] As the white supremacist Dominion Party gains in strength by playing on European fears of ultimate black domination, the United Federal Party has been increasingly forced to take a less liberal position by making publicly explicit its own belief in white supremacy. Given the uncertainty regarding the Federation's future and the increasing radicalization of African attitudes, party competition within the oligarchy is bound to remain intense for some time to come.

In this survey of the general characteristics and patterning of political parties in Sub-Saharan Africa two features stand out with striking clarity. One is the diversity and complexity of African political systems, the other the highly transitional character of political phenomena. Africa is rapidly breaking out of the rigid steel grid which a variegated European colonialism imposed upon an even more diverse aggregation of indigenous societies. In most instances this great transformation is not occurring within the boundaries or the framework of established societies; rather, entirely new political systems and new societies are in the process of birth. Politically, the essence of this dynamic movement is that power is rapidly gravitating into the hands of entirely new social groups unaccustomed to its exercise. As a consequence there is a generalized instability, and particularly an unpredictability regarding political authority. This generates desperate fear or despair among groups less favored, or among those clearly destined for displacement; it also stimulates and agitates the reckless ambitions of the *nouveaux riches* and those who sense the manifold opportunities for acquiring prestige, influence, and power previously denied. These fears and ambitions are all the more intense because they are the emotions of peoples who feel themselves to be the victims of history. There is a passionate urge for self-justification, for racial-justification.

[34] In 1957 the United Rhodesia Party of Southern Rhodesia merged with the Federal Party, the majority party controlling the government of the Federation, to which Europeans in both of the Rhodesias and Nyasaland have belonged. The United Federal Party, the new party created by the merger, was intended to function in both Southern Rhodesian and federal elections. Immediately before the 1958 elections in Southern Rhodesia, however, the liberal wing of the new United Federal Party under Garfield Todd was superseded by the conservative faction, whereupon Todd reactivated the United Rhodesia Party, which suffered complete defeat in the elections. The Dominion Party is the latest organizational embodiment (earlier forms being the Democratic and Confederate Parties) of rightwing attitudes on the racial question. It draws the bulk of its support from a mixture of Afrikaner and English-speaking white supremacists.

Given this maelstrom of moving and struggling social forces, political parties tend to be the instruments of particular groups concerned not primarily with questions of public policy, but with the very nature of a new social and political system in which they find themselves imprisoned by historical accident. Not being part of a society whose boundaries and institutions are relatively stable, they are forced to be preoccupied with the relative position their group will occupy in the new order. This illuminates again the highly futuristic aspect of African politics referred to earlier. Yet there is also the traditionalist aspect. Although the dynamic unfolding character of the political scene compels political leaders to be future-oriented, in many instances the process of differentiation (whether by class, occupation, or otherwise) has not occurred to an extent sufficient to provide modern social bases for party alignments; hence the primary reference group for party formation is frequently some traditional group. Thus, as African leaders reach into the future in their efforts to create new societies, they are compelled to look to their past for their basic political support.

Interest Groups and Interest Group Systems

In evaluating the role of institutional groups in Sub-Saharan Africa, one must at the outset distinguish between two different categories of political systems. In authoritarian-oriented systems such as Liberia, Ethiopia, and northern Nigeria, or in purely colonial systems such as Belgian, Portuguese, and Spanish Africa, the effective center of political gravity lies in authoritative institutional groups. In the new African states the appearance of militant nationalist parties and the evolution of competitive party systems shattered the predominating role of the colonial bureaucracy and shifted the center of politics to extra-institutional arenas. As we have seen, however, in the post-independence period there is a tendency for it to shift back. In the emergent and transitional systems, the extraordinary fluidity of the situation, coupled with the residual presence or influence of colonial authority, justifies only the most tentative generalization at this stage.

In Colonial Africa, armies are the neutral instruments of civilian authorities in the imperial or colonial governments.[35] Except for the

---

[35] While there is strong Gaullist sentiment among many Europeans in what was formerly French tropical Africa, particularly in Chad, the small size of the European population and the substantial authority now exercised by African leaders makes it extremely unlikely that the French army could play the independent political role it has done in Algeria. In Spanish and Portuguese Africa there are army officers in the colonial bureaucracy, but they do not play a political role independent of the army hierarchy in

Sudan, none of the new African states has an army capable of exerting a political role. The armies of the European oligarchic states are all firmly under civilian control. Thus, compared to other non-Western areas, the army has until now been an insignificant factor in African politics. In looking to the future, however, there is evidence that the army could become a political force of increasing and perhaps decisive importance in certain countries. The assumption of power by the military in the Sudan is a case in point. In South Africa the Nationalist Party has departed from the British tradition of a politically neutral army by concentrating heavily on a program of Afrikanerization of the officer corps. In Ethiopia the Emperor has placed high priority upon the creation of a modern air force and army officered by young Western-educated Ethiopians. These young officers, together with their counterparts in the Ethiopian government service, could become a class capable of independent political action. Also, it is not impossible that if the European oligarchy in the Federation of Rhodesia and Nyasaland were to force a showdown with the United Kingdom government on the issue of independence, the settler-controlled army could become the decisive force in winning independence and in maintaining the oligarchy in power.

For most of Africa, institutionalized religion is part of the ensemble of innovations introduced by the Western impact. This does not mean that traditional African societies were lacking in religion; on the contrary, religion permeated every aspect of life, and in many societies ultimate authority was vested in an essentially religious institution or person, such as a diviner or priest-king. Here we are concerned, however, with the position of institutionalized religious groups in modern African politics. In general, most of Africa's new societies are religiously pluralistic as a result of the intermixture of Islam, traditional African religions, and the missionary activities of the various competing Christian sects and churches. As a result, no single church has become an institutionalized interest group.

There are three important exceptions, however, which deserve special comment. Two of these are found in the special role played by the Dutch Reformed Church in the Afrikaner community of South Africa and by the Coptic Church in Ethiopia. In both cases, the overwhelming

---

Madrid and Lisbon. Contingents of the British army are rigorously under the control of civilian authority in British territories, although during the Mau Mau Emergency in Kenya they played a transitory political role.

majority of Afrikaner and Ethiopian peoples accept their respective churches as national institutions. The church is not only one of the principal supports for political authority; it is also a powerful integrative factor in the two communities. In neither case, however, is the church an independent political force. The Emperor of Ethiopia is the recognized and effective head of the Coptic Church. The Nationalist Party and the Dutch Reformed Church are but the political and religious wings, respectively, of Afrikaner nationalism, at the head of which one finds an "interlocking directorate of personalities."[36] Although the Dutch Reformed Church has provided the Nationalist Party leadership with a theological rationalization of apartheid, a small but influential group of theologians have emerged who are also among the principal critics of that policy on both theological and practical grounds.

The other exception is the role of the Catholic Church in Spanish and Portuguese Africa, and, to a certain extent, Belgian Africa. Here church and state have reinforced the authority and influence of each other. In general, the religious authoritarianism of Catholicism, like that of Calvinism, tends to strengthen political authoritarianism when Catholicism is the religion of the majority and is supported by the state. It could be argued, for example, that Catholicism in Spanish and Portuguese Africa has contributed to political quiescence, while in British Africa, where it has been in a competitive and frequently minority position, it has not had this effect. Where Islam has taken institutional form, as in the emirates of northern Nigeria, authoritarianism has also been strengthened. Apart from its supporting role, the Catholic Church, where institutionalized, has exerted a powerful influence in the field of education, and, in certain respects, upon social policy.

Until comparatively recently, Sub-Saharan Africa could legitimately claim to be the continent of bureaucratic government, of administrations and *administrés*, where the political process and the administrative process are synonymous. Politics had a seditious implication. Even today the very word "politics" is spoken in whispers by many Africans in what remains of Colonial Africa. This administrative outlook is reflected in existing literature which is saturated with such concepts as "native administration," "colonial administration," "administrative powers," "urban administration," and so forth. Moreover, the bureaucratic domination of the political process was strengthened and perpetuated by

---

[36] Carter, *op.cit.*, p. 280. The rigid Calvinism of the Dutch Reformed Church has led to an authoritarian philosophy of government supporting the divine right of the "elect" to rule, and the religious duty of the governed to conform.

the fact that government employment tended to absorb, and thereby immobilize politically a large percentage of the Western-educated elements—of all groups, the most predisposed to political activity. This situation, of course, is now rapidly changing. But it does provide a clue to the volatile and unpredictable quality of contemporary political change. The bureaucratic grid is being shattered by the emergence of new political arenas into which are being drawn and activated millions of people unaccustomed to "politics" in a large-scale society.

Once these general observations are made, the role of the bureaucracy in different type systems requires special comment. In the African oligarchic states of Ethiopia and Liberia, there is little concept of a civil service. In both states the bureaucracies dominate the society and are the arenas in which the political struggle occurs. The bureaucracy in Liberia is the permanent preserve of the dominant elements in the True Whig Party; in Ethiopia it is staffed by personal appointees of the Emperor, who shrewdly transfers or rotates officials in order to avoid the creation of separate and possibly disloyal centers of power. With the expansion in government activities consequent upon economic development and modernization, the bulk of young university-educated Ethiopians and Liberians are entering the subaltern ranks in the bureaucracy. Thus, it is probable that for some time to come the bureaucracy will remain the center of the political process, and that as the size and influence of this new class of younger men expands it will become the principal active element of politics in the two states concerned.

In the two European oligarchic states of Southern Rhodesia and the Union of South Africa the bureaucracy has been developed in the British tradition of a politically neutral public service. This feature has far wider applicability, however, for in all British territories the dominant concept has been that of a professional civil service in which recruitment and promotion are in principle based upon merit and performance under rules administered by a neutral public service commission. The degree to which this principle leads to a durable service tradition and persists after the displacement of the professional colonial bureaucracy varies according to the situation. In South Africa it is being rapidly undermined as a result of the Nationalist Party's policy of Afrikanerization of the higher posts in the army, police, and civil service. In both states it is operative only as regards the political process within the white oligarchy; for the African mass, the European bureaucracy is the principal instrument for maintaining white supremacy, playing a role not dissimilar to colonial bureaucracies elsewhere. In the government of Northern Rhodesia and of the Federation of Rhodesia and Nyasaland a concerted effort is being made to recruit into the bureaucracies "local" rather than "overseas" Europeans, ostensibly to economize and to give public servants "roots" in the country. This will have the effect, whether intended or not, of replacing a comparatively neutral colonial bureaucracy with one which identifies itself with the principle of white supremacy. In Kenya such an identification already exists in those many instances where colonial civil servants have acquired land with the intention of becoming "settlers" upon their retirement.

In the new African states it is still too early to evaluate the extent to which the concept of a neutral public service has caught on and will endure. In the Sudan and Ghana, the only two fully independent states, the principle still commands general acceptance. In part this is due to the recency of their independence, and in part to the fact that in both instances the intense nationalist drive to "Africanize" or "Sudanize" the higher civil service has resulted in the induction into that service of Africans who are qualified and available without special reference to their political affiliation. In Ghana supporters of the dominant Convention People's Party (CPP) have been appointed to most boards and commissions, but the civil service has continued as an essentially neutral instrument of public policy, the latter being formulated by the majority party leadership. For both countries this might well be a transitional phenomenon, a post-colonial hangover, and in due course the bureaucracy will become the preserve and instrument of the dominant party.

In the Northern Region of Nigeria the dominant party (Northern People's Congress) and the bureaucracy are fused through an interlocking directorate of personalities. Most of the leading members of the Congress are also emirate officials. The bureaucratic structure of the emirate system down to and including the level of the district head has provided strong institutional support for Congress. All members of the bureaucracy are expected to be Congress supporters, and all Congress activists are usually ensured a suitable post in the bureaucracy. Through this monolithic fusion of the emirate bureaucracy and the dominant party, the latter has been able to acquire complete control over the new institutions of the northern regional government. Once in control of that government the party initiated a policy of thoroughgoing "northernization," that is, northerners are progressively displacing British officials and southerners who heretofore have predominated in the northern colonial bureaucracy.

As we turn to the role of non-institutional interest groups in modern Africa, it should be clear from earlier analysis that interests centered upon race, tribe, and nationality, and in some instances class and religion, are the most decisive factors in contemporary African politics. European colonialism and Westernism have initiated and fostered a process of social and economic change which has led to the rise of new social and political groupings. The interests of the latter should in theory cut across and transcend original bonds of identification; in actual fact, it has in many instances strengthened such bonds.[37] Moreover, although nationalism has served to aggregate and integrate the interests of many diverse groups in the drive to terminate colonialism, this has proved to be transitory. The actual approach of self-government has in many instances tended to activate latent particularistic interests and to sharpen status, racial, and tribal cleavages. There is, of course, an awareness of status, tribal, racial, or class interests under colonialism. But the bureaucratic authoritarianism characteristic of a colonial milieu enforces quiescence and minimizes the self-consciousness and political expression of the groups concerned. Once the colonial regime is seriously challenged and there is movement toward a new but indeterminate structure of authority, the interest groups become increasingly self-conscious and assertive.

Associational and party development in Africa reflects the tenacity and primacy of racial, tribal, religious, and regional interests. In multiracial Africa, race is the principal basis for the organization of both political parties and associational interest groups. The names of most associations carry the prefix "European," "Asian," or "African." Within each race, however, there is considerable variation in the character of the secondary basis according to which associational interest groups are organized. Among Europeans, nationality (e.g., Afrikaner vs. English in South Africa) or religion (e.g., Protestants vs. Catholics in the Belgian Congo) have been overriding considerations in certain situations.

---

[37] Indirect rule and differential administrative policies are partly responsible for the awakening or strengthening of tribal or regional interests. Although a general phenomenon of British Africa, it is best illustrated by the differential administration of the Hausa-Fulani area of Northern Nigeria and the Nilotic area of the southern Sudan. In both areas there were profound ethnic and religious differences between the groups concerned and other groups in the territory, but the policy of separate administration tended to perpetuate and accentuate these differences. Of even greater significance, however, has been the differentiating effect of modernity. Economic development, for example, did not create the difference between Europeans, Asians, and Africans in multiracial Africa, nor the differences between tribal groups such as the Yoruba, Baganda, and Chagga and their respective neighbors. Nevertheless, its uneven incidence (like that of Christianity and Western education) has sharpened and aggravated those differences.

But in general the associational structure of the European community is functionally specific in character. Particular interests have their own associations, such as chambers of commerce, farmers' unions, professional societies, labor unions, and so forth. Among Asians the associational pattern has been largely determined by the communalism of Asian groups in Africa. Hindus, Muslims, Goans, Sikhs, and Ismailis have their own associations espousing all of the interests of their respective communities. African associations fall roughly into three main categories: comprehensive (racial) nationalist parties discussed previously; associations centered upon tribal, kinship, or lineage ties; and associations based upon the new occupational, professional, and economic interests created by the impact of modernity. Associations of the third type are functionally specific, whereas the first two are functionally diffuse in that they aggregate and articulate the ensemble of interests of the groups concerned.

Most Africans in urban centers belong to a kinship or tribal association. Organized initially as mutual-aid and self-help societies, some have assumed a variety of significant political functions, including the representation and protection of interests of the village or tribal community concerned. In British territories they have been encouraged by government, in some instances being used officially as instruments for representation and taxation. At the level of local government in both the urban center and the tribal homeland these associations have acted as pressure groups agitating for political reform, greater representation, and other measures to protect or enhance their group interests. In some areas pan-tribal federations have been organized at the territorial level. In this larger political arena they have played a pressure group role and in some instances provided the infrastructure for comprehensive nationalist movements and laterally competitive political parties.[38] Elsewhere I have noted the reasons for this phenomenon:

"It is the result of the gravitation of the politically conscious educated elements to their tribe of origin not only because of the persistence of tribal loyalties and obligations or their new appreciation of African culture, but also because the tribe could provide them with a relatively secure political base, a fairly reliable personal following, and masses whose aspirations, belief systems, grievances, and tensions they

[38] The outstanding examples of such organizational links are the Yoruba Egbe Omo Oduduwa and the Action Group, the Ibo State Union and the National Council of Nigeria and the Cameroons, and the Luo Union and the Central Nyanza District Association in Kenya.

knew intimately and therefore could most easily and legitimately appeal to or manipulate. Moreover, in many cases tribal unions have taken on the political functions of organized pressure or bargaining groups on behalf of tribes placed in a minority or disadvantageous position as a consequence of constitutional developments at the territorial level. Finally, tribal unions were 'organizations in being' which territorial politicians found highly useful not only as a structure in which they could climb to positions of leadership in territorial politics but also as an immediately available, developed organizational apparatus and a cadre of political activists."[39]

One of the several features differentiating Sub-Saharan Africa from other non-Western areas is the fact that most of its peoples have been the beneficiaries of programs of positive social, economic, and political development initiated and carried through by colonial powers not only chastened and reformed by imperial disintegration elsewhere but subject to ever-increasing pressure of a critical world opinion and growing African nationalism. Most other areas terminated their colonial experience without the benefit of such programs. During the past decade the tempo of social and political change has been vastly accelerated and the influence of modernity has become ever more pervasive. This has had the effect of greatly expanding the number of Africans participating in modern institutions and processes. Moreover, policies have been deliberately aimed at bringing about radical changes in the mode of life in the bush and the village through programs of mass education, rural agricultural development, and the democratization of local government. It is likely that the rate of social mobilization has been higher in parts of Africa than in any other underdeveloped area of the world.

This distinctive feature of African modernization has many implications relevant to this study. One is that it has accelerated the organization of associational interest groups that are functionally specific. In British territories, governments have taken the initiative in organizing cooperative societies and labor unions.[40] Moreover, full-time government officials have been appointed, not only to render advice and assistance, but also to ensure that these societies and unions perform

---

[39] "Current Political Movements in Africa," *The Annals*, No. 298, March 1955, p. 102.

[40] One of the clauses inserted in the Colonial Development and Welfare Act under pressure from the U.K. Labour Party was that no grants would be made to territories in which labor unions were not given encouragement.

the specific functions prescribed by legislation. In the former French territories the *société indigene de prevoyance* reflected a similar policy. These actions at the official level have been strengthened and extended by the energetic overseas activities of the British Trade Union Congress and the French CGT, and such international organizations as the ILO and ICFTU, which have given substantial financial and organizational assistance to labor unions in Africa.[41]

The associational development resulting from these special factors in the African situation has had variable consequences. In Northern Rhodesia the African Mineworkers' Union has emerged as an association embracing and representing virtually all the interests of its members. Many of its leaders, until recently, were members of the National Executive of the African National Congress. Thus, the union has served the dual role of representing the interests of workers vis-à-vis management and at the same time providing a structure and leadership cadres through which a comprehensive nationalist party could mobilize support for nationalist objectives. In other territories there also exists an interlocking directorate exercising control over both the central organization and the nationalist movement (e.g., Kenya, Tanganyika, and Guinea). Yet, in still other territories (e.g., Sierra Leone, Nigeria, and the Sudan) this close link between an associational interest group and dominant political parties has not been achieved, although repeated efforts have been made by leaders to bring it about.

Rapid social change has not only created and differentiated new social groupings having particular interests requiring articulation and representation; it has also created situations of profound psychological tension and frustration which have found expression in witchcraft cults, riots, and politico-religious mass movements of an anomic character. These take a variety of forms, among which the most common have been puritanical or chiliastic religious movements or nativistic movements. The distinguishing feature of the latter is not the existence of a simple material dissatisfaction (though this may be the provocation which ignites the movement), nor the feeling that alien rule is oppressive or ethically intolerable, but rather a generalized predisposition to escape from the insecurity, hopelessness, and frustrations of the present by a return to the past, or at least the past as it has been idealized.

[41] During the decade 1947-1957 French African labor unions were directly affiliated with the three major labor federations of metropolitan France. The competition between these metropolitan associations in their effort to expand their strength in French Africa has greatly accelerated the process of labor unionization.

Situations of this order have been inflamed and converted into politically consequential forms of non-programmatic mass action by any one of a number of immediate provocations, including particularly actual or rumored economic disabilities or deprivations, the appearance of a prophet or messiah, or the harangues of a political agitator. They are not exclusively a phenomenon of colonialism, as evidenced by the riots in 1958 in Eastern Nigeria.[42]

IV. POLITICAL FUNCTIONS

In the discussion thus far our attention has been repeatedly directed to the diversities and the pluralism of Africa's territorial societies. These attributes are largely the consequences of (1) the imposition of highly differentiated alien authority structures upon a mosaic of traditional societies; (2) the uneven incidence of the impact of Westernism and modernity arising from differences in the purposes and policies of the mediating political elites and from variations in the assimilative or adaptive capacities of traditional cultures; (3) the gross cultural disparities between the indigenous African peoples and the alien races who have made Africa their home; and (4) the comparative brevity of the European presence. As the political systems of the territorial societies are progressively refashioned in the move toward self-government the discontinuities created by the foregoing factors not only define the central issues of politics but decisively affect the character of political structures and the performance of key political functions.

Another striking feature of contemporary African politics which has been stressed is the extraordinarily transitional character of most political systems. In the new and emergent African states, the peoples have moved in one short decade from a purely colonial status toward variant forms of self-government. The Sudan, the first in this group to become independent, has yet to adopt a constitution defining the character of its new political order. In the past seven years, Nigeria, now on the threshold of independence, has had four constitutions (and a fifth now under negotiation), each of which has prescribed a different set of political structures and pattern of role relationships. In multiracial Africa existing constitutions are officially defined as transitional, and none of the principal actors (Britain, the Africans, or the settlers) can speak

---

[42] Eastern Nigeria has been one of the principal centers of anomic movements. Two occurred during the 1920's after British pacification, another in 1952 as a protest against a technological innovation (palm-oil mills), and another in 1958 as a protest against the termination of free universal primary education.

with confidence regarding the ultimate character of the political order.

Given the highly ephemeral and indeterminate character of most territorial political structures at this stage in African development, how valid are generalizations regarding the nature of Africa's political systems *qua* systems? From the purist's point of view, they could be seriously questioned, since a system implies a set of ordered relationships having stable boundaries and a certain persistence over time. Again, when there are gross discontinuities, fleeting structures, and rapidly changing patterns of rule-making, for example, can one systematically analyze the structures of the system in which these are found and meaningfully compare them with those in other systems? As long as structures, and particularly authoritative structures, are the focus of analysis, the answer is in the negative. If one postulates, however, that in every society, no matter how transitory its structures, certain key political functions are performed, then it can be validly claimed that a system exists and that comparisons can be made. Once this proposition is stated, however, it should be emphasized that from the analyst's point of view a distinction must be drawn between a comparatively stable and settled polity and one in which rapid structural change is occurring. In the latter situation, which includes most of Africa, functional categories are used to illuminate the dynamic forces of change that are eroding old systems and conditioning the character of new political systems now in gestation or the process of birth. This is, in any event, the way in which they are employed in the following analysis.

The Function of Articulation of Interests

In our earlier survey of interest groups and interest group systems we discussed in general terms the character of interests demanding recognition as well as the agencies through which they found expression. Here we are concerned with more specific issues of interest specification and interest representation. At the outset we must distinguish between the character of interests and their articulation in traditional African political systems and in the larger territorial societies. As for the first, all traditional societies, like modern societies, have some form of stratification and differentiation, whether it be by sex, race, age, wealth, occupation, class, lineage, or locality. Among traditional societies there are wide variations in the degree to which different types of differentiation are given an articulative emphasis. In many societies the lineage is the basic socio-economic unit and the ensemble of economic and religious interests in the land and the ancestors are the interests of the

lineage as a corporate group. But a village is not merely an aggregation of autonomous corporate lineages making separate and specific
economic demands upon the authority structure; rather, as Fallers has
pointed out for the Busoga of Uganda, "ties of personal loyalty were
established between the headman and leading members of peasant lineages and these ties were reinforced by ties of marriage. . . . Thus,
the headman, as head of the village or sub-village, like the ruler as
head of the state, balanced his position within his own corporate lineage
group with personal ties with important members of other corporate
groups."[43]

In more highly stratified societies marked by considerable division
of labor and occupational specialization, like the Hausa-Fulani states
of northern Nigeria, the lineage is of lesser importance than craft groups.
Yet in the rigidly hierarchical authoritarianism characteristic of these
societies, the interests of individual crafts have not been articulated
through guild organizations or structure. Rather, one finds the phenomenon of occupational class, in which the members of a particular
occupation constitute a class differentiated from other occupational
classes in a highly stratified system of prestige ranking. These occupational classes were graded in order of prestige as follows: aristocracy
by birth, aristocracy by appointment, Koranic teachers, successful merchants, craftsmen, small traders, brokers, farmers, blacksmiths, hunters,
musicians, and butchers.[44] There were relations between craft groups,
but normally sons inherited their father's occupation (unless by chance
they became commoner clients to the chief), the interests of which
found representation within the limits of a deferential and hierarchical
society. These are but two examples of the variant forms of interest
articulation in traditional societies.

The impact of modernity has had a dual effect upon those traditional
systems. It has altered the traditional modes of interest expression as
a result of the erosion of traditional authority and lineage bonds and
the progressive decline in traditional crafts.[45] It has also given birth

[43] Lloyd A. Fallers, *Bantu Bureaucracy*, Cambridge, 1957, p. 128.
[44] M. G. Smith, *The Economy of Hausa Communities of Zaria*, London, 1955, pp. 15-16.
[45] The decline in traditional craft organization is but a general tendency resulting
from the sudden impact of modern technology; there are, however, many instances
where new craft organizations have emerged from the old, performing the same functions, but have a structure based not upon the lineage but upon the territorial division
of society. As Lloyd describes it: "The structure (of the traditional organizations) was
the lineage structure, the lineage meeting was the craft meeting; the craft head was the
compound head, the oldest man in the lineage. The modern craft guild has precisely

to specific interests requiring new modes of expression consonant with a secular authority structure and appropriate to a modern territorial society. It is clear from our earlier analysis, however, that neither of these twin processes of disintegration and restructuring has been completed. The urban worker is aware that in the modern sector he has common occupational interests with other workers not his kinsmen, and that to protect and advance these interests it is necessary to support a labor union; but he is also sensitive to both the responsibilities imposed, and the security provided, by his lineage. African farmers or traders participating in the modern economy recognize the need for the articulation of their specific agricultural or trading interests; but they are also impressed by the fact that in many instances lineage and clan loyalties and organizations are useful, if not indispensable, aids in larger-scale enterprise and in the amassment of capital. Even some of the most acculturated urban barristers active in a panoply of modern social, economic, professional, and political associations maintain a strong interest in the economic and political affairs of their lineages and home villages. Family obligations, ties of sentiment, and a secure political base for a political career in the territorial society are some of the considerations involved. In any event, the existence of these multiple interests, embracing both the traditional and the modern, makes it necessary to soften the implication of opposition or discontinuity in such dichotomies as urban-rural or modern-traditional. Most Africans still have interests in both worlds. This has had the practical effect of retarding both the disintegration of the old and full-scale involvement in the new.

Another consideration affecting the articulation of specific interests is the comparative instability of individual career or occupational interests among Africans either in or entering the modern sector of the society. In the unskilled ranks of labor the rate of turnover is extremely high, mainly because most of the Africans concerned regard wage employment as a temporary measure for securing enough money to get married and for acquiring a few prestige items like a bicycle or phonograph. Among other social categories, however, the explanation is largely found in the intense ambitions to move to other and higher careers coupled with the tremendous expansion in career opportunities

---

the same economic functions as the lineage meeting . . . but the workers are drawn from all parts of the town by their common interest, and are not related by blood." Peter Lloyd, "Craft Organization in Yoruba Towns," *Africa*, Vol. XXIII, January 1953, p. 43.

in the late stages of terminal colonialism and the early stages of independence. Among most educated Africans in the emergent African states the rate of occupational mobility is extraordinarily high. Thus, the individual interests of members of those groups most likely to perform the articulating function for special interests are unstable mainly because of a preoccupation with their own rapid upward climb to positions of affluence and power in the new national society.

The articulation of interests has also been affected by African attitudes regarding both the utility and the legitimacy of specific interests making separate demands upon the political system. In most traditional societies the idea of having specific interests articulated separate from those of the lineage or other corporate grouping was largely absent, although in some instances lineages were, in effect, special interest groups because of the specialization of their members in a single craft. Most colonial powers have given consideration to certain special interests in early forms of representation, but the idea that the organization of functionally specific interest groups could meaningfully affect public policy under colonialism did not take hold. Rather, it gave way to the more convincing notion that special interests could be advanced only through a common nationalist front under which all interest would be subsumed. Once colonialism commenced to be seriously questioned by rising nationalism, pressure-group activity by special interests was considered useless, if not accommodationist. Thus, until comparatively recently, the articulation of special interests has been deterred by perspectives shaped by traditional culture as well as by the nationalist drive for independence.

This latter point brings us back to the fundamental fact that in contemporary Africa the articulation of functionally specific interests is, with few exceptions, transcended by and considered to be the function of the articulation of the general interests of one's race, tribe, region, or other group whose survival or primacy has first priority. In multiracial Africa the two frequently coincide. As most Asian residents in East Africa are *commerçants*, it could be argued that Asian associations organized to defend Asian interests are not only racial or communal groups but also special-interest trader's organizations. Similarly, on the Copperbelt in northern Rhodesia, the African National Congress could be regarded as an association articulating the specific occupational interests of African miners. In such situations, where a specific interest is the virtual monopoly of one race, its articulation is bound to intensify racial consciousness. Similarly, where, by the very nature of the socio-economic structure of the society, the ensemble of special interests of one race is in flat opposition to the ensemble of special interests of another race, which is the situation in most of multiracial Africa, then all interests are bound to be articulated as a general racial interest. The basic causal factor, of course, is not merely the enforced coexistence of different races within one political system. It is the fact that the processes of stratification and occupational differentiation which create functionally specific interests have been operative only *within* each racial community or *between* racial communities as wholes, and not on a multiracial or non-racial basis. Were territorial societies racially or tribally homogeneous, the process of differentiation and articulation of special interests would follow a more conventional pattern. In fact, in Africa's uniracial territories this is now occurring, although under the limitations previously described.

The Function of Aggregation of Interests

The subsumption of specific and limited interests under the more general interest of race or tribe is one way in which the aggregative process is being performed. But it is a way that is dysfunctional to the development of consensus in the new territorial political systems. This compels us at once to distinguish levels of analysis and types of territories. If our focus is upon the aggregative process at the level of the territorial system, then an African nationalist movement in a uniracial African society would be performing an aggregative function for the whole system, but in a multiracial society, only for a sub-system. If the tribe were our focus, then the chief would be fulfilling the aggregative function. With this caveat entered, we will analyze the principal aggregators, namely, chiefs, colonial governments, and political parties.

In African chiefdoms the chief was more than an aggregator; he embodied the unity of interests of the whole society. Fallers has described a Busoga chieftaincy: "The authority of the ruler, as representative of the royal group, extended over members of all clans; the royal ancestors were in a sense 'national' ancestors and the royal group, through the ruler, had interests in all the land of the state and its products. The royal group was . . . the structural manifestation and the symbolic embodiment of the unity of the whole state. . . . (The chief's) special relationship with the royal ancestors and nature spirits served both to support the ruler's position and to prevent his misuse of power, for these supernatural forces were believed to favour the general welfare and to punish rulers who became cruel or tyrannical."[46] Under the impact of modernity the supernatural powers, previously a source of strength, are now of little consequence.

This special image of the nature of political authority and of the chief as the embodiment of all of the interests of the group has shaped or conditioned the political perspectives of many Africans of the present generation. Entering the modern political arena with such an image helps to explain the apparent widespread predisposition to accept and support nationalist leaders as the embodiment of all the interests of the new society. Indeed, in one recent experiment in the measurement of prestige of leadership positions, "tribal chief" and "African Congress Leader" were accorded the highest rank by a selected sample of African secondary school students.[47] This suggests a second exploratory hypothesis regarding the effect of traditional authority systems upon the political orientation of Africans in the modern scene, namely, that Africans coming from traditional societies in which there were no chiefs or other institutions of centralized government, and in which the political process was found in ever-shifting *ad hoc* alignments between competing groups, are more predisposed to view politics at the modern territorial level as an aggregative and brokerage process. The political behavior of modern Ibo politicians lends some support to this hypothesis, though it should also be noted that a substantial number of these politicians received their education and spent considerable time in the United States. In any event, this is a hypothesis which further systematic study might prove fruitful.

Among the several rationalizations of colonial rule in Africa two arguments have stood out: the paternal argument, namely that Europeans, as representatives of the more advanced civilization to which Africans ought to aspire, know best what is in the African interest; and the representative argument, namely, that given the state of social forces in the new African societies only a neutral colonial administration, unencumbered by kinship or tribal ties, can protect and aggregate the interests of all the people at this stage of development. The latter argument has received special emphasis in the efforts of colonial authorities to counter the influence of nationalist leaders. The latter have been stigmatized by colonial spokesmen as self-appointed and self-seeking political careerists representative of only the educated

[46] *Op.cit.*, pp. 127, 134.
[47] Cf. J. C. Mitchell and A. L. Epstein, "Occupational Prestige and Social Status among Urban Africans in Northern Rhodesia," *Africa*, Vol. XXIX, January 1959, pp. 22-39.

urban minority. As the Governor of Nyasaland stated in 1947, ". . . it is most necessary that the educated African be brought into the picture [but he does not form] the whole of that picture [nor does he] represent the whole of the African element."[48] On the other hand, virtually the whole acculturative process—conscious indoctrination as well as unconscious imitation—has been directed toward stimulating a consciousness among educated Africans that they are superior and more advanced than their compatriots. The distinctive appelations accorded this group in French and Belgian Africa (*elite noire*) are a testimony to this build-up. European rule was also defended in terms of the intellectual and technological superiority of Europeans—a superiority derived from education, and therefore within the grasp of the educated African. This strand in colonialism is responsible for the necessary link believed to exist between Western education and the legitimacy of claims to political authority, which has furthered the belief common among educated Africans that it is inevitable, if not a divine right, that the educated few should rule.

Most colonial administrations have made provisions for the representation of special interests in advisory and legislative councils. In British Africa, special provision for interest representation has been a characteristic feature of constitutions governing the make-up of legislative councils. In the West Coast territories the special interests included chiefs, as representatives of tribal groups, and economic enterprise of European expatriates. In the prewar Gold Coast constitution, for example, there was a nominated "Mercantile Member" representing the European Chamber of Commerce and a "Mining Member" representing the mining industry. Similarly, in Nigeria, there were four nominated representatives of chambers of commerce, one for European banking and shipping interests, and a nominated member for the "Niger African Traders." In British Central and East Africa representation has tended to be on a communal basis. African interests were regarded as monolithic and in Kenya, the Rhodesias, and the Union of South Africa, Europeans were appointed to represent those interests. In Kenya, Asian communal interests have been given formal representation (e.g., a Hindu member, a Muslim member, an Arab member, etc.).

Prior to the introduction of universal suffrage in the former French territories special interests were accorded specific representation via the electoral system. *Citoyens de statut francais* (mainly Frenchmen) were all entitled to the vote, but among *citoyens de statut local* (entirely

[48] *The African Weekly*, October 15, 1947.

African) only selected categories had suffrage. These included *notables evolués*; members or former members of local councils, chambers of commerce, chambers of agriculture and industry, agricultural unions, cooperatives or trade-unions; permanent employees of commercial, industrial, craft, or agricultural establishments; ministers of religion, licensed traders and planters; chiefs, etc. In the Belgian Congo, functional representation has been the distinguishing feature of the central and provincial advisory councils instituted by the Belgian government in 1953. The interests given formal recognition fall into four categories: capitalist enterprise, the independent African middle classes, employees of firms and enterprises, and a residual category consisting of "notables."[49] They represent the interests which the Belgian administration thinks are important, or the ones they want to cultivate for political reasons.

The aggregation of interests under colonialism shows a fairly common pattern. In the initial stages of pacification and stabilization colonial governments exercise unfettered authority. In due course this gives way to variant forms of advisory or consultative bodies, although the ultimate authority of the colonial power remains absolute. In this second stage the members of these bodies are selected by governments from those interests, mainly European, which are functionally specific and already articulated, and from those categories of the African population which the colonial power favors (chiefs, *notables evolués*, middle classes, etc.), as well from communal groups. During this period of stabilized colonialism the colonial administration arrogates to itself the exclusive right to determine the character of the interests to be aggregated. This stage, in turn, is succeeded by the third, or nationalist phase, during which the system of special-interest representation is subjected to increasing attack by nationalist leaders for several reasons: their exclusion from the categories being represented; the fact that many of the particular interests represented are those either of the European economic oligopoly which they deem oppressive, or of African groups they consider collaborationist; their ideological commitment to, and espousal of, the principle of universal suffrage; and their insistence upon the

[49] For the period 1957-1959 nominated members of the Conseil de Gouvernement of the Congo included the following: for capitalist enterprise, a president of a Chamber of Commerce and Industry, a director of a factory, and a director-general of a large firm (all European); for the independent Middle Classes, a director of a travel agency, an "entrepreneur," and a trader (all African); for employees, a university professor (European), a European accountant, and an African accountant; and for the notables, a European barrister, an African chief, and an African executive in a firm. See *Ordonnance no. 12/126*, May 4, 1957.

legitimacy of their own right to represent all interests in the new society.

Nationalist leaders have been generalists, however special their own economic and political interests. They do not deny the legitimacy of special interests; on the contrary, they argue that only through a common national party can all particular interests be advanced. Like all revolutionary groups seeking power, they are compelled to appeal to the interests, and to mobilize the support, of all possible groups. Tactical considerations weigh heavily in their calculations, and are made all the more imperative because their principal opponents, the colonial administrations, are also generalists. Moreover, being strongly futuristic, their main objective is to create an image of a post-colonial Golden Age in which all interests will find complete fruition. Although their programs frequently mention the grievances and aspirations of particularly critical groups (e.g., cocoa farmers, traders, plantation workers, etc.), they nevertheless essay to identify all particularities with the "national interest." The latter is not the symbol of a way of life to be preserved; rather, it is the embodiment of their collective aspirations. As such, their principal emphasis is upon general goals, such as universal education, higher standards of living, racial dignity, and "life more abundant."

In those territories where self-government remains a distant objective, the aggregative function is performed either exclusively by the colonial governments or by the comprehensive nationalist parties which have emerged to challenge them. Where self-government has been achieved, or is assured, as in the emergent African states and the French territories, competing political parties are the principal aggregators. Particularistic parties, of course, are by definition aggregative only of the interests of tribe or region or other communal grouping. Competing territorial parties, however, even though based upon a political core area of a tribe or region, are forced to appeal to all groups by the very nature of their pretensions and of the majority rule principle. Whether the antagonists are colonial governments and nationalist movements, or competing political parties, the factor of competition tends to accelerate not only political recruitment, but also the processes of differentiation and articulation of interests, and, paradoxically, of political integration as well.

The character of the aggregators is only one aspect of the way in which the function of aggregation is being performed. Of equal importance is the character of the interests being aggregated. Here we are brought back to the fundamental fact that in most of Africa interests continue to be identified with race or tribe for reasons already explained. In many instances this may prove to be but a transitional phenomenon of the present generation and situation. The expansion of education, greater social mobility, and economic development should lead to ever-increasing differentiation on non-communal lines. Moreover, tribalism and racialism are aggravated in the period of terminal colonialism because of the indeterminacy of political systems. Once the general character of the new political order has been determined, there is likely to be some abatement of communalism either because of enforced conformity to the new structure of society or because communalism ceases to be an effective basis for political action in territorial politics. Much will depend upon the character of governmental structures and the manner in which authoritative functions of the political process are performed by those structures.

Political Socialization and Recruitment

In turning to the functions of political socialization and recruitment, we should keep in mind two types of distinctions. The first is the conceptual distinction made by Almond between political socialization as the process of induction into the political culture and the inculcation of basic attitudes toward the political system, on the one hand, and political recruitment as the process of induction into specialized political roles, on the other. The two are very closely related; as Almond states, "the political recruitment function takes on where the general socialization function leaves off." Indeed, the same structures or processes may perform both functions simultaneously. The second type of distinction to be made is that between traditional African societies and political systems on the one hand and the new territorial societies and political systems created by, and progressively emerging from, European colonialism on the other. Here our primary focus will be upon socialization to the political culture of the territorial societies, including in particular the inculcation of basic attitudes toward the territorial political system, as well as upon recruitment to the specialized political roles of that system.

As we focus upon the territorial systems, two special observations regarding the character of the socialization process are particularly in point. One is the overwhelming predominance of particularism. For the vast majority of Africans socialization is to the kinship, lineage, tribal, or status group, which for all practical purposes continues to be regarded as the terminal political community. This means that political socialization to the territorial system is mainly latent, that attitudes toward authority are largely shaped by the structures and characteristic socialization processes prevailing in a multitude of different sub-systems, and that participation in the larger systems tends, as Almond has suggested, to be constituent and not direct. Where policies of indirect rule have prevailed, this phenomenon is particularly pronounced.

In the modern, mainly urban, sector of the territorial societies, socialization is characteristically more manifest and direct not only because the socializing structures are more explicitly concerned with the larger territorial systems, but also because of the progressive weakening of primary ties. An ever-increasing number of Africans are being drawn into the modern sector as a result of the acceleration of the several processes of change. Moreover, as will be seen, various political events, experiences, and institutional innovations are serving to widen political perspectives and deepen an awareness of citizenship in the larger system. This does not mean that an African moves abruptly from the traditional to the modern sector. Indeed, the traditional-modern dichotomy is in many respects deceptive. Nowhere is this more evident than in the crucial role played by urban tribal and kinship unions—socializing structures which have at once preserved and fostered particularistic attachments to traditional subsystems while at the same time inculcating loyalty to and stimulating involvement in the territorial society.

The second noteworthy feature of the socialization process in a large part of contemporary Africa is the generalized instability of attitudes regarding both the nature and the locus of political authority. The rapid and multidimensional character of the changes now occurring are the obvious explanation. While change does occur in established polities, it usually occurs without an abrupt and fundamental alteration of the basic socializing structures, or of the attitudes toward the political system they seek to inculcate. In such polities there is a determinate political system, which tends to be safeguarded and perpetuated through the ensemble of key socializing structures in the society. In much of Africa, however, many aspects of the political systems are indeterminate —boundaries are in flux, existing structures are being abolished or radically transformed, new institutions are being introduced, and roles are undefined, or defined by their incumbents, who are fleeting—or fleeing. Indeed, given the amorphous character of some of the emergent polities, it is difficult even to conceptualize a "political system" at the territorial level, or to talk in terms of a single political culture or a single process of socialization to that culture. Rather within the emergent societies there are fragmented cultures, and a variety of socialization processes through which peoples are inducted into an array of sub-systems. There has not yet emerged a recognizable process of political socialization through which a loyalty to and an awareness of member-ship in the territorial political system is created.

During the period of stabilized colonial rule, now rapidly drawing to a close, the key structures involved in the socialization process—schools, religious organizations, media of communication, and govern-mental institutions—were concerned in various ways with rationalizing, perpetuating, and fostering loyalty or conformity to the colonial regime. The attitudes that were inculcated included acceptance of the idea of white superiority and the beneficence of European tutelage, the tran-scendent imperative of "law and order," and the notion that if any change were to occur it must represent the free gift of the trustee made in terms of his estimate of the capacities of the ward, and not be a response to popular political action. The school curricula were carefully controlled by government education officers, missionaries were enjoined from political comment or involvement, the press was rigidly controlled by stringent libel and sedition laws, all subordinate political structures were integrated into a monolithic bureaucratic unity, and "voluntary" associations were allowed to exist only if they were non-political and performed "useful" ameliorative functions. There were, of course, wide variations in this general pattern; in British uniracial territories, for example, the system was much more liberal and flexible than the model suggests. Nevertheless, under colonialism all secondary socializing struc-tures participated in various degrees in the inculcation of attitudes of conformity and acceptance.

African nationalism emerged to challenge, compete with, and ulti-mately to displace these structures as the effective elements in the socialization process. African nationalist leaders were the first to recog-nize the priority of what Azikiwe called "mental emancipation" from a servile colonial mentality. They attached great importance to the establishment of African independent schools, the organization of Afri-can separatist churches, the creation of a nationalist press, and the or-ganization of comprehensive nationalist movements aimed explicitly at the inculcation of a very different set of attitudes, namely, the il-legitimacy and exploitative character of alien rule, the right to seek political freedom irrespective of how one's actions challenged "law and order," and the duty to take positive action to force fundamental changes in the political formula. Thus, from the first appearance of nationalism until the achievement of independence, Africans have been involved in two highly competitive processes of socialization regarding the creation of attitudes toward the territorial political system. This accounts in large measure for the instability of attitudes regarding the nature and locus of authority in the political system.

The manner in which this basic transformation has occurred has created a special problem in the new African states. The nationalist struggle tended to inculcate attitudes of disrespect, contempt, and even defiance, toward government and political authority in general. It has been an experience—not unlike a great war or depression, as Almond notes—which has had a profound impact on the political socialization of the present generation of political actors. The political leaders in the new states are obliged to counter attitudes of defiance and resistance they themselves fostered in the preindependence period, and to restore some of the value standards stressed by their predecessors, namely, "law and order" and an acceptance of tutelage. But if the new political system is to be stabilized and preserved, something more than mere law-abidingness must be created. Special efforts have to be made to maximize the affective component of the political socialization process. Respect for the police power must be supplemented by positive sentiments of loyalty, pride, and respect toward the territorial political system. The schools, media of communication, and associations must supplement the authoritative structures in fostering these sentiments in the political socialization of the upcoming generation.

With these preliminary observations regarding selected aspects of the political socialization function, we turn to an analysis of the ways in which Africans have been drawn into the political arena and recruited to political roles. In a little more than a decade the number of Africans drawn into modern political processes has increased from the tiny cadres of self-appointed intellectuals found in the capital cities of a few of the British and French territories to the hundreds of thousands now participating in elections and other forms of political activity. This phenomenal increase in such a short time-span is both a symptom and a cause of the rapidity of social and political change. It illuminates the fact that the bulk of the peoples of Africa are either in or only recently removed from the agitational phase of political development—an intermediate stage on a continuum stretching from prenationalist colonialism to full independence. In our analysis of patterns of political recruitment in contemporary Africa, therefore, we are compelled to place our main focus upon recruitment processes in a nationalist situation.

In the several decades preceding the formal appearance of nationalist movements, two of the main carriers of the Western impact—colonial administrations and missionary societies—were responsible for inducting a substantial number of Africans into structures and roles which either were explicitly political, such as the civil service, or were springboards that later facilitated rapid entry into politics. Moreover, in British indirect rule territories, the "native administrations" provided legitimate arenas for local political activity, as well as political structures in which certain types of political education and bureaucratic training could take place. A strikingly large percentage of the members of Africa's new political elite began their careers as government clerks, mission school-teachers, and, in British territories, local government employees or councillors.

In most of Africa the principal agencies of direct political recruitment have been comprehensive nationalist parties. Leaders of such parties have usually been political entrepreneurs par excellence. Unencumbered by specific programs of public policy or by a restrictive ideology, they have been interest aggregators and collectors of grievances. They have sought to induct all elements of the population into the political arena in support of the goal of self-government. Among the several strategies they have employed, three stand out. One has been to create a party organization having full-time officials, branches, and dues-paying members. Another has been to politicize and to link with the nationalist movement, whether by formal federation or by an interlocking directorate, all types of associations ranging from youth clubs and literary societies to tribal and labor unions. Such organizational amalgamation and proliferation, when successful, explains in part the extraordinary speed and ease with which nationalist parties have appeared, and the strength they have been able to display. A third approach has been for nationalist parties in a few instances to precipitate or tacitly to support nativistic or anomic movements.

Nationalist parties have been responsible for accelerating political recruitment not only as a result of their direct efforts to politicize the masses, but also because of the counter-nationalist activity they have provoked and the constitutional reforms they have compelled governments to concede. The leaders and main activists in the nationalist parties have tended to come mainly from the more acculturated, urbanized, Western-educated sections of the population. Despite their pretensions to national leadership, and their thoroughgoing efforts to aggregate and articulate all interests as parts of an ensemble called the "national interest," there have been at least three groups who have felt that their interests would be threatened, if not extinguished, by the nationalist's accession to power: (1) chiefs and other elements among the traditional elites or aristocracy whose interests had been safeguarded, if not enhanced, under colonialism; (2) the so-called "moderate and responsible" Africans who had acquired status and prestige during the colonial period either as civil servants, government nominees on commissions and councils, or in some similar honorific role, and who favored and even defended accommodationism and gradualism; and (3) colonial administrators and settlers who obviously had a deep vested interest in the status quo and felt the threat of displacement most keenly. As nationalist forces gathered strength, these counter-nationalist elements, acting individually or collectively, have endeavored to mobilize variant forms of popular opposition to those forces, utilizing in many instances the full weight of government authority and propaganda. As in any competitive situation, this has operated to accelerate the recruitment process.

The political development of northern Nigeria illuminates the effect of this particular phenomenon upon political recruitment. Until 1950 northern Nigeria was largely unaffected by the growing forces of nationalism then centered in the cities of southern Nigeria. As southern nationalists cast their recruiting nets ever wider and sought an alliance with incipient nationalist forces in the north, the Fulani aristocracy, aided by the British administration, organized a counter-nationalist party into which northerners were inducted to defend gradualism and the emirate system. Officials were expected to use their influence to activate northerners in this defense. In the ensuing struggle, the northern political scene was transformed. Political quiescence gave way to ever wider popular involvement in the political arena.

Although this development has been most dramatic in northern Nigeria, one finds similar situations in the northern sections of Sierra Leone, Ghana, Togoland, and the Cameroons. In Tanganyika the government used its influence to support (both overtly and covertly) the counter-nationalist United Tanganyika Party. More recently it organized the Conference of Chiefs as a counterweight to the modernists. In the Rhodesias and Nyasaland the government and the settlers have pursued a similar course, favoring and supporting the "moderate and responsible African leaders" and multiracial organizations as counter-nationalist forces. In these and other instances the interplay and competition has vastly expanded the number of persons actively engaged in politics.

This is primarily a phenomenon of the early stages of nationalist development. As nationalist forces have been goaded into greater activity by various opposition elements, a point has usually been reached where nationalist victory appears to be not only inevitable but more immediate than even the nationalists had anticipated. At this point the counter-nationalist opposition has tended to crumble, and its African elements have either switched their support to the nationalists or have withdrawn from political activity. This has usually meant an immediate accession in strength for the nationalists, and subsequent concessions by government. With the approach of self-government, however, latent groups have been activated and fresh competition engendered between political parties formed by groups differentiated on ethnic or tribal lines, or by level of development. This competition has led to further political mobilization. Thus by the time a territory approaches and crosses the threshold of self-government a variety of crosscutting and interacting forces has elevated a substantial proportion of its peoples to varying levels of active political consciousness.

This process of political mobilization has been furthered by two special, if not unique, factors in African political development. One is the fact that democratic processes have been introduced before the termination of colonialism. In most of the non-Western world, the peoples have moved immediately from the heat of agitational politics to the letdown of independence. During the agitational phase both the rate and degree of recruitment may have been high, but independence in most instances led to considerable political demobilization. The pattern has been somewhat different in the new and emergent African states. In these countries the peoples are moving from a predominantly agitational phase into a terminal colonial phase during which recurrent elections are held and competitive party activity allowed full play. Prior to independence, two elections were held in the Sudan, and three in Ghana. Indeed, the British government made Ghanaian independence conditional upon the holding of a national election under universal suffrage. In the former French territories there have been nine elections, with many more in the offing. The peoples of Nigeria have already been drawn into three elections, with a fourth one scheduled for the eve of independence in 1960. Other territories of British Africa at lower levels of the constitutional ladder are scheduled for the same sort of progressive mobilization through electoral development. This distinctive process of graduated independence during which democratic elections have been recurrently held has meant not only that the peoples have been introduced, and possibly semi-habituated, to democratic processes for registering popular choice, but also that competitive groups have been allowed full play, in a ring held by the colonial powers, to mobilize their respective followings on such issues as the character of the national elite and the future form of government they prefer. There can be little doubt that this structured political competition during terminal colonialism has had a powerful lift-pump effect upon political recruitment and socialization.

The second special factor in the African situation has been the effect that the United Nations Trusteeship System has had upon political recruitment in the seven African trust territories. Two institutions in that system (the triennial Visiting Mission and the Oral Hearing granted petitioners by the Trusteeship Council and the Fourth Committee of the General Assembly) have had a marked stimulus upon political awakening in the territories concerned. The tours of the Visiting Missions have had an especially provocative effect. Their visits have been regarded as open invitations to all groups to present their grievances and aspirations, and to nationalist groups, in particular, to mobilize and display their "mass" followings. Moreover, as trust territories approach self-government the United Nations has thus far favored a final plebiscite, supervised by United Nations observers, in which the peoples are allowed full freedom of expression. This has resulted in intensive popular campaigns by competing groups (and the administration in the French territories), in which the whole population, one way or another, has been compelled to join in the rendering of a political decision regarding the territory's future.

Thus far we have focused primarily upon the agencies and situations that have fostered political recruitment. These have been operative primarily, if not exclusively, in British and French Africa. But there are also strong deterrents to recruitment, such as the paternalistic and repressive policies found in Belgian, Portuguese, and Spanish Africa, as well as in Southern Rhodesia and the Union of South Africa. The prohibition or strong discouragement of nationalist activity, the absence of national elections, and the generalized notion that politics among Africans is illegitimate—all these result in surface conformity and comparative political quiescence. Beneath the surface little is known of the political process either because of government hostility to objective inquiry or because of the understandable but incorrigible suspicion of the

African. Only when covert activity breaks into the open, as in the case of the Mau Mau, can we gain any insight into these phenomena. What we do know suggests that political recruitment leans heavily upon the use by modernists of traditional sanctions or associations which they seek to harness to a mafia-type movement. In using traditionalism as an instrument, however, influence tends automatically to be limited to one tribal group.

Apart from repression or punishment, there are other deterrents affecting recruitment. In British Africa the indiscriminate application of the principle of political neutrality of the civil service has immobilized a substantial proportion of the very class most attracted to national politics, namely, Western-educated clerks and artisans. "Government service" has frequently been very broadly interpreted. Thus, in the 1951 elections, in Eastern Nigeria, the miners in the Enugu coal fields were automatically excluded because the latter were owned and operated by the government. Again, in Northern Rhodesia until recently all schoolteachers (government or mission) were prevented by a government order from participating in territorial politics. In some territories similar restrictions have been imposed upon African employees by private business firms. In Southern Rhodesia, the presumably independent urban class of African traders and shopkeepers are effectively deterred from political activity because of their fear that government will cancel their licenses or terminate the leases on their business plots. These are but a few examples of ways in which potential activists have been prevented or dissuaded from participation in agitational politics. The exclusion of such groups has obviously had a marked effect upon the character of the African political elite.

In considering the change which occurs in patterns of political recruitment when a country passes from the agitational phase of politics to independence, we can only draw on the brief experience thus far of the Sudan and Ghana. In both cases the party competition which characterized the terminal stages of alien rule has persisted after independence, although in Ghana the groups opposing the dominant CPP were perhaps more active in their efforts to mobilize support immediately prior to independence in order to impress and influence the British government. Again, in both cases, the governments of the independent states have placed the highest priority on the Africanization ("Sudanization") of the higher civil service. Elsewhere I have noted three possible consequences of this determined drive for total Africanization:

"A decline in efficiency and probity, and hence of popular respect for government, is possible, in view of the slight experience and the absence of service traditions. The absorption of the developing educated class into bureaucratic office will prevent them . . . from participating in the political activities of the unofficial sector of society. A third consequence will be the absence of a normal age spread within the administrative hierarchy. Europeans of varying ages in the higher civil service are giving way to young African university graduates, all roughly of the same age set. When all these positions are 'Africanized,' there could be virtual stagnation for nearly a generation because of the absence of normal attrition. This has very disquieting implications. Government posts tend to carry higher salaries and perquisites, and to confer more prestige than other positions in these countries. The absence of career outlets for the subsequent generation could lead to instability within the bureaucracy and in the society at large. The difficulties could be avoided only by developing new and attractive careers both in government and the private sectors of the economy."[50]

The Sudanese civil service is completely Sudanized, except for certain technical positions, whereas a considerable number of the higher positions in the Ghana civil service are still occupied by expatriates (i.e., Europeans).

One of the remarkable features of the new political elites in Ghana and Nigeria is the similarity in social background of their members. In an analysis of selected aspects of the background of members of the legislatures of Ghana and the two southern regions of Nigeria (see Table 8) several points emerge which provide considerable insight into political recruitment in these two countries. The most striking fact is that in both countries 30 per cent of the members of the legislatures are teachers. Most of these are from the rural areas and constitute what Lucian Pye has called the "provincial elite." One observer of the Ghanaian scene argues that this heavy representation of teachers is "mainly attributable to the fact that the primary school teacher enjoys a position in the bush village which gives him a high social standing and great influence."[51] This is also true in Nigeria. In both cases it is a reflection of the high prestige attaching to Western education, as well as the fact that effective participation in the national legislature is believed to require someone who can hold his own in the English lan-

[50] "The Character and Viability of African Political Systems," *The United States and Africa*, New York, The American Assembly, 1958, pp. 47-48.
[51] J. H. Price, "The Gold Coast's Legislators," *West Africa*, May 26, 1956, p. 325.

TABLE 8

Selected Aspects of the Social Background of the Political Elites
in Ghana and Nigeria and
the United States and United Kingdom
(All figures in per cent, except age)

Category	Ghana[a]	Nigeria[b]	United States[c]	United Kingdom[d]
OCCUPATIONS				
Education (teacher or headmaster)	30	30 ⎫		8
Professional (barrister, doctor, etc.)	16	20 ⎬	69	38
Private enterprise (trader, businessman)	17	27 ⎭	22	23
Farmer	4	6	4	3
Workers (manual and clerical)	6	3	3	20
Local government (chiefs, officials)	16	11	_e	_e
All other	11	3	2	8
EDUCATION				
University	14	30	88	52
Secondary	42	37	12	35
Presecondary	44	33	0	13
AVERAGE AGE	38	39	51	49
TURNOVER IN LEGISLATIVE MEMBERSHIP[f]	51	74[g]	25	9

[a] 1954 Legislative Assembly.

[b] House of Assembly of Eastern (1953) and Western (1956) Regions. Were data on Northern Region included the percentages would be considerably different.

[c] 1949 House of Representatives, except education, 1941.

[d] 1951 House of Commons.

[e] Included under professional.

[f] Figures are percentages of the members of the previous legislatures who were not re-elected.

[g] Western region only.

Sources: J. H. Price, "The Gold Coast Legislators," West Africa, May 26, 1956, p. 34; James S. Coleman, Nigeria, Background to Nationalism, Los Angeles, 1958, pp. 380-381; Donald R. Matthews, The Social Background of Political Decision-Makers, New York, 1954, pp. 29-30; Congressional Quarterly Almanac, 1949, Washington, 1949, v, 20-21; David E. Butler, The British General Election of 1951, London, 1952, pp. 37-41.

guage, the official language for legislative debate. It is likely that with the spread of education in rural areas, the teacher will in time lose his present inflated status.

The professions also account for a substantial share of legislative membership (16 per cent in Ghana and 20 in Nigeria). The predominance of barristers in earlier councils and in nationalist leadership, however, is not reflected in their present representation (5 per cent in Ghana and 8 in Nigeria). One reason is that the electoral laws have made representation democratic and national; hence the earlier preponderance of urban centers (and of groups, such as barristers, based on those centers) has been diminished. Another is that barristers are preoccupied elsewhere, either by the demands of a lucrative law practice or because they have taken high posts in the civil service or judiciary. When the latter are completely Africanized and when the profession becomes saturated by the flood of students now studying at the London Inns of Court, it can be expected that barristers will become increasingly prominent in the national political elite.

Since both Ghana and Nigeria are overwhelmingly agricultural, it is interesting to note that only a small percentage of the members are farmers (4 in Ghana and 6 in Nigeria). The fact that most farmers lack the requisite education, or are busy farming, are obvious explanations. That farming interests are not represented is not a valid conclusion. The provincial elite of schoolteachers and local government officials defends those interests. In any event, the issue falls into perspective when it is noted that the per cent of farmers in Ghana's Legislative Assembly is identical with that of the United States House of Representatives, namely 4 per cent. As the data on education show, members of the legislatures tend to be drawn from the ranks of the better educated, although the percentage of university graduates is rather low, particularly in Ghana. It is not necessarily low when compared to other countries (e.g., note the remarkable correlation between the educational qualifications of Nigeria's legislators and those of the British House of Commons) but low when one considers the extraordinarily high prestige accorded those with higher education. This low ratio is partly explained by the almost wholesale induction of university graduates into high bureaucratic office, and partly by the political inactivity of African faculty members of the universities of Ghana and Nigeria.[52] One reason for the latter is the prevailing notion that participation in politics at this stage tends to involve the young universities, whose biggest problem is the establishment of their complete independence from politics. Another is that most African faculty members are preoccupied with their rapid advance up the academic ladder, at the top of which are high prestige positions now occupied by Europeans, but to which they are clearly the heirs presumptive. Finally, some of the leading intellectuals at the universities are biding their time, awaiting a more propitious (and predictable) moment to enter the political arena.

[52] In Ghana only one African professor (Dr. Kofi Busia, leader of the opposition) has entered politics. In Nigeria, one faculty member (Dr. E. Njoku) had a brief but tragic experience in politics, and has since withdrawn to academic life; another (Dr. Chike Obi) has sought, thus far unsuccessfully, to enter politics as leader of the Dynamic Party, which advocates a Nigerian brand of "Kemalist" authoritarianism.

Thus, at the moment doctors of philosophy are scarce on the political scene, but as the flow of new degree holders increases one can expect to see, as with barristers, their progressive gravitation into politics. The idea of the divine right of the educated to rule (and of the best-educated to rule the most) still commands no little acceptance.

There are two respects in which the character of the national elites in Ghana and Nigeria can be regarded as transitional. The first concerns the changes now taking place in the social categories from which leaders are most likely to be drawn. Here the most striking change is the rapid induction of most available talent (university graduates, barristers, doctors, etc.) into government service to replace Europeans, to fill new vacancies created by the expansion of government activity, or, for those who have held government scholarships, to complete their required term of service to satisfy the bond. Recruitment to bureaucratic office is furthered by the attractions of comparatively high salaries and perquisites, as well as the prestige and psychological satisfaction of being able at last to sit in the "Master's chair." Set against this denudation of the political arena of much of its talent is the fact that an ever-increasing number of career-seeking university graduates are returning from overseas or leaving territorial universities. In due course an equilibrium will be established in the supply-demand situation; thereafter, the incoming stream of career seekers will perforce be turned upon the society at large. This could, in turn, lead to great expansion in the number of aspirants for political careers.

The discontents and claims of the new generation are, in fact, already apparent. This leads us to the second main consideration affecting political recruitment in these countries, namely, the growing evidence of a generational cleavage between the incumbent leadership made up mainly of nationalist carryovers and old party henchmen, on the one hand, and the upcoming generation of youth—mainly university students—on the other. The fact that the average age of legislators in Ghana and Nigeria is thirty-eight years illuminates the youthful character of the present national elite when compared to more developed countries; it also indicates, however, that the incumbents are one generation removed from the new generation. Many members of this new generation are disenchanted with the old leadership and the post-independence state of affairs. They are also ambitious to attain the high offices now held by the older generation of nationalist agitators whose meteoric rise from lowly status to great power and affluence has been watched with a mixture of adulation and envy. The extravagance of their own career expectations is a reflection of their belief, or hope, that such rapid upward mobility can be repeated in their case. They are confronted, however, with an entrenched elite determined to hold on to high office and the affluence derived therefrom—a determination made all the more desperate because the obvious alternative, in many instances, would be a return to the low status from whence they came. Thus, at the very time that large numbers of a new and politically ambitious generation are commencing to flow into the political arena, there is likely to be increased restrictiveness in admission to the ranks of the national political elite.

The Function of Communication

The problem of integration and the building of a consensus in Africa's new territorial political systems is largely a problem of developing patterns of communication which transcend, rather than coincide with, prevailing discontinuities and communal divisions. Although there are important exceptions subsequently noted, existing communications processes serve to reinforce those divisions, whether they are tribal, regional, urban-rural, educated-uneducated, or racial (African-European-Asian). This fact underscores again the unassimilated (and, in the view of some, unassimilative) character of the groups composing these societies. Until recently, of course, the very conception of a larger integrated society at the territorial level did not exist.

The character of the communication process in any individual territory is determined by several factors. One major consideration is the policy of the government regarding freedom of the press and movement, and the degree to which government seeks to develop or influence the communication system. Another is the language pattern, and particularly the extent to which vernacular languages have been developed as media of communication; whether there exists a lingua franca such as Arabic, Swahili, or Hausa; and the degree of acceptance and use of European languages. A third is the racial pattern, and particularly the degree to which mass media tend primarily to be vehicles for communication within, rather than between, the different racial communities. These and other factors are the criteria by which we can categorize the several African territorial systems according to their different patterns of communication.

According to these criteria, African territories fall roughly into four categories. In the authoritarian polities (Ethiopia, Liberia, and Portuguese and Spanish Africa) the mass media are characteristically either instruments of government or non-political and highly deferential toward government. In view of the official assimilationist policies prevailing in these countries, however, the mass media further the process of national integration. In the absence of countervailing influences, an *assimilado* in Angola, or an educated Galla in Ethiopia, or Mandingo in Liberia, who is touched by these media, is likely to have his sense of identification with the dominant culture strengthened. Set against this possible integrative effect is the fact that the communications systems in these countries are comparatively undeveloped, barely extending beyond the confines of the principal cities and the dominant cultural minorities. In the relatively untouched groups of the hinterland autonomous, tribally bound communications systems predominate.

The second distinctive category embraces most of so-called Bantu Africa (the Union of South Africa, the Rhodesias and Nyasaland, Tanganyika, and the Belgian Congo). Here one finds in varying degrees a very highly developed European press and radio network; the virtual non-existence of an independent African-owned press; and newspapers and other literature addressed to Africans but owned either by government or missionary societies, or by Europeans deferential to government policies. The European press caters almost exclusively to European interest, but nonetheless commands a sizable African readership. Lacking their own independent press, Africans prefer European newspapers to those published for them by government or missionary societies because of their higher quality and broader news coverage. The political effects of this predominant role of European newspapers are mixed. They are essential media for communication within the European community and for the functioning of that community's near-autonomous political process. They are also a media furthering African acculturation to European models in style, dress, speech, tastes, and social norms, and to that extent they further emulative urges and a measure of assimilation. Indeed, they have been highly influential in the inculcation of accommodationist attitudes among certain segments of the African community.

But they have also been instruments for ceaseless affirmation of white supremacy, and no group reads their anti-African editorials or slanted news more avidly than do the Africans. The major European papers outside the Union have accepted in theory the concept of multiracialism, a stance they feel to be liberal. But most African nationalists discriminate between theoretical and applied multiracialism, and in their eyes "multiracialism" is only the latest and most euphonious slogan for perpetuating white supremacy. Thus, the papers serve as agencies of alienation, reminding the educated African daily of his subordinate role and confirming in his mind the hopelessness of his political future. In this respect they are malintegrative as regards the territorial society and serve mainly to pluralize the communication process by quickening the urge among Africans to establish their own press.

The absence of an African press in these areas is only partly attributable to obstacles and liabilities (both subtle and explicit) imposed by governments. Another factor has been the lack of capital to finance the initial plant and early losses suffered by any new paper. This is, of course, but a reflection of a more general feature of most of these societies, namely, the absence of an independent African middle class. A second explanation is the comparatively undeveloped state of education in these territories, which obviously has affected the number of Africans capable of operating a publishing enterprise as well as the number of potential African readers. Finally, from the standpoint of news coverage and other features to attract a readership, it is doubtful if they could financially compete with the European press. Nevertheless, the upsurge of nationalist sentiment has intensified African determination to create an independent vehicle for African opinion. The comprehensive nationalist parties in most of these territories (the Union and Belgian Congo excepted) already publish a propaganda newssheet for their members, and the Tanganyika African National Union (TANU) has recently launched its own paper. This movement to create a separate African communications system will undoubtedly continue. Politically it has had and will continue to have the effect of defining and interpreting all issues in racial terms.

In most of these territories, missionary societies and governments have played an active role in the development of mass media, the former to spread their particular brand of the gospel, and the latter to further programs of mass literacy and rural development, as well as to counter nationalist activity. In Tanganyika this has been carried farthest: there are 5 mission newspapers and 28 government newspapers. Of the latter, 6 are published by the Public Relations Department for territorial circulation, and 22 by district commissioners for circulation in each district. Although most of these are particularistic in the sense that they are designed to serve distinct subgroups within the system, nevertheless, they enable the African reading public throughout the territory to relate itself to developments in its own area as well as to the emerging territorial society.

The development of the vernacular press among the Kikuyu of Kenya and the Baganda of Uganda place these two territories in a category separate from the rest of Bantu Africa, although the European press of Kenya has played a role identical to its counterpart in the Rhodesias and the Union of South Africa. Between 1945 and 1952 a virulent and highly-nationalistic vernacular press developed among the Kikuyu of Kenya. By the time the emergency was declared in 1952, there were around 40 newssheets (mainly mimeographed and in the vernacular) being published and circulated in Kikuyu country. Since few Europeans could read Kikuyu and government monitoring services were underdeveloped, these papers went largely unchecked. This rapid development of a communications network among the Kikuyu was one of the critical factors in the nationalist build-up eventuating in the Mau Mau movement. Although it fostered social and political cohesion among the Kikuyu, it was obviously malintegrative for Kenya territorial society.

The development of the vernacular press in Uganda has further strengthened the predominant position of the Baganda. When the Kabaka of Buganda was deposed, Buganda-owned and edited newspapers (written in Luganda) emerged as a powerful political force in the awakening and growth of Buganda nationalism and anti-British sentiment. Indeed, the Uganda National Congress was largely based on its press rather than mass membership. The higher educational development among the Baganda was one factor making this growth possible. It is estimated that about 70,000 Africans buy a paper at least once a week and that the number of readers, mainly Baganda, is more than 300,000. With one exception all African papers are published in Kampala, the cultural and political center of both Buganda and Uganda societies. Although this development in communications has sharpened separatist and autonomist sentiment of the Baganda, it has had a significant secondary effect upon educated elements in neighboring Bantu groups. Luganda, because of the historic cultural dominance exercised by the Baganda, is accepted as a regional, if not national, medium of communication. Thus, whereas the expansion of the Kikuyu press affected only the Kikuyu, the growth of the Buganda press had a wider impact.

In Kenya, Tanganyika, and Zanzibar, Swahili is a lingua franca not only for Africans but for all races. It is taught in all African schools, and most European and Asian residents of these territories use it as a second language. Swahili is the principal medium of political communication among Africans in their mass meetings, at party conferences, in political pamphlets, and in the press. Whereas an African nationalist leader at a political rally in Lusaka, Northern Rhodesia, is frequently obliged to have his remarks in English interpreted into Chinyanja, Bemba, and Lozi, a political leader in Nairobi or Dar-es-Salaam can through Swahili communicate effectively with large gatherings of peoples coming from diverse tribes, with emphases and idioms understood by all. *Baraza*, the principal Swahili newspaper catering to African interests, has as large a circulation in Tanganyika as it has in Kenya, where it is published. Unlike Luganda or English, or Bemba on the Copperbelt, it is not burdened with the stigma of being the language of a dominant group. Moreover, it is not merely the language of the literate elite; a Swahili-speaking African can communicate almost as effectively in an upcountry bush market as he can in Dar-es-Salaam, Nairobi, Mombasa, or Zanzibar. The rapid rise and spread of nationalism in Tanganyika, one of the most tribally diverse territories in Africa, is partly explained by the existence of Swahili as a lingua franca.

In the remaining territories and countries of Sub-Saharan Africa (the Sudan, British West Africa, and French tropical Africa) one finds variant forms of a fourth pattern in the development of modern mass media of communications. The distinctive feature of this pattern is the early growth and overwhelming predominance of African-owned and edited newspapers. This is but a reflection of two more general characteristics of these areas, namely, the earlier and, in most instances, more extensive development of education, and the prevalence of greater freedom for political activity and expression, partly because of British and French liberalism, and partly because of the absence of a European settler oligarchy whose repressive influence and press monopoly have elsewhere acted as a deterrent. On each of these counts, however, British territories have been ahead of the French. Except for Hausa (northern Nigeria) and to a lesser extent Yoruba (western Nigeria) the vernacular languages have not been significant in the modern communications process. French, English, and Arabic (in the Sudan) have emerged as the dominant and accepted media. Although in British territories a recurrent demand has been made by cultural nationalists for a "national" language, the manifest practical difficulties and disadvantages, not to mention the tribal jealousies which would be aroused, have thus far, as in India, confined this demand to a romantic fringe.

The press in the Sudan, Ghana, Nigeria, and Sierra Leone has been the principal medium of agitational politics. It is partly responsible for the recruitment of most literate Africans into the political arena and for the inculcation of nationalist sentiment. Its influence in the communication of ideas and of interpretations of events has been far greater than in most countries. In view of the extraordinarily high prestige attaching to education, the written word has tended to command great authority. Thus, the press has served as the main vehicle to political power. Nationalist organizations have grown up around the press, rather than around organized membership. During the period 1948-1951, for example, the National Council of Nigeria and the Cameroons, then the leading nationalist organization in Nigeria, existed only in the pages of Nnamdi Azikiwe's chain of newspapers; organizationally it was moribund. The continuity of the press agitation helped to compensate for the discontinuities in organizational development.

Given this determinative role of the press, the ownership or the support of a newspaper has been indispensable to any person aspiring to national leadership. As a consequence, newspapers have developed as organs of individual political leaders and of the parties of which they are head.[53] This had two residual effects. One is that a new entrant into the political arena found it necessary to organize his own newspaper if he seriously wanted to compete with existing leaders. The other is that the highly personalized character of the press led to frequent and extremely vituperative press wars between competing candidates for leadership.

During the past few years there have been at least two developments which have brought about a change in this earlier pattern. One has been the emergence of an independent press whose influence upon political developments and popular attitudes has been profound. In the three British West African territories the *London Daily Mirror* has used its vast financial and technical resources to establish three West Coast dailies in Nigeria (*Daily Times*), Ghana (*Daily Graphic*), and in Sierra Leone (*Daily Mail*). From the beginning the policy of these papers has been vigorous neutrality as between the competing parties, objective reporting of news gathered by professionally trained reporters from all points of the country, constructive criticism wherever it might fall, volume production, and territory-wide distribution, using air transport for remoter areas. Whereas the circulation of the most popular nationalist paper seldom exceeded 10,000, the two dailies in

[53] Seven of the 12 Sudanese papers are organs of the principal parties and the two religious sects; 8 of the 13 principal Nigerian papers are organs of the main leaders and their parties.

Ghana and Nigeria command an expanding readership of now over 60,000, with a wider audience of several hundred thousand. This infusion of external capital and expertise, devoted not only to profits but to the creation of new national communities and a discerning public opinion, has both revolutionized the pattern of communications and furthered the process of political maturation. Literate Africans in the remotest areas have been linked with their new national governments and made to feel themselves an integral part of the developing national societies to which they belong.

The second change which has affected the communications process has been the expansion in the public relations activities of governments. At the height of agitational politics, when colonial governments were subjected to unrelenting invective by the nationalist press, the British government gave high priority to the development of public relations departments specifically charged with the task of countering nationalist propaganda and explaining government policies and programs to the masses. This engendered intense competition between nationalist propagandists and colonial governments, which led to a progressive widening and deepening of the communications process. When nationalists finally approached the threshold of political power they were determined that one of their first acts would be the dissolution of all government public relations activities. Once in power, however, they saw the utility of the official apparatus of mass communication which had been developed during terminal colonialism, particularly as they became increasingly impressed with the difficulties in realizing their ambitious programs and the consequent need to rationalize and explain postponements or non-fulfillment. The result is that public relations departments acquired a new lease on life, and had their activities expanded. This growth has been matched by the mass education programs carried out by departments of education, agriculture, forestry, and health, among others. Of even greater significance is the creation of national radio networks, controlled by public corporations, exempted from politics, which give continuous coverage of events and developments throughout the new national society. With the great increase in literacy, these activities have operated to create a unified communications process, transcending existing discontinuities and pluralism, at least for certain strata of the population.

These features of the former territories of British West Africa draw our attention once again to the special circumstances under which many African countries are moving toward independence. The introduction of democratic institutions and universal suffrage during the terminal phase of colonialism has, in the balance, furthered the evolution of a unified communications process. Party competition in recurrent territory-wide elections has forced national political leaders to mobilize support in rural areas; it has also compelled elected representatives to keep in close touch with their constituencies. Preindependence agitational politics were urban-centered; but competitive democratic politics—wherein rural constituencies by the very nature of the population structure exercise preponderance—have weakened the urban-rural cleavage. Beneath the superstructure of modern political activity there undoubtedly remain large numbers of village-bound Africans only intermittently aware of the larger world. Yet two ongoing processes are making this awareness less intermittent; namely, the introduction of free universal elementary education, and the democratization of local government bodies integrated through a hierarchy of councils with regional and central government. Both of these processes have already been instituted in Ghana and the two southern regions of Nigeria.

An African-owned press emerged sooner in British West Africa than in French tropical Africa because of earlier educational development and, until recently, greater freedom. Another factor has been the presence of a larger number of Europeans in French territories. As elsewhere (e.g., the Belgian Congo and British multiracial Africa) this resulted in the founding of European newspapers in the main urban centers catering to European interests and read by literate Africans; but it has operated as a deterrent to African newspaper enterprise. Unlike British multiracial Africa, however, the European press in French areas served as a medium furthering the process of assimilation of the educated African elite to French culture. In this respect it reinforced the Gallicizing influence of the French African educational system. Most educated French Africans are far more at home in the French language and the French cultural milieu than are British Africans with the English language and culture. As between the upper stratum of the French African elite and European Frenchmen one could argue that a unified communications process tended to develop. This suggests the existence of a marked discontinuity in communication between the African elite and the French African mass. Compared to the British territories, this is probably true. On the other hand most French African political leaders have emerged as effective mediators, as communications nexus. Leopold Senghor and Felix-Houphouet-Boigny, for example, were able to communicate effectively with their

Wolof and Baoulé compatriots, respectively, as well as their French associates in the French Parliament.

The pattern of acculturation in French territories has produced a distinctive cosmopolitan-minded African elite. As noted, this is largely the product of the educational system and the communications media. Participation in metropolitan political institutions has also been a factor. Members of this elite, representing widely separated territories and differing in religion and tribe, have been brought together in central structures and subjected to a common pattern of political acculturation. With the growth of nationalism and autonomist sentiment in French Africa, however, the unifying links between them and the French are being challenged. The concept of *Negritude* is acquiring wider acceptance and support. African parties have broken their links with metropolitan parties; African labor federations have severed their ties with their metropolitan counterparts; and African newspapers, articulating the African point of view and inculcating the idea of an African personality, have been founded.

Throughout Africa territorial colleges and secondary schools have exercised a unifying influence in the perspectives and associations of members of the present political elites. In most territories there has usually been only one leading institution of higher learning, at which a substantial percentage of the present leaders were contemporaries. In certain respects one might say they constitute a modern age-set. A study of the social background of the present military and bureaucratic elite of the Sudan shows the heavy stamp of Gordon Memorial College. Indeed, the first political organization in the Sudan was named the Graduates Congress, of which many of Sudan's leading politicians were members. A similar identification exists regarding Achimota College in Ghana, Fourah Bay College in Sierra Leone, King's College in southern Nigeria and Katsina Training College in northern Nigeria, Tabora Secondary School in Tanganyika, Alliance High School in Kenya, Makerere College in Uganda, Munali Secondary School in Northern Rhodesia, and so forth. Many of the most prominent African political leaders in Kenya, Tanganyika and Zanzibar were contemporaries at Makerere College. All of these have been boarding schools. Thus members of the present territorial elites are not only of the same generation, but many of them have lived and schooled together for four or more years, although tribally they were drawn from all parts of the territory. This is now changing, of course, as a result of the expansion of educational facilities; but for the present generation this

353

phenomenon has been of tremendous significance in the development of territorial political parties and unified communications processes.

V. GOVERNMENTAL STRUCTURES AND AUTHORITATIVE FUNCTIONS

The general characteristics of Africa's territorial systems of government have been briefly delineated in Table 2 and the discussion related thereto. Those of Ethiopia and Liberia reflect the unique historical evolution of a medieval monarchy and an insecure alien oligarchy respectively. Although the mediating political elites have adopted the form of many Western institutions, the latter have remained largely a façade behind which a divine right autocracy and a culturally differentiated oligarchy have endeavored to carry out, sometimes only intermittently, the authoritative functions of government.

The governmental structures of Portuguese and Spanish Africa are but overseas extensions of the authoritarian institutions of the respective metropolitan countries. Until very recently, those of the Belgian Congo have been purely colonial in character, designed specifically to enable the Belgian government to pursue an unfettered policy of benevolent paternalism.[54] The formal institutional structure of the new states which formerly made up French Afrique Noire has tended to reflect the indiscriminate extension of the unitarian metropolitan structures to the African scene. Only in British Africa do we find a self-conscious effort being made not only to adapt British institutions to the peculiar requirements of the new territorial societies, but also, in the words of Lord Hailey, "to maintain African social and political institutions in being until such time as they merge into a modified series of institutions reflecting the adjustment of the usages of Africa to the purposes of Western civilization."[55] Even here, however, there has been a progressive gravitation to purely Western forms. Thus, the formal governmental structures in Africa's political systems represent

[54] On January 13, 1959, the Minister of the Belgian Congo and Ruanda-Urundi informed the Belgian Senate of the government's new policy concerning the political future of the Congo. The key elements in this radically new policy were (1) that "Belgium intends to organize a democracy in the Congo which will be capable of exercising the prerogatives of sovereignty and of deciding upon its independence;" (2) the creation of a legislative council, which in due course would become a senate for the Congo; and (3) the abolition of the purely advisory government council, and the creation of a general council—a future Congolese house of representatives—which will be given legislative powers.

[55] Lord Hailey, *An African Survey Revised, 1956*, New York, 1957, p. 618.

at the territorial level a virtually wholesale superimposition of Western forms and concepts.

All traditional societies had means by which the basic authoritative functions of government were fulfilled, although there were marked variations in structural complexity and explicitness. The distinctive conceptual and institutional innovations of the West have been the concept of the rule of law; the concept of a crime being an offense against an impersonal community, rather than an affair to be settled by compensation between the parties concerned; the concept of legislation, or rule-making, as a positive instrument for satisfying claimant interests within the society and for bringing about social and economic change; and the creation of specific institutions explicitly endowed with distinctive responsibility for the fulfillment of the basic functions of rule-making, rule enforcement, and rule adjudication. Here we are concerned with how these basic functions are being carried out in Africa's modern territorial systems.

The Function of Rule-Making

Until the Second World War the function of rule-making in most African territories was the exclusive preserve of professional bureaucracies headed by European colonial ministries, with territorial governors, provincial commissioners, and district officers serving thereunder in a quasi-military hierarchy. In Belgian, Portuguese, and Spanish territories this rigid centralization of the rule-making function persists. All policies, laws, and decrees are made by the metropolitan governments and then passed on to the colonial bureaucracies in the African territories for administration and execution. Until 1956 this orderly and simplified rule-making procedure was also a characteristic of the former French territories. Under the *loi-cadre* of that year, however, a substantial degree of rule-making authority on specified subjects was delegated to territorial governments; and in 1958, except for certain reserved powers for the Community, full authority was devolved upon those governments.[56]

The British pattern has differed considerably from the foregoing in at least two important respects. One has been the British practice of

[56] The Constitution of the Fifth Republic of September 1958 fundamentally altered the relationship between France and its territories in *Afrique Noire*. Among other things it provided for the right to independence; it terminated French African representation in the National Assembly; and it endowed the "member states" with the powers of full self-government, excepting those powers (Foreign Affairs, Defence, Currency, Financial and Economic Policy, Justice and Higher Education) reserved for the Community in whose organs the member states have equal representation.

creating local legislative councils and of devolving from the very beginning substantial legislative authority to local territorial governments. As Lord Hailey observes, "there has been a tendency to meet the expanding needs of the Colonies and Protectorates not by the further extension to them of Imperial legislation, but by the issue of local regulations, which as the dependencies came to be endowed with Legislatures, took increasingly the form of enactment of local legislation."[57] Thus, most existing law in British territories is the result of local enactment by territorial legislatures. In the early stages of colonial rule these legislatures were largely advisory and dominated by an official majority, but as each territory proceeded up the constitutional ladder popular participation was progressively increased until the stage of full responsible government (i.e., where the executive is drawn from and responsible to the legislature) has been achieved. Among British territories there have been wide variations in the pace of advance up the constitutional ladder and in the character of representation at each stage, but in all instances there has existed the assumption of progressive advance toward the final goal of responsible self-government.

The second distinctive feature of British territories has been the statutory devolution of subsidiary rule-making powers to "native authorities." The degree of devolution has been determined by the character of the traditional structures. Where they were highly developed, as in the Buganda and Barotse Kingdoms and in the emirates and chieftaincies of northern and western Nigeria, it has been substantial, elsewhere somewhat less. In any event, these two features have meant that the rule-making function in British territories has been divided among institutions operating at three levels—the imperial government, the territorial government, and native authorities. As British territories approach self-government, however, the function becomes increasingly focused upon the territorial government as a result of its absorption of residual imperial authority.

Among the democratic colonial powers, metropolitan parliaments have exerted a decisive influence upon the rule-making function. Although constitutional instruments in the British system are issued as Orders in Council, the House of Commons has invariably debated all major policy issues affecting African territories, and its consent has been necessary to all principal legislation governing those territories, individually or collectively. Despite recurrent demands for a united imperial front, the two major parties in the United Kingdom have fre-

[57] *Op.cit.*, p. 591.

quently disagreed over specific legislative proposals. Behind the scenes, a well-organized system of consultation has been developed, and on certain occasions there has been marked pressure-group activity in London by settler organizations, European commercial firms, and African nationalist associations. Moreover, a small group of MP's have regularly acted as spokesmen for the African position during Question Hour, in the debate on an adjournment motion, or in the annual debate on colonial affairs. They have frequently compelled the government of the day, and indirectly territorial governments, to desist from, or to initiate, various types of action.

Until recently the role of the metropolitan parliaments in the highly centralized Belgian and French systems has been even more determinative. The Belgian Parliament has had full control over the Congo budget, and its agreement is required for the grant of concessions. The annual parliamentary debate on the report of the Governor-General of the Congo has usually involved a lively and penetrating critique of colonial policy. In addition, the Minister for the Belgian Congo and Ruanda-Urundi has had to consult an independent advisory body (Conseil Colonial) before the issuance of decrees. In the French system, the National Assembly of the Fourth Republic undoubtedly exerted a stronger influence upon the rule-making process than did the legislature of any other metropolitan country. This was so not only because it was constitutionally the source of all legislation, but also because a critical part of its membership was made up of elected African deputies. Thus, until the De Gaulle reforms of 1958, the rule-making process in the French system was part of the larger decision-making process in metropolitan France.

The data in Table 9 set forth general characteristics of the authoritative structures of government in Sub-Saharan Africa. They point up the contrast between British and French territories, in which there has been the introduction of parliamentary institutions, and all other territories wherein an authoritarian or colonial-bureaucratic pattern prevails. But the British territories are not uniform; in fact, they fall into three categories: the white oligarchic states, such as Southern Rhodesia, in which rule-making is the function of an all-European cabinet responsible to an all-European parliament; the new African states, such as Ghana and Nigeria, in which rule-making is constitutionally the function of a cabinet responsible to an all-African parliament; and the in-between territories in which members of the colonial bureaucracy and elected Europeans and Africans in varying ratios participate in the legis-

TABLE 9

Authoritative Structures of Government in African Political Systems

Political Systems	Central Representative Organs	Executive Organs	Judicial Organs	Higher Bureaucracy
AFRICAN CONTROLLED SYSTEMS				
Historic African States				
Ethiopia	Elected national parliament; parliament non-functional in rule-making	Absolute monarchy; cabinet responsible to monarch	Instrument of executive	Personal instrument of executive
Liberia	Elected national parliament; limited suffrage; ratifying role in rule-making	Elected president; limited suffrage; cabinet responsible to president	Instrument of executive	Instrument of executive
New African States				
Ghana Guinea	Elected national parliament; universal suffrage; mainly ratifying role in rule-making	Prime minister and cabinet responsible to parliament; President (Guinea)	Independent judiciary	Non-political; mainly Africanized (Ghana), complete (Guinea)
Nigeria Cameroons Togoland Somalia	Elected national parliament; universal suffrage, except Northern Nigeria; variable participation in rule-making	Prime minister and cabinet responsible to parliament; residual colonial control	Independent judiciary	Non-political; partially Africanized
Sudan	Elected national parliament abolished in November 1958	Army-controlled	Independent judiciary	Non-political; completely Sudanized
Senegal Sudanese Republic Upper Volta Ivory Coast Mauritania Dahomey Niger Chad Central Afr. Republic Republic of Congo Gaboon	Elected national parliament; universal suffrage; variable participation in rule-making; electoral college for representatives to the Senate of the Community	Prime minister and cabinet responsible to parliament; certain reserved powers (defence, foreign affairs, *etc.*) exercised by President of the Community	Independent judiciary	Non-political; partially Africanized

TABLE 9 (continued)

Political Systems	Central Representative Organs	Executive Organs	Judicial Organs	Higher Bureaucracy
AFRICAN CONTROLLED SYSTEMS (continued)				
Emergent African States				
Sierra Leone	Mainly elected national parliament; universal suffrage; participant in rule-making	Prime minister and cabinet responsible to parliament; residual colonial control	Independent judiciary	Non-political; partially Africanized
Uganda	Partially elected national parliament; broad suffrage; participant in rule-making; prescribed multiracial representation	Colonial governor, with a cabinet drawn from but not responsible to parliament	Independent judiciary	Non-political; partially Africanized
TRANSITIONAL SYSTEMS				
Tanganyika Kenya	Partially elected national parliament; restricted suffrage; participant in rule-making; prescribed multiracial representation	Colonial governor, with a cabinet drawn from but not responsible to parliament	Independent judiciary	Non-political; mainly European
Belgian Congo Ruanda-Urundi	Nominated advisory council; non-functional in rule-making	Colonial governor	Independent judiciary	Non-political; mainly European
EUROPEAN CONTROLLED SYSTEMS				
Union of So. Africa Federation of Rhodesia & Nyasaland	Elected national parliament; universal European suffrage; very limited African suffrage; in union no African members	Prime minister and cabinet responsible to parliament	Independent judiciary	Non-political; entirely European
Angola Mozambique	None; although limited representation in advisory national assembly in Lisbon	Colonial governor	Instrument of executive	Instrument of executive; entirely European

lative process, with ultimate authority residing in the governor as representative of the United Kingdom government. In all of these territories, the British cabinet system of government is the model for emulation. The essence of this system is the transcendent power of the cabinet in initiating all major legislation and in administering, through a professional civil service, all rules made thereunder. Although parliamentary debate and committee discussions may produce modifications, so long as the cabinet commands the confidence of the legislature it is the center of the rule-making function.

In the new African states formerly under British control tendencies toward executive predominance in rule-making, inherent in the British concept of "cabinet government," have been furthered by other factors —the tradition of executive-bureaucratic predominance derived from the colonial experience, the notion that in the post-independence period a political opposition is an unnecessary luxury, and the fact that dominant parties in power have emerged from nationalist movements, whose leaders—charismatic or otherwise—are still endowed with or pretend to possess a very special legitimacy. Thus, while parliaments play a variable role in the rule-making process, there is a tendency for them to be ratifiers of decisions already taken by party leaders and the bureaucracy. In the new states formerly under French administration this same tendency is in evidence, although it is far too early to discern a settled pattern.

Another aspect of the performance of the rule-making function is the development of variant types of federalism. Although differing radically in form and in the motives which inspired them, these federal experiments are all designed to distribute the performance of that function among two or more levels of government. They fall roughly into three types: one of these is inter-African in character; that is, federalism is used as a device to preserve or to secure the political unity of African territories in the post-independence period. The best example of this type is the Federation of Nigeria. The effort here is to preserve the integrity of British-created Nigeria for a variety of economic, political, and psychological reasons all related to the manifest advantages of largeness in scale, while at the same time making maximum provision for Nigeria's complex diversity and the autonomist pressures from ethnic and regional groups therein. The movement for "primary federations" (e.g., the Federation of Mali) in the former French territories, and for a federal structure in the Sudan and Uganda, are other examples of this same type.

Another type of federal experiment is "Euro-African" in character, and is designed to preserve a measure of political unity between metropolitan countries and African territories. This type is represented by the functional division of powers between the organs of the new (French) Community and the governments of the eleven autonomous republics of the former French Afrique Noire. The recently announced reforms for the Belgian Congo point toward a similar formula to govern the relations between Belgium and the Congo. It is still far too early to judge these developments or to evaluate, in the French case, the functional division that has been made as well as the character of the rule-making process at the federal (i.e., "Community") level. It should be noted, however, that the division of powers between territorial governments and the Community weakens the movement for "primary federations." The obvious reason is that African territorial governments desiring to federate can delegate to the government of a prospective primary federation only such of those residual powers as they possess. In order to establish a primary federation as a meaningful political entity, therefore, they are obliged to make grave inroads into the powers of territorial governments. Indeed, it is doubtful whether two federations can exist within the same political order.

A third type of federation, also "Euro-African" in character, is represented by the Federation of Rhodesia and Nyasaland. Here the effort is to create a large-scale politico-economic order with a federal government controlled by a resident European minority and with the two northern territorial governments controlled transitionally by the colonial power, and ultimately by African majorities. It is designed to accommodate two objectives—the maintenance of European supremacy and economic enterprise, and the protection of Africans in two of the three territories from complete domination by the European minority. Official efforts to create a similar federation among the East African territories of Uganda, Kenya, and Tanganyika have been frustrated by African nationalist opposition. An extreme variation of this type of territorial division of rule-making functions is represented by the current efforts of the Nationalist government of the Union of South Africa to create "Bantustans" in the African Reserves, to the governments of which would be given limited powers of local self-government. An important element in the European community of the Rhodesias is currently arguing in favor of a similar pattern for the two northern territories of the federation.

Two observations should be made regarding these various efforts to divide the rule-making function on a federal basis. The first is that they illuminate again what has been repeatedly stressed throughout this study, namely, the highly transitional and unstable character of governmental structures and the performance of governmental functions. Rather than concerning ourselves with the rule-making process, we are forced to focus upon the changing character of transitional structures in which no regularized pattern of rule-making has yet been established. Our analysis is thus heavily burdened with qualifications and speculation. The second observation is that in the case of the two types of "Euro-African" federalism ultimate success will depend upon the extent to which there is full and equal participation by Africans in the federal rule-making organs. Where this does not prevail, or is not a prospect, the experiment would seem to be doomed to failure.

The Function of Rule Application

It has been observed previously that Africa has been *the* continent of bureaucratic rule. Colonial bureaucracies, staffed by Europeans recruited in metropolitan countries according to merit, not only applied rules but participated in their making. Bureaucratic behavior was governed by service traditions which decreed impersonality and social detachment, a comparatively high ethical code, political neutrality, and career advancement according to merit. The exceptions to this fairly uniform pattern are Ethiopia and Liberia, where bureaucracies have been the personal instruments of the respective heads of state who personally participate very actively in the petty details of rule application, and the Union of South Africa, where the Nationalist Party has undermined the prevailing British concept of a politically neutral civil service through its policy of thoroughgoing "Afrikanerization."

The colonial bureaucratic legacy has been mixed in character. It includes not only the tradition of political neutrality, but also the tradition of a unitary, monolithic, quasi-military administrative structure completely controlled by central government and functioning in a non-political milieu. The "administration" has both staff and line components, and the career histories of most administrators included tours of duty both in the bush and on the staff at the central, regional, or provincial levels of government. Government at all levels was regarded as "administration"; politics had no place in the general scheme of things—an assumption that served to preserve if not strengthen the non-political character of the administrative service. With the birth of agitational politics and the subsequent transfer of control over central power to African political leaders, both of these elements in the bureaucratic legacy have undergone change. This was to be expected, for there has not been simply a transfer of power but a more fundamental shift from an almost exclusively bureaucratic order to one based upon the primacy of politics.

In the new and emerging political systems one can discern a trend toward increased politicization of the bureaucracies, and hence of the rule-application process. In the new African states the political neutrality of the administrative service is being rapidly weakened as a result of intrusions by the political executive into the mechanisms of appointment and promotion. In new European oligarchic states such as the Federation of Rhodesia and Nyasaland, there has been a shift from a politically neutral expatriate civil service to one recruited locally, and hence one which in its application of rules will tend more to reflect the interests and assumptions of the European oligarchy. In both there is a strong predisposition to preserve the tradition of strong central administrative control of the country, with government administrative officers exercising authority in local areas. It is likely, therefore, that the pattern most likely to be established will be a prefect-type system. Thus far there have been few fundamental changes made in the monolithic quasi-military administrative structures bequeathed by colonialism. The basic change is to substitute, at what some consider a recklessly suicidal rate, local "national" recruits for expatriate administrators. These characteristics of the emerging systems portend the continued application of rules by a distinctive bureaucratic structure, but one highly responsive to, if not the personal instruments of, the political leaders in power.

The Function of Rule Adjudication

In turning to the function of rule adjudication we should note three points. The first is that modernity has done much to weaken both supernatural and moral sanctions previously operative in traditional African societies. A second point is that a new set of legal sanctions has been created which do not necessarily, and in many cases do not in fact, reflect the African concept of what is right or wrong. As a consequence, many of the rules being adjudicated and enforced do not have the backing either of custom or a moral consensus, and therefore they lack what most modern legal theorists consider to be the essence of law. Finally, a distinction must be drawn between the rural mass,

TABLE 10

Selected Aspects of Structures of Rule Adjudication in Certain African Political Systems

Country	Structure (descending order)	Jurisdiction		Method of Selection of Judiciary	Persons Recruited
		Law Applied	Persons		
HISTORIC AFRICAN STATES					
Ethiopia	Single-hierarchical national high court; local courts plus special courts convened at govt. convenience	National law (statutes & royal decrees)	Criminal for all persons Civil for all except Muslims	Personal appointment of emperor	Administrators and *ulama* favorable to emperor
Liberia	Single-hierarchical supreme court coastal county courts hinterland provincial courts —district courts —chiefs' tribunals	Liberian national law	"Civilized" persons	Personal appointment by president	Whig administrators and lawyers
		Customary law	"Uncivilized" persons		"Civilized" persons and chiefs
NEW AFRICAN STATES					
Ghana	Dual-hierarchical supreme court district courts	Ghanaian law (British common law; Ghanaian statute & common law)	All citizens	Appointment by ministry of justice	Non-political lawyers
	Native courts	Ghanaian and customary law	Tribal groups	—	Native authorities

TABLE 10 (continued)

Country	Structure (descending order)	Law Applied	Jurisdiction		Method of Selection of Judiciary	Persons Recruited
			Law Applied	Persons		
Guinea	Dual-hierarchical-mixed high court district courts local courts	Guinea law (statutes & decrees)		Guineans not under jurisdiction of native or mixed courts	Ministry of justice	Non-political; lawyers and administrators
	Native courts chiefs' courts Muslim courts Mixed tribunals (magistrate and local assessors)	— Customary and conventions Maliki law Customary law according to subject		Tribalized Africans Muslims Mixed	— Government Administrators	Administrators Chiefs *Ulama*
TRANSITIONAL Belgian Congo	Dual-hierarchical-mixed Cour de Cassation Provincial high courts Tribunaux de Police	Charte Coloniale & Belgian statute law	Belgians		Belgian government	Non-political; Belgian lawyers
	Parquet Tribunaux de Territoire Tribunaux de Centre (mixed population areas) Tribunaux de Secteur Tribunaux de Chefferie	— Customary law	Africans	—	— Provincial governors and district commissioners	— Chiefs, elders and appt'd assessors

(The "*Parquet*" is a corps of professional judges and lawyers appointed by the governor general for service throughout Congo. Members act as prosecutors in criminal courts, judges in courts of first instance in civil cases, judges in criminal cases in limited instances. Serves as highest court of revision for native courts.)

which is still influenced to varying degrees by both supernatural sanctions and moral sanctions derived from custom, and the urbanized and so-called "detribalized" elements, physically removed from the traditional milieu and subject mainly to the new legal sanctions.

The distinction noted elsewhere between British policy and that of other colonial powers regarding the maintenance of indigenous institutions is less evident in the case of authoritative structures performing the function of rule adjudication. As the data in Table 10 show, the French and Belgian governments have also recognized a dualism in the structures of rule adjudication, namely, territorial courts adjudicating according to European law and native courts adjudicating according to customary law. The crux of the distinction is that the British have been far more self-conscious and determined in their efforts to base the native court system upon traditional structures of authority, and far more willing to permit the native courts to adjudicate rules of both a customary and statutory character.

There is increasing evidence that in the new states the dualism characteristic of the administration of justice will be replaced by a single hierarchy of courts in which officials at all levels are professional lawyers. African barristers have always strongly opposed the native court system, partly because they believe that a modern court system is a necessary attribute of the new society they wish to build, and partly because they have a strong personal interest in the expansion of professional opportunities in the judicial machinery of the new states. Moreover, most modernists are opposed to the native authority system not only because they believe the colonial administration has used native authorities as part of a policy of divide and rule, but also because it has become in their eyes a symbol of backwardness. Finally, unification of the judicial system is considered necessary for the consolidation of the new national society. In this sense it can be viewed as another means through which the new political elites can weaken or destroy the power of chiefs and other traditional elements which have a tendency to resist central control.

VI. POLITICAL INTEGRATION

The Western impact has produced fundamental changes not only in the class structure of Africa's societies and in the values and institutions of its peoples, but also in the scale of political societies. The accidental and arbitrarily imposed boundaries of colonial Africa have, with few exceptions, been adopted uncritically as the boundaries of the emergent political systems.[58] Given the racial and tribal heterogeneity of these new political entities, and the relatively short period during which the steel grid of European colonialism has kept these disparate groups bunched together, it is clear why issues and problems of national unification are at the center of politics in the new and emergent societies.

As noted earlier, the processes of urbanization, commercialization, and Western education have furthered the widening of perspectives, accelerated social mobility, created new reference groups, as well as a nationally minded educated class. In some instances, however, these processes have operated to sharpen previous lines of cleavage or to create new ones, thereby obstructing the process of national unification around new territorial symbols and institutions. This differential development of groups or areas within territories has been malintegrative in two ways: the less-developed groups fear domination in the new territorial systems, and the more highly developed groups do not want either their affluence diluted, or their traditional status lowered, through merger with economically depressed and lower status groups.[59]

[58] Elsewhere I have noted the several factors which have operated to focus African political energies and passions upon the territory as the framework for the new political community: "In the modern world mere 'bigness' has a seductive attraction. It is not only a symbol of power, equality and respectability but also a means by which to 'make one's voice heard.' Largeness in scale is also considered essential for rapid industrialization and economic development. Also, except for such large cultural groups as the Yoruba, Ibo, Ewe, Hausa, Baganda, Kikuyu, few African tribes are so constituted or situated in the eyes of educated Africans themselves as to become independent national states. Again, in some instances simple imitation and emulation, or the irrepressible expansiveness of thought and aspirations characteristic of a 'liberation' mood, are not negligible factors. Moreover, the social groups most actively working for change have frequently been those whom circumstances have placed closest to the territorial superstructure (students and teachers, clerks, and artisans employed by colonial government and foreign firms, and so forth) or those elements, such as traders and merchants, who have benefited most from a broad area of economic interchange. All of these groups find it comparatively easy, if not attractive, to think and act in 'territorial' terms. Furthermore, there is the obvious fact that only a territorial movement can seriously challenge the power and legitimacy of a colonial government. Perhaps the most decisive factor, however, has been the coercive influence of territorial representative institutions—Legislative Councils, Regional Assemblies, Assemblées Territoriales, or Grands Conseils—which have compelled African political leaders to organize and act with a territorial frame of reference if they want to act meaningfully." "Current Political Movements in Africa," *The Annals*, No. 298, March 1955, p. 106.

[59] The Buganda *lukiko* (parliament) in 1958 demanded that their *Kabaka* (king) be recognized as head of the new territorial state of Uganda, although the Baganda people constitute only 19 per cent of the population of Uganda: "We pointed out that it was meaningless to attempt to unite Uganda without a head, and that the Kabaka of Buganda was the head, because in the agreement the Queen recognized the other rulers in the Protectorate through the Kabaka of Buganda. We are agreeable to the other rulers being recognized in their countries, provided the Kabaka is the head of the Protectorate." *East Africa and Rhodesia*, June 5, 1958, p. 1246.

European colonialism is largely responsible for the "territorialization" of Africa, not only by the creation of boundaries within which the intensity of social communication and economic interchange has been greater than across boundaries, but also by the imposition of a common administrative superstructure, a common legal system, common political institutions, and a common national (European) model to emulate. The British policy of bestowing extensive local powers and budgetary autonomy upon territorial governments has furthered the process of territorialization; on the other hand, the differential application of the policy of indirect rule, and the disproportionate power given to alien racial communities, have had malintegrative consequences for the building of new political communities within the territories concerned.

Although the racial and tribal pluralism of the new political communities tends to retard the process of national unification, it is not a barrier to their survival, nor is it necessarily unhealthy in terms of the development of competitive societies. The multiplicity of tribes within a state is not everywhere an obstacle to the creation of a broader political nationality. Indeed, the larger their number and the smaller their size, the better are the chances for effective amalgamation. Moreover, it could be argued that such a rich pluralism makes dictatorship less likely by providing countervailing power centers which cannot be coerced into a single authoritarian system.

4. THE POLITICS OF

The Near East:

SOUTHWEST ASIA AND NORTHERN AFRICA

DANKWART A. RUSTOW

••

I. BACKGROUND

THE PERVASIVE INSTABILITY of the Near Eastern region not only mani-
fests itself in wars, revolutions, riots, and assassinations but seems to
extend to the very delimitation and even the name of the area. The
terminological confusion—Near East, Middle East, or Near *and* Middle East—is of little significance, and I shall without further apology
give preference to the term "Near East." But the uncertainty about
the region's boundaries is no mere accident. Unlike the Americas, Australia, or the Indian subcontinent, the Near East is not set off from
neighboring regions by vast oceans or impassable mountains. On the
contrary, it is situated at the hub of the three Old World continents
and is intersected by major branches of two oceans. Political boundaries
within this focal region, moreover, have been less stable over the last
century and a half than in any other part of the world. If a minimal
definition of the Near East would restrict it to the area from Turkey
to Yemen and from Egypt to Iran, persuasive pleas can be entered
for its extension westward to Libya or as far as Morocco, southward
to the Sudan or Ethiopia, eastward to Afghanistan and Pakistan or
even India and Sinkiang, and northward to Turkestan, Transcaucasia,
or the Balkans. Of two of the standard reference works on the region,
The Middle East: A Political and Economic Survey, by the Royal
Institute of International Affairs,[1] adheres to the minimal definition,
and the *Middle East Journal*[2] to the maximal. In the present essay
I shall understand the Near East to include the countries from Mo-

[1] London and New York, 1950, third edition, 1958.
[2] Washington, D.C., 1947–, quarterly.

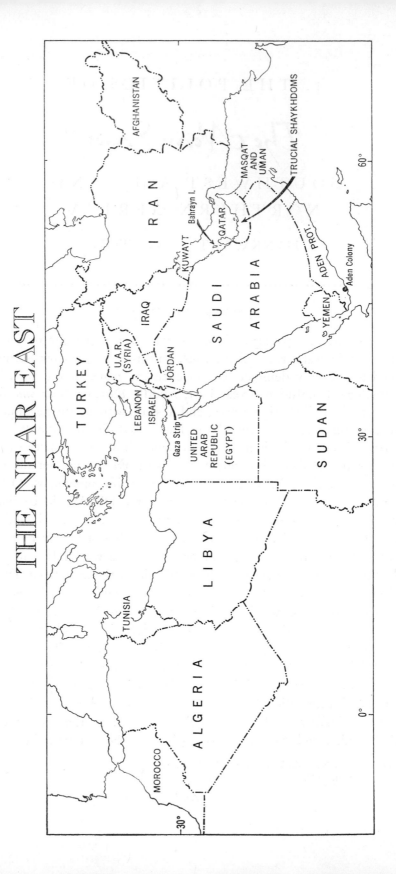

THE NEAR EAST

rocco to Afghanistan and from Turkey to Yemen and the Sudan. The Near East within this intermediate definition is distinguished from other world regions by the fact that the vast majority of its peoples adhere to the Islamic faith, speak one of the three great Islamic languages—Arabic, Persian, or Turkish—and, for most of the past millennium, have been ruled by Arabic, Persian, and Turkish rulers. Again, as thus defined, the Near East is wholly bounded by world regions distinct in their ethnic, religious, and historical backgrounds, yet of comparable size and significance: Europe, Russia, the Indian subcontinent, and Tropical Africa.

The nature of contemporary Near Eastern politics can best be understood as the interplay of three sets of factors: the geography of the region, its indigenous cultural tradition, and the recent cultural impact of other regions—specifically, of modern Western civilization. The following sections will briefly examine each of these factors in turn.

The Physical and Human Setting

The Near East forms a broad east-westerly belt of just over 5,000,000 square miles, about 75 per cent larger than the continental United States. (See Table 1.) The air distance from Casablanca to Kabul is about 4,000 miles, that from Istanbul to Aden 2,000 miles. Although few parts of the region are more than 500 miles from the sea, imposing mountain ranges along the coasts cut across the prevailing direction of moist winds: the Atlas range in northwestern Africa, the highlands of Yemen and 'Uman in southern and western Arabia, the Lebanon and Anti Lebanon ranges, and the Tauros-Zagros and Pontus-Elburz ranges (intertwined in the so-called Armenian Knot) along the southern and northern rims of the Anatolian-Iranian plateau. Hence there is abundant rainfall along narrow coastal strips: 35 inches per year in Beirut, 29 in Istanbul, 27 in Algiers, 25 in Jerusalem, 21 in Rabat, 16 in Tunis. In the interior there is little precipitation, or none: 10 inches in Tehran, 7 in Baghdad, 5 in Khartum, 1.27 in Cairo, and none in Aswan. (By comparison, annual precipitation in El Paso is 8 inches, in Las Vegas 4.8.) Large river systems provide ample irrigation for two of the dry regions—the Nile in Egypt, and the Euphrates and Tigris in Mesopotamia, the "Land between the Rivers" (i.e., northeastern Syria and Iraq). The remainder of the area forms an enormous expanse of steppe, semi-desert, and desert matched in extent or aridity only by the Sahara and parts of Australia and Central Asia. Variations in elevation and rainfall make for extreme climatic contrasts within

TABLE 1

Area, Population, and Ethnic Composition of
Near Eastern Countries

Country	Area (000 sq. km)	Population 1955 (millions)	Inhabitants per sq. km	Linguistic Groups (% of population)	Religious Groups (% of population)
Morocco	411	9.7	24	Berbers (60+) Arabs (30+) French (6)	Sunni Muslims (93) Christians (6)
Algeria	2,191	9.6	4	Arabs (72) Berbers (14) French (14) (1948)	Sunni Muslims (89) Christians (11) (1954)
Tunisia	156	3.7	24	Arabs, Berbers, French (7)	Sunni Muslims (91) Christians (7)
Libya	1,760	1.1	1	Arabs (94) Italians (6)	Sunni Muslims (94) Christians (6)
Sudan	2,506	10.2[b]	5	Arabs (70) Nilotic and Negro tribes (30)	Sunni Muslims (70) Pagans (30)
United Arab Republic[a]	1,180	27.0	23	Arabs	Sunni Muslims (89) Shi'i Muslims (2) Christians (9)
Turkey	777	24.1[b]	30	Turks (91) Kurds (6)	Sunni Muslims (99)
Iran	1,630	18.9[c]	13	Persians (67+) Turks (15+) Kurds (7±) Arabs	Shi'i Muslims (94) Sunni Muslims (4) Bahais (2)
Afghanistan	650	12.0	18	Pushtuns (50+) Tajiks Hazara	Sunni Muslims (80±) Shi'i Muslims (20±)
Israel	21	1.7	85	Hebrew (54) Arabic (12) Yiddish (10)	Jews (89) Muslims (7) Christians (2)
Gaza Strip	.2	.3	1,609	Arabs	Muslims
Lebanon	10	1.4	137	Arabs	Sunni (21) and Shi'i (15) Muslims Maronite (29) and other (25), Christian Druzes (6)
Jordan	97	1.4	15	Arabs	Sunni Muslims (94) Christians (6)
Iraq	444	5.2	12	Arabs (80) Kurds (18)	Shi'i (50+) and Sunni Muslims (50— Christians (3)
Saudi Arabia	1,600	7.0[d]	4	Arabs	Sunni Muslims

Country	Area (000 sq. km)	Population 1955 (millions)	Inhabitants per sq. km	Linguistic Groups (% of population)	Religious Groups (% of population)
Yemen	195	4.5e	23	Arabs	Shi'i Muslims
British Dependencies f	624	1.8	3	Arabs	Sunni Muslims
Near East Thereof	13,476	139.6	11		
N.W. Africa	2,758	23.0	8		
N.E. Africa	5,266	34.2	7		
S. W. Asia	5,452	82.4	15		

a Formed in 1958 by merger of Egypt (1,000,000 km²; 22.9 million inhabitants) and Syria (181,000 sq. km and 4.1 million).
b 1955 census.
c 1956 census.
d 1952 estimate.
e 1949 estimate.
f i.e. (clockwise along Arabian coast), Kuwayt, Bahrayn, Qatar, Trucial Shaykhdoms, Masqat and Uman, Aden Protectorate and Colony.
Sources: The first three columns according to United Nations, *Demographic Yearbook, 1955*, New York, 1956, except as indicated. The last two columns have been adapted from various sources; some of the figures are rough estimates and/or refer to earlier years.

a short compass. The dense tropical vegetation of Iran's Caspian coast, called *jangal* in Persian, has supplied the word "jungle" to other languages. But this rain forest, 92 feet below sea level, is overlooked by the 19,000-foot snow-capped peak of Mount Demavend in the Elburz range only 40 miles to the south. Another 50 miles inland, just southeast of Tehran, is the beginning of the Dasht-i Kavir sand desert, adjoined 200 more miles to the south by the salty waste of Dasht-i Lut, perhaps the most barren and inhospitable spot on the entire globe.

At present less than 5 per cent of the land area of the Near East is cultivated. While there is room for considerable expansion, especially in the Sudan and (with proper irrigation) in Mesopotamia, water is the inexorable factor that limits potential cultivation everywhere. Even the projected gigantic Aswan dam, which would increase Egypt's cultivable area by about one-third, could no more than slow down the steady decline of living standards imposed by current explosive population-growth rates.

With one single exception, the Near East is equally poor in mineral resources. Metals, such as iron, chromium, copper, and manganese, are found in Northwest Africa and in Turkey, potash near the Dead Sea, and some coal on the Turkish Black Sea coast; yet none of these mineral resources suffices to provide an adequate base for indigenous heavy industry. The only abundant subsoil resource is petroleum. According to current estimates, around 70 per cent of the world's petroleum reserves are located in the Near East. Most of this oil is located within a 200-mile radius around the head of the Persian Gulf, but the Near East's share of estimated world reserves is likely to increase as exploration proceeds in the older petroleum fields in Saudi Arabia, Kuwayt, Iraq, and southern Iran, and as the recently discovered pools in the northern Sahara are more fully developed. The abundance of these oil deposits may be gauged by the facts that the presently known oil deposits of the Near East, at the unprecedented rates of pumping which prevailed in the mid-1950's, were expected to last for about a century, whereas presently known deposits in the United States on the same assumption will be exhausted in a dozen years. In addition to these enormous proved reserves, low costs of extraction and processing in the Near East give the Near Eastern producers a great advantage over American firms, as evidenced by the fact that American independent petroleum producers are forever clamoring for import quotas to forestall competition with Near Eastern oil in their home market. Since the conclusion of equal profit-sharing agreements between the operating companies and the local Near Eastern governments, countries like Saudi Arabia and the Persian Gulf principalities have derived nearly all their revenues, and Iran and Iraq a majority of them, from this single source. The aggregate sum paid to Near Eastern governments out of oil profits has recently been in the neighborhood of a billion dollars a year; and in view of upward price trends and of the rapid postwar pace of European industrialization, it is not hard to foresee a time—perhaps in a decade—when that sum will reach the billion-and-a-half or two-billion mark.

But neither the abundance of oil nor of the money paid for it by fuel-hungry industrial countries is a substitute for scanty agricultural resources. Plants will not grow on a diet of gasoline, and men cannot eat dinars or riyals. The contrast between mineral riches and agricultural poverty is most starkly illustrated in the 6,000-square-mile

Shaykhdom of Kuwayt. The Shaykh's oil revenues of $300 to $400 million a year give Kuwayt's population, estimated at 200,000, one of the highest per capita incomes in the world. The ruler's revenue, after providing free schooling and up-to-date welfare facilities for most of his subjects, is still ample enough to make him the largest depositor in the Bank of England; yet Kuwayt's fresh water supply—for car radiators, air conditioners, and humans alike—is derived entirely from three huge seawater distilling plants. Of the large-scale oil-producing countries, only Iraq and Iran have enough population, water, and topsoil to allow them to channel their income into extensive agricultural development. Besides, only five or six Near Eastern countries have any substantial amounts of oil; the United Arab Republic, Jordan, and Lebanon derive a minor share of the oil income from pipeline and canal transit fees; and Afghanistan, Turkey, the Sudan, Morocco, and Tunisia go empty-handed.[3]

The economic plight of much of the Near Eastern region is aggravated by the fact that many of the mineral-poor and arid countries have the highest population densities and the highest rates of population increase. The birth rate in most countries of northern Africa far exceeds that of India, and is in turn exceeded only in some Middle American countries. Although infant mortality rates are also high, recent improvements in sanitation have tended to accelerate the population explosion.[4] Egypt's population, huddled in the narrow irrigable trough that is the Nile Valley and in the adjoining Delta, was estimated at 2.5 million in 1798; by 1897 it had nearly quadrupled to 9.7 million; and since then the range of the net increase has been between 11.5 and 19.4 per thousand per decade, making for a total of 23 million in 1955. If such rates were to continue, the population toward the end of the century would be somewhere between 40 and 50 million—or five times the present population of Belgium in a habitable area only a trifle larger.

[3] The disruption of oil transport through the Suez Canal and Syria as a result of the Sinai-Suez War of 1956 spurred tentative plans for building two new major pipelines, one from Iraq or Kuwayt, the other from Qum in Iran, to the Turkish Mediterranean coast. These lines, once built, would transfer Turkey from the have-not to the get-a-little category.

[4] The following are selected figures for crude birth rates and for excess of crude births over crude deaths: Algeria (Muslim population, 1954): 43.2, 29.5; Jordan (1955): 40.7, 31.4; Egypt (1953): 40.0, 21.6; Iran (1955): 34.6, 26.6; Tunisia (1954): 32.5, 24.0; Syria (1955): 20.9, 15.3; Iraq (1954): 13.0, 7.1. This compares with the following figures for 1955 outside the Near East: Mexico: 46.2, 32.5; India (1954): 25.8, 12.7, United States: 24.6, 15.3; United Kingdom: 15.4, 11.7. See United Nations, *Demographic Yearbook, 1955, op.cit.*, pp. 610ff. and 634ff.

Along with poverty of agricultural resources and uneven distribution of the only major mineral asset go low levels of income and of education. Annual per capita incomes are generally in the $50 to $150 range. Israel alone, with a per capita income of $389, has a standard of living—until now largely subsidized from abroad—approaching that of European countries. Again, literacy rates are highest in Israel (90-95 per cent), followed at a considerable distance by Lebanon (45-50 per cent), Turkey (30-35 per cent), and the United Arab Republic (20-25 per cent). Elsewhere less than one-fifth of the population is literate and the traditional monarchies of Afghanistan, Saudi Arabia, and Yemen have minimal literacy rates of 5 per cent or less.[5] Israel and Lebanon are the only countries of the region where the non-agricultural population constitutes a majority. In Egypt agricultural and non-agricultural occupations are almost evenly balanced. Elsewhere from two-thirds to nine-tenths of the population derive their livelihood from the scanty soil as peasants or nomads.

About nine Near Easterners out of ten are Muslims. Islam is the predominant religion in all countries except Israel and Lebanon (the latter having an almost even balance of Muslims and Christians); elsewhere the three million pagan Nilotic and Negro tribesmen of the Sudan constitute the largest non-Muslim group. Arab Christians belonging to a variety of Eastern churches (Copts, Maronites, Greek Orthodox, Gregorians, Jacobites, etc.) are scattered through Egypt, Lebanon, Syria, and Jordan. The once-substantial Jewish minorities of Yemen, Morocco, Iran, and Iraq during the last decade have largely migrated to Israel. The vast majority of Near Eastern Muslims in turn belong to the Sunni, or orthodox, branch of Islam. Shi'i Islam, on the other hand, is the faith of the majority in Yemen, Iran, and Iraq—although the Sunni half of the population in the last-named has long been the politically predominant group—and of important minorities in Syria, Lebanon, and Afghanistan.[6]

Of the Near East's total population of approximately 140 million, nearly 70 million—or just under one half—speak Arabic, the major

[5] See UNESCO, *World Literacy at Mid-Century*, 1957, pp. 38-44.

[6] The many minor faiths of the Near East include the Druzes in Lebanon, Syria, Jordan, and Israel, and the Bahais of Iran—eleventh-century and nineteenth-century offshoots of Islam, respectively. (The former are at times improperly classified as Muslims.) In Central Iran, from 10,000-12,000 persons preserve Zoroastrianism, the pre-Islamic religion of Iran; in Iraq an even smaller group of Mandaeans, or followers of St. John the Baptist, survive; and in Turkey, the Dönmes, descendants of a Jewish sect converted to Islam in the eighteenth century, play a role of some importance in the country's intellectual life.

extant Semitic tongue. While local colloquial dialects—such as North-west African or Maghribi Arabic, Egyptian Arabic, Syrian Arabic, and the dialects of the Arabian peninsula—do not always permit immediate intercommunication, the classical Arabic of the Qur'an and other great literature, and the modified classical idiom used today for formal dis-course in print, on the lecture platform, and over the radio, provide a language common to all Arabs with a rudimentary education. The 70 million non-Arabic speakers are concentrated along the periphery of the region. Turkish (the Ottoman Turkish of Turkey proper and the related Turkic dialects of Azarbayjan and of scattered Turkomans of Iraq and Iran) accounts for about 25 million, and Persian, together with related Iranian languages (Pushtun, Kurdish, and Tajik), for about an equal number. Of these, Turkish is an agglutinative language of the Ural-Altaic group, while the Iranian languages belong to the Indo-European family. Approximately 10 million Northwest Africans speak one of the many distinct Berber languages—although Arabic is the common language of education, commerce, and politics even in Morocco, where Berber-speakers form a substantial majority. In the southern Sudan, a variety of Negro and Nilotic dialects are prevalent. In Israel, Hebrew has been revived as the official language, although it is today the main tongue of only a bare majority of the population.

If the divisions among Arabs, Turks, Persians, Berbers, and other linguistic groups, and among Sunni and Shi'i Muslims, Christians, and other religious denominations are taken together, the following scale of national homogeneity emerges: in Saudi Arabia and Yemen the population consists almost exclusively of Arabs of the Sunni and Shi'i creeds, respectively. Turkey has a 94 per cent majority of Sunni Turks, while Sunni Arabs constitute 94 per cent of the population in Libya and 89 per cent in the United Arab Republic. In Morocco the Sunni Berbers and in Algeria and the Sudan the Sunni Arabs constitute a majority of from 70 to 80 per cent. In Iran the predominant Shi'i Persian group amounts to about two-thirds of the population. Four other countries, finally, are almost evenly divided either in language or in religion: predominantly Sunni Afghanistan between Pushtuns, on the one hand, and the Tajiks and Hazara, on the other;[7] Arab Lebanon between Muslims and Christians; predominantly Jewish Israel between Hebrew and non-Hebrew speakers; and predominantly Arab Iraq be-tween Shi'is and Sunnis.

[7] In addition, Persian still retains its traditional position as the language of govern-ment and literature.

Traditional Culture

The traditional structure of Near Eastern society before the concentrated impact of the modern West[8] was based on a loose agglomeration of autonomous units held together by economic interdependence, by a framework of common religious beliefs, and by the power of political authority. With some convenient oversimplification the constituent units within this structure may be divided into villages, nomadic tribes, and towns. The villagers specialized in the raising of crops, the tribesmen in livestock products—milk and cheese, meat, leather and wool, as well as animals for transport—and the townspeople in handicrafts, as well as in trade in all three types of product. Communication among these separate groups rarely went beyond the necessities of economic intercourse.

The legal rules and institutions of Islam provided a common framework for this existing diversity. Under the so-called *millet* (or denominational) system in the Ottoman Empire, for instance, each of the non-Muslim confessions—Latin, Greek, Armenian, Maronite, a variety of other Christian groups, and Jews—were left free to regulate their own laws of marriage, inheritance, and other community relations. Among the Muslims themselves, certain categories—such as the *ashraf* (descendants of the Prophet), the *'ulama* (learned in canon law), the followers of various religious orders, and members of the Janissary corps—enjoyed special privileges, and again the tendency was, in law or in practice, for each of these groups to adjudicate disputes among its members autonomously. Different tax systems applied to many of these groups, and often each group was collectively responsible for its payments. While all these groups engaged freely in economic exchange and cooperation, their personal and social contacts (especially in the case of the various denominations) were often restricted to their own group. Even in the productive process each of these groups had its own specialty, so that the traditional Near Eastern economic organization has been aptly described as one based on an "ethnic division of labor."

The authority of government, based almost entirely on taxation, the maintenance of an army, and an age-old tradition of dynastic rule, was felt most immediately in the towns, less directly in the villages, and

[8] For a comprehensive survey of that traditional structure, see H. A. R. Gibb and Harold Bowen, *Islamic Society and the West*, Vol. I: *Islamic Society in the Eighteenth Century*, 2 parts, London, 1950-1957.

hardly at all among the tribes. The provinces were ruled by military governors or landed feudatories with only occasional interference from the capital. The nomadic tribes lived in what an apt Arabic idiom calls the "land of insolence," respecting no outside authority. The city economies were largely regulated by the autonomous guilds of the craftsmen. In the country at large, each village was a self-contained unit economically as well as politically. The principal emissary of authority to the village, the tax-gatherer, was less of a government official than a private contractor or subcontractor who recompensed himself as liberally as he could for the advances he had paid to his employers. Often the village was responsible for tax payments collectively—a circumstance which further reduced the control of authority over the *individual* peasant. Law itself was largely beyond the scope of the ruler, whose decrees in a few points supplemented or modified a universal structure of religious law and local custom. As late as the mid-nineteenth century almost all of the sultan's revenues were spent on the army, the navy, the civil list, and the servicing of the public debt, with but an insignificant fraction reserved for education, public works, and other economic and social functions of government.[9]

Islam was the faith both of the rulers of the traditional Near East and of the vast majority of their subjects; in theory at least, its tenets and traditions controlled the entire structure of government, law, and society. The historical impact of Islam on the politics of the region therefore deserves special emphasis. Muhammad, almost alone among the world's great religious leaders, was not only a prophet but also a highly successful statesman. Islam both in its early history and in its later doctrine has been a polity as well as a religion, and to the true believer the two aspects are all but indistinguishable. There is no systematic distinction in Qur'anic revelation between the things that are God's and the things that are Caesar's. Muhammad's successors, the Caliphs, were both spiritual and temporal heads of the Muslim community—both *imams* and commanders of the faithful. This merger of religion and politics has had important consequences.

First, it has meant that the religious hierarchy of Islam could assert no effective autonomy from the temporal rulers; nor does theological doctrine accept them as indispensable mediators between the believer

---

[9] The preceding two paragraphs are adapted from my essay on *Politics and Westernization in the Near East*, Princeton, N.J., Center of International Studies Monograph, 1956, pp. 21ff. and 17. For descriptions of the traditional "ethnic division of labor" and of the "land of insolence," see Carleton S. Coon, *Caravan: The Story of the Middle East*, New York, 1951, pp. 27, 295ff.

and his God. In Europe the medieval conflict between empire and papacy helped to crystallize traditions of constitutionalism and natural law. In the Near East, by contrast, an individual *mufti* (jurisconsult) might inveigh against the immoral ways of his sultan or even conspire in the sultan's deposition, but the *mufti's* own tenure was ultimately at the pleasure of the sultan or his successor. The *muftis* and other *'ulama* were not an independent priesthood but rather a branch of government officialdom.

Second, sectarian organization *within* Islam was for centuries the chief idiom in which political and social protest came to be expressed. The earliest and most important theological division in Islam—that between the orthodox Sunnis and the schismatic Shi'is—arose over an essentially political question, the succession in the early Caliphate. Even in our own day this Islamic potential for sectarian organization seems far from spent, and it has frequently acted as an important regenerative force.

Third, classical Muslim constitutional theory has tended to turn almost entirely on the proper personal qualifications which the legitimate ruler is to possess—to the neglect of any institutional safeguards that might limit his authority. In part at least, this concern with personality may be attributed to the religious functions which the legitimate Caliph was expected to exercise.

Fourth, Islamic doctrine has always held that the true faith may be spread both by individual conversion and by conquest. This has been true even though Muslim conquerors in practice have been far more tolerant of other faiths among their subjects than were medieval Christian rulers—witness the survival of important Christian and Jewish populations in the Near East and in the Balkans under centuries of Muslim rule, in contrast to the extinction of Islam in Southern Spain and in Sicily. Still, the Muslim doctrine of *jihad*, or Holy War, has accorded to warfare a high degree of legitimacy which it possesses in few other religions. Emphasis on personal leadership—what the Latin Americans call *personalismo*—and prominence of the military are features common to the politics of many non-Western countries today, and many factors can be adduced to explain them; in the Near East, however, both are reinforced by these theological traditions.

Finally, the conviction that God has promised to Muslims not only the enjoyment of paradise in the hereafter but also prosperity in their temporal realms on earth has magnified the psychological shock of the political decline of Islam in its contest with the Christian West. The Qur'an says, "Power belongs to God, and to His Apostle, and to the

Believers."[10] The fact that unbelievers of varying descriptions seem well on their way to inheriting the earth has called for an urgent reexamination of the traditional Islamic justification of the ways of God toward man. The decline of Muslim power has thus implied a spiritual as well as a political crisis.

While the Western impact on the Near East has had its negative effects in weakening the Islamic tradition and impairing Muslim self-confidence, it has also, on the positive side, led to the release of many new and dynamic forces on the Near Eastern political stage. Let us examine this Western impact on the Near East a little more closely.

Patterns of Western Impact

Although many Near Eastern countries have had intense and bitter experience with Western colonial or semi-colonial rule, the colonial impact on the Near East, by comparison with other areas, was late and brief. The first colonial outposts were established in the Near East just over a hundred years ago—Algeria in 1830, Aden in 1839—but the significant imperialist penetration came only in the late nineteenth and early twentieth centuries: Egypt in 1882, Libya in 1911, Syria, Palestine, and Iraq after the First World War. Thus the Near East remained largely untouched by European domination until after colonialism had reached its maximum extent in Asia and Africa, and long after it had been liquidated in the Americas. The recognition that Western Colonialism in the Near East was only a late and brief—if intense and painful—interlude opens up several important perspectives.

The Near East—of all major non-Western regions the closest to Europe in history and geography—had been subjected to important Western modernizing influences ever since the late eighteenth century, when the Ottoman Turks were expelled from the Danubian basin and Napoleon attempted his abortive invasion of Egypt. The desire of the rulers of Ottoman Turkey, of Egypt, and of Iran to imitate the superior military techniques of Europe provided the initial stimulus to Westernization. Yet reorganization of the defense system, by an irresistible logic, soon went far beyond the army itself. In rapid sequence it encompassed public works for improved communication, manufacture of military supplies, advanced training of physicians and engineers, improved tax collection, attempts at centralized administration, and a sweeping reform of the entire system of higher education. It meant the calling of numer-

[10] Cf. Wilfred Cantwell Smith, *Islam in Modern History*, Princeton, N.J., 1957, p. 54.

ous European military instructors to the Near East, and the dispatch of an even greater number of Near Eastern students to Europe.

The new class of Western-trained army officers and civil servants which thus grew up in the nineteenth century was thoroughly committed, both by education and by vested interest, to the cause of further modernization. It was only natural that they should become devoted not only to the European technology of warfare and industry but also to European forms of poetry and literature, and to the European political ideologies of nationalism and constitutionalism. This spread of nationalism among educated Near Easterners was reinforced by the colleges established by Western missionary and philanthropic organizations in the Arab countries, for it was in these institutions that Arabic-speaking Muslims and Christians, drawn into a close association that transcended their narrow local and sectarian loyalties, rediscovered the bond of their common Arab cultural heritage.[11] Significantly, it was a Presbyterian mission school which set up the first Arabic printing press in Beirut in 1834.

From fifty to one hundred years of Western cultural influence thus preceded the full impact of colonialism. Following the Ottoman collapse in the First World War, the Turkish rump of the Empire, through the determined efforts of the Turkish nationalists and a combination of favorable external circumstances, retained its independence. Under the resolute leadership of Atatürk, the new Turkish Republic embarked on a course of political, cultural, and social reform unparalleled in its broad sweep elsewhere in the Near East. Farther east, Iran also managed to escape the twofold threat to her independence from Russia and Britain—although the modernization program of Riza Shah brought far less impressive results. But in the Arab parts of the Ottoman Empire the soaring ambition of youthful nationalists for a unitary or federated Arab state was bitterly disappointed. A belt of British and French mandates was established over Iraq, Palestine, Transjordan, Syria, and Lebanon. In neighboring Egypt the organized force of nationalism was locked in an acrimonious and unequal duel with the British occupying power. British sponsorship of Zionist immigration into Arab Palestine added greatly to Arab animosity toward the West.

Colonialism came to the region after the Near East's educated elite had been converted to Western ideals of nationality, constitutionalism, and self-determination. It came, moreover, at a time when Western public opinion itself had developed a sensitive conscience about Europe's

[11] For a historical survey of the Western impact on Arab nationalism, see George Antonius, *The Arab Awakening*, London, 1946. Cf. p. 440 and note 44 *infra*.

earlier colonial expansion. Specifically it came in the wake of solemn pronouncements, such as Wilson's Fourteen Points, in which Western statesmen had committed themselves to the universal principle of national self-determination. The institutional cloak of the mandate never fully concealed this basic Western self-contradiction, for the educational theory of the mandate form of government was belied by the extensive military measures required to impose and maintain it. The implicit promise of early self-government was sure to fan nationalist aspirations which the reality of colonial or semi-colonial rule was bound to frustrate. In practice, an attitude of non-cooperation on the part of the Arabs, accentuated by periodic revolts, proved to be the most effective means of hastening the pace toward independence. In this mounting atmosphere of coercion, each side tended to conclude that the other would respond not to reason but to force alone.

Today, as a result of European exhaustion after the Second World War, all but the last traces of colonial domination in the Near East have disappeared. Even in most of the former colonial or mandated areas, imperial hegemony was never securely enough established—nor did it last long enough—to confer in full measure its incidental benefits of large-scale public works, improved standards of health and education, and orderly administration. It is this short, late, and unhappy experience with colonialism—along with the continuing irritation produced by the Palestine question—that has so embittered relations between the West and many of the Arab countries. As Professor Bernard Lewis of the University of London has put it: "There is a case to be made for and against imperial rule as a stage in political evolution. . . . But there is little that can be said in defense of the half-hearted, pussy-footing imperialism encountered by most of the peoples of the Middle East— an imperialism of interference without responsibility, which would neither create nor permit stable and orderly government."[12]

It is tempting at this point to classify Near Eastern countries according to the impact which European expansionism had on their political development and integration. Three broad categories may be distinguished—countries where a high degree of modernization was achieved entirely under indigenous auspices; countries where Westernization resulted from the interaction of foreign and indigenous efforts; and countries which have experienced neither Western colonial rule nor any

[12] "Democracy in the Middle East—Its State and Prospects," *Middle Eastern Affairs*, Vol. VI, April 1955, p. 105.

notable degree of self-directed Westernization.[13] (1) The first category includes Turkey. Her experiment in rapid Westernization was favored not only by the country's relatively balanced economic endowment and the legacy of political experience left by the Ottoman Empire, but also by her ability, demonstrated in the War of Independence of 1919-1922, to thwart European designs of subjugation and hence to reestablish political relations with Europe on a basis of mutual respect. Her political system today demonstrates a degree of integration which is high by Near Eastern standards, and rests on a predominantly modern basis. (2) The second category includes the large number of Near Eastern countries which experienced shorter or longer periods of European domination. It may in turn be divided into three subcategories. (a) In the first—including Tunisia, Morocco, and the Sudan—European power was firmly established for a half-century or more. Interference was not divorced from responsibility, and while modern and traditional patterns coexist within government and society, a fairly high degree of political integration has been maintained. (For Algeria, see below.) (b) In the second—including Egypt, Libya, and the Fertile Crescent countries of Lebanon, Syria, Jordan, and Iraq—foreign rule was only briefly or tenuously established. The evenly matched contest between indigenous and foreign political forces, lasting anywhere from one to two generations, generally has had a severely disruptive effect on the integration of the political process. (c) In the third—including Iran and Saudi Arabia—European hegemony never took the form of colonial or mandatory rule, but its disruptive effect on the traditional integration of the political process has been quite comparable. Iran from 1907 to 1921, and again from 1941 to 1946, was subject to military occupation by a variety of European powers. In 1919 she narrowly avoided a treaty arrangement that would in effect have made her a British protectorate. The emotional climate of the contest over control of her oil resources after the Second World War was not unlike that of Egypt and Syria at the time of their fight against European colonial rule. In Saudi Arabia, the sudden growth of a foreign-operated petroleum industry within a nomadic Bedouin society has had profoundly unsettling effects on traditional patterns of integration. (3) The third category includes Yemen and Afghanistan, which, in the absence of colonial domination

---

[13] The first and third categories are analogous to category 3 and the second to category 5 in Cyril Black's classification of countries according to their patterns of modernization. See Cyril E. Black, "Political Modernization in Historical Perspective," Princeton, N.J., Center of International Studies, 1959, mimeographed.

and of any profound commercial impact from abroad, still retain their traditional patterns of political integration.

The preceding classification indicates that Near Eastern countries which have escaped European control have maintained the highest degrees of political integration, but that, by extension of Bernard Lewis' theorem, precarious foreign control has proved more disruptive than firmly entrenched control. The case of Algeria, however, suggests that the correlation is less than perfect: here the introduction of a substantial proportion of European settlers into an indigenous Near Eastern population has injected a severely disintegrating factor not present elsewhere in the Near East.[14]

An incidental consequence of the twentieth-century Western impact on the Near East has been the establishment, under auspices of a British mandate, of a Jewish community in Palestine which, upon the withdrawal of the mandate in 1948, constituted itself into the state of Israel. In international affairs Israel is very much, and from all appearances lastingly, a part of the Near East. Indeed the political aftermath of the Palestine War of 1948 in countries like Syria and Egypt indicates that Israel's presence has also become a dynamic ingredient in the Arab domestic political scene. Yet the politically, socially, and culturally dominant elements of Israel's population were transplanted to their present locale only within the last generation. As a result, Israel's domestic political processes differ very sharply from those of her immediate neighbors and instead offer striking similarities to many political systems of continental Europe. The following analysis of Near Eastern political processes will therefore largely omit Israel—for the sole reason that few useful generalizations could be made that would apply with equal validity to Israel and to other countries of the Near East.

II. PROCESSES OF CHANGE

Because of the Near East's central location within the land mass of the Old World, social change within the region has been throughout history the result of the interplay between indigenous and exogenous forces. Cultural innovations such as the mathematical and scientific discoveries of the ancient Babylonians and the medieval Arabs have radiated outward. The monotheistic creeds of Moses, Jesus, and Muhammad

---

[14] The situation under the Palestine Mandate was in important respects analogous to that in Algeria. On the other hand, Israel, which includes only a small non-Jewish minority, has been highly integrated as a result of its far-flung program of assimilation of its immigrant population. In Black's scheme, Algeria comes under category 4.

have spread to other regions of the globe. The land-and-sea lanes from the Indian Ocean via the Persian Gulf and the Red Sea to the Mediterranean have been major trade routes, whether for medieval spice caravans or for modern oil pipelines and tankers. The Near East has played a prominent and often a decisive role in strategic and political calculations of conquerors and statesmen in Europe, Asia, and North America—from Alexander the Great, Pompey, Caesar, Genghis Khan, Timur, Catherine the Great, Napoleon, and Palmerston to Wilhelm II, Wilson, Stalin, Hitler, Churchill, Truman, Eisenhower, and Khrushchev. The Near East has been the center of empires from the Pharaohs and Achaemenids to the Umayyads, 'Abbasids, and Ottomans. It is strewn with ancient and recent battlefields. In historical times it has been the most frequently invaded region of the globe.

The three most recent invasions of the region have largely shaped its present cultural pattern and dynamics—that of the Arabs from the core of the region itself; that of the Central Asian Turks and Mongols from the northeast; and that of Europe from the northwest. In the seventh century A.D. the religious revelation received by Muhammad in the caravan trading towns of Mecca and Medina temporarily gave the Bedouin Arabs of the peninsula a unified social structure and political purpose, making them forget their tribal raids and feuds and releasing them in triumphant conquest across northern Africa into Spain and southern France and across the Iranian highlands into northern India. For the first time in history the Near Eastern region as here defined—from the Atlas to the Pamirs—was culturally and politically unified. While political unity crumbled after a century, cultural unity has remained. The entire area was permanently converted to Islam and most of it to the Arabic language. Only in Iran did Persian language and culture reassert themselves in a fruitful blend with Arabic-Islamic elements. The Turkish and Mongolian conquerors of the eleventh to the fifteenth century were largely absorbed into this Islamic-Arab-Persian culture—although the political power of the 'Abbasid caliphs in Baghdad and the elaborate irrigation system of Mesopotamia emerged ruined from the encounter. To the north, the Islamized Turks first pushed back and at length conquered the Byzantine Empire, thus spearheading the second major wave of Islamic advance toward Europe. For more than three centuries, Ottoman administration gave to Islamic religion and to Arabic-Persian civilization the most stable institutional forms they had yet attained. Once again (with the exception of Morocco to the west, of Iran and Afghanistan to the east, and of the restless Bedouins of inner Arabia) the entire Near Eastern region was unified.

In the seventeenth and eighteenth centuries Ottoman power was driven back—from the Danubian basin by Austria, and from the northern Black Sea coast by Russia—and its decline continued relentlessly until its final demise in the aftermath of the First World War. But the most important and lasting aspect of the European and Western impact on the Near East was not the imposition of a new political rule. Throughout the nineteenth century, in fact, European political divisions and rivalries provided the best guarantee for Ottoman and Iranian political survival. Only in the Arab-speaking part of the Near East—from Morocco to Iraq and 'Uman—was European rule imposed for periods ranging from a decade to a century. But the need for defense against superior Western military and economic power prompted the adoption— at first fitful and reluctant and later eager and systematic—of major elements of modern Western technology, ideology, and social organization. Most important among the new cultural features thus emerging in the Near East have been the ideal of the nation-state—with its corollaries of civic equality and obligation, of universal schooling and conscription, of centralized taxation and administration—and the products and practices of modern technology, including the use of inanimate energy, intensified communication and trade, and vastly improved standards of sanitation.

The most important elements of social dynamics resulting from this process of modernization are a tendency toward national unification in politics, industrialization in economics, secularization in thought and social and legal organization, and a population explosion in demography. (See Table 2.) National unification has gone furthest in Turkey. It has been held up in Iran by linguistic and religious heterogeneity and a lack of intensive communication. It has been delayed and complicated in the Arab countries by recent (or, in the case of Algeria, continuing) colonial rule, and by persisting uncertainties as to the geographic definition of nationality.

Industrialization has gone furthest in Turkey, Egypt, Lebanon, and Northwest Africa; it is rapidly increasing in Iraq. Urbanization is accelerated both by the growth of industry and commerce in metropolitan centers and by population pressure from rural areas. Before the Second World War, among major Near Eastern cities only Cairo had a population of over a million. Today its population is around three million, and Istanbul, Tehran, and Alexandria have passed the million mark. Casa-

TABLE 2

Selected Socio-Economic Characteristics of Near Eastern Countries

Country	Population % Rural % Urban		Cities over 200,000 (population in thousands)	Per Capita Income in $	Annual Rate of Population Increase (%)
(1)	(2)	(3)	(4)	(5)	(6)
Morocco	80.6	19.4	Casablanca 742	160	1.89
			Marrakech 220		
Algeria	76.4	23.6	Algiers 361	170	2.95
			Oran 299		
Tunisia	70.1	29.9	Tunis 410	138	2.4
Libya	*	*	(none)	*	*
Sudan	*	*	Greater Khartum 228	*	*
U.A.R. Egypt	69.9	30.1	Cairo 2,600		
			Alexandria 1,200		
			Assiut 250	100	2.16
Syria	*	*	Aleppo 400		
			Damascus 395		
			Homs 293	*	1.53
Turkey	78.1	21.9	Istanbul 1,215		
			Ankara 453		
			İzmir 286		
Iran	*	*	Tehran 1,513		
			Tabriz 290		
			Isfahan 254		
			Mashhad 242		
			Abadan 226	85	2.66
Afghanistan	*	*	Kabul 300	*	*
Israel	66.2	33.8	Tel Aviv-Jaffa 391	389	2.31
Gaza Strip	*	*	(none)	*	*
Lebanon	*	*	Beirut 450	125	2.32
Jordan	*	*	Amman 202	*	3.14
Iraq	*	*	Baghdad 656	85	.7
Saudi Arabia	*	*	Jiddah 250	40	*
Yemen	*	*	(none)	40	*
British Dependencies	*	*	Kuwayt 200	*	*

* No data available.

Sources: Columns 2 and 3: *United Nations Demographic Yearbook, 1955*, New York, 1956, pp. 185-197; figure for Morocco calculated from data for French and Spanish Zones.

Column 4: *The American Annual 1959, passim*; and *World Almanac 1959*, pp. 395-396.

Column 5: United Nations, *National and Per Capita Income of Seventy Countries, 1949*, New York, 1950, pp. 14-16; for Morocco, United Nations, *Structure and Growth of Selected African Countries*, New York, 1958; for Algeria and Tunisia, Tunisia, Secretary of State for Information, *Tunisia*, Tunis, 1957, p. 150.

Column 6: *United Nations Demographic Yearbook, 1955, op.cit.*, pp. 610ff. and 634ff.

The author is indebted to Professor Douglas E. Ashford, Indiana University, for his able assistance in compiling the above data.

blanca, Baghdad, Ankara, Beirut, and Aleppo have populations of half a million or more apiece, and other cities, like Tunis, Damascus, Algiers, Tel Aviv, Kabul, Oran, İzmir, Homs, Greater Khartum, Tabriz, Isfahan, Mashhad, Abadan, and Marrakech have moved into the quarter-million class. Despite this increase in the industrial and urban proportion of the population, the Near East remains predominantly rural and agricultural. The sharp traditional cleavage between the urban-educated ruling class and the rural lower class persists—although it is perhaps least pronounced in prosperous cash-crop regions such as Lebanon, and the İzmir and Adana districts of Turkey, where the ascent from small or medium-sized farming into trade and manufacturing is easy and frequent. Government programs such as easy agricultural credit and high crop supports in Turkey, or the collectivized agriculture of Egypt's Liberation Province, cause a sharp deviation from the traditional pattern of family subsistence farming or tenant farming on large estates. If such policies are continued and extended and, above all, if the resulting forms of production can be economically maintained over sufficiently long periods, they may become the prelude to a social revolution in the Near East whereby the farming population for the first time in recorded history would be propelled as a major active force onto the political scene.

Whatever the future role of the rural population in the Near East, there is no doubt that the overwhelming majority of the urban population—both upper and lower class—live in an increasingly modern and secularized context. The Westernizing reforms of the late eighteenth and early nineteenth centuries were largely imposed by autocratic rulers and their energetic ministers on reluctant and bewildered populations. Today, by contrast, the desire for modernization has become a potent and irresistible force to which the entire ruling class and the increasing numbers who aspire toward it are thoroughly committed. The process of modernization has been aided in the years since the Second World War, as colonial rule has given way to solicitude for what are patronizingly called "underdeveloped" countries, and as the global conflict between Russia and the United States has come to focus on the Near East. American philanthropic organizations have been setting up model village programs in Jordan and Iran; throughout the region American, and more lately Russian, engineers have been constructing dams, laying roads, building airports, improving telephone systems, and erecting grain elevators.

But this peaceful and beneficent competition is also a constant reminder of the Near East's lack of indigenous strength in the international power struggle. The Near Eastern frontier from the Caucasus to the Pamirs is the only line at which Russian power is today still contained within its pre-1939 and pre-1914 boundaries. The threat of Russian expansion through diplomatic deals, through subversion, through small-scale war, or through a combination of the three is ever present. The international constellation thus remains far and away the most important potential force for change in the Near East. Within the region itself the merger and federation movements begun in early 1958 also indicate the importance of political dynamics.

The processes of change just outlined have worked far from uniformly throughout the Near Eastern region. The cultural and social transformation set off by the Western impact and the closely related forces of industrialization, secularization, and urbanization has gone furthest in Turkey, followed by Lebanon, the U.A.R., Algeria, and Tunisia. Iran, Iraq, the Sudan, Morocco, Saudi Arabia, and Libya may be considered an intermediate group, where major segments of the rural or nomadic population still remain unaffected by these changes. Yemen and Afghanistan once again are at the traditional end of the spectrum. Population growth has been most rapid in Northwest Africa and in Egypt. In the latter country in particular, the resulting pressure on limited economic resources has become enormous. More recently Turkey and Iran also have entered on spurts of population growth, accompanied by large-scale migration from village to city. In the remainder of the area the population still is sparse and is expanding at a far more leisurely rate. In Iraq, Northeast Syria, and the Sudan, appropriate development of water resources could provide a secure economic basis for far larger populations. The purely political forces of change—including the drive for national unification and the region's growing involvement in the East-West conflict—at the moment focus on the Arab parts of the Near East. Except for Iran, the rapidly expanding petroleum industry of the region and its transport routes toward Europe are also located in the Arab countries. Current and possible future political realignments and mergers almost certainly will have a profound impact on cultural and social developments, whatever their immediate consequences in political turmoil and violence. One long-range possibility is that the relatively well-trained manpower of countries like Egypt and Syria will be combined with the oil income of the Arab countries on the Persian Gulf to ensure a large-scale and more uniform process of economic development throughout the region, with its attendant consequences of progressive secularization, industrialization, and urbanization. On the other hand, a country like

Iraq may be able, through a concerted effort in education and technical training, to bring the skills of its manpower up to the level of its other economic resources. At any rate, major questions of social and economic policy are sure to vie with questions of defense and international affairs for the attention of Near Eastern powerholders.

III. POLITICAL GROUPS AND POLITICAL FUNCTIONS

Political Groups

(1) *Parties and party systems*. A party is a group of competitors rivaling with other such groups for power. In modern Europe parties have generally emerged in two related types of power contest: the parliamentary contest for control of legislation and of executive policy, and the contest among candidates for election. But the term "party" also applies to conspiratorial groups aiming at the violent overthrow of existing regimes, and to the dominant political organizations within authoritarian or totalitarian societies. In the Near East, well into the nineteenth century, competition for power was narrowly confined by the decentralized patriarchal structure of society, by traditional religious beliefs, and by the dynastic structure of government. Elected parliaments—except for the short-lived Ottoman Assembly of 1877-1878— came to the area only during the first quarter of the twentieth century. While there have been numerous overthrows of governments and of entire regimes, most of these were until recently carried out not by specific competitive groups but rather by such existing political structures as the clergy, merchant guilds, and the army, or else by spontaneous mob action.

An exhaustive listing of all known political parties and similar associations in the Ottoman Empire[15] begins with a number of conspiratorial societies formed after 1859 in opposition to the despotism of the sultans. Few of these attracted any considerable membership, and most of them were forced to operate in exile. It was only after 1908 that one of these—the Society of Union and Progress—established itself with the help of the military as the controlling party of the Ottoman Empire. In the following decade (1908-1919) four parliamentary elections were held, governments were formed with the confidence of the Assembly and overthrown upon its censure, and new parties were formed among

[15] Tarık Zafer Tunaya, *Turkiyede Siyasi Partiler, 1859-1952*, Istanbul, 1952; cf. E. E. Ramsaur, *The Young Turks: Prelude to the Revolution of 1908*, Princeton, N.J., 1957.

the Unionists' disenchanted followers and among its antagonists. In Egypt the bid of a consultative assembly for greater control over expenditures in the early 1880's and the military coup of 'Urabi Pasha were the first steps toward systematic political organization; yet both movements were thwarted by the British occupation of 1882. In Iran the revolution of 1905-1906, which resulted in the adoption of a constitution providing, inter alia, for elected parliaments, does not seem to have been preceded or followed by any large-scale organized party activity.

If the despotism of nineteenth-century sultans, shahs, and khedives called to the scene the first modern political associations, the imposition of colonial regimes (or of semi-colonial regimes, disguised as protectorates, mandates, or bilateral treaty arrangements) supplied a continuing incentive for organization. The establishment of full independence often gave added impetus to the formation of political groupings and to active competition between them. Today political parties in one form or another are an established part of political life in all Near Eastern countries, except for the most remote patriarchal areas—Afghanistan and the Arabian peninsula. (See Table 3.)

TABLE 3

Survey of Political Regimes in the Near East

AFGHANISTAN
Independent Kingdom (Amirate)
ALGERIA

-1830	Under (nominal) control of Ottoman Empire
1830-	Part of French Empire
1946-	Northern part declared to be integral part of Metropolitan France
1954-	Open warfare between French forces and National Liberation Front
1958	Nationalist Provisional Government formed in exile

BRITISH DEPENDENCIES
Aden Colony: A British Crown Colony since 1839
Aden Protectorate: 22 tribal areas, most of them in "treaty relations" with United
      Kingdom
Masqat and 'Uman: Sultanate with "close ties" to United Kingdom
Persian Gulf States (viz. Bahrayn, Kuwayt, Qatar, and 7 Trucial Shaykhdoms):
      principalities "protected" by United Kingdom
EGYPT

-1914	*Part of Ottoman Empire*, but de facto independence established in 1805 under dynasty of Muhammad 'Ali, whose members successively take the titles Pasha, Khedive (1867), Sultan (1914), and King (1922)
1881	Military coup of 'Urabi Pasha, in alliance with constituionalists, suppressed by British occupation
1882-1922	*British occupation* places power in hands of British Residents (e.g., Lord Cromer, 1882-1907)
1919-1922	Widespread nationalist revolt prompts British to negotiate for adoption of independent constitutional regime

1922-1953 *Independent monarchy* under Fuad I (1922-1935) and Faruq I (1935-1952) ; successive constitutions proclaimed and suspended; British occupation continues until 1936 and 1939-1946; protracted power struggle between King and Wafd party with repeated and decisive British interventions

1946-1952 Quick alternation of (pseudo-) parliamentary governments of anti-Wafd coalitions (1944-1950) and Wafd (1950-1952) replaced by military coup under Najib in 1952; British occupation limited to Suez Canal Zone

1953- Republic (Presidents Najib, 1952-1953; and Abdul Nasser ['Abd al-Nasir], 1954-)

1952- Power of military junta (Revolutionary Command Council) gradually concentrated in person of Abdul Nasser, British occupation of Canal Zone terminated by 1956

1958- Egypt merged with Syria in *United Arab Republic*

GAZA STRIP

-1948 Part of Palestine Mandate (cf. Israel, below)

1949- Under Egyptian administration

1957- A United Nations contingent guards border between Gaza Strip and Israel

IRAN

-1925 *Qajar dynasty*

1906-1921 Adoption of parliamentary constitution followed by contest between constitutionalists and monarch; repeated political or military intervention by Russia, Britain, Ottoman Empire, and Germany

1921-1925 Military dictatorship of Riza Khan

1925- *Pahlavi dynasty* founded by Riza Khan (Shah)

1925-1941 Personal rule of Riza Shah

1941-1946 British-Russian occupation legalized by tripartite alliance in 1942; Riza Shah replaced by son, Muhammad Riza (1941-)

1946-1951 Successive pseudo-parliamentary governments (Qavam 1946-1947, Razmarra 1950-1951) ; Russian-inspired separatist regime in province of Azarbayjan (1945-1947) collapses after withdrawal of Russian troops

1951-1953 Government of Mossadegh (Musaddiq), who consolidates dictatorial powers after brief interregnum in 1952

1953- Rule of Shah and pseudo-parliamentary governments restored after General Zahidi's coup overthrows Mossadegh

IRAQ

-1917 *Part of Ottoman Empire*

1917-1920 British occupation; widespread rebellion suppressed in 1920

1920-1930 *British Mandate*: Faysal I (ousted earlier as King of Syria) proclaimed King of Iraq under British auspices in 1921; parliamentary constitution adopted in 1924

1930-1958 *Independent Kingdom* (Hashimite dynasty: Faysal I -1933, Gazi 1933-1939, Faysal II 1936-1958, at first with regency of 'Abd al-Ilah) ; pseudo-parliamentary constitution with rapidly revolving governments and persistent influence of General Nuri al-Sa'id

1936-1941 Seven successive military coups interrupt normal constitutional operations

1958 Arab Federation with Jordan formed in February and dissolved by republican regime in July

1958- *Independent Republic* established in bloody revolution; its President, Colonel 'Abd al-Karim Qasim

ISRAEL

-1918 Part of Ottoman Empire; British occupation after 1918

1920-1948 Part of British Mandate over Palestine

1948- *Independent Republic*; present boundaries established in 1949 armistice agreements following Palestine War; parliamentary constitution with multiparty coalition governments

JORDAN

    -1918   *Part of Ottoman Empire*

    1920-1923 *Part of British Mandate* over Palestine

    1923-   Amirate (since 1946 Kingdom) in Transjordan under Hashimite dynasty ('Abd Allah 1923-1951, Husayn, 1952-   )

    1946-   *Independent Kingdom*; parts of Arab Palestine incorporated and name changed to Hashimite Kingdom of Jordan, 1949; close treaty relations with United Kingdom severed, 1957

    1958   Joins Arab Federation with Iraq; following its dissolution in July, British troops temporarily recalled to Jordan

LEBANON

    -1943 See Syria

    1943-   *Independent Republic* with parliamentary constitution; French occupation ended in 1946; constitutional government restored after bloodless ouster of President Bishara al-Khuri in 1952. Civil war between supporters and opponents of President Kamil Sham'un in 1958 leads to intervention of American forces. Internal peace restored under President Fuad Shihab.

LIBYA

    -1911   *Part of Ottoman Empire*

    1911-1943 *Italian Colony*, but resistance centering around Sanusi order in Cyrenaica continues until 1930's

    1943-1952 Occupation by British (Cyrenaica, Tripolitania) and French (Fezzan)

    1952-   *Independent monarchy* (composed of three federal units) under Sanusi dynasty (Idris II, 1952-   ); continued dependence on British and other outside aid; parliamentary constitution

MOROCCO

    -1912   *Independent Sultanate* under Sharifi dynasty

    1912-1956 Protectorate: French Zone, Spanish Zone in North, and International Zone of Tangiers; resistance continues in Rif area into 1920's

    1956-   Independent monarchy (Muhammad V, 1927-1953, 1955-   ); constitutional government with strong royal influence

OTTOMAN EMPIRE

See Turkey, Algeria, Egypt, Iraq, Israel, Jordan, Lebanon, Libya, Syria, Tunisia, Yemen

PALESTINE

See Israel, Jordan, Gaza Strip

SAUDI ARABIA

Traditionalist absolute monarchy of House of Su'ud, originating in central Arabian region of Najd, expanded during rule of 'Abd al-'Aziz Ibn Su'ud (1897-1953) to include Persian Gulf and Red Sea coasts; present ruler Su'ud ibn 'Abd al-'Aziz, 1953-   ; major part of royal revenues since 1930's derived from operations of American-owned Arabian-American Oil Company.

SUDAN

    -1899 See Egypt

    1899-1955 *British occupation* (nominally Anglo-Egyptian Condominium, in fact British colonial rule)

    1956-   *Independent republic* with parliamentary, and since 1958 military, regime

SYRIA

    -1918   *Part of Ottoman Empire*

    1918-1920 Occupation by British and Arab forces; Faysal I proclaimed King of (Greater) Syria

    1920-1945 *French Mandate* established after expulsion of Faysal and reasserted after periodic rebellions in mid-1920's; separate administration for Lebanon (q.v.); remainder divided into three (1920), four (1922), two (1925), and again three (1930) separate units. Constitutions adopted for

Syria (1930-1939, 1943-   ) and Lebanon (1926-1932, 1934-1939). Control by Vichy (1940-1941) and De Gaullist forces (1941-1946)

1943-1958 Independent Republic

1943-1949 Unstable parliamentary governments

1949-1954 Military regimes established by successive coups (Colonels Za'im, March 1949; Hinnawi, August 1949; and Shishakli, December 1949)

1954-1958 Parliamentary governments under increasing control of left-wing groups and army officers

1958-   Merged with Egypt in *United Arab Republic* under President Abdul Nasser

TRANSJORDAN

See Jordan

TUNISIA

-1881 *Dependency of Ottoman Empire*

1881-1956 *French Protectorate,* with continued nominal rule of native monarch (Bey)

1956-   *Independent Monarchy* and (since 1957) *Republic;* parliamentary regime under Prime Minister (since 1957 President) Habib Bourguiba (Abu Raqiba)

TURKEY

-1923 *Ottoman Empire*

1808-1839 Mahmud II inaugurates program of Westernizing centralizing reforms (*Tanzimat*)

1876-1878 Parliamentary constitution adopted, then suspended

1878-1908 Autocratic rule of Sultan Abdülhamid II

1908-1918 Second constitutional period under Young Turks, by 1913 converted into de facto military dictatorship under Enver Paşa

1918-1922 Shadow government of Mehmed VI in Istanbul under Allied occupation; Sultanate declared abolished by Ankara government in 1922

1920-1923 Provisional government of Grand National Assembly in Ankara under Mustafa Kemal (Atatürk) wins victory in War of Independence (chiefly against Greece)

1923-   *Republic of Turkey*

1923-1945 One-party rule of Republican People's Party under Presidents Kemal Atatürk (1923-1938) and İsmet İnönü (1938-1950)

1946-   Competitive party system; governments of Republican People's Party (until 1950) and Democratic Party (1950-   , President Bayar, Prime Minister Menderes)

UNITED ARAB REPUBLIC

Formed in 1958 by merger of Egypt and Syria (qqv.)

YEMEN

Traditional autocracy under rulers (with title Imam) who also are heads of Zaydi sect of Shi'i Islam

-1918 Nominally part of *Ottoman Empire*

1918-   *Independent monarchy*: Imam Yahya, murdered in 1948, succeeded by his son Imam Ahmad

---

Despite this recent proliferation of political parties, there has been little durability in the resulting patterns of organization. The history of most independent Near Eastern regimes has been punctuated by dictatorships, military coups, riots, and states of siege. The short breathing spells of constitutional and electoral government often allowed the formation of no more than loose, ephemeral coteries in the capitals that were quick to adopt solemn programs and elaborate bylaws but unable or unwilling to set up local branches in the provinces, to attract a mass following, or to influence policy. Of all the Near Eastern countries, only Turkey and Egypt have developed durable party alignments persisting for several decades. Turkey has had a one-party system dominated by the Society of Union and Progress (1908-1918), a dictatorial one-party system under the Republican People's Party (1923-1945), and a two-party system of Republicans vs. Democrats (1946–   ).[16] In Egypt, the Wafd Party won every free election from 1924 to 1950; yet its dominance was restricted not only by the existence of other parties but also by an almost continuous power contest among the Wafd, the Royal Palace, and the British Residency. Lebanon since the end of World War II has had governments accountable to parliamentary majorities; yet rivalry of religious sects and traditional patriarchal loyalties tend to overshadow political alignments based on party organization. The Arab countries in Northwest Africa (Morocco, Tunisia, and Algeria) developed strong nationalist parties during their colonial days that may furnish the basis for stable one-party systems. Similarly, the Sudan during the first few years following independence seemed headed for a two-party system. Nonetheless, the advent of a military regime in the Sudan in 1958 proves how brittle such incipient tendencies often are, and also that, after a mere three or four years of independence, long-range predictions of the evolution of political regimes are risky and premature. In the other Arab countries and in Iran parties have been even more ephemeral and unorganized.

The early growth of political parties coincided in the Near East with the rise of the principle of nationality, which toward the turn of the twentieth century began to displace earlier dynastic-traditional structures. The desire for establishment or preservation of a nation-state thus has been among the commonest motives of party formation. Other European-derived ideologies—none of them rivaling the predominant position of nationalism—have also from time to time attracted a following: Socialism, Fascism, and, above all, Communism. Muslim fundamentalism, stimulated by resentment of the rapid advance of Westernization, has provided another important point of ideological attachment. Other parties were founded by the defenders of oligarchic privilege. Finally, at times when both the country's boundaries and its form of government

---

[16] For the classification of party systems, see Austin Ranney and Willmoore Kendall, "The American Party Systems," *American Political Science Review*, Vol. XLVIII, No. 2, 1954, pp. 480ff.

were sufficiently settled to allow for such preoccupations, differences of outlook, interest, or ambition have produced parties concerned predominantly with the pragmatic pursuit of power and its perquisites.

In order to introduce some clarity into the often bewildering and changeable array of parties in the Near East, it is helpful to classify them by their function or role in the over-all socio-political process. In other words, we should distinguish first among various types of party system and, within each of these, among the major types of party commonly associated with it. The classification to be applied may be outlined as follows:

I. ONE-PARTY SYSTEMS in which all, or nearly all, the politically articulate elements of a country are enlisted in a single organization. The single parties prevalent in this system in turn may belong to one of the following types:

A. Comprehensive-nationalist parties, whose exclusive position results from the rallying of all forces for the attainment or maintenance of independence; here the power contest is primarily between the society as a whole and an actual or potential foreign ruler.

B. Dictatorial parties, whose monopoly is ensured through various open or disguised means of coercion.

II. COMPETITIVE PARTY SYSTEMS, where two or more parties vie for the allegiance of the articulate public—each of them, as a rule, restricting its appeal to some particular social group or interest, or combination of groups and interests. Among competitive parties, the following types may be distinguished:

A. Pragmatic parties, whose appeal is based chiefly on economic interest, desire for patronage, or other concrete policy questions. Among these, in turn, it is useful to differentiate between:

(1) *Broadly based pragmatic parties*, which have a wide mass appeal and are generally eager to extend their social base; and

(2) *Narrowly based pragmatic parties*, which are formed by the alignment and realignment of leaders within a small ruling group, compete for power only within the limits imposed by the existing oligarchic regime, and are generally confined to the personal following of some particular individual.

B. Ideological parties, whose appeal is based largely on a theoretical doctrine. In the Near East, the following ideologies have enjoyed the widest currency among organized competitive political parties:

(1) *Muslim fundamentalism*—a doctrine, variously formulated,

397

which opposes the prevalent tendency toward secularization with a self-conscious reassertion of the Islamic heritage in ethics and politics.

(2) *Nationalism.* Note here that nationalist parties competing with other pragmatic or ideological parties should be clearly distinguished from comprehensive-nationalist parties in one-party systems (I-A, above). In the Near East the competitive nationalist parties have generally tended to greater intransigence. Since they typically developed at a time when national independence was largely or completely attained, their campaign slogans often have been divorced from concrete policy proposals—a circumstance which favors tactical shifts and appeals to direct action. At the time when German and Italian influence stood at their zenith in the Near East (*ca.* 1936-1942), some of these groups displayed Fascist sympathies; since the late 1940's they have at times cooperated closely with the Communists.

(3) *Communism* (whose role as an ideological and political force in the Near East will be discussed in detail in a later section).

(4) *Socialism*—with emphasis on progress toward social equality and of full use of governmental powers for industrialization and agricultural development.

It should be noted that the scheme of classification as employed in other chapters of this study calls for two additional categories: I-C. *Dominant non-dictatorial parties*—which maintain their dominance without resort to coercion. II-C. *Particularistic parties*—i.e., the political organizations of ethnic or regional minorities which do not, or do not fully, recognize the legitimacy of the existing regime. There are, nevertheless, so few clear-cut examples of either of these types in the Near East that these two classes may conveniently be omitted in the present context. Some observers might place the Tunisian Neo-Dustur Party or even the Egyptian Wafd of the 1920's and 1930's in category I-C. But while the struggle against French rule in neighboring Algeria and against its vestiges in Tunisia itself continues, the Neo-Dustur is more properly classed as a comprehensive-nationalist party. Again the Wafd, engaged in a continuous two-front struggle against the British and the Royal Palace, can hardly be characterized as "dominant." An example of a particularistic party might be seen in the Azarbayjan Democratic Party of 1945-1947. In fact, however, it was only a temporary and tactical metamorphosis of the Iranian Communist movement. The short-lived Armenian nationalist movement in the last years of the Ottoman Empire was the only clear Near Eastern example of this class, but it has long been defunct. The most notable particularistic

movement in the Near Eastern state system that emerged in the 1920's
—the Kurdish independence movement in Iraq, Turkey, and Iran—
was based on tribal rather than party organization.[17]

Before we proceed to a survey of the various types of party—or such
of them as are found in the Near East—a number of general caveats
should be recorded. First, the distinctions here employed are generally
quite fluid. The difference between a narrowly based and a broadly
based party clearly is one of degree rather than of kind. Similarly,
the distinction between pragmatic and ideological parties should be seen
as part of a continuum. Even the most pragmatic patronage parties tend
to reflect a number of theoretical assumptions about the nature of politics and to make use of ideological tenets in their propaganda; conversely, the most doctrinaire ideological parties frequently make tactical
concessions to the pragmatic requirements of the moment. Second, the
scheme of classification highlights the differences between major types
of political groupings as they have empirically arisen; viewed in the
abstract the scheme somewhat lacks in symmetry. The broadly based–
narrowly based continuum, for example, could be applied with equal
theoretical validity to ideological parties and within single-party systems.
Similarly, the contrast between pragmatic and ideological emphases
can be traced within all types of party. Third, both parties and party
systems change their social and political attributes in time, and it is
therefore quite common for one and the same empirical party to move
from one analytical category to another. Indeed, the major aim of
some competitive parties, such as the Communists and certain oligarchic
groups, is typically to transform themselves into dictatorial parties. But
the example of the Turkish Republican People's Party illustrates that
a reverse transition is also possible. Finally, it should be emphasized
that the distinctions and designations applied here are meant to serve
purposes of description and analysis, not of praise or condemnation.

A schematic listing of major Near Eastern parties by country and
type will be found in Table 4.

Comprehensive nationalist parties. Typically a party's commitment
to nationalism, in the early stages of development toward a nation-state,
involves it in a fight on two fronts—externally, against existing or
threatened foreign rule, and, domestically, against the traditional political structure and its defenders. The party's comprehensive character

[17] Similarly, agrarian populism, which has been of considerable importance in other
parts of the world, and might be listed as category II-B-5, has not developed as a distinct ideology in the Near East.

arises from the need to secure support in this two-front fight among the widest possible combination of social strata. But the party is also comprehensive in the further sense that it desires not merely a political regeneration but, beyond this, a far-reaching reshaping of society. Its major socio-cultural aims commonly are mass education, economic development—particularly of industry—and secularization; in short, a hastening of the process of modernization of which the rise of national consciousness itself is but one facet.

The stimulus for the formation of comprehensive nationalist parties may be negative or positive, based on fear or on hope. The sudden threat of foreign domination may galvanize the politically articulate elements of a hitherto independent country. Or, a new favorable constellation of circumstances may suggest the possibility of shaking off established colonial rule. Nationalism spread throughout the Near East in the wake of the Balkan and First World Wars, just as it did in Europe during the Napoleonic Wars a century before. Wherever the struggle for independence was directed against European rulers, the two European civil wars (1914-1918 and 1939-1945) provided an important incentive to nationalist action. The changing fortunes of war exposed the vulnerability of colonial rulers (e.g., the French collapse in 1940) and tempted the belligerents to promise independence both to their own and to their enemies' subjects (e.g., Britain's promise in 1914 of postwar independence for Egypt and, in 1915-1916, of support for Arab independence in the Ottoman territories; Wilson's Fourteen Points; the Anglo-French promise of Syrian and Lebanese independence in 1941). The advent of the French Popular Front government in the mid-1930's similarly encouraged nationalism in Syria and in Northwest Africa. More recently, the dissolution of colonial empires in the wake of the Second World War accentuated the nationalist struggle in Morocco and Tunisia; and the attainment of independence in those two countries intensified nationalist guerrilla warfare in neighboring Algeria.

Those background dates give meaning to a simple chronological listing of the origins of Near Eastern nationalist movements. The Young Turk movement, which started in the late nineteenth century as a conspiracy against the despotism of Sultan Abdülhamid II, was propelled into revolutionary action in part by the prospect of partition of the Ottoman Empire resulting from the Anglo-Russian agreement of 1907. The Turkish nationalist movement of Mustafa Kemal (Atatürk) crystallized in 1919 in opposition to the Allied attempt at partition of the

TABLE 4

Major Political Parties in the Near East

COUNTRY	ONE-PARTY SYSTEMS		COMPETITIVE PARTY SYSTEMS	
	Comprehensive-Nationalist Parties	Dictatorial Parties	Pragmatic Parties	Ideological Parties
Turkey	Society of Union and Progress, 1889-(1913) Society for the Defense of Rights, 1919-1923: Kemal Atatürk	Society of Union and Progress, (1913)-1918: Enver, Talât Republican People's Party, 1923-(1945): Kemal Atatürk, İnönü	Freedom and Accord Party, 1911-1913 Second Group, 1922-1923 Progressive Party, 1924-1925 Free Party, 1930 Republican People's Party (1945-); İnönü Democratic Party, 1946: Bayar, Menderes	*Nation Party, 1949
Iran		National Front, 1951-1953: Mossadegh	National Will Party, 1944-1946: Tabatabai Iran Democrat Party, 1946: Qavam	*Devotees of Islam (Fidaiyan-i Islam) †Tudah Party, 1941 †Azarbayjan Democratic Party, 1945-1947
Syria	Young Arabs, 1911 Arab Revolt, 1916-1920 Independence Party People's Party, 1924 National Bloc, 1928	Arab Liberation Movement, 1952-1954: Shishakli	People's Party National Party Syrian National Social Party 1934: Sa'adah Arab Renaissance Party, 1940: Hawrani Arab Socialist Renaissance Party	*Muslim Brethren ‡Arab Socialist Renaissance Party: Hawrani (see previous column) †Communist Party: Bakdash

TABLE 4 (continued)

COUNTRY	ONE-PARTY SYSTEMS		COMPETITIVE PARTY SYSTEMS	
	Comprehensive-Nationalist Parties	Dictatorial Parties	Pragmatic Parties	Ideological Parties
Lebanon	See Syria		Phalanges Libanaises Progressive Socialist Party, 1949: Junblat	‡Progressive Socialist Party (see previous column)
Iraq	Iraqi Covenant, 1914		Iraqi Covenant People's Party National Brotherhood, 1931 Ahali Group, 1931 (later National Democratic Party, 1946-1954): Chadirji Independence Party, 1946-1954 Constitutional Union 1949-1954: Nuri al-Sa'id Socialist Party of the Nation, 1951-1954: Salih Jabr	‡Ahali (see previous column) §People's and National Brotherhood Parties (see previous column)
Egypt	'Urabi Revolt, 1881-1882 National Party 1897-1907: Mustafa Kamil Wafd, 1918-(1936): Zaghlul, Nahhas	National Union: Abdul Nasser	Wafd (1936)-1952: Nahhas Sa'dist Wafd, 1938-1952 Wafdist Bloc, 1942-1952 Liberal Constitutional Party, 1922 Union Party, 1925 People's Party, 1931: Isma'il Sidqi	‡Muslim Brethren, 1928: Hasan al-Banna §Young Egypt (Green Shirts)

		National Union Party:
Sudan	White Flag League, 1922-1924	Mirghani, Azhari
	Graduates' General Congress, 1937	People's Party: 'Abd al-Rahman al-Mahdi
Tunisia	Dustur Party, 1920	
	Neo-Dustur Party, 1934: Bourguiba	
Algeria	Algerian People's Party, 1937: Masali al-Hajj	
	Friends of the Declaration, 1943: Farhat 'Abbas	
	National Liberation Front	
Morocco	National Party 1937	
	Independence (Istiqlal) Party, 1944: 'Allal al-Fasi	

Explanation: Dates following party names represent the years of the party's founding and disbanding; dates in parentheses indicate the (approximate) year a party shifted from one category to another. Names after colons are those of prominent party leaders. In the last column, the following types of ideological party have been distinguished:
* Islamic-Fundamentalist
† Communist
‡ Socialist
§ Nationalist-Fascist

Turkish-Anatolian rump of the Empire.[18] That same year a self-appointed Egyptian committee (or Wafd, i.e., "delegation") set out to plead Egyptian nationalist claims before the Paris Peace Conference and, upon its return, furnished the nucleus for the Wafd Party. In Arab Southwest Asia, nationalist organization was stimulated by the repressive centralizing policies of the Young Turk regime of 1908-1918, and by wartime agreements between the British and Sharif Husayn, guardian of the Holy Places of Mecca and Medina. The result was the celebrated Arab Revolt of 1916-1918.[19] In Northwest Africa the Tunisian Constitutional (Dustur) Party formed in 1920 (its more vigorous successor, the Neo-Dustur, splitting off in 1934); the Algerian People's Party and the Moroccan Nationalist Party in 1937; a moderate Algerian group known as the Friends of the Proclamation in 1943; and the Moroccan Independence (Istiqlal) Party—an expansion of the earlier Nationalist Party—in 1944.[20]

In addition to the comprehensive nationalist parties just listed, there are a number of others which under the pressure of external circumstances never developed in fully comprehensive fashion. The Egyptian nationalist movement of 'Urabi Pasha, which was suppressed by the British occupation of 1882, has already been mentioned. Another nationalist group formed in Egypt toward the turn of the century around a journalist, Mustafa Kamil.[21] After some ten years of activity, it was officially constituted in 1907 as the Nationalist Party (Hizb al-Watani). Although the party survived until the suppression of all political parties by the Najib (Naguib) regime in 1952, it never attracted the mass following later accorded to the Wafd, and the campaign inaugurated by Kamil petered out shortly after his death in 1907.

In the Fertile Crescent, the Arab nationalist movement was thwarted by the partition of the area into French and British mandates after

[18] The movement was constituted in 1919 as the Society for the Defense of Rights of Anatolia and Rumelia (i.e., Asiatic and European Turkey); in 1923 it was transformed into the People's Party, which, in 1924, changed its name to the Republican People's Party. In 1921 the title Gazi (Victor) was conferred upon Mustafa Kemal Paşa, and in 1934 he adopted the family name Atatürk, omitting henceforth the titles Gazi and Paşa (i.e., General).

[19] See Antonius, *op.cit.* For Britain's role, see Elie Kedourie, *Britain and the Middle East, 1914-1920*, London, 1956.

[20] See Alal al-Fasi, *Independence Movements in Arab North Africa* (American Council of Learned Societies Translation Series), Washington, D.C., 1954.

[21] Not to be confused with the Turkish leader Mustafa Kemal (Atatürk). On Mustafa Kamil, see Jacob M. Landau, *Parliaments and Parties in Egypt*, Tel Aviv, 1953; and Fritz Steppat, "Nationalismus und Islam bei Mustafa Kamil," *Welt des Islams*, N.S. Vol. IV, 1956, pp. 242-341.

1920. In Syria and Lebanon the French policy of suppression and divide-and-rule weakened and split the nationalist movement. (Syrian supporters of the Arab Revolt and of the short-lived nationalist regime of King Faysal in Damascus formed the Independence Party. A People's Party was founded in 1924, and elements from both groups in 1928 joined the Nationalist Bloc, which led the struggle against French domination during the next two decades.) In Palestine five of six loosely organized Arab parties joined in 1936 to form the Arab Higher Committee under Hajj Amin al-Husayni, better known as the Mufti of Jerusalem. The Committee took a prominent part in organizing Arab resistance to Jewish settlement in the late 1930's and again in the mid-1940's. Its hopes for an Arab-controlled Palestine government were thwarted not only by the proclamation of the State of Israel and its victory in the Palestine War, but also by the incorporation of most of the remnants of Arab Palestine into Jordan.

The concentration of all articulate political forces upon a single task, which is the essence of comprehensive nationalist parties, can generally be maintained only during periods of head-on collision between the forces of independence and suppression—as during the Arab Revolt in the Hijaz and in Syria (1916-1920), the War of Independence in Turkey (1919-1922), the Egyptian Revolution (1919), and the post-World War II struggle against French rule in Northwest Africa. Once the political focus shifts to issues other than independence, the appeal for comprehensive unity is likely to lose its potency. The disenchantment may come about when the goal of independence is reached —as in Turkey in 1922, and in Morocco and Tunisia in 1955—or when it seems to elude, for the foreseeable future, the grasp of the nationalists—as in Egypt and in Syria in the 1920's. At this point the very comprehensiveness of the nationalist movement, which is its strongest asset in its fighting days, tends to become a liability. The heterogeneous political interests included in the organization engage in factional quarrels or, as a result of expulsions and secessions, form separate parties. For the original comprehensive-nationalist group the transition may lead in one of two directions. It may maintain its earlier ascendancy by assuming dictatorial powers—as in Turkey under Kemal Atatürk and İsmet İnönü. Or else it may remain in the political arena as one of several competing parties—as did the Egyptian Wafd after 1922 and 1936. (Once again, the Northwest African experience is too recent to reveal ultimate trends.) To the extent that the original nationalist party was truly comprehensive, later political groupings will, in one way or another, be descended from it.

Comprehensive dictatorial parties. Dictatorial parties in the Near East have originated in one of three ways. First, they have resulted from the transformation of a comprehensive-nationalist party; second, they have been the result of a competitive party assuming dictatorial powers; third, they have been created *ad hoc*, usually by dictators who came to power through a military coup. Although the evidence is somewhat limited, it is significant that the first kind of dictatorial party has been the most durable, and the third the most ephemeral.

Turkey furnishes the only clear examples of a dictatorship based on a prior comprehensive-nationalist movement. Both the Society of Union and Progress and the Kemalist movement eliminated their competitors after their victorious revolutions. In the first instance, a young Unionist officer, Enver Paşa, occupied the war ministry in a brash military coup in 1913, displaced the bureaucratic cabinet which the CUP had hitherto allowed to remain in office, and in effect set up a dictatorial triumvirate consisting of himself, Cemal Paşa, and Talât which with the support of the Society's party organization ruled Turkey until the defeat of 1918. Following the victory in the Turkish War of Independence, Mustafa Kemal retained power for himself and his party organization, abolished the sultanate (1922) and caliphate (1924), and proclaimed a republic (1923). Early opposition movements, such as the Progressive Party, the Kurdish Revolt of 1925, and the conspiracy which led to an attempt on Kemal's life in 1926, were crushed with the aid of extraordinary tribunals. Yet the prestige which Kemal and his Republican People's Party (RPP) enjoyed as liberators of the country was great enough to enable him to consolidate his rule without further overt use of violence, and to carry out a legal and cultural reform program unsurpassed in scope or rapidity. (Kemal's personal prestige was symbolized by the name Atatürk, or Father of the Turks, which the Turkish National Assembly bestowed on him in 1934.) The smooth transition by which, after Atatürk's death, his long-time collaborator İsmet İnönü assumed the succession is further evidence of the movement's vigor and unity of purpose. İnönü readmitted many of the erstwhile dissidents (such as the surviving Progressive Party leaders) into the RPP. In 1945 he took the further step of allowing the formation of opposition parties. Following an almost continuous four-year campaign, the leading one among these, the Democratic Party of Celâl Bayar and Adnan Menderes, won by a landslide in Turkey's first free and honest election in 1950. The RPP since then has assumed the role of leading opposition party. The original Kemalist movement thus underwent two major transitions: from comprehensive-nationalist to comprehensive-dictatorial party in the early 1920's and from dictatorial to competitive party in the late 1940's.

Although competitive parties, once in power, have often ridden roughshod over the opposition, there are few clear examples in the past of a competitive party transforming itself into a dictatorial one; yet additional examples may be in the making. Probably the clearest case—other than that of the Union and Progress Party—is that of Muhammad Mossadegh's National Front in Iran. Mossadegh entered politics as a typical representative of the educated landowning aristocracy of Iran, but won fame in 1944 as sponsor of a law (then clearly directed against Russian aspirations) which forbade the granting of any oil concessions without parliamentary approval. The National Front originated in the late 1940's as a small band of nationalist deputies dissatisfied with the existing oligarchic regime and its moderate foreign policies. It rode into power in 1951 on a platform of nationalization of the Anglo-Iranian Oil Company. Following his temporary dismissal in the summer of 1952, Mossadegh attempted systematically to centralize power in his hands and those of the party. Within a year Mossadegh had dissolved the senate and the house of deputies, broken with his erstwhile Muslim fundamentalist followers under Kashani, and attempted to curtail the powers of the Shah and the army. At this point it turned out that he had overreached himself, and even the eager support of the Communist Tudah Party was not enough to keep him in power. An army countercoup under General Zahidi displaced him in 1953, restored the Shah to power, brought Mossadegh to trial, and dissolved his party.

Examples of dictatorial parties established *ad hoc* and *ex post facto* by military dictators are Adib Shishakli's Arab Liberation Movement (1952-1954) and Jamal Abdul Nasser's National Union, created in 1956. Both dictatorships, at least in their early stages, were supported by a combination of military force and of nationalist and reformist sentiment among the intelligentsia; in addition, Nasser has had intermittent support from organized labor and until 1958 from Communists. Shishakli's Liberation Movement, after sweeping a controlled election in 1953, elected a mere two deputies the next year, when the dictator had fallen from power. Clearly the Liberation Movement had been little more than a smoke-screen for personal despotic rule. Nasser has confronted the difficult task of welding into an effective unit not only his supporters among the military, the middle class, the workers, and the peasantry of Egypt, but also his followers in other Arab countries who have joined in his drive for Arab unity. What organizational changes his National Union may undergo in the process, and whether it will survive its founder, it is too early to predict.

Competitive-pragmatic parties. While comprehensive parties of either the nationalist or the dictatorial variety run to a few well-defined types, the competitive-pragmatic classification includes a wide variety of disparate political movements and pseudo-movements. As suggested earlier, they may be thought of as constituting a spectrum extending from those with well-organized mass support to those which are merely the temporary agglomeration of personal followers of this or that leader in a ruling oligarchy. Today, the parties of Turkey clearly stand at the well-organized, broadly based end of the spectrum, while party competition in a country such as pre-1958 Iraq did not break the grip of the traditional oligarchy.

In Turkey, there was a brief interval of party competition in the period before the First World War. In 1911, a number of dissidents who opposed the extreme centralizing tendencies of the Union and Progress Party split off to form the Freedom and Accord Party (Hürriyet ve İtilâf Firkasi, sometimes translated "Liberal Entente"). They were powerless, however, to prevent the establishment of the wartime Unionist dictatorship, and a reconstituted Freedom and Accord Party came to power only as a result of the country's defeat in 1918. Hopelessly discredited by their support of the Sultan's policy of cooperation with the Allied occupying powers, it disappeared completely with the collapse of the Sultan's government in Istanbul. Three early opposition groups which split off from the Kemalist movement were even more short-lived. Of these, the so-called Second Group of 1921-1923 and the Progressive Republican Party of 1924-1925 opposed the establishment of Kemal's personal dictatorship. The third, the Free Republican Party of 1930, originated as a "loyal" opposition party set up by one of Kemal's close collaborators and with his approval; it was suppressed four months later, once again at Kemal's behest, apparently because its appeal to opposition sentiment had been too successful for comfort. The Democratic Party of 1946, like its predecessors, split off from the RPP on the basis of such obvious opposition demands as greater attention to religion and to private enterprise, in contradistinction to the RPP program of secularism and etatism. Unlike those earlier party ventures, however, the Democrats could develop in complete freedom. Within four years of opposition campaigning (1946-1950) they extended their organization to cities and towns in most provinces, founding many times the number of local branches that the RPP had founded in the preceding decades. As a result of growing contact with the peasant majority of the electorate, the party emphasized increasingly the demands for a limited Islamic restoration and for rapid agricultural development under state auspices, and it was on the basis of these demands that the Democratic Party won its sweeping election victory of 1950.[22] A succession of good harvests, large-scale rural development, and high cash supports for wheat and other crops solidified this agrarian backing for the Democratic Party, which in 1954 was reelected by an even greater majority. In the meantime, Premier Menderes and other Democratic Party leaders became increasingly intolerant of criticism in the press and at public meetings; nevertheless, the campaign techniques of the Republican People's Party, under the vigorous leadership of İsmet İnönü, Kasim Gülek, and others, improved sufficiently to turn the 1957 election into a very close race, which Menderes' Democrats won only by a popular plurality.

The early years of opposition to the RPP in the late 1940's attracted to the Democrats a heterogeneous following, including urban intellectuals, large landowners and small farmers, industrial workers, and various religious-conservative groups. This heterogeneous character led to a series of splits in proportion as control of the party organization was tightened in the hands of Adnan Menderes. The first such split led to the formation in 1949 of the Nation Party, a religious-conservative group with solid local following in certain parts of Central Anatolia and in the poorer districts of the large cities. Another split in 1955 resulted in the formation of the Liberty Party, composed of dissident Democrats who opposed Menderes' heavy-handed treatment of the opposition press. The Liberty Party, like the Nation Party, showed only limited local strength; in 1958 it merged with the RPP.

The Sudan, like Turkey, has shown certain tendencies toward a two-party system—except that the Sudanese parties have been far more limited in their organizational base. The concrete issue which, in 1946, led to a clear alignment of two party coalitions was that of the country's political future, with the People's Party favoring complete independ-

---

[22] On the religious question, see Dankwart A. Rustow, "Politics and Islam in Turkey, 1920-1955," in *Islam and the West*, ed. Richard N. Frye, 's Gravenhage 1957, pp. 69-107.

ence, and the National Union Party advocating a close political connection with Egypt. Following the liquidation of the British-controlled
condominium regime at the end of 1955, however, both groups in fact
agreed on complete independence. There is considerable evidence that,
underneath the surface of party politics, the crucial political divisions
were those between rival Muslim sects. Of these the Ansar, led by
Sayyid 'Abd al-Rahman al-Mahdi, were aligned with the People's
Party, while the National Unionists claimed the support of the Khatmiyah sect and its leader Sayyid 'Ali al-Mirghani.

Egyptian political life between the two world wars produced numerous parties. Of these some were "broadly based"—notably the Wafd,
which was discussed earlier as a comprehensive-nationalist party. The
original Wafd's aspirations for national independence clashed with the
hard reality of British military occupation, and the so-called Egyptian
Declaration of Independence of 1922 was a document issued unilaterally
by the British government and encumbered with so many reservations
as to deny the substance of independence. For more than a decade the
Wafd, both in and out of government, continued its agitation for withdrawal of British troops. By 1936, however, it agreed to a bilateral
treaty regularizing the presence of British troops in the Suez Canal
Zone in peacetime, and in the rest of Egypt in wartime. Six years later
the British, by rolling up tanks before the Royal Palace, forced King
Faruq to replace a pro-Axis government with one of the Wafd under
its leader Mustafa Nahhas. During this period of uncomfortable *de
facto* alliance with the former "national enemy," the Wafd gradually
was converted from a comprehensive-nationalist movement into a party
machine for the pursuit of patronage, nepotism, and graft. Two dissident groups split off after the 1936 and 1942 turning points—one,
founded in 1938, calling itself the Sa'dist Wafd (after the parent party's
founder, Sa'd Zaghlul); the other, founded in 1944, the Wafdist Bloc
(al-Kutlah al-Wafdiyah). The period from 1945 to 1950 developed
largely into a three-cornered contest among the Wafd, the Sa'dists and
allied groups, and the Muslim Brethren (of whom more below), each
trying to outdo the other in radical and nationalist oratorical appeal to
the masses and in direct action and violence. In the 1950 elections the
Wafd once again was swept into power—to carry out a program of uni-
lateral denunciation of the Anglo-Egyptian Treaty that their leader
had signed fourteen years earlier. But its victory was short-lived: early
in 1952 the Nahhas government was dismissed by the King, and follow-

ing the military coup of July the Wafd and all other political parties were banned altogether.

The three other competitive-pragmatic parties of Egypt between the wars had in common their narrow organizational base in the traditional land-holding and financial aristocracy, their antagonism to the Wafd, and their ability to cooperate with the Royal Palace and the British Residency. Three brief quotations from a recent study of Egyptian party movements[23] may suffice to characterize these groups. The Party of Constitutional Liberals, founded in 1922, "published manifestoes and arranged meetings, but it was a foregone conclusion that they would enjoy the support of neither the urban nor the rural masses." The Union Party, formed in 1925, "numbered few adherents [and] derived its support almost exclusively from the King and the Palace. . . . The Union Party served the King by aiding him to govern by royal decree instead of ruling by Parliamentary government. Otherwise its role was insignificant, nor did it leave an important imprint on Egyptian political life." The formation of the People's Party in 1930 preceded the suspension of the 1923 constitution by the anti-Wafdist premier Isma'il Sidqi; it was "an insignificant . . . party . . . founded by Sidqi in order to afford him at least a pretence of popular support." Except for its patent lack of comprehensiveness, the last-named party therefore might perhaps have been classified as a dictatorial party within a single-party system.

In Syria, Lebanon, and Iraq we can distinguish two sets of competitive parties. The first set originated in the division of the original nationalist groups of the First World War period into moderates, inclined to cooperate with the mandatory power, and into radicals, persisting in opposition. In Syria the moderate group was known as the People's (Sha'b) Party, and the more radical as the Nationalists (Ummah Party). Following the acquisition of full independence after the Second World War, the quest for greater Arab unity became the foremost issue of domestic politics, with the Populists leaning toward cooperation, or union, with Iraq and Jordan, and the Nationalists toward cooperation with Saudi Arabia and especially with Egypt. In Iraq the more radical group in the 1930's formed the People's (Sha'b) Party, not to be confused with its Syrian namesake, and the National Brotherhood Party. In 1946 their place was taken by an Independence Party of similar tendency. The more moderate group in the 1930's called itself the Iraqi Covenant, and in 1949 reemerged after a considerable interval as the Constitutional Union, both groups being led by General Nuri Sa'id. In 1951 a rival

[23] Landau, *op.cit.*, pp. 170, 173, 184.

group, known as the Socialist Party of the Nation (Hizb al-Ummah al-Ishtiraki), was organized by a prominent Shi'i politician, Salih Jabr. These and all other parties were dissolved by decree in 1954. Prior to the Iraqi revolution of 1958 none of these groups had any visible effect on parliamentary or cabinet politics. "The rank and file of the Deputies, elected as supporters of White, would complacently sustain Black; their seats, rather than any body of principles, were at stake."[24] The 1958 uprising, on the other hand, had the support of a broad range of opposition groups, among whom the military and the Independence Party appear to have played leading roles.

Dissatisfaction with the restrictive oligarchic character of these more traditional parties gave rise to the formation, among the younger urban educated groups, of parties with a more militant and more ideological tinge. In Syria these included Akram Hawrani's Arab Socialist Party (1940) and Michel Aflaq's Arab Resurrection (Ba'th) Party, subsequently merged under Hawrani's leadership into the Arab Socialist Resurrection Party. Its program committed the party to revolutionary action for its two stated goals—Arab unity and socialism. Hawrani's group, together with the Nationalist (Ummah) Party, provided much of the impetus for the Arab unity movement set off by the merger of Egypt and Syria in the United Arab Republic early in 1958. A rival group, known as the Syrian People's Party (or Syrian National Social Party) was founded by a Lebanese Christian emigrant, Antun Sa'adah, in 1934. In contrast to the resurrection Party's pan-Arab program, it advocated a Syrian nationalism based on the merger of Lebanon and Syria. The party has been illegal in Lebanon since Sa'adah's execution on charges of high treason in 1949, and in Syria as a result of the assassination of a leading military figure, Adnan Malki, in 1955 which was traced to members of the group. A third group, advocating an exclusively Lebanese nationalism, formed in 1936 under the name Phalanges Libanaises; its following was mostly limited to the Maronite Christian group in Lebanon. Among both the older and the more recent parties of Syria and Lebanon, the question of the territorial definition of the future ideal political unit has thus played a paramount role. Still another Lebanese group, the Progressive Socialist Party, combined an abstract Socialist platform with solid regional support among the Druze tribesmen loyal to its leader Kamal Jumblat.

In Iraq, the more youthful radicals in the early 1930's joined in a

---

[24] S. H. Longrigg, *Iraq, 1900-1950*, London, 1953, p. 230; cf. Majid Khadduri, *Independent Iraq*, London, 1951, p. 78.

Socialist study circle, known as the Ahali Group. Later the Ahali and their leader Kamil Chadirji provided some of the civilian support for the military regimes that followed the coup of 1936, thus foreshadowing the Socialist-military alliance in Syria in the mid-1950's. After the Second World War the former Ahali Group provided the nucleus for the National Democratic Party (1946), dissolved along with the other Iraqi parties in 1954.

The clearest example of parties formed loosely around members of an established oligarchy is provided by Iran, where the end of Riza Shah's dictatorship in 1941 led to a proliferation of political organizations. With the notable exception of the Tudah (see below), these parties were generally "formed from above—a few people grouping themselves around some prominent personality, or publishing a newspaper with funds provided by an anonymous capitalist. Their programs were virtually interchangeable, and were confined to a series of pious platitudes, of which the 'integrity and independence of Iran' was usually the first. Their names gave even less indication of their policy. . . . Parties of this type seldom spread their influence beyond their own circle of intellectuals and professional men, and their fortunes, being dependent on the whims of individuals, fluctuated widely."[25]

Competitive-ideological parties. Ideological parties in the Near East, in contrast to Europe, have not been the expression of clear social alignments or well-thought-out integral domestic reform programs. The various "Socialist" groups just surveyed, for instance, have not been workers' parties aiming at a reorganization of the industrial economy. Like most other parties they have rather originated among the urban intelligentsia. As the merger of the Arab Socialist and Arab Resurrection parties in Syria indicates, ideological labels such as pan-Arabism and socialism are to a large extent interchangeable. What these pseudo-ideological movements have in common is their feeling of frustration with static oligarchic regimes within their country, and their country's relative impotence on the international scene. Above all, they share an inclination toward flamboyant oratory, mass demonstrations and, frequently, organized violence. No career demonstrates this fickleness of aim, combined with constancy in method, better than that of Ahmad Husayn, leader of a Fascist youth movement in the 1930's known as Young Egypt, who founded, successively, a "Nationalist Islamic Party" and an "Egyptian Socialist Party"—which in the 1950's closely co-

[25] L. P. Elwell-Sutton, "Political Parties in Iran, 1941-1948," *Middle East Journal,* Vol. III, 1949, p. 49.

operated with the Communists and the Muslim Brethren. Of the latter party, one observer stated that it "has little about it that is socialist except its name. In fact, it is the old Fascist Green Shirt Party . . . which has in the last fifteen years changed its name, the colour of its shirt, and its tactics, but not its revolutionary nature."[26]

The most highly organized political ideologies in the Near East have been Muslim fundamentalism and communism. The first tendency has been represented in Egypt and Syria by the Muslim Brethren and in Iran by the Devotees of Islam (Fida'iyan-i Islam). Communism also has been strongest in Iran, where it is organized in the Tudah Party (Party of the Masses), and in Syria. The Muslim Brethren originated as a religious, non-political organization founded in Egypt in 1928 by a schoolteacher, Hasan al-Banna. Their major aim was the revival of Muslim piety in faith and in works, in opposition to the prevalent trend of secularization and Westernization. They organized workshops to secure employment for indigent members, and set up dispensaries to care for the sick. In contrast to many other political parties in the Near East, they raised their funds exclusively by subscriptions from the membership rather than from government patronage, foreign embassies, or wealthy sponsors. Toward the end of the Second World War their membership in Egypt was estimated at anywhere between 200,000 and 2.5 million,[27] and they also began to build up a following in Syria. About this time the Brethren began increasingly to shift to political action, and they found that their secret initiation rites and tight hierarchical organization could be adapted extremely well to the growing atmosphere of violence. In 1948 they countered an edict dissolving their organization with the assassination of the Egyptian premier, Nuqrashi Pasha, and sent organized bands of armed volunteers into the Arab-Israeli war of 1948. When the military regime of Najib and Abdul Nasser dissolved all political parties early in 1953, the Brethren, claiming to be a non-political association, escaped the ban and found the field free of former competitors such as the Wafd Party. Some of the members of the military junta, indeed, were known to have been members or sympathizers of the Brotherhood. But apparently the initial honeymoon gave way to a contest for power; and following an assassination attempt on Colonel Nasser by a Muslim Brother in 1954, the organization was forcefully suppressed.

[26] Charles Issawi, *Egypt at Mid-Century*, London, 1954, p. 264. Cf. Walter Z. Laqueur, *Communism and Nationalism in the Middle East*, 2nd ed., New York, 1957, pp. 58ff.

[27] Laqueur, *op.cit.*, p. 238 (and note on p. 344).

The ideological importance of communism in the contemporary Near East will be more fully discussed in the following section. Suffice it here to say that Communist parties, except for brief periods, have been illegal throughout the Near East, but that they have been active in nearly every country despite such prohibitions. The greatest asset of the Communists has been their organizational talent, their singlemindedness, and their ability to set up front groups and to cooperate with other movements according to tactical exigencies. Today the strongest Communist parties appear to be those in Syria and in Iran (in the latter, known as the Tudah Party, or Party of the Masses).[28] In Syria, Khalid Bakdash—probably the ablest Communist leader in the region—became an independent member of parliament in 1954. Except for Turkey and Israel, Communist organization seems to be growing in strength and numbers throughout the area. It seems likely, for instance, that the current ban on all political party organizations in countries like Iran, Iraq, Jordan, and Egypt hurts the Communists, who have long been accustomed to illegal operation, far less than it does rival opposition groups.[29] As in other non-Western regions the Communists in the Near East have wavered from time to time between advocating broad "national fronts" with nationalist groups and denouncing them as "bourgeois reactionaries." Significantly, the current attempt at creating an image of Soviet-Muslim solidarity had its parallel after the First World War—with the difference that the main Communist bid for influence was then directed at Turkey and Iran, whereas today it is aimed at the Arab countries.

(2) *Ideological tendencies*. The four most important ideologies which vie today for the allegiance of politically articulate Near Easterners are (1) nationalism, (2) Islam in its political aspect, (3) Communism, and (4) constitutionalism. In practice, of course, elements of more than one of these ideologies are frequently combined in the same individual or the same political organization.

Of these four ideologies, nationalism enjoys by far the widest currency. Every Near Eastern political leader is, or at the very least professes to be, an ardent and sincere nationalist. This verbal unanimity, however, merely indicates that the significant ideological battles tend to be fought over the implications and applications of "true" nationalism.

Many of the inner tensions and logical contradictions of Near Eastern

---

[28] For Iran, which is not included in Laqueur's study, see George Lenczowski, *Russia and the West in Iran*, Ithaca, N.Y., 1949.

[29] For Egypt in particular, see Laqueur, *op.cit.*, pp. 358ff.

nationalism can readily be attributed to its relative youth. Throughout the Near East, down to the nineteenth century, the primary loyalties were dynastic and religious, local and tribal—rarely, if ever, national. The Ottoman Empire was a dynastic structure based on a close economic partnership of Muslims, Christians, and Jews, of Turks, Arabs, Greeks, Armenians, Bulgarians, Kurds, and a score of other ethnic groups. The very word "Turk," today a proud designation of nationality, down to the nineteenth century was employed by the Ottoman elite as a term of contempt for the unlettered peasants of Anatolia. Throughout the Near East, nationalism as an ideal supported by small groups of political leaders dates back only to the 1880's; as an ideological commitment of large masses it emerged as late as the 1920's.

Just as modern nationalism in countries like Germany and Spain was stimulated by the Napoleonic invasions, so Near Eastern nationalism began as a defensive and imitative response to the impact of the Western powers. As a result, the typical nationalist attitude toward the West is ambivalent—compounded in varying degrees of admiration and hate, of eager emulation and indignant rejection. Again as in Europe, the emergence of national consciousness in the Near East was accompanied by a radical transformation of society's image of its own history. The avid nationalist search for historical antecedents must be sharply distinguished from any conservative defense of living historical tradition. On the contrary, the glories of a distant past—whether it be the early Islamic history of the Arabs, the pre-Islamic history of the Turks and Iranians, or even that of the Phoenicians, the Pharaohs, the Babylonians, and the Hittites—are eagerly seized upon as an ally in the present struggle against the stranglehold of the more immediate cultural tradition.[30]

While Near Eastern nationalism shares this ambivalence toward its antagonists and toward its own history with youthful nationalisms everywhere, it also confronts a number of problems characteristic of Asian and African rather than European nationalism. For the nationality that is so emphatically proclaimed from the rostrum is not always as easily delimited on the map or as deeply etched within the civic consciousness of the nationals. Indeed, the less securely nationalism is based in reality, the louder tend to be its verbal proclamations. Turkey and Iran here are in a relatively fortunate position. Turkey's boundaries conform to

[30] For Turkey, cf. Dankwart A. Rustow, "Politics and Islam in Turkey," *loc.cit.*, pp. 81ff.; and Bernard Lewis, "History-Writing and National Revival in Turkey," *Middle Eastern Affairs*, Vol. IV, 1953, pp. 218-227.

the explicit limits set in the original nationalist program of 1919-1920, and over 90 per cent of her population speaks the same language and adheres to the same faith. And although Iran includes very sizable ethnic and religious minorities, it is heir to a national historical tradition going back to classical Persian literature of the tenth to fourteenth centuries and reinforced by the acceptance of Shi'i Islam as the predominant faith in the sixteenth century.

The Arab countries, however, face a serious dilemma amenable to no rapid or easy solution. Arabic is the exclusive or predominant language in over a dozen different countries from Morocco to 'Uman and from Syria to the Sudan. In an age of intensifying communication and social independence, language universally tends to become the primary criterion of nationality, and large groups in each of these countries profess their adherence to the ideal of Arab nationalism. Most of the present political boundaries among the Arab countries command little historical respect, since they were often imposed by European colonial powers. The boundaries in the Fertile Crescent, in particular, were the result of the partition of the Arab-Ottoman territories into British and French mandates after the First World War. Yet, while European hegemony lasted, it set up effective barriers to unification. For a generation or more, political energies in each country were fully absorbed in the struggle against foreign rule within these particular boundaries. Thus Egyptian nationalists in the 1920's and 1930's showed scant concern with the problems of their Arab neighbors east of Sinai. Even after the European withdrawal in the 1940's and 1950's, formidable obstacles to unification remained. Ruling dynasties and oligarchies had established powerful vested interests in the existing separate states. The dynastic feud between the Saudis of Arabia and the Hashimites of Iraq and Jordan abated, but was soon overshadowed by the intense political rivalry between populous Egypt and oil-rich Iraq. Such schemes of unity as were put forward in the 1940's—Nuri Sa'id's Fertile Crescent plan of 1942, King 'Abd Allah's perennial Greater Syria proposal, and the Egyptian-sponsored Arab League of 1945—played up to popular pan-Arab sentiment but were primarily designed to further the sponsor's personal ambition or to thwart those of his rivals. In the mid-1950's, the slogan "Unity of the Nile Valley" foundered against Sudanese resentment of Egyptian highhandedness. The continued animosity between Nasser's United Arab Republic and General Qasim's republican regime in Iraq indicates that rivalry between these two Arab population centers was no mere dynastic accident but has profounder geopolitical causes.

A new impetus was furnished by Colonel Nasser's success in exploiting the rivalry between the Soviet and Atlantic blocs for the enhancement of his prestige. The Syrian decision early in 1958 to merge with Nasser's Egypt in the United Arab Republic constituted the first positive move toward unity after decades of mere vociferation, and as such set off a powerful chain reaction. Distant Yemen, seeking help in its perennial border conflict with the British in Aden, associated herself with the new state, and in Arabia King Saud yielded most of his powers to his pro-Egyptian brother Faysal. The Hashimite countermove of a federation between Iraq and Jordan was thwarted by the Iraqi revolution in July 1958. Pro-Western regimes in Lebanon and Jordan precariously survived with the assistance of hastily summoned United States and British troops. By the summer of 1958 the goal of Arab unity from Cairo to the Persian Gulf and from Damascus to the Bab al-Mandab seemed at least a distant possibility. The Arab countries of Northwest Africa were not associated with these developments; yet here, too, the possibility of a Mahgrib Federation was being explored in contacts between Tunisian Premier Bourguiba, on the one hand, and Algerian nationalist and Libyan leaders, on the other.

Next to nationalism, Islam is undoubtedly still the most important ideological force in Near Eastern politics today. In some countries relatively untouched by modern industry and urbanization, the ruler's claim to religious authority tends to make for a harmonious reinforcement of religious and political loyalties among his subjects. This has been true in Libya, whose king is the head of the Sanusi sect that predominates in the eastern half of the country, as well as in Yemen and Morocco, whose kings claim lineal descent from the Prophet. Until recently Saudi Arabia might have been put into the same category, because of the close historical association between the House of Saud and the puritanical Wahhabi sect; yet the growth of the oil industry and the powerful appeal of Arab unity under Nasser's leadership have severely strained this traditional balance. In the Sudan, as pointed out earlier, the political scene was long dominated by the contest between two major Islamic sects—the Khatmiyah and the Ansar—whose role far overshadows that of the constantly shifting party alignments.

These traditional Islamic sects, such as the Wahhabis or Sanusis, must be sharply distinguished from the newer fundamentalist movements, such as the Muslim Brethren, which have militantly reasserted Islamic theocratic ideals against a prevailing trend of secularist nationalism. This type of neo-religious movement typically enlists those segments of the population which have been torn out of their traditional social context by urbanization and industrialization without having found a satisfactory place in the modern order of things. Their strength will thus depend largely on the success or failure of the social reform policies of their secularist rivals.

One may hesitate to list Communism as a third major ideological force in the Near East today. The number of card-holding Communists certainly is infinitesimally small—in the Arab countries it was recently estimated at around 30,000. Yet experience indicates that such small numbers may wield an entirely disproportionate power at crucial moments;[31] this is the lesson of the Bolshevik advent to power in Russia herself, and in the Near East the same rule has been illustrated by the recent role of the Communist Tudah Party in Iran and by that of fellow-traveling officers in Syria. Indeed, Communist power seems far more likely to come to the Near East today through foreign-policy alliances with nationalist regimes than through any domestic expansion of card-holding Communist membership.

The appeal of Communism to the Near East is not based on classical Marxian doctrines of surplus value, of the iron law of wages, or of proletarian revolution. It is based almost entirely on accumulated resentment of the West, and on the example of the Russian challenge to that same West. For, as Arnold Toynbee strikingly put it some years ago, Communism can say to the masses of Asia and Africa: "If you follow the Russian example, Communism will give you the strength to stand up against the West today."[32] This Communist appeal has been weakest in Turkey, where memories of Russian expansionism from the days of the Czars to those of Stalin and Khrushchev are vivid, where relations with the West have been based on mutual respect, and where constitutional processes have proved their strength both under a benevolent dictatorship and under a competitive two-party system. It has been strongest in Arab countries such as Syria, Iraq, Jordan, and Egypt, where nationality is still insecure, and where anti-Western resentment is nourished by continuing hostility toward Israel. Ultimately the progress of Communism in the Near East will depend largely on the West's ability to maintain or reestablish relations of mutual respect with Near Eastern leaders, and on the ability of these same leaders to devise and operate orderly constitutional forms of government that will command the loyalty of their subjects.

[31] Laqueur, *op.cit.*, pp. 276f.
[32] *The World and the West*, London, 1953, p. 15.

Certainly the prospects for constitutionalism, which I have listed as the fourth ideological force in the Near East, looked far brighter fifty years ago than they do today. The rise of a Western-educated elite in the nineteenth century went hand in hand with an enthusiastic faith in Western political institutions that is hard to imagine from our present perspective. If the sultans' early reform schemes produced no tangible increments in political power, the rising elite was inclined to blame, not Western cultural patterns, but rather the half-heartedness of the sultans' reformist zeal. Above all, it blamed the despotic system itself which allowed spendthrift monarchs to contract ruinous debts and thereby to deliver their countries into the hands of foreigners. Throughout the Near East—in Turkey, in Egypt, in Iran—the nineteenth-century nationalists rallied around the demands for written constitutions, for elected parliaments, for responsible ministers.

This overconfident and perhaps naïve belief in the beneficial effect of political institutions transplanted from the West gave way in many places to quick disillusionment. First, far from protecting the Near East against the Western onslaught, the adoption of constitutional forms—in the Ottoman Empire in 1876 and 1908, in Egypt in 1881, in Iran in 1906—was quickly followed by the full impact of colonialism on the region. Secondly, the newly acquired constitutional instruments proved difficult, if not impossible, to operate in the absence of a strong tradition of voluntary political organization. In Europe the growth of such voluntary associations had paralleled the expansion of modern state power since the sixteenth century and had served to subject it to the control of a widening political community. In the Near East, the cultural alienation of the Westernized intellectuals from the rural masses tended to delay such development of a sense of political responsibility.

Today the constitutionalist tradition is strongest in Turkey, which inherited an Ottoman bureaucratic machinery with long experience in self-government and orderly administration. The military played a crucial role in saving the country's independence after the defeat of the First World War. Yet Atatürk and İnönü upon the founding of the Republic gave up any direct control over the armed forces and insisted that other army personnel make a similar choice between a political and military career.[33] The far-flung educational program of Atatürk's People's Party broadened the base of support for the new regime in the small

[33] On the role of military leadership in the transition from the Ottoman Empire to the Kemalist regime, see my essay on "The Army and the Founding of the Turkish Republic," *World Politics*, 11, 513-552, July 1959.

towns and villages. The introduction of a competitive party system since 1945 has sped up this process of induction of the villagers into politics. And although the ruling Democratic Party has shown a distinct tendency to revert to authoritarian techniques, the third competitive Turkish elections of October 1957 seemed to demonstrate the vitality of the Turkish two-party system.

Elsewhere in the Near East the lack of indigenous political experience, combined with the legacy of coercion left by the contest between nationalist movements and mandate regimes, has largely endangered or undermined the basis for orderly constitutional development. Iraq experienced a half-dozen military coups between 1936 and 1941, and Syria since 1949 has been on the way to surpassing that record. Egypt after the Second World War descended into a period of political assassinations, endemic riots, and near civil war, followed by the firm military rule of the Najib-Nasser regime. By the late 1950's, the monarchical regimes in Iraq, Jordan, and Iran were crumbling under, or at best tenuously asserting themselves against, mounting popular pressure. In Lebanon, constitutional procedures had long been guaranteed by a precarious balance among a dozen or more rival religious denominations and by the prevalent preoccupation with commerce which tended to restrain the more destructive political instincts. But, even here, the civil war of 1958 threatened the earlier constitutional foundations.

Yet the picture was not altogether bleak. Tunisia, under the enlightened leadership of Bourguiba, was embarked on a course of constructive secularist reform closely reminiscent of Atatürk's example. In Morocco, Sultan Muhammad V used his traditional, religiously sanctioned prestige to smooth the transition toward a more secular culture and more representative patterns of government. In the eastern Arab countries, rapidly rising oil revenues were introducing a positive sense of self-reliance in place of the age-old feeling of impotence against the outside forces of nature and of international politics. In the short run, the drive for Arab unity and the replacement of dynastic-oligarchic with revolutionary middle-class regimes were introducing an element of instability. Yet if a stable political framework should emerge from the critical transition period, there is at least a possibility that a closer integration of the various Arab regions and of the disparate social classes in each of them will result. In that event, there may thus be a second chance for representative and constitutional government—rising this time on more solid foundations than did the premature hopes of the turn of the century.

(3) *Interest groups and interest group systems.* Despite the great

proliferation of political parties in the Near East, much power is in fact still exercised by other groups—above all, by institutional groups such as armies and bureaucracies and ascriptive groups such as kinship and lineage systems.

Both historical and sociological reasons may be adduced to account for the prominent role of armies and their officer corps in the politics of many Near Eastern countries.[34] The legitimacy accorded to warfare in traditional Islamic doctrine has already been referred to. But the prominence of the armies on the contemporary political scene has been reinforced by a number of additional factors:

1. The reform attempts of the nineteenth-century Near Eastern rulers were prompted by military defeat and hence began with the army. The officer corps thus came to have early and privileged access to social and political ideas and organizational techniques taken over from Europe. Army officers, therefore, were among the earliest spokesmen of constitutionalism and nationalism in the Near East. It is important to note that, in this close association with middle-class ideas of egalitarianism and reform, Near Eastern army officers follow the radical Bonapartist rather than the conservative Prussian tradition.

2. While in Turkey the military withdrew from an active role on the political scene after the establishment of an independent republic, the imposition of foreign regimes in the Arab countries accentuated the tradition of violence in politics. In Egypt, in Syria, in Iraq—everywhere postwar British and French rule was imposed by concerted military action. Yet violent nationalist resistance in many cases prompted a more conciliatory policy on the part of the European rulers than might otherwise have been adopted. The Egyptian revolution of 1919 resulted in the Milner Report, urging agreement with the nationalist leaders; the Iraqi rebellion of 1919-1920 was followed by the installation of an Arab monarch under British auspices; and the Syrian revolt of 1925-1926 was followed in 1928 by the calling of the first Syrian constituent assembly. Similarly, the British in 1948 relinquished the Palestine mandate as a result of competitive terrorist campaigns by Arab and Jewish groups. Generally, the first definite moves toward evacuation followed the European powers' military exhaustion in the Second World War. Clearly

---

[34] Cf. Majid Khadduri, "The Role of the Military in Middle East Politics," *American Political Science Review*, Vol. XLVII, June 1953, pp. 511-524 (also in Sydney N. Fisher, ed., *Social Forces in the Middle East*, Ithaca, N.Y., 1955, pp. 162-184); for a particular example, see my essay, "The Army and the Founding of the Turkish Republic," *loc.cit.*

experience seemed to demonstrate that, in politics, only force could be counted upon to achieve decisive results.

3. The last, and probably the most important, factor prompting the rash of Near Eastern military coups in the last two decades has been the feeling of frustration caused by the inefficiency, weakness, disorganization, and corruption of civilian regimes—a feeling accentuated by the high hopes which were earlier attached to independence as a universal panacea. Once again the sequence is striking: in Iraq, Syria, and Egypt the first military coup followed from four to six years after the withdrawal of the foreign occupying power (1932-1936 and again 1955-1958 in Iraq, 1945-1949 in Syria, and 1946-1952 in Egypt). In Syria and Egypt the fresh impression of defeat in the Palestine War contributed to the prevalent sense of frustration. Typically, armies that made a poor showing on the battlefield thus were not only able but also eager to overpower their domestic antagonists. Only two of the resulting military regimes have shown any degree of durability—that of Colonel Adib Shishakli, who ruled Syria from 1949 to 1954, and that of his colleague Jamal Abdul Nasser in Egypt, who has been in power since 1952.[35] In many cases, by contrast, a first military coup, in the fashion of a breeder-reactor, led to a whole series of coups. Few of the military leaders were able, as was Kemal in Turkey, to remedy the basic weakness of Near Eastern representative government by building up a genuine political movement. Facing their first serious difficulties in the unfamiliar political arena, the military juntas soon tended to lose the reputation for efficiency and the enthusiastic popular support that had swept them into power. But since none of the underlying causes that led to the original coup were removed, and since military force is difficult to remove by non-military means, the stage was set for a new armed coup. Perhaps the military at times were genuinely surprised to see how easy the overthrow of the legal government turned out to be and found it hard henceforth to resist the temptation. Once a few generals or colonels have been propelled into power, a good many captains and lieutenants will indulge similar ambitions. Some of the Iraqi coups of the thirties turned out to be highly ritualized affairs: a declaration of disobedience by a few commanders placed strategically near the capital, a few planes over the capital itself, sometimes not even a shot fired—and the startled citizenry might learn from the morning radio bulletin that the government had

---

[35] Or, more properly, since 1954, when he won out in his see-saw contest with General Muhammad Najib. The remainder of the paragraph is adapted from my *Politics and Westernization, op.cit.*, pp. 32 ff.

surrendered to another self-appointed clique of officers. Some coups, however—notably, those in Iraq in 1936 and 1958—shocked all observers by the brutality shown toward their opponents.

The role of the bureaucracy in Near Eastern politics varies greatly from country to country both in extent and character. It has perhaps been greatest in Turkey and Egypt, which inherited indigenous administrative systems from Ottoman and Mamluk times, respectively. The Kemalist regime, which had its roots in a popular movement with military leadership, increasingly acquired a bureaucratic character; thus from 1920 to 1943, the proportion of civil servants in the Turkish National Assembly rose from about 60 to nearly 75 per cent. In Egypt, the civil service, recruited from among Western-educated personnel and working for a long time with British advisers, provided a good deal of political continuity throughout the rapid changes of cabinets and regimes after 1922.

In addition to armies and bureaucracies, the *'ulama* (or learned in Islamic religious and legal doctrine; the singular is *'alim*) may be listed as an institutional interest group—although their importance has sharply declined in recent decades and is nowhere as strong as it was in the early years of Pakistani political development. Islam, as mentioned before, does not have any "church" independent of secular authority, nor any "priests" who mediate between the believer and his God or whose ministrations are considered essential to salvation. An *'alim* in practice is simply a person who has received the prescribed training in Qur'anic exegesis, canon law, and related subjects, and who thus qualifies for such posts as prayer leader, preacher, or jurisconsult in matters of canon law (*mufti*); but all these appointments are, directly or indirectly, made by the secular state authorities.[36] Sunni *'ulama*, like any other professional class, often display a certain corporate spirit which may take occasional political expression. The leading theological scholars (such as the professors of al-Azhar in Cairo, the leading Sunni seminary, and the Wahhabi *'ulama* of Saudi Arabia) are at times invited by state authorities to give advisory opinions on pending legislative proposals in the field of civil law.

The Shi'i *'ulama* (also known as *mullahs*) of Iran, on the other hand, play a more distinct political role—partly because of their tighter hierarchical organization, and partly because of the greater authority which

---

[36] In Turkey, the office of *mufti* lapsed automatically with the adoption of Western codes in 1926; appointments of preachers and other mosque officials, however, continue to be made by the Presidency of Religious Affairs, an independent agency within the prime minister's office.

Shi'i doctrine accords to them in theological and legal matters. Thus the first successful resistance against the spendthrift autocracy of the late Qajars centered around the *mullahs*, who in the 1890's organized a tobacco boycott that forced the shah to cancel an odious foreign commercial concession. A clause (never implemented) of the 1906 constitution of Iran even envisaged a process of judicial review of parliamentary legislation by a college of *'ulama*. In the popular agitation at the time of the Iranian oil crisis, the Iranian *mullahs* led by Kashani once again played a prominent role. The Shi'i *'ulama* of Iraq also have been active on the political scene, although government authority has been concentrated largely in Sunni hands.

In the decentralized structure of traditional Near Eastern government, *non-associational interests* based on kinship and lineage played a crucial role. In the more or less autonomous village communities, and particularly among the nomadic tribes, the patriarchal kinship system generally supplied the only effective political authority. Even in the towns, family ties and family feuds tended to determine political activity and allegiance. Under the impact of industrialization and urbanization, these non-associational interests have lost most of their old power. In Lebanon, on the other hand, the coexistence of a large number of Christian and Muslim sects, as well as a distinct Druze group, has given rise to a recognized and intricately balanced system of religious group politics. The proportion of Maronites, Sunnis, Shi'is, Greek Orthodox, Druzes, and others within parliament is predetermined by law, and custom prescribes a similar proportional allocation of executive positions (with the President of the Republic drawn from the Maronite, the Prime Minister from the Sunni community).

In areas such as Saudi Arabia, Afghanistan, Libya, Morocco, and Jordan, nomadic tribes continue their age-old autonomy. In eastern Turkey, southern Iran, Syria, and Iraq, on the other hand, progressive sedentarization and administrative centralization have brought them increasingly within the purview of national authority. The transition, however, has been accompanied by intense conflict, which at times threatened the integrity of the newly established states. The rebellious Kurdish mountain tribes in Turkey and Iraq constituted a powerful challenge to central authority in the 1920's and 1930's, and in the late 1950's Iraq's Kurdish mountaineers, in alliance with Communist elements, continued their disruptive activity. Iranian nomads dramatically intervened in Central Iranian politics on at least two occasions—in 1907 when the powerful Bakhtiari tribe marched on Tehran to forestall a royalistic coup against the newly instituted constitutional regime, and in 1947, when action by the Qashqais prompted Premier Qawam to dismiss three Communists from his coalition government. In the Khuzistan province of oil-rich southern Iran, the British long maintained an amicable relationship with the local Arab shaykh without reference to the central government at Tehran. On the other hand, some of the fiercest resistance against foreign occupation in parts of the Near East was led by nomads in their mountain or desert refuges. The Berber leader 'Adb al-Karim in the Rif region fought the French for two decades after their occupation of Morocco, and in Libya the Sanusi tribesmen of Cyrenaica carried on a similarly tenacious war against the Italians. The 1921 Iraqi rebellion against British rule was spearheaded by the tribes of the Middle Euphrates, and the Syrian uprising against French rule in 1925 by the Druze mountaineers. In Morocco, the powerful and aging Berber chieftain of Marrakech, Thami al-Glawi, in two dramatic moves in the early 1950's first enabled the French to oust Sultan Muhammad V and later forced them to reinstate him.

Associational interest groups are comparatively undeveloped in the Near East, but again there are significant variations between the more Westernized and the more traditional countries. Where the traditional landed oligarchies retain their power, they feel little need for formal association. The vast peasant majority is still completely unorganized, even where, as in Turkey, its vote is eagerly courted by city politicians.

Trade unions have become a political force of some moment in a few of the countries—Egypt, Lebanon, Turkey, Iraq, Tunisia, and the oil region of Iran. Frequently their growth was encouraged by advanced labor and social welfare legislation adapted with few changes from European models. The adoption of a policy of etatism (or state sponsorship of industrial development) in Turkey and other countries further accentuated the government's role in the labor relations field. Conversely, nascent unions unable to assert their autonomous strength have sought to advance their cause by association with a political party or by pleas for legislative relief. In Tunisia, for example, the Neo-Dustur Party has derived considerable support from its association with the union movement. But it can also be argued that the emphasis on political action has unnecessarily involved the labor movement in the fortunes and misfortunes of ephemeral politics and has delayed the search for independent strength through better organization. Demonstrations by Egyptian workers at a crucial turning point in 1954 helped swing the political balance from Najib to Nasser, but in the subsequent period of consolidation of dictatorial power labor reaped little tangible benefit in return for its services.

Business as an articulate political interest group is perhaps even less organized than labor. In many countries this is due in part to the state's prominent role in the establishment and control of important industries. In the oil-producing countries such as Saudi Arabia, Kuwayt, Iran, and Iraq, the petroleum companies are an obvious and important political factor; yet the disparity in size and outlook between the foreign-owned petroleum companies and the much smaller domestic industrial and commercial firms tends to discourage formal interest organization. But even in the non-oil countries, businessmen are more likely to make use of family or personal connections to individual legislators or administrators to obtain favors for their individual firms rather than to resort to organized group action in behalf of an entire economic class.

Civic associations of a wide variety of types have greatly proliferated in recent decades in such countries as Turkey, Egypt, and Syria. In Egypt, for example, a feminist organization known as the Daughters of the Nile has conducted a much-publicized campaign for woman suffrage; since it was not considered a political party, it survived the ban placed on such organizations by the Nasser regime. As a rule, associations of university students tend to be the most vocal in politics; where political authority has been weak, as in most of the Arab countries, demonstrations by college students have been a familiar accompaniment of political unrest. The university students share with the officer corps a wide social and geographic base of recruitment and a privileged position of access to the knowledge, techniques, and orientations associated with modernization. Just as the army officers enjoy a reputation for purposeful action which contrasts with prevalent governmental inefficiency, the students are at an age and in a social position where idealism has not yet succumbed to the temptations of self-interest that go with a government job and responsibility for a growing family. Yet, in contrast to the armies, which generally control the coercive means of imposing a new regime, the students whose demonstration has brought down a government have little choice in the end but to go back to their classes. Their role thus tends to be more purely disruptive.

The frequency of revolutions, riots, mass demonstrations, and sporadic violence in the Near East testifies to the importance of *anomic groups*. In the absence of detailed studies and in view of the inherent scantiness of evidence, it is hard to determine in each particular case to what extent such phenomena are truly spontaneous or anomic, and to what extent they are instigated by secret organization. Frequently advance planning and spontaneous activity would seem to intermingle. In an emotionally charged situation, such as that in Egypt in the late 1940's and early 1950's, or in Iran during the Mossadegh period, a few determined and vociferous organizers could quickly assemble a mob. Or else a demonstration planned or encouraged by government authority on a minor or peaceful scale may quickly degenerate into an uncontrollable outburst of destructive passion. This may have been the case in the incendiary Cairo riots of 1952 and in the violent anti-Greek riots in Istanbul in 1955.

Political Functions

Any systematic analysis of the Near Eastern political process is complicated by the fact that, in most of the countries, that process is as yet far from perfectly integrated. Cultural and economic changes are rapidly involving ever larger segments of the population in the national political process, which has so far been dominated almost entirely by the urban elites. Yet a myriad of distinct political processes in villages and tribes survive. In addition, national politics are disrupted by the uncertainty of boundaries and of national sentiment. During periods of strong central rule, the outlying districts of Iran—such as Azarbayjan, Khuzistan, and the nomadic areas in the Zagros range—grudgingly yielded to Tehran authority. Yet such periods of tenuous political integration have been far too intermittent to allow for the emergence of a single, unified political process. The Kurds in Iran, Iraq, and (until recently) Turkey have put tribal over national loyalty. Most of Libya and Afghanistan, the inland portions of Saudi Arabia, and the mountain regions of Morocco are occupied by loose tribal confederations which still maintain all or most of their autonomy. In many of the Arab countries, urban agitators and their mass audiences live in the pan-Arab political context, oriented increasingly toward Cairo, whereas the more traditional elements of the ruling class have strong vested interests in the preservation of existing inter-Arab boundaries.

This imperfect integration of the political process profoundly affects specific political functions, such as articulation and aggregation, recruitment and communication.

(1) *Interest articulation.* A discussion of the articulative function in the Near Eastern political process may conveniently be centered around two themes—the level of articulation and the range of articulation.

It is clear from what has been said in earlier sections about the development of political parties and interest groups that the general level of political articulation in the Near East is low when compared with that of the countries of Western Europe or North America. At the same time, the Near Eastern level of articulation varies widely with time and place. It is appropriate at this point to attempt a more systematic discussion of these variations.

First, there are, of course, pronounced differences among Near Eastern countries. At one end of the spectrum are Turkey, Lebanon, the United Arab Republic, and Tunisia, where literacy rates are comparatively high, transport and communications well developed, and parties and other groups relatively well organized. Here something of a continuous debate on national political issues becomes possible in the press of the capital cities, over the radio, in pamphlets, and in political speeches. As a result, a wide range of views and interests can be heard and expressed. At the other end are the patriarchal monarchies, where fragmentation of the political process into tribal, village, or clan compartments, minimal rates of literacy, and scarcity of transport severely inhibit the possibilities of articulation.

Second, the extent and nature of articulation vary with the character of political regimes. In dictatorships, the repressive power of government and the opportunism of political participants keep articulation within well-regulated channels. Particularly in countries with a highly developed system of communication, a repressive regime will do its utmost to ensure an effective monopoly of such media as journalism and broadcasting. (Conversely, the radio station in the capital generally is among the first targets of any revolutionary attack against the regime.) In competitive political situations, a far wider range of articulation prevails *ex hypothesi*, and the process of competition generally leads to a further widening.

Third, there are important local variations within any given country. The metropolitan resident of Cairo, Istanbul, and Tehran is exposed to, and himself likely to form, more political views than his small-town cousin in Zagazig, Diyarbekir, or Yazd—who in turn is an expert articulator compared with the villager in the hinterland. These sharp differences in levels of articulation make any true representation of interests difficult even in otherwise competitive political situations.

Fourth, the level of articulation and of other political activity varies markedly over time. In the short run, articulation is intermittent and fitful, reaching a high pitch of intensity almost overnight in times of election, riot, or revolution, and dying down equally suddenly in their wake. Such short-run fluctuations are of course rarely synchronized from

one country to the next, except as the success of a revolutionary movement in one country sets off an emulative chain reaction among the
neighbors. (Think of the encouragement which Algerian nationalists derived from the proclamation of independence in neighboring Tunisia
and Morocco; or of the wave of coups, riots, and rebellions set off in
countries like Jordan, Syria, and Iraq by the Egyptian revolution of
1952.) Broadly speaking, however, a look at the last hundred years of
Near Eastern history reveals a fairly consistent temporal sequence for
most of the region. Prolonged and intensive commercial, political, and
ideological contact with Europe started a strong tide of nationalist-con-
stitutionalist articulation near the turn of the century—culminating in
the Egyptian revolution of 1881-1882, the Persian revolution of 1905,
and the Young Turk revolution of 1908. Another intense wave of political activity followed the First World War, as Near Eastern countries
struggled with varying success to shake off or avert foreign domination.
The establishment of semi-colonial or indigenous dictatorial regimes in
the Arab countries, Turkey, and Iran resulted in comparative quiescence
during the interbellum period. The years since the Second World War,
in turn, have brought an unprecedented level of articulation—accompanying the withdrawal of foreign rule, the intensification of industrial
development and urbanization, and the growing involvement of the area
in the East-West conflict.[37] The two major periods of articulation—from
the turn of the century to the aftermath of the Great War of 1914, and
again since 1945—coincide, of course, with periods of rapid political development in other respects, including the induction of first the urban
and now the rural populations into the political process, and the drawing
and redrawing of political boundaries with their obvious implications for
national integration.

The range of political articulation is severely limited by a variety of
factors, many of which have been discussed in earlier contexts. The precarious hold of governments and entire regimes over the loyalty of their

[37] For Turkey, Dr. Tunaya's comprehensive survey makes possible something approaching statistical measurement of this ebb and flow of political activity. The 152 parties
and similar political associations founded in the century from 1859 to 1952 are distributed as follows among various periods (calculated from *op.cit.*, pp. 773-777):

	Total Number	Average Per Year
Despotic period (1859-1908)	17	.35
Second constitutional period (1908-1918)	25	2.5
Armistice and Defense of Rights periods (1918-1922)	55	11
Republican (one-party) period (1923-1945)	5	.23
Republican (multi-party) period (1945-1952)	30	3.75
Total (1859-1952)	152	1.39

subjects has prompted the enactment of numerous legal restrictions on association and expression and hence articulation. Beyond this, the insecure sense of nationality inhibits articulation of many interests even in the absence of legal obstacles. Above all, the traditional cultural gap between urban elite and peasant mass, reinforced in the early stages of Westernization, prevents any genuine and continuous articulation of the views and interests of a vast majority in each population.

The latent divisions which are particularly prone to suppression and repression are those among ethnic or denominational groups and those among socio-economic classes. Lebanon is the only Near Eastern country whose representative system is frankly based on a recognition of religious-denominational differences. In Iraq, on the other hand, the token presence of individual Kurds or Shi'is in the cabinet (see below) served to appease rather than to articulate ethnic and denominational differences. Bitter experiences of the past—such as the ethnic conflicts of the dying Ottoman Empire, the various Kurdish rebellions of the 1920's and 1930's, and the Soviet regime in Azarbayjan in 1945-1946—demonstrate how quickly ethnic articulation can turn into separatism and hence, in the eyes of nationalist regimes, into high treason. Even in a relatively well-integrated country such as Turkey, legislators have resorted to a long list of specific prohibitions on political articulation that might endanger national unity. A law of association, adopted in the late Ottoman period and continued with little modification to the present day, specifically prohibits political associations based on distinctions of race, language, religion, locality, or social class. But this legal provision is reinforced by psychological taboos dating back to the formative years of the Republic. Census data record the proportion of Muslim Turkish citizens who speak Kurdish, Arabic, Circassian, Laz, or other dialects. Yet while practical politicians are keenly aware of the importance of these groupings, any open reference to such distinctions in the press or in public speech would meet with cries of indignation. In addition, the distinction between Sunni and Alevi (or Shi'i) Muslims seems to be of considerable social and political significance in some localities of Anatolia. But here the inhibition against admitting to any sectarian differences among the Muslim population is so strong that even elementary census data on the proportion of Alevis in Turkey are lacking.

Articulation of economic or class interests once again is a rare phenomenon in the Near East. Here legal sanctions and psychological inhibitions are reinforced by the traditional monopoly held by the urban educated class on political activity at the national level. It hardly needs to be stressed, however, that any sudden and organized irruption of the urban and rural masses into the political process would have unsettling effects far beyond those of ethnic diversity or regional separatism. At present the trade unions, as noted earlier, are ill organized and often expect fulfillment of their demands not through concerted group action but through legislative or administrative beneficence. The peasantry is still very largely outside the national political process. Such recent phenomena as the organization of Persian oil workers by the Tudah Party and the strong appeal of the Turkish Democratic Party to the village electorate may foreshadow a fundamental change in this respect.

Within the ruling upper class itself, on the other hand, differences of interest are subdued and attenuated and face-to-face relations are generally too close to create any need for organized articulation. Large landowners or large business enterprises can rely on family ties, personal acquaintance, and direct or indirect bribery to influence individual legislators or civil servants. The establishment of a legislative lobby or the conduct of a nationwide political publicity campaign would therefore seem cumbersome and wasteful by contrast. Smaller firms, without any leadership from the giants, have little prospect of successful organization and instead must try to apply the same means of influence at correspondingly lower administrative levels.

With some oversimplification, it may be said that differences susceptible of articulation are either too small to warrant elaborate organization (as those within the ruling class) or so fundamental as to threaten national integrity and hence likely to invite legislative or psychological repression (as those among ethnic groups or among the major socio-economic classes).

A word may be added here on the significance for articulation of the four major ideological tendencies present in the Near East. As noted earlier, nationalism is the most prevalent of these. Since it provides the idiom for all types of articulation, it cannot become a differential criterion of one movement as opposed to its competitors. No avowedly anti-national movement has a chance: the only question is whether its founders would be jailed first or lynched. Liberal constitutionalism has many dedicated supporters among the professional segment of the urban elite. But in the current situation it more frequently serves as a self-interested posture of those temporarily out of power rather than as a vehicle for systematic articulation of organized interests. In addition, a number of other Western ideologies, notably Socialism, provide little more than convenient reservoirs of oratorical imagery for the urban articulator.

Islam, like nationalism, is widely respected as an ideological symbol; the articulator may dilute, or reinterpret, or ignore it—but oppose it only at his peril. Even in the secularist Turkish Republic of Atatürk, ostentatious agnosticism never became fashionable, and the targets of secularist attack have always been carefully identified as "fanaticism" or "reaction" rather than as religion or Islam. On the other hand, Islamic fundamentalism does provide the basis for the only truly ideological movements of the present-day Near East, such as the Muslim Brethren and the Fida'iyan-i Islam. Communism, finally, appeals to the Near East not in terms of its own ideology but rather through support of extreme nationalism, through vague hopes of social reform, and through the lure of foreign-policy cooperation with the powerful Soviet Union.

Once again, the range of political articulation faces a double limitation. Of the readily available ideologies, some (like nationalism and Islam) are accepted in word, if not in deed, by nearly all citizens; others (such as Communism) are palatable only when disguised beyond ready recognition. Only in rare cases do ideological distinctions therefore result in differential articulation.

The Near Eastern process of political articulation often appears to be floating in mid-air. It commonly lacks the solid fundament of any genuine interest representation. In turn it rarely provides the basis for any impressive superstructure of national policy. The divorcement of articulation from interest and policy is of course a striking reflection of the discontinuities in other political functions—such as communication and recruitment—all due in large part to the cultural discontinuity between urban elite and rural mass. The interests of the organized peasantry are voiced, if at all, by large landowners, teachers, journalists, or army officers—not because their interests coincide with those of the peasantry but because they are more adept at the techniques of articulation. The contrast is even sharper in the case of the dissident aristocrat whose oratory launches the city mob into violent action. The vagueness of the verbal symbols which enjoy the widest currency—positive symbols such as nationalism, justice, progress, unity; or negative ones such as feudalism, imperialism, exploitation—aggravates the imperfections in the relay system within the articulative process. As a result, established leaders can often carry out sudden shifts or turnabouts with little risk to their careers. The verbal content of articulation and the associated techniques of agitation remain fairly constant; the ostensible purpose of agitation varies erratically, and increasingly its only justification is a crude quest for power in the abstract. Here then is one of the prime factors in the political instability prevailing in many Near Eastern countries today.

(2) *Interest aggregation.* The character of the aggregative function varies widely from the more traditional to the more modernized countries, from monarchies to oligarchies, from dictatorships to competitive systems; it is at all times intimately related, of course, to the pattern established by other functions such as articulation, communication, and recruitment.

In the patriarchal monarchies, the task of interest aggregation resolves itself largely into the preservation of tranquility by forestalling sedition among the outlying tribes. In Saudi Arabia, religious sanction for polygyny and for instantaneous divorce at the husband's pleasure enabled King Ibn Saud (1897-1953) to conclude successive marriages with the daughters of large numbers of tribal chiefs. The sudden spurt of oil revenues further eased the king's task by allowing him to disburse subsidies among tribal leaders from whom he had once exacted tribute. As ever larger numbers of tribesmen, however, are involved in the sedentary patterns of the oil industry and related enterprises, this system of connubial and financial aggregation of tribal interests becomes increasingly inadequate.

A quite different pattern of interest aggregation may be observed in the changing composition of the political inner circle from which Iraqi cabinets were commonly recruited during the monarchical period (1921-1958). The central core of this oligarchy was the group of former Ottoman army officers who formed the nationalist society known as the Iraqi Covenant and subsequently rallied around Amir Faysal, later King Faysal I of Iraq. From the beginning of the mandate period, this group of officers of middle-class background was joined by members of the old Baghdad families. The inclusion of individual members of various ethnic or religious minority groups helped to establish a modicum of political unity in one of the more heterogeneous countries of the region. Thus, Sasun Hasqayl, a Jewish financier from Baghdad, was a frequent cabinet member during the mandate period. One or another member of the Baban family—descended from a long line of Kurdish chiefs in Sulaymaniyah and hence considered "a Kurd for ministerial purposes"[38]—was usually included in the cabinet list. The growing restlessness of the Shiʻi half of the population under entrenched Sunni rule has prompted the admission, since the 1940's, of

[38] In Stephen Hemsley Longrigg's apt phrase; see *Iraq 1900-1950, op.cit.*, p. 229.

individual Shi'is to government office. The challenge of incipient party movements with a strong rhetorical appeal to the intelligentsia and the urban masses was diverted in the late 1940's by the promotion of some of their leaders to an occasional cabinet portfolio. Through the entire period from 1920 until the overthrow of the regime, Nuri al-Sa'id, co-founder of the original Iraqi Covenant, retained his position at the center of the political stage. Moving in and out of the premiership more than a dozen times in a quarter-century, he skillfully guided Iraqi affairs through the conclusion of the 1930 treaty which replaced the British mandate, the restoration of constitutional government after the pro-Axis Rashid 'Ali coup of 1941, the conclusion of the 1952 profit-sharing agreement with the Iraq Petroleum Company, the adoption of the Development Board Law which has allocated a minimum of 70 per cent of the increased oil income to major public works, and the ratification of the Baghdad Pact of 1955. This oligarchic pattern survived with minor variations until the Iraqi revolution of 1958 in which, moreover, the key figures, such as Nuri Sa'id and Crown Prince Abd al-Ilah, lost their lives.

In the dictatorships the process of aggregation is far less visible and also is kept within narrower limits by potential or actual coercion. Generally, the initial years of a dictator's rule are devoted to the task of devising a working combination among various divergent groups of supporters, or else of training more docile cadres of followers to take the place of recalcitrant former allies. The years following the initial installation of Kemal in Turkey, of Riza in Iran, and of the Revolutionary Command Council in Egypt all brought a rapid turnover of top or next-to-the-top personnel. Kemal broke with his erstwhile religious-conservative followers even before the final victory in the Greek-Turkish war of 1919-1922; and the civilian and military leaders who had helped him organize the first nationalist Anatolian resistance of 1919-1920 joined the opposition Progressive Party in 1924 almost to a man. Not until about 1927 did he find a stable and reliable group of supporters who assisted in the execution of his ambitious reform program during the next decade. The Egyptian officers' junta at first tried to induce a voluntary purge among the existing parties while enlisting the services of individual leaders of the *ancien régime*. When this plan was abandoned and power concentrated more directly in military hands, the Command Council was soon split by internal tensions which, in 1954, led to the replacement of Najib with Nasser. The Muslim Brethren, as noted earlier, were suppressed after the initial tacit alliance had given way to rivalry and open hostility, climaxed by the 1954 assassination attempt on Colonel Abdul Nasser.

Once securely in power, a dictatorship is likely to attempt to bring all effective interest organizations under the indirect control of its political machinery. Nasser's success in using labor demonstrations in his contest with Najib has already been referred to. Army officers associated with the Revolutionary Command Council came to fill not only cabinet posts and other key administrative positions, but also editorships of newspapers and directorships of corporations. In Turkey, by contrast, Atatürk and his closest military associates gave up their army connections to enter political life as members of parliament and cabinet ministers, thus effecting a close working partnership with civilian nationalist leaders recruited from the civil service and the professions. But here, too, the inner circle of political leadership gradually extended its control. The exodus of Greek and other non-Muslim businessmen after the War of Independence prompted the formation of the İş Bankası, a private commercial and investment bank formed by members of the People's Party leadership. The Türk Ocağı, or Turkish Hearth, a nationalist political-cultural association founded in the Young Turk period, was taken over by the People's Party in 1931 and its local branches converted into the so-called People's Houses. A Press Association formed in the 1930's issued informal directives to its member journalists and thus kept press debate within broad limits acceptable to the regime. Coordination between the People's Party and the administrative arm of government was achieved not so much by partisan appointments within the bureaucracy as by the increasing recruitment of civil servants into the party and into parliament. At the same time the etatist economic policy of the 1930's gave the government and its industrial holding companies, such as the Etibank and the Sümerbank, a crucial share in the industrial development of the country. Finally, the Turkish Historical Association and the Turkish Language Association, both founded under the personal aegis of Atatürk, strove to reshape the younger generation's image of history and its language in conformity with nationalist ideology.

With Turkey's transition to a competitive political system after the Second World War, a new pattern of aggregation developed which in some of its features is strongly reminiscent of the United States scene. Turkey's multiple-member plurality system of elections—even more than the American system of single-member plurality elections for Congress combined with nationwide presidential elections—provides a powerful incentive for the maintenance of a nationwide two-party system. On the other hand, the persisting inadequacy of coverage by the communication media and wide local variations in economic and cultural development encourage a pattern of semi-autonomous provincial politics. In the economically advanced urban and Western districts, parties campaign through mass meetings and emphasis on major national issues. In Istanbul, a party ticket, in good New York fashion, must represent a careful balance—achieved in this case by including among thirty-odd candidates on each party's list at least one Greek, one Armenian, one Jew, one woman, one labor union official, and one prominent businessman. In the Eastern rural and tribal areas, by contrast, the political process still resolves itself into a pattern of *ad hoc* local alliances with tribal chiefs, powerful landlords, and leading urban families. In this more traditional setting, mass meetings would be self-defeating, and politicians must operate by informal private contact. Competing for the votes of a heterogeneous electorate in a situation of rapid cultural change, the political actors, to use Professor von Grunebaum's apt phrase, must "play to two galleries at the same time."[39] Within a party's national committee and at national congresses, these divergent tendencies must be reconciled and integrated by careful selection of personnel and frequent readjustment of policies.

(3) *Political recruitment and socialization.* Patterns of political recruitment vary as widely in the Near East as does political aggregation. In the patriarchal societies, the problem of political recruitment in its modern form hardly exists. Among the Bedouins of the Arabian peninsula, leadership in the clan, tribe, or federation of tribes is generally handed down within a single family for a number of generations. Occasionally, however, a clash in a desert raid may lead to the secession of one clan or to the subjugation of another, and a new "ruling family" will have been established. The ancestors of the present king of Saudi Arabia, for example, ruled in the central Arabian region of Najd from the early eighteenth century. In the late nineteenth century they were displaced by the Ibn Rashid family of neighboring Shammar; young Ibn Saud, growing up as a refugee in the palace of the Shaykh of Kuwayt, then set out to reconquer his ancestral domain, and by 1926 he had unified most of the peninsula. Similar patterns are prevalent among the nomadic tribes of the Iranian mountains and of Afghanistan. In sedentary Yemen, the ruling family is that of the *imams*, or reli-

[39] Gustave E. von Grunebaum, "Problems of Muslim Nationalism," in *Islam and the West, op.cit.,* p. 26.

gious leaders, of the Zaydi sect of Shi'i Islam. In Cyrenaica, the descendants of Sayyid Muhammad ibn 'Ali al-Sanusi, founder of a religious order in the Kufra oasis, were called in as mediators in tribal disputes and by stages became the recognized chiefs of the area they had succeeded in pacifying. Below the highest level, the problem of political recruitment in patriarchal societies reduces itself largely to one of obtaining the ruler's favor.

In the non-patriarchal societies it is convenient to distinguish between more traditional and more recently emerging patterns of recruitment. The traditional political leaders in most areas of the Near East were the large landowning families, the chief clans of sedentary or semi-nomadic tribes, and the old patrician families in the towns; to these must be added the *'ulama* who traditionally performed a religious-legal administrative and judicial function, but have in recent times often become spokesmen for protest movements against Westernization. Within this general pattern there seem to be some significant differences of regional shading. In Iran leading politicians from the landowning class include a number of descendants of the prolific Qajar family, whose eldest line was the ruling house until 1925: Muzaffar Firuz, right-hand man of Premier Qawam in the late 1940's; Iraj Iskandari, a prominent sponsor of the Tudah Party; and, through his mother, Muhammad Mossadegh. In the Arab countries of the Fertile Crescent, and in parts of Turkey, landowning families resident in the cities, some of whom can trace their descent to the period of the Crusades, have been the most prominent traditional group. Any Iraqi government down to the mid-1950's was replete with old Baghdad names such as Gaylani,[40] Pachachi, Haydari, Chadirji, and Suwaydi, together with a sprinkling of Mosul and Basrah families such as the 'Umaris and Bash-Ayans. In Arab Jerusalem the local scene has for a long time been dominated by the rivalry of the Nashashibis and Husaynis. Since the position of these urban patricians has firm local roots, their support is courted by successive regimes and competing national factions; at times, such families have been known to assign each brother or cousin to a different faction as a method of insurance against unforeseen reversals.[41]

[40] The Gaylanis are descended from the medieval Muslim saint and founder of the Qadiriyah order, 'Abd al-Rahman al-Gaylani; they have traditionally held the post of *naqib al-ashraf*, a supervisory position of honor among the authenticated descendants of the Prophet in each city.

[41] Even in the comparatively egalitarian and competitive setting of recent Turkish politics, the same family names tend to recur on the provincial nomination lists of all three or four principal parties.

It should not be assumed that the scions of old families always play a socially conservative role in contemporary politics. Many of them, on the contrary, have tended to radicalism of one sort or another— as the examples of Muzaffar Firuz, Mossadegh, and Kamil Chadirji indicate; in Jordan today the Communist Party includes a number of Western-educated sons of old Arab-Palestinian families.[42] The same division into conservative and radical politicians applies to the leaders with a traditional background—such as Sayyid 'Abd al-Rahman al-Mahdi and Sayyid 'Ali al-Mirghani, Sudanese party leaders and heads of the two leading religious sects; Abu al-Qasim Kashani, the Iranian clerical leader and sponsor of the Fida'iyan-i Islam; and the well-known Mufti of Jerusalem, al-Hajj Amin al-Husayni.

Within the more recent pattern, political leaders are recruited increasingly from the urban-professional classes—army officers, civil servants, lawyers and other professional persons, and, rather more recently, some leaders in business and finance. The early nationalist movements were often led by army officers (such as 'Urabi, Enver, Kemal, and Nuri Sa'id), whose special role was discussed earlier. During the interwar period, on the other hand, the civilian professions came increasingly to the fore. In Turkey the Young Turk and Kemalist revolutions were spearheaded by the military, but subsequently obtained strong support from civilian elements, especially the government bureaucracy and the professions. Among the prominent members of the Union and Progress Party ministry of 1913-1918, in addition to Enver and Cemal Paşas, were Talât, a telegraph clerk; Cavid, a school director who as finance minister freed the tax system of the last vestiges of tax farming; and Şükrü, a government clerk who as minister of education reformed the University of Istanbul. Talât, who succeeded to the premiership in 1917, once remarked on his modest origins to a friend: "Once I became minister," he said, "everybody began nursing the same ambition." In the Arab countries, whose armies (except in Iraq) were long commanded by foreigners and whose bureaucracies (except in Egypt) had to be developed *ab ovo* after the First World War, lawyers have held an entrenched position, from Mustafa Kamil and Sa'd Zaghlul in Egypt to Kamil Chadirji in Iraq and Bourguiba in Tunisia. In Lebanon, Emile Boustani, head of a large construction firm, and other businessmen have been prominent; in Egypt, financiers associated with the Banque Misr and other large enterprises played an important role; and a Turkish industrialist, Nuri Demirağ, founded

[42] See Laqueur, *op.cit.*, pp. 131f. and notes.

the first small opposition party after the loosening of the one-party regime in 1945.

In the Near East, as in most areas of the world, little can be said in detail about the function of political socialization. The impact of family and kinship groups, education, religion, work experience, the media of communication, and political organizations and participations of one kind or another have not as yet been studied in the major social constellations of the area—city, village, and tribe. Daniel Lerner's recent book on cultural modernization in the Middle East[43] is most useful in specifying the attitudes of the "modernized," "traditional," and "transitional" strata and some of the conditions associated with these attitude patterns. But depth studies of the political socialization processes among the various sub-cultures; studies of the major agents of political socialization, such as teachers, religious leaders, and the like; and extensive studies specifying the resultant patterns of political culture in the individual political systems of the area are still to be made.

The earlier discussion of traditional cultures, of the impact of modern ideas and practices, and of the various ideologies at work in the region tell us something of the content of the new political culture which is permeating the Middle East. Some further comments are in order regarding the spread of modern education as one of the major institutions imparting these new tendencies to the younger generation.

Educational changes were a crucial factor in preparing the advent of the modern state system of the Near East. The contribution to the growth of Arab nationalism of higher schools established by European and American missionaries in Lebanon and elsewhere has already been referred to. Often they provided the first setting where Arabs of diverse religious denominations and local backgrounds came into intimate contact—and, ultimately, came to think of themselves as Arabs.[44] Even

[43] *The Passing of Traditional Society: Modernizing the Middle East*, Glencoe, Ill., 1958.

[44] Edward Atiyah, a Syrian Christian, in *An Arab Tells His Story* (London, 1946, p. 54) gives a vivid autobiographical account of an encounter soon after his arrival at Victoria College, Alexandria:

"A stocky, athletic-looking boy, with ruffled hair, came along asking boys if they wanted to play football, and jotting down their names. I asked Kfouri who he was when he had gone.

" 'Oh, that's the head boy of the school, and Captain of the First Eleven,' he answered; 'a very nice chap, and plays soccer awfully well; his name is Amin Osman.'

" 'He's a Moslem, then?' I commented in some surprise.

" 'Oh, yes, but Good Lord, nobody takes any notice of that here. We're all just Victorians.' "

And a few weeks later, after the college's first soccer victory: "New Loyalties for

more important was the growth of an indigenous educational system. In Egypt the religious reform movement of Muhamad 'Abduh in the late nineteenth century concentrated its attention on the reform of religious education at al-Azhar, traditional center of Muslim learning. And one of the highlights of the career of the founder of the Egyptian National Party, Mustafa Kamil, was the creation, through private contributions, of a secular Egyptian University in 1907. Today Egypt has the leading teachers' colleges in the Arab Near East and supplies a large proportion of the teachers for neighboring countries as well.

In the Ottoman Empire, the most lasting achievement of the reformers of the mid-nineteenth century was the establishment of a comprehensive system of secular education, including a medical school, a general staff school, a school for government administrators (known as the Mülkiye), and a system of preparatory schools. During the Young Turk and Kemalist periods, great numbers of European teachers were called in to help set up and expand the Universities at Istanbul (1917, 1933) and Ankara.[45]

While the number of centers of higher education was thus being expanded, a scholarship system was developed whereby any qualified high-school graduate could study at the university at state expense, on condition that he serve the government—as a teacher, judge, engineer, country doctor, and so forth—two years for every year of scholarship received. This system has had a twofold integrating effect: young men and women from the small towns and villages of all sections of Turkey are given access to higher education. Having received a common training and adopted the outlook of the relatively closely knit educated class, they are sent back as administrators into the remote areas of the country—and, if they remain in the public service, are rotated periodically from locality to locality. In the 1940's this system of higher education in Istanbul and Ankara was supplemented by a series of village institutes. These were centers where teachers for village schools, themselves recruited from the peasantry, were trained in a rural setting, without being exposed to the influence of large cities which almost inevitably would alienate them culturally from their future

---

Old . . . Under the unifying roof of a common school, the Moslem Egyptian, Amin Osman, was dearer to me now than all the Syrian Christians of the world" (p. 58).

[45] The nucleus of the University of Ankara, significantly, was a school of humanities, officially called the Faculty of Language, History, and Geography—three disciplines which, in Atatürk's conception, constituted the essence of civic education. Inscribed over the Faculty's portal is Atatürk's often-quoted dictum: "The truest guide in life is learning."

pupils.[46] At the same time, a large number of "People's Houses" were set up in the larger towns and cities under the auspices of the Republican People's Party as centers for adult education and cultural and artistic activities. The same connection between party and educational activity can be observed in present-day Morocco, where the Istiqlal Party soon after independence inaugurated a nationwide network of literacy circles.

(4) *Political communication.* The Near Eastern communication process is sharply divided. On the one hand, there is the more or less unified communication system of the educated urban class in each country; on the other, there are the largely autonomous systems of face-to-face communication in the villages and among the tribes. Taking each country as a whole, the intensity of communication in the Near East is low compared with that of modern societies in Europe or North America. Among the village majority of most Near Eastern countries, hardly more than 10 or 20 per cent are literate. Yet, in the highly oral-verbal culture of the Near East, literacy is by no means the only avenue to knowledge. Qur'anic quotations and couplets from the classical epics or from contemporary nationalist poetry are on the lips of even those without formal education. The small-town bazaar continues its age-old function as a center not only for commercial exchange but for news dissemination. In addition, the radio in the village square today reaches the large number of villagers, however illiterate, who while away their idle hours over coffee or tea. Similarly, the battery-powered short-wave set keeps the camel-borne shaykh abreast of the world's events. The rapid development of roads in countries like Turkey over the last decade has begun to break down the ancient pattern of village self-sufficiency and isolation. The truck farmer who sells his produce in the city comes into weekly contact with the Westernized ways of the urban population. The terminal of the overland bus lines at the cobblestone corner has joined the bazaar, and in part replaced it, as a center for urban-rural communication.

Among the urban educated population, communication is aided not only by high literacy rates—as high as 75 per cent in the larger metropolitan centers—but also by the fact that every Near Eastern country has a clearly recognized national language which dominates the press, radio, and literature. Berber, Kurdish, and Nilotic dialects survive as

[46] On the frustrating cultural tensions between institute graduate and village pupil which even this arrangement could produce, see the absorbing autobiographical account of Mahmut Makal, *A Village in Anatolia*, London, 1954.

the first language of sizable groups in Northwest Africa, the mountain areas of Iran and Iraq, and the Sudan, respectively; yet Arabic, and in Iran Persian, are clearly accepted as the languages of culture and education. Literate communication is further unified and centralized by the predominance of the press of the capitals over that of the provincial centers. European languages are used as a medium of habitual intercourse among the educated elite only in Northwest Africa, and among the non-Muslim groups in commercial centers such as Beirut and Istanbul. No Near Eastern country therefore has to cope with the perplexing problems of linguistic fragmentation that are the rule in South and Southeast Asia.

Near Eastern journalism dates back only to the turn of the century. But printing costs have remained low, and most papers get by with a skeleton staff of one or two editorial writers, two or three part-time printers, a subscription to a wire service or two, and a roving leg-man who rarely deserves the dignified name of correspondent. Where the government does not, by outright censorship or systematic harassment, impose strict conformity, journalistic opposition is likely to be vociferous and varied. A city such as Istanbul, with a population only one-sixth that of New York, boasts three or four times more daily newspapers. In many newspapers, to be sure, editorial opinion and satirical cartoons make up for the lack of solid news. The marginal economics of journalism makes the poorer papers vulnerable to pressure from advertisers, gratefully receptive to publicity handouts from foreign embassies and at times susceptible to outright bribery. The better papers, on the other hand, however poor their layout by Western standards, maintain a high intellectual and literary position. In the early years of this century, periodicals such as Rashid Rida's *al-Manar* in the Arab countries and Ziya Gökalp's *Yeni Mecmua* in Turkey contributed much to the intellectual ferment of Islamic modernism and incipient nationalism. Istanbul papers such as *Cumhuriyet* and *Tanin* in the 1930's and 1940's periodically published important historical memoirs of the Young Turk and early Kemalist periods. The People's Party organ *Ulus* in Ankara had an important influence in promoting Atatürk's attempt to purify the Turkish language of Arabic-Persian elements. In contrast to the press, which alternates between periods of anarchic freedom and stern repression, broadcasting suffers from the obvious handicaps of state control. Yet, in the hands of the Turkish reformers, such state control could become a potent instrument to promote new cultural tastes, such as that for European classical and contemporary music.

The richness of communication afforded by the press obviously varies widely in dictatorial and in competitive political situations. The Nasser regime has enforced on the Egyptian press a monotonous degree of uniformity, making it a willing tool for his shifting propaganda tactics. Nuri al-Sa'id, before leading Iraq into the Baghdad Pact, took the even more radical step of closing down all papers in the capital and then individually relicensing a handful. On the other hand, where pressure on newspapers stops short of such drastic means, as in Menderes' Turkey, newspapermen are developing a remarkable ingenuity in combating the government's repressive tactics. Periodicals like *Forum, Akis,* and *Kim* in the mid- and late 1950's rose to a record level of circulation on the basis of detached factual reports and analyses of the news which contrasted starkly with the vituperative tone of much of the daily press. The daily press, in turn, with the exception of party-owned papers such as *Ulus* and *Zafer,* has always tended to champion the opposition in its fight against government harassment—whether it was the Democratic Party fighting against the İnönü regime before 1950, or the People's Party attacking Premier Menderes since then. Official denials forced on newspapers by the district attorney's office are introduced with sly comments, or with obviously inferior layouts, which let the victimized journal have the last laugh. The lavish monies spent on subsidizing provincial papers through liberal allocations of official notices have little effect on the established press of Istanbul and Ankara. A year's jail term in the Ankara prison rapidly became a mark of distinction for any self-respecting journalist, and even the outright confiscation of *Ulus* in 1953 deprived the People's Party of an official mouthpiece for only a few months. While Turkish journalists serve more jail terms and pay more fines today than they ever did under the one-party regime of the interwar period, a vastly wider range of critical opinion is expressed than anyone could have imagined a quarter-century ago.

It is only natural that within such an increasingly competitive context, the newspapers with top circulation should become an independent force to be reckoned with on the political stage. A good illustration is provided by the systematic campaign on the Cyprus issue conducted by the Istanbul paper *Hürriyet* in the 1950's. For several years the Turkish government denied that any such issue existed, so far as Turkey was concerned. But later, under the constant barrage of banner headlines about Greek atrocities against the Turkish minorities in Cyprus and Western Thrace, the government reversed itself and initiated a major propaganda campaign of its own under the successive slogans

"Cyprus Is Turkish" and "Partition or Death" which persisted until the peaceable settlement of the dispute in 1959.

Aside from the press, poetry and pamphlets make up a substantial part of politically relevant written communication. The role of poets in expressing new political ideals such as nationalism should be emphasized. In the Ottoman Empire, for example, the writings of the poet Şinasi, who founded the first private newspaper in Istanbul in 1860, the performance of Namïk Kemal's patriotic play *The Fatherland, or Silistria* in 1873, and the publication in 1897 of Mehmed Emin's poem "Going to Battle" (in which the word "Turk" for almost the first time is used as a proud designation of nationality) mark the major stages of crystallization of national sentiment. In the last few decades, however, there has been a marked revulsion against the earlier role of poetry as the handmaiden of politics, and more purely artistic forms of description of nature, of philosophical introspection, and of social criticism have increased. The steady growth of indigenous novels, along with a veritable flood of translations from Western languages in the same genre, has contributed to the same development of a new social consciousness.

IV. GOVERNMENTAL STRUCTURES AND AUTHORITATIVE FUNCTIONS

Rule-Making

In discussing the governmental processes and governmental functions in the Near East, we must bear in mind how fluid the basic geographic definition of most of its political units still is. At the beginning of the twentieth century there were only five major spheres of political control in the region: the indigenous governments of the Ottoman Empire, Iran, and Afghanistan, and foreign control in Egypt and the Sudan (by Britain) and Northwest Africa (by France). The collapse of the Ottoman Empire in the First World War greatly increased this number, adding spheres of British (Palestine, Transjordan, Iraq), French (Syria and Lebanon), and Italian (Libya) control, and creating new indigenous states in Turkey, Yemen, and Saudi Arabia. The Second World War and its aftermath resulted in the successive withdrawal of European control, and by 1955 there were no less than sixteen separate major political units in the region (Morocco, Algeria, Tunisia, Egypt, the Sudan, Libya, Turkey, Iran, Afghanistan, Israel, Syria, Lebanon, Jordan, Iraq, Saudi Arabia, and Yemen). Recently, however, there has been a tendency toward amalgamation in the Arab countries, initiated by the formation of the United Arab Republic of Egypt and Syria early in 1958, so that the number of political units may be once again on the decline. Political independence, moreover, has been established throughout most of the area. Of the larger units, only Algeria continues under foreign control, but maintenance of that control since the outbreak of the Algerian war in 1954 has required a supreme military effort that has placed a formidable strain on French economic resources—and, incidentally, on France's domestic political integration and international prestige. Foreign rule or tutelage in a variety of legal guises also remains in effect in the various British dependencies along the southern shore of the Persian Gulf and the southern and western coasts of the Arabian peninsula. (Developments such as the Buraymi oasis dispute between Saudi Arabia and the British-protected Trucial shaykhs, the continuous border warfare between Yemen and Britain's Aden protectorate, and contacts between the Shaykh of Kuwayt and the United Arab Republic have been a clear indication, however, that the current drive toward boundary realignments and Arab unity may soon engulf these meager remnants of a once powerful imperial position.) In addition, the Gaza Strip—a small refugee-crammed remnant of the former British Palestine mandate which since 1949 has been administered by Egypt—occupies a special and anomalous position.

Most of the present political units of the Near East began as monarchies; indeed, after the toppling of European thrones in the first half of the present century, the Near East for a time stood out as the remaining major citadel of the monarchical form of government. But in the Near East, too, the trend is toward republics. The first republic, Turkey, was formed in 1923, to be joined two decades later by Syria and Lebanon, and, upon their attainment of independence, by Israel (1948) and the Sudan (1956). Other countries abolished monarchy as a result of revolutionary or peaceful changes (Egypt in 1953, Tunisia in 1957, Iraq in 1958; in the latter country, monarchy already had had a narrow escape in 1941). In Jordan and Iran, monarchy has been precariously surviving in the face of similar revolutionary forces. The Shah of Iran, in 1953, had already fled the country when the Zahidi countercoup unexpectedly returned him to power; and King Husayn of Jordan, after suppressing a long series of attempted revolts from 1955 to 1958, at length saw himself forced to call for the temporary return of British troops whose departure he had been forced to demand only the year before. In Saudi Arabia, Libya, Morocco monarchy still seems fairly secure—particularly so in Morocco. In Yemen and Afghanistan, finally, the monarchical form of government appears never to have been seriously questioned.

A more important line than the somewhat formalistic one between monarchies and republics is that which divides the traditional autocracies of Yemen, Afghanistan, and Saudi Arabia from the rest. Here the plenitude of the ruler's power is restricted not by formal constitutional limitations, but rather, in theory, by the sovereignty of the law of God as revealed in the Qur'an and interpreted by the *'ulama* of the recognized school, and, in practice, by the lack of communication and the self-sufficiency of tribal groups.[47]

Most of the remaining independent countries have written constitutions which generally vest legislative power in elected parliaments, executive power in cabinets appointed by the heads of state and responsible to the legislatures, and judicial power in separate judiciaries. The constitutional monarchies generally have bicameral legislatures, with the senate as a rule appointed by the king; in Libya the senate represents the three federal units of Tripolitania, Cyrenaica, and Fezzan. Suffrage is limited to males, except in Turkey, Lebanon, Syria, and Israel. Strict and prolonged observance of the spirit, or even the letter, of these constitutional rules has been characteristic only of Israel, Lebanon, and Turkey. In most of the other countries, brief and hesitant periods of parliamentary government have alternated with dictatorial or royal rule, when the legislatures were in fact responsible to, and often selected by, the executive. The 1958 constitution of the United Arab Republic was the first to lay down this procedure in law. Even where they are competitively elected, parliaments, in the absence of well-organized parties or interest groups, have frequently been representative of only a small articulate segment of the population.

Rule Application

It is obvious, then, that throughout the Near East the executive tends to be far stronger, especially in relation to the legislature, than the official constitutional enactments would indicate. In the traditional monarchies, the powers of rule-making, rule application, and even central adjudication are merged in the head of state. Elsewhere the constitutional relationship between executive and legislature has often been neatly inverted. In Turkey, for example, the 1924 constitution

[47] For a perceptive analysis of governmental process in these three countries, see George Lenczowski, "Political Institutions," in Ruth Nanda Anshen, ed., *Mid-East: World Center*, New York, 1956, especially pp. 119-135.

envisaged a system of popular sovereignty and legislative supremacy. The adult male (and, since 1934, female) population was to elect a Grand National Assembly, which in turn was to elect a President of the Republic for the duration of its own term. The President selected a Premier, and the latter a cabinet that was to be fully responsible to the legislature. But during the dictatorship of Atatürk and İnönü, the President of the Republic, as permanent chairman of the Republican People's Party, had the right of final approval of that party's nomination lists. Since no other parties were allowed to compete in the elections to the Assembly, it was in fact the President who selected the legislature—his own election by that body being a mere formality. Similarly, during the constitutional monarchy period of Iraq (1920-1958), the cabinet, according to official constitutional theory, was expected to resign in the face of a vote of no confidence in the parliament. In fact, no such votes ever occurred. Cabinets changed frequently, but these changes were due either to disagreements among the ministers, or to disagreements with the monarch, or, finally, to military coups. When an important difference arose between the major branches of government, it was the cabinet that dissolved the legislature—not vice versa—and the ministry of the interior generally employed a large array of indirect means of coercion to ensure the election of an acceptable parliament. Similar observations could be made of the *de facto* form of government in Egypt, especially in the 1920's and early 1930's, and in Iran under Riza Shah and again after the Second World War.

It has been noted earlier that the historical tradition of bureaucratic government was strongest in Turkey and Egypt. The nineteenth-century reforms of such rulers as Muhammad 'Ali and Mahmud II introduced a measure of European training and organization, and administrative services were further expanded and tightened toward the turn of the century—particularly during the Egyptian administration of Lord Cromer and during the Young Turk government of the Ottoman Empire. In some of the Arab countries, notably the Sudan, Morocco, Tunisia, and Iraq, British and French rule left an important legacy of administrative personnel and services whose efficiency and honesty were high by regional standards, and whose presence has been an invaluable asset to succeeding independent regimes.

The task of bureaucratic rule application in the Near East is greatly complicated by the enormous expansion of the functions of government, which has been one of the most notable consequences of the Western political and cultural impact in the last century and a half. As late as the mid-nineteenth century, Near Eastern rulers spent roughly nine-tenths of their income on the armed forces and the civil list; central government, that is to say, consisted chiefly of an army and a court establishment. Today, by contrast, universal military training, universal education, extensive public works programs, and a wide array of economic controls, individual income taxes and social welfare legislation, state-owned transportation networks and state-controlled broadcasting systems—all these have become facts or urgent aspirations throughout most of the Near East. Taken together, these innovations confer on modern Near Eastern administrations a power—and a responsibility—which eighteenth-century sultans in their boldest dreams of omnipotence could scarcely have imagined. Uneven as this development of public services has been from country to country, it has generally been far more rapid than the corresponding development of civic organizations, political parties, and economic interest groups; and this disparity tends to widen the traditional gulf between administrators and the citizenry. As a result, there is a further disparity between administrative theory and practice. The arm of government in most Near Eastern countries has only recently reached out from the capitals into the more remote village and tribal areas. Although the Near Eastern bureaucracies from decade to decade are setting new regional records of skill and dedication, legislative autocracy is still softened by bureaucratic laxity. The edicts from the capital are wholly dedicated to centralization; at the local level, on the other hand, a good deal of the traditional autonomy of rule application by tribal or village custom remains. The widespread use of states of siege, and other executive emergency powers, further divorces the process of rule application from official constitutional theory.

The foregoing remarks emphasize the important and varied role which coercion plays in the Near Eastern governmental process—a role already referred to in our earlier discussion of constitutionalism as an effective political ideology and of the army as an institutional political group. Near Eastern evidence confirms the notion that coercion can be kept to a minimum under two vastly different sets of conditions. The first is one where political rules, elaborated and sanctioned by religious or other traditional beliefs, are accepted by the vast majority of the community, rulers as well as subjects. The other is one where the habit of tolerating diversity and criticism has become established within a clearly defined and accepted political structure. In the West, the medieval traditional order broke down in the fourteenth and fifteenth centuries, but toleration within the resulting territorial nation-states was not established until the nineteenth century at the earliest. In the intervening half-millennium, the emergence of new states was accompanied by coercion from above (the Tudors, Louis XIV, Frederick II, Bismarck, etc.) and by revolt and civil war from below (the night of St. Bartholomew, the Fronde, the French Revolution, the Puritan Revolution, the German peasant wars, the Thirty Years' War, etc.). Moreover, the emergence of each new European state was accompanied by a prolonged contest for continental preeminence with the rest.

In the Near East, the traditional religious-political order survives unchallenged only in Yemen and Afghanistan, but nowhere has modern political order based on freedom of expression and toleration of criticism fully crystallized, except possibly in Israel. In the transition period, a prolonged though tenuous truce among conflicting groups may reign—as in the commercial atmosphere of Lebanon. Or else the emergence of a comprehensive-nationalist movement, or of a leader whose superior guidance is voluntarily accepted by large segments, may reduce —though not eliminate—coercion. Even then, the rapidly shifting tensions of the international scene and the relentless pressures of cultural change endanger any temporary adjustment.

Rule Adjudication

The formal legal orders of the Near East range from the system of European secular codes adopted in Turkey in 1926 to the unrestricted rule of the *shari'ah*, or Muslim canon law, in the traditional monarchies. In most of the Arab countries, as well as in Iran, two distinct legal systems coexist. Muslim religious law still determines such matters as marriage, divorce, and inheritance, whereas commercial and penal law are patterned on Western models. Even here the tendency has recently been toward the abolition of separate religious jurisdictions—as in Egypt —or toward a Westernization of the traditional system—as in the new Tunisian code. The underlying shift in legal philosophy is striking and unmistakable. Where once religious law, all-engulfing in theory, made grudging concessions to the ruler's secular power of decree, the surviving remnants of traditional Islamic law now almost invariably derive their formal validity from the enactment of secular parliaments. Conservative lawyers in countries such as Egypt no longer deny the legislative power of elected or appointive assemblies; rather they plead for the enactment by such assemblies of codes which will blend some religious-traditional elements into the prevailing pattern derived from the Code Napoléon or other European models. Or else they tackle a task at once more imaginative and more modest—that of searching the rich literature of canon law for tolerably plausible precedents that seem to anticipate what secular legislatures enact on utilitarian grounds. A specific example may illustrate the underlying pattern of reasoning, which was already adopted by modernist theologians in the later nineteenth century. For more than a millennium, faithful Muslims had accepted the explicit option of the Qur'an that a man might marry as many as four wives. But observe, says the modern jurist, that this provision, in Muhammad's time, restricted rather than increased the permissible number of marriages. Besides, the Qur'an enjoins the true believer to marry several wives only if he can treat them equally—and what mortal can be *sure* that he will give *exactly* equal treatment even to two wives in *all* respects at *all* times? Hence monogamy, the modernist triumphantly concludes, is the clear precept of Scripture.

The secular attitudes toward law-making often reveal an almost naïve faith in the curative powers of legal fiat, which reflects simultaneously the region's history of despotism, the deep-seated commitment of a verbal-oral culture to the power and self-justifying value of the word, and the reformist rationalism of Western utilitarian theory. If literacy is found to be shockingly low, let there be a law requiring universal education. The lack of trained teachers, the shortage of school buildings, the resistance of traditionalist peasants who may prefer to send their sons to work in the field or to recite the Qur'an before the village preacher—these are details of application that need not detain the legislator. If advanced industrial countries have strong trade union movements, let there be a labor law specifying the conditions under which unions are to be formed and what standards of pay and safety the workers are to enjoy. If a steady oversupply of labor enables employers to circumvent such provisions, let there be drastic penalties for the evaders.

Aside from these difficulties, and occasional incongruities, of legal theory, the process of adjudication in most Near Eastern countries differs from European, and particularly Anglo-American, patterns in important respects. The independence of the judiciary from the executive, which is laid down in many constitutions, is in practice often vitiated by patronage appointments or punitive transfers of judges. The theory or practice of judicial review is unknown. Claims against the state are commonly heard by administrative tribunals rather than in the judiciary proper. In criminal cases, once the prosecution has specified its charges, it usually devolves on the defendant to establish his innocence. Charges of high treason are generally tried in secret by military tribunals. And the frequent proclamation of states of siege, already referred to, periodically serves to deprive the civilian courts of much other jurisdiction as well.

V. POLITICAL INTEGRATION

As suggested in an earlier context, political integration is easiest to achieve within a predominantly traditional or a predominantly modern setting. Although modernity of itself brings no assurance of political integration, the current fragmentation or disintegration of many Near Eastern political systems is in large part a result of the coexistence of modern and traditional patterns. Specifically, the socio-cultural contrast between city and village, and especially between settled and nomadic populations, emerges as one of the most important barriers to political integration.

A number of further observations, however, are in order. The terms "traditional" and "modern," as used in this context, cover in fact a wide variety of cultural patterns. Traditional culture in the contemporary Near East rests everywhere on an Islamic basis. But doctrinal distinctions between Sunnah and Shi'ah; socio-economic differences among the settled agriculture of Yemen, the irrigation economy of the river valleys, and the nomadic pastoralism of the desert fringes and the arid mountains; historical variations among the Ottoman imperial tradition of Turkey and the Arab and the Iranian literary heritages—all these and a host of other historical and geographic facts superimpose a scintillating variety upon this common traditional base. Similarly the experience of Western Europe, and North America, indicates that "modern" cultural patterns when combined with traditional patterns produced a variety of individually unique political systems. Even if at some future stage politics, society, and culture throughout the Near East should have become thoroughly modernized, there is no reason why this should make the countries of the region into replicas of any Western country or of each other—any more than Norway is a replica of France, or Canada of Austria. Most of the political systems of the Near East present mixtures of modern and traditional components. But what we mean by mixture is in need of further differentiation. A "mixture" of modern and traditional patterns can take the form of a geographic division into city, village, and tribal areas, or of a class division between professional persons and laborers in the same city. But the interaction of tradition and modernity not only leads to such more or less unrelated coexistence; it also gives rise to new cultural patterns which are neither part of tradition or of the modern culture, nor a mere transition between the two. For these I have in an earlier study suggested the term "amalgamate" patterns.[48] In Near Eastern politics examples of such amalgamate patterns are legislation which combines an Islamic content with the European practice of paragraph codification; the emergence of movements like the Muslim Brethren which use modern propaganda techniques for the reassertion of (presumed) traditional values; and the prevalence of student riots.

In an assessment of the effect of various combinations of modern and traditional political patterns, these should be viewed in a dynamic context of historical development. It is quite true that political integration is favored by situations where political and governmental functions are in unison—i.e., where both are traditional, or both mixed, or both modern. But in the many situations where they do not accord, the comparative rates of change make a crucial difference. Integration fares better where the authoritative functions move from traditional to mixed to modern ahead of the political group functions—or, in other words, where the political precedes the social transformation. This clearly was the case in Kemalist Turkey, where Westernizing constitutional and legal changes set a much faster pace than the more gradual changes in social group structure. Tunisia under Bourguiba, the Sudan under its largely British-trained political leadership, and Morocco under the cooperative rule of Muhammad V and the Istiqlal Party seem to be embarked on a similar course—although the specific levels of traditionalism and modernity vary considerably among these countries. Conversely, where rising elements of a modernized middle class feel thwarted in their aspirations by a government which they consider excessively traditional, a potentially revolutionary situation arises. This clearly has been the case in pre-1958 Iraq, in Jordan, and in Iran. A similar trend can be discerned in Saudi Arabia, although it may not be irreversible there.

Furthermore, there are other factors which crucially affect the political integration of a society. These include technological changes and, above all, developments in the international situation. Major petroleum discoveries, for example, have in the past quickly revolutionized the social and political structure of some Near Eastern countries, and may have similar effects elsewhere in the future. On the other hand, a global

[48] See Rustow, *Politics and Westernization in the Near East, op.cit.,* p. 6.

displacement of oil by other sources of power may in the long run return the oil-rich countries of the Persian Gulf region to their previous desert poverty. The merger of Transjordan with Eastern Palestine in 1949 transformed the once peaceful and traditional Bedouin protectorate of Britain into a restless hotbed of revolutionary ferment. A Soviet military intrusion into the Near East may impose a coercive pattern of integration on the region. Prolonged Western military occupation of parts of the Near East may cause the further spread of anti-Western attitudes which could adversely affect the further course of Westernization and the political integration of the area. A concerted and successful campaign for national independence, such as Turkey conducted under Atatürk, may promote the political cohesion of a country. Any large-scale drive for Arab unification, finally, is sure to have not only political but also social, cultural, and economic repercussions.

5. THE POLITICS OF

Latin America

GEORGE I. BLANKSTEN

....

I. IN THE BACKGROUND

The Physical Setting

SCHOLARS IN THE UNITED STATES generally use the term "Latin America" to embrace the twenty sovereign countries which have joined with the United States in the Organization of American States. Thus used, the term excludes not only the political units in the Western Hemisphere lying north of Mexico, but also Puerto Rico and the British, French, and Dutch possessions in the region.

It is sometimes convenient to think of the twenty states of Latin America as falling into two major geographic categories. The first of these, the continent of South America, contains Argentina, Bolivia, Brazil, Chile, Colombia, Ecuador, Paraguay, Peru, Uruguay, and Venezuela. The second, sometimes called "Middle America," includes Mexico, the five states of Central America,[1] Panama,[2] and the Caribbean island republics of Cuba, the Dominican Republic, and Haiti. Of the entire Latin American group, only four countries have populations numbering more than 10,000,000 (see Table 1). These are Brazil (52,645,000), Mexico (25,791,000), Argentina (17,108,000), and Colombia (11,477,000). The largest of these, Brazil, has an area (3,288,383 square miles) greater than even that of the United States (3,022,387). The remaining sixteen countries of Latin America are relatively small, having an average population of 3,186,000 and an average area of 139,000 square miles.

Some basic characteristics of the physical geography of Latin America are worth noting, since many of these, in one way or another, affect political patterns in the area. In the first place, there is the matter of climate. Approximately three-fourths of the area lies in the tropics. It is an inter-

---

[1] Costa Rica, El Salvador, Guatemala, Honduras, and Nicaragua.

[2] Geographers frequently include Panama in Central America, although other social scientists often do not because many of Panama's historical, cultural, and political orientations are toward South rather than Central America.

MEXICO

CUBA

DOMINICAN
REP.

HAITI

HONDURAS

GUATEMALA
EL SALVADOR   NICARAGUA

COSTA RICA

PANAMA

VENEZUELA

COLOMBIA

ECUADOR

PERU

BRAZIL

BOLIVIA

PARAGUAY

LATIN
AMERICA

C H I L E

ARGENTINA

URUGUAY

EQUATORIAL SCALE 1:30,000,000
(SCALE VARIES WITH LATITUDE)

Don Goldman

TABLE 1

Latin America: Some Basic Data

Country	Area (sq. miles)	Population	Population Density Persons per sq. m.	Capital City
SOUTH AMERICA				
Argentina	1,079,965	17,108,000	18	Buenos Aires
Bolivia	419,470	3,990,000	8	La Paz
Brazil	3,288,383	52,645,479	18	Rio de Janeiro
Chile	296,717	5,930,809	24	Santiago
Colombia	447,536	11,477,495	30	Bogotá
Ecuador	171,874	3,383,654	37	Quito
Paraguay	157,047	1,405,627	10	Asunción
Peru	482,258	8,405,000	19	Lima
Uruguay	72,153	2,353,000	38	Montevideo
Venezuela	352,143	5,400,000	17	Caracas
MIDDLE AMERICA				
Mexico	763,944	25,791,017	40	Mexico City
CENTRAL AMERICA				
Costa Rica	19,695	803,084	51	San José
El Salvador	13,173	2,179,249	280	San Salvador
Guatemala	42,042	2,788,122	79	Guatemala City
Honduras	44,880	1,365,605	40	Tegucigalpa
Nicaragua	57,143	1,057,023	24	Managua
Panama	28,575	805,285	32	Panama City
ISLAND REPUBLICS				
Cuba	44,164	5,870,904	132	Havana
Dominican Rep.	19,332	2,135,872	131	Cuidad Trujillo
Haiti	10,204	3,111,973	309	Port-au-Prince
TOTALS	7,810,698	158,007,198		

Source: William W. Pierson and Federico G. Gil, *Governments of Latin America*, New York, 1957, p. 15.

esting and probably significant circumstance that the greatest degree of economic development and "Westernization" to be found in Latin America occurs, for the most part, in the sections which are *not* in the tropics—that is, in Mexico, Argentina, Uruguay, Chile, and southern Brazil. The reasons for this are not clear, although the nature of the relationship between climate and human behavior is a question which has interested scholars for centuries. Despite recent attempts to renew inquiry into this problem,[3] it remains essentially unresolved. The probability

[3] See, for example, Douglas H. K. Lee, *Climate and Economic Development in the Tropics*, New York, 1957.

seems quite high that, when and if the patterns of interplay between climate and human behavior are isolated and analyzed, considerable light will be thrown on political questions in most of the countries of Latin America.

The spectacular physical terrain of the region not only enchants the tourist but also has social and political consequences. The immense jungles, towering mountains, and even important sectors of the great river systems have operated as formidable barriers to transportation and communication in Latin America, and are frequently regarded by Hispanic Americans as virtually unsurmountable obstacles to the realization of their political ambitions. Political fragmentation—eighteen sovereign states now administer the territory once comprising only eight Spanish colonies—and an intense regionalism or sectionalism are among the more salient contemporary aspects of this problem.

Physical geography, of course, governs the major economic activity of Latin America—agriculture. The productivity of the soil ranges from the highly fruitful conditions to be found in Argentina to the bare subsistence agriculture of, say, Ecuador. Agriculture and other types of land use are central to many of the political patterns of the American nations. Almost no Latin American state is free of the question of land tenure as an extremely severe *political* problem; and in many of the countries, especially in Central America, one-crop economies and monoculture are integrally linked to politics.

Further, the natural resources of Latin America make the area one of the world's major suppliers of certain raw materials. The political implications of this source of wealth lie most obviously in the international field, although the ramifications in the domestic politics of the area should not be overlooked. Consider, for example, Bolivia, where political power was long held by the so-called "tin barons." The gold and silver of places like Mexico and Peru were, of course, among the original magnets drawing the Spanish *conquistadores* to the New World. In more recent times gold and silver have diminished in significance, but today new forms of mineral wealth preserve the importance of subsoil deposits in Latin American politics. In addition to the tin of Bolivia, oil—perhaps the most political of all minerals—is crucial in the politics of countries like Mexico and Venezuela. In other countries, other minerals perform a similar political function. Brazil, in particular, possesses one of the most remarkable endowments of diverse and valued minerals of any country on earth.

With respect to the economy of the area, four chief points should be noted. In the first place, the economies of most of the Latin American countries are underdeveloped. That is to say, largely in consequence of problems of technology, a relatively large input into the productive process yields a relatively small output. This condition of the productive arts results in low standards of living and widespread poverty; in much of Latin America industrialization has hardly begun.

Next, land plays a disproportionately large role in the region's economy. It is generally regarded as the chief source of wealth, and land ownership is a mark of prestige. Other sources of wealth, such as industry and commerce, are generally undervalued throughout the area. Uneconomically worked in many of the countries, land is a widespread economic problem. Were the five major economic problems of each of the twenty states of Latin America to be itemized, the role of land in the economy would be on at least three-quarters of the lists.

In the third place, as we have mentioned, Latin America is one of the world's major sources of raw materials, particularly of minerals. This is especially true of oil, tin, and other materials sought, sometimes desperately, by the more industrialized states. Latin America's role in international affairs derives in large part from this situation; in times of war, the area is a leading supplier of strategic and critical materials.

Finally, foreign companies and capital play a large role in the development and exploitation of the natural resources of Latin America. A curious dividing line separates southern South America—Argentina, Uruguay, Chile, and Paraguay—where the largest single source of foreign capital has traditionally been British, from the rest of Latin America, where the largest single foreign source is the United States. Foreign capital plays a large role not only in the economies but also in the politics of Latin America and is the basis of most charges of "imperialism." It is worth noting that, with the single major exception of Central America, foreign investment generally tends *not* to be in land.

Traditional Culture

It is possible to write an essay on the politics of the United States without mentioning the American Indian; a similar feat cannot be performed in the case of Latin America. Two basic considerations underlie this sharp contrast. First, the cultures of some of the pre-Hispanic Indian societies of Latin America differed significantly from the ways of life of the indigenous peoples of British North America. In the second place, the policies and practices adopted by the European settlers toward the

Indians in the two areas differed. Each of these points deserves a further word.

So far as the first is concerned, the pre-Columbian cultures of the Western Hemisphere differed considerably from area to area. Indeed, anthropologists have divided indigenous America into fourteen so-called "culture areas."[4] Those in what later became the United States were essentially nomadic and variously warlike in character, with little capacity for long-term survival. The same could be said of some of the indigenous culture areas of Latin America, to be sure; but a few stand as striking exceptions. One of these is the area embracing what are now Mexico and Guatemala. Here, in pre-Columbian times, the Mayas, Aztecs, and Toltecs developed remarkable civilizations of such durability that many Mexicans and Guatemalans today still live as Indians. A second such area centered in Peru, and included parts of what are now Ecuador, Bolivia, and northwestern Argentina. Again, the survival potential of the early civilization has been such that about one-half the populations of Peru, Ecuador, and Bolivia still live as Indians.

Secondly, in British North America there was very little incorporation of the Indians in the society of the European settlers. Rather, the indigenous peoples were at first driven back and later placed on reservations. The Latin American experience differed markedly. There the Indian became the serflike servant of the European. Partly because the Spaniards brought few women with them from Europe, and partly because of a differing pattern of race prejudice, miscegenation was far more widespread in Latin than in British North America.

With the exception of the Caribbean islands, where the Indians were wiped out shortly after the Spanish conquest, the American Indian remains a major element in the political pattern of Latin America.

In 1494, shortly after Columbus discovered the New World, Pope Alexander VI drew a line of demarcation in an attempt to divide the lands eligible for colonial exploitation between Spain and Portugal. In the Western Hemisphere the line ran from north to south through South America; Spain was free to occupy the lands west of the line, and Portugal was assigned the territory to the east. Despite frequent border squabbles and differences of interpretation as to where the line lay in certain localities, the demarcation was in general respected by the Spanish and Portuguese governments. Under its general formula, Brazil became Portuguese and the remainder of Latin America Spanish.[5]

[4] See, for example, A. L. Kroeber, *Anthropology*, New York, 1923, pp. 335-339.
[5] Two chronic controversies between Spain and Portugal grew out of the line of de-

In 1697, Spain acknowledged French sovereignty over Haiti. Thus the major European influences in Latin America came to be Spanish, Portuguese, and French.

The meeting of the Indian and European civilizations produced a class system which is of fundamental importance in the political patterns of Latin America. This system of classes, with the passing of generations, has become highly rigid and formalized. The order varies somewhat from country to country, but in general the upper class—called "creoles" or "whites"—is European in historic, linguistic, and cultural orientation. In many of the states—particularly in northwestern South America, Mexico, and portions of Central America—Indians constitute an appreciable portion, in some cases the majority, of the population (see Table 2). In these Indo-American countries, the In-

TABLE 2

Indians in the Populations of Latin America

Country	Number	Percentage
Argentina	50,000	0.38
Bolivia	1,650,000	50.00
Brazil	1,117,132	2.70
Chile	130,000	2.58
Colombia	147,300	0.91
Costa Rica	4,200	0.64
Ecuador	1,000,000	40.00
El Salvador	348,907	20.00
Guatemala	1,820,396	55.44
Honduras	105,732	9.54
Mexico	5,427,396	27.91
Nicaragua	330,000	23.90
Panama	64,960	10.90
Paraguay	40,000	4.16
Peru	3,247,196	46.23
Venezuela	100,000	2.79

Source: Pierson and Gil, *op.cit.*, p. 9.

dians tend to make up the lower class. A middle group—variously called *mestizos* or *cholos*—is found in the Indian countries; this group represents a species of cross or fusion of the European and Indian cultures.[6] Negroes are found in appreciable numbers in the Caribbean

marcation. One involved dispute over the western extremity of Brazil. The other, called the "Banda Oriental" question, was the issue of whether what is now Uruguay should be considered Spanish or Portuguese. The latter controversy was resolved through agreement in 1828 to consider Uruguay as independent of both claimants.

[6] The *mestizos* are a middle class in the social and cultural senses rather than in the

461

island republics and in some regions of Brazil, but are rare elsewhere in Latin America. Where Negroes exist in large numbers, they tend to be associated with the lower class.

It is common, in the non-technical parlance of Latin America, to refer to the component part of this class system as "races." In the interest of precision of analysis, however, it is of crucial importance to note that they are classes rather than races. The bases of differentiation among them are social rather than biological; an individual's learned behavior, his way of life rather than his physical characteristics, determine the group with which he is identified. Thus, the director of the Peruvian government's statistical bureau has said: "The way they live determines whether a family is Indian. There is a family of German descent near my home who live as 100 percent Indians in a hut on a small *finca*.[7] They speak only Quechua[8] and think only Quechua. Thus a language is another criterion of race. Speech determines culture. A Peruvian who knows no Spanish may be called an Indian."[9] Hispanic Americans who speak Indian languages at home and Spanish elsewhere are normally counted as *mestizos* or *cholos*. And those who use Spanish and/or other European tongues—especially if they are literate in these languages—at home as well as in other contexts are, virtually by definition, "whites" or creoles. Urban dwellers are frequently counted as "whites," and rural folk as *mestizos* or Indians, often depending on the extent of their contacts with the "whites." Many anthropologists hold that an individual's style of dress is the basic key to whether he should be classed as a "white," *mestizo*, or Indian. Criteria such as these, in differing combinations, are used throughout Latin America in assessing the ethnic composition of populations. The point cannot be overemphasized that these terms—"white," *mestizo* or *cholo*, Indian —refer to groups defined in fundamentally social and cultural rather than biological ways, despite the frequent loose use of the word "race."

This extremely important consideration has two significant aspects. First, the class system is a rough measure of the distribution of political power in Latin America. The "whites" and creoles—constituting from 15 to 30 per cent of the population of many of the countries—are a species of ruling class. They are the landowners, the political leaders

---

economic sense of the term. The economic middle class is small, weak, and—in some countries of the area—virtually non-existent.

[7] A *finca* is a small plot of land in a rural area.

[8] Quechua is a major language of the Andean Indians.

[9] W. Stanley Rycroft, *Indians of the High Andes*, New York, 1946, p. 33.

and government officials, the clergymen, almost all of the voters and army officers, and about 90 per cent of the people counted as literate. *Mestizos* and *cholos* constitute about one-third of the population of many of the countries, and in some of them the Indians account for almost half of the population. Many of the countries have what might be called oligarchical political systems, with the "whites" and creoles functioning as the ruling group and the *mestizos* and Indians as the ruled.

Secondly, just as these classes are not races, neither are they castes. Under the rules of a caste system, an individual may not move from caste to caste. In Latin America, Indians may become *mestizos, mestizos* may become "whites." Indeed, no field investigator can remain in the area very long without encountering a "white" fond of reminiscing about his experiences "when I was an Indian." Upward mobility from class to class occurs more frequently than downward mobility, but the latter is also a Latin American phenomenon. Movement from class to class may be accomplished by becoming literate, learning a new language, changing one's style of dress, moving from a rural to an urban area (or vice versa), or becoming a landowner, a priest, or an army officer. When intermarriage occurs, husband and wife become members of the same group, depending on which partner's way of life the household adopts. Instances are not infrequent of Indians who leave their villages to become educated in urban centers and later return—as "whites"—to their villages.

This is not to say that, since it is *possible* for a Latin American to move from class to class, it is therefore *easy* for him to do so. Although it does occur, class mobility is a slow process for two general types of reasons. The first concerns values. Typically, each class values its own way of life. Indians generally have a deep and intense love for their communities and villages; the "white" who would prefer to be an Indian or a *mestizo* is rare.[10] Secondly, the remaining barriers to interclass mobility are still formidable. It is not a simple task for an Indian to learn to speak Spanish, let alone read or write it, or to move to a big city, or to buy a large landed estate, or to become a priest. As might be expected, interclass mobility occurs at different rates in different regions of Latin America.

[10] Apparently *mestizos* tend to place a lower value on the *mestizo* way of life than Indians and "whites" ascribe to their respective systems. See John Gillen, *Mestizo American*, Chapel Hill, N.C., *passim*.

Patterns of Western Impact

Westernizing influences upon Latin America have been exercized in a wide variety of ways. These have ranged, historically, from the dramatic imposition of Spanish and Portuguese rule during the conquest of the area in the sixteenth century, through the subsequent introduction of some phases of European culture during the colonial period, to the European immigration, influence of the United States, and Latin American participation in international affairs of more contemporary times. All of these patterns of Western impact have made their peculiar contributions to the types of political systems to be found in Latin America today.

As has been noted, indigenous civilizations were several centuries old in the area when the first Spaniards arrived. The Caribbean islands felt the first concentrated impact of the West.[11] This impact was violent and conclusive. In an attempt to repel the invaders, the Indians of the Caribbean gave battle to the Spaniards but, largely for technological reasons, were no military match for them. War characterized the relationship between the Spaniards and the Indians during the generation following Columbus' voyages, and during this period the Caribbean Indians were not only militarily defeated but literally wiped out. Today there are no indigenous Indians in the Caribbean islands. After the conquest, when the Spaniards wanted to import laborers into that region, Negro slaves were brought from Africa. Caribbean society is thus characterized by European and African elements, with no Indian admixture.

On the mainland, the pattern differed. The Indians there—particularly in Mexico and in Peru—were better equipped to defend themselves against the Spaniards. Nevertheless, had military events been permitted to run their course, the outcome might have resembled the Caribbean experience. Under the initial leadership of Fray Bartolomé de las Casas, the Church intervened to prevent the extermination of the mainland Indians. Las Casas, who had himself witnessed some of the slaughter in the Caribbean, was able to persuade the Church and the Spanish government to adopt policies designed to save the Indians from extinction. Under the celebrated "Laws of the Indies," dating from the 1530's, Indians were not to be killed if they accepted the Roman Catholic religion; they were to live under the protection of the Church, then a major arm of the Spanish government. The "Laws of the Indies"

[11] The center of Portuguese impact, of course, was in Brazil, claimed for Portugal by Cabral in 1502.

set the basic pattern for the subsequent development of relations between Spaniards and Indians. The Spanish *conquistadors* formed the nucleus of the ruling class; the humiliated and conquered Indians took their place as the lower class under the aegis of the Church. Today the Indians may be counted among the most loyal and devout followers of the Church in Latin America.

A third variation occurred in Chile. There the culture of the Araucanian Indians differed from the ways of the Indians whom the Spaniards had earlier encountered in the north. Unlike the Aztecs or the Incas, the Araucanians were a nomadic and warlike people who proudly refused to accept the Church or anything else the Spaniards brought with them. Somewhat reminiscent of the Sioux of the North American plains, the Araucanians stubbornly resisted the advance of the Europeans into Chile. That advance has persisted, with the Indians being progressively driven toward the south. Thus, like the United States in the nineteenth century, Chile has had its historic problem of the Indian frontier, resolved in a manner similar to the solution in the United States. The Araucanians live in southern Chile today under arrangements resembling the Indian reservations in North America.[12] In striking contrast to those in the rest of the South American mainland, the Indians of Chile live apart and have not been incorporated into Latin American society as a lower class or in any other capacity.

The Spanish government treated its American colonies as a collection of cities. The Europeans who settled in the colonies tended to gather in urban centers, and most of the decrees and other laws which flowed from Madrid during the colonial period governed urban rather than rural life.[13] This circumstance set the pattern for a basic contrast between the urban centers and the rural areas which remains a fundamental characteristic of contemporary Latin America. The major municipalities were, and are, "Westernized"; the indigenous or "non-Western" systems retreated to the rural areas. Today this deep division separating urban from rural life is still a basic element of the Latin American scene. The "Westernized" cities look to Europe and mimic its culture; rural Hispanic America, for the most part, remains the land of the

[12] Throughout this chapter, the term "North America" is used, in the Latin American sense, to refer to the United States.

[13] The sole major Hispanic-American exception to this general pattern is to be found in Argentina, which was "Westernized" on a regional or provincial rather than municipal basis. The explanation for this Argentine deviation lies at least in part in the fact that Argentina was settled not in the Hapsburg, but in the Bourbon period of Spanish rule, when a number of French colonial practices were employed in the empire.

Indians. In this division lies one of the major elements of the pattern of Westernization of the area.[14]

Another of the elements of this pattern dating from the colonial period is what may be referred to as the problem of the frontier. The physical barriers to transportation and communication have not been surmounted in Latin America. European civilization has not yet penetrated effectively into the regions shielded by these natural barriers, and the problem of the frontier underlies the ecology of Westernization in the area. Everywhere the frontier is significant; in some of the countries it is one of the most romanticized sectors of national life. For example, in Brazil—where the vast Amazon jungle lands beyond the frontier are known as the *sertão*—the idea of this wilderness has acquired a mystical quality. The *sertão*, in a sense, terrorizes Brazilians. Who knows what it contains? To Brazilians, to travel from one city to another is merely to have undertaken a journey; but to have gone to or from the *sertão* is to have had the adventure of a lifetime.[15] The influence of the West may be great in the cities, but it is virtually unknown in the rural areas and beyond the frontier.

The mercantilistic policies of Spain should also be included among the colonial conditions establishing the pattern of Westernization in Latin America. Spain was not alone in practicing mercantilism; it was pursued by most of the colonial powers of the time. Essentially, mercantilism rested on the proposition that colonies exist for the benefit of the mother country. In a mercantilistic system, colonies were not permitted to produce goods that would compete with those of the governing country; and colonies were, in general, forbidden to trade, or to engage in many other forms of intercourse, with other European states. As it found expression in colonial Latin America, mercantilism had the effect of limiting the Westernizing influences upon the area to those emanating from Spain, Portugal, and—later—France.

Partly in consequence of the mercantilism of the era, the new colonists who arrived in Latin America came almost exclusively from the mother countries. This pattern was enforced, and curiously underscored, by the laws of Spain governing immigration to her American colonies. Under these laws, non-Spaniards could make their homes in Hispanic America only if they (a) were Roman Catholics and (b) were nationals of coun-

[14] See Harold E. Davis, ed., *Government and Politics in Latin America*, New York, 1958, pp. 368-392.

[15] Recently, this writer was privileged to attend a gathering of Brazilians that included a recent returnee from the *sertão*. Upon completing his travels, Marco Polo could not have been accorded greater deference.

tries not considered to be colonial rivals of Spain. As a result, Irish emigrants were virtually the only non-Spanish Europeans eligible to move to the colonies. Irish influence remains significant in Hispanic America, where names like that of O'Higgins, the first president of Chile, abound.

Since their achievement of political independence early in the nineteenth century, the Latin American countries—with the exception of Argentina—have not been particularly attractive to immigrants from Europe. A number of such immigrants have nevertheless arrived, and their incorporation into Hispanic American life has had a Westernizing effect upon it. During the nineteenth and twentieth centuries, the Europeans emigrating to the area have fallen into three major classes. The first of these is the remarkable stream of immigrants who began pouring into Argentina in the late 1860's and who have continued to move into that country during the twentieth century, partly because Argentina since the colonial period has been the most Western of the sectors of Hispanic America, and partly in consequence of the country's immigration laws, which after the 1860's had the effect of inviting immigration. Indeed, Argentina has been second only to the United States among the American countries attracting European immigrants. During the nineteenth century the immigrants to Argentina were chiefly Spaniards and Italians; in the twentieth century these were joined by large numbers of Germans.

The second major class of European immigrants journeying to Latin America includes the refugees fleeing the disruptive effect of World Wars I and II. Each of these conflicts created a large number of stateless, displaced, or otherwise uprooted Europeans. Refugees from Nazism, including many Jews, came to Hispanic America shortly before the outbreak of World War II; during and immediately after that conflict, the American republics continued to absorb refugees from the strife of Europe.

The third major group of European immigrants embraces the refugees from the political turmoil of Spain. Since the outbreak of the Carlist Wars in the 1840's, the former mother country has been involved in more or less constant internal strife. On a number of occasions these difficulties have led to upheavals causing Spaniards to leave the country and make their homes elsewhere, often in Latin America. Two major instances of this have occurred during the twentieth century. The first was the Spanish Revolution of 1930; the second was the Spanish Civil War (1936-1939). Both drove impressive numbers of Spanish immigrants to Latin America. When the Fascist-like Spanish regime of Primo de Rivera fell in the Revolution of 1930, many of Primo de Rivera's supporters fled to Hispanic America. They became significant carriers of Fascism into the area, and their post-1930 political roles have been important particularly in Argentina.[16] The later Spanish Civil War drove significant numbers of Spanish Republicans to Latin America. These too have had politically impressive roles in the area, particularly in Mexico, where a Spanish Republican government-in-exile was maintained for many years after General Francisco Franco seized power at Madrid in 1939.

Regardless of which stream of immigration brought them to the area, the Europeans who made their homes in Latin America during the nineteenth and twentieth centuries have contributed to its Westernization. As they have been absorbed into its society, the immigrants have generally settled in the cities rather than in the rural areas and have become creoles or "whites"; only in isolated instances have European immigrants become *mestizos* or Indians.

Further, the internal population dynamics of Latin America have had a Westernizing tendency. The population figures suggest that, even if there were no European immigrants in the area, with each succeeding generation the proportion of Indians would become smaller, and that of *mestizos* and of creoles or "whites" larger. Through its normal internal processes of intermarriage and other forms of social mobility, Latin America Westernizes itself: Indians become *mestizos, mestizos* become creoles or "whites," and the "whites" are the carriers of Western ways in Latin America. This is one of the more subtle and slower forms of Westernization in the area—the process may take generations—but it is nevertheless significant.

And then there is the "Colossus of the North." More than any other great power, the United States is in constant contact with Latin America. This contact has had its Westernizing effect. The forms of United States contact with the area have been many and varied, ranging all the way from invasion and military occupation through cultural and constitutional influences as well as financial investment, to trade and technical assistance. It is true of virtually every Latin American state that its major contacts outside the area are with the United States: in Mexico, the money spent by *gringo* tourists is the fourth largest source of national income. The effects in Latin America of "Yankee" influence—

[16] See George I. Blanksten, *Perón's Argentina*, Chicago, 1953, pp. 276-305 and 316-328.

whether it be represented by the United States armed forces, the borrowing of *gringo* constitutional and legal institutions and practices; the *imperialismo yanqui* of the oil, rubber, and fruit companies; the pattern of imports and exports; the operation of technical assistance programs; or the annual flood of *gringo* tourists—are generally Westernizing. Although United States influence is not the same in all twenty of the states of the area, it can nevertheless be said that relations with the "Yankees" are among the more significant forms of Western impact in Latin America.

Economic development, a process of rapidly growing significance in the area, also has Westernizing effects. Industrialization has begun in many of the countries, and everywhere there is evidence of economic change. This process is abetted by the technical assistance programs—whether supported on a bilateral basis by the United States or multilaterally through the United Nations—which have been operating on a large scale in Latin America since the 1940's. These programs, chiefly in agriculture, education, public administration, and industrial productivity, have elevated the standards of living in the participating countries and have imported Western technology. While the effect of interplay between levels of economic development and political patterns is as yet unclear, it is undoubtedly true that Westernization of the economy has significant repercussions on the political scene. In any case, the process of economic development can be regarded as one of the most spectacular forms of Westernization in Latin America during the mid-twentieth century.

Finally, the area's involvement in international politics has had some Westernizing implications. Eight of the countries were belligerents in World War I,[17] and all twenty took part in World War II; further all twenty have been members of both the League of Nations and the United Nations. Although Latin America has experienced its share of isolationism, the area has become increasingly involved in international affairs. These have their influences, many of them Westernizing. To be a weaker partner of a Western wartime ally is to be exposed to his influence; to sit with him at the council table of an international organization has a similar effect. In the foreign policy of present-day Latin America—as elsewhere—isolationism is increasingly recognized as unworkable. As Latin Americans expand their dealings with other states of the world, many of them Western, the area opens its doors still further to the processes of Western impact.

[17] Brazil, Cuba, Costa Rica, Guatemala, Haiti, Honduras, Nicaragua, and Panama.

II. PROCESSES OF CHANGE

Urbanization

As has been noted, the rural areas have historically been the least, and the urban areas the most, Westernized parts of Latin America. In a very real sense, the rural dweller who moves to an urban center takes a long step toward becoming Westernized. The Indian who migrates to the big city becomes a *mestizo* almost in so doing; he has not lived there very long before he is counted as a creole or a "white." To put the proposition in another way—in Latin America, the rural civilization is non-Western and the urban civilization is Western. In virtually all of the countries of Latin America, urbanization has been one of the major social phenomena of the late nineteenth and the twentieth century. It has been intensified by the tendency of European immigrants to locate in the major cities.

There is no Latin American country in which there has been a trend away from urbanization; everywhere the impressive fact has been the movement toward the city, the swelling of urban populations. This trend has given rise to what is sometimes referred to as the problem of *la cabeza de Goliat* (Goliath's head), characterizing a country in which a giant urban head rests upon a dwarflike rural body. This situation is most acute in Cuba and Uruguay, where more than half the national populations live in the metropolitan areas of Havana and Montevideo; Argentina, where a little more than one-fourth of the people are located in Greater Buenos Aires; and Venezuela, where approximately 20 per cent of the population lives in Caracas. In any case, urbanization, with its attendant problems, is a major process in contemporary Latin America and a principal means of Westernization.

Commercialization and Industrialization

Trade and commerce have been among the major vehicles of Westernization in Latin America for more than a century. They have operated in a number of ways. For one thing, commercialization stimulates trade contacts with the outside world, much of it Western. Whoever buys the physical commodities of the West imports with them other aspects of Western culture, including the political. Commercial relations among peoples have long been recognized as a significant stimulus to other types of contact, and the Latin American experience demonstrates the effectiveness of this process.

Further, there are more subtle, if no less significant, patterns of the synergistic relationship between commercialization and Westernization in Latin America. Among these is the effect of commerce upon the role of land in the economy of the area. In the more non-Western parts of Hispanic America, land is regarded as the chief source of wealth—in extreme cases, as the only major source. By generating an alternative source, trade and commerce challenge, and change, the economic positions of the land and the landowners. This also has political ramifications. Many observers have noted that in Latin America both liberal and conservative parties represent propertied interests; some have made the mistake of concluding from this that these parties are merely the opposite sides of the same coin. It should be noted that wealth derived from the land functions differently from that derived from trade and commerce. The latter compete with the landed estate for labor, and lure the workingman from his traditional serflike status. Commercialization spurs land reform and undermines the political status of the Church, historically associated in the area with the system of land tenure. Further, commerce stimulates the beginnings of industrialization and technological change.

Roughly since the early 1940's, technological change and economic development have been among the most spectacular forms for Westernization in Latin America. A close correlation exists between economic underdevelopment and non-Westernization; indeed, the underdeveloped areas of the world are frequently defined as its non-Western parts. While a generally acceptable theory of the pattern of interplay between levels of economic development and political culture has not yet been formulated, it has nevertheless been established that technical innovation, insofar as it renders the productive arts more efficient, is a major vehicle of economic development. The international exchange of technology, of course, is a process as old as international relations itself. But since the early 1940's steps have been taken, at first in Latin America and later in other underdeveloped areas, to structure or channel these exchanges through public policies designed to contribute to the more immediate and effective economic development of the participating countries.

These policies have generally been known as technical assistance, "Point Four," or technical cooperation. Whatever the designation, the objectives of the policies are essentially the same. These are, through the introduction of technical changes in the underdeveloped areas, to alter their productive arts or technologies to increase the productivity of their economies, thus stimulating economic development. Today all twenty of the countries of Latin America are participating in programs of technical cooperation, in the form of bilateral arrangements with the United States, multilateral arrangements with the United Nations, or—the most common pattern—some mixture of both the bilateral and the multilateral approach. While the results of these programs have not been the same in all of the states of Latin America, the current, impressive economic development in a number of them—notably, Brazil, Peru, and Mexico—has operated in conjunction with effective programs of technical cooperation.

In much of Latin America, economic development may be regarded as the most effective avenue of change in the mid-twentieth century. Where it has taken hold, it has stimulated industrialization. Economic development weakens the once-rigid lines separating the social classes; class mobility becomes easier and more rapid; the pastoral Indian moves from the *hacienda* to employment in the emerging industries. As economic development multiplies the opportunities open to the peoples of Latin America, it broadens their horizons, gives them new roles, alters their patterns of expectation. It is argued in some quarters that this process is the whole of Westernization of the underdeveloped areas; if that position is too extreme, the more moderate proposition that economic development is a major element of the transition is incontrovertible.

Westernized Education

If the term "education" is understood to refer to an essentially institutionalized process, resting heavily on the inculcation of the ability to read an established literature and to produce contributions to it, this process has played a crucial role in the Westernization of Latin America. It is generally true throughout the area that literacy is, virtually by definition, the ability to read *European* languages.

In this context, two points are central to the Westernizing role of education. First, in much of the area formal education, as measured by literacy rates, comes close to being a monopoly of the upper class. Large percentages of the populations of Latin American countries are illiterate. This in itself is significant, to be sure; but the figures assume added importance when viewed in terms of the class distribution of literacy. Very few of the "whites" or creoles of post-school age are illiterate, whereas the ability to read and write is rare among the *mestizos* or *cholos*, and virtually non-existent among the Indians. Indeed, the correlation between literacy and the class systems is so close that it is frequently used in Latin American statistical work to develop figures on either of the two in situations where data on only one are available. Further, it is the established practice of the census officers in many of the countries to employ literacy as a major criterion in determining whether to classify persons as "whites," *mestizos*, or Indians.

Second, education has always been "Western" in the area. To chart the major trends in the history of education in Latin America is to examine some of the major directions that Westernization has taken there. Formal education was originally introduced by the Roman Catholic Church. From the earliest colonial times until well into the nineteenth century, Latin American education was administered and controlled by the Church. Indeed, the record contains numerous instances of men who went into the Church because it provided the only Latin American opportunities for scholarship.

During the nineteenth and twentieth centuries, education in Latin America experienced a general secularization. This has taken two forms, corresponding roughly to the course followed by the humanities, on the one hand, and by the sciences, on the other. The secularization of the humanities has been reflected in expanding French influences upon Latin American education, whereas the growing role of the sciences has responded to German and, later, North American educational forces. These influences have been exercized in a number of ways, ranging from the translation of French, German, and English works into the languages of Latin America, through curricular changes, to travel abroad by Latin American students.

The political implications of these patterns of education are for the most part, clear. Doctrines of authority—strong in most of Latin America—can usually be traced to Spanish and Church-oriented intellectual sources. Where the questioning of, or outright revolt against, authority assumes respectability in academic and intellectual circles, this generally reflects the inroads made by French influences, particularly in such doctrinal matters as democracy and constitutionalism. North American ideas contribute somewhat secondarily in a similar fashion, but the chief influence of the United States in this field, like the German influence, is primarily in the realm of the sciences rather than the humanities. That the intellectual environment of the more highly educated Latin Americans remains far more humanistic and artistic than scientific no doubt reflects the fact that religious, Spanish, and French educational influences in the area are still stronger than the North American and German.

A word should be said about Portuguese and Italian elements in Latin American education. The first, of course, are dominant in Brazil. In the realm of political ideas, teachings of Portuguese origin resemble the Spanish and the French in their strong inclination toward humanism and art. Doctrines of authority in the Portuguese tradition are less Church-oriented and, indeed, less authoritarian than in the case of Spanish influences, but contain more of both elements than the French. Italian intellectual currents are to be found in a few of the Latin American countries—notably, Argentina, Uruguay and, to a lesser extent, Brazil. Like the Spanish and the French, Italian educational values place greater emphasis on the humanities than the sciences; unlike either, the Italian intellectual tradition encourages a form of individualism so extreme in some cases as to border on anarchism. To describe the ideal of Italian-oriented teaching as "every man his own political party" no doubt exaggerates the situation, but it has more than a grain of validity.

Changes in educational developments of course occur in Latin America. Nevertheless, two general propositions remain true. Formal education is, and always has been, restricted primarily to the upper classes; it is, and always has been, "Western."

Restratification

Westernization is also stimulated by changes in class structure. The most dramatic instance of this is social revolution. In Latin America, despite the frequency of its so-called "revolutions,"[18] only one state, Mexico, has experienced a true, thoroughgoing social revolution. This has indeed restratified Mexican society, multiplied the opportunities open to the Indians and *mestizos*, and hastened their Westernization. Economic development also brings about restratification and stimulates Westernization. Beyond these processes, class lines alter very slowly in Latin America, the reduction of the proportion of Indians and the increase of the proportion of *mestizos* and creoles or "whites" requiring several generations to make themselves felt.

Secularization

In Latin America, secularization takes two forms, both contributing to the process of Westernization. One is the release of the hold upon the Indians of their indigenous religious and traditional systems. The other is the reduction of the influence of the Roman Catholic Church. The first of these forms has been in process for a longer period of time than the second. In a sense, the secularization of the Indians began

[18] See Davis, ed., *op.cit.*, pp. 119-146.

with the arrival of the first Europeans, and it has continued with each succeeding generation. Although the process is by no means completed, it is well advanced, and there is every indication that it will persist.

The second form of secularization—the diminution of the influence of the Church—began more recently, roughly with the achievement of political independence from Europe early in the nineteenth century. This form of secularization is not as far advanced as the first. Mexico, where the Church was disestablished by the Revolution, is atypical of the area. Elsewhere, the power of the clergy is closely associated with large Indian populations and the persistence of quasi-feudal systems of land tenure. Where Indian civilization retreats and where land systems change—through agrarian reform programs, commercialization, and industrialization—the Church loses its hold. These trends are afoot everywhere in Latin America, at a rate that differs from country to country.[19]

Political Impact of Processes of Change

It may be well at this point to inquire into some of the political implications of the processes of change discussed in the foregoing pages. How do such developments as urbanization, restratification, secularization, commercialization, trends toward national unification, technical innovation, and movements in education affect political integration in Latin America? What is their impact upon such political functions as the recruitment of personnel, communication, articulation, political aggregation, rule-making, rule application, and rule adjudication?

Many of the processes of change influence the character of the patterns of *integration* in the area. Urbanization, for example, contributes to the development of common sets of political attitudes and experiences on the part of the people who live in the growing cities of Latin America. Although in some instances urbanization aggravates political conflict between large municipal centers and rural areas—as in Cuba, Uruguay, and Argentina—the over-all effect of the movement to the cities is integrative, and Westernizing, so far as the urban folk are concerned. Restratification—changes in class structures—also produces an integrative result. The impressive social distances separating the "white," *mestizo*, and Indian groups from each other have already been noted. In the countries where these class systems are rigidly maintained, each of their components is in a sense a separate world. Where the class systems

---

[19] See J. Lloyd Mecham, *Church and State in Latin America*, Chapel Hill, N.C., 1934, *passim*.

change, greater contacts among the groups may occur, and they may be expected to share more political experiences. Secularization, whether it takes the form of the detribalization of the Indian or the relaxation of the hold of the Church, likewise encourages greater social mobility. Two aspects of this should be noted, one internal and the other external. Secularization within a Latin American country facilitates expanded interaction between Indians and non-Indians, and between Catholics and non-Catholics. Externally considered, secularization hastens the assimilation into Latin American life of newly arrived immigrants. Both aspects, of course, have largely integrative consequences. Further, the growing rate of commercialization not only feeds upon urbanization, restratification, and secularization, but also, in multiplying the business for the transaction of which the previously separated sectors of society find frequent contact with each other indispensable, is significantly integrative in itself. As noted elsewhere in this chapter, technological change also exercises a similar influence, particularly insofar as it accompanies urbanization and tends to accelerate such processes as secularization and commercialization. Finally, these processes, largely Westernizing in their effects, are acquiring some of the necessary elements of an intellectual undergirding through developments in education, which in Latin America has always been, and continues to be, "Western."

With respect to the *recruitment* of new personnel into politics, it should be remembered that, in traditional society in the area, careers in government and politics are a species of monopoly of the "whites" or creoles, being generally closed to *mestizos* and Indians. As has been pointed out, it is possible for Indians to become *mestizos*, and *mestizos* to become "whites." This interclass mobility occurs where populations become literate, move to the cities, and become property owners. Many of the processes discussed here have the effect of manufacturing new "whites." Under the rules of the class systems of the area, an urbanized, restratified, secularized, commercialized, skilled, and literate Indian is entirely acceptable in any Latin American country as a completely pedigreed "white." Insofar as the "whites" enjoy a virtual monopoly of political power and activity in these societies, to manufacture new "whites" is to render them eligible for recruitment into politics. In essence, these processes, by increasing the percentage of the population classed as "whites," make possible the selection of political actors from a broader sector of the society than where the "white" group remains proportionately small.

Moreover, these changes have had dramatic effects upon the Latin

American patterns of *communication*. Nowhere is this more sharply clear than in the case of urbanization. Historically, the area has been divided along urban versus rural lines. The former have been European-oriented and "Western"; the latter, indigenous and "non-Western." In the classic formulation of Domingo Faustino Sarmiento, Latin America's Benjamin Franklin, the difference between urban and rural life has been the difference between civilization and barbarism. The basic environment which has prevented the spread of Westernization in rural Latin America has been physical isolation, fostered by impressive barriers to transportation and communication. Urbanization supplants this isolation with a communication network carrying implications for greater involvement in the national political life.

Restratification, of course, weakens the barriers between classes and opens the possibility of greater communication and other forms of interaction among them. Secularization opens a previously tradition-bound people to contacts with other cultures and other traditions. Commercialization and technical innovation render continued isolation economically unfeasible and place material values on the establishment of broader communication networks. Finally, the spread of education facilitates the development of the mass media of communication.

Further, these processes of change have implications for the patterns of *interest articulation*. It is typical of Latin America that, with the exception of the landowners and the Church, few interests arising in the rural areas are capable of making themselves heard in national politics. In the cities, however, interest groups form more readily and give voice to the demands of urbanized sectors of the population. Similarly, new interests find organized expression in consequence of the processes of restratification, secularization, and commercialization.

These processes affect not only the articulation but also the *aggregation of interests*. In traditional Latin American society there is a tendency for each interest group—often with little voice—to fend for itself. With the movement to the cities, however, and with the changing of class structure, previously isolated interests more readily make common cause, joining together to form larger groups with more effective roles in political life. Similarly, secularization, commercialization, and technological change contribute to the formation of larger communities of interest.

Urbanization and the changing of class structure also exert influences upon problems of *rule-making*. Not only does it become necessary to state in the form of explicit policy and law what was once unwritten custom and tradition, but also the processes of change create a host of new questions about which rules must be made. Secularization frees man from the laws of his indigenous community and of the Church to place him before still another law-giver; the rise of commerce and new techniques of production expands the range of problems demanding regulation and statements of public policy.

The function of *rule application* is similarly affected. One of the more notorious political problems of Latin America is the great number of laws which are "on the books" but unenforced. This condition stems in part from colonial origins, when Spain treated her colonies as a collection of cities and regulated them to the comparative neglect of rural areas. Today it remains generally true that there is more actual enforcement of the laws in the urban centers than beyond their limits. Where the rules are differentially enforced in different classes—and this is generally the case in the area—restratification will encourage more equal application of the laws. Secularization, weakening the force of custom and tradition as law, and reducing the role of ecclesiastical regulation, renders larger sectors of the various countries subject to the actual implementation of the laws emanating from constituted political authority. Economic changes such as commercialization and technological development tend to create new problems for which rules must be devised and to which they must be applied.

Rule adjudication is likewise affected by the processes of change. Class bias in adjudication has been so widespread in Latin America for so long that in many of the countries it has come to be accepted as one of the more common facts of life. "The Indian knows about the judicial function if he or his friends have ever been haled into court," it has been noted. "The judiciary is where 'the law' is; the courts dispense justice. 'Justice' is a word which means that the Indian always loses."[20] The movement to the cities and the altering of class lines point to the expansion of adjudicatory situations in which fewer Latin Americans "always lose" on class grounds. Differentiated organs of the state set up for the purpose of adjudication acquire larger roles, as secularization and economic development deliver to civil tribunals much of the work once done on a traditional and undifferentiated basis. The expansion of Westernized education should include among its consequences the giving of ideological content to "justice" as dispensed by the adjudicators.

[20] George I. Blanksten, *Ecuador: Constitutions and Caudillos*, Berkeley, California, 1951, p. 142.

In short, the processes of change bring with them implications of far-reaching revolution in Latin America. All of these processes do not move at the same rate or in the same combination in all of the countries of the area; but the extent to which they are under way is the extent to which the Americas are in a period of political transition of a basic and fundamental nature.

III. POLITICAL GROUPS AND POLITICAL FUNCTIONS

Political Groups

(1) *Parties and party systems.* Among the objects of fairly general interest to political scientists, Latin American political parties are outstanding in that very little research has been done on them. Indeed, only one Latin American party has been the subject of a full-scale monographic study.[21] "The field is one which needs a vast amount of spade work of a primary sort and on top of that additional synthesis in order to put the raw materials in proper arrangement and perspective," Fitzgibbon has said. "I commend the field of Latin American political parties to a whole generation of prospective graduate students in political science."[22]

Not only the political parties, but also the types of party systems, are many and varied in Latin America. It would therefore appear to be helpful at this point to attempt a rough classification of the area's political party systems. Although the existing literature of political science contains a number of fairly elaborate attempts at categorization, nothing more complicated seems necessary for the present purpose than a simple dichotomy distinguishing one-party systems from competitive party systems. Both types are to be found in Latin America.

(a) *One-party systems.* In this type of system, a single political party holds an effective monopoly of public power and controls access to government office. In some one-party systems, this may be provided for by law, in which case other political parties are considered illegal or subversive; in another type of one-party system, other parties may exist legally but—for reasons largely unrelated to legal questions or government coercion—find themselves unable to challenge effectively the dominant party's hold on public power.

[21] Harry Kantor, *The Ideology and Program of the Peruvian Aprista Movement,* Berkeley, California, 1953.

[22] Russell H. Fitzgibbon, "The Party Potpurri in Latin America," *Western Political Quarterly,* Vol. x, No. 1, March 1957, pp. 21-22. See also Federico G. Gil, "Responsible Parties in Latin America," *Journal of Politics,* Vol. xv, 1953, pp. 333-348.

Thus conceived, it is theoretically possible for three types of dominant political parties to hold power in one-party systems. One of these is the *comprehensive nationalist* party. Although such parties are common in many of the countries with non-Western political systems, the contemporary Latin American scene offers no instance of a comprehensive nationalist party in power. In large part, no doubt, this is due to the fact that such parties generally are found in emerging states—colonies struggling for political independence, or newly created states that have recently achieved it. Political independence is more than a century old in Latin America, and it is therefore likely that no political environment conducive to the rise of comprehensive nationalist parties exists in the Americas outside of the remaining colonies or dependencies, such as Puerto Rico and the British, Dutch, and French West Indies.

A second type of theoretically possible dominant party in a one-party system is the *dictatorial* party. This is found where two elements are present. First, an official attempt is made to obscure the distinction between the party in power and the government of the country, and to render opposition to the party virtually synonymous with treason against the state. Secondly, the party in power is the only legal party, all others being considered subversive. Party systems of this variety may be found in Latin America. The best current illustration is in the Dominican Republic. Such a system also operated in Venezuela. Paraguay's arrangement is a borderline case—other parties than the *Colorado* are theoretically legal, but the price of participating in them is frequently imprisonment or exile.

Finally, the group in power in a one-party system may be a *dominant non-dictatorial* party. In this situation, one party holds a monopoly of political power in the sense that it is victorious in virtually all elections, but other parties are legal and do exist. The "Solid South" in the United States might be offered as an example of this system. The leading Latin American case is in Mexico, where the Party of Revolutionary Institutions (PRI)[23] is without a serious rival. Other Mexican parties exist legally, but they exercise virtually no authority in government. Uruguay's system may also be included here, if one agrees with Fitzgibbon that it cannot be regarded as a two-party affair. Further, it has been noted that the situation in Paraguay's case is borderline—if one Para-

---

[23] *Partido Revolucionario Institucional.* This translates as "Institutional Revolutionary Party"; "Party of Revolutionary Institutions" is a more intelligible, though freer, translation.

guayan foot is in the dictatorial party camp, the other is in the dominant non-dictatorial party.

(b) *Competitive party systems.* These exist where two or more parties, none of them a dominant or "official" organization, contend among themselves. In general, there are two types of competitive systems: multiparty and two-party systems.

A multiparty system may be defined as containing three or more major political parties, normally making it impossible for any one of them to command a majority of the seats in a representative assembly. Politics in these systems frequently operates through coalitions or blocs involving two or more parties, and such arrangements are designed to produce working majorities. Latin America's best illustration of a multiparty system is found in Chile, where there are at least six major political parties, none of which controls a legislative majority. The multiparty arrangement also exists in Argentina, Bolivia, Brazil, Costa Rica, Cuba, Guatemala, Panama, and Peru.

Two-party systems contain two major political parties sufficiently matched in strength to permit their alternation in power. "Third" or "minor" parties are legal in these systems, but are rarely serious rivals of the two major parties at the polls. Thus conceived, two-party systems are rare in Latin America: indeed, they are rare outside the English-speaking world. The best Latin American illustration of a two-party system is to be found in Colombia, where the Conservative and Liberal parties, roughly evenly matched, have held power alternately. Uruguay also has two major political parties—the Colorados and the Blancos—but there is some question as to whether this is a clear case of a two-party system. Fitzgibbon, for example, believes that, since the Colorados have been victorious in all national elections since 1868, it cannot be said that Uruguay's is a true two-party arrangement.

Most of the major parties in the competitive systems of Latin America are what might be called "traditional" political parties. In general, they have two characteristics. First, the issues which concern them have troubled Latin Americans as long-range political problems of their respective countries. Primarily, these issues have involved questions of land tenure and the temporal role which should be exercised by the Roman Catholic Church. Second, the traditional parties draw their membership, in terms of the class systems of Latin America, primarily from the upper class, with *mestizos* and Indians virtually excluded from direct participation in these parties. Roughly speaking, the traditional ideological parties may be branded as conservative or liberal. Conservative parties generally defend the interests of the large landowners and advocate an expanded temporal role of the Church, sometimes including union of Church and State. Such parties have been in power in most of the countries of Latin America during most of the years of their national history. Representative Conservative parties include the Conservative Party of Argentina, the Conservatives of Colombia, the Conservative Party of Ecuador, the Blanco Party of Uruguay, and COPEI of Venezuela. Liberal parties, on the other hand, have generally advocated some species of land reform, separation of Church and State, and a general reduction in the temporal influence of the Church. Representative liberal parties are the Radical Party of Argentina, the Radicals of Chile, the Liberals of Colombia, the Radical-Liberal Party of Ecuador, and the Colorados of Uruguay.

The parties which participate in the competitive systems of Latin America may be classed as pragmatic, ideological, and particularistic. *Pragmatic* parties are those which make no major ideological or philosophical demands upon their membership. Such parties are far more interested in commanding the votes than the minds of their followers, who may enter or leave them without undergoing the trauma of ideological, philosophical, or religious conversion.

Pragmatic parties may be broad- or narrow-based, depending on how large a sector of the politically articulate population is appealed to by the group. Perhaps Latin America's best illustrations of the broad-based pragmatic party are the Argentine Radical Party (UCR)[24] and the Chilean Radical Party. The UCR has endeavored, with some success, to appeal for the electoral support of organized labor, commercial and industrial interests, associations of university students, and professional and intellectual organizations. Indeed, under the leadership of Arturo Frondizi in the presidential election of 1958, the UCR, which had bitterly fought the Perón dictatorship (1946-1955), successfully campaigned for the votes of those who had formerly supported Perón! In Chile, the Radical Party has joined together university students, labor organizations, teachers' associations, and the smaller commercial and industrial interests.

Narrow-based pragmatic parties are more numerous in the area. In general, these are of two types—personalistic and *ad hoc* parties. Personalistic parties are an outgrowth of *personalismo*, a long-standing ingredient of Latin American politics. *Personalismo* may be defined as the tendency to follow or oppose a political leader on the basis of his

[24] Unión Cívica Radical (Radical Civic Union).

personality rather than on ideological grounds—to be swayed by personal, individual, and family motivations rather than by an impersonal political idea or program. This historic attribute of the politics of the area has been noted by many students of Latin America. Pierson and Gil, for example, point to "the high value placed on the individual and personal leadership," promoting "a disposition to vote for the man rather than the party or the platform."[25] Another student has said: "From earliest days the Latin Americans . . . have always been more interested in their public men than in their public policies. They have tended to follow colorful leaders, to the subordination of issues. . . . A picturesque demagogue is virtually assured a large following."[25]

Latin Americans like to say—and this exaggerates the situation—that "Every 'ism' is a somebody-ism." Personalist parties are "Somebody-ist" groups organized in support of the political ambitions of strong personal leaders. Paraguay has its Franquista Party, composed of the followers of General Rafael Franco;[27] Brazil had a Querimista[28] Party; Ecuador a Velasquista organization, made up of the followers of Dr. José María Velasco Ibarra; and Uruguay a Batllista "faction," founded by the nineteenth-century statesman, José Batlle y Ordóñez.[29] There is some evidence that personalist parties are currently declining in number and influence in Latin America.

Finally, there are *ad hoc* parties. These are fluid organizations created to achieve short-range political objectives and disappearing when these ends have been accomplished or defeated. These parties are particularly important in the politics of Bolivia, Ecuador, and Paraguay. "In these times," a Bolivian wrote in 1942, "nothing is simpler than to found a political party. To form a political party only three people and one object are necessary: a president, a vice-president, a secretary, and a rubber stamp. The party can get along even without the vice-president and the secretary. . . . There have been cases in which the existence of only the rubber stamp has been sufficient."[30] Parties of this type are especially important in times of political instability and so-

[25] Pierson and Gil, *op.cit.*, p. 31.
[26] Austin F. Macdonald, *Latin American Politics and Government*, 2nd ed., New York, 1954, p. 2.
[27] Not connected with Spain's General Francisco Franco.
[28] Literally, "We-wantist," a popular abbreviation of "We want Vargas."
[29] Argentina's Peronista Party, the followers of General Juan Domingo Perón, is not a clear illustration of a personalist party, as the Peronistas had more of an ideological base than is usual with personalist parties. See Blanksten, *Perón's Argentina*, pp. 276-356.
[30] Luis Terán Gómez, *Los Partidos Políticos y su Acción Democrática*, La Paz, 1942, pp. 60-61.

called "revolution"—which are not infrequent in a number of the countries of Latin America.

Ideological parties are also to be counted among the actors in the competitive party systems of the area. Communist parties, for example, exist throughout the Americas. The most important Communist organizations are in Argentina; Bolivia, where the party has long been known as the Leftist Revolutionary Party (PIR);[31] Brazil; Chile; Cuba; Guatemala; and Mexico, where the group is called the Popular Party. Although the Mexican party system is not a competitive one, the Mexican Communists are nevertheless worth mentioning here. Despite indications that the party is small and weak from the standpoint of influence upon domestic politics in Mexico, the Communist organization in that country does perform a noteworthy international function in serving as a point of liaison, and as an informational clearing-house, between European Communists and those of Central America and the Caribbean islands. Meetings of the Communist leaders of the smaller countries of Middle America are occasionally held in Mexico.[32]

Also, Socialist parties exist in virtually all the countries of Latin America. The membership of these parties is generally dominated by middle-class intellectuals with a strong interest in Marxism. Despite their avowed interest in the problems of the working classes, the Socialists of Latin America have, in fact, developed little genuine influence over the masses. In country after country, the Socialists "have become increasingly doctrinaire, academic, and intellectualized."[33] Ray Josephs once remarked that "the socialist weakness lies in addiction to theory and philosophy and what we might call their lack of practical, sound common sense."[34] It need hardly be added that Socialists have never been in power for any appreciable length of time in any country of Latin America.

A number of Church-oriented parties are to be found in the area, and these may also be regarded as largely ideological. The best current illustrations are the Conservative parties of Colombia and Ecuador. Heavily Catholic in doctrinal orientation, Church parties have participated in most of the competitive systems of Latin America during the past century. Not since the regime of Gabriel García Moreno in Ecuador (1859-1875) has a Church group been the dominant party

[31] Partido Izquierdista Revolucionario.
[32] See Robert J. Alexander, *Communism in Latin America*, New Brunswick, N.J., 1957.
[33] Fitzgibbon, *op.cit.*, p. 13.
[34] Ray Josephs, *Argentine Diary*, New York, 1944, p. xxxiii.

in a one-party system. In that case, religious intolerance was revived; only practicing Catholics were permitted to be citizens of the country, then called the "Republic of the Sacred Heart"; and government was heavily authoritarian in character.[35]

Nationalist groups also exist among the ideological parties of Latin America. It should be noted that, while many nationalist groups are to be found in the area, none of them currently is of the comprehensive type. The typical Latin American nationalist party is narrow-based, addressing a concerted appeal to a small sector of society. Indeed, it is not unusual for two or more small nationalist parties to function as rivals in the same country. While anti-clerical nationalists are not unheard of—one such group once effectively employed "We are Ecuadorans, not Romans!" as its slogan—the nationalist parties more frequently embrace the Church, demand religious intolerance, oppose secularization, and attempt to eradicate foreign influence in the countries in which they operate. Often such parties are active centers of anti-Semitism. In recent times, the most important nationalist parties of Latin America—all of them narrow-based rather than comprehensive—have operated in Argentina, Bolivia, Paraguay, and Venezuela.

The area also has its share of Fascist parties. With respect to many of these, "Fascist-like" or "quasi-Fascist" would probably be a better designation, since these parties generally combine selected elements of Fascist ideology with enough indigenous Latin American ingredients to render the organizations difficult to equate with European Fascist parties. During World War II most of such organizations in Latin America pursued pro-Axis foreign policy objectives. Representative parties of this type are the Peronista Party of Argentina, the Nationalist Revolutionary Movement (MNR)[36] of Bolivia, the Integralist Party of Brazil, the Nacista Party of Chile, and the National Sinarquist Union of Mexico.

Also occupying a significant place on the roster of the area's ideological parties are those comprising the agrarian-populistic group. In Latin America, these have come to be called Aprista parties. They have two distinguishing characteristics. First, they seek far-reaching social and economic change, usually including radical land reform and the integration of the lower classes into the political process. Indeed, there is a greater percentage of lower-class adherents in the membership of

[35] See Richard Pattee, *Gabriel García Moreno y el Ecuador de su Tiempo*, Mexico City, 1944, *passim*.
[36] Movimiento Nacionalista Revolucionario.

Aprista groups than in any other type of Latin American party. Second, Aprismo is indigenous to the area. Such international connections as the movement has—and they are not many—are entirely within Latin America. The chief prototype of this class of political party is the celebrated Aprista Party, or APRA,[37] of Peru.[38] Other Aprista parties include Acción Democrática of Venezuela, the Auténtico Party of Cuba, the National Liberation Party of Costa Rica, and, in a sense, Mexico's PRI.[39]

Particularistic parties have on occasion appeared in the competitive systems of Latin America, although there is no clear illustration of a particularistic party operating in the area today. Such organizations, concerned in a separatist fashion with selected ethnic groups or regions and including some form of secession among their statements of political objectives, have from time to time filled major roles in the Americas. Indeed, this is one of the reasons why what were once only eight Spanish colonies are now eighteen independent states. In the past, particularist parties have been led by such personalities as General José Antonio Páez, who directed the secession of Venezuela from Gran Colombia; General Juan José Flores, who presided over the similar secession of Ecuador; and Dr. Amador, prominent in the detachment of the isthmus of Panama from Colombia. Particularistic parties were also active in the reduction of the former Central American Confederation to its present five separate heirs. So far as the contemporary scene is concerned, no major particularistic parties are functioning in the area, although there are significant instances of the presence of some of the ingredients of which such groups may be fashioned. In Brazil, for example, the two states of São Paulo and Minas Gerais, which had stubbornly opposed the regimes of President Getúlio Vargas (1930-1945, 1951-1954), have fallen into a political collaboration against the rest of the country which approximates particularism. Again, in the countries where regionalism is a major political force—such as Peru, Ecuador, and Bolivia—there is a tendency for political parties to become regionally based. It is therefore apparent that, whereas no clearly particularistic party is active in Latin America today, the record of the past and the current scene combine to suggest the reappearance of such organizations in the area from time to time in the future.

[37] Alianza Popular Revolucionario Americana (American Popular Revolutionary Alliance).
[38] See Kantor, *op.cit.*
[39] See Robert J. Alexander, "The Latin-American *Aprista* Parties," *Political Quarterly*, Vol. xx, 1949, pp. 236-247.

(2) *Ideological movements.* Since the 1820's, when most of Latin America achieved its independence of Europe, an impressively wide variety of political ideas and philosophical systems has found adherents in the area. So many of these ideological movements have, at one time or another, enjoyed strongly organized support—often by groups which have come to power and attempted to implement the ideologies—that it may well be true that the governments of Latin America have experimented with a wider range of ideological systems than has any other area of the world. "In America," a recent Ecuadoran President has said, "there exist almost all formulae and systems."[40]

It is important to bear in mind, in assessing the roles of ideological systems in Latin America, that the area is characterized by high illiteracy rates, and that literacy in general is a species of monopoly held by the upper class. The effect of systems of ideas is felt primarily by the literate; and, in a major sense, the ideological movements discussed here have been largely localized among the "white" or creole groups, with *mestizos* and Indians participating at best in only a peripheral and narrowly limited fashion. The political implications of this are, of course, worthy of exploration, and an attempt at such analysis is made at a later point in this chapter. However, it is worth mentioning at this juncture that the lower classes—in some of the countries, the majority of the population—are largely innocent of the doctrinal bases of the ideological movements discussed here.

Authoritarian political doctrines are among the most deeply entrenched in Latin America. It is literally true that these were the first Western ideas brought to the area by the Spaniards, the Portuguese, and the French. Authoritarianism was assiduously cultivated throughout the colonial period, and its mark is to be found on many aspects of contemporary Latin American life. Two institutions prominent in the colonial era did much to cultivate authoritarian thought. One of these was the Church, which, it must be remembered, was an arm of colonial government. Introducing education in the colonies and remaining to dominate it, the Church has fostered heavily authoritarian thinking in the area. Where this institution has been active in politics, it has stressed the preservation of the notion that authority should not be challenged. In a political campaign speech, a Catholic priest running

---

[40] "Almost all," he added, "are men in regimentation." José María Velasco Ibarra, *Conciencia o Barbarie*, Buenos Aires, 1938, p. 15.

for office in twentieth-century Latin America declared: "You must shut your mouths because Jesus Christ Himself was a great dictator."[41]

A second institution sponsoring authoritarian thought in the colonial period was government. Until the French Revolution, Spain, Portugal, and France were absolute monarchies. In preaching the desirability of loyalty to the mother countries on the part of the Latin American colonists, these governments indoctrinated their subjects with the authoritarian theory of the divine right of kings. So thoroughly was this done that when the independence movements were launched early in the nineteenth century, many of the leaders of these movements believed that monarchy should be retained as the basic governmental form of the newly independent states of Latin America.

An insight into the role that authoritarian political thought had acquired in the area by the time of the independence movements may be gained from the ideas of General Simón Bolívar, regarded in much of South America as the father of independence from Spain. "I have never been an enemy of monarchy, as far as general principles are concerned," Bolívar said. "On the contrary, I consider monarchies essential for the respectability and well-being of new nations. . . . The new states of America . . . need kings with the name of presidents."[42] In the famous Constitution of 1826, which he wrote for the emerging Republic of Bolivia, Bolívar made provision for a president with not only lifelong tenure but also the authority to choose his successor. "The President of the Republic becomes in our constitution the sun, which, firm in the center, gives life to the universe," said Bolívar. "This supreme authority should be perpetual. . . . A life-term President with the power of naming his successor is the most sublime addition to the republican system."[43]

Thus authoritarian thought not only flourished throughout the colonial period in Latin America, but was also an active ingredient of the independence movements and the creation of the new American nations in the nineteenth century. Indeed, upon the achievement of independence, three of the countries—Mexico, Haiti, and Brazil—openly adopted

[41] Padre Virgilio M. Filippo, quoted in Associated Press dispatch, October 7, 1943. See also Filippo, *El Plan Quinquenal Perón y los Communistas*, Buenos Aires, 1948, *passim.*

[42] See Victor Andrés Belaunde, *Bolívar and the Political Thought of the Spanish American Revolution*, Baltimore, 1938, pp. 243, 244, 246, and 283. See also Vicente Lecuna, *Cartas del Libertador*, New York, 1948, Vol. XI, pp. 44, 50-51, 189, 222-223, and 267; and Pío Jaramillo Alvarado, *El Régimen Totalitario en América*, Guayaquil, 1940, p. 107.

[43] Belaunde, *op.cit.*, pp. 243-246.

monarchy as their system of government. While this failed in Mexico and Haiti, the monarchical period in Brazil (1822-1889), particularly the remarkable reign of the celebrated Emperor Dom Pedro II (1831-1889), is still widely regarded by that country's historians as Brazil's "Golden Age."

Today no Latin American country is governed by monarchy, and nowhere in the area is there a major political group seriously advocating the restoration of the monarchical system. Authoritarianism, however, remains very much alive as an ideological movement in the Americas. Dictatorships (monarchies in republican dress) and dictators ("kings with the name of presidents") are to be found throughout Latin America. Many political groups, ranging from the Church and, in some countries, military organizations, to such political parties as the Peronistas of Argentina, the Integralistas of Brazil, the Conservative parties of Colombia and Ecuador, and the Sinarquistas and PAN[44] of Mexico, retain some measure of authoritarianism in their doctrinal bases.

It may well be that a major point of contrast between Latin America and the areas discussed in the other chapters of this volume lies in the ideological circumstances under which political independence from Europe was achieved. Independence from Spain was not so much a consequence of popular revolutionary movements in the American colonies as it was of the pattern of international politics during the first quarter of the nineteenth century. "The independence of the Latin American nations," two recent students have pointed out, "was precipitated prematurely by events in Europe."[45] During the course of the Napoleonic Wars, both Spain and Portugal were defeated and occupied by France. Napoleon Bonaparte's brother, Joseph, was named King of Spain by the invading forces, and promptly dubbed the "Intruder King" by the resentful and rebellious Spaniards. Rebellion, when it came in Latin America, was initially directed not so much against the old system of empire as against Bonapartist attempts to exercise authority over it. Indeed, some of the independence movements in Hispanic America specifically expressed ideological rejection of the principles of the French Revolution. The text of one of the first Latin American declarations of independence, for example, proclaimed defiance of the "Intruder King" and the desire of the rebels to restore a system of government

[44] Partito Acción Nacional (Party of National Action).
[45] Donald E. Worcester and Wendell G. Schaeffer, *The Growth and Culture of Latin America*, New York, 1956, p. 423.

"in conformity with the very principles of the ancient and wise constitution of Spain."[46]

Nevertheless, some of the ideas of the French Revolution did find their way to receptive Latin American ears to become the basis for ideological movements opposed to the authoritarianism which had long dominated the political thought of the area. It is of some significance that political independence came to most of Latin America during a fifty-year period—1775 to 1825—which also witnessed both the North American and the French revolutions. This was an era in the history of political thought which endowed the revolutionary movements of the time with a species of ideological commonality. Among the elements of this rubric were the rejection of divine-right monarchy and its replacement by a dedication to the principles of constitutionalism and constitutional government; a redefinition of the relationship between Church and State, which in the United States took the form of separation of the two, but in France and in much of Latin America was expressed in terms of a strong political anticlericalism; and a belief in some philosophical formulations of the rights of man, as well as acceptance of a number of principles of democracy. The Latin American ideological movements committed to this orientation are by no means dead so far as the twentieth-century scene is concerned. They are represented by such contemporary political parties as the Radicals of Argentina, the Radical Party of Chile, the Liberal Party of Colombia, the Radical-Liberal Party of Ecuador, and the Colorado Party—particularly its Batllista wing—of Uruguay. Moreover, most of the written constitutions currently in force in Latin America reflect this ideological orientation.[47]

Ideological life in Latin America has been characterized by an ambivalence between the extremes of authoritarian thought, still deeply embedded in the area, and the ideological bases of democracy and constitutional government, which, after all, provided the foundations upon which the independent states of the area were erected. This ambivalence has taken a number of forms. The most common of them is an eclecticism, which may appear curious to the North American, in which elements of authoritarianism and constitutionalism—often logically incompatible with each other—are combined in a single sys-

[46] Pierson and Gil, *op.cit.*, p. 88.
[47] The reader may wish to consult William Rex Crawford, *A Century of Latin American Thought*, Cambridge, Mass., 1944; José Luis Romero, *Las Ideas Políticas en Argentina*, Mexico City, 1946; Ricardo Donoso, *Las Ideas Políticas en Chile*, Mexico City, 1946; and William H. Calcott, *Liberalism in Mexico*, London, 1931.

tem. Thus a strong dictator may preside over an arrangement equipped with a democratically oriented written constitution; a small landowning oligarchy may rule a state while vigorously proclaiming the rights of man; and Church and State may be united in a system espousing some philosophical elements of the French Revolution.

New ideological ingredients have been introduced into Latin America in more recent times, particularly during the late nineteenth and early twentieth centuries. Marxism is among the most significant of these. Socialism came to the area in the 1890's. Socialist parties remain active in most of the countries, particularly in Argentina, Chile, Ecuador, and Uruguay. In general, the Socialists have been noteworthy for their participation in programs directed toward land reform, the emergence of a labor movement, and an accelerated rate of secularization. Communism, another ideological child of Marxism, also has its organized adherents in the area. The most important Communist parties are to be found in Argentina, Brazil, Chile, Colombia, Cuba, Guatemala, and Uruguay. Finally, Fascism, introduced into Latin America in the 1930's, has also produced ideological movements there—notably the nationalist organizations which were embraced by the Peronistas in Argentina, the Integralistas of Brazil, and the Sinarquista and PAN of Mexico.

The Latin American tendency toward ideological eclecticism—combining elements of diverse philosophical systems to form a new unit—has contributed to two types of phenomena in the area. The first of these involves native ideological movements which contain ingredients borrowed from the sources discussed above. Many of these movements, for example, have taken some elements of Marxism, joined them with ingredients indigenous to Latin America, and produced ideological systems that have often acquired great political strength. The two leading illustrations of this in contemporary Latin America are the Apristas of Peru and the PRI of Mexico. Thus, the ideological base of Aprismo is essentially a mixture of the nationalism of the indigenous Peruvian Indian, the anticlericalism of the French Revolution, and a demand for land reform and a resistance to imperialism stemming from Marxism. Similarly, the doctrine of the Mexican PRI is compounded of Indian nationalism, eighteenth-century French anticlericalism, and those elements of Marxism contributing to land reform, a strong interest in the development of a labor movement, and opposition to imperialism.

A second Latin American phenomenon encouraged by the tendency toward eclecticism is the development of spurious ideological movements. These borrow small fragments—often only slogans—of established systems of ideas and incorporate them into new movements. It is characteristic of the spurious phenomenon—and this is what distinguishes it from the native ideological movement—that it is a superficial borrowing of the vocabulary and slogans, rather than the ideas, of diverse philosophies; in the typical spurious system there is little or no consistent political thought. Essentially a political tool, the spurious ideology is often "used by a leader in order to enlist greater obedience among his followers or to obtain new otherwise inaccessible recruits, but the leader does not himself believe in the ideology propagated by him, unless this happens unbeknownst to himself—having repeated the same words once too often, he finally believes in them."[48]

Regardless of their logical and philosophical indefensibility, spurious ideologies have been of growing importance in Latin America, and movements of this type have seized power in a number of the countries of the area. Two such movements—both of which came to national power—may be cited here. The first of them, called "sociocracy," supported the dictatorship of Getúlio Vargas during Brazil's *Estado Novo*. Consider the diversity of the sources of sociocratic slogans: "In the great French shock of 1789, the bourgeoisie . . . called itself the people and its regime democracy. . . . This . . . system . . . ought to be called 'bourgeoicracy.' . . . Awaken, proletariat! This is a snare for a return to the past, when your aspirations were matters for the police. Awaken, capitalists! You cannot wish to return to the reign of strikes and revolutions. . . . Democracy, middle-class rule, and selfishness are synonyms. Sociocracy is altruism; it is living for others."[49] A second spurious ideology, called *Justicialismo*, developed in Argentina in 1949 in support of the Perón regime, which endured until 1955. The diverse and mutually incompatible sources of *Justicialismo* are revealed by this partial list of its slogans: "Dignification of Labor," "Elevation of Social Culture," "Humanization of Capital," "Faith in God," "Solidarity among Argentines." What was the ideology? As one famous answer had it: "*Justicialismo* is that doctrine before, during, and after which nothing happens."[50]

The growing importance of spurious ideological movements in Latin America has in some of the countries caused the leaders of the move-

[48] Robert Strausz-Hupé and Stefan T. Possony, *International Relations*, New York, 1950, p. 421.
[49] From an unpublished translation of the writings of Viriato Vargas, 1943.
[50] See Blanksten, *Perón's Argentina*, pp. 293 and 282.

ments from which the slogans are borrowed to take steps to halt this process. This endeavor has taken the form of what might be called new departures in political education, designed to encourage the followers of an ideological movement to engage in study of its ideas as well as its vocabulary and slogans, in the hope that more people would thus be better equipped to distinguish readily between genuine and spurious uses of the jargon of political ideas. Perhaps the leading exponent of this formula is Américo Ghioldi, chief of the Socialist Party of Argentina. Alarmed by the success with which Perón had used the vocabulary without the ideas of Marxism, Ghioldi turned his party to the task of keeping its terminology wedded firmly to its ideational base. What are the Marxist meanings of words like "capitalism" and "imperialism"? Do they mean that Socialists must shake their fists at the Yankees and the British? Not at all, according to Ghioldi: the Socialists must "not make a tabu and a street slogan of the word 'imperialism.' "[51] The terms must be precisely defined. It is Peronism, *Justicialismo*, and not Socialism, to pin the political label of "foreign imperialist" on the North Americans and the British. It is *Justicialismo*, and not Marxism, to hate the United States and the United Kingdom.[52] Such an educational endeavor, however laudable, is not likely to meet with large-scale success in Latin America. Spurious ideological movements remain a major potential force in the area's politics.

Another major point of contrast between Latin America and the areas discussed in the other chapters of this book involves the role of nationalism in ideological movements. Little has been said in this chapter about Latin American nationalism. It exists, to be sure; but this type of movement does not have as much, or the same kind of, significance in the Western Hemisphere as in other parts of the world. One reason for this contrast has already been suggested. In the so-called "non-Western" areas, nationalist movements frequently accompany struggles for political independence from colonial powers. Most of Latin America not only has been independent since the 1820's, but acquired that status more as an outcome of international politics than through internal movements within colonies fighting for national identification. In short, there was little if any functional role for nationalism to play in the achievement of Latin American independence. This consideration places the area in sharp contrast with such regions as Southeast Asia, the

---

[51] Américo Ghioldi, *Marxismo, Socialismo, Izquierdismo, Comunismo y la Realidad Argentina de Hoy*, Buenos Aires, 1950, p. 146.
[52] See Blanksten, *Perón's Argentina*, pp. 383-386.

Middle East, and Africa, where nationalism is integrally tied to independence movements.

Such nationalism as exists in Latin America is, essentially, addressed to other objectives. Latin American nationalist movements may be divided into two categories. The first is class-oriented. In the rigid class systems of the area, Indians form the lower class of many of the countries. In some of them—notably, in Peru and in pre-Revolutionary Mexico—what might be called nationalist movements have developed among the Indians and have been directed against the upper classes, particularly the "whites" or creoles. These have been nationalist movements in the sense that, in much of the area, the Indians participate in a culture differing significantly from that of the upper classes. Although occasionally of political consequence—witness Peru and Mexico—Indian nationalist movements more typically have made little headway, owing primarily to the particularistic nature of Indian society, with little political organization or communication existing among Indian communities.

A second form of Latin American nationalism resembles the European variety which was associated in the 1930's with Fascism and Nazism. This is a racist type of elitist doctrine, again geared to the class system. In this brand of nationalism, the people of the upper classes are urged to look upon their " 'white'-ness" or "creole-ness" as involving a form of racial purity, and to regard themselves as inherently superior to the Indians and other lower classes. Argentina is the Latin American country in which this brand of nationalism has been particularly significant as an ideological movement. There the nationalists joined with the army and the Church to produce the beginnings of Peronism. Indeed, such nationalism remains of high importance in Argentine politics. On balance, however, Latin American nationalism—even in Argentina—should not be assigned the same type or degree of significance that nationalist movements have acquired in areas like Southeast Asia, the Middle East, and Africa.

Two final points should be made regarding ideological movements in Latin America. In the first place, in recent times—especially since the 1930's—these movements have devoted increasing attention to the problems and aspirations of the lower classes. They have made growing appeals to the Indians, to organized labor, to the *descamisados* (literally, the "shirtless ones") and to the landless. These movements have, on an expanding scale, included among their demands shorter hours, higher wages, and other labor benefits, as well as social security programs and other measures designed for the benefit of the lower classes. This social welfare orientation has been held by three types of ideological movements, all of them relatively recent arrivals upon the Latin American scene. The first of these have been the Marxist movements, embracing Socialism and Communism; the second, the native ideological movements, such as the Apristas or the PRI of Mexico; and the third, the spurious ideological movements, such as those presided over by Vargas in Brazil and Perón in Argentina. To gauge trends in this field is not a simple task. It would appear that there is no fourth major type of Latin American ideological movement making appeals to the lower classes. Of the three types sharing a virtual monopoly in this field, the Marxist movements appear to be holding their own, the native movements to be diminishing in strength (except in Mexico), and the spurious movements to be growing in potential. If this be accepted as even a rough guide to the future, it may well help to locate an enlarging aspect of political instability in the area.

Finally, it should be remembered that Latin America is an area of high illiteracy rates, that the class distribution of literacy gives the upper class something of a monopoly of formal education, and that the ideological movements discussed here have centered on political ideas held by the "whites" or creoles, ideas of which the lower classes—in most of the countries, the overwhelming majority of the population—are essentially innocent. In many of the countries, the participants in, and even some of the leaders of, ideological movements are not schooled in the fundamentals of the doctrines around which their movements are centered. This writer has had a good deal of field experience in Latin America interviewing members and leaders of Church parties who do not know the Church's own political doctrine; Socialists and Communists who have not read Marx, or even about him, and cannot discuss Marxism; and Peronista party leaders ignorant of the elements of *Justicialismo*. Surely most political scientists who have worked in Latin America have had similar experiences. Two implications of this appear to be especially significant. In the first place, once politics reaches the realm of ideology in Latin America, it strengthens the hand of the upper classes. The phenomenon of upper-class leaders heading movements designed for the lower classes is not unknown, of course, and the Apristas and the PRI furnish good illustrations. But ideological movements are essentially upper-class movements, sometimes created *for*, but never *by*, the lower classes. Secondly, ideological movements in societies characterized by widespread illiteracy can easily be spurious. As already pointed out, this has often been the case in Latin America, and there is some indication that in the immediate future spurious ideological movements are likely to be of growing importance.

(3) *Anomic movements.* Various spontaneous activities, carried on outside the framework of established political institutions and channels, are sometimes significant in the politics of Latin America. The most publicized manifestation of this sort is the so-called "revolution." Others include demonstrations, riots, mob action, and political assassination.

Two major propositions should be stressed with respect to Latin American anomic movements. In the first place, they arise almost exclusively from politics among the "whites"—that is, within the upper class. Rarely indeed do Indians or *mestizos* become involved in these activities, and, when they do, it is only to enter an action already begun by the "whites." Indian uprisings are very infrequent. When they occur, they are sporadic, unorganized or badly organized, restricted to a small number of easily isolated communities or villages, and readily put down by the armed forces of the "whites." Thus the only anomic movements of any serious consequence in Latin American politics are those which have their origin in—and usually remain within the confines of—the upper class.

The second proposition involves a problem in perspective. Revolutions, riots, and assassinations are dramatic and exciting, and make good newspaper copy, especially if press photographers are fortunate enough to be upon the scene at the proper moment. Thus, anomic movements in Latin America are given so much publicity that they are frequently assigned distorted and disproportionately large roles in the politics of the area. In perspective these movements are not as crucial in the Americas as our newspapers would lead us to believe; indeed, most of the movements and processes discussed in other sections of this chapter—though less spectacular and less newsworthy—are of greater significance in Latin America.

Take, for example, the problem of revolution. The area is famous for its "revolutions." Indeed, the Brazilian Emperor Dom Pedro II is said to have remarked, when he visited the Philadelphia Exposition in 1876, that many of the Latin American countries had more revolutions per minute than the machines he saw on display at the exposition. However, few words are more loosely and promiscuously used in the area than "revolution." An amazing array of dissimilar and unrelated occurrences go by this name in Latin America. The Wars of Independence have been so dubbed, as well as minor changes in government, the promulgation of new constitutions, political violence of almost any variety—in Latin America, even revolutions are called "revolutions."

If the term is used precisely, true revolution—a basic change in the political system, a recasting of the social order—is surprisingly infrequent in Latin America. Indeed, revolutions are at least as rare there as anywhere else in the world, and probably less common in this area than in any of those discussed in the other chapters of this book. It may well be true that only one unquestionably real revolution has occurred in Latin America thus far in the twentieth century—the Mexican Revolution, which began in 1910.

Nevertheless, there is a type of anomic movement, popularly called a "revolution" although it is not a true one, which occurs often in Latin America and should be examined here. For present purposes let us refer to this phenomenon as the "typical Latin American revolution." This may be defined as a change in government brought about by other than constitutional means, but not accompanied by a fundamental change in the social or political order. Violence, or the threat of it, is often present in such a movement, but it is not essential to its definition. In the typical Latin American revolution, the changes are usually restricted to the replacement of the president and his immediate aides, with the basic political system remaining intact. Revolutions of this character are frequent in the area, sometimes occurring as often as four times in a single year. Basically, the typical Latin American revolution springs from two major conditions. The first relates to the nature of the written constitutions of the area. Fundamentally, these revolutions are violations of constitutions; in Latin America, these documents are peculiarly susceptible to defiance. Their texts tend to be normative or anticipatory —expressions of what the constitution-writers hope will eventually come to pass rather than of what is, or can be, actuality. The typical revolution is often merely a statement that tomorrow's ideals have not yet been achieved. Secondly, constitutional fragility in the area is aggravated by such divisive forces among the "whites" as *personalismo* and family rivalries, regionalism, and other conflicts of intra-class interests, sometimes translated into doctrinal and ideological terms. These conflicts are frequently sufficiently disruptive to give the *coup de grace* to a weak and unworkable constitution.[53] They are normally followed by the promulgation of a new—and equally weak and unworkable—constitution, with

[53] See Russell H. Fitzgibbon, "Constitutional Development in Latin America: A Synthesis," *American Political Science Review*, Vol. xxxix, No. 3, June 1945, pp. 517-518.

the political system, fundamentally unchanged, settling down to await its next "revolution."[54]

Since the 1930's the general strike has come to be a movement of growing importance in Latin America. Having more of an organizational base than the anomic movements discussed here, the general strike usually rests on labor unions and associations of university students, frequently acting in coalition. The general strike is especially important in Central America, where it has been a major factor in the overthrow of governments, particularly in Guatemala, El Salvador, and Honduras. Military dictators have found this type of movement, when employed by their opposition, peculiarly difficult to cope with. Indeed, General Maximiliano Hernández Martínez, whose government was overthrown through a general strike in El Salvador in 1944, said upon his arrival in his North American exile that he resigned the presidency because "I couldn't shoot everybody."

Demonstrations are among the more time-honored of anomic movements in Latin America. These, too, usually have at least something of an organizational base. Normally, demonstrations in the area occur in opposition to the regimes in power. However, demonstrations organized and directed by governments as instruments of their own support are not unknown. The clearest Latin American illustrations of the government-sponsored demonstration were found in Brazil's *Estado Novo* (1930-1945), where a bureau of a major government agency—the DIP[55] —had as its function the organization and conduct of pro-government demonstrations; and in Argentina during the Perón regime (1946-1955), where they were likewise carefully directed and administered by government agencies, despite President Perón's constant protestations that his demonstrations were "spontaneous." It should be stressed, however, that Latin American demonstrations are more typically instruments of opposition groups and, as such, are not as well-organized or controlled as the pro-government variety. A number of groups contribute to the opposition demonstrations. Communists sometimes participate in them, but it is easy to exaggerate the Communist role in Latin American demonstrations. Other opposition political parties are active in them, as is the Church when it finds itself opposed to a given regime, and as are labor unions and university students.

[54] See Russell H. Fitzgibbon, "Revolutions: Western Hemisphere," *South Atlantic Quarterly*, Vol. LV, July 1956, pp. 263-279; and George I. Blanksten, "Revolutions," and "Constitutions and the Structure of Power," in Davis, ed., *op.cit.*, pp. 119-146, and 225-251.

[55] Departamento de Imprense e Propaganda (Department of Press and Propaganda).

A long-established phenomenon, the opposition political demonstration has acquired a status of its own in Latin America. In general, it is respected. While governments often do what they can to prevent a demonstration from taking place, once it is underway it is normally permitted to run its course. Official attempts to break up demonstrations are rare, and persons who are arrested in connection with them are ordinarily released almost immediately, usually without even a reprimand. When demonstrations are successful, in the sense that they draw large sympathetic crowds, governments typically attempt to—or give the appearance of attempting to—meet the demonstrators' demands. It is the practice in much of Latin America to regard a successful demonstration as the voice of the people, and government officials seldom feel that they can ignore it safely.

Mob action and riots—more violent, having less of an organizational base, and less controlled or controllable than demonstrations—are unusual in Latin America. Indeed, they are far more uncommon in the area than any of the other anomic movements discussed here. Whereas it can be held that "revolutions," general strikes, demonstrations, and even political assassinations have an established or systematic place in the normal functioning of Latin American politics, this cannot be said of political rioting. When this occurs, it is symptomatic of a serious malfunctioning of the political system. Large-scale mob riots in Latin America are so rare that all of them which have occurred in the twentieth century can probably be counted on the fingers of one hand. The most noteworthy have been the 1911 rioting in Panama; the extreme violence accompanying the fall of the Bolivian government in July of 1946, when President Gualberto Villarroel's body was hanged from a lamppost at La Paz; and the celebrated *bogotazo*, which took place in Bogotá in April of 1948, when an estimated 5,000 Colombians were killed. All of these riots were characterized by a lack of organization and a serious breakdown in the normal functioning of the political system. In the case of the *bogotazo*, for example, Colombia's established political party system had begun to collapse in consequence of the unprecedented results of the presidential election of 1946; this breakdown was dramatized in 1948 by the assassination of the Liberal Party leader, Jorge Eliecer Gaitán, which touched off the *bogotazo*.[56] Thus mob action and riots, so far as Latin America is concerned, stand in a separate class from the other anomic movements discussed here. Unlike them, rioting does not

[56] See Vernon L. Fluharty, *Dance of the Millions*, Pittsburgh, 1957, *passim*, especially pp. 84-117.

recur more or less regularly. Certainly it would be an error to include riots among Latin American political styles. On the few occasions when they have occurred, they represented departures from the usual pattern of Latin American politics.

With respect to the role of political assassination in Latin American systems, four chief points should be emphasized. First, here again the problem of perspective becomes important. It is well to bear in mind the caveat that, while political assassinations do occur in Latin America, they neither happen every day nor are as significant as a number of less highly publicized Latin American processes.

Next, there are two countries in the area where political assassination has responded to forces and processes atypical of Latin America as a whole: Cuba and Mexico. In Cuba, especially during President Fulgencio Batista's first period in power (1933-1944),[57] assassination was frequent, but followed a peculiarly Cuban rather than a generally Latin American pattern. In that epoch, Cuban opposition political leaders were on occasion "taken for a ride" in a fashion reminiscent of Chicago gangster practices during the prohibition era, the bullet-ridden corpses of the victims being found some time after their disappearance. A partial explanation of this practice lies in Cuba's peculiar susceptibility to North American influences, including those emanating from the underworld, coupled with the circumstance that during the relevant period Cuba was in a condition of political transition, with older practices disintegrating and the system unusually receptive to experimentation with diverse new alternatives. In the Mexican case, political assassinations occurred relatively often during the 1910-1920 stage of the Revolution. That phase is known to Mexicans as *la tormenta*, which may be freely translated as the "time of trouble" or the "reign of terror." As has been pointed out above, the Mexican Revolution was one of the very few true revolutions to take place in modern Latin America. The violence of *la tormenta* responded far more to the process of revolution than to any property of Mexican or Latin American politics as such. As the extensive use of the guillotine and the violent fate of men like Robespierre arose from the nature of revolution rather than from French political culture, so the assassinations of Madero, Zapata, and other Mexican revolutionary leaders were the product of the revolutionary process and not of Mexican or Latin American political systems.[58]

[57] Batista returned to the presidency in 1952, and continued in office until 1959.
[58] See Crane Brinton, *The Anatomy of Revolution*, New York, 1938, *passim*; and Blanksten, "Revolutions," in Davis, ed., *op.cit.*, pp. 121-122, and 131-138.

Third, political assassination, like mob action and rioting in the area, is sometimes a symptom of the malfunctioning of a system or the breakdown of one or more of its component parts. In such instances the analysis is essentially the same as that advanced in the case of riots, and need not be repeated here. Illustrative of this form of political murder are the assassinations of Bolivian President Villarroel in 1946 and of the Colombian leader Gaitán in 1948.

Finally, assassination is sometimes a product of what we have called the "typical Latin American revolution." As pointed out above, violence, or the threat of it, is often present in such a movement. When this is the case, assassination is but one of the forms this violence takes. Legislative leaders and cabinet members are the victims of assassination in such "revolutions" more often than chief executives, but the latter are also fair game and sometimes fall. Among the more recent instances of this are the late General Anastasio Somoza and Colonel José Remón, Presidents of Nicaragua and Panama, respectively, both of whom were assassinated in 1956, and Colonel Carlos Castillo Armas, whose career as President of Guatemala was terminated by an assassin's bullet in the following year. It should be pointed out, however, that presidents who have been ousted from office normally are permitted to go into exile without suffering physical harm. Capital punishment does not exist legally in much of Latin America, where public opinion has reacted strongly against political assassination. Imprisonment and exile for political reasons are quite acceptable and generally practiced in the area, but the taking of lives in such causes is normally considered to be an infraction of the rules of the game.[59]

(4) *Interests and interest groups.* In the politics of the United States and of the United Kingdom, it is possible to draw a sharp distinction between political parties and political interest groups. In those "Western" countries, "political parties tend to be free of ideological rigidity, and are aggregative, that is, seek to form the largest possible interest group coalitions by offering acceptable choices of political personnel and public policy."[60] In those same countries, "interest groups articulate political demands in the society, seek support for these demands among

---

[59] This consideration was no doubt prominent among the factors underlying the widespread Latin American expressions of protest against the execution of about 500 suspected supporters of overthrown President Batista (who himself escaped) after the seizure of power in Cuba by Fidel Castro in 1959.

[60] Gabriel A. Almond, "A Comparative Study of Interest Groups and the Political Process," unpublished paper, Committee on Comparative Politics, Social Science Research Council, 1957, p. 20. See also Sigmund Neumann, *Modern Political Parties*, Chicago, 1956.

other groups by advocacy and bargaining, and attempt to transform these demands into authoritative public policy by influencing the choice of political personnel, and the various processes of public policy-making and enforcement."[61]

In Latin America—and, no doubt, in many of the so-called "non-Western" countries—this differentiation of functions cannot be drawn quite so sharply. Many Latin American political parties act as interest groups would in Western Europe, and interest groups in a number of the American republics approach the functions of European political parties. In short, in Latin America the functional line between parties and interest groups is hardly recognized, let alone observed.

Many of the interest groups in Latin America are of types similar to those found in Western Europe. Some, however, are of varieties which are rare there. What follows is not an exhaustive census of the groups of the area, but an attempt to indicate the major types of political interest groups of Latin America, with emphasis upon bases of comparison with those operating in the so-called "West."

(a) *Institutional interest groups.* One of the major political interest groups of Latin America is the *Roman Catholic Church*. Historically, Church and State were united in the Spanish tradition. This was true throughout the colonial period in Latin America; indeed, the movement for separation of Church and State may, in a sense, be regarded as a relatively recent development in the area. In most of the countries, the Church pursues political objectives, and in some of them its functions resemble those of a political party. Some Latin American political parties are essentially Church parties—as, for example, the Conservative parties of Colombia and Ecuador. Consider this statement of its *political* program by the Conservative Party of Ecuador: "Man is essentially a religious being and religion, consequently, is a natural phenomenon . . . . The end of man is God, whom he should serve and adore in order to enjoy after death the beatified possession of divinity. . . . The purpose of the state is to facilitate religious action so that its subjects will not lack the necessities of the spirit and will be able to obtain in the next life the happiness which can never be achieved in this."[62] The power of the Church as a political interest group varies, of course, from country to country. It is perhaps strongest in Ecuador and weakest in Mexico, but there is no Latin American state in which the Church is not

[61] Almond, *op.cit.*, pp. 19-20.
[62] Jacinto Jijón y Caamaño, *Política Conservadora*, Riobamba, 1934, Vol. I, pp. 26, 32.

to be counted as a major political group.[63] The Church, of course, has been studied from several points of view, but published assessments of it as an interest group are rare.

Similarly, there are few studies of the *armed forces*, particularly the armies, of Latin America as political groups, although militarism has long been recognized as a fundamental characteristic of Latin American politics. "The last step in a military career is the presidency of the republic" is a well-known and frequently practiced precept in the area. Rather than in the defense of the community, the basic function of the Latin American military lies in domestic politics. Everywhere high-ranking army officers are important politicians; everywhere the military provides a species of backdrop for politics. Generally this is more true of the army than of the other armed services, although in a few of the countries—notably Argentina[64] and Paraguay—the navy also operates as a significant political group. Political studies of the Latin American armed services are sorely needed. Questions especially requiring investigation include the process of political clique-formation among military and naval officers, and the relationship between militarism and the class system; certain military ranks—major, lieutenant colonel—appear to be of peculiarly critical political significance.

Few studies have been made of *bureaucracy* in Latin America and, consequently, little can be said of the roles of bureaucratic cliques, or of associations of public workers as interest groups. In some of the countries government work, like other types of occupations, is organized on the basis of part-time jobs. Moreover, few of the republics have developed effective merit systems of civil service, and a spoils system is generally characteristic of the area. These considerations would suggest patterns of action differing from what is to be found in Western Europe or the United States. Associations of government workers, of course, exist in Latin America, and may be regarded as interest groups. However, the current state of research on this problem does not permit evaluation at this time of the political significance of these organizations.

(b) *Non-associational interests*. Interests which are not formally or consciously organized as groups abound in Latin America, as they do in other areas of the world. For the most part, these coalesce around such symbols as class, status, ethnic groups, kinship and lineage, and regionalism.

[63] See Mecham, *op.cit.*
[64] See Blanksten, *Perón's Argentina*, pp. 314-316; and Arthur P. Whitaker, *Argentine Upheaval*, New York, 1956, *passim*.

Much has been said in the earlier pages of this chapter about the *class* systems of Latin America. These are fairly rigid in most of the countries of the area. Classes, of course, are not formally or consciously organized groups; yet significant political interests arise from them. Although the structure of the class system varies somewhat from country to country in Latin America, the typical class system is composed of three levels. The highest class is usually referred to as the creoles or "whites"; the middle group is known as the *mestizos* or, in some countries, *cholos*; and, in the countries with large Indian populations, the Indians have constituted the lowest class. The interests of the scholars who have examined these classes in Latin America have been such that they have devoted more attention to the creoles or "whites" and to the Indians than they have to the *mestizos* or *cholos*. Consequently, fewer data are available concerning the middle group than is the case with respect to the highest and lowest classes.

The highest class—creoles or "whites"—are the most politically articulate of the three, and, in most of the countries of the area the interests of the "whites" are the best protected and most adequately espoused. These interests involve such matters as the preservation of the system of land tenure, the wielding of control by the Church and the high military ranks, and the maintenance of a European rather than an indigenous cultural orientation. Where commercialization and industrialization have taken hold, these create new interests, primarily among the "whites." In some of the countries, this has a divisive effect upon "white" interests, which also include land ownership, sometimes held to be threatened by commercialization and industrialization. Conscious of themselves as the ruling group in most of the countries of the area, the "whites" share an interest in the avoidance of revolution and, in general, oppose political reforms believed to imperil their ruling position.

As has been said, less is known about the *mestizo* or *cholo* than about either of the other major classes in Latin America. A detribalized Indian but not yet a "white," the *mestizo* constitutes over 30 per cent of the population of some of the countries. He is not politically articulate, and rarely organizes. He is interested in working his way into the "white" group and, usually, in severing his ties with the Indians. He is frequently employed as an artisan or a tradesman. In some of the countries of the area, the *mestizos* are an important source of the labor supply. Given the paucity of available data about them, little more can be said here regarding their non-associational interests without making a major excursion into the realm of speculation.

As for the Indian, entire libraries have been written about him. Indian communities and villages are tightly organized, and the Indians feel strong loyalties to them, but the Indian class as a whole is not organized in any of the Latin American countries. In general, the Indians resist incursion upon their way of life by the "whites"; they want to be left alone. They seek decentralized, loosely organized, or inefficiently administered government, if by these terms is meant a system under which the number of "white" government officials entering the Indian communities bearing rules and regulations from the national capital is held to a minimum. Further, the Indians normally have a strong love for their villages and communities, and strongly resist resettlement programs involving relocation of the lower classes. Typically, the Indian does not own much, if any, land. Many writers have argued that in Latin America the Indian problem is basically a land problem, and have urged land reform programs which would deliver holdings to Indian ownership.[65] The Indians, however, have rarely expressed this sentiment themselves, and have been slow to respond to land redistribution programs on the few occasions when these have been adopted by governments. It should probably be added that the Indian is quite inarticulate politically, and rarely communicates his desires to the "white" officials of the governments which rule him. However, in recent times the Indian has acquired impressive experience and skill in communicating with North American anthropologists.

In addition to the question of class, interests also arise from the concept of *status*. This is especially important within the "white" group. In colonial times, the upper class was acrimoniously divided within itself, with the creoles (persons born in the colonies) pitted against the *peninsulares* (born in Europe) who enjoyed higher status. Indeed, this intra-class struggle was one of the factors giving alignment to some of the fighting during the Wars of Independence. Since then, the *peninsulares* have dropped from the Latin American class structure, but the concept of the "old families" or "good families" remains. These—when they can establish themselves as such—enjoy considerable prestige within the ruling class. Although the "whites" are at least as racially mixed as any other group in Latin American society, the "old families" are con-

[65] See, for example, José Carlos Mariátegui, *Siete Ensayos de Interpretación de la Realidad Peruana*, Lima, 1934; W. Stanley Rycroft, ed., *Indians of the High Andes*, New York, 1946; Eyler N. Simpson, *The Ejido: Mexico's Way Out*, Chapel Hill, N.C., 1937; Moisés Sáenz *Sobre el Indio Ecuatoriano*, Mexico City, 1933; Sáenz, *The Peruvian Indian*, Washington, D.C., 1944; and Sáenz, *The Indian: Citizen of America*, Washington, D.C., 1946.

stantly engaged in heraldic research designed to demonstrate their un-
mixed Spanish descent. To be accepted as an "old" or "good" family
is to be the aristocracy of the aristocracy. The families which have
achieved this enviable position have a strong interest in preserving those
elements of the system—particularly the older patterns of land tenure—
lending security to the prestige system, and in making it difficult for
other "new" families to become "old" and share the higher status.

Again, in view of the paucity of research on the *mestizo* or *cholo*
group, little can be said here of the prestige patterns within that class.
In general, however, the *mestizos* strive to become "whites," in order
to enjoy the benefits of higher status.

Status is at least as important among the Indians as it is among the
"whites." A significant difference, however, should be noted. Whereas
those who acquire high prestige among the "whites" enjoy it on a
national—and, in some cases, international—basis, status among the
Indians has meaning only on a local village or community level. As in
the case of the "whites," status among the Indians rests more on ascriptive than on achievement considerations. Village elders and their rela-
tives enjoy prestige, as do witch doctors and medicine men. To hold high
status in the Indian community is to exercise some power—frequently,
power of government—within it, and those who have this prestige are
interested in preserving it and preventing its adulteration.[66]

Non-associational interests also arise among some of the *ethnic groups*
in Latin America. For example, Negroes—numerous in the Caribbean
island republics, and in some parts of Brazil—have developed strong
interests on an unorganized basis. So, too, have a number of the European immigrant groups, notably the Italians, Germans, Spaniards, and
Jews. The roles of these groups in Latin American life are discussed at
another point in this chapter. It may be noted here, however, that the
European immigrant groups are normally more articulate than many of
the indigenous groups, particularly the Indians and *mestizos*, and that
they have developed interests that are usually directed toward the preservation of their social and economic positions in society, and often
toward the expansion or improvement of these positions.

Patterns of *kinship and lineage* also produce systems of non-associational interest in Latin America. This is especially true among the
"whites" and Indians, with the *mestizos* again, for the time being at
least, standing as an unknown quantity. Among the "whites," reference
has already been made to the "old" or "good" families. High values

[66] See Aníbal Buitrón and John Collier, *The Awakening Valley*, Chicago, 1950.

are assigned to being members of them or, if that is impossible, to being related to or connected with them. The extensive use made of letters of introduction among the "whites" and the exaggerated importance given to them have frequently reached the proportions of a joke. A letter of introduction from a well-known member of an established "good" family is, in many of the countries, indispensable to the candidate seeking employment or some other favor from government. "The Municipal Departments had become a perfect teeming house of *recomendados*— persons for whom jobs had been found whether jobs were to be had or not," an observer has said of politics among the "whites" in Argentina. "In the old days of the Municipal Council, it used to be a standing joke that business offices could be wallpapered with the notes of introduction given to job applicants by the Municipal Councillors."[67] Although this particular reference is to local government, the practice is general.

Three generalizations can be made regarding the role of kinship and lineage among the Indians of Latin America. First, they are of even more basic importance in this class than among the "whites" as determiners of interest. Next, in many Indian groups, kinship and lineage are more centrally and directly related to politics and government than is the case in the upper class. Finally, in contrast to the situation among the "whites," the political role of kinship and lineage is confined primarily to the level of village and community, where the older forms of Indian culture persist.

Practices in this field have varied widely among the indigenous peoples of the area, for two major reasons. First, it is in many senses unrealistic to lump all of the Indian groups together and treat them as a unit. These people have differing cultures, languages, and social, economic, and political systems. Secondly, the extent to which "white" practices have penetrated Indian systems varies considerably, not only from country to country but also within many of the countries. Kinship and lineage functioned as an important determinant of political station and interest in the overwhelming majority of the indigenous Indian systems of Latin America. In some areas, where these systems have been interfered with relatively little by the "whites," this is still true. Indeed, instances exist in which Indian systems of village government continue to function with little outside intervention, despite the fact that the "whites" have promulgated written constitutions providing for very different patterns of local government.[68] But there are cases—often in

---

[67] Josephs, *op.cit.*, p. 26.
[68] See, for example, Manning Nash, "Relaciones Políticas en Guatemala," in Jorge

other regions of the same countries—where acculturation has taken the form of Indian responses to "white" influences which have fundamentally altered, or even obliterated, the indigenous practices. A number of monographic studies of this situation in specific Indian communities have been published. Short of reporting those detailed findings—which cannot be done in the scope of this chapter—little more can be said here than to stress the point that kinship and lineage are, in general, even more crucial among the Indians than among the "whites" as determinants of interest. Also, it should be remembered that, as a rule, Indian groups are markedly less politically articulate than the upper class. Thus, this type of interest, while often more crucial in the lower classes, typically receives far less of a hearing when emanating from the Indians than when originating among the "whites."

Non-associational interests also arise on *regional* bases. Two major aspects of this should be stressed here. First, regionalism is characteristically an important feature of the pattern of Latin American politics, owing not only to the role of regional loyalties in Spanish culture, but also to the historic difficulty of transportation and communication across the mountains and through the jungles. Living in a species of isolation from each other, the regions of Latin America have developed their own sets of interests. In Peru and Ecuador, for example, the regions known in each country as the "Coast" (located west of the Andes Mountains) are receptive to secularization and commercialization, fostering commercial and industrial interests; whereas, in both countries, the less secularized "Sierra" (lying between the eastern and western cordilleras of the Andes) cultivates the interests of the landowners and the Church. In both countries, the sometimes bitter conflict of interests between these regions is a major element of the national political pattern.[69] In Argentina, to cite another illustration, the interests of the landowners and the Church in the "interior" have been pitted against those of the secularized and far more commercialized metropolitan region of Greater Buenos Aires.

A second major aspect of the regional base of non-associational interests arises from the process of urbanization. In some instances in Latin

Luis Arriola, ed., *Integración Social en Guatemala*, Guatemala City, 1956, pp. 137-156; K. H. Silvert, *A Study in Government: Guatemala*, Part 1, New Orleans, 1954, *passim*, especially pp. 62ff.; George I. Blanksten, "Problems of Local Government in the Caribbean," in A. Curtis Wilgus, ed., *The Caribbean: Its Political Problems*, Gainesville, Fla., 1956, pp. 215-231; and Blanksten, *Ecuador: Constitutions and Caudillos*, pp. 154-156.

[69] See Blanksten, *Ecuador: Constitutions and Caudillos*, pp. 28-31.

America, as much as half the national population lives in the country's one large city. Here again the secular, commercial, and sometimes industrial interests of the urban center are in chronic conflict with those of the religious and quasi-feudal "interior." The major illustrations of this pattern are to be found in Argentina, Cuba, and Uruguay.

(c) *Associational interest groups.* In addition to non-associational interests, there are many formally or consciously organized interest groups in Latin America. These also play an important role in the politics of the area.

Associations of landowners, in one form or another, exist in all countries of the area. In view of the role of the land in the economy of Latin America and the predominance of feudal-like systems of land tenure, these groups are of high importance. In Argentina, for example, the combined land holdings of fewer than two thousand families cover an area greater than England, Belgium, and the Netherlands put together; and statistics produced by some of the American republics indicate that approximately three-fourths of their land is owned by about two per cent of their respective populations. Landowning groups wield considerable political as well as economic power in Latin America. The best-known landowners' association in the area is the Argentine Jockey Club; similar organizations operate in most of the other states of the Western Hemisphere.

Foreign companies function as political interest groups in some of the countries. In northern Latin America—particularly in the Caribbean area—United States corporations are prominent among the interest groups. Excellent illustrations can be found in the United Fruit Company as it operates in a number of the states of Central America, and in the influence of several North American oil companies in Venezuelan politics. In southern South America—Argentina, Uruguay, Paraguay, and Chile—British firms function in a similar fashion.

Labor organizations, though still small, are of growing importance as Latin American interest groups. Their role is expanding as industrialization begins to take hold in the area. From the standpoint of political interest groups, the most important labor organizations are Argentina's CGT,[70] Chile's CTCH,[71] Cuba's CTC,[72] and Mexico's CTM.[73] Organized labor in Latin America is, in general, quite politically articulate, and its support has long been sought by Socialist and Communist parties.

[70] Confederación General del Trabajo (General Confederation of Labor).
[71] Confederación de Trabajadores Chilenos (Confederation of Chilean Workers).
[72] Confederación del Trabajo Cubano (Confederation of Cuban Labor).
[73] Confederación de Trabajadores Mexicanos (Confederation of Mexican Workers).

Student associations are vigorously active interest groups in all the countries of the area. In the words of two writers familiar with Latin America: "The . . . university, traditionally, is a miniature battleground of national politics. Students strike, riot, and stage political demonstrations on the slightest provocation." Politics "becomes a passion that invades and confuses everything. I myself remember many postponed examinations; many study hours disturbed; countless meetings, discussion strikes—a whole year lost in them—elections that ended with gunfire. . . ."[74] As a general proposition, it can be stated that, as political interest groups, student associations are far more significant in Latin America than is the case in the United States.

Professional associations should also be counted among the active groups. Lawyers' associations are perhaps the most long-standing of these. It should be noted that, with the growing economic development of Latin America, associations of engineers, though still small, are of rising importance. *Business groups* are also small in the area; however, they may be expected to grow in influence as industrialization and economic development continue.

Veterans' associations, important in the United States, are of little significance as Latin American political interest groups. Exceptions to this generalization should be noted in the cases of Bolivia and Paraguay, where organizations of veterans of the Chaco War (1928-1935) have become major pressure groups. Indeed, in Bolivia, such a group served as the nucleus for the MNR Party. In most of the region, however, veterans' organizations have done little to make themselves felt. In the absence of systematic studies of this circumstance, any explanatory statement can be little more than conjecture. The guess of this writer—and it is only a guess—is that in most of Latin America the influence that veterans' groups might have had has been more than engulfed by the interest groups representing the armed services. International wars producing veterans are, after all, rare in contemporary Latin America; on the other hand, militarism and the military are ever-present.

The techniques employed by political interest groups to achieve their objectives in Latin America, as in other areas of the world, vary. They include appeals to public opinion, which may take the form of anything from advertisements in the newspapers to painted signs and slogans on public walls and buildings; the latter is a time-honored publicity device in most of the countries involved. Also, the groups seek to influence, and

[74] Ysabel F. Rennie, *The Argentine Republic*, New York, 1945, p. 212; and Luis Guillermo Piazza, "There'll Always Be a Córdoba," *Américas*, January 1950, p. 27.

sometimes capture, political parties. Interest groups most successful at this in Latin America include the Church, the military, the landowners, and, less frequently, foreign companies. Further, interest groups may purchase public decisions through the direct or indirect use of "political money"; in some of the countries, the foreign companies excel particularly in the use of this technique. And there is always the so-called "revolution," which can be made or bought by interest groups. The associations to which this technique is most readily available are, of course, military. It should be noted, however, that military groups often make revolutions in coalition with other organizations.

Finally, a word is in order on the patterns of coalition among Latin American interest groups. He who attaches labels—e.g., "reactionary," "conservative," liberal," or "radical"—to them is treading dangerous ground. He is in a still worse predicament if he assumes that "reactionary" or "radical" groups enter into coalitions or combinations only with other groups bearing the same or similar labels. The investigator working in Latin American politics soon becomes accustomed to finding the Church in alliance with labor, foreign companies in association with the military, or the military joined with either the landowners or those seeking land reform. One need look no further afield than Perón's Argentina, for example, to find the military in alliance with organized labor.[75]

Political Functions

(1) *Interest articulation.* The pattern of formulation and expression of political interests in Latin America in a sense reflects the class system. Where this is especially rigid, the illiterate lower classes are largely inarticulate in national politics. Few instruments exist for the seeking-out, formulation, and expression of their interests. For the most part, the effectively articulated interests are those of the creoles and "whites."

Among the most effective agencies for the articulation of interests in Latin America are the Church and the armed forces. Each endows the interests it expresses with a virtually irresistible legitimacy. Both—the Church more regularly than the army—are often spokesmen for the landowners; both command a respectful hearing. Although the army occasionally wanders from this path, both represent generally conservative interests in that they defend the class system and resist reforms, particularly in the field of land tenure. Both have a powerful press; both have at their disposal most of the effective media of communication.

[75] See Robert J. Alexander, *The Perón Era*, New York, 1951, *passim*.

Interests are also articulated by the political parties. These, too, are spokesmen for the creoles and "whites" more often than for the lower classes. "Conservative" parties generally represent the Church and the landowners; "liberal" parties represent commercial and, where they have appeared, industrial interests. Whether dubbed "conservative" or "liberal," most of the political parties are agents of, and operate in, the upper class. Some political parties seeking to articulate lower-class interests do exist, but these are more rare and, in general, less effective than those at the service of the upper class. As an agency of articulation, the press conforms to a similar orientation. This, in part, reflects the class distribution of literacy, largely a monopoly of the creoles or "whites."

What is impressive about this phase of the Latin American scene is the vast array of interests which are unrepresented, unformulated, and often not even expressed. Political apathy is widespread. Indian communities exhibit little interest in national politics, and the local interests and problems of these groups go largely unnoticed by the nation as a whole. Only on rare occasions does an effective spokesman for the Indian arise. The *mestizo* is in a similar situation. The one major exception to the general inarticulateness of lower-class interests lies in the field of labor. Where unions exist, they are political representatives of their membership, and occasionally political parties woo them. With this exception, little evidence can be found of the national articulation of interests outside the creole or "white" group.

(2) *Interest aggregation.* In Latin America, as in other regions of the world, much of the function of interest aggregation is performed by political parties. These institutions are, no doubt, less aggregative in Hispanic America than in the West, as most of the Latin American states have multi-party systems, with each party representing a relatively small number of interests. Nevertheless, the parties do aggregate interests.

The simplest and most common illustrations in the area are the "conservative" and "liberal" parties, both of which function almost exclusively among creoles or "whites." The typical Latin American conservative party joins together the Church and the landowners, with military cliques frequently included in the combination. Parties representative of this brand of aggregation of interests include the conservative parties of Argentina, Colombia, and Ecuador. Liberal parties, also operative in the upper class, tend to group together commercial and industrial—as opposed to landowning—interests; the Church is rarely included in a liberal aggregation, although military cliques are on occasion found there. The Liberal Party of Colombia and the Radical-Liberal Party of Ecuador are illustrative of this form of Latin American liberalism.

Broadly aggregative, or catch-all, political parties are rare in the area, although they do exist. The leading instances are the Mexican Party of Revolutionary Institutions (PRI), the Argentina Radical Party (UCR), and the Chilean Radical Party. In Mexico, the PRI has brought together such diverse interests as organized labor, the army, the bureaucracy, and, more recently, commercial and industrial interests. The Argentine UCR has endeavored, with some success, to accommodate in one party the right wing of the labor movement, commercial and industrial interests, associations of university students, and professional and intellectual organizations. In Chile, the Radical Party has joined together university students, labor organizations, teachers' associations, and the smaller commercial and industrial interests. The point to stress is that while such broad aggregations do occur in some Latin American political parties, they are atypical; far more representative of the general pattern are the "liberal" and "conservative" combinations.

The aggregative function is also performed, to some extent, by the press. The Hispanic American newspaper which speaks for a number of interests and attempts to combine them is fairly common. *La Prensa* of Buenos Aires joins the landowners with commercial and industrial interests; *El Tiempo* of Bogotá groups coffee growers with labor unions and trade associations.

Some aggregation also involves the Church, the landowners, and the army. These often join together in political movements and sometimes political parties are based on aggregations of this type. However, coalitions of this order are generally short-lived.

(3) *Political recruitment.* The selection of new participants in Latin American politics is governed by a number of characteristics and institutions of the area. In the first place, the class system is among the primary determinants of the identity of political personnel. In most of the countries—particularly, the more "non-Western"—membership in the upper class is a virtually indispensable prerequisite of eligibility for induction into a major political role. Most of the major government officials and the key members of the political parties are drawn from the creole or "white" group. For the most part, direct or active political roles are denied to the Indians, and are open on only a minor scale to the *mestizos*. As has been pointed out, it is possible—although nor-

mally it is not easy—for Indians and *mestizos* to become creoles or "whites." In most of Latin America, this is a necessary first qualification for recruitment into direct political roles.

Economic development and revolution also affect the induction process. Usually, this operates through the influence of these developments upon the class system. Both economic development and revolution, where they occur, weaken the lines separating the classes and facilitate restratification. In such cases, new elements of the population become eligible for political careers.

Further, the Latin American systems of formal education also govern political recruitment. In this region—as, indeed, in other "non-Western" areas—illiteracy figures are quite high. In largely illiterate societies, literacy performs a function essentially unknown in the West. Where only a small minority of the population has received a formal education, the ability to read and write confers prestige and, indeed, power. In most of the countries of Latin America, between 60 and 65 per cent of the population is illiterate. Raw illiteracy figures do little more than underscore, sometimes dramatically, this sharp contrast with the West, but when they are related to the class system, these statistics acquire greater significance, as the correlations are quite instructive. In many of the countries, two questions—"What percentage of the population are creoles or 'whites'?" and "What percentage of the population is literate?"—produce as answers strikingly similar sets of figures. As we have emphasized, the upper classes in much of the area enjoy a virtual monopoly on formal education. The class distribution of literacy becomes even more significant when it is realized that, in some of the countries, learning to read and write Spanish is one of the ways in which Indians and *mestizos* may become "whites" or creoles. In terms of its relationship to the class system, then, the educational system of Latin America may be regarded as an agency of political recruitment.

Moreover, let it be remembered that "the last step in a military career is the presidency of the republic." No doubt recruitment is more familiar as a military than as a political term, but in much of Spanish America this distinction is hardly worth making. In highly militaristic situations, such as abound in the area, to be a high-ranking army officer is to be a politician. Recruitment into the commissioned officer class is, in many Latin American cases, recruitment into politics.

The Roman Catholic Church is another time-honored recruiting agency. Although the general pattern of the history of the area points toward the gradual reduction of the influence of the Church in politics,

Church and State are still formally united in no fewer than eight of the twenty states of Latin America.[76] In these, Roman Catholicism is the official state religion, and in some of them membership in the Church is a prerequisite to eligibility for some or all government positions. Endorsement by the Church frequently legitimizes a man's political ambitions, and—in all of the countries except Mexico—to have incurred the public opposition of the clergy is to have received the kiss of political death. Although this is less certain and occurs less frequently than in the case of the military, a Church career is often a means of achieving a leading role in politics. Latin America's most celebrated example of this is Gabriel García Moreno, who, in the nineteenth century, rose through the Church hierarchy to become dictator of Ecuador. In contemporary affairs, the Church is often the primary sponsor of political parties, and roles in these are governed by the clergy. The best current illustrations are provided by the Conservative parties of Colombia and Ecuador.

To these, of course, should be added the more common political recruiters, such as political parties and interest groups. Political parties recruit political personnel in much the same fashion in Latin America as in the "West," while Latin American interest groups play a somewhat more direct role in this process than do similar groups in "Western" countries. Lawyers' associations are worth singling out here as interest groups of especial significance as recruiters of non-military and non-clergical political personnel.

Political socialization incorporating the Indians and *mestizos* into the pattern of politics dominated by the ruling groups occurs on a limited scale in Latin America. Where this process is operative, of course, it is a vehicle of integration. It is difficult to generalize about the nature of this process in all twenty of the countries of the region, but it can be said that it operates everywhere in Latin America. However, this statement is in itself not very useful, as socialization takes different forms and moves at varying rates of speed in the various countries.

Four major forms of political socialization may be distinguished in Latin America—social mobility, economic development, political agitation, and revolution. The major characteristics of social mobility are, first, that it operates throughout the area, and, second, that it proceeds at a slower rate than the other forms of political socialization. The Indian who learns a new language, changes his style of dress, becomes

[76] The eight: Argentina, Bolivia, Costa Rica, Ecuador, Peru, Paraguay, Colombia, and Venezuela.

literate, acquires a new occupation, moves from his village, or marries a *mestizo* or a creole or "white," may himself become a *mestizo*. Similarly, *mestizos* may become "creoles" or "whites." If no other socialization process were at work in Latin America, it would still be true that, with each successive generation, the proportion of Indians would become smaller, that of *mestizos* larger, and that of "whites" or "creoles" larger, too, with the last group enlarging its ranks at a somewhat slower rate than the *mestizos*. Indeed, it has been said that the *mestizo* is the Latin American of the future. Everywhere this process can be seen in the area; everywhere it moves slowly.

Economic development, the second form, is also to be found throughout the region, but its impact—from the standpoint of socialization—differs according to country. In some, economic change is taking place at an extremely, even spectacularly, rapid rate. At the other end of the spectrum, there are Latin American states where industrialization is just beginning and where economic development has not yet taken hold on a substantial scale. Brazil and Mexico are leading illustrations of Latin American countries in which economic development is moving rapidly—indeed, São Paulo, Brazil, is the fastest-growing city in the world. At the other extreme, Paraguay, Bolivia, and Ecuador are representative of the states in which this process has hardly begun and appears to be moving slowly. In the rapidly developing states, economic change has contributed markedly to political socialization. Industrial development weakens the once-rigid lines separating the social classes; class mobility becomes more easy and rapid; the pastoral Indian moves from the *hacienda* to take employment in the emerging industries. In his new role he becomes a member of a labor union which involves him in issues and activities new to him, many of them political. As economic development multiplies the opportunities open to the peoples of Latin America, it broadens their horizons, gives them new roles, alters their patterns of expectation. Here is, in a sense, socialization which is often traumatic in nature. Where this process has taken hold, the active membership of political parties swells, political apathy wanes, and the percentage of the national population counted as voting citizens grows impressively. As has been suggested, the Latin American countries in which this form of political socialization is most significant are countries like Brazil and Mexico; it is least important in such states as Paraguay, Bolivia, and Ecuador.

Agitation may be regarded as a third form of political socialization where this technique is used to change the expectations of the lower classes and to arouse them to political action previously unfamiliar to them. Like economic development, political agitation is not uniformly effective throughout Latin America. It has been of high importance in some of the countries, almost non-existent in others. Peru and Bolivia present the clearest illustrations in the area of the achievement of effective political socialization through agitation. In both countries this has been the work of opposition political parties. In Peru, the agitating party is the American Popular Revolutionary Alliance (APRA) popularly known as the Aprista Party; in Bolivia, the group concerned is the Nationalist Revolutionary Movement (MNR). The Peruvian party has long demanded political recognition of what it calls the "true Peru," seen by the Apristas as the culture and civilization of the Indians. During much of the twentieth century, the Apristas have engaged in political agitation among the lower classes, seeking to rouse them to action in the service of APRA. The party reached the peak of its strength in the middle 1930's, and again during the administration of President José Luis Bustamante (1945-1948). There can be little doubt that the work of the Aprista Party, largely agitation, can be counted among the major factors in the political socialization of the Peruvian Indian during the last generation.[77]

In the Bolivian case, the work of the MNR has been primarily directed toward the unionization of the lower classes and the political direction of their labor organizations. These unions have been, for the most part, composed of tin miners. Led by the MNR, a miners' union staged a strike in December 1942 at the Catavi mine, operated by the Patiño tin interests. The government used armed force to terminate the strike in an action labeled by the MNR—then an opposition party —as the "Catavi Massacre."[78] Seizing upon the incident, the MNR stepped up its political agitation on behalf of the miners, and overthrew the Bolivian government on December 20, 1943, the first anniversary of the "Catavi Massacre." Since the revolution of 1943, the MNR has been in power on two occasions. The first (1943-1946) was a hectic reign of terror brought to a close by a bloody counterrevolution. The second was inaugurated by the revolution of 1952, again made by the MNR, which was still in power when these lines were written. During the second MNR period, the tin mines were nationalized and im-

[77] See Kantor, *op.cit.*, *passim.*
[78] The number of strikers killed at the time will probably never be known. Estimates range from the government claim of only four to the MNR charge of more than one hundred casualties.

pressive steps were taken in the direction of land reform. This activity has contributed substantially to the more direct incorporation of a sector of the lower classes into the national political life of Bolivia. In comparing the Peruvian with the Bolivian experience, it should be noted that the former has directed its attention to a broader category of the lower classes than has the latter: the Apristas have considered their clientele to include all the Indians of Peru, whereas the MNR has concentrated primarily upon organized labor. In both cases, however, the agitational work of these parties has brought a large proportion of previously apolitical people, mostly Indians, into direct participation in the national political cultures.

Revolution may be regarded as the fourth major form of political socialization in Latin America, and the clearest illustration of its use in this respect is to be found in Mexico. The upheaval which began in that country in 1910 and dominated the lives of the ensuing generation of Mexicans has been a revolution in as real and as profound a sense as the French and Russian revolutions. The Mexican venture has found a new place for the Indians and *mestizos* in the life of the nation. It has attacked illiteracy and even engineered a renaissance of Indian culture. Class stratification has been made more flexible, and the older class system has been modified to multiply the opportunities available to the lower classes. Restrictions have been placed upon the ability of foreigners to acquire property in the country. Expropriation and other revolutionary measures have deprived non-Mexicans of their holdings in such areas of the national economy as land, oil, and transportation. The Roman Catholic Church has been disestablished and its place in the temporal life of Mexico severely curtailed. New sectors of the population of the country have been brought into direct participation in its politics. Political socialization, in short, has been stimulated on a grand scale in Revolutionary Mexico.

(4) *Political communication.* The barriers to communication in Latin America are as impressive as the resistances to integration. The lack of cultural homogeneity—especially in the Indo-American countries, where large sectors of the populations do not even speak the language of the dominant groups—poses a substantial obstacle to effective communication. The rigid class system, with articulate interaction between the strata held to a minimum, produces a similar effect. This is also true of the particularism and regionalism of the area, abetted by mountains, jungles, and other physical barriers to transportation and communication. Economic problems hindering the construction of satisfac-

tory highways, railroads, and other avenues of transportation likewise obstruct communication. To these inhibiting factors must be added the effects of widespread illiteracy.

Thus, communication is limited and difficult in many parts of Latin America. One of its major historic agencies is the Roman Catholic Church. More than any other element of the Hispanic American scene, the Church has communicated a common set of values to large masses of the populations and is the major architect of such consensus as exists. Often, in outlying rural sections the clergy is the major instrument of communication between local communities, the national capital, other major urban centers of the country, and the outside world—particularly the Catholic world—in general. It is worth noting that the depth of the historical roots of this function of the Church is to be measured in centuries in Latin America.

Political parties also function as communicators in the area. These institutions not only keep their membership informed on national political questions, but also perform a communicating function in their appeals for the electoral support of non-members. Fundamentally, this aspect of the work of political parties is not greatly different in Latin America from that in other areas. The major difference is an expression of the role of the class system: the parties communicate with the already politically articulate. In much of Latin America, this limits the parties' communicating role primarily to their relationship with the upper classes.

The chief of state is also a major instrument of communication. In Latin America, this function of the executive is more significant than in many other areas, particularly in the West. It should be remembered that the Hispanic American political tradition has historically embraced a strong authoritarianism. The chief of state is generally regarded as the focal point of politics—for many Latin Americans, he is government personified. As such, he is a major vehicle of political consensus throughout the area.

Finally, it should be noted that such familiar Western media of communication as the press, radio, television, and motion pictures also operate in Latin America, although their communicating function is more limited. It is unrealistic, for example, to treat the Latin American press as a medium of communication without taking into account the high rate of illiteracy. Illiteracy does not prevent Latin Americans from listening to the radio, of course, but technical and economic factors do have this effect on a significant scale. The distribution of electric power is such that radio reception is still rare in many of the rural areas. Moreover, in the Latin American economy a radio receiving set is a highly expensive item, normally beyond the reach of the bulk of the *mestizos* and the Indians. The same is in general true of television, which is just beginning to be introduced in the urban centers of Latin America. Counterbalancing the inhibiting effects of technical and economic problems is another factor suggesting an expanding future role for radio and television in Latin America. In these media, many Hispanic American leaders see a method of communicating information and ideas to a population which cannot read or write. Indeed, it has even been suggested that they will make it possible—some say feasible—to bypass formal education in the difficult task of incorporating the masses of the people into the national political culture. As for motion pictures, the situation is different. The Latin American community—almost no matter how small or rural—without at least one motion picture theater is rare, and the price of admission is normally not prohibitive to the lower classes. The problem here is that, with the exception of Argentina, Mexico, Cuba, and, to a lesser extent, Brazil, the Latin American countries do not have film-producing industries of consequence. Accordingly, the ideas and information communicated in the motion-picture theaters of the area emanate, for the most part, from Hollywood, and are the products of an alien culture.

IV. GOVERNMENTAL STRUCTURES AND AUTHORITATIVE FUNCTIONS

Governmental Structures

All twenty of the Latin American states boast written constitutions describing formal structures of government. These basic laws function in different ways from country to country—indeed, it is often said that in some of them the constitutions are more frequently honored in the breach than otherwise—but in all of the political systems the formal structure acts as a species of backdrop against which the political process moves. Accordingly, there may be some virtue in noting a few of the salient features of the written constitutions of Latin America.

The formal frames of government that these constitutions provide reflect the strong constitutional influences exercised on the area by France and the United States. Most of the reasons for this are not difficult to find. The fifty-year period which came to a close in 1825 was crucially formative in the development of France, the United States, and Latin America, and tended to impose a curious species of constitutional commonality upon Frenchmen, North Americans, and Latin Americans. Between 1775 and 1825 the United States won its independence from Britain, France suffered a great revolution, and the Latin Americans achieved independence from Spain, Portugal, and France.[79] These events, decisively formative in the political development of the countries involved, were subject to the same intellectual and ideological influences. Whether they be called the ideas of the French Revolution, of the American Revolution, or of Latin American independence, they were, essentially, the products of the same stage in the evolution of political philosophy; and this common heritage is reflected in the written constitutions of the countries involved.

There are, of course, other factors entering into the constitutional influence of France and the United States upon Latin America. France has long been regarded as the cultural center of the Latin world. Mesmerized by the notion that civilization radiates from Paris, Latin Americans are prone to adopt ideas and practices having vogue among Frenchmen. Some of these ideas and practices have been political and constitutional.

As for the United States, the influence of the "Colossus of the North" upon its southern neighbors is a theme constantly occupying the attention of Latin Americans. "Poor Mexico," General Porfirio Díaz is said to have remarked, "so far from God—so close to the United States!" Partially a function of geographic propinquity, the influence of the North Americans is considerable. In discoursing upon it, Latin Americans are apt to dwell, frequently in a spirit of complaint, upon economic influences, upon "imperialism," big companies, and intervention. This should not obscure the fact that some of the influence of the United States in Latin America is also political and constitutional.

Thus much of what is written in the constitutions of Latin America can readily be traced to French and North American origins. In contemplating the provisions of these documents, we should bear in mind that no constitution, anywhere in the world, functions precisely as written; everywhere there is some divergence between the text of the basic law and actual practice. In most of the states of Latin America, this divergence is considerably greater than is the case in the United States.[80]

---

[79] The sole exception to this general formulation is Cuba, which was not separated from Spain until 1898.

[80] See Fitzgibbon, "Constitutional Development in Latin America: A Synthesis," *op.cit.*, pp. 517-518.

The following paragraphs are therefore an abstract of what the written constitutions say rather than a description of political life as it is lived in Latin America.

Although some of the states of the area have experimented with monarchy and with parliamentary government,[81] the basic form employed throughout Latin America since independence is the presidential system, characterized by a separation of powers on the national level among the executive, legislative, and judicial branches of government.

The spread of the presidential system through the area stands as a striking index of the constitutional influence of the United States in the Western Hemisphere. The constitutions of nineteen of the Latin American countries provide that the executive branch be headed by a single individual, called the president of the republic.[82] He is elected for a fixed term of office.[83] The president is indefinitely eligible for reelection only in the Dominican Republic, Paraguay, and Venezuela. The other seventeen constitutions prohibit the incumbent president from immediately succeeding himself, and in Mexico no president may ever be reelected. Eleven constitutions provide for the office of vice presi-

---

[81] Monarchy was a common form of government among the pre-Columbian American Indians. After the achievement of independence early in the nineteenth century, three Latin American states—Mexico, Haiti, and Brazil—experimented with monarchical systems. The Mexican and Haitian experiments are generally judged to be failures, as the reigns of Emperors Agustín de Iturbide (1822-1823) and Maximilian Hapsburg (1864-1867) in Mexico and of Emperors Jean Jacques Dessalines (1804-1806), Henri Christophe (1808-1820), and Faustin Soulouque (1849-1861) in Haiti were characterized by extensive disorder, political instability, and civil war, ending in all cases in the violent deaths of the monarchs. The monarchical period in Brazil (1822-1889), however, is generally regarded as successful, particularly the reign of Emperor Dom Pedro II (1830-1889).

In the case of parliamentary government, the most noteworthy instance is the Chilean experience from 1891 to 1924. Seven other Latin American states (Brazil, Bolivia, Cuba, Haiti, Honduras, Uruguay, and Venezuela) have also, from time to time, employed selected aspects of the parliamentary system. See William S. Stokes, "Parliamentary Government in Latin America," in Asher N. Christensen, ed., *The Evolution of Latin-American Government*, New York, 1951, pp. 458-459.

[82] Since 1952, Uruguay, the sole exception, has employed the plural executive. This arrangement preserves the separation of powers but provides for the administration of the executive branch by a committee or *colegiado* of nine elected members. This Uruguayan system is described in Russell H. Fitzgibbon, "Adoption of a Collegiate Executive in Uruguay," *Journal of Politics*, Vol. xiv, November 1952, pp. 616-642, and in Fitzgibbon, *Uruguay: Portrait of a Democracy*, New Brunswick, N.J., 1954, pp. 156-159.

[83] Four years in Costa Rica, Cuba, Ecuador, and Panama; five years in Brazil, the Dominican Republic, Paraguay, and Venezuela; and six years in Argentina, Bolivia, Chile, Colombia, Guatemala, Haiti, Honduras, Mexico, Nicaragua, Peru, and El Salvador.

dent.[84] Latin American presidents are assisted by cabinets similar in composition and function to the cabinet of the President of the United States.

National legislatures in Latin America also reflect the North American model. Bicameral congresses exist in fourteen of the countries.[85] Their constitutional powers are similar to those of the Congress in Washington.

Both French and United States influences are evident in the judicial systems of Latin America. The North American model is reflected primarily in the constitutional notion of an independent court system standing as one of the three branches of government. In other respects, the courts of Latin America lean more toward the French pattern. Judges have many administrative as well as judicial duties, and the law applied is code law or Roman law rather than common law. Judicial review is virtually unknown in Latin America. Some Mexican and Colombian practices resemble it, but should not be confused with judicial review.[86]

The French pattern is predominant in Latin American constitutional approaches to the distribution of power between national and regional levels of government. The unitary system, under which the national or central government possesses unlimited legal power over all territory in the state, is employed in sixteen of the Latin American constitutions. The other four—those of Argentina, Brazil, Mexico, and Venezuela— distribute legal power between the national and state or provincial governments on a federal basis. The constitutional theory of Brazilian, Mexican, and Venezuelan federalism resembles Canadian more than United States practice; the federalism of Argentina is more closely patterned after that of the United States.[87] Local government operates as the creature of the national authorities in the unitary systems, and as the agent of the state or provincial governments in the federal arrangements.[88]

[84] The office does not exist in Chile, the Dominican Republic, Guatemala, Haiti, Mexico, Nicaragua, Paraguay, Uruguay, and Venezuela. Costa Rica, Panama, and Peru each have two vice presidents.

[85] The national legislatures of Costa Rica, Guatemala, Honduras, Panama, Paraguay, and El Savador are unicameral.

[86] See Association of American Law Schools, ed., *Latin American Legal Philosophy*, Cambridge, Mass., 1948.

[87] See Blanksten, *Perón's Argentina*, pp. 133-149.

[88] See *ibid.*, pp. 149-157; and Blanksten, "Problems of Local Government in the Caribbean," in Wilgus, ed., *op.cit.*, pp. 215-231. For English translations of the constitutions of Latin America, see Russell H. Fitzgibbon, *et al.*, eds., *The Constitutions of the Americas*, Chicago, 1948.

Authoritative Functions

(1) *Rule-making.* Constituent assemblies in Latin America play a role in rule-making probably unparalleled anywhere else in the world. While all of the states of the area have written constitutions, as a rule they do not enjoy longevity. The constitution which lasts for more than a quarter of a century is rare in the area, where each of no fewer than eight countries[89] has had ten or more constitutions. Indeed, more than twenty of them have been promulgated in the Dominican Republic and Venezuela.

Thus, the meeting of a constituent assembly to write a new constitution is not the sort of event which occurs only once or twice in the national history of the typical Latin American country. Rather, it recurs fairly frequently—one might almost say regularly—approximating the ideal of the "constant constitutional convention." The basic rules are rewritten often by elected assemblies in which the interests of the landowners, the Church, and the military are usually represented.

All the written constitutions produced at these meetings provide for national legislatures. According to the texts of the documents, these bodies have fundamental legislative or rule-making power. However, one of the chronic constitutional problems of Latin America is that this power is in fact rarely exercised by legislative bodies. There are exceptions to this, of course—the most notable being in Uruguay, Costa Rica, and Chile. In most of the states, however, it is necessary to look elsewhere to find the makers of the laws. Almost everywhere, the chief of state—usually called the President—is the basic rule-maker. This springs in part from the fundamentally authoritarian political tradition of the area. It is commonly believed by Latin Americans that the chief executive makes the laws, and in much of the area this is not far from the truth. The President and the groups that have influence upon him, including his supporting bureaucracy, not only initiate but in many cases make the rules.

There are, of course, limits within which the executive acts. One of the basic institutions setting these limits is the army, which must be counted as a chief Latin American rule-maker. In this capacity, the military functions in two ways. First, it is often an active rule-maker, taking the initiative in creating and establishing policy. Secondly, it sometimes operates as a veto-wielder. This is true in situations where

[89] Bolivia, Colombia, the Dominican Republic, Ecuador, Haiti, Honduras, Peru, and Venezuela.

the active policymakers are other than military men but nevertheless keep the interests of the military in mind. In such cases, no decision that the army is known to oppose can be made with impunity. Though the army may appear to be politically passive in such instances, its potential veto can almost never be overridden.

The Church functions as a rule-maker in a similar fashion. The principal difference between the clergy and the military in this regard is that, while the army is often the active policymaker as well as the passive veto-wielder, the Church rarely plays the active role, serving more normally as the veto group. So long as government officials realize that to invite Church opposition is to incur the kiss of death, there is no need to employ the veto. Normally the threat of its use is enough, and this, too, sets the limits within which rules can be made.

(2) *Rule application.* The rules are applied in four major types of contexts—constitutional, religious, military, and cultural. There are, of course, a number of procedures laid down in the constitutional systems of Latin America, and these play a role in rule application. The executive branch of the national governments performs this function, for example. It is worth noting in this regard that, particularly in the unitary states of the area, chief executives often give close personal attention to administrative matters, many of them minute, on regional and local levels of politics. It is in a sense characteristic of Latin American patterns that higher-echelon officials are reluctant, or unable, to delegate many types of functions to personnel occupying lower positions in hierarchical structures. The Hispanic American scene abounds in illustrations of presidents giving personal attention to small local questions. Mexico's President Lázaro Cárdenas (1934-1940) was famous for his penchant for hurrying off to rural areas to aid personally peons whose crops had failed, whose animals were ill, or who were in similarly unfortunate circumstances. No Latin American country is without its repertoire of stories about presidents who personally attended to matters because they were characterized as "nothing," or who gave audiences to unexpected callers because they announced themselves as "nobody." In a sense, to be "nobody" is a significant credential in the area. While these instances often involve suspending or making an exception to the rules in particular cases, this pattern is especially evident in the general process of rule application. Latin American constitutions are not unusual in that they give the president over-all administrative and enforcement responsibility; what *is* unusual is the extent to which these national executives attend personally to such matters.

Constitutionally, the court systems of the area also take part in the application of the rules. The general pattern here involves hierarchies of tribunals enforcing codes established by the national legislatures. Higher courts exercise administrative and other jurisdictions over lower courts, and in most of the countries the Ministry of the Interior is the point of liaison between the court system and the national executive. While there are exceptions to this, generally the courts are more free of executive intervention than are other rule-applying institutions.

The Church also figures in rule application. Here the function of the clergy is to endow the rules with legitimacy and provide them with moral and political sanctions. Rules publicly supported by the Church often appear to enforce themselves; it is difficult in most of the countries to apply rules to which the clergy are known to be opposed. In a similar sense, the army also takes part in this process. While the armed forces can and do use violence in the enforcement of the rules, more frequently the potential or implied threat of the use of force is sufficient to give the military a place among the major appliers of the rules.

The cultural aspects of rule application are of especial significance in rural areas, particularly in the Indo-American countries. While creoles or "whites" are normally appointed as the officers of civil government—variously called intendants or political chiefs or political intendants—in these communities, these officials are unable to function unless they establish a viable relationship with the local community systems. To illustrate what happens when such a relationship is lacking: "The Indians . . . recruited [by the political lieutenant for public service] may clean a public plaza, a street or road, or a private garden, orchard, or corral without receiving pay. . . . Every year in each community the political lieutenant sponsors what . . . are called free elections, at which he appoints an Indian committee composed of president, vice-president, and secretary. . . . The Indians do not understand these names and call all the members of the committee mayors. Very few Indians care to have these positions. Many refuse to accept them upon being appointed, first because they lose time in the constant walking about from house to house, and second because the jobs will gain them enemies and the disapproval of other members of the community."[90]

Life in an Indian community would be curious indeed if the above were a total description of its government. Actually, the Indians have their own political systems, largely ignored in the texts of the consti-

[90] Buitrón and Collier, *op.cit.*, pp. 34-35.

tutions and statutes written by the creoles or "whites" in the national capital. In the indigenous communities, the chief enforcers of the rules are the village elders or other functionaries endowed with legitimacy by the Indian systems. The "white" intendant or political chief or political lieutenant sent into the community by the national government is forced to operate a system resembling that described above if he can make no other contact with the local authority system. Often, however, he establishes a relationship with the elders or other indigenously legitimate authorities which permits him to govern through them in a fashion somewhat reminiscent of the British colonial practice of indirect rule. Where this is the case, the indigenous authorities are among the most effective agents of rule application to be found on the local level in Latin America.

(3) *Rule adjudication.* Constitutionally, of course, much of the rule-adjudication function falls to the courts in Latin America. While the methods of selecting judges vary from country to country, these officials generally represent the creoles or "whites" rather than the lower classes. We have mentioned the fact, almost without exception, the dispensing of "justice" means that the Indian loses. In view of this class bias, it can be said that a portion of the adjudicating function is performed by the judicial systems of the various countries.

Also, in recent years there has been a growth of what are called "special courts"—that is, tribunals established to deal with specific categories of disputes. These are usually labor courts and tribunals with specialized jurisdiction in some classes of commercial controversy. The trend toward the development of labor courts is a phenomenon of some significance in Latin America. These tribunals do not exist in all of the countries, but are growing rapidly where industrialization is beginning to take hold, and where labor unions are emerging as major interest groups. Particularly important as illustrative of countries developing labor courts under these circumstances are Mexico since 1910, Cuba, Brazil, and Argentina, where the labor court movement was especially stimulated during the Perón period (1943-1955). It should be noted that, in general, the class bias of the labor court is the reverse of what has been noted above for the judiciary in general, as the decisions of labor tribunals often favor the interests of workers' organizations.

In much of the West, administrative agencies operate as significant rule adjudicators. It should be stressed that this is a major area of contrast between the West and Latin America. In most of the countries of the region, administrative agencies are few, small, weak, and not to be counted among the important adjudicators. Brazil represents the sole major Latin American exception to this generalization. During the administrations of President Getúlio Vargas (1930-1945, 1950-1954), Brazilian administrative agencies grew rapidly and chaotically, and the country's bureaucratic problems became sharply atypical of the situations in other states of the area. These agencies came to be major rule adjudicators. Brazil remains, in this regard, unique in Latin America.[91]

The final arbiters of the area are the executive, the Church, and the military. Everywhere in Latin America, the presidents are regarded, with considerable accuracy, as government personified. Frequently, Hispanic Americans do not think of the work of legislative bodies and courts as government, too. The president is the government, and he is a major adjudicator. As for the Church, Mexico is the only country in the region where the clergy has been ousted from its powerful position. Elsewhere, the Church is unrivaled in its ability to endow one side or another in a controversy with legitimacy, and the adjudicating force of the clergy is in most cases irresistible. The same is in general true of the army.[92] Historically, arms have been the court of last resort in Latin America. This pattern has become so firmly embedded in the political culture of the area that appeal to arms to decide fundamental questions is generally an accepted procedure. Indeed, the armies in many of the countries regard rule adjudication as an official function of the military in cases where division on an issue is deep and strong. There have been instances of attempts to indoctrinate Latin American armies with the proposition that they should be apolitical, but these have not been effective.[93] At any given moment, anywhere from ten to fifteen army officers may be counted among the nineteen incumbent Latin American presidents. "Oh, people of Paraguay, how long will

[91] See Karl Loewenstein, *Brazil under Vargas*, New York, 1942, *passim*.

[92] This writer hesitates to speculate on the classic riddle of the "two irresistible forces" by positing a situation in which the Church and the army oppose each other. While it is true that this type of division has on occasion taken place in Latin America, the instances have not been sufficiently frequent to justify the formulation of a general proposition.

[93] For example, during the United States occupation (1909-1933), the Nicaraguan Army, which had been heavily political, was disbanded. A new organization, the Nicaraguan National Guard, was created and trained by the United States Marines, and indoctrinated with the idea that the National Guard must be above politics. Having governed Nicaragua since 1937, the National Guard is today at least as political as the former Nicaraguan Army ever was.

you remain idiots?" a president once asked his people. "Bullets are the only saints you have."[94]

V. POLITICAL INTEGRATION

For the most part, the states of Latin America embrace unintegrated or culturally heterogeneous societies. Throughout most of the nineteenth and twentieth centuries, the countries of the area have been making slow and troubled progress toward national unification. This trend usually involves an expansion of the hold of the upper class, already largely Westernized, upon the rest of the country, which gradually becomes subject to the greater control, influence, and cultural direction of the ruling group. Thus the advance in the area toward national cohesion is in a sense synonymous with Westernization. It should be noted that while this process moves slowly in some parts of Latin America, it is afoot everywhere and is one of the fundamental aspects of the spread of Western political culture.

Resistance to integration has long been one of the major political characteristics of Latin America. Indeed, the centrifugal forces often appear to have been stronger than the integrative. What in colonial times were only four Spanish viceroyalties have today become nine independent states.[95] The area once administered through the single captaincy-general of Guatemala is now occupied by the five independent governments of Central America. The political fragmentation of the Caribbean region is not only one of its leading characteristics but is often cited among its chief problems. In countries with especially rigid class systems—particularly in Indo-America—the social distances separating the strata of society are so great that it is only a minor exaggeration to say that different classes in the same country live in different worlds. Everywhere in Latin America extreme regionalism—often producing secessionist movements—is an established element of

[94] Paraguayan President José Gaspar Rodríguez de Francia, quoted in J. Fred Rippy, *Historical Evolution of Hispanic America*, New York, 1940.

[95] The colonial viceroyalty of New Granada has become the separate states of Colombia, Venezuela, Ecuador, and Panama; the viceroyalty of the United Provinces of the Plata River has been divided into Argentina, Paraguay, and the southern third of Bolivia; and what was the viceroyalty of Peru is now the Republic of Peru and the northern portion of Bolivia. Uruguay, once territory disputed by Brazil and the viceroyalty of the United Provinces of the Plata River, is now a separate state. The major exceptions to this divisive process have been the viceroyalty of New Spain (which, with the exception of the area lost to the United States, remains essentially intact in contemporary Mexico) and the former Portuguese colony of Brazil.

the political pattern. Illustrations of these centrifugal manifestations could be multiplied, but perhaps what has been said here will suffice to demonstrate that resistance to integration has been a historic political characteristic of the region.

This is not to say, however, that integrative processes have not been at work in Latin America. These, of course, exist. Perhaps the most obvious of them is coercion. It has been noted earlier that the armed forces in many of the countries play a role in domestic politics at least as basic as the defense of international frontiers. Many Latin American secessionist movements have been suppressed by armed force or by the threat of its use. And use of arms has accompanied attempts by national governments to suppress in outlying areas various indigenous practices such as head-hunting or head-shrinking or the production of certain types of powerful beverages, and to substitute for them practices more integrally related to those of the more politicized groups.

Constitutional and legal arrangements are also prominent among the politically integrative functions in Latin America. Sixteen of the twenty states of the area currently have constitutions providing for unitary or centralized systems of government. Unitary practices often perform integrative functions. Centralized formal patterns tend to discourage regional and local autonomy and to inhibit secessionist movements. Operating as a pressure toward political uniformity on a nationwide basis, unitary arrangements tend to limit regional differences and to promote the absorption of variant indigenous systems, particularly in outlying areas, into a more integrated over-all pattern.

Some legal practices traceable to the French Revolution are common throughout Latin America. Many of these tend to perform integrative functions. Among them is a highly centralized system of administrative law, contributing to generally unified administration in most of the countries. Judicial uniformity may also be cited as a force contributing to integration. This is abetted by various forms of the Roman code law system, in which the courts apply legislatively determined codes on a fairly uniform basis throughout each of the countries in the area.

A strongly authoritarian political tradition also performs something of an integrative function in Latin America. Two points should be stressed in this connection. First, the political tradition brought to the Americas by the Spanish *conquistadores* was characterized by a strongly centralized authoritarianism. Second—and this is frequently forgotten— the same was in a sense true of the political tradition of the indigenous Indian groups. This is especially significant in those parts of contem-

porary Latin America where Indians still account for important proportions of the national population. For the Indians in some areas,
"life has been controlled by indisputable law for at least a thousand
years, regardless of whether the particular political unit happened to
be called the Kingdom of Quito, the Inca Empire, the Audiencia of
Quito, the Presidencia of Quito, the Department of the South," or
a twentieth-century republic.[96] It is worth noting that the Spanish and
the Indian political traditions in this regard have been so similar that
in some degree they have constituted a bond linking the two ethnic
groups together, in contrast to the many differences between the Spanish and Indian cultures which have functioned as barriers between them.

Further, the Roman Catholic Church performs an integrative function in Latin America. Among the oldest of the integrative forces in
the area, the Church arrived in the Western Hemisphere early in the
sixteenth century with the avowed purpose of Christianizing the indigenous peoples of the Americas. In the early years of the colonial
period, force and other coercive measures associated with the Inquisi-
tion were freely employed to achieve that end. Subsequent developments stand as eloquent evidence of the effectiveness of the Church
in this field. For the most part, the Indians have indeed been Christianized. Although essentially unsophisticated in religious doctrine and
in theology, the Indians may today be counted among the most loyal
and devout Catholics in Latin America. Statistics for the individual
states indicate that approximately 90 per cent of their populations are
Catholics; there is no country in the area where this figure falls significantly below 85 per cent. Thus the Church has contributed a variety
of religious consensus to the area, and in many phases of Latin American life this consensus promotes political integration.

Thus, although resistance to integration remains among the historic
characteristics of the Latin American pattern, integration has indeed
occurred in the area. The process has moved at varying rates of speed
in different parts of the region, and it has taken a number of forms.

[96] Blanksten, *Ecuador: Constitutions and Caudillos*, pp. 32-33.

CONCLUSION:

THE POLITICAL SYSTEMS
OF THE DEVELOPING AREAS

JAMES S. COLEMAN

....

I. INTRODUCTION

The purpose of this final chapter is to summarize briefly the modal characteristics of the political systems covered in this survey, to analyze the range of variation among these systems, and, where possible, to suggest propositions regarding relationships and developmental patterns in the process of modernization.

It is important at the outset not only to make the analytical distinction between society and polity, but also to be explicit regarding the concept of "modernity" as used herein. A *modern society* is characterized, among other things, by a comparatively high degree of urbanization, widespread literacy, comparatively high per capita income, extensive geographical and social mobility, a relatively high degree of commercialization and industrialization of the economy, an extensive and penetrative network of mass communication media, and, in general, by widespread participation and involvement by members of the society in modern social and economic processes. The degree of modernization of the societies covered in this survey will be examined in greater detail in our discussion of the processes of change.

The properties of a *modern political system* have been described at length in the Introduction and need be only summarized briefly here. The most general characteristic of such a system is the relatively high degree of differentiation, explicitness, and functional distinctiveness of political and governmental structures, each of which tends to perform, for the political system as a whole, a regulatory role for the respective political and authoritative functions. In the political socialization process, the manifest, secondary, system-wide structures serve to create a distinct loyalty to the general political system, not only by their direct impact upon the individual citizen, but also by their penetration and regulation of primary structures. In political recruitment, ascriptive elements are present, but they tend to be contained within or limited by general performance criteria. In the articulation of interests, associational interest groups perform a system-wide regulatory role by processing raw claims and directing them in an orderly way and in aggregable form through the party system, the legislature, and the bureaucracy—thus helping to maintain the boundary between the society and the polity. In the aggregation of interests, a party system—characterized by competing, pragmatic, and bargaining parties—regulates and gives order to the performance of the aggregative function by other structures in the system. Political communication is performed by autonomous and specialized media which tend to penetrate all other structures and to transmit a steady flow of information within the polity. Finally, in the performance of authoritative functions by governmental structures, boundaries between the latter tend to be more sharply delineated and more effectively maintained; and informal, particularistic structures throughout the system tend to be penetrated and acculturated to the secondary formal structures.

It is clear from this list of attributes that the Anglo-American polities most closely approximate the model of a modern political system described in the Introduction and Shils's model of a "political democracy."[1] Competitiveness is an essential aspect of political modernity, but not all competitive systems are "modern" in terms of the characteristic structures and styles of performance of functions found in the model presented in this book. Similarly, non-competitiveness or authoritarianism is usually associated with nonmodern (i.e., "traditional") polities; yet not all authoritarian regimes are "traditional." Actually, as Almond has emphasized, every political system is dualistic or "mixed," falling somewhere along a continuum between "modern" and "traditional." The distinguishing features of "modern" polities are the greater differentiation of the secondary structures and the fact that they tend to penetrate and "modernize" the primary structures.

The political systems covered in this survey are listed in Table 1 according to the degree of competitiveness (competitive, semi-competitive, and authoritarian) and degree of political modernity (modern, mixed, and traditional). These classifications have been made with a profound awareness of the gross character of the judgments they represent, as well as of the fact that most of the systems concerned are

---

[1] See Gabriel A. Almond, "Comparative Political Systems," *Journal of Politics*, Vol. XVIII, August 1956, pp. 391-409; and Edward Shils, "Political Development in the New States," unpublished manuscript.

TABLE 1

Classification of Political Systems in Underdeveloped Areas

CLASSIFICATORY CRITERIA		COUNTRIES BY AREAS				
Degree of Competitiveness	Degree of Political Modernity	Southeast Asia	South Asia	Near East	Africa	Latin America
Competitive	Modern					
	Mixed	Malaya Philippines	Ceylon India	Israel Lebanon Turkey		Chile Argentina Brazil / Uruguay Costa Rica
Semi-competitive	Mixed	Burma Indonesia Thailand		Algeria Iran Jordan Morocco Tunisia	Cameroons Central African Republic Chad Dahomey Gabon Ghana Guinea Ivory Coast Mali Federation Mauritania Niger Nigeria No. Rhodesia Nyasaland Rep. of Congo Sierra Leone Somalia So. Rhodesia Tanganyika Togoland Uganda Upper Volta Union of So. Africa	Colombia Ecuador Mexico / Panama Peru
Authoritarian	Mixed	Cambodia Laos	Pakistan	Iraq Libya Sudan U.A.R.	Angola Belgian Congo Liberia Mozambique Ruanda-Urundi	Bolivia Cuba Dominican Republic El Salvador Guatemala / Haiti Honduras Nicaragua Paraguay Venezuela
	Traditional			Afghanistan Saudi-Arabia Yemen	Ethiopia	

in transition. The present classification is regarded as both tentative and disputable. Its only purpose is to bring all of the systems together in one framework for the analysis that follows.

Given the array of disparate systems shown in Table 1, it is only at the highest level of generalization that one can make statements about their common properties. At that level, at least three features stand out. One is the "mixed" character of their social, economic, and political processes. Most of the countries are still overwhelmingly rural; the majority of the populations are illiterate. Per capita income in these countries remains very low. Social and geographical mobility is relatively high in the modern sector but very low in the rest of the society. The subsistence element persists as an important factor in most of the societies, and industrialization is either just getting underway or remains only an aspiration. The central structures of government are in most instances modern in form, but the authoritative as well as the political functions tend to be performed through a variety of "mixed" structures embodying both modern and traditional elements. These admixtures of modernity and traditionality are in some instances fusional, in others, isolative in character.

A second common feature of these societies is their lack of integration. This is due in part to the ethnic, religious, racial, and cultural pluralism characteristic of the societies, in part to the limited and uneven operation of the processes of modernity. The critical fact, however, is not that these societies are pluralistic—pluralism is one of the key attributes of most modern societies—but that interests still tend to be defined predominantly in terms of tribe, race, religion, or communal reference group. The persistence and the predominance of such groups retards assimilation into the new national societies. Moreover, so long as interests are primarily rooted in and find expression through communal groups, they are far less amenable to aggregation in a competitive and bargaining process. Only in the modern sector of these mixed societies does one find the emergence of non-communal functionally specific interest groups.

A third modal characteristic is the wide gap which exists between the traditional mass and the essentially modern subsociety of the Westernized elite. The latter controls the central structures of government and essays to speak and act for the society as a whole. This elite subsociety is the main locus of political activity and of change in the society at large. The character of the principal actors and participants in the elite subsociety is variable: in the new states and colonies of Africa, and in the new states of Asia, they constitute the urbanized, Western-educated minority; in the white oligarchic states of Africa and Latin America they constitute to varying degrees a culturally defined elite. The principal differences among the societies sharing this characteristic are the degree of access to the elite subsociety, and the extent to which there is communication between the two sectors in the form of such mediators as provincial elites, or an intermediate class in transition between the traditional and modern sectors. The gap between the two sectors illuminates the mixed character of the social and political processes in these countries as well as the degree of malintegration on the vertical plane.

In addition to these general characteristics common to most of the seventy-five countries covered in this study, there are others which can be more appropriately summarized under the headings of the common outline the area authors have employed, namely, the processes of change and their political implications, and the functions of the political system.

II. PROCESSES OF CHANGE AND THEIR POLITICAL CONSEQUENCES

The processes of change examined in the varying contexts of the five areas are major aspects of the broader process of modernization. Analysis of the character and consequences of this process illuminates the interrelated character of the several subprocesses and supports Daniel Lerner's thesis that modernization as a process has a distinctive quality of its own, that the various elements in this process "do not occur in haphazard and unrelated fashion," and that they have gone together so regularly because "in some historical sense they *had* to go together."[2]

The political consequences of the operation of the several processes of change have been many and varied. While in general the changes have brought the countries concerned nearer to the model of a modern society, their effect has by no means been uniform. At the most general level the more significant political consequences can be stated in propositional form:

1. National politics tend to be primarily if not exclusively centered in urban areas; usually they are a phenomenon of capital cities. The

[2] Daniel Lerner, *The Passing of Traditional Society*, Glencoe, Ill., 1958, p. 438.

latter are the principal political arenas because they are the centers in which the modern elite subsociety is concentrated.

2. The gap between the modern-oriented urban subsociety and the larger national society of which it is the political center is not unbridged. A substantial number of the urban dwellers maintain close ties with their rural homeland; as a consequence, they constitute a very significant medium through which modernity is pumped into rural areas and the rural population becomes involved in or identifies itself with the drama of national politics. Such participation, however, tends to be intermittent.

3. The gross disparities between the standard of living and career opportunities in the urban centers and in the village areas has accelerated a movement into the urban centers far beyond the capacity of the latter to provide employment. As a consequence there exists in most urban centers, particularly the capital cities, elements predisposed to anomic activity.

4. The processes of commercialization and industrialization of the economies of these societies have not everywhere contributed to social or political integration, or to the emergence of a politically relevant entrepreneurial or middle class. One reason is that in the initial stages at least commercial activity has been in the hands of alien groups: the Indian and Chinese middleman in Southeast Asia, the Hindu entrepreneurs in the Muslim areas of preindependence India, Lebanese and Jews in North Africa, Levantines in West Africa, Indians in South and East Africa, and various alien groups in Latin America.

5. Although modernity has introduced basic changes in the social structure of many of these countries, these changes have frequently intensified intergroup tensions. Education and economic wealth have not been acquired by nor distributed evenly among all groups, but differentially along communal, racial, or tribal lines. Thus, there is not a positive correlation between economic development and greater social and political integration.

6. Wherever the modernization process has had an impact, it has contributed to secularization, both social and political. But in most countries religion is still a factor of great significance in the political process. In the daily lives of the masses living in the traditional sector, religion is still a vital force. The new secular elites frequently feel compelled, for various reasons, to respect, or even to use, religion as a political force. In most countries there are political parties having a religious basis. The politicization of religion aggravates communal tensions; it

also perpetuates the struggle between those demanding a greater role for religion in the state and those demanding a secular polity.

In addition to these very general statements regarding the political consequences of the modernization process, it is in point here to examine briefly the relationship between economic development—one crucial dimension of that process—and political competitiveness—an essential attribute of a democracy. The most recent study of this issue is that of Seymour Martin Lipset, who uses selected indices of economic development to compare West European and Latin American democracies and dictatorships.[3] Despite the many serious reservations one can and should make regarding the accuracy, comparability, and significance of available economic statistics, as well as the validity of gross judgments regarding the competitive or authoritarian character of political systems, it is believed that a similar effort for the seventy-five political systems covered in this survey can, at the least, be suggestive. Drawing upon many of the categories used by Lipset, as well as others for which data could be obtained, such an effort has been made and the results are set forth in Tables 2, 3, and 4 and in Appendix 1. Following Lipset, our major working hypothesis is that there is a positive correlation between economic development and political competitiveness.

The data in Appendix 1 are the raw scores for each country on eleven indices of economic development used to measure the degree of wealth, urbanization, education, and industrialization. In Table 2 mean scores computed from these data are shown in terms of major area (Latin America and Africa-Asia) and degree of competitiveness (competitive, semi-competitive, or authoritarian). In Tables 3 (Latin America) and 4 (Africa-Asia) the countries are listed in terms of composite rank order on the eleven indices of economic development and categorized according to the competitiveness of their respective political systems.

Two general observations can be made from the data in Table 2. The first relates to the substantial differences between the countries of Latin America and the countries of Africa-Asia. On each of the eleven indices the average level of economic development in the countries of Latin America as a group is higher than the average level of development in the countries of Africa-Asia as a group. This differential between the two major areas is further illuminated by the fact that on five out of the eleven indices of economic development Latin American countries, irrespective of the degree of political competitiveness, consistently rank

[3] Seymour Martin Lipset, "Some Social Requisites of Democracy: Economic Development and Political Legitimacy," *American Political Science Review*, Vol. LIII, March 1959, pp. 69-105.

higher as a group than the countries of Africa-Asia. Put another way, on five indices authoritarian Latin American countries rank higher than competitive countries of Africa-Asia. The five indices concerned relate to wealth (doctors, vehicles, telephones, and radios) and per capita energy consumption. On the other hand, on all indices other than those relating to wealth (i.e., urbanization, education, and labor unionization), the average of competitive countries in Africa-Asia is higher than the average of Latin American countries in one or more of the three categories of competitiveness. In the case of one of the educational indices (primary enrollment ratio) competitive countries of Africa-Asia and Latin America have the same average.

Once these inter-area differences are noted, the second general observation that emerges from the data in Table 2 relates to the degree of consistency between level of economic development and the competitiveness of political systems. In both major areas a pattern is found which is consistent with the hypothesis, namely, on ten out of eleven indices the competitive countries have the highest average score, the semi-competitive countries the next highest, and authoritarian countries the lowest.

The significance and validity of the foregoing general observations can be elucidated, and should be qualified and interpreted, in the light of several additional findings revealed by these data. One point of special relevance is whether the positive relationship between economic development and political competitiveness, established by analyzing the mean scores of countries grouped according to degree of competitiveness, continues to exist when the scores of individual countries are considered. An analysis of the ranking of the countries in Tables 3 and 4 illuminates several striking deviations from the ranking which would be expected if economic development and competitiveness were perfectly correlated.

In the case of the colonies listed in Table 4, three types of deviation should be noted. One type is represented by the cluster of semi-competitive systems ranking very low on the scale of economic development (Tanganyika through Togoland). These polities might be called "terminal colonial democracies," whose competitiveness is a reflection of colonial policies directed toward the establishment of competitive systems; none of them has yet had the opportunity to demonstrate its capacity to run a competitive system on its own. The Sudan, which had this opportunity, passed under military rule after three years of independence. The second type of deviation is represented by two semi-competitive colonial systems ranking very high on the scale of economic development (Algeria and Southern Rhodesia). The higher ranking

TABLE 2

Average Level of Economic Development
by Major Area and Type of Political System

INDICES OF DEVELOPMENT	COMPETITIVE		SEMI-COMPETITIVE		AUTHORITARIAN	
	Latin America	Africa & Asia	Latin America	Africa & Asia	Latin America	Africa & Asia
WEALTH						
Per capita gross national Product (US $)	338	254	242	123	239	102
Number of persons per doctor	1,862	4,800	2,834	21,828	4,542	41,988
Number of persons per vehicle	63	260	91	362	164	592
Number of persons per telephone	49	353	110	688	273	986
Number of persons per radio	12	92	29	496	66	730
Number of persons per newspaper copy	11	50	20	547	80	528
INDUSTRIALIZATION						
Per capita energy consumed (in tons)	.70	.37	.42	.24	.39	.12
Per cent of population in labor unions	8.3	5.0	2.6	2.0	4.2	.5
URBANIZATION						
Per cent of population in cities over 100,000	29.3	17.1	13.7	5.9	11.0	5.6
EDUCATION						
Per cent of population literate	77	52	60	22	45	13
Primary enrollment ratio (in per cent)	51	51	43	24	35	17

economic position of these countries is largely explained by the existence of a substantial settled European population. The countries are classified semi-competitive because, despite the very considerable competition within the dominant racial oligarchy, there is very limited participation by the indigenous inhabitants in the political process. The third type of deviation is represented by the Belgian Congo, which ranks higher on the economic scale than would be expected in the light of its classification as an authoritarian system. This is explained by Belgian policy, which has fostered economic development but has restricted political participation.

In order to interpret two other types of deviations, a brief explanation should be made of the two broken horizontal lines appearing in Tables

TABLE 3

Composite Rank Order
of Latin American Countries
on Eleven Indices of Economic Development

RANK		TYPE POLITICAL SYSTEM	
	Competitive	*Semi-Competitive*	*Authoritarian*
1	Argentina		
2	Uruguay		
3			Cuba
4	Chile		
5			Venezuela
6		Panama	
7		Mexico	
8	Costa Rica		
9	Brazil		
10		Colombia	
11			Paraguay
12		Peru	
13		Ecuador	
14			Nicaragua
15			Dominican Republic
16			Bolivia
17			El Salvador
18			Honduras
19			Guatemala
20			Haiti

3 and 4. The position of these lines has been determined quite arbitrarily, namely by a calculation of the number of competitive, semi-competitive, and authoritarian political systems in each major area classified in Table 1. In that table it will be noted that five Latin American countries are classified as competitive, five as semi-competitive, and ten as authoritarian; thus a broken horizontal line has been drawn after rank 5 and another rank 10 in Table 3. The rationale for the nine-cell matrix thus created is that if there were a perfect correlation between economic development and competitiveness, and if statistics and judgments were accurate, the five most competitive countries would occupy the first five ranks and be in the competitive column, the five next most competitive countries would occupy the succeeding five ranks and be in the semi-competitive column, and the ten least competitive countries would fill the remaining ranks and be in the authoritarian column. The same type of lateral division has also been made for the political systems of Africa-Asia in Table 4.

TABLE 4

Composite Rank Order
of Asian and African Countries
on Eleven Indices of Economic Development*

RANK	COMPETITIVE	SEMI-COMPETITIVE		AUTHORITARIAN	
	Independent	Independent	Colony	Independent	Colony
1	Israel				
2		Union of So. Africa			
3	Lebanon				
4	Malaya				
5			Algeria		
6				United Arab Republic	
7			Southern Rhodesia		
8	Turkey				
9	Ceylon				
10		Morocco			
11		Tunisia			
12	Philippines				
13				Iraq	
14		Jordan			
15		Ghana			
16			Northern Rhodesia		
17			Kenya		
18		Iran			
19	India				
20		Indonesia			
21		Thailand			
22				Libya	
23					Belgian Cong
24		Viet Nam			
25			Cameroons		
26		Burma			
27			Uganda		
28				Saudi Arabia	
29					Angola
30				Pakistan	
31				Liberia	
32			Tanganyika		
33			Nigeria		
34					Mozambique
35				Laos	
36			French West Africa		
37			Nyasaland		
38			Somalia		
39				Sudan	
40			French Equat. Africa		
41			Sierra Leone		
42				Cambodia	
43			Togoland		
44				Afghanistan	
45					Ruanda-Urur
46				Ethiopia	

*Note: The discrepancy in the number of systems listed here and in Table 1 is explained by the omiss in this table of Yemen, due to insufficient data, and of the former individual eight territories of Fre West Africa and four territories of French Equatorial Africa, due to the fact that statistics on which ra ings are based were available only for the two federations.

One set of deviations revealed by the position of countries in the cells of the two matrices comprises those countries which fall significantly far outside the cell in which they would fall were economic development and competitiveness perfectly correlated. The most striking examples of this type of deviation are the authoritarian states of Cuba, Venezuela, and the United Arab Republic. All rank economically among the top six countries in their respective areas. In the case of Cuba and Venezuela there may be special factors (e.g., Cuba's proximity to the United States and its very unique historical development; Venezuela's great oil wealth; and the fact that both have been unstable dictatorships) which could account for their position; nevertheless, such deviations tend to weaken the major hypothesis. The same could also be said for the United Arab Republic.

Another example of this type of deviation concerns the competitive systems of Latin America (Costa Rica and Brazil) and of Asia (Turkey, Ceylon, Philippines, and India), regarding which several observations could be made. The three Latin American countries are not gross deviants, ranking as they do 7th, 8th, and 9th among the twenty countries in the area. The character of Costa Rica's population, the legacy of Mexico's revolution, and the great size and diversity of Brazil's population are also considerations that are in point. Turkey stands by itself as a country which was economically transformed under authoritarianism and subsequently moved toward a competitive polity. As for Ceylon, the Philippines, and India, there is much in their comparatively unique development under Western colonialism, as illuminated by the analyses of Pye and Weiner, which would explain why they tend to be more competitive than their level of economic development would indicate.

A second set of deviations is discernible where the relative economic rank of countries falling within a single category of competitiveness correlates negatively with the relative competitiveness of those same countries. Among Latin American competitive countries, for example, Costa Rica is generally recognized as being more competitive than Argentina, although the former ranks 8 and the latter 1 on the scale of economic development. Again, among Latin American authoritarian systems Paraguay (economic rank 11) is more authoritarian than Bolivia (economic rank 16); and in Africa-Asia, Cambodia (economic rank 42) is less authoritarian than Saudi Arabia (economic rank 28). Once these obvious cases of negative correlations are noted, however, it must be pointed out that for the majority of countries the inadequate state of our knowledge makes it impossible for us to differentiate more finely the degree of competitiveness within the present three categories.

The analysis in the preceding paragraphs leads to two conclusions: (1) the major hypothesis that economic development and competitiveness are positively correlated is validated when countries are grouped into major differentiating categories of competitiveness and when mean scores of economic development are employed; but (2) the hypothesis is weakened by negative correlations found when the economic scores and relative competitiveness of individual countries are considered. To this should be added the caveat that economic modernization constitutes only one dimension of the ensemble of determinants shaping political institutions and behavior in the countries with which we are concerned.

III. THE FUNCTIONS OF THE POLITICAL SYSTEM

Political Socialization and Recruitment

In the Introduction, political socialization has been defined as the process of induction into the political culture. As we have seen, one of the most striking features of all but a few of the seventy-six countries covered in this study is the fragmented character of their political cultures. Those few polities whose political culture even approximates homogeneity are quite exceptional: Argentina, Chile, Costa Rica, and Uruguay in Latin America; and Turkey, Israel, the Philippines—and, in a very special sense, Saudi Arabia and Yemen—in Africa-Asia. Elsewhere the degree of cultural fragmentation is marked, although there are wide variations in the extent to which it affects the political process and in the rate at which a homogeneous political culture is developing.

The cultural fragmentation of most of these countries is a reflection of two basic types of internal cleavage. One is the gap, previously noted, between the predominantly urban, modern subsociety of the Westernized elements, whose members are oriented toward political values and institutions representative of an exotic—usually Western—political culture, on the one hand, and the traditional societies, into the political cultures of which a large segment of the population continues to be socialized, on the other. This gap on the vertical plane is compounded by the horizontal divisions among the melange of indigenous political cultures which, by the accidents of colonialism or recent history, are included within the boundaries of larger territorial political systems. A very considerable number of persons in these countries, of course, are in a transitional stage, being subject to the socializing processes in both spheres. Where the traditional cultures are adaptive to rather than isolative from the modern territorial system, the task of creating a unified socialization process is obviously much easier.

The governing elites of the "new states" are engaged in the development and strengthening of system-wide secondary structures that not only impinge directly upon the individual but also penetrate the primary socializing structures. They are seeking to create, by an act of will, an integrated process of political socialization in which at all levels there is an inculcation of positive sentiments of respect, loyalty, and pride in the new polities. Their efforts are being met with strong resistance, especially from particularistic forces—forces which modernization itself ironically tends, in many situations, to strengthen. Moreover, there are distinct limits to which a political culture can be deliberately created in a single generation; such a culture is a reflection of the ensemble of predispositions and orientations toward authority and politics, most of which are the product of socializing experiences and influences antedating the contemporary drive toward modernization.

In the remaining political systems (except for the few having fairly homogeneous political cultures) the character of the socialization process varies according to the goals of the governing elite and the nature of the cultural pluralism. Although differing in many ways, the elite in such established states as Thailand, Iran, and Ethiopia are endeavoring, through the manipulation of both old and new socializing structures, to adapt the traditional political culture to modernity. In the Union of South Africa one finds the strikingly atypical situation of the governing oligarchy deliberately bending every effort not only to maintain but to strengthen a dualistic political culture. In most of the other countries, and particularly in the culturally pluralistic states of Latin America, the dominant oligarchy is less purposive in this regard, being more inclined to let the processes of assimilation gradually bridge existing cultural discontinuities.

With these general observations regarding political socialization, it is in point to note the patterns of recruitment into the political arena and into political roles in the systems covered in this study. It is clear from the area chapters that there are wide variations in these patterns. These variations are a reflection of several differences: (1) the character, and particularly the breadth, of the social bases from which entrants into the political arena are drawn; (2) the circumstances under which, and the avenues through which, members of the society become politically participant; (3) the degree to which the recruitment process is undergoing change; (4) the rate of political activation; and (5) motivations for entering politics.

The range of variations in the patterns of recruitment extends from the largely ascriptive patriarchal systems such as Saudi Arabia, Yemen, and Ethiopia, through the narrow-based oligarchies of Liberia and the Dominican Republic, to the broad-based competitive systems such as the Philippines and India. In most of these societies, however, the ongoing processes of social change are continuously producing, in varying degrees and at different tempos, fundamental alterations in the recruitment pattern.

In the narrow-based patriarchies and oligarchies, as well as in several of the colonial territories on the threshold of independence, the social categories from which participants are drawn reflect the mixed character of the societies. Traditional leaders are recruited by ascriptive criteria from social groups which historically have been predominant in the system (wealthy families, dominant lineages and clans, etc.). Other leaders came from the modern sector, in which university students, the urban educated classes, army officers, civil servants, and professional and business groups characteristically predominate. In the patriarchal societies professional, business, and other modern groups are largely non-participant, although the continuous increase in their numbers indicates the potentiality for change. In the other narrow-based societies modern elements are increasingly assertive and in several cases are already engaged in efforts to extinguish the influence of the traditional elements.

In those societies where political participation is broadly based, a useful distinction can be drawn, for reasons previously noted, between the countries of Latin America and of Africa-Asia (a contraction used herein to refer to Africa, the Near East, and South and Southeast Asia). In the new states and the terminal colonial systems of Africa-Asia there appears to be a fairly common pattern of development in the recruitment process. For analytical purposes four distinct periods can be distinguished: (1) the period of accommodation and petition; (2) the period of agitation and assertion; (3) the period of maneuver, characteristic of terminal colonialism, where the goal of self-government is in sight and competing groups struggle to establish a favorable position in the new order; and (4) the period of adjustment and consolidation following independence. Each of these are stages in the evolution of political participation, commencing with the initial activities of a small

Westernized minority and ending with the mass popular involvement via universal suffrage and periodic elections. Not all countries have gone through all stages; indeed the terminal colonial phase has tended to be a distinctive feature of the emergence of Africa's new states. Nevertheless, in the majority of these countries there has been a progressive broadening of the social and geographical bases of recruitment.

There are at least three special features of this process which are common to most of the countries of Africa-Asia. One concerns the extreme variations in the rate of recruitment. During the age of petition the rate was comparatively slow, due to the limited degree of social mobilization, the limited horizon of political expectations, and the absence of meaningful political roles to which the ambitious could aspire. The age of agitation and assertion characteristically has been one of extremely rapid upward mobility and of a high rate of recruitment because of the heightened expectations generated by the vision of self-government. As Pye notes, "national freedom became closely related to strong personal career interests and ambitions."

During the post-independence period of adjustment and consolidation there has been a progressive decline in the rate of recruitment into authoritative and bureaucratic roles, and a tendency toward political demobilization of large segments of the population activated during the struggle for independence. At the same time the number of new entrants into the political arena—representative of a new generation—has increased and will continue to grow as a consequence of the acceleration of the processes of change. The cleavage between generations—between the older generation of victorious nationalists holding prestigeful roles and a younger post-independence generation whose career ambitions appear thwarted—is the second special feature stressed by the authors of the chapters on the political systems of Africa-Asia.

A third common feature has been the emergence of rural or "provincial" political elites whose influence has become increasingly determinative in the political process. As Weiner points out, there has been a progressive shift in the geographical bases of recruitment. The same phenomenon has been noted by Pye for Southeast Asia; and it is also observable in the new states of Sub-Saharan Africa. These new rural politicians tend to be vernacular-speaking and less educated; they are also more securely rooted in the traditional social structure than are the urban-based, Western-educated politicians who constituted the vanguard in political action in the preindependence period.

Interest Articulation

In most of the countries included in the five major areas covered by this survey there are similarities in the character of interests and in the degree and manner in which interests are articulated. Ascriptive, communal, and similar groups (i.e., those in which membership is defined by ethnic, racial, linguistic, tribal, religious, or status criteria) continue to predominate and to determine the character of political issues and the lines of political cleavage. Particular economic or occupational interests are mainly latent or in gestation and are not articulated by functionally specific associations. Where the latter exist, they have not become crucial units in the political process. In many countries, institutional interest groups (armies, religious groups, or bureaucracies) play a predominant role.

These three modal characteristics—the persistence and importance of non-associational groupings of an ascriptive or communal character, the limited development of associational interest groups, and the predominant role of institutional interest groups—have a reciprocal dependence. The strength and tenacity of communal and similar groupings militates against the emergence of functionally specific groups as the foci of interest identification and expression. The fact that the latter are either non-existent or undeveloped serves not only to perpetuate the former but also to invite, if not to compel, institutional interest groups to assume a preponderant role.

Armies and bureaucracies in particular tend to play a predominant role for several reasons: they have a special responsibility for the maintenance of law and order, a major desideratum both in the stabilization of the new states and in the maintenance of oligarchic politics. In the new states their ranks are filled mainly by statist and nationally minded modernists, including some of the most able and sophisticated elements in the Western-educated class. For special reasons linked to the rationalization of colonialism, this class supports the idea of the "divine right" of the educated to rule; and its members have not been unaffected by bureaucratic-authoritarian predispositions derived from traditional society or from the colonial experience.

This common syndrome of interests is to a large degree a reflection of the limited and uneven impact of modernity. The modernization process tends to give birth to new, functionally specific interests; yet in many cases the provocations and uneven incidence of its impact have preserved or even strengthened pre-existing tribal, communal, racial, and status cleavages, as well as the urban-rural gap.[4] As Weiner has noted, the growth in mass communication extends and often deepens the network of communal ties, and the introduction of universal suffrage and a national political arena often pushes communal interests into politics. As the degree of functional specificity of associational interest groups is one of the key attributes of political modernity, the prevalence of this phenomenon in much of Sub-Saharan Africa and South and Southeast Asia means that in the initial stages at least the modernization process strengthens antimodern forces and institutions.

The patterning of interests in many of the countries has been partly determined by the character of the colonial experience and of the movements for national independence. In both instances, the legacy has been mixed in character. Under colonialism it was not uncommon for the colonial authorities to recognize and to deal with specific organized interest groups, particularly in the modern sector. At the same time the colonial policies of most European powers had the effect, sometimes intended, of strengthening and preserving communal, ascriptive, ethnic, and racial divisions, as well as of creating religious or status differences. Colonialism was also the medium for introducing and for habituating the mass of the population to government through highly developed structures controlled by a bureaucratic elite. The latter claimed to be responsible not only for governing in the interest of all the people but also for modernizing the society.

The legacy of movements for national independence has also been varied. In countries such as India or Nigeria, where nationalist movements acquired a mass base, the organization of all types of interests was stimulated. One of the most effective techniques employed by nationalist leaders in the mobilization of the population was to work through the network of associations which had emerged from the impact of modernity and the processes of social change. The interests that were activated, articulated, and organized in this process were both functionally specific (e.g., labor unions and student groups), and functionally diffuse (e.g.,

[4] For Latin America, Ralph L. Beals notes that "Industrialization and the rise of new values have been accompanied by an accentuation of the rural-urban contrast in most countries. A disproportionate amount of national income has usually gone into the improvement of cities, making them increasingly desirable, in contrast with the undeveloped or unmodernized countryside. Moreover, the strong feudal class barriers have decayed much more rapidly in the city. Rural individuals or groups aspiring upward find the penetration of barriers easier in the impersonal atmosphere of the city, even though the elites may still successfully maintain their social integrity." "Social Stratification in Latin America," *The American Journal of Sociology*, Vol. LVIII, January 1953, p. 329.

tribal unions, status associations, and other communal groupings) in character. Nationalist leaders aggregated the disparate interests of this melange of participating groups, not by compromises aimed at the immediate satisfaction or accommodations of their respective interests, but rather by subsuming the goals of all interests under the rubric of a new "national interest." When the latter was secured through independence, all specific interests, it was assumed, would automatically be satisfied. This had two consequences. As Pye has observed, it fostered the idea that national leaders, like the rulers of traditional Asian and African societies, were the embodiment of all interests of their people. It also served to create organizational linkages or identifications between interest groups on the one hand and nationalist movements or political parties on the other. Both of these developments tended to minimize and to weaken the autonomy of interest groups in pressing their demands upon the political system.

Post-independence efforts to stabilize the new political systems, to create a sense of national unity, and to accelerate the modernization of societies, have served to perpetuate the idea that the national interest not only transcends but embodies all specific interests and that public policy is not the product of competing claims of specific interests, but rather a reflection of the "national will" of the modernizing national elite. The notion of the "creative state," coupled with a statist mentality derived from traditional culture or from the colonial experience, has tended to strengthen attitudes of hostility or indifference toward special-interest economic groups (especially business and landlord groups), and, as a consequence, to minimize their role in the public policy process.

Over against these elements in the situation have been other developments in the post-independence period having different consequences. Once independence has been achieved (and in some instances even before it is achieved) functionally diffuse groups of all types (ethnic, racial, linguistic, status, and underdeveloped regions) have become activated and have asserted their claims, which in general have taken the form of implied or threatened separatism and the insistence upon safeguards to insure their continuing integrity. Moreover, even in the case of functionally specific groups linked to nationalist movements or political parties there has been a tendency for the new generation of interest-group leaders to seek greater autonomy in the articulation of the specific interests of the groups they represent.

There are other respects in which the character and articulation of interests in these countries are distinctive. One is the active and frequently crucial role played by student groups, and particularly by university students. Another is the extremely limited degree to which the economic interests of the great mass of the population—the peasantry—find associational expression. In Latin American countries, however, ideological parties (Socialist, Communist and Aprista) are to an increasing extent articulating agrarian interests, as well as those of organized labor.

Interest Aggregation

A second attribute of a modern political system is the existence of a party system in which competing parties, broadly based in structure and pragmatic in program and tactics, perform the function of aggregating the major interests in the society. The countries most closely approximating this model of a modern party system are the Philippines and Turkey. Elsewhere one finds an array of variant patterns, although one or more of the attributes of the foregoing model may be present. More characteristically, one finds that political groups are narrow-based and serve essentially as vehicles for competition between different elements drawn from the modern sector. *Personalismo* (the tendency for political groups to be organized in support of particularly strong personal leaders) is common not only in Latin America, where it has flourished for generations, but also in many countries of Africa, the Near East, and South and Southeast Asia. One-party systems tend to predominate, although there are important differences in this type, ranging from the comprehensive nationalist movements found in several African countries, through the broadly aggregative non-dictatorial party systems of Uruguay, Mexico, and India to such narrow-based dictatorial systems as in Paraguay, the Dominican Republic, and Liberia.

Once these general observations are made regarding the character of political groups, it is useful, if not necessary, to emphasize again the major contrast between the political systems of Latin America on the one hand, and those systems of Africa, the Near East, and South and Southeast Asia, on the other. For while there are wide variations in the patterning of the political groups in these latter four areas, most of the countries therein share an historical experience which the countries of Latin America have missed, and which is of decisive significance, namely, modern Western colonialism. By making this distinction it is easier to explain differences found in at least four aspects of political groups: their origin and pattern of development, the issues on which they are divided, their social bases, and their ideology.

The political history and pattern of political development of the countries of Latin America differ considerably from that of Africa-Asia. As

Blanksten points out, most of the countries of Latin America achieved their independence in a predemocratic period, and largely as a consequence of diplomatic events in Europe. By contrast, many of the countries of Africa-Asia secured their independence as a result of the progressive mobilization of the populations in nationalist movements of a populist character inspired by mid-twentieth century ideals of democracy, equality, and the social welfare state. These differences, and the circumstances under which independence was achieved in the two areas, provide a partial clue to the following elements of contrast:

1. With few exceptions (e.g., Uruguay and Chile) politics in Latin America is almost exclusively an affair of the upper classes, with variable but insignificant participation by *mestizos*, Indians, and Negroes. The closest analogy to this pattern in Africa-Asia is found in the European oligarchic states of southern Africa. The African majorities in the latter, however, have organized mass movements of a nationalist character on a scale not found among the Indian and other non-white groups in Latin America, although the phenomenon of Aprismo is a close approximation.

2. The two traditional issues dividing political parties in the competitive systems of Latin America are the role of the Catholic Church and land tenure. By contrast, the dominant issues dividing political groups in most of the countries of Africa-Asia are either communal in derivation or character, or they involve questions of the tempo and manner in which national independence will be achieved and the new national society modernized.

3. There are ideological movements in both major areas, but those of an authoritarian character can be traced to very different traditions. Authoritarian ideologies in Latin America tend to reflect the authoritarianism of early modern Europe, characterized by a rigid stratification system and the preservation of the status quo. By contrast, the authoritarian ideologies of Africa-Asia represent the influence of the modernizing authoritarianism of Atatürk or of Soviet Communism.

In Africa-Asia the character and development of political groups show the influence of the twin stimuli of modernity and of recent colonial rule. The incidence of the impact of modernity, and the objectives and character of modern European colonialism, have resulted in several different patterns of development, although the following similarities should be noted:

1. In most of the countries of Africa-Asia the first formally organized political groups were extremely narrow-based and reflected primarily the interests and aspirations of the small Westernized elite. The functions

of such groups were to press for increased political representation and for the removal of the special grievances of that class.

2. As a result of the spread of education and the acceleration of the several processes of change introduced and furthered by Western colonialism, new associations were formed which were both communal and functionally specific in character. Subsequently, nationalist movements were organized for the purpose of mobilizing the population in the drive for national independence. Although primarily the creation and instrument of the Western-educated minority, the determined efforts of the latter to make the movements comprehensive both broadened and deepened popular involvement in political affairs.

3. Nationalist movements ushered in the era of agitational politics. In most countries it was also an era of competitive politics. Despite the determined efforts of leaders to make nationalist movements comprehensive and to create a new single "national will," the appearance of such movements served in most cases as a stimulant to the organization of competitive opposition parties. The latter tended to be of three types: (a) parties organized, with or without the open support of colonial authorities, by that element in the Western-educated elite, frequently in alliance with traditional authorities, which opposed early independence on grounds of principle or because their privileged status or careers under colonialism would be adversely affected; (b) bodies organized by dominant personalities who were rivals of, but who did not necessarily differ ideologically with, incumbent leaders in the main nationalist party—the issue being a struggle for power among different factions or strong personalities of the nationalist movement; (c) parties organized by tribal, religious, or communal groups, or by less-developed groups, to advance or protect their interests, which they believed would be threatened if the leaders of the nationalist movement were to assume power. The main reason for the activation and proliferation of competing parties is that the nationalist leaders consciously sought to undermine and destroy an existing status quo and to create a new status quo in which it was not at all certain the interests of certain elements in the society would be secured. Thus the appearance and growth of nationalist movements intensified popular involvement in political affairs, not only because such movements aimed specifically at widespread political mobilization, but also because their activities stimulated the organization of opposition groups which, although they may have desired the objective of national independence, held different views regarding the methods

by which independence should be obtained and the character of the new regime it would establish.

4. Thus, during the preindependence period of agitational politics in most countries of Africa-Asia some of the more important political lines of cleavage had already become manifest. As a country approached the threshold of independence, however, certain changes usually occurred in the character of political alignments and in the state of political forces. Moderates and evolutionists either retired into silence, or they switched their support openly to nationalist movements, the certain victory of which became increasingly evident. Competition between rival leaders either subsided as the result of temporary alliances or party fusion—depending upon the calculation of relative power position—or it was intensified in a final struggle for power in the emergent order. With the approach of independence, opposition communal parties either intensified their resistance because of their growing conviction that their interests would be neglected in the new polity, or they suspended their opposition for reasons not unlike those of the moderates and evolutionists, namely, the assumption that their interests could be most effectively secured by joining, or accommodating themselves to, the nationalist movement. In the period of terminal colonialism whichever of these changes occurred depended upon the degree to which the nationalist leaders were able to make the main nationalist party broadly aggregative of all major interests in the society. Indian Congress leaders were successful; Sudanese leaders were not.

5. In the post-independence period the character of political alignments has characteristically undergone further changes. When the *raison d'être* of nationalism—the attainment of political independence—has no longer existed, leaders have endeavored in various ways to perpetuate nationalism as an active and unifying force: by demanding a positive role for their new state in world affairs, by creating new external enemies or threats, and by dramatizing the vision of a new society through monumental public works and other such symbols. Despite such measures the cohesion provided by nationalism has been gravely weakened after independence. This has furthered a characteristic process of disintegration and proliferation of groups.

6. The introduction of universal suffrage has been an added factor fostering particularism and a persistence or an activation of communalism or tribalism. In the electoral struggle candidates find it advantageous, if not necessary, to manipulate local issues in order to establish the most

secure political base possible, which is normally their tribal, communal, or religious group of origin.

In many cases, these strong centrifugal tendencies have been countered by actions taken by the dominant party which inherited power from the colonial regime. Dominant parties, where they exist, have tended to be confronted with two principal types of opposition: (a) unreconciled tribal, communal, or regional groups demanding greater local autonomy or threatening secession; and (b) new parties organized by the younger generation, more ideological in outlook, and more determined to push the "revolution" to its conclusion. The emergence of this new line of cleavage represents the reappearance of the moderate-radical split in a new context—the former "radical" nationalists are now conservative or moderate officeholders and the new entrants into the political arena are the radicals, whose ranks continue to grow as a consequence of the expansion of education and the operation of other processes of change.

The developmental syndrome described above is characteristic of only one category of countries in Africa-Asia (i.e., India and Burma in Southeast Asia; Morocco and Tunisia in the Near East; and Ghana, Guinea, Sierra Leone, Somalia, Tanganyika, and Nyasaland in Sub-Saharan Africa). The distinguishing feature of this category is the emergence of a dominant nationalist movement, comprehensive in character, which has provided or currently offers the basis for modified one-party systems in the post-independence period. Elsewhere, the pattern of party development has been somewhat different as a result either of government policy (colonial or indigenous), the special circumstances prevailing in the terminal colonial period, and the communal or racial composition of the country concerned. Thus, the broadly based competitive party system in the Philippines is in large measure the product of official American policy encouraging such a pattern, just as the absence of parties in the traditional authoritarian states of Afghanistan, Saudi Arabia, Yemen, Libya and Ethiopia, Thailand, Cambodia and Laos reflects an official policy opposed to parties. The party systems in such countries as Malaya, Indonesia, Lebanon, and the Sudan (prior to the military coup) reflect the special ethnic or religious composition of the populations of these countries as well as the special circumstances under which they obtained independence. In the European oligarchic states of Algeria, Kenya, the Rhodesias, and the Union of South Africa the peculiar pattern of competitive parties within the oligarchy and comprehensive nationalist movements organized by the masses are a reflection both of official colonial policies as well as the distinctive racial character of the population.

The party systems in Latin America have emerged from a very different historical experience. As Blanksten points out, only two states (Colombia and Uruguay) have a two-party system, but neither conforms to the model of a two-party system in which there is an alternation in office between competing parties. The more typical pattern is that of narrow-based pragmatic parties, or personalistic or *ad hoc* parties. Unlike most of the countries of Africa-Asia, particularistic parties having an ethnic, racial, or tribal basis are either non-existent or insignificant in Latin America. Of far greater importance is the ever-increasing number of parties that are ideological in character (Socialist, Communist, or Aprista) which appeal to organized labor and their variant elements. These latter types are still relatively insignificant in many of the countries of Africa-Asia, although they are clearly growing in strength. This difference between the two major areas is explained in part by the differences in levels of economic development analyzed earlier.

A political phenomenon found throughout the countries of Africa-Asia, and to a lesser extent in Latin America, are anomic movements. These are sudden, sporadic, and unprogrammatic outbursts of political activity engendered by the insecurity and frustrations universally characteristic of societies undergoing rapid change. As Pye points out, the participants in the anomic movements tend to be the newly urbanized elements not fully integrated into either the modern or the traditional sectors of society. The most characteristic type of anomic movement is the highly suggestible urban mob whose passions are readily ignited and whose energies are frequently manipulated by those out of office. Their prevalence helps to account for the volcanic and unpredictable character of politics in these areas. As Weiner suggests, their appearance is probably the result of the fact that more discontent exists in the society than has been articulated through organized groups.[5] Where functionally specific interest groups are undeveloped, anomic movements tend to occur and organized institutional groups tend to be dominant.

[5] Cf. Dorothy L. Meier and Wendell Bell, "Anomia and Differential Access to the Achievement of Life Goals," *American Sociological Review*, Vol. 24, April 1959, pp. 189-202: ". . . in American society anomia results when individuals lack access to means for the achievement of life goals. Such lack of opportunity follows largely as a result of (among other things) the type and amount of association in both formal organizations and in informal groups. . . ."

Political Communication

In all but a few of the countries of Africa-Asia and Latin America there are gross discontinuities in political communications. These discontinuities tend to be of two types and coincide with the fragmentation in political cultures noted earlier, namely, the cleavages between communal groups and the gaps between the modern and traditional sectors of the societies. In many instances the two coincide, one reinforcing the other. Within communal groups (whether defined by race, tribe, religion, or culture) one frequently finds near-autonomous communications systems strengthened in their isolative tendencies by linguistic distinctiveness. Equally fundamental is the cleavage between the predominantly urban, commercialized modern sector of these societies, in which mass media are developed and political participation is high, and the rural, predominantly traditional sector where, as Pye notes, "the communications process coincides with patterns of personal relationships."

The degree to which these discontinuities have been bridged and a single unified network of political communication created is directly related to several factors, among the most important of which are (1) the extent, and particularly the evenness of the geographical incidence of modernization and social change; (2) the structure of political groups, and particularly the extent to which political organization, recruitment, and participation are national in scope; (3) the linguistic pattern, and particularly the extent to which vernacular languages persist as the main vehicle for communication; and (4) the character and level of development of transportation systems and of the media of mass communication. Thus, in countries such as Israel, Chile, and the Philippines, where the impact of modernity has been widespread, where broadly based political parties have emerged, where a single language commands general acceptance, where the output of the press, radio, and other media of mass communication impinges upon a national audience, a single system of political communication is found. In the remaining countries, however, the communications processes reflect in varying degrees the two major cleavages already noted.

Because the development of a single, unified communications system appears to be so heavily dependent upon processes and situations characteristic of modernity, including comprehensive political organization and highly developed mass media, it would seem to follow that the trend toward increased modernization in all of these countries will lead to the progressive extinction of the discontinuities in the communications processes. Although as a general position this is presumptively true, two special observations should be made. One is the point previously made that under certain circumstances increased modernization can aggravate existing discontinuities—much depends upon the tempo and the incidence of its impact. The other is that in the more static societies, such as the patriarchal monarchies of the Near East and Africa and certain countries in Latin America, modernization—which means secularism—will weaken and ultimately extinguish the unifying role played by the Ulama and clergy in the existing systems of political communication.

The Authoritative Functions: Rule-Making; Rule Application; Rule Adjudication

For all but a few of the countries of Africa-Asia, Pye's observations regarding the formal structures of government are valid, namely, the Western impact has been felt greatest at the level of formal structure, and opposition to Western rule has not usually meant opposition to Western institutions. Even in those countries least affected by that impact, such as the monarchies of Southeast Asia and the Near East, there has been a progressive gravitation toward the establishment of formal Western institutions. In most instances the model for emulation has been the parliamentary system of the Western country with whom contact has been most direct. Among Latin American countries, the formal structures of government are also an importation, with the French and American influence predominant. The American influence is particularly noticeable in the predominance of the presidential system, and the constitutional separation of powers at the national level which this system implies. Thus, although there are variations as regards the particular type of structure selected as a model by the countries covered in this survey, the heavy impact of the West at the level of formal structure is everywhere evident.

The two types of formal structure which represent the most distinctive innovation are central representative parliaments endowed with a determinative role in the rule-making function and secular independent judicial structures through which rules are authoritatively adjudicated. Most of the countries have had long experience with executive-bureaucratic government, either through traditional or colonial structures. The concepts of legislation and independent adjudication are distinctly exotic importations, which does much to explain a pattern common to all but a few of the polities concerned, namely, the under-participation by parliaments in the rule-making function, the fragility of the independent judiciary, and executive-bureaucratic predominance. For the countries of South and Southeast Asia and of Sub-Saharan Africa, particularly those which have experienced British colonial rule, this characteristic pattern is modified by a colonial experience in which great emphasis was placed upon the political neutrality of the civil service and the independence of the judiciary. In several of the new states these elements in the colonial legacy have been forces sustaining constitutional government in the post-independence period. How much they are a transitional phenomenon characteristic of the present generation has yet to be seen.

Another common feature, also in part a legacy of the traditional past and of colonialism is the tendency toward unitary government and heavy centralization of decision-making. This is true even in systems such as India and the several countries of Latin America, where federalism has been attempted. In the new and emergent states of Sub-Saharan Africa one finds Africans replacing Europeans as provincial commissioners and district officers in the role of rural agents of central government. The strong centrifugal forces pressing for separatism or greater local autonomy tend to provoke central governments to strengthen their control in terms of national unification and stabilization of the polity. Moreover, the pressures for rapid modernization perpetuate and strengthen the tendency toward centralism. The concept of strong local government, passionately encouraged by British colonial administrators, is not likely to command general acceptance. The general trend throughout the non-Western world is therefore toward centralism.

IV. FUNCTIONAL PROFILES OF TYPE POLITICAL SYSTEMS

In the introduction to this chapter it was pointed out that a modern political system was characterized by a fairly clear differentiation between governmental and political spheres and by a relatively high degree of functional specificity of structure, both governmental and political. The degree of differentiation of spheres and functional specificity of structures in the political systems covered in this survey are indicated by the entries made in Tables 5 and 6. These entries are based on judgments made by the authors of the five area memoranda regarding the respective political systems with which they have dealt. Such judgments have been based on a model of a modern political system which assumes that governmental and political functions are performed by specific structures: rule-making primarily by parliaments and secondarily by executives; rule application by bureaucracies functioning under political executives; rule adjudication by an independent judiciary; interest articulation by associational interest groups and/or competing parties; interest aggregation by competing parties and/or parliaments; political socialization and recruitment by system-wide secondary structures that penetrate primary structures; and political communication by autonomous and differentiated media of communication. It further assumes that armies and religious organizations are non-participant in the performance of governmental and political functions, and that the locus of change in the society is in the activities of competing parties. In those political systems where there is a reasonable approximation of this model an *x* is placed in the "Model" column.

Where in the performance of governmental functions there is, in terms of the model, over-participation by either governmental structures (executive or bureaucracy) or institutional interest groups (army or religious organizations), or by the dominant party, an *x* is placed in the appropriate column. In order to illuminate the absence or non-participation by parliaments in the rule-making process, a column "parliament absent or non-functional" has been included to cover such cases where there either is no parliament (e.g., the Belgian Congo) or where, if one exists, it in fact performs no authoritative function (e.g., Ethiopia). Similarly, where there is in the performance of political functions over-participation—in terms of the model—by governmental structures, institutional groups, or the dominant party, an *x* has been placed in the appropriate column. In order to show the non-existence or the non-functional character of the press as a medium of political communication, a column "press non-functional" has been added.

The patterning of the entries in Tables 5 and 6 confirms and points up observations already made in the area memoranda and at previous points in this chapter regarding the relationship between structures and functions in the several political systems examined. The predominance of certain structures in the performance of both governmental and political functions is very striking: the army in Latin American systems (Table 5), the bureaucracy in African-Asian systems (Table 6), and the executive in both major areas. Very few countries approximate the model; and even among those which come close there are instances where religious organizations and armies intermittently play a preponderant role. Moreover, there is not only an over-participation by certain structures in the performance of particular functions; there is also a multiplicity of structures involved in the performance of the several functions.

The patterning of entries in these two tables also suggests profiles characteristic of different types of polities in terms of the degree of functional specificity of their governmental and political structures. It will be noted that the Latin American countries (Table 4) are classified according to degree of competitiveness, while the African-Asian countries (Table 5) are categorized in terms of a different and more detailed typology. At earlier points in this chapter some of the crucial differences between the systems of the two major areas have been noted. Although many of the Latin American countries could perhaps be fitted into the more detailed typology, the differences between the two major areas are such that the inclusion of those countries in the following analysis of functional profiles would tend to dilute the distinctiveness of the categories. Hence, the focus here will be only upon the African-Asian systems.

For the analyst the most distinctive phenomenon of the African-Asian area is the "new state." Broadly defined, the latter includes all those political systems which since the end of World War II have either received, or have advanced toward the threshold of attaining, their political independence. All but 15 of the 56 African-Asian polities fall in that category. The 15 exceptions include the 4 traditional oligarchies (Afghanistan, Ethiopia, Saudi Arabia, and Yemen), 6 of the colonial or racial oligarchies (Angola, Mozambique, Belgian Congo, Ruanda-Urundi, Algeria, and the Union of South Africa), and the older established states of Thailand, Turkey, Iran, Iraq, and Liberia.

The African-Asian countries listed in Table 5 are grouped according to a classificatory scheme adapted from Edward Shils's political typology referred to in the Introduction. To four of Shils's categories—political democracy, tutelary democracy, modernizing oligarchy, and traditional oligarchy—have been added two others: "terminal colonial democracy" and "colonial or racial oligarchy." The first is a special case of tutelary democracy; the second is a mixed class which does not fall into any one of Shils's categories. The purpose of this six-fold classification is to enable us to describe the distinguishing characteristics of some of the major types of systems in terms of the functional concepts used in this study. From each of the following categories a representative system has been selected and its functional characteristics briefly summarized in order to provide us, in a very general way, with a functional profile of the political type concerned: political democracy (Philippines), tute-

TABLE 5
Functional Specificity of Structure in Latin American Political Systems

COUNTRIES BY TYPE OF POLITICAL SYSTEMS	MODEL	PERFORMANCE OF GOVERNMENTAL FUNCTIONS					*Parliament Absent or Non Functioning*
		OVER-PARTICIPATION BY					
		Executive	*Bureaucracy*	*Army*	*Religious Organization*	*Dominant Party*	
COMPETITIVE							
Uruguay	x						
Chile	x						
Costa Rica		x					
Brazil			x				
Argentina			x	x			
SEMI-COMPETITIVE							
Ecuador		x			x		
Mexico		x	x			x	x
Colombia				x	x		
Peru		x	x	x			x
Panama		x		x			x
AUTHORITARIAN							
Nicaragua		x		x			x
Venezuela		x		x			x
Guatemala				x			x
Cuba		x		x			x
Haiti		x		x			x
Dominican Republic		x		x			x
Paraguay		x		x			x
El Salvador		x	x	x			x
Honduras		x		x			x
Bolivia		x		x		x	x

lary democracy (Indonesia), terminal colonial democracy (Nigeria), modernizing oligarchy (Pakistan), colonial or racial oligarchy (Southern Rhodesia), and traditional oligarchy (Ethiopia).

Any classificatory scheme creates difficulties, and often provokes legitimate controversy among area specialists. As every political system is *sui generis*, generalizers are invariably confronted with the purist's argument that no system can be regarded as representative of other systems. Many of the countries concerned could be regarded as marginal in the category to which they have been assigned, and, approached with a different purpose, could justifiably be shifted to another. The distinctions between categories are rather fine: for example, there is not a great difference between a "tutelary democracy" and a "modernizing oli-

TABLE 5 (Cont'd)

COUNTRIES BY TYPE POLITICAL SYSTEMS	MODEL	PERFORMANCE OF POLITICAL FUNCTIONS OVER-PARTICIPATION BY					Press Absent or Non-Functioning
		Executive	Bureaucracy	Army	Religious Organization	Dominant Party	
COMPETITIVE							
Uruguay	x						
Chile	x						
Costa Rica	x	x					
Brazil		x		x			
Argentina				x	x		
SEMI-COMPETITIVE							
Ecuador		x			x		
Mexico			x	x		x	
Colombia		x		x	x		
Peru		x		x	x		
Panama		x	x				x
AUTHORITARIAN							
Nicaragua		x		x			x
Venezuela		x		x			x
Guatemala		x		x			x
Cuba		x		x		x	x
Haiti		x		x	x		x
Dominican Republic		x		x		x	x
Paraguay		x		x		x	x
Salvador		x		x	x		x
Honduras		x		x	x	x	x
Bolivia		x		x	x	x	x

garchy," and a "terminal colonial democracy" is really one form of "tutelary democracy." Depending upon which features are stressed, Lebanon could be classified as a "tutelary" rather than a political democracy, Ethiopia as a "modernizing" rather than a traditional oligarchy, and so forth. There is always the problem of relating empirical systems to analytical models, particularly when those systems are in transition. Finally, there is above all the lamentable state of our knowledge regarding all these systems. Once these several qualifications are made, however, it is believed that an exploratory functional approach to political systems, which the present endeavor represents, should at least attempt to differentiate those systems on the basis of functional profiles constructed from existing knowledge, however inadequate the latter may be.

TABLE 6
Functional Specificity of Structure in Asian and African Political Systems

COUNTRIES BY TYPE OF POLITICAL SYSTEMS	MODEL	PERFORMANCE OF GOVERNMENTAL FUNCTIONS OVER-PARTICIPATION BY					Parliament Absent or Non Functioning
		Executive	Bureaucracy	Army	Religious Organization	Dominant Party	
POLITICAL DEMOCRACY							
Ceylon	x						
Israel	x						
Philippines	x				x		
Lebanon					x		
India						x	
Malaya						x	
Turkey		x					
TUTELARY DEMOCRACY							
Tunisia		x	x			x	
Morocco		x	x			x	
Ghana		x	x			x	x
Guinea		x	x			x	x
Vietnam		x	x				x
Indonesia		x	x	x			x
Burma		x	x	x			x
TERMINAL COLONIAL DEMOCRACY							
Cameroons		x	x				
Chad		x	x				
Dahomey		x	x				
Gabon		x	x				
Niger		x	x				
Republic of Congo		x	x				
Togoland		x	x				
Upper Volta		x	x				
Nigeria		x	x				
Sierra Leone		x	x				
Central African Rep.		x	x			x	
Ivory Coast		x	x			x	
Kenya		x	x				
Mali Federation		x	x			x	
Mauritania		x	x			x	
Somalia		x	x				
Tanganyika		x	x				
Uganda		x	x				
MODERNIZING OLIGARCHY							
Pakistan		x		x			x
Iraq		x		x			x
United Arab Republic		x	x	x			x
Sudan		x	x	x	x		x
Thailand		x	x	x			x

TABLE 6 (Cont'd)

COUNTRIES BY TYPE POLITICAL SYSTEMS	MODEL	Executive	Bureaucracy	Army	Religious Organization	Dominant Party	Press Absent or Non-Functioning
POLITICAL DEMOCRACY							
Ceylon	x						
Israel	x				x		
Philippines	x						
Lebanon					x		
India						x	
Malaya						x	
Turkey		x	x			x	
TUTELARY DEMOCRACY							
Tunisia		x				x	
Morocco		x				x	
Ghana		x	x			x	
Guinea		x	x			x	x
Vietnam		x					x
Indonesia		x	x				x
Burma		x			x	x	
TERMINAL COLONIAL DEMOCRACY							
Cameroons		x	x				
Chad		x	x				
Dahomey		x	x				
Gabon		x	x				
Niger		x	x				
Republic of Congo		x	x				
Togoland		x	x				
Upper Volta		x	x				
Nigeria		x	x				
Sierra Leone		x	x				
Central African Rep.		x	x			x	
Ivory Coast		x	x			x	
Kenya		x	x				
Mali Federation		x	x			x	
Mauritania		x	x			x	
Somali		x	x			x	
Tanganyika		x	x			x	
Uganda		x	x		x		
MODERNIZING OLIGARCHY							
Pakistan		x		x			
Iraq		x		x			x
United Arab Republic		x	x	x			x
Sudan		x	x	x	x		x
Thailand		x					x

TABLE 6 (cont'd)

TABLE 6 (Cont'd)

Functional Specificity of Structure in Asian and African Political Systems

COUNTRIES BY TYPE OF POLITICAL SYSTEMS	MODEL	PERFORMANCE OF GOVERNMENTAL FUNCTIONS					*Parliament Absent or Non-Functioning*
		OVER-PARTICIPATION BY					
		Executive	*Bureaucracy*	*Army*	*Religious Organization*	*Dominant Party*	
COLONIAL AND RACIAL OLIGARCHY							
Southern Rhodesia		x	x				
Northern Rhodesia		x	x				
Nyasaland		x	x				
Union of South Africa		x	x			x	
Belgian Congo		x	x		x		x
Ruanda-Urundi		x	x		x		x
Angola		x	x		x		x
Mozambique		x	x		x		x
Algeria		x		x			x
CONSERVATIVE OLIGARCHY							
Jordan		x	x	x			
Iran		x	x	x			
Cambodia		x					x
Laos		x					x
Liberia		x					x
Libya		x					x
TRADITIONAL OLIGARCHY							
Afghanistan		x			x		x
Ethiopia		x					x
Saudi Arabia		x	x				x
Yemen		x		x			x

Political Democracy: Philippines

Among the mixed systems of Africa-Asia, the Philippines stands out as the most advanced and integrated. Lucian Pye has noted that although the performance of both the governmental and political functions in the Philippine political system reflects a combination of modern concepts and traditional practices, the mixture is approximately equal in both spheres. The governmental structures reflect a strong Western influence, but they also demonstrate the adaptability of traditional customs and practices. In the performance of the political functions of socialization and recruitment, articulation, aggregation and communication, there is the same blending of modernity and the traditional. Moreover, the dynamics for change in the society are centered as much in the political as in the

TABLE 6 (cont'd)

COUNTRIES BY TYPE POLITICAL SYSTEMS	MODEL	PERFORMANCE OF POLITICAL FUNCTIONS					Press Absent or Non-Functioning
		OVER-PARTICIPATION BY					
		Executive	Bureaucracy	Army	Religious Organization	Dominant Party	
COLONIAL AND RACIAL OLIGARCHY							
Southern Rhodesia		x	x				
Northern Rhodesia		x	x				
Nyasaland		x	x			x	
Union of South Africa		x	x		x		
Belgian Congo		x	x		x		x
Ruanda-Urundi		x	x		x		x
Angola		x	x		x		x
Mozambique		x	x		x		x
Algeria		x		x		x	x
CONSERVATIVE OLIGARCHY							
Jordan		x					
Iran		x	x				
Cambodia		x					x
Laos		x					x
Liberia		x					x
Libya		x					x
TRADITIONAL OLIGARCHY							
Afghanistan		x					x
Ethiopia		x	x		x		x
Saudi Arabia		x			x		x
Yemen		x			x		x

governmental structures. As he puts it: "The requirements of public administration lead to the demand for many changes, but all initiative does not rest with government as in countries committed to government-directed planning. Popular demands for change are reflected in a competitive political process and thus much of the dynamics for change is to be found in the operation of the political functions."

Thus, the Philippine system reflects a fusional adaptation of the modern and traditional sectors and the consequent emergence of a fairly homogeneous political culture. The discontinuities between the modern elite subsociety and the mass are much less marked than in other transitional systems. Moreover, there is a comparatively high degree of differentiation and functional distinctiveness of the political and governmental structures. Most of the latter tend to function in the distinctive orbits characteristic of a modern system where competing parties are instruments through which political "brokers" endeavor to aggregate the largest possible number of interests, and where a relatively autonomous system of political communication exists. In the performance of the governmental functions the Philippine legislature is fully participant, the bureaucracy is far less dominant in the performance of political functions than in most other African-Asian systems, the judiciary is independent, and the army is apolitical.

The Philippine system, however, is still one in transition, and there are factors which could retard or frustrate the consolidation and stabilization of a fully modern polity. Although it ranks high in literacy and education, it is less advanced economically than several other countries in the area. Indeed, this very imbalance, which elsewhere has created havoc with democratic experiments, could introduce tensions and strains in the system beyond its capacity to handle them. Moreover, as Pye has noted, there are few organized interest groups, and "Philippine parties, for all their historical continuity, still represent primarily the network of personal ties and obligations of the particular politicians of the moment." This element of personalism in Philippine politics may, as in certain Latin American countries, be but a transitional phenomenon. In the balance, however, the Philippines has started its career as a new state with certain distinct advantages—its long exposure to external influences, its comparatively homogeneous culture, and the intensive political acculturation which characterized its colonial experience with the United States. These have been factors of no little significance in its success thus far.

Tutelary Democracy: Indonesia

Of the seven new states classified as tutelary democracies, Indonesia stands out as a country whose leaders have been most articulate in advancing the concept of tutelage. Although the structural forms of a democratic polity have been adopted, and political leaders have repeatedly affirmed their dedication to the formal norms of democracy, both political and governmental functions are performed by structures and in a style reflecting an isolative mixture of modern and traditional elements, a fragmented political culture, and an undeveloped political infrastructure. The Indonesian parliament has been relatively non-functional in the rule-making process, and there is a heavy concentration of power in the executive and the army. Both of the latter have tended to exert a dominant influence in the performance of political as well as governmental functions; a clear distinction between the two spheres has yet to emerge. But even the army, a predominating institutional group, is not the monolithic structure characteristic of modern armies; rather, it is an aggregation of quite diverse elements born out of the experiences of World War II and the military action against the Dutch forces.

In the political socialization process the secondary structures of the new state have not yet effectively penetrated—hence, they do not regulate —the primary structures. Associational interest groups have only begun to emerge as articulators of functionally specific interests. Recurrent anomic activity has become a characteristic feature of the political process and continues to have a high future potential. A class of politicians has emerged, but these principal actors have sought mainly to advance the interests of distinctive communal or regional groupings, or to gain support for a particular total ideology they espouse. Thus political parties have been ineffective as system-wide aggregators of interests. Indeed, in introducing the concept of "guided democracy," President Sukarno observed that tutelage was necessary because the political parties had failed to represent the real interests of the society. Finally, there are gross discontinuities among the structures of political communication. The heavy concentration of mass media in the urban centers of Java, the geographical dispersion of the many islands forming the new state, and the unbridged gap between what Pye has termed the "provincial elite" and the national elite have been obstacles to the development of a unifying system of political communication.

These attributes of the Indonesian case serve to explain why Indonesia is one of the least effectively integrated of the new states, and why, despite the strong determination to create a modern polity, the system depends for its survival upon executive-army dominance. In comparing it to India, with which it ranks about equally on the scale of economic development, at least three factors are in point—their differing colonial experiences, the different circumstances under which they achieved their independence, and the patterning of political groups. India emerged from the colonial experience in a relatively orderly manner with a well-trained cadre of skilled administrators and an officer corps steeped in the British tradition of apolitical service to the state. Moreover, a not unimportant segment of the populace had developed political skills at the state level. Above all, however, it had a comprehensive political party, which not only provided the new state with a national leadership commanding wide acceptance in governmental roles, but which has also been a structure capable of performing several of the crucial political functions for the system as a whole. The Indonesian experience has been quite different, partly because of Dutch colonial policy and partly because of the Japanese occupation and the confused and disorganizing circumstances under which the island republic secured its independence. From a functional standpoint the really striking feature about Indonesia is the extremely underdeveloped character of its political infrastructure, and particularly the absence of political structures— whether pragmatic competing parties as in the Philippines, or a multifunctional comprehensive party as in India—through which the varied interests of the society can be articulated, aggregated, and communicated to the government.

Terminal Colonial Democracy: Tanganyika

With few exceptions (for example, Malaya until its independence, and the new West Indies Federation), the terminal colonial democracy is a political type found only in contemporary Sub-Saharan Africa. In both theory and fact it is a tutelary regime, differing from the preceding type in at least two important respects, namely, tutelage is by an alien colonial power, and there is a far greater certitude that in due course it will be terminated. It is a transitional regime in which the residual power of the colonial government ensures law and order while the new indigenous elite progressively assumes responsibility for the governmental functions. A colony usually enters this final phase when it becomes clear to all concerned that indigenous political forces are in control of the timetable. The regime terminates, of course, with independence. The Belgian Congo is on the threshold of entering this phase. Nigeria is on the threshold of independence, having entered the terminal phase in 1952. The other 17 polities of this type are at various stages in between. Tanganyika, whose functional profile is briefly described below, is in the early stages of the terminal colonial phase.

The British colonial bureaucracy in Tanganyika continues to be ultimately responsible for the performance of the governmental functions, but the largely elected legislative council exerts a growing influence on both the rule-making and rule-application process at the central level. The police and the army are apolitical instruments of the central government, and the judiciary is independent.

The governmental functions at the central level are performed by modern structures in a modern style. At the local level, however, they are very mixed in character, reflecting a thoroughgoing policy of indirect rule in which colonial administrators, acting in accordance with rational-legal bureaucratic assumptions, direct and guide the modernization of traditional or mixed structures performing the functions of rule-making (local government councils), rule application (local administration), and rule adjudication (native courts). There is, therefore, a fairly systematic penetration and regulation of local structures by central government. This local pattern is being progressively altered by the democratization of local councils, and hence the attenuation of traditional authority; by the modernization of traditional adjudicative procedures and their integration into a system-wide legal structure; and by the Africanization of local administrative cadres, including in particular the agents of central government. In short, while policy during the colonial period was directed toward maximizing the traditional element in the local government functions, during the terminal colonial phase policy is aimed at rapid modernization.

In the political sphere, the colonial regime previously undertook to perform, for the system as a whole, the functions of political socialization, interest aggregation, and political communication. Except for the exceedingly small modern sector of the society, the "chiefs and elders" were endowed with the function of articulating the interests of their respective tribal groups. Since the end of World War II, however, a comprehensive political party, TANU (Tanganyika African National Union), has emerged as a competitive structure in the political realm, asserting its right and competence to articulate and to aggregate what it claims to be the real, and previously neglected, interests of the society. TANU has also endeavored to penetrate and influence other structures so as to socialize the populace to a new Tanganyikan political culture, to recruit into its ranks political activists from all sectors of society, and to create alternate media and channels of political communication to offset the government and European-controlled press and other media in both the modern and traditional sectors.

When it became evident, through the results of free elections and other events, that TANU commanded wide acceptance, the way was opened for its leaders and its European and Asian supporters to move into roles in the central governmental structures where they are now in a position to assert progressively greater control over the performance of the governmental functions at both the central and local levels. While the British administration is still in control of the "commanding heights" of the system, and although competition continues to be intense between the colonial bureaucratic structure and TANU in the political sphere, there is clearly a gravitation toward a form of diarchy now characteristic of the terminal colonial democracy. In terms of political infrastructure, Tanganyika is a decade or more behind such new states as Ghana and Malaya. The intensive modernization of its political system during its current terminal colonial period may rapidly narrow the gap. In any event, it is too early to be able to judge whether on independence Tanganyika will become a political democracy, a tutelary democracy under an indigenous elite, or a modernizing oligarchy.

Modernizing Oligarchy: Pakistan

The thin line dividing a modernizing oligarchy from a tutelary democracy is nowhere more evident than in the case of Pakistan. Yet there is an important respect in which Pakistan differs from Burma and Indonesia, two of the other Asian countries in which the army currently plays a dominant role. This difference is found in the considerably weaker determination and effort in Pakistan to establish the forms and practices of a modern democratic polity. The fact that both Burma and Indonesia have held national general elections, while Pakistan has not, is particularly in point. Also, as Weiner has noted, in its program and goals the Muslim League was from the beginning far less committed to parliamentary institutions than were, for example, the Indian National Congress or the Ceylonese nationalist leaders. The Pakistan army came to power not with the self-conscious purpose of guiding the new state to a more democratic polity, but to "purify" the political process of corruption and to replace the politicians and political confusion with authority, order, and rationality.

Since its emergence as a state the performance of the governmental functions in Pakistan has been dominated by the executive, bureaucracy, and army. The Constituent Assembly was comparatively non-participant in the rule-making process prior to its dismissal by the governor-general in 1954, and since 1958 the judiciary has lost its independence through the establishment of dual judicial structures, army and civil, in which the army is supreme.

The political infrastructure of Pakistan, like that of Indonesia, is relatively undeveloped. Although the Muslim League emerged as a comprehensive party in the decade preceding independence, it failed to develop either an effective organization or enduring loyalties on the part of its members and adherents. Unlike the Indian Congress party, the League did not appeal to and seek to aggregate the interests of the major groups in the society; indeed, as Weiner notes, it had no program at all. As a consequence of these and other factors, the League progressively disintegrated after independence. Nothing has replaced it since as the integrating element in the new society, except the coercion of the army and a strong executive. Such political groups as have existed have been split on the critical issues of East-West Pakistan and secularism versus an Islamic state. Thus divided, the parties were incapable of performing the function of system-wide aggregation. Moreover, because of the relatively limited degree of economic development in Pakistan, there are few modern associational interest groups. Indeed, some of the major interests making claims upon the new polity have been largely non-aggregable.

Despite its religious homogeneity—which is, of course, virtually its sole *raison d'être*—Pakistan has a highly fragmented political culture. It is deeply divided geographically, linguistically, culturally, and between secular and orthodox wings of Islam. These internal cleavages, coupled with the comparatively high levels of illiteracy, and the authoritarian controls in the society have prevented the emergence of an autonomous system of political communication. These same discontinuities also affect the process of political socialization. Except for Islam, which spans three continents, and anti-Hinduism, there are no symbols or distinctive institutions of the society which can endow the secondary structures with the prestige and penetrative qualities necessary to create a sense of national unity and purpose. It is this ensemble of elements in the Pakistani functional profile which have invited, if indeed they have not compelled, the heavy intrusion into the political process of the executive and the army.

Colonial and Racial Oligarchy: Southern Rhodesia

Like the "terminal colonial democracy," this type of system is unique to contemporary Africa, although Peru, with its racially defined elite, is a close approximation. Even within this type, however, there are vast differences, such as the conservative authoritarianism of Portuguese Africa versus the development-oriented paternalism of the Belgian Congo, and the rigid racial separation in the Union of South Africa versus the gradual assimilation implicit in the concept of "partnership" prevailing in the Federation of Rhodesia and Nyasaland. Despite these differences, and particularly the fact that some of them are undergoing fundamental political change (for example, Northern Rhodesia and the Belgian Congo), they currently constitute a special type. They are really dualistic political societies distinguished by the fact that the overwhelming majority of the population is excluded on racial or cultural grounds from the political process.

Within the subsociety of the European oligarchy in Southern Rhodesia one finds an essentially modern political system. An elected legislature participates actively and meaningfully in the rule-making function; the bureaucracy is apolitical and serves as the neutral instrument of the executive; and the judiciary is independent. A fairly dense network of functionally specific associational interest groups exist to articulate the interests of the various economic, social, and occupational groups in the European subsociety. An autonomous system of political communication penetrates the entire subsociety, and the secondary structures penetrate and influence primary structures in a process of political socialization into the fairly homogeneous political culture of the European oligarchy. All of these functions are performed, however, in a manner which assumes the indefinite continuation of the dualistic system, and particularly European supremacy in that system.

There is a very different pattern of performance of functions within the African subsociety. Rules are made and authoritatively applied and adjudicated by central organs of the European bureaucracy, which is recruited from and reflects the interests of the resident European population. There is a symbolic delegation of limited authority to local African councils, chiefs, and headmen, but it does not extend to spheres beyond local regulation. The central agents of the European oligarchic government are charged with the task of ascertaining the needs and interests of the African rural mass, which they in turn communicate to the central government. The functional pattern among the urban African groups is essentially similar, although they are permitted to form associations to articulate their peculiar urban interests. There are strong deterrents to the formation of political parties as vehicles for aggregating and pressing upon government the ensemble of African interests. Individual Africans, however, are permitted to join the predominantly European political parties where it is argued they can present the African point of view and possibly exert some influence upon public policy.

In the African sub-society there is not a differentiated system of communication; indeed, there is by design of the European authorities extremely little communication between the urban African and the rural mass. The European communications media, and a press catering particularly to the urban African, aim at inculcating African attitudes of deference and accommodation to the dualistic society. The same is true of all manifest secondary structures of political socialization. The European oligarchy maintains that there is only one legitimate political culture for the participant citizen, and that until the African is qualified to participate, he must remain in the African subsociety. The crucial feature of this dualistic system is that the resident racial oligarchy defines the qualifications and judges eligibility for full acceptance.

Traditional Oligarchy: Ethiopia

A measure of the magnitude and pervasiveness of the impact of modernity upon Africa and Asia is the surprisingly few traditional polities that remain. Perhaps Yemen is the closest approximation of a purely traditional system, but the outside world knows very little about the character of its regime. Despite its energetic modernizing emperor, Ethiopia still has a predominantly traditional system, about which somewhat more information is available.

As an absolute monarch, supported by a legend of descent from Solomon, the Ethiopian emperor is the supreme authority in the state. There is a parliament, personally created by him, but it plays a relatively insignificant part in the rule-making function. Rules are applied through a bureaucratic process in which the emperor personally plays a very active role. The higher bureaucracy, guided by shrewdly selected foreign advisers, is staffed by personal appointees of the emperor, and in most instances they have some traditional status. Thus, recruitment to most of the higher governmental roles is still largely ascriptive, with the young university graduates filling the subaltern ranks. There is a judicial system that is quite modern in structure, but judges are selected by ascriptive criteria, they have no tenure, and much of Ethiopian law is still largely customary.

Despite its long history of independent existence, Ethiopia does not have a homogeneous political culture. The dominant Amharas constitute a minority of the population, and in the provinces traditional tribal institutions among the non-Amharic peoples function largely as they have done for centuries. The provincial governors representing the emperor exercise their authority almost entirely through the traditional tribal chiefs (*balabats*), upon the good will of which they depend very heavily.

It is in the political sphere that one finds a complete vacuum. There are neither associational interest groups (except among the small foreign contingents), nor political parties. The press, which is limited to government newspapers and in which much space is devoted to adulation of the emperor, has very little circulation beyond Addis Ababa. Outside the capital city the pattern of communications is very much like what it has been for generations, namely, widely dispersed and autonomous communications systems, linked only through the agents of central government and the large number of priests of the Ethiopian Orthodox Church.

One of the most remarkable features of the Ethiopian system is that the emperor, whose position depends heavily upon the preservation of tradition, has been and remains one of the most powerful modernizing influences in the country. On his own initiative he has introduced modern constitutional structures; he is using the resources of the state deliberately to create a new class of educated Ethiopians to staff the expanding bureaucracy and a modern army. He is, in a word, setting in motion processes of change which will most likely eventuate in profound tensions in the society, and which could lead in time to a shattering of the whole traditional structure. However, it is still too soon to evaluate the extent to which the response of the traditional to the impact of modernity will be isolative or fusional in character. Much depends upon the emperor's successor.

The propositions which have been developed and applied in the course of this book have had as their major purpose improving our capacity to order the phenomena of non-Western political systems, and to compare them with the Western ones, and with one another. From this point of view our work represents a contribution to the general theory of political systems. A second purpose, which has been fulfilled only to a very limited extent, is to improve our understanding of the processes of political change or modernization. We have contributed to our understanding of these processes by classifying the political systems of the non-Western areas, specifying their properties, and analyzing the impact on politics of the various factors making for change. But the development of a rigorous theory of political modernization is still unfinished business. Here the interests of political theory and political practice converge in such a way as to invite the best efforts of political scientists. If this book stimulates such efforts and provides useful intellectual tools for those concerning themselves with these problems, it will have served its purpose.

APPENDIX

Economic Development in Underdeveloped Countries

COMPETITIVENESS OF POLITICAL SYSTEM BY ECONOMIC RANK AND MAJOR AREA	Per Capita Gross National Product (US $)	WEALTH — Number of Persons					INDUSTRIALIZATION		URBANIZATION Per Cent of Population in Cities over 100,000	EDUCATION	
		Per Doctor	Per Vehicle	Per Telephone	Per Radio	Per Newspaper copy	Per Capita Energy Consumed (in tons)[a]	Per Cent of Population in Labor Unions		Per Capita Population Literate	Primary Enrollment Ratio (in per cent)[b]
COMPETITIVE											
Latin America											
Argentina	374	780	32	17	7	6	.97	21.6	37.2	87	68
Uruguay	569	862	31	22	7	5	.83	6.9	31.8	85	45[e]
Chile	180	2,010	66	46	11	13	.99	7.7	30.7	81	56
Costa Rica	307	3,100	103	88	19	11	.32	1.0	33.5	80	51
Brazil	262	2,560	83	71	17	20	.39	4.2	13.2	50	34
Africa-Asia											
Israel	540	448	49	25	5	5	1.10	22.8	45.6	93	78
Lebanon	269	1,189	45	38	32	13	.49	1.7	16.0	50	n.d.
Malaya	298	8,350	80	109	34	71	.38	4.1	25.0	38	48
Turkey	276	3,510	348	166	24	31	.23	.8	8.2	35	33
Ceylon	122	5,330	109	308	87	32	.08	4.1	4.7	58	62
Philippines	201	9,250	169	360	103	52	.19	.5	10.6	62	60
India	72	5,525	1,022	1,460	360	143	.12	1.2	9.5	28	22
SEMI-COMPETITIVE											
Latin America											
Panama	350	3,265	41	43	10	9	.40	.2	15.9	72	56
Mexico	187	2,245	55	80	12	20	.75	6.4	15.1	65	47
Colombia	330	2,879	86	65	26	25	.50	3.2	14.7	55	30
Peru	140	2,915	93	140	19	25	.31	1.3	8.4	50	42
Ecuador	204	2,865	181	224	76	20	.14	2.0	14.6	56	42

[a] Gross inland consumption of commercial fuels and water power, expressed in terms of coal equivalent.
[b] Primary enrollment ratio is defined as the primary school en-rollment taken as a percentage of children age five to fourteen.
[e] Based on public school enrollment only.

Economic Development in Underdeveloped Countries (cont'd)

COMPETITIVENESS OF POLITICAL SYSTEM BY ECONOMIC RANK AND MAJOR AREA	W Per Capita Gross National Product (US $)	E A L T H — Number of Persons					INDUSTRIALIZATION		URBANIZATION Per Cent of Population in Cities over 100,000	EDUCATION	
		Per Doctor	Per Vehicle	Per Telephone	Per Radio	Per Newspaper copy	Per Capita Energy Consumed (in tons)a	Per Cent of Population in Labor Unions		Per Cent of Population Literate	Primary Enrollment Ratio (in per cent)b
Semi-Competitive (Cont'd)											
Africa-Asia											
Union of So. Africa	381	2,070	17	21	18	18	2.39	2.5	27.7	45	46
Algeria	176	5,100	58	68	27	42	.24	3.3	6.0	20	n.d.
Southern Rhodesia	134d	3,990	31	67	103	48	.58e	.8d	6.7	25	n.d.
Morocco	159	10,150	56	85	22	43	.24	8.6	15.0	15	10e
Tunisia	131	6,720	72	113	29	45	.18	5.9	10.8	20	20
Jordan	96	7,050	187	133	37	111	.12	.8	13.7	15	42e
Ghana	135	22,600	180	296	151	48	.13	2.9	3.5	25	42
Northern Rhodesia	d	10,240	57	359	55	125	e	d	.0	25	n.d.
Kenya	61f	9,460	109	209	257	200	.16	.7	3.4	25	27
Iran	100	8,160	366	296	103	166	n.d.	.1	16.6	15	15
Indonesia	127	75,620	642	1,060	258	143	.12	2.4	7.9	46	35
Thailand	100	7,020	408	1,759	191	275	.04	.6	4.5	54	54
Vietnam	133	63,600g	259	996	1,270g	45	n.d.	3.7	7.6	23g	7
Cameroons	n.d.	18,500	151	881	1,063	n.d.	.04	1.1	3.8	10	23
Burma	52	8,400	649	2,682	1,320	125	.04	.8	5.2	57	16e
Uganda	f	21,050	234	523	n.d.	800	.04	.1	.0	30	30
Tanganyika	f	20,100	375	736	1,129	470	.05	.5	1.1	10	14
Nigeria	70	57,900	942	1,295	455	230	.04	.5	4.3	15	13
French West Africa	58	29,520	277	703	379	590	.04	.5	1.9	5	5
Nyasaland	d	33,400	366	1,080	897	n.d.	n.d.	d	.0	10	39
Somalia	n.d.	20,000	294	n.d.	650	1,080	n.d.	2.5	.0	5	n.d.
French Equat. Africa	58	21,500	244	840	482	6,030	.03	n.d.	2.1	5	10
Sierra Leone	n.d.	33,830	2,210	n.d.	345	300	.03	1.2	.0	10	8
Togoland	n.d.	27,900	505	941	2,176	1,090	.02	n.d.	.0	10	22

d Data is for Southern Rhodesia, Northern Rhodesia, and Nyasaland combined.
e Data is for Southern Rhodesia and Northern Rhodesia combined.
f Data is for Kenya, Uganda, and Tanganyika combined.
g Includes North Viet Nam.

COMPETITIVENESS OF POLITICAL SYSTEM BY ECONOMIC RANK AND MAJOR AREA	Per Capita Gross National Product (US $)	Number of Persons					INDUSTRIALIZATION		URBANIZATION	EDUCATION	
		Per Doctor	Per Vehicle	Per Telephone	Per Radio	Per Newspaper copy	Per Capita Energy Consumed (in tons) a	Per Cent of Population in Labor Unions	Per Cent of Population in Cities over 100,000	Per Cent of Population Literate	Primary Enrollment Ratio (in per cent) b
Authoritarian											
Latin America											
Cuba	361	865	29	39	6	8	.70	20.6	21.9	76	43
Venezuela	762	1,615	25	54	27	14	2.18	5.5	20.6	69	43
Paraguay	108	2,080	267	281	21	83	.04	2.8	15.2	69	57
Nicaragua	254	2,695	161	224	43	19	.12	.7	10.3	38	n.d.
Dominican Republic	205	5,530	192	222	27	41	.17	2.6	8.5	43	45
Bolivia	66	4,060	91	276	22	43	.18	7.7	9.9	31	28
El Salvador	244	5,730	135	220	108	30	.19	.6	8.7	42	33
Honduras	137	4,960	222	312	66	280	.17	1.4	.0	43	27
Guatemala	179	6,430	126	316	97	34	.15	.1	10.2	30	23
Haiti	75	11,450	396	782	246	250	.04	.2	4.3	11	20
Africa-Asia											
United Arab Rep.	133	3,696	226	126	30	41	.24	1.1	19.4	25	28
Iraq	195	5,820	128	116	74	48	.48	.0	16.6	15	19
Libya	90	10,420	939	149	64	167	n.d.	.4	15.0	10	n.d.
Belgian Congo	98h	21,000	253	903h	996h	n.d.	.18h	.1h	4.1	40	37h
Saudi Arabia	166	n.d.	n.d.	436	603	600	n.d.	.0	8.4	5	n.d.
Angola	70i	24,800	164	1,090	180	290	.05	.5	4.3	5	1e
Pakistan	56	15,220	1,660	1,615	768	111	.05	.5	5.9	19	n.d.
Liberia	103	20,160	n.d.	n.d.	500	1,040	.03	4.0	.0	10	n.d.
Mozambique	i	37,000	289	713	437	470	.09	.4	1.6	5	13
Laos	n.d.	31,500	481	n.d.	1,320	n.d.	n.d.	.0	6.9	20	11
Sudan	100	68,800	514	552	1,704	350	.04	.5	3.5	10	5e
Cambodia	n.d.	89,700	n.d.	1,442	614	300	.04	.1	.0	20	18
Afghanistan	54	60,320	n.d.	1,937	1,500	920	n.d.	.0	1.2	5	n.d.
Rwanda-Urundi	h	62,400	1,100	h	h	n.d.	h	h	.0	10	h
Ethiopia	54	137,000	763	2,753	1,429	2,000	.01	.0	2.6	5	n.d.

h Data is for Angola and Mozambique combined.

h Data is for Belgian Congo and Ruanda-Urundi combined.   i Data is for Belgian Congo and Ruanda-Urundi combined.

INDEX